BASIC
MANAGERIAL
FINANCE

1817

HARPER & ROW, PUBLISHERS, New York
Cambridge, Philadelphia, San Francisco, Washington,
London, Mexico City, São Paulo, Singapore, Sydney

BASIC MANAGERIAL FINANCE

Lawrence J. Gitman
Wright State University

Sponsoring Editor: John Greenman
Development Editor: Nat LaMar
Project Editor: David Nickol
Text Design: Barbara Bert/North 7 Atelier
Cover Design: Robert Bull/Design
Text Art: Vantage Art, Inc.
Production: Paula Roppolo
Compositor: Progressive Typographers
Printer and Binder: R. R. Donnelley & Sons Company

BASIC MANAGERIAL FINANCE

Library of Congress Cataloging in Publication Data

Gitman, Lawrence J.
    Basic managerial finance.

    Includes index.
    1. Business enterprises — Finance.   2. Corporations —
Finance. I. Title.
HG4026.G59   1987   658.1'5   86-25666
ISBN 0-06-042366-8

87 88 89   9 8 7 6 5 4 3 2

To John Greenman
Editor Extraordinaire

CONTENTS IN BRIEF

CONTENTS IN DETAIL

12   RISK, RETURN, AND VALUATION   332

13   THE COST OF CAPITAL   379

Part Five
LONG-TERM FINANCIAL DECISIONS   **411**

 CAPITAL BUDGETING AND CASH FLOW PRINCIPLES   413

TO THE INSTRUCTOR

Finance is the important and dynamic field of study concerned with the management of money. *Basic Managerial Finance* has been carefully developed to provide a stimulating first exposure to the basic concepts and practices of managerial finance used by financial managers in the business world. It is intended for use in the first undergraduate managerial finance course at both two-year and four-year schools. It may also be used with good results in introductory MBA finance courses emphasizing broad concepts and practices rather than theories and detailed computations. In addition, the text works well in technical and continuing education courses in finance offered through management development and adult education programs and seminars.

The text's streamlined, straightforward, and easily understandable approach blends a traditional accounting orientation with modern valuation techniques. Numerous examples and illustrations clarify basic concepts, and several pedagogical aids make learning the materials easier and more enjoyable.

Organization

The text's organizational structure was carefully designed to assure a smooth transition from accounting to managerial finance topics. It is structured around the corporate balance sheet, with linkages to share price. Various financial decisions are examined as they relate to the balance sheet, and in terms of their impact on return, risk, and share price. The text contains twenty chapters broken into six parts. It is divided evenly between short-term and long-term aspects of managerial finance. Although the book is intended to be read as a continuum, almost any chapter may be taken out of sequence and studied as a self-contained unit. Since each instructor has particular topic preferences, the book's coverage is intentionally both extensive and flexible.

The first three parts include ten chapters emphasizing the accounting and short-term aspects of managerial finance. Part One covers career opportunities in finance; the role of the financial manager; the operating environment of the firm — *including a description of the key tax and depreciation requirements of the Tax Reform Act of 1986*, which are applied throughout the text—and a review of the key aspects of accounting and cash flow. Part Two presents the basics of financial analysis and planning, and Part Three describes the major areas of short-term (or working capital) decisions. The last three parts include ten chapters concerned with the long-term aspects of managerial finance. After presenting basic long-term financial concepts in Part Four, Part Five describes important long-term financial decisions, including expansion and failure. In Part Six, basic features of primary sources of long-term financing are described.

Appendix A is an optional section concerned with international perspectives. It explores the international ramifications of major short-term and long-term financial decisions presented in the text. The international finance material is included as an appendix for the sake of flexibility. For those instructors wishing to emphasize the international dimensions of managerial finance, this material may be covered toward the end of the course.

Teaching and Learning Aids

All chapters in *Basic Managerial Finance* employ a managerial decision-making perspective. Once each concept has been described, it is related to the financial manager's goal of wealth maximization and is demonstrated in specific situations. In addition, the following teaching and learning devices are incorporated in each chapter.

LEARNING OBJECTIVES Each chapter begins with five action-oriented learning objectives that preview and guide the student's understanding of the material presented.

EXAMPLES Numerous demarked examples are interspersed in each chapter to demonstrate potentially troublesome concepts and practices. The examples are detailed, and quite often the reason for choosing a particular instance or situation is included along with the demonstration.

RUNNING GLOSSARY When new terms are first introduced in the text they appear in bold type and are defined. Additionally, their definitions are given in the running glossary included in the margins of text pages. Each such term is also included in the index, along with the text page number on which it is defined, for easy reference.

BOXED ITEMS Each chapter contains two boxed essays describing real-world events or actual company situations that further demonstrate text concepts, illustrate practices, or describe career opportunities.

BULLETED SUMMARIES   The summary at the end of each chapter appears as a bulleted list of major points for quick review.

END-OF-CHAPTER QUESTIONS AND PROBLEMS   A comprehensive set of questions and problems included at the end of each chapter enables students to test their understanding of chapter content. More than one problem is provided for each concept in order to assure multiple self-testing opportunities and to give instructors a wide choice of assignable material. Where applicable, integrative problems that tie related topics together are included. A short tagline in parentheses at the beginning of each problem identifies the concept that the problem tests.

Special Appendixes

Several special text appendixes facilitate and enrich student learning. They are concerned with international finance, career opportunities, the computer disk keyed to this text, financial tables, calculator use, and selected answers to text problems.

INTERNATIONAL PERSPECTIVES   As noted earlier, Appendix A is actually an optional chapter concerned with the international dimensions of managerial finance. It includes the same basic teaching and learning aids as the text chapters and may be used by those wishing to emphasize international finance materials.

CAREER OPPORTUNITIES   Appendix B includes a summary of career opportunities in managerial finance and in financial services. It profiles eighteen different financial careers: what they are, where to find them, and what they're paying. A review of the appendix should allow students to get a "feel" for various career opportunities.

COMPUTER DISK KEYED TO TEXT   The text's interconnection with *The Basic Managerial Finance (BMF) Disk* — a user-friendly, menu-driven personal computer disk containing ten problem-solving routines (described in detail later) — is flagged by a disk symbol in pertinent text discussions and before appropriate end-of-chapter problems. These passages are identified by the symbol: 🖫. Instructions for using the disk are given in Appendix C.

FINANCIAL TABLES   A complete set of financial tables for percentage rates between 1 and 50 percent is included in Appendix D. In order to more easily find these tables, the outer edge of each of their pages has been darkened. Also included for students' convenience is a removable, laminated present-value table card that may be used in working problems.

CALCULATOR USE Appendix E illustrates procedures for performing routine financial calculations using the most basic four-function calculator. With a little practice, students following these procedures should improve their speed and accuracy in doing financial calculations described in the text.

SELECTED ANSWERS Answers to selected end-of-chapter problems appear in Appendix F. These answers provide "check figures" to help students evaluate their progress toward finding correct problem solutions.

Supplements

A number of ancillary materials have been developed to assist students and instructors using this text.

STUDY GUIDE An important learning aid for the student, *Study Guide to Accompany Basic Managerial Finance*, prepared by Cherie Mazer of Wright State University, contains a variety of features to enhance the student's learning experience. For each text chapter it includes a summary, an outline, a programmed self-test, helpful hints, exercises with detailed solutions, and an equations and techniques summary. Where appropriate, discussions and problems are keyed to *The BMF Disk*.

THE BASIC MANAGERIAL FINANCE (BMF) DISK A computerized supplement for use with the Apple II and the IBM-PC, *The Basic Managerial Finance (BMF) Disk*, has been specifically developed by Frederick Rexroad to accompany this text. All routines are written in BASIC and can be transferred easily to other computers with little or no modification. *The BMF Disk* includes ten short programs, presented in a user-friendly, menu-driven format, for use in solving financial problems. Applicability of the disk throughout the text and study guide is always keyed by a printed disk symbol like that shown above. Each routine on the disk includes page references to the text discussion of the technique being applied. *The BMF Disk* is available free to adopters. A detailed description of the disk and its use is given in Appendix C.

INSTRUCTOR'S MANUAL The *Instructor's Manual*, prepared by Cherie Mazer of Wright State University and me, has been designed to reduce the preparation time and effort required of instructors and provide supplemental teaching materials. Each chapter includes a review of the teaching objectives, an outline of the key concepts covered in the text, a discussion of the text, lecture notes, and comprehensive detailed answers to all end-of-chapter problems. Great care has been taken to ensure the accuracy of all answers and solutions. The lecture notes sections contain some combination of additional teaching or homework exercises, excerpted articles from the financial press relating to the chapter's topics, ideas for projects to assign to students, and a listing of films and videos available for augmenting chapter topics.

COMPUTERIZED TEST BANK A test bank containing 1,000 multiple-choice questions and 100 problems with solutions has been carefully developed by Cherie Mazer of Wright State University and is available free to adopters. The test bank is available in two formats: as a computer software package and as a separate printed test-bank manual. The software package is designed to help the instructor create and customize tests and solution keys. The difficulty level and solution for each question are among the descriptors that enable an instructor to design a customized test. The software is compatible with the Apple II and IBM-PC microcomputers.

TRANSPARENCY ACETATES A pack of over 100 transparency acetates of key exhibits and problem solutions is available free to adopters. The *Instructor's Manual* includes a complete list of the available transparencies.

Acknowledgments

Many people have made significant contributions to the development and production of this book. Without their classroom experience, advice, and professional expertise, I could not have produced this textbook. Especially important has been feedback received on prepublication drafts from students, instructors, and practicing financial managers. If you are moved to write to me about any matters pertaining to this text package, please do. I welcome constructive criticisms and suggestions for improving the book and its adjuncts.

Harper & Row obtained the experienced advice of a large group of excellent reviewers who participated at various stages in the text's development. My special thanks go to the following people who reviewed all or part of the writing plan and various drafts of the manuscript.

Holland Blades (Texas Women's University)
Brian Belt (University of Missouri-Kansas City)
Louis E. Bonanni (Siena Heights College)
Paul J. Corr (Skidmore College)
Maurice P. Corrigan (Post College)
Thomas P. Czubiak (Mercy College of Detroit)

Fred J. Ebeid (Western Illinois University)
Keith Wm. Fairchild (University of Texas-San Antonio)
Alvin Kelly (Livingstone College)
Theodore T. Latz (Lakeland Community College)
John L. Lohret (SUNY-Cobleskill)
Martin I. Lowy (Harrisburg Area Community College)
Clifford D. Mpare (Wingate College)
Dimitrios Pachis (Eastern Connecticut University)
Janice L. Pitera (Broome Community College)
Ralph A. Pope (Illinois State University)
J. J. Quinn (Camden County College)
Abu Selimuddin (Berkshire Community College)
Jean L. Souther (Cape Cod Community College)
Alice Steljes (Illinois Valley Community College)
Bev S. Stevenson (Owens Technical College)
A. M. Tuberose (West Virginia University)
Dean R. Vickstrom (Iowa Western Community College)
John Washecka (Mesa College)

I am especially indebted to Mehdi Salehizadeh of San Diego State University for the outstanding job he did in preparing and revising the chapter on International Perspectives included as Appendix A. Special thanks is due Cherie Mazer of Wright State University for her splendid assistance in preparing Appendix B on Career Opportunities, the *Student Study Guide,* the *Instructor's Manual,* and the *Test Bank.* Her expertise and experience significantly affected the quality and timeliness of each of these items. I also wish to thank Fred Rexroad for developing *The Basic Managerial Finance (BMF) Disk.* Thanks is also due Pieter A. Vandenberg of San Diego State University for preparing and revising the material on calculator use appearing in Appendix E. The assistance of Ronald S. Pretekin of Coolidge, Wall Co., LPA, in developing the discussions of business failure is greatly appreciated. My colleagues, tax experts Russel H. Hereth and John C. Talbott, deserve a special word of thanks for helping me interpret and incorporate the *Tax Reform Act of 1986* into all applicable text discussions. Thanks is also due my colleagues Peter W. Bacon, Nicolas Gressis, Daniel J. Kaufman, Jr., Charles E. Maxwell (now of Hofstra University), and Richard E. Williams for their continuing advice, assistance, and support. Special mention is due Teresa Mayfield for her outstanding efforts in typing the manuscript, running numerous errands, and generally keeping things in order.

The staff of Harper & Row — particularly John Greenman, Lauren S. Bahr, Judy Rothman, and David Nickol — deserve special thanks for their professional expertise, creativity, enthusiasm, and commitment to this text. I am particularly indebted to freelance editor Nat LaMar for his many unique contributions to this book, especially his critical evaluation of both content and presentation, which helped me achieve a new level of clarity and conciseness. An extra word of thanks is due David Nickol for tolerating and accommodating my obsession for perfection.

Finally, my wife, Robin, and our children, Zachary and Jessica, have played most important parts in patiently providing the support and understanding I needed during the writing of this book. To them I will be forever grateful.

Lawrence J. Gitman

TO THE STUDENT

Dear Student,

Twenty years ago I took my first finance course. It was tough! The blending of basic accounting with new and more quantitative financial concepts challenged my classmates and me. Although the text we used was the most popular at that time, it seemed boring and abstract. It presented concepts confusingly and failed to relate them to actual business practice. You may have already had a similar experience in your studies. I hope not.

I wrote this text for you. My objective was to convey the important concepts and practices of managerial finance in an interesting and understandable fashion. As I wrote, I constantly kept in mind the unnecessary difficulty I had in my first finance course. Based on feedback from students and reviewers, I feel that this text meets my objective. If it does, you should find your first exposure to managerial finance an enjoyable educational experience. If it doesn't, I apologize and hope that you will not give up on the study of finance. I didn't! In either case, you will find the *Study Guide to Accompany Basic Managerial Finance* helpful in studying this subject.

I sincerely hope you enjoy learning the basics of managerial finance and earn an "A" in the course. Best of luck!

Sincerely,

Lawrence J. Gitman

CHAPTERS IN THIS PART

THE FINANCIAL MANAGER AND THE FIRM

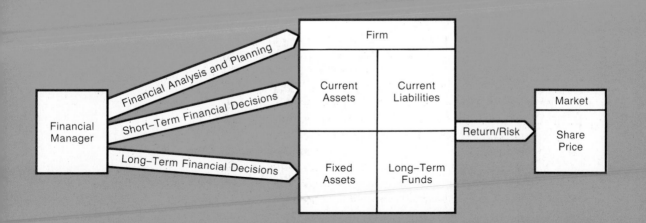

1

THE ROLE
OF THE
FINANCIAL
MANAGER

After studying this chapter, you should be able to:

- Define *finance* and describe its major areas and opportunities.

- Describe the managerial finance function and differentiate managerial finance from the closely related disciplines of economics and accounting.

- Identify the wealth maximization goal of the financial manager and explain why it is preferred over profit maximization.

- Discuss the key activities of the financial manager within the firm.

- Understand the text's approach to the key managerial finance concepts, tools, and techniques.

The financial manager plays an extremely important role in the operation and success of business. All key employees of any business organization, however large or small, should understand the duties and activities of its financial manager. Developing such an understanding begins with some basic questions: What is finance? What career opportunities exist in the field of finance? What is the managerial finance function, and what are the goals and activities of the financial manager? Answering these basic questions sets the stage for discussion of the basic concepts, tools, and techniques of managerial finance.

FINANCE AS AN AREA OF STUDY

The field of finance is broad and dynamic. It directly affects the lives of every person and every organization, financial or nonfinancial, private or public, profit-seeking or not-for-profit. Many areas of finance can therefore be studied, and a large number of career opportunities are available.

What Is Finance?

finance The art and science of managing money.

Finance can be defined as the art and science of managing money. Virtually all individuals and organizations earn or raise money and spend or invest money. Finance is concerned with the processes, institutions, markets, and instruments involved in the transfer of money among and between individuals, businesses, and governments.

Major Areas and Opportunities in Finance

financial services The area of finance concerned with design and delivery of advice and financial products to individuals, business, and government.

The major areas of finance can be summarized by reviewing the career opportunities in finance. These opportunities can, for convenience, be divided into two broad categories: financial services and managerial finance.

FINANCIAL SERVICES **Financial services** is the area of finance concerned with the design and delivery of advice and financial products to individuals, business, and government. It is one of the fastest-growing areas of career opportunity in our economy. Financial services includes banking and related institutions, personal financial planning, investments, and real estate and insurance. Exciting career opportunities available in each of these areas are described briefly in Table 1.1.

managerial finance Concerns the duties of the financial manager in the business firm.

financial manager Actively manages the financial affairs of any type of business, whether financial or nonfinancial, private or public, profit or not-for-profit.

MANAGERIAL FINANCE **Managerial finance** is concerned with the duties of the financial manager in the business firm. **Financial man-**

TABLE 1.1 Career Opportunities in Financial Services

Opportunity	Brief description
Banking and related institutions	Banks, savings and loan associations, mutual savings banks, finance companies, and credit unions all offer challenging career opportunities for those trained in financial services. Because of the many services offered by these institutions, a wide choice of careers is available. Loan officers handle installment, commercial, real estate, and/or consumer loans. Trust officers administer trust funds for estates, foundations, and business firms. Many of these institutions have begun to offer new services in insurance brokerage, real estate, and personal financial planning.
Personal financial planning	Career opportunities for personal financial planners have increased dramatically in recent years, largely due to increasingly complicated tax laws, new investment vehicles, and a relaxed regulatory environment. Financial institutions, brokerage firms, insurance companies, and consulting firms are all interested in hiring individuals who can provide sound advice to consumers regarding the management of their personal financial affairs.
Investments	Careers in investments include working as a securities broker or as a securities analyst in a brokerage firm, insurance company, or other financial institution. Investment specialists are involved in analyzing securities and constructing portfolios that will achieve their clients' objectives. Related opportunities to work in investment banking, which involves developing and marketing security offerings for corporate and government issuers, are also available.
Real estate and insurance	Real estate is a field with varied career opportunities. Careers include real estate broker, appraiser, mortgage banker, and real estate developer. There are also highly rewarding career opportunities for insurance specialists, such as sales agents, statisticians, and underwriters. Insurance companies also need personnel well-trained in finance to help them manage their vast investment portfolios.

agers actively manage the financial affairs of many types of business — financial and nonfinancial, private and public, profit-seeking and not-for-profit organizations. They perform such varied tasks as budgeting, financial forecasting, cash management, credit administration, investment analysis, and funds procurement. In recent years the changing economic and regulatory environment have increased the importance and complexity of the financial manager's duties. As a result many top executives in industry and government have come from the finance area.

The Study of Managerial Finance

An understanding of the concepts, tools, and techniques presented throughout this text will fully acquaint you with the financial manager's activities and decisions. In the process of studying the material presented, you will learn about various career opportunities in managerial finance. For convenience, Appendix B of the text provides a summary of career opportunities in managerial finance as well as financial services. For most students this first exposure to the exciting field of finance provides the foundation and initiative for further study and possibly even a future career.

THE MANAGERIAL FINANCE FUNCTION

Since most business decisions are measured in financial terms, the financial manager plays a key role in the operation of the firm. People in all areas — accounting, manufacturing, marketing, personnel, operations research, and so forth — need a basic understanding of the managerial finance function. To gain this understanding, we will now look at the organizational role of the finance function and its relationship to economics and accounting.

An Organizational View

The size and importance of the managerial finance function depend on the size of the firm. In small firms the finance function is generally performed by the accounting department. As a firm grows, however, the importance of the finance function typically results in the evolution of a separate department linked directly to the company president or chief executive officer (CEO) through a vice-president of finance. Figure 1.1 is an organizational chart showing the structure of the finance activity within a typical medium-to-large-size firm. Reporting to the vice-president of finance are the treasurer and the controller. The **treasurer** is commonly responsible for handling financial activities, such as financial planning and fund raising, managing cash, making capital expenditure decisions, managing credit activities, and managing the investment portfolio. The **controller** typically handles the accounting activities, such as tax management, data processing, and cost and financial accounting. The activities of the treasurer, or financial manager, are the primary concern of this text.

treasurer The officer responsible for the firm's financial activities, such as financial planning and fund raising, managing cash, capital expenditure decisions, managing credit activities, and managing the investment portfolio.

controller The officer responsible for the firm's accounting activities, such as tax management, data processing, and cost and financial accounting.

Relationship to Economics

The field of finance is closely related to economics. Since every business firm operates within the economy, the financial manager must

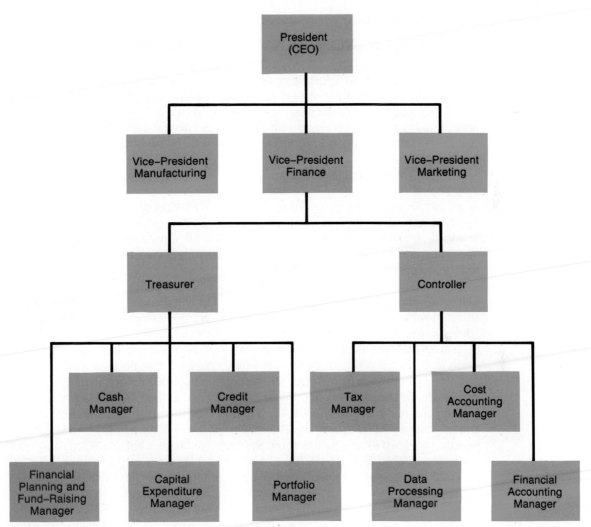

FIGURE 1.1 Organization of the Finance Function
The treasurer and controller typically report to the vice-president of finance. The treasurer commonly handles financial activities and the controller handles accounting activities.

understand the economic framework and must be alert to the consequences of varying levels of economic activity and changes in economic policy. The financial manager must also be able to use economic theories as guidelines for efficient business operation. Examples include supply-and-demand analysis, profit-maximizing strategies, and price theory. The primary economic principle used in managerial finance is **marginal analysis:** financial decisions should be made and

marginal analysis States that financial decisions should be made and actions taken only when added benefits exceed added costs.

PERSONAL FINANCIAL PLANNING: A HOT NEW BUSINESS

Some 200,000 insurance agents, brokers, accountants, bankers and lawyers have flocked into the hot new business of financial planning. . . .

Note that few planners merely plan. For most, it's a sideline to the insurance, brokerage, banking or other businesses. So planners are paid in one of three ways — by commissions on products they sell you, by an hourly or flat fee or by a combination of both.

Anyone can claim to be such a planner. But there are designations showing educational qualifications. The College for Financial Planning confers the certified financial planner (CFP) designation. The American College confers the chartered financial consultant (ChFC) designation. Several universities also offer degrees in financial planning. A person who sells investment advice must register with the Securities and Exchange Commission as a registered investment adviser (RIA) although no courses or tests are required.

The Institute of Certified Financial Planners (ICFP), whose members are CFP's, has educational standards for membership and a code of ethics. The International Association of Financial Planners (IAFP) is a trade association whose members abide by a code of ethics. IAFP recently instituted a registry of planners who meet certain educational and experience requirements. Finally, the National Association of Personal Financial Advisors (NAPFA) is a new group of "fee only" planners. . . .

Fees range from $40 or $50 an hour up to $200 or more, depending on the complexity of the plan. Minimum fees generally run around $400. Mary Malgoire, a fee-only planner in Washington, D.C., says that most clients should have both income and assets of $50,000 to warrant a full-scale plan. David King, a planner in Hays, Kans., says that the least expensive plans, usually made for families with $30,000 to $40,000 combined income, cost from $300 to $400. Complex plans can cost from $1,000 to $10,000 and up — sometimes based on a percentage of the client's income or assets.

Computerized plans are least expensive. Brokerages such as Merrill Lynch sell them for around $250. The Consumer Financial Institute, 288 Walnut Street, Newton, Mass. 02160, offers a computerized plan for $175 and will send a free brochure.

Source: John W. Hazard, "Before Picking Your Financial Planner," *U.S. News & World Report*, November 12, 1984, p. 85.

actions taken only when the added benefits exceed the added costs. A basic knowledge of economics is therefore necessary to understand both the environment and the decision techniques of managerial finance.

Relationship to Accounting

The firm's accounting (controller) and finance (treasurer) activities, as noted in Figure 1.1, are typically within the control of the financial vice-president. These functions are closely related and generally overlap; indeed, managerial accounting and finance are not often easily distinguishable. In small firms the controller often carries out the finance function, and in large firms many accountants are intimately involved in various finance activities. However, there are two basic differences between finance and accounting; one relates to the method of funds recognition and the other to decision making.

METHOD OF FUNDS RECOGNITION   The accountant's primary function is to develop and provide data for measuring the performance of the firm, assessing its financial position, and paying taxes. Using certain standardized and generally accepted principles, he prepares financial statements that recognize revenue at the point of sale and expenses when incurred. This approach is commonly referred to as the **accrual method.**

> **accrual method** Recognizes revenue at the point of sale and recognizes expenses when incurred.

The financial manager, on the other hand, places primary emphasis on *cash flows*, the intake and outgo of cash. He maintains the firm's solvency by analyzing and planning the cash flows necessary to satisfy its obligations and acquire assets needed to achieve the firm's goals. The financial manager uses this **cash method** to recognize the revenues and expenses only with respect to actual inflows or outflows of cash.

> **cash method** Recognizes revenues and expenses only with respect to actual inflows and outflows of cash.

A simple analogy may help to clarify the basic difference in viewpoint between the accountant and the financial manager. If we consider the human body as a business firm in which each pulsation of the heart represents a transaction, the accountant's primary concern is *recording* each of these pulsations as sales revenues, expenses, and profits. The financial manager is primarily concerned with whether the resulting flow of blood through the arteries reaches the cells and keeps the various organs of the whole body functioning. It is possible for a body to have a strong heart but cease to function due to the development of blockages or clots in the circulatory system. Similarly, a firm may be profitable but may still fail due to an insufficient flow of cash to meet its obligations as they come due.

EXAMPLE

Thomas Distributing Company in the calendar year just ended made one sale in the amount of $100,000 for merchandise purchased during the year at a total cost of $80,000. Although the firm paid in full for the merchandise during the year, it has yet to collect at year end the $100,000 from the customer to whom the sale was made. The accrual-based accounting view and the cash-flow-oriented financial view of the firm's performance during the year are given by the following income and cash flow statements, respectively.

Accounting View

**Thomas Distributing
Company
Income Statement
for the Year Ended 12/31**

Sales revenue	$100,000
Less: Expenses	80,000
Net profit	$ 20,000

Financial View

**Thomas Distributing
Company
Cash Flow Statement
for the Year Ended 12/31**

Cash inflow	$ 0
Less: Cash outflow	80,000
Net cash flow	($80,000)

It can be seen that whereas in an accounting sense the firm is quite profitable, it is a financial failure in terms of actual cash flow. The Thomas Distributing Company's lack of cash flow resulted from the uncollected account receivable of $100,000. Without adequate cash inflows to meet its obligations the firm will not survive, regardless of its level of profits. ■

The example above shows that accrual accounting data do not fully describe the circumstances of a firm, and thus the financial manager must look beyond financial statements to obtain insight into developing or existing problems. The financial manager, by concentrating on cash flow, should be able to avoid insolvency and achieve the firm's financial goals. Of course, while accountants are well aware of the importance of cash flows and financial managers use and understand accrual-based financial statements, the primary emphasis of accountants is on accrual methods and the primary emphasis of financial managers is on cash flow methods.

DECISION MAKING We come now to the second major difference between finance and accounting: decision making. Whereas the accountant devotes the majority of his or her attention to the collection and presentation of financial data, the financial manager evaluates the accountant's statements, develops additional data, and makes decisions based on subsequent analyses. The accountant's role is to provide consistently developed and easily interpreted data about the firm's past, present, and future operations. The financial manager uses these data, either in raw form or after making certain adjustments and analyses, as an important input to the decision-making process. Of course, this does not mean that accountants never make decisions or that financial managers never gather data; but the primary focuses of accounting and finance are distinctly different.

GOAL OF THE FINANCIAL MANAGER

In the case of corporations, the owners of a firm are normally distinct from its managers. The goal of the financial managers should be to achieve the objectives of the firm's owners (the stockholders). Presumably, if the managers are successful in this endeavor they will also achieve their own financial and professional objectives.

Some people believe that the owners' objective is always the maximization of profits; others believe it is the maximization of wealth. While a number of arguments can be offered in favor of the wealth maximization goal, the key factor linking profit and wealth maximization is risk. We explain the relationship of profit and risk to wealth maximization in the sections that follow.

Profit Maximization?

To achieve the goal of profit maximization the financial manager takes only those actions that are expected to make a major contribution to the firm's overall profits. Thus for each alternative being considered the financial manager would select the one expected to result in the highest monetary return. For corporations, profits are commonly measured in terms of **earnings per share (EPS),** which represent the total earnings available for the firm's common stockholders—the firm's owners—divided by the number of shares of common stock outstanding.

earnings per share (EPS) The firm's total earnings available to stockholders divided by the number of shares of common stock outstanding.

EXAMPLE

The financial manager of Harper's, Inc., is attempting to choose between two alternative investments, X and Y. Each is expected to provide the following earnings per share over its three-year life.

	EARNINGS PER SHARE (EPS)			
Investment	Year 1	Year 2	Year 3	Total for years 1, 2, and 3
X	$1.40	$1.00	$ .40	$2.80
Y	.60	1.00	1.40	3.00

Based on the profit-maximization goal, investment Y would be preferred over investment X since it results in higher earnings per share over the three-year period ($3.00 EPS for Y is greater than $2.80 EPS for X). ■

Two weaknesses of profit maximization can be highlighted. The first is concerned with the timing of EPS. Because the firm can earn a return on funds it receives, *the receipt of funds sooner as opposed to later is preferred.* In our example, in spite of the fact that the total earnings from investment X are smaller than those from investment Y, X may be preferred due to the greater EPS it provides in the first year. These earlier returns could be reinvested in order to provide greater future earnings.

The second weakness of profit maximization stems from the fact that a firm's earnings do not represent cash flows available to the stockholders. These owners receive realizable returns either through cash dividends paid them at regular intervals or by selling their shares for a higher price than initially paid. A greater EPS does not necessarily mean that dividend payments will increase, since the payment of dividends results solely from the action of the firm's board of directors. Furthermore, a higher EPS does not necessarily translate into a higher stock price. Firms often experience earnings increases without any correspondingly favorable change in stock price.

risk The chance that actual outcomes may differ from those expected.

PROFIT AND RISK Another weakness of profit maximization is its disregard for **risk** — the chance that actual outcomes may differ from those expected. (Wealth maximization, on the other hand, considers risk.) A basic premise in managerial finance is that a trade-off exists between return (profit) and risk. *Return and risk are in fact the key determinants of share price, which at any time represents the wealth of the owner in the firm.* Profit and risk affect share price differently: Higher profit tends to result in a higher price while higher risk tends to result in a lower price since the stockholder must be compensated for the greater risk. In general, stockholders are **risk averse** which means they seek to avoid risk. Where risk is involved, stockholders expect higher returns from investments of higher risk and vice versa.

risk averse The tendency of stockholders to avoid risk.

FINANCIAL OFFICERS IN HIGH DEMAND

The premium on expertise has made it harder for companies and accounting firms to retain their financial whizzes. "The good ones are approached daily," says Roger K. Williams, a recruiter with Williams, Roth & Krueger in Chicago.

Jack M. Greenberg left his job as a partner with Arthur Young & Co. to become executive vice president and chief financial officer of McDonald's Corp. "It was rare that a partner in an accounting firm ever left," says Mr. Greenberg. "I think you're seeing more people doing that over the years."

The demand for financial talent has helped make the chief financial officer the third highest-paid officer at many companies, recruiters say. A 1981 survey by Heidrick & Struggles Inc., a Chicago recruiting firm, found that the average financial chief earned $146,284, plus perquisites such as stock options and extra life insurance. Other headhunters say financial officers earn as much as $350,000 a year.

Financial officers get a greater percentage of their compensation from performance-related bonuses than do most top employees, according to a study by Hewitt Associates, a Chicago consulting firm. The company says short-term rewards can add between 40% and 50% to a financial officer's compensation, and long-term rewards can add another 35% to 40%.

Source: Heywood Klein, "Financial Officers Often in Demand As Companies Seek Cost-Cutters," *The Wall Street Journal,* November 22, 1982, p. 1. Reprinted by permission of *The Wall Street Journal.* © Dow Jones & Company, Inc. 1982. All rights reserved.

Maximizing Shareholder Wealth

The goal of the financial manager is to maximize the wealth of the owners for whom the firm is being managed. The wealth of corporate owners is measured by the share price of the stock, which in turn is based on the timing of returns, cash flows, and, most important, on risk. In considering each decision alternative or possible action in terms of its impact on the share price of the firm's stock, only those actions that are expected to increase share price should be undertaken. Financial managers rely on the two dimensions, return and risk, to link decisions to share price. (Figure 1.2 depicts this process.) Since share price represents the owners' wealth in the firm, share-price maximization is consistent with owner-wealth maximization. Note that while profit (return) is considered in the wealth maximization process, it is not the key decision variable.

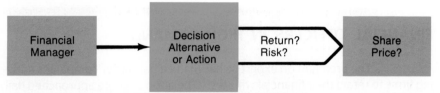

FIGURE 1.2 Financial Decisions and Share Price
The financial manager, when evaluating decision alternatives or potential actions, must consider both return and risk and their expected impact on share price. Actions expected to increase share price should be undertaken.

KEY ACTIVITIES OF THE FINANCIAL MANAGER

The financial manager's activities, all of which are aimed at achieving the goal of owner wealth maximization, can be evaluated in terms of the firm's basic financial statements. His or her primary activities are (1) financial analysis and planning; (2) managing the firm's assets; and (3) managing the firm's liabilities and equity. Figure 1.3 relates each of these financial activities to the firm's **balance sheet,** which shows the firm's financial position at a given point in time.

balance sheet Record that shows the firm's financial position at a given point in time.

Financial Analysis and Planning

Financial analysis and planning is concerned with 1) transforming financial data into a form that can be used to monitor the firm's financial condition; 2) evaluating the need for increased productive capacity; and 3) determining what additional financing is required. These func-

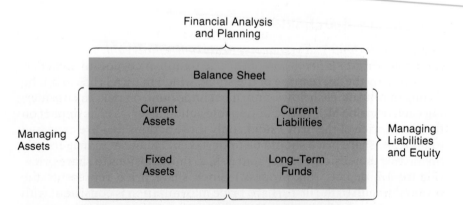

FIGURE 1.3 Key Activities of the Financial Manager
The financial manager's key activities—(1) financial analysis and planning; (2) managing assets; and (3) managing liabilities and equity—can be related to the firm's balance sheet.

tions encompass the entire balance sheet as well as the firm's income statement and other financial statements.

Managing the Firm's Assets

The financial manager determines both the mix and the type of assets found on the firm's balance sheet. This activity is concerned with the left-hand side of the balance sheet. *Mix* refers to the number of dollars of current and fixed assets. Once the mix is determined, the financial manager must establish and attempt to maintain certain optimal levels of each type of current asset. He or she must also decide which are the best fixed assets to acquire and know when existing fixed assets need to be modified or replaced.

Managing the Firm's Liabilities and Equity

This activity deals with the right-hand side of the firm's balance sheet and involves two major decisions. First, the most appropriate *mix* of short-term and long-term financing must be determined. This decision is important because it affects the firm's profitability and overall liquidity. A second and equally important concern is which individual short-term or long-term sources of financing are best at a given point in time. Many of these decisions are dictated by necessity, but some require an in-depth analysis of the available alternatives, their costs, and their long-run implications.

AN OVERVIEW OF THE TEXT

The text's organization is structured around the corporate balance sheet, with linkages to share price. The activities of the financial manager in the areas of financial analysis and planning, short-term financial decisions, and long-term financial decisions are presented in relation to the firm's balance sheet, with primary attention given to the return/risk tradeoffs involved and their potential impact on share price. This framework is depicted in Figure 1.4.

Keyed to various parts of the text is *The Basic Managerial Finance (BMF) Disk,* a menu-driven computer disk compatible with most personal computers that can be used as an aid in performing many of the routine financial calculations and procedures presented. Appendix C describes this decision aid, which for convenience is keyed to text discussions and end-of-chapter problems that can be solved with it.

These sections are clearly marked with a disk symbol:

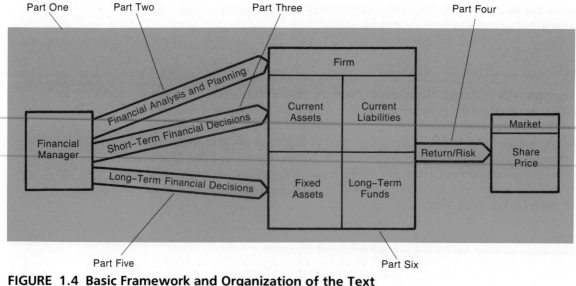

FIGURE 1.4 Basic Framework and Organization of the Text
This text is organized around the balance sheet, which is linked to share price via the return/risk mechanism. Each of the six parts of the text can be keyed to this model.

A brief description of each of the text's six parts is given below. These descriptions are keyed to Figure 1.4, which relates each part of the text to the share-price-oriented decision framework.

Part One: The Financial Manager and the Firm

Part One sets the stage for subsequent discussion of the managerial finance function. The present chapter discusses finance as an area of study, describes the managerial finance function, and examines the goal and key activities of the financial manager. Chapter 2 describes the operating environment of the firm. Chapter 3 reviews corporate financial statements and discusses depreciation and cash flow.

Part Two: Financial Analysis and Planning

Part Two describes the basic tools of financial analysis and planning. Chapter 4 emphasizes the use of financial ratios to analyze financial statements. Chapter 5 describes the use of breakeven analysis and the important leverage concepts. In Chapter 6 we discuss the use of cash budgets and pro forma statements in short-term financial planning.

Part Three: Short-Term Financial Decisions

Part Three, Chapters 7 through 10, is devoted to the management of the firm's current accounts (working capital management). The focus is on the management of the firm's key current assets (cash, marketable securities, accounts receivable, and inventory) and current liabilities (both unsecured and secured sources of short-term financing). The relationship between current assets and current liabilities is discussed along with strategies for their efficient management.

Part Four: Basic Long-Term Financial Concepts

Part Four presents the basic long-term financial concepts underlying the principles and practices of going concerns. Chapter 11 introduces the time value of money. In Chapter 12 the concepts of risk and return are developed and linked to bond and stock valuation. Chapter 13 describes the important concept of cost of capital.

Part Five: Long-Term Financial Decisions

Part Five considers the major long-term decisions confronting most firms. Chapter 14 presents the basic principles of capital budgeting — long-term investment decisions — and cash flows. Chapter 15 continues the discussion of capital budgeting by describing the key decision techniques available in both certain and risky situations. Chapter 16 discusses capital structure — the mix of long-term financing — and dividend policy. In Chapter 17 expansion through business combination and the alternatives available to the failed firm are briefly discussed.

Part Six: Sources of Long-Term Financing

Part Six describes the major sources of long-term financing. Chapters 18 through 20 discuss the cost, availability, inherent characteristics, and pros and cons of each of the following: long-term debt and leasing, preferred and common stock, and convertibles, warrants, and options.

SUMMARY

- Finance, which is the art and science of managing money, affects the lives of every person and every organization.
- Major opportunities in finance exist in financial services — banking and related institutions, personal financial planning, investments, and real estate and insurance — and in managerial finance, which is concerned with the duties of the financial manager in the business firm.
- In large firms the managerial finance function might be handled by a separate department headed by the vice-president of finance, to whom both the treasurer and controller report; in small firms the finance function is generally performed by the accounting department.

● The financial manager must have a knowledge of both economics and accounting. The accountant devotes primary attention to the accrual method and gathering and presenting data; the financial manager concentrates on cash flow methods and decision making.

● The goal of the financial manager is to maximize the owner's wealth (dependent on stock price) rather than profits. Profit maximization ignores the timing of profit, does not consider cash flows to owners, and, most importantly, ignores risk.

● Return and risk are the key determinants of share price. Both must be assessed by the financial manager when evaluating decision alternatives or actions.

● The three key activities of the financial manager are (1) financial analysis and planning, (2) managing the firm's assets, and (3) managing the firm's liabilities and equity.

● The text is divided into six major parts. Its organization uses a simple balance sheet structure to link the firm's activities to its share price.

QUESTIONS

1-1 What is *finance?* Explain how this field affects the lives of everyone and every organization.

1-2 What is the *financial services* area of finance? Briefly describe each of the following areas of career opportunity:
a Banking and related institutions
b Personal financial planning
c Investments
d Real estate and insurance

1-3 Describe the field of *managerial finance.* Compare and contrast this field with financial services.

1-4 How does the finance function evolve within the business firm? What financial activities does the financial manager perform in the mature firm?

1-5 Describe the close relationship between finance and economics, and explain why the financial manager should possess a basic knowledge of economics.

1-6 What are the major differences between accounting and finance with respect to:
a The method of funds recognition?
b Decision making?

1-7 What is the goal of the financial manager? Discuss how one measures achievement of this goal.

1-8 Briefly describe three basic reasons why profit maximization is not consistent with wealth maximization.

1-9 What is *risk?* Why must risk as well as return be considered by the financial manager when evaluating a decision alternative or action?

1-10 What are the three key activities of the financial manager? Relate them to the firm's balance sheet.

2

THE OPERATING ENVIRONMENT OF THE FIRM

After studying this chapter, you should be able to:

- Identify the key participants in financial transactions, and identify the basic activities and changing role of the major financial institutions.

- Understand the relationship between institutions and markets, and the basic function and operation of the money market, capital markets, and major securities exchanges.

- Discuss the fundamentals of interest rates and required returns—their role, the term structure, and risk and rates of return.

- Describe the basic forms of business organization and their respective strengths and weaknesses.

- Understand the fundamentals of corporate taxation of ordinary income and capital gains. Understand the role of S corporations.

A firm operates not as an isolated entity but in a close and dynamic interrelationship with various financial intermediaries, markets, and the government. Financial institutions, financial markets, interest rates and required returns, legal forms of business organization, and corporate taxation are all key aspects of the firm's *operating environment*. In this chapter we will study these important aspects in order to understand how they both limit and create opportunities for the financial manager.

FINANCIAL INSTITUTIONS

financial institution An intermediary that channels the savings of individuals, businesses, and governments into loans or investments.

Financial institutions are intermediaries that channel the savings of individuals, businesses, and governments into loans or investments. Many financial institutions directly or indirectly pay savers interest on deposited funds; others provide services for which they charge depositors (for example, the service charges levied on checking accounts). Some financial institutions accept savings and lend this money to their customers, while others invest customers' savings in earning assets such as real estate or stocks and bonds, and still others both lend money and invest savings. Financial institutions are required by the government to operate within established regulatory guidelines.

Key Participants in Financial Transactions

The key suppliers and demanders of funds are individuals, businesses, and governments. The savings of individual consumers placed in certain financial institutions provide these institutions with a large portion of their funds. Individuals act not only as suppliers of funds to financial institutions but also demand funds from them in the form of loans. However, the important point here is that individuals as a group are the *net suppliers* for financial institutions: They save more money than they borrow.

Business firms also deposit some of their funds in financial institutions, primarily in checking accounts with various commercial banks. And firms, like individuals, also borrow funds from these institutions. As a group business firms, unlike individuals, are *net demanders* of funds: They borrow more money than they save.

Governments maintain deposits of temporarily idle funds, certain tax payments, and social security payments in commercial banks. They do not borrow funds directly from financial institutions, although by selling their securities to various institutions governments indirectly borrow from them. The government, like business firms, is typically a *net demander* of money: It borrows more than it saves.

Major Financial Institutions

The major financial institutions in the U.S. economy are commercial banks, mutual savings banks, savings and loans, credit unions, life insurance companies, pension funds, and mutual funds. These institutions attract funds from individuals, business, and government, combine them, and perform certain services to make attractive loans available to individuals and businesses. They may also make some of these funds available to fulfill various government demands. Table 2.1 provides brief descriptions of the major financial institutions.

Changing Role of Financial Institutions

Passage of the **Depository Institutions Deregulation and Monetary Control Act of 1980 (DIDMCA)** signaled the beginning of the "financial services revolution" that continues to change the nature of financial institutions. By eliminating interest-rate ceilings on most accounts and permitting certain institutions to offer new types of accounts and services, the DIDMCA intensified competition and blurred traditional distinctions among these institutions. What is evolving is the **financial supermarket,** at which a customer can obtain a full array of financial services, such as checking, deposits, brokerage, insurance, and estate planning. The emergence of the financial supermarket is evidenced, for instance, by Sears, Roebuck and Company's "Sears Financial Network." In addition to its credit and insurance (Allstate) and home mortgage (Sears Mortgage) operations, Sears now owns a national real estate brokerage firm (Coldwell Banker), a major stock brokerage firm (Dean Witter), and a West Coast savings and loan (Allstate Savings and Loan). It offers all these financial services in a growing number of "Financial Networks" housed within its retail stores.

> **Depository Institutions Deregulation and Monetary Control Act of 1980 (DIDMCA)** Signaled the beginning of the "financial services revolution" by eliminating interest-rate ceilings on most accounts, permitting certain institutions to offer new types of accounts and services, such as checking, deposits, brokerage, insurance, and estate planning.

> **financial supermarket** An institution at which the customer can obtain a full array of the financial services now allowed under DIDMCA.

FINANCIAL MARKETS

Financial markets provide a forum in which suppliers of funds and demanders of loans and investments can transact business directly. Whereas the loans and investments of institutions are made without the direct knowledge of the suppliers of funds (savers), suppliers in the financial markets know where their funds are being lent or invested.

> **financial markets** Provide a forum in which suppliers of funds and demanders of loans and investments can transact business directly.

The Relationship Between Institutions and Markets

It is quite common to find financial institutions actively participating in the money market and the capital market as both suppliers and de-

TABLE 2.1 Major Financial Institutions

Institution	Brief description
Commercial bank	Accepts both demand (checking) and time (savings) deposits and also offers negotiable order of withdrawal (NOW) accounts, which are interest-earning savings accounts against which checks can be written. In addition, currently offers money market and "super" NOW accounts, which pay interest at rates competitive with other short-term investment vehicles. Makes loans directly to borrowers or through the financial markets.
Mutual savings bank	Similar to commercial banks except that it may not hold demand (checking) deposits. Obtains funds from savings, NOW, and money market account deposits. Generally lends or invests funds through financial markets, although some residential real estate loans are made to individuals. Located primarily in New York, New Jersey, and the New England states.
Savings and loan	Similar to mutual savings banks in that it holds savings deposits, NOW accounts, and money market accounts. Also raises capital through the sale of securities in the financial markets. Lends funds primarily to individuals and businesses for real estate mortgage loans. Some funds are channeled into investments in the financial markets.
Credit union	A financial intermediary that deals primarily in transfer of funds between consumers. Membership is generally based on some common bond, such as working for a given employer. Accepts members' savings deposits, NOW account deposits, and money market accounts and lends the majority of these funds to other members, typically to finance automobile or appliance purchases or home improvements.
Life insurance company	The largest type of financial intermediary handling individual savings. Receives premium payments that are placed in loans or investments to accumulate funds to cover future benefit payments. Funds are lent to individuals, businesses, and government or channeled through the financial markets to those who demand them.
Pension fund	Set up so that employees of various corporations or government units can receive income after retirement. Often employers match the contributions of their employees. Money is sometimes transferred directly to borrowers, but the majority is lent or invested via the financial markets.
Mutual fund	A type of financial intermediary that pools funds of savers and makes them available to business and government demanders. Obtains funds through sale of shares and uses proceeds to acquire bonds and stocks issued by various business and governmental units. Creates a diversified and professionally managed portfolio of securities to achieve a specified investment objective, such as liquidity with a high return. Hundreds of funds, with a variety of investment objectives, exist. Money market funds, which provide competitive returns with very high liquidity, are currently quite popular.

manders of funds. Because of the importance to the firm of these two key financial markets—the money market and the capital market—the next two sections of this chapter are devoted to these topics.

The Money Market

The **money market** is created by a financial relationship between suppliers and demanders of *short-term funds*, which have maturities of one year or less. The money market is not an actual organization housed in some central location, such as a stock market, although the majority of money market transactions culminate in New York City. Most money market transactions are made in **marketable securities,** which are short-term debt instruments, such as U.S. Treasury bills, commercial paper, and negotiable certificates of deposit issued by government, business, and financial institutions, respectively. (Marketable securities are described in Chapter 8.)

The money market exists because certain individuals, businesses, governments, and financial institutions have temporarily idle funds that they wish to place in some type of liquid asset or short-term, interest-earning instrument. At the same time, other individuals, businesses, governments, and financial institutions find themselves in need of seasonal or temporary financing. The money market thus brings together these suppliers and demanders of short-term liquid funds. Figure 2.1 depicts the general flow of funds through and between financial institutions and financial markets; private placement transactions are also shown.

The Capital Market

The **capital market** is a financial relationship created by a number of institutions and arrangements that allows the suppliers and demanders of *long-term funds*—funds with maturities of more than one year—to make transactions. Included among long-term funds are securities issues of business and government. The backbone of the capital market is formed by the various securities exchanges that provide a forum for debt and equity transactions. The smooth functioning of the capital market, which is enhanced through the activities of *investment bankers,* is important to the long-run growth of business.

KEY SECURITIES   Major securities traded in the capital market include bonds (long-term debt) and both common and preferred stock (equity, or ownership). **Bonds** are long-term debt instruments used by business and government to raise large sums of money, generally from a diverse group of lenders. *Corporate bonds* typically pay interest *semiannually*

---

money market
A financial relationship between suppliers and demanders of *short-term funds.*

marketable securities
Short-term debt instruments, such as U.S. Treasury bills, commercial paper, and negotiable certificates of deposit issued by government, business, and financial institutions.

capital market
A financial relationship created by institutions and arrangements that allows suppliers and demanders of *long-term funds* to make transactions.

bond Long-term debt instrument used by businesses and government to raise large sums of money, generally from a diverse group of lenders.

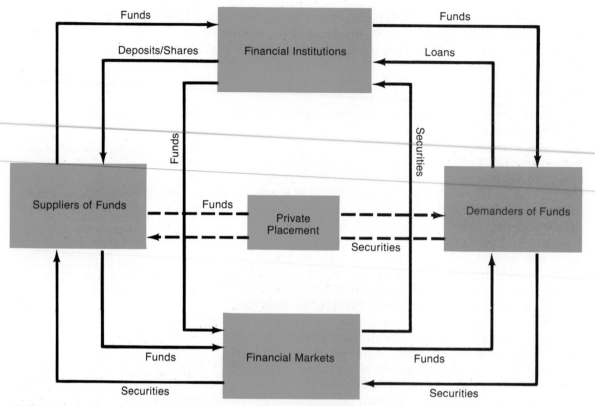

FIGURE 2.1 Flow of Funds for Financial Institutions and Markets
Financial institutions and financial markets as well as private placements are the mechanisms used to transfer funds between individual, business, and government suppliers and demanders. These mechanisms allow savings to be converted into investment.

(every six months), have an initial *maturity* of from 10 to 30 years, and have a *par*, or *face*, *value* of $1,000 that must be repaid at maturity. Bonds are described in detail in Chapter 18.

EXAMPLE

Lakeview Manufacturing has just issued a 12 percent, 20-year bond with a $1,000 par value that pays interest semiannually. Investors who buy this bond receive the contractual right to (1) $120 annual interest (12 percent × $1,000 par value) distributed as $60 (½ × $120) at the end of each six months for 20 years and (2) the $1,000 par value at the end of year 20. ■

common stock Collectively, units of ownership interest, or equity, in a corporation.

Shares of **common stock** are units of ownership interest, or equity, in a corporation. Common stockholders expect to earn a return by receiving **dividends** — periodic distributions of earnings — or by realizing gains through increases in share price. **Preferred stock** is a special form of ownership that has features of both a bond and common stock. Preferred stockholders are promised a fixed periodic dividend that must be paid prior to payment of any dividends to the owners of common stock. In other words, preferred stock has "preference" over common stock. Preferred and common stock are described in detail in Chapter 19.

dividends Periodic distributions of earnings to the owners of stock in a firm.

preferred stock A special form of stock having a fixed periodic dividend that must be paid prior to payment of any common stock dividends.

THE ROLE OF THE INVESTMENT BANKER In order to raise money in the capital market, firms can make either private placements or public offerings. **Private placement** involves the direct sale of a new security issue, typically debt or preferred stock, to an investor or group of investors, such as an insurance company or pension fund. However, most firms raise money through a **public offering** of securities; this takes the form of a nonexclusive issue of either bonds or stock. In making a securities offering, whether public or private, most firms hire an **investment banker** to find buyers for new security issues.

The term *investment banker* is somewhat misleading, because an investment banker is neither an investor nor a banker; furthermore, he or she neither makes long-term investments nor guards the savings of others. Instead, acting as a *broker* between the issuer and the buyer of new security issues, the investment banker purchases securities from corporations and governments and sells them to the public. Investment bankers, in addition to bearing the risk of selling a security issue, advise clients. In the United States, for example, Salomon Brothers and Merrill Lynch Capital Markets are two of the largest investment banking firms.

private placement The direct sale of a new security issue, typically debt or preferred stock, to a selected investor or group of investors.

public offering A nonexclusive issue to the general public of either bonds or stock by a firm in order to raise funds.

investment banker A financial institution engaged by a firm to solicit purchasers for new security issues.

Major Securities Exchanges

As we noted earlier, **securities exchanges** provide the marketplace in which firms can raise funds through the sale of new securities and purchasers of securities can maintain liquidity by being able to easily resell them when necessary. Many people call securities exchanges "stock markets," but this label is somewhat misleading because bonds, common stock, preferred stock, and a variety of other investment vehicles are all traded on these exchanges. The two key types of securities exchange are the organized exchange and the over-the-counter exchange.

securities exchanges Provide the marketplace in which firms raise funds through the sale of new securities and in which purchasers can resell securities.

ORGANIZED SECURITIES EXCHANGES **Organized securities exchanges** are tangible organizations on whose premises outstanding securities are resold. Organized exchanges account for over 72 percent of *total* shares traded. The dominant organized exchanges are the New York

organized securities exchanges Tangible organizations on whose premises outstanding securities are resold.

THE FINANCIAL MANAGER AND THE FIRM

INVESTMENT BANKING: SHARP, CREATIVE, FLEXIBLE PEOPLE NEEDED

Investment banking used to be a business where clients were loyal, the markets were predictable and the skills required to make it as a fat cat on Wall Street were minimal. Nowadays the financial rewards are still alluring, but stock and bond issues and corporate takeovers take place in an arena that pits one investment banking firm against another as never before. And the successful deal-makers are men and women who must possess the creativity of an artist, the fortitude of an athlete and the timing of a trader.

In recruiting new investment bankers out of colleges and business schools, in fact, the big banks and brokerage firms look much more closely at candidates who combine those aptitudes rather than ones who have simply mastered their courses in business and finance and can make pleasant conversation. Indeed, they are looking more and more for candidates whose strong suits are flexibility and a sharp mind but who might not have any financial background.

For those who can fill the bill, however, investment banking is among the highest-paying professions. Starting salaries of $50,000 a year with a likely bonus of $10,000 are commonplace for recruits with a master of business administration degree and little or no work experience to their credit.

Demand is also strong for those with only undergraduate degrees, whose starting salaries are in the $30,000 range, and for graduates of business schools. That is because, in addition to heightened competition among Wall Street firms in take-overs and in the underwriting of securities, many large commercial banks are getting into the business of mergers and acquisitions, private placements and international bond deals, and their demand for people to staff these departments is soaring. "All the big banks are trying to become players in the capital-markets area," said Kevin Sullivan, senior vice president of Warren Management Consultants, a New York executive-recruiting firm. "It is causing the supply/demand ratios to go through the roof, both for new people and for seasoned Wall Streeters."

Source: Fred R. Bleakley, "Newer Ingredients Sought for Investment Bankers," *New York Times 1986 National Employment Report,* October 13, 1985, p. 18. Copyright © 1985 by The New York Times Company. Reprinted by permission.

Stock Exchange (NYSE) and the American Stock Exchange (AMEX), both headquartered in New York City. There are also regional exchanges, such as the Midwest Stock Exchange and the Pacific Stock Exchange.

Most exchanges are modeled after the New York Stock Exchange, which accounts for over 80 percent of the shares traded on organized exchanges. To make transactions on the "floor" of the New York Stock

Exchange an individual or firm must own a "seat" on the exchange. There are a total of 1366 seats on the NYSE, most of which are owned by brokerage firms. In order to be listed for trading on an organized stock exchange, a firm must file an application for listing and meet a number of requirements. Trading is carried out on the floor of the exchange through an *auction process*. The goal of trading is to fill *buy orders* (orders to purchase securities) at the lowest price and to fill *sell orders* (orders to sell securities) at the highest price, thereby giving both purchasers and sellers the best possible deal. Information on the trading of securities is reported in various media, including financial publications such as *The Wall Street Journal*.

THE OVER-THE-COUNTER EXCHANGE   The **over-the-counter (OTC) exchange** is not an organization but an intangible market for the purchasers and sellers of securities not listed by the organized exchanges. Active traders in this market are linked by a sophisticated telecommunications network. The prices at which securities are traded "over the counter" are determined by competitive bids and negotiation. The OTC, in addition to creating a resale market for outstanding securities, is the market in which new public issues are sold. The OTC accounts for nearly 28 percent of *total* shares traded.

INTEREST RATES AND REQUIRED RETURNS

Financial institutions and markets create the mechanism through which funds flow between savers (suppliers) and investors (demanders). When funds are lent, the cost of borrowing the funds is the **interest rate.** When funds are invested to obtain an ownership, or equity, interest—as in stock purchases—the cost to the demander is commonly called the **required return.** In both cases the supplier is compensated for providing either debt or equity funds. Generally, the lower the interest rate or required return, the greater the flow of funds, and therefore the greater the economic growth and vice versa.

The Term Structure of Interest Rates

For any class of similar-risk securities, the **term structure of interest rates** relates the interest rate or rate of return to the time to maturity. At any point in time, the relationship between the rate of return or **yield** —the annual rate of interest earned on a security if purchased on a given day and held to maturity—and the remaining time to maturity can be represented by a **yield curve.** In other words, the yield curve is a graphic depiction of the term structure of interest rates.

Figure 2.2 depicts two yield curves for all U.S. Treasury securities,

over-the-counter (OTC) exchange Not an organization, but an intangible market for the purchasers and sellers of securities not listed by the organized exchanges.

interest rate When funds are lent, the cost of borrowing funds.

required return The cost paid by the demander of funds to the owner of an equity interest, such as stock, in the firm.

term structure of interest rates Relates the interest rate or rate of return on similar-risk securities to the time to their maturity.

yield The annual rate of interest earned on a security if purchased on a given day and held to maturity.

yield curve A graph depicting the term structure of interest or return rates for similar-risk securities. (It shows the relationship between the rates and time to maturity.)

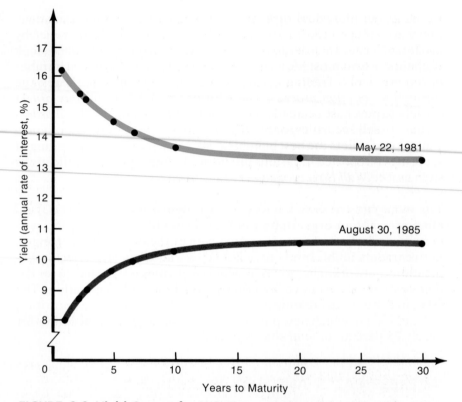

**FIGURE 2.2 Yield Curves for U.S. Treasury Securities, May 22, 1981,
and August 30, 1985**

The May 22, 1981, yield curve was downward-sloping reflecting an expected
long-run decline in interest rates, while on August 30, 1985, the upward-sloping
yield curve reflected an expected increase in interest rates.
Source: Data from *Federal Reserve Bulletin*, June 1981, p. A25, and November 1985, p. A24.

one at May 22, 1981, and the other at August 30, 1985. On May 22, 1981,
the yield curve was *downward-sloping*, reflecting expected lower future
interest rates. On August 30, 1985, the yield curve was *upward-sloping*,
reflecting the expectation of higher future rates due primarily to the
looming record budget deficit. Occasionally the yield curve is flat, indicating a stable expectation.

Risk and Rates of Return[1]

A positive relationship exists between risk and return. After assessing
the risk embodied in a given security, an investor would tend to pur-

[1] Detailed discussions of risk and return and their linkage to value are included in Chapter 12.

chase that security if it is expected to provide a return commensurate with the risk involved. Furthermore, the actual return earned on the security will affect subsequent actions—whether to sell, hold, or buy additional quantities of the same. In addition, most investors look to certain types of securities to provide a certain range of risk-return behaviors.

ACTUAL AND EXPECTED RETURN The **actual return** on an investment, like interest rates and other financial costs, is measured as a percentage return on the initial price or amount invested. Equation 2.1 presents the basic expression for calculating actual return.

$$\text{Return} = \frac{\text{ending value} - \text{initial value} + \text{cash distributions}}{\text{initial value}} \quad (2.1)$$

actual return The percentage return on the initial price or amount of an investment.

Basically the equation expresses the sum of the change in value and any cash distributions as a percentage of the initial value. This method of calculating investment return is commonly applied over annual periods or expressed as an annual rate of return.[2]

EXAMPLE

Janet Holmes purchased 20 shares of Armadillo, Inc., common stock for $37.00 per share one year ago. During the year she received cash dividends on the stock of $3.00 per share. This stock is currently selling for $41.50 per share. To find the rate of return earned by Janet, we first need to calculate the initial and ending value as well as the amount of cash distributions.

$$
\begin{aligned}
\text{Initial value} &= \$37.00 \times 20 \text{ shares} = \$740 \\
\text{Ending value} &= \$41.50 \times 20 \text{ shares} = \$830 \\
\text{Cash distributions} &= \$\ 3.00 \times 20 \text{ shares} = \$\ 60
\end{aligned}
$$

Substituting these values into Equation 2.1 yields:

$$\text{Return} = \frac{\$830 - \$740 + \$60}{\$740} = \frac{\$150}{\$740} = \underline{\underline{20.3\%}}$$

Over the one-year holding period, Janet earned a 20.3 percent rate of return. ■

The return calculated using Equation 2.1 is typically an actual rather than an expected return. When estimating **expected return,** the decision maker must forecast the ending value and cash distribution, thus introducing an element of risk or uncertainty as to the real outcome.

expected return The sum of the change in an investment's value and any cash distributions expressed as a percentage of the initial value.

[2] The measurement of return over longer periods of time using present value techniques is presented in Chapters 13 and 15. For now this single time period measure is assumed.

THE BASIC TRADE-OFF A *risk-return trade-off* exists such that investors must be compensated for accepting greater risk with the expectation of greater expected returns. Figure 2.3 illustrates the typical relationship between risk and return for several popular securities. Clearly, higher returns (costs to the issuer) are expected with greater risk. Financial managers must attempt to keep revenues up and costs down, but they must also consider the risks associated with each investment and financing alternative. Decisions will ultimately rest on an analysis of the impact of risk and return on share price.

LEGAL FORMS OF BUSINESS ORGANIZATION

The three basic legal forms of business organization are the *sole proprietorship*, the *partnership*, and the *corporation*. The sole proprietorship is the most common form of organization; however, the corporation is by far the dominant form with respect to receipts and net profits. Corporations are given primary emphasis in this text.

Sole Proprietorships

sole proprietorship
A business owned by one person and operated for profit.

A **sole proprietorship** is a business owned by one person who operates it for his or her own profit. About 75 percent of all business firms are sole proprietorships. The typical sole proprietorship is a small firm, such as a neighborhood grocery, auto-repair shop, or shoe-repair business. Typically the proprietor, along with a few employees, operates the

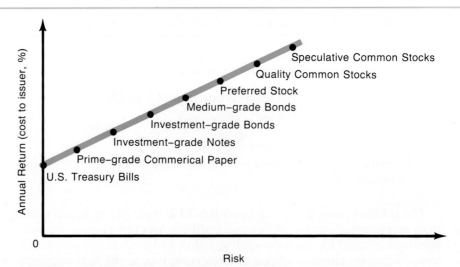

FIGURE 2.3 Risk-Return Profile for Popular Securities
The greater the risk of a given security, the higher the expected return (cost to the issuer). Low-risk securities include U.S. Treasury bills and prime-grade commercial paper, while high-risk securities include all types of common stocks.

proprietorship. He or she normally raises capital from personal resources or by borrowing and is responsible for all business decisions. The sole proprietor has **unlimited liability,** which means that his total wealth, not merely the amount originally invested, can be taken to satisfy creditors. The majority of sole proprietorships are found in the wholesale, retail, service, and construction industries. The key strengths and weaknesses of sole proprietorships are summarized in Table 2.2.

unlimited liability The condition imposed by a sole proprietorship (or general partnership) allowing the owner's total wealth to be taken to satisfy creditors.

TABLE 2.2 Strengths and Weaknesses of Legal Forms of Business Organization

	LEGAL FORM		
	Sole proprietorship	**Partnership**	**Corporation**
Strengths	• Owner receives all profits as well as losses • Low organizational costs • Income taxed as personal income of proprietor • Secrecy • Ease of dissolution	• Can raise more funds than sole proprietorships • Borrowing power enhanced by more owners • More available brain power and managerial skill • Can retain good employees • Income taxed as personal income of partners	• Owners have *limited liability,* which guarantees they cannot lose more than invested • Can achieve large size due to marketability of shares • Ownership is readily transferable • Long life of firm—not dissolved by death of owners • Can hire professional managers • Can expand more easily due to access to capital markets • Receives certain tax advantages
Weaknesses	• Owner has *unlimited liability* —total wealth can be taken to satisfy debts • Limited fund-raising power tends to inhibit growth • Proprietor must be jack-of-all-trades • Difficult to give employees long-run career opportunities • Lacks continuity when proprietor dies	• Owners have *unlimited liability* and may have to cover debts of other less financially sound partners • When a partner dies, partnership is dissolved • Difficult to liquidate or transfer partnership • Difficult to achieve large-scale operations	• Taxes generally higher since corporate income is taxed and dividends paid to owners are again taxed • More expensive to organize than other business forms • Subject to greater government regulation • Employees often lack personal interest in firm • Lacks secrecy since stockholders must receive financial reports

Partnerships

partnership A business owned by two or more persons and operated for profit.

A **partnership** consists of two or more owners doing business together for profit. Partnerships, which account for about 9 percent of all businesses, are typically larger than sole proprietorships. Finance, insurance, and real estate firms are the most common types of partnership. Public accounting and stock brokerage partnerships often have large numbers of partners.

articles of partnership The written contract used to formally establish a business partnership.

Most partnerships are established by a written contract known as the **articles of partnership.** In a *general* (or *regular*) *partnership,* all the partners have unlimited liability. In a **limited partnership,** one or more partners can be designated as having limited liability as long as at least *one* partner has unlimited liability. A **limited partner** is normally prohibited from being active in the management of the firm. Commonly cited strengths and weaknesses of partnerships are summarized in Table 2.2

limited partnership Business relationship in which one or more partners can be assigned to have limited liability but in which one partner must assume unlimited liability.

limited partner A partner having limited liability and normally prohibited from active management participation in the firm.

Corporations

corporation An intangible business entity created by law (often called a "legal entity").

A **corporation** is an artificial being created by law. Often called a "legal entity," a corporation has the powers of an individual in that it can sue and be sued, make and be party to contracts, and acquire property in its own name. Although only 16 percent of all businesses are incorporated, the corporation is the dominant form of business organization. It accounts for 88 percent of business receipts and 78 percent of net profits. Since corporations employ millions of people and have many thousands of shareholders, their activities affect the lives of everyone. Although corporations are involved in all types of business, manufacturing corporations account for the largest portion of corporate business receipts and net profits. The key strengths and weaknesses of corporations are summarized in Table 2.2.

stockholders The true owners of the firm by virtue of their equity in the form of common and/or preferred stock.

board of directors Group elected by the firm's stockholders and having ultimate authority to guide corporate affairs and make general policy.

president or chief executive officer (CEO) Corporate official responsible for managing the firm's day-to-day operations and executing the policies established by the board of directors.

The major parties in a corporation are the stockholders, the board of directors, and the president. Figure 2.4 depicts the relationship among these parties. The **stockholders** are the true owners of the firm by virtue of their equity in common and preferred stock. They vote periodically to elect the members of the board of directors and to amend the firm's corporate charter. The **board of directors** has the ultimate authority in guiding corporate affairs and in making general policy. The directors include key corporate personel as well as outside individuals who typically are successful business persons and executives of other major organizations. Outside directors for major corporations are typically paid an annual fee of between $5,000 and $20,000. The **president** or **chief executive officer (CEO)** is responsible for managing day-to-day operations and carrying out the policies established by the board. He or she is required to report periodically to the firm's directors.

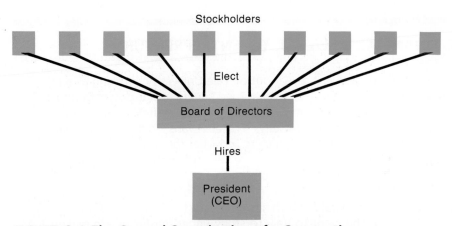

FIGURE 2.4 The General Organization of a Corporation
The stockholders are the owners of the firm. They elect the board of directors, who establish policies and hire the president, or chief executive officer (CEO), to manage the firm and implement their policies.

TAXATION OF CORPORATIONS

In order to make sound financial decisions, a financial manager must understand the manner in which corporate income is taxed. The major changes introduced by the *Tax Reform Act of 1986* are reflected in the following discussions. Corporations can earn either of two types of income, ordinary and capital gains; both are taxed the same under current law. A special type of corporate tax-reporting entity is the S Corporation, which we will also discuss.

Ordinary Income

The **ordinary income** of a corporation is income earned through the sale of a firm's goods or services. Ordinary income is currently taxed at the following rates:

ordinary income
Income earned through the sale of a firm's goods or services.

15 percent on first $50,000
25 percent on next $25,000
34 percent on the amount over $75,000

Corporations with taxable income in excess of $100,000 must, in addition, increase the tax calculated from the above rate schedule by the lesser of $11,750 or 5 percent of the taxable income in excess of $100,000.

FROM FINANCIAL ANALYST TO ENTREPRENEUR

Myra Evans was just a year out of Yale University, working as a financial analyst in New York City, when ice cream turned her life upside down. During a 1982 trip to San Francisco, her brother introduced her to a frozen Italian treat called *gelato.* "It was so good I had it twice in three days," recalls Evans. So good, in fact, she made it her career. Her company, Gelato Modo Inc., now has four shops in Manhattan, sales that will top $1 million in 1985, and plans to set up franchises across the U.S.

Considering the effort it took to start her business, success is the just dessert for Evans, 25. At first she worked all day at Goldman, Sachs & Co. and spent nights testing recipes for *gelato,* which has less butterfat, less air, and stronger flavor than ice cream. Then she went to Italy to study under master *gelato* makers. "My friends thought I was crazy," she says.

She talked a childhood friend from Cleveland, Derek Jones, into becoming her partner and persuaded 30 investors to put up a total of $200,000 in just six weeks. The company is now capitalized at more than $1 million. Evans, Jones, and relatives maintain 50.5% ownership.

Evans believes authenticity is at the heart of Gelato Modo's success. At the flagship store, which opened in June, 1983, "even the spoons were imported." She is enthusiastic about the company's future — she has already received 2,500 requests for information on franchising and hopes to open about 10 outlets this year. But with 40 years until retirement, Evans says *gelato* may someday be just a dessert instead of a way of life for her. "If Pillsbury or Kraft Foods said they wanted to buy us tomorrow," she says, "I wouldn't mind."

Source: "Turning a *Gelato* Obsession into Sweet Success," *Business Week,* June 10, 1985, p. 72. Reprinted from the June 10, 1985, issue of *Business Week* by special permission, © 1985 by McGraw-Hill, Inc.

EXAMPLE

Jessie Manufacturing, Inc., has before-tax earnings of $250,000. The tax on these earnings can be found by taking:

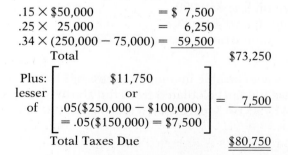

$$.15 \times \$50,000 = \$\ 7,500$$
$$.25 \times \ 25,000 = \ \ 6,250$$
$$.34 \times (250,000 - 75,000) = \ \underline{59,500}$$

Total $73,250

$$\text{Plus:} \\ \text{lesser} \\ \text{of} \left[\begin{array}{c} \$11,750 \\ \text{or} \\ .05(\$250,000 - \$100,000) \\ = .05(\$150,000) = \$7,500 \end{array} \right] = \underline{\ \ 7,500}$$

Total Taxes Due $\underline{\$80,750}$

The firm's total taxes on its before-tax earnings are therefore $80,750. If the firm had earned only $20,000 before taxes, its total tax liability would have been .15 × $20,000, or $3,000. ▪

AVERAGE TAX RATES   The *average tax rate* paid on the firm's ordinary income can be calculated by dividing its taxes by its taxable income. The average tax rate ranges from 15 to 34 percent, reaching 34 percent when taxable income equals or exceeds $335,000. The average tax rate paid by Jessie Manufacturing, Inc., in our preceding example was 32.3 percent ($80,750 ÷ $250,000). Table 2.3 presents the firm's tax liability and average tax rate for various levels of pretax income; it can be seen that the rate approaches and finally reaches 34 percent. To simplify calculations, *a fixed 40 percent tax rate is assumed to be applicable to ordinary corporate income.*

TAX-DEDUCTIBLE EXPENSES   Corporations are allowed to deduct operating expenses, such as advertising expense, sales commissions, and bad debts as well as interest expense in calculating their taxes. The tax-deductibility of these expenses reduces their after-tax cost, making them less costly than they might at first appear. The following example illustrates the benefit of tax-deductibility.

EXAMPLE

Companies X and Y each expect to have earnings before interest and taxes of $200,000 in the coming year. Company X during the year will have to pay $30,000 in interest, while Company Y has no debt and therefore will have $0 of interest expense. Calculation of the earnings after taxes for these two firms, which pay a 40 percent tax on ordinary income, are shown below.

	Company X	Company Y
Earnings before interest and taxes	$200,000	$200,000
Less: Interest expense	30,000	0
Earnings before taxes	$170,000	$200,000
Less: Taxes (40%)	68,000	80,000
Earnings after taxes	$102,000	$120,000
Difference in earnings after taxes		$18,000

The data demonstrate that while Company X had $30,000 more interest expense than did Company Y, Company X's earnings after taxes are only $18,000 less than those of Company Y ($102,000 for Company X versus $120,000 for Company Y). ▪

TABLE 2.3 Pretax Income, Tax Liabilities, and Average Tax Rates

Pretax income (1)	Tax liability (2)	Average tax rate [(2) ÷ (1)] (3)
$ 50,000	$ 7,500	15.00%
75,000	13,750	18.33
100,000	22,250	22.25
200,000	61,250	30.63
335,000	113,900	34.00
500,000	170,000	34.00
1,000,000	340,000	34.00
2,500,000	850,000	34.00

The tax-deductibility of certain expenses can be seen to reduce their actual (after-tax) cost to the profitable firm. Note that *interest is a tax-deductible expense, whereas dividends are not.* Because dividends are not tax-deductible, their after-tax cost is equal to the amount of the dividend. Thus a $30,000 cash dividend would have an after-tax cost of $30,000.

Capital Gains[3]

capital gain The amount by which the price at which an asset was sold exceeds the asset's purchase price.

If a firm sells a capital asset such as stock held as an investment for more than its initial purchase price, the difference between the sale price and the purchase price is called a **capital gain.** For corporations, capital gains are added to ordinary corporate income and taxed at the regular corporate rates, with a maximum tax rate of 34 percent. To simplify the computations presented in later chapters of the text, like for ordinary income, *a 40 percent tax rate is assumed to be applicable to corporate capital gains.*

EXAMPLE

The Commodore Company has operating earnings of $500,000 and has just sold for $40,000 a capital asset initially purchased two

---

[3] To simplify the discussion, only capital assets are being considered here. The full tax treatment of gains on depreciable assets is presented as part of the discussion of capital budgeting cash flows in Chapter 14.

years ago for $36,000. Since the asset was sold for greater than its initial purchase price, a capital gain of $4,000 ($40,000 sale price − $36,000 initial purchase price) results. The corporation's taxable income will total $504,000 ($500,000 ordinary income plus $4,000 capital gain). Since this total is above $335,000, the capital gain will be taxed at the 34 percent rate resulting in a tax of $1,360 (.34 × $4,000). ■

S Corporations

Subchapter S of the Internal Revenue Code permits corporations with 35 or fewer stockholders to be taxed like partnerships. That is, income is normally taxed as direct personal income of the shareholders, regardless of whether it is actually distributed to them. The **S corporation** is a tax-reporting entity rather than a tax-paying entity. The key advantage of this form of organization is that the shareholders receive all the organizational benefits of a corporation while escaping the double taxation normally associated with the distribution of corporate earnings. (**Double taxation** results when the already once-taxed earnings of a corporation are distributed as cash dividends to stockholders, who must pay taxes on these dividends.) S corporations do not receive other tax advantages accorded regular corporations.

S corporation
A tax-reporting entity whose earnings are taxed not as a corporation but as the incomes of its shareholders, thus avoiding the usual double taxation on corporate earnings.

double taxation Occurs when the already once-taxed earnings of a corporation are distributed as dividends to the firm's stockholders, who are then taxed again on these dividends.

SUMMARY

- Financial institutions, such as banks, savings and loans, and mutual funds, channel the savings of various individuals, businesses, and government into the hands of demanders of these funds.
- The role of the financial institution is changing as a result of relaxed legislation, permitting competition and ushering in the era of the "financial supermarket."
- The financial markets provide a forum in which suppliers and demanders of loans and investments can transact business directly. These institutions include the money market, where short-term securities are traded, and the capital market, where long-term debt (bonds) and equity (common and preferred stock) are traded.
- Investment bankers are hired to bear the risk of finding buyers for new security issues as well as advising clients. They help firms make both private placements and public offerings.
- The backbone of the capital market is formed by the securities exchanges, which provide a forum for trading outstanding securities. The organized securities exchanges are the dominant exchanges involved in the resale of outstanding securities. In addition to creating a resale market for outstanding securities, the over-the-counter (OTC) exchange is the market in which new public issues are sold.

- The flow of funds between savers (suppliers) and investors (demanders) is regulated by the interest rate or required return. For any class of similar-risk securities, the term structure of interest rates reflects the relationship between the interest rate, or rate of return, and the time to maturity. Yield curves can be downward-sloping, flat, or upward-sloping.
- Since investors must be compensated for taking risk, they expect higher returns for greater risk. Each type of security offers a range of potential risk-return trade-offs.
- The basic forms of business organization are the sole proprietorship, the partnership, and the corporation. Although there are more sole proprietorships than any other form of business organization, the corporation is dominant in terms of business receipts and net profits.
- Corporations are subject to corporate tax rates. The average tax rate paid by a corporation ranges from 15 to 34 percent. For our purposes, a 40 percent tax rate is assumed.
- Corporations can deduct certain expenses when calculating taxes. The tax-deductibility of expenses in effect reduces their actual (after-tax) cost to the firm.
- If a firm sells a capital asset for more than its initial purchase price, a capital gain results. Capital gains are added to ordinary corporate income and taxed at the regular corporate rates, with a maximum tax rate of 34 percent. In this book, a 40 percent rate is assumed.
- The government permits a business with 35 or fewer stockholders to file as an S corporation, which is taxed as a partnership with certain accompanying advantages.

QUESTIONS

2-1 Who are the key participants in financial transactions? Indicate who are net savers and who are net borrowers.

2-2 Briefly describe each of the following financial intermediaries:
   a Commercial banks
   b Savings and loans
   c Life insurance companies
   d Mutual funds

2-3 What relationship exists between financial institutions and financial markets? Why does it exist?

2-4 What is the *money market?* Where is it housed? How does it differ from the *capital market?*

2-5 How does the over-the-counter exchange operate? How does it differ from the organized securities exchanges?

2-6 What is the *term structure of interest rates,* and how does it relate to the yield curve? For a given class of similar-risk securities, what expectation causes the yield curve to be downward-sloping, flat, or upward-sloping?

2-7 How are actual and expected returns measured, and what is the difference between them? What is meant by the *risk-return trade-off?*

2-8 What are the three basic forms of business organization? Which form is most common? Which form is dominant in terms of business receipts and net profits?

2-9 How do the various legal and organizational aspects of corporations facilitate their growth into large business?

2-10 Briefly describe the structure of taxation of ordinary corporate income. What is the average tax rate? How is it determined?

2-11 What benefit results from the tax-deductibility of certain corporate expenses? Compare and contrast the tax treatment of corporate interest and dividends.

2-12 What is a *capital gain?* Describe the tax treatment of capital gains.

PROBLEMS

2-1 **(Yield Curve)** A firm wishing to evaluate interest rate behavior has gathered yield data on five U.S. Treasury securities, each having a different maturity and all measured at the same point in time. This data is summarized below.

U.S. Treasury security	Time to maturity	Yield (%)
A	1 year	12.6
B	10 years	11.2
C	6 months	13.0
D	20 years	11.0
E	5 years	11.4

a Draw the yield curve associated with the data given above.

b Describe the resulting yield curve in **a**, and explain the general expectations embodied in it.

2-2 **(Term Structure of Interest Rates)** The following yield data for a number of highest-quality corporate bonds existed at each of the three points in time noted.

Time to maturity (years)	YIELD (%)		
	5 years ago	2 years ago	Today
1	9.1	14.6	9.3
3	9.2	12.8	9.8
5	9.3	12.2	10.9
10	9.5	10.9	12.6
15	9.4	10.7	12.7
20	9.3	10.5	12.9
30	9.4	10.5	13.5

a On the same set of axes, draw the yield curve at each of the three points in time given.

b Label each curve in **a** as to its general shape (downward-sloping, flat, upward-sloping).

c Describe the general interest rate expectation existing at each of the three points in time.

2-3 **(Actual Rate of Return)** Alex Williams wishes to estimate his returns during the past year on a number of securities he owns. Using the data summarized in the table below, find the actual rate of return Alex would have earned during the year had he purchased the securities at the beginning price and sold them at the ending price.

| | Cash dividends or interest paid ($) | MARKET PRICE | |
| | | Beginning ($) | Ending ($) |
Security			
A	2.00	30.00	34.00
B	0.00	25.00	27.00
C	2.50	17.50	16.00
D	1.00	86.00	89.50
E	3.00	63.50	54.00

2-4 **(Actual or Expected Return)** The following data describe the actual return inputs as well as the expected returns on five securities for the year just ended.

| | Cash dividends or interest paid ($) | MARKET PRICE | | Expected return (%) |
| | | Beginning ($) | Ending ($) | |
Security				
A	4.50	22.50	21.00	15
B	2.00	17.00	19.00	20
C	0.00	64.00	67.50	8
D	1.50	25.00	26.50	12
E	3.20	30.00	26.00	10

a Calculate the actual return on each security for the year just ended.

b Evaluate each security's actual return in view of the expected return.

c If you owned each of the securities, what action, if any, would you take in view of your findings in **b**?

2-5 **(Liability Comparisons)** Marilyn Smith has invested $25,000 in the Research Marketing Company. This firm has recently become bankrupt and has $60,000 in unpaid debts. Explain the nature of payments, if any, by Ms. Smith in each of the following situations.

a The Research Marketing Company is a sole proprietorship owned by Ms. Smith.

b The Research Marketing Company is a 50-50 partnership of Ms. Smith and Arnold Jones.

c The Research Marketing Company is a corporation.

b The Research Marketing Company is a 50-50 partnership of Ms. Smith and Arnold Jones.

c The Research Marketing Company is a corporation.

2-6 **(Corporate Taxes)** Kim Supply, Inc., is a small corporation acting as the exclusive distributor of a major line of sporting goods. During 1987 the firm earned $92,500 before taxes.

a Calculate the firm's tax liability using the actual tax rates given in the chapter.

b How much is Kim Supply's 1987 after-tax earnings?

c What was the firm's average tax rate, based on your findings in **a**?

2-7 **(Average Corporate Tax Rates)** Using the corporate tax rates given in the text, perform the following:

a Calculate the tax liability, after-tax earnings, and average tax rates for the following levels of corporate earnings before taxes: $10,000; $80,000; $300,000; $500,000; $1.5 million.

b Plot the average tax rates (measured on the y-axis) against the pretax income levels (measured on the x-axis). What generalization can be made concerning the relationship between these variables?

2-8 **(Interest versus Dividends)** The Randy Company expects earnings before interest and taxes to be $40,000 for this period. Assuming an ordinary tax rate of 40 percent, compute the firm's after-tax net profits and earnings available for common stockholders under the following conditions:

a The firm pays $10,000 in interest.

b The firm pays $10,000 in preferred stock dividends.

2-9 **(Capital Gains Taxes)** Waters Manufacturing is considering the sale of two nondepreciable assets, X and Y. Asset X was purchased for $2,000 and will be sold today for $2,250. Asset Y was purchased for $30,000 and will be sold today for $35,000. The firm is subject to a 40 percent tax rate on capital gains.

a Calculate the amount of capital gain, if any, realized on each of the assets.

b Calculate the tax on the sale of each asset.

2-10 **(Capital Gains Taxes)** The table below contains purchase and sale prices for the capital assets of a major corporation. The firm paid taxes of 40 percent on capital gains.

Asset	Purchase Price	Sale Price
A	$ 3,000	$ 3,400
B	12,000	12,000
C	62,000	80,000
D	41,000	45,000
E	16,500	18,000

a Determine the amount of capital gain realized on each of the five assets.

b Calculate the amount of tax paid on each of the assets.

3

FINANCIAL STATEMENTS, DEPRECIATION, AND CASH FLOW

After studying this chapter, you should be able to:

- Describe the purpose and basic components of the stockholders' report.

- Identify the format and key components of the income statement and the balance sheet, and interpret these statements.

- Recognize the purpose and basic content of the statement of retained earnings and the statement of changes in financial position.

- Understand the effect of depreciation on cash flow, the depreciable value and life of an asset, and the methods used to depreciate assets for tax purposes.

- Discuss the funds flow through the firm and develop and interpret the statement of changes in financial position.

Every corporation has many and varied uses for the standardized records and reports of its financial activities. Periodically, reports must be prepared for regulators, creditors (lenders), owners, and management. Regulators, such as federal and state securities commissions, enforce the proper and accurate disclosure of corporate financial data. Creditors use financial data to evaluate the firm's ability to meet scheduled debt payments. Owners use corporate financial data in assessing the firm's financial condition and in deciding whether to buy, sell, or hold its stock. Management's concerns center on regulatory compliance, satisfying creditors and owners, and on monitoring the firm's performance.

The guidelines used to prepare and maintain financial records and reports are known as **generally accepted accounting principles (GAAP).** These accounting practices and procedures are authorized by the accounting profession's rule-setting body, the **Financial Accounting Standards Board (FASB).** In the sections that follow we will examine the most important of the various corporate documents that depend upon the application and interpretation of these fundamental accounting principles.

THE STOCKHOLDERS' REPORT

Publicly held corporations are those that have their stock traded either on an organized securities exchange or on the over-the-counter exchange. These corporations are required by the **Securities and Exchange Commission (SEC)** — the federal regulatory body governing the sale and listing of securities — and by state securities commissions to provide their stockholders with an annual **stockholders' report.** This report, which summarizes and documents the firm's financial activities during the past year, begins with a letter from the firm's president or chairman of the board followed by the key financial statements. In addition, other information about the firm is often included.

The President's Letter

The **president's letter** is the primary communication from management to the firm's owners. Typically the first component of the stockholders' report, it describes the events considered to have had the greatest impact on the firm during the year. In addition, the letter generally discusses plans for the coming year and their anticipated effects on the firm's financial condition. Figure 3.1 includes excerpts from the president's letter to the stockholders of Harper & Row, Publishers, Inc., from its 1985 stockholders' report. The letter summarizes

generally accepted accounting principles (GAAP) Authorized accounting practices and procedures used as guidelines in preparing and maintaining corporate financial records and reports. Authorized by Financial Accounting Standards Board (FASB).

Financial Accounting Standards Board (FASB) Rule-setting body of the accounting profession. Authorizes generally accepted accounting principles (GAAP).

publicly held corporations Corporations that have their stock traded either on an organized securities exchange or on the over-the-counter exchange.

Securities and Exchange Commission (SEC) Federal regulatory body governing the sale and listing of securities.

stockholders' report Annual report that summarizes and documents the firm's financial activities during the past year.

president's letter The first component of the annual stockholders' report, and the primary communication from management to the firm's owners.

Fiscal 1985 was an eventful year for Harper & Row. We sold a major division that had been part of the company for many years, discontinued a second that was a recent start-up, and made a substantial acquisition in one of our major growth areas.

The result at year-end was a company that was slightly smaller but significantly more profitable than a year ago. And that year was itself a record year for the company — a year in which we had the benefit of one of the best-selling trade book titles in recent publishing history.

Finally, it was a year in which our books and authors won more than their fair share of prizes and awards — including a clean sweep of four of the major awards for literary excellence given for adult trade books in this country. . . .

The General Books group did extremely well, improving both revenues and profits despite the lack of a single runaway bestseller such as *In Search of Excellence* last year. Exceptionally strong performances were turned in by our Junior Books division and our San Francisco division, sales of which grew 20 percent and 14 percent respectively. Most gratifying of all was the fact that our adult books and their authors were winners of every major award in the industry: a Pulitzer, an American Book Award, a National Book Critics Circle Award, and the Bancroft Prize. Replications of their covers grace the front of this report; a full list of prizes and awards won this year appears elsewhere in these pages. . . .

Our major disappointment was in College text publishing, where revenues were essentially flat for the third year in a row. Despite our successful efforts to publish more titles for the hard sciences and engineering, we have been plagued by continued erosion of our substantial backlist in the humanities and social sciences. Industry-wide problems with returns and the increasing use of used books and illegal copying have also been factors. We are making a major effort to break out of this pattern, and have been investing heavily in new editorial resources and product. The list being published this spring is the largest the department has ever had, and our editorial pipeline of future projects is also at an all-time high. College text publishing remains an attractive and profitable business, and we are determined to have for it the same leadership position in the industry that our other major product groups enjoy. . . .

The outlook for the new year is opaque. Heavy returns continue to be a problem for the industry, and for college used books as well. The strength of our retail markets is spotty and could deteriorate further as the year progresses. Despite these portents we expect a year of moderate if unspectacular growth. Adult trade books will be hard put to extend the gains of the last two years, but we expect our junior books to do well. Professional publishing will benefit from a full year of Gower, and we expect journal sales to continue strong. Medical and nursing bound book sales will be more affected by the pressure being exerted on health care costs. The big question mark — as always at this time of year — is the fate of our college text list, which will be tested during July and August. With the biggest new list in our history we have more to gain, and to lose, than usual. . . .

I would like to thank all of our authors, employees, and stockholders for their help in making this another record-setting year for the company. I hope to see many of you at our Annual Meeting in Philadelphia in August.

BROOKS THOMAS

SOURCE: Harper & Row, Publishers, Inc., *1985 Annual Report*, pp. 4–5.

FIGURE 3.1 Excerpt from Harper & Row's 1985 President's Letter

The president's letter is the first component of an annual report. It describes the key events — both positive and negative — affecting the firm's recent performance and discusses plans and expected outcomes for the coming year.

key events of the fiscal year ended April 30, 1985 and discusses the outlook for fiscal 1986.

Financial Statements

Following the president's letter will be, at minimum, the four key financial statements required by the Securities and Exchange Commission (SEC). Those statements are (1) the income statement, (2) the balance sheet, (3) the statement of retained earnings, and (4) the statement of changes in financial position. The annual corporate report must contain these statements for at least the two most recent years of operation. Historical summaries of key operating statistics and ratios for the past five to ten years are also commonly included with the financial statements. (Financial ratios are discussed in Chapter 4.)

Other Features

The stockholders' reports of most widely held corporations also include discussions of the firm's activities, new products, research and development, and the like. Most companies view the annual report not only as a requirement, but as an important vehicle for influencing owners' perceptions of the company and its future outlook. Because of the information it contains, the stockholders' report may affect expected risk, return, stock price, and ultimately the viability of the firm.

BASIC FINANCIAL STATEMENTS

Our chief concern in this section is to understand the factual information presented in the four required corporate financial statements. The financial statements from the 1987 stockholders' report of a hypothetical firm, the Elton Corporation, are presented and briefly discussed below.

Income Statement

The **income statement** provides a financial summary of the firm's operating results during the period specified. Most common are income statements covering a one-year period ending at a specified date, ordinarily December 31 of the calendar year. (Many firms, however, operate on a 12-month financial cycle, or *fiscal year*, that ends at a time other than December 31.) In addition, monthly statements are typically prepared for use by management, and quarterly statements must be made available to the stockholders of publicly held corporations.

income statement
Provides a financial summary of the firm's operating results during a specified period.

**TABLE 3.1 Elton Corporation Income Statement ($000)
for the Year Ended December 31, 1987**

Sales revenue		$1,700
Less: Cost of goods sold		1,000
Gross profits		$ 700
Less: Operating expenses		
Selling expense	$ 80	
General and administrative expense	150	
Depreciation expense	100	
Total operating expense		330
Operating profits		$ 370
Less: Interest expense[a]		70
Net profits before taxes		$ 300
Less: Taxes (rate = 40%)		120
Net profits after taxes		$ 180
Less: Preferred stock dividends		10
Earnings available for common stockholders		$ 170
Earnings per share (EPS)[b]		$ 1.70

[a] Interest expense includes the interest component of the annual financial lease payment as specified by the Financial Accounting Standards Board (FASB).

[b] Calculated by dividing the earnings available for common stockholders by the number of shares of common stock outstanding ($170,000 ÷ 100,000 shares = $1.70 per share).

Table 3.1 presents Elton Corporation's income statement for the year ended December 31, 1987. The statement begins with *sales revenue* — the total dollar amount of sales during the period — from which the *cost of goods sold* is deducted. The resulting *gross profits* of $700,000 for Elton Corporation represents the amount remaining to satisfy operating, financial, and tax costs after meeting the costs of producing or purchasing the products sold. Next *operating expenses*, which includes sales expense, general and administrative expense, and depreciation expense, is deducted from gross profits.[1] The resulting *operating profits* of $370,000 for Elton Corporation represents the profit earned from producing and selling products; it does not consider financial and tax costs. (Operating profit is often called *earnings before interest and taxes* or *EBIT*.) Next, the financial cost — interest expense — is subtracted from operating profits in order to find *net profits (or earnings) before taxes*. After subtracting $70,000 in 1987 interest Elton Corporation had $300,000 of net profits before taxes.

After applying the appropriate tax rates to before-tax profits, taxes

---

[1] Depreciation expense can be, and frequently is, included in manufacturing costs — costs of goods sold — in order to calculate gross profits. Depreciation is shown as an expense in this text in order to isolate it as an important cash flow component.

are calculated and deducted to determine *net profits (or earnings) after taxes*. Elton Corporation's net profit after taxes for 1987 was $180,000. Next, any preferred stock dividends must be subtracted from net profit after taxes to arrive at *earnings available for common stockholders*. This is the amount earned by the firm on behalf of the common stockholders during the period. Dividing earnings available for common stockholders by the number of shares of common stock outstanding, *earnings per share (EPS)* is obtained. EPS represents the amount earned during the period on each outstanding share of common stock. In 1987 Elton Corporation earned $170,000 for its common stockholders, which represents $1.70 for each outstanding share. (The earnings per share amount rarely equals the amount, if any, of common stock dividends paid to shareholders.)

Balance Sheet

The **balance sheet** presents a summary statement of the firm's financial position at a given point in time. The statement balances the firm's *assets* (what it owns) against its financing, which can be either *debt* (what it owes) or *equity* (what was provided by owners). Elton Corporation's balance sheets on December 31 of 1987 and 1986, respectively, are presented in Table 3.2. They show a variety of asset, liability, and equity accounts. An important distinction is made between short-term and long-term assets and liabilities. The **current assets** and **current liabilities** are *short-term* assets and liabilities. This means that they are expected to be converted into cash within one year or less. All other assets and liabilities, along with stockholders' equity, which is assumed to have an infinite life, are considered *long-term*, or *fixed*, since they are expected to remain on the firm's books for one year or more.

In reviewing Elton Corporation's balance sheets, a few points need to be highlighted. As is customary, the assets are listed beginning with the most liquid down to the least liquid. Current assets therefore precede fixed assets. *Marketable securities* represents very liquid short-term investments such as Treasury bills or certificates of deposit, held by the firm. *Accounts receivable* represent the total monies owed the firm by its customers on credit sales made to them. *Inventories* include raw materials, work-in-process (partially finished goods), and finished goods held by the firm. The entry for *gross fixed assets* is the original cost of all fixed (long-term) assets owned by the firm.[2] *Net fixed assets* represents the difference between gross fixed assets and *accumulated*

balance sheet Summary statement of the firm's financial position at a given point in time.

current assets Short-term assets, expected to be converted into cash within one year or less.

current liabilities Short-term liabilities, expected to be converted into cash within one year or less.

---

[2] For convenience the term *fixed assets* is used throughout this text to refer to what, in a strict accounting sense, is captioned "property, plant, and equipment." This simplification of terminology permits certain financial concepts to be more easily developed.

TABLE 3.2 Elton Corporation Balance Sheets ($000)

	DECEMBER 31	
Assets	**1987**	**1986**
Current assets		
Cash	$ 400	$ 300
Marketable securities	600	200
Accounts receivable	400	500
Inventories	600	900
Total current assets	$2,000	$1,900
Gross fixed assets (at cost)		
Land and buildings	$1,200	$1,050
Machinery and equipment	850	800
Furniture and fixtures	300	220
Vehicles	100	80
Other (includes certain leases)	50	50
Total gross fixed assets (at cost)	$2,500	$2,200
Less: Accumulated depreciation	1,300	1,200
Net fixed assets	$1,200	$1,000
Total assets	$3,200	$2,900
Liabilities and stockholders' equity		
Current liabilities		
Accounts payable	$ 700	$ 500
Notes payable	600	700
Accruals	100	200
Total current liabilities	$1,400	$1,400
Long-term debt	600	400
Total liabilities	$2,000	$1,800
Stockholders' equity		
Preferred stock	$ 100	$ 100
Common stock—$1.20 par, 100,000 shares outstanding in 1987 and 1986	120	120
Paid-in capital in excess of par on common stock	380	380
Retained earnings	600	500
Total stockholders' equity	$1,200	$1,100
Total liabilities and stockholders' equity	$3,200	$2,900

depreciation — the total expense recorded for the depreciation of fixed assets. (The net value of fixed assets is called their *book value*.)

Like assets, the liabilities and equity accounts are listed on the balance sheet from short-term to long-term. Current liabilities includes: *accounts payable,* amounts owed for credit purchases by the firm; *notes payable,* outstanding short-term loans typically from commercial banks; and *accruals,* amounts owed for services for which a bill may not or will not be received. (Examples of accruals include taxes due the

EVALUATING AN ANNUAL REPORT

Back in 1866 when the New York Stock Exchange first asked listed companies for regular financial reports, the Delaware, Lackawanna and Western Railroad replied. "This company makes no reports and publishes no statements."

Things are vastly different now. Large companies publish annual reports with pictures in color—and what may be an overly colorful report from the chief executive officer (CEO). . . .

The typical format has a letter from the CEO followed by pictures of company operations; financial statements followed by footnotes; management's analysis of financial conditions and, finally, a certificate by the independent auditors.

Start from back. "Forget the front," says a seasoned investment analyst. "The meat is in the back, so read the report backward, starting with the auditor's report." If it says that "in our opinion, the statements present fairly the company's financial position in conformity with generally accepted accounting principles," O.K.

But if there is an "except for" or a "subject to," look out. This red flag should send you forward to the footnotes, which may show large contingent liabilities, a big debt coming due, a suit for damages, or possible dilution of common stockholders' equity from conversion of convertible securities.

Next read the analysis of operations. In this section the Securities and Exchange Commission requires management to level with the shareholders. Ideally, management tells whether or not it is doing well and how it intends to do better. It might, for example, describe whether it follows a policy of keeping dividends at a flat amount or of increasing them each year to keep ahead of inflation.

This material can vary widely from the CEO's blurb in the front. For example, in one report the CEO states: "Your company's utility operations continued to show excellent progress during the past year. . . . Net earnings of the utility segment increased 38 percent. . . ." What the letter does not say is that losses by a wholly owned subsidiary caused consolidated earnings to fall from 76 cents a share to 55 cents.

The "Dear Stockholder" letter from a large savings and loan association reports significant improvement in earnings for fiscal year 1984 over the "prior fiscal period, which was nine months." The company had changed fiscal periods, but earnings for the 12 months ended Sept. 30, 1984, were only 13 percent of those for the 12 months ended Dec. 31, 1982.

. . .

Going on to the balance sheet and the income statement, some of the key figures show whether earnings and dividends have been increasing, whether current assets are safely larger than current liabilities—for most companies the ratio should be 2 to 1—and various other ratios measuring financial soundness.

Source: John W. Hazard, "How to Read Annual Reports," *U.S. News & World Report*, Feb. 18, 1985, p. 74.

par value Per-share value arbitrarily assigned to an issue of common stock primarily for accounting purposes.

paid-in capital in excess of par The amount of proceeds in excess of the par value received from the original sale of common stock.

retained earnings The cumulative total of all earnings retained and reinvested in the firm since its inception.

government and wages due employees.) *Long-term debt* represents debt for which payment is not due in the current year. *Stockholders' equity* represents the owners' claims on the firm. The *preferred stock* entry shows the historic proceeds from the sale of preferred stock ($100,000 for Elton Corporation). Next, the amount paid in by the original purchasers of common stock is shown by two entries — common stock and paid-in capital in excess of par on common stock. The *common stock* entry is the **par value** of common stock, an arbitrarily assigned per-share value used primarily for accounting purposes. **Paid-in capital in excess of par** represents the amount of proceeds in excess of the par value received from the original sale of common stock. The sum of the common stock and paid-in capital accounts divided by the number of shares outstanding represents the original price per share received by the firm on a single issue of common stock. Elton Corporation therefore received $5.00 per share [($120,000 par + $380,000 paid-in capital in excess) ÷ 100,000 shares] from the sale of its common stock. Finally, **retained earnings** represents the cumulative total of all earnings retained and reinvested in the firm since its inception. It is important to recognize that retained earnings *are not cash,* but rather have been utilized to finance the firm's assets.

From Elton Corporation's balance sheets in Table 3.2 it can be seen that the firm's total assets increased from $2,900,000 in 1986 to $3,200,000 in 1987. The $300,000 increase was due primarily to the $200,000 increase in net fixed assets. The asset increase in turn appears to have been financed primarily by an increase of $200,000 in long-term debt. Better insight into these changes can be derived from the statement of changes in financial position, which we will discuss shortly.

Statement of Retained Earnings

statement of retained earnings Reconciles the net income earned in a given year, and any cash dividends paid, with the change in retained earnings between the start and end of that year.

The **statement of retained earnings** reconciles the net income earned during a given year, and any cash dividends paid, with the change in retained earnings between the start and end of that year. Table 3.3 presents this statement for Elton Corporation for the year ended De-

TABLE 3.3 Elton Corporation Statement of Retained Earnings ($000) for the Year Ended December 31, 1987

Retained earnings balance (January 1, 1987)		$500
Plus: Net profits after taxes (for 1987)		180
Less: Cash dividends (paid during 1987)		
Preferred stock	($10)	
Common stock	(70)	(80)
Retained earnings balance (December 31, 1987)		$600

$180,000, from which it paid a total of $80,000 in dividends, resulting in year-end retained earnings of $600,000. Thus the net increase for Elton Corporation was $100,000 ($180,000 net profits after taxes minus $80,000 in dividends) during 1987.

Statement of Changes in Financial Position

The **statement of changes in financial position** provides a summary of the flow of funds over the period of concern, typically the year just ended. The statement, which is sometimes called a "source and use statement," provides insight into operations and financing. Elton Corporation's statement of changes in financial position for the year ended December 31, 1987, is presented in Table 3.10. However, before demonstrating the preparation of this statement it will be helpful to understand various aspects of depreciation.

statement of changes in financial position Provides a summary of the flow of funds over the period of concern, typically the past year.

DEPRECIATION

Business firms are permitted to systematically charge a portion of the cost of a fixed asset against the annual revenues it generates. This allocation of historic cost over time is called **depreciation.** For tax purposes, the depreciation of corporate assets is regulated by the Internal Revenue Code, which underwent major changes under the *Tax Reform Act of 1986.* Because the objectives of financial reporting are sometimes different from those of tax legislation, often a firm will use different depreciation methods for financial reporting than those required for tax purposes. (The student should thus not jump to the conclusion that a company is attempting to "cook the books" simply because it keeps two different sets of records.) Tax laws are used to accomplish economic goals such as providing incentives for corporate investment in certain types of assets, whereas the objectives of financial reporting are of course quite different.

depreciation The systematic charging of a portion of the cost of a fixed asset against the annual revenues generated by the asset.

Depreciation for tax purposes is determined using the **Accelerated Cost Recovery System (ACRS),**[3] while for financial reporting purposes a variety of depreciation methods are available. Before discussing the methods of depreciating an asset, we must understand the relationship between depreciation and cash flows, the depreciable value of an asset, and the depreciable life of an asset.

Accelerated Cost Recovery System (ACRS) Used to determine the depreciation of assets for tax purposes.

Depreciation and Cash Flows

The financial manager is concerned with cash flows rather than net profits as reported on the income statement. To adjust the income statement to show *cash flow from operations,* all noncash charges must

[3] This system was first established in 1981 with passage of the *Economic Recovery Tax Act.* The *Tax Reform Act of 1986* revised this system, which is sometimes referred to as the "new" or "modified" accelerated cost recovery system (ACRS). For convenience, the new system is called "ACRS" throughout this text.

noncash charges
Expenses deducted on the income statement that do not involve an actual outlay of cash during the period.

be *added back* to the firm's *net profits after taxes*. **Noncash charges** are expenses that are deducted on the income statement but do not involve an actual outlay of cash during the period. Depreciation, amortization, and depletion allowances are examples. Since depreciation expenses are the most common noncash charges, we shall focus on their treatment; amortization and depletion charges are treated in a similar fashion.

The general rule for adjusting net profits after taxes by adding back all noncash charges is expressed as follows:

$$\text{Cash flow from operations} = \text{net profits after taxes} + \text{noncash charges} \quad (3.1)$$

Applying Equation 3.1 to the 1987 income statement for Elton Corporation presented earlier in Table 3.1 yields a cash flow from operations of $280,000 due to the noncash nature of depreciation:

Net profits after taxes	$180,000
Plus: Depreciation expense	100,000
Cash flow from operations	$280,000

(This value is only approximate since not all sales are made for cash and not all expenses are paid when they are incurred.)

Depreciation and other noncash charges shield the firm from taxes by lowering taxable income. Some people do not define depreciation as a source of funds; however, it is a source of funds in the sense that it represents a "nonuse" of funds. Table 3.4 shows the Elton Corporation's income statement prepared on a cash basis as an illustration of how depreciation shields income and acts as a nonuse of funds. Ignoring depreciation, except in determining the firm's taxes, results in cash flow from operations of $280,000 — the value obtained earlier. Adjust-

TABLE 3.4 Elton Corporation Income Statement Calculated on a Cash Basis ($000) for the Year Ended December 31, 1987

Sales revenue		$1,700
Less: Cost of goods sold		1,000
Gross profits		$ 700
Less: Operating expenses		
Selling expense	$ 80	
General and administrative expense	150	
Depreciation expense (noncash charge)	0	
Total operating expense		230
Operating profits		$ 470
Less: Interest expense		70
Net profits before taxes		$ 400
Less: Taxes (from Table 3.1)		120
Cash flow from operations		$ 280

ment of the firm's net profits after taxes by adding back noncash charges such as depreciation will be used on many occasions in this text to estimate cash flow.

Depreciable Value of an Asset

Under the basic ACRS procedures, the depreciable value (amount to be depreciated) of an asset is its *full* cost including outlays for installation. No adjustment is required for expected salvage value.

> ### EXAMPLE
>
> Elton Corporation acquired a new machine at a cost of $38,000, with installation costs of $2,000. Regardless of its expected salvage value, the depreciable value of the machine is $40,000: ($38,000 cost + $2,000 installation cost). ∎

Depreciable Life of an Asset

The time period over which an asset is depreciated (its **depreciable life**) can significantly affect the pattern of cash flows. The shorter the depreciable life, the more quickly the cash flow created by the depreciation write-off will be received. Given the financial manager's preference for faster receipt of cash flows, a shorter depreciable life is preferred to a longer one. Unfortunately, the firm must abide by certain Internal Revenue Service (IRS) requirements for determining depreciable life. These ACRS standards, which apply to both new and used assets, require the taxpayer to use as an asset's depreciable life the appropriate ACRS **recovery period**, except in the case of certain assets depreciated under the *alternative depreciation system*.[4] There are six ACRS recovery periods — 3, 5, 7, 10, 15, and 20 years — excluding real estate. As is customary, the property classes (excluding real estate) are referred to in accordance with their recovery periods, as 3-year, 5-year, 7-year, 10-year, 15-year, and 20-year property. The first four property classes — those routinely used by business — are defined in Table 3.5.

depreciable life Time period over which an asset is depreciated.

recovery period The appropriate depreciable life of a particular asset as determined by ACRS.

Depreciation Methods

For *tax purposes*, using ACRS recovery periods, assets in the first four property classes are depreciated by the double-declining balance (200%) method using the half-year convention and switching to straight line when advantageous. Although tables of depreciation percentages are not provided by law, the *approximate* (i.e., rounded to nearest whole percent) *percentages* written off each year for the first four property

---

[4] For convenience, the depreciation of assets under the *alternative depreciation system* is ignored in this text.

TABLE 3.5 First Four Property Classes under ACRS

Property class (Recovery period)	Definition
3 year	Research and experiment equipment and certain special tools.
5 year	Computers, typewriters, copiers, duplicating equipment, cars, light-duty trucks, qualified technological equipment, and similar assets.
7 year	Office furniture, fixtures, most manufacturing equipment, railroad track, and single-purpose agricultural and horticultural structures.
10 year	Equipment used in petroleum refining or in the manufacture of tobacco products and certain food products.

classes are given in Table 3.6. Rather than using the percentages in Table 3.6, the firm can either use straight-line depreciation over the asset's recovery period with the half-year convention or use the alternative depreciation system. For purposes of this course, we will use the ACRS depreciation percentages given in Table 3.6, since they generally provide for the fastest write-off and therefore the best cash flow effects for the profitable firm.

TABLE 3.6 Rounded Depreciation Percentages by Recovery Year Using ACRS for First Four Property Classes

Recovery year	PERCENTAGE BY RECOVERY YEAR[a]			
	3-year	5-year	7-year	10-year
1	33	20	14	10
2	45	32	25	18
3	15	19	18	14
4	7	12	12	12
5		12	9	9
6		5	9	8
7			9	7
8			4	6
9				6
10				6
11				4

[a] These percentages have been rounded to the nearest whole percentage in order to simplify calculations while retaining realism. In order to calculate the *actual* depreciation for tax purposes, be sure to apply the actual unrounded percentages or directly apply double-declining balance (200%) depreciation using the half-year convention.

Because ACRS requires use of the half-year convention, assets are assumed to be acquired in the middle of the year and therefore only one-half of the first year's depreciation is recovered in the first year. As a result, the final half year of depreciation is recovered in the year immediately following the asset's stated recovery period. In Table 3.6 it can be seen that the depreciation percentages for an n-year class asset are given for $n + 1$ years. For example, a 5-year asset is depreciated over 6 recovery years. (*Note:* The percentages in Table 3.6 have been rounded to the nearest whole percentage in order to simplify calculations while retaining realism.)

For financial *reporting purposes* a variety of depreciation methods— straight-line, double-declining balance, and sum-of-the-years'-digits[5] —can be used. Since primary concern in managerial finance centers on cash flows, *only tax depreciation methods will be utilized throughout this text*. The application of the tax depreciation percentages given in Table 3.6 can be demonstrated by a simple example.

EXAMPLE

The Elton Corporation acquired for an installed cost of $40,000 a machine having a recovery period of five years. Using the applicable percentages from Table 3.6, the depreciation in each year is calculated below.

Year	Cost (1)	Percentages (from Table 3.6) (2)	Depreciation [(1) × (2)] (3)
1	$40,000	20%	$ 8,000
2	40,000	32	12,800
3	40,000	19	7,600
4	40,000	12	4,800
5	40,000	12	4,800
6	40,000	5	2,000
Totals		100%	$40,000

It should be clear from column 3 that the total cost of the asset is written off over six recovery years. ■

ANALYZING THE FIRM'S FUNDS FLOW

The statement of changes in financial position, briefly described earlier, summarizes the firm's funds flow over a given period of time.

[5] For a review of these depreciation methods as well as other aspects of financial reporting, see any recently published financial accounting text.

Because it can be used to capture historic cash flow, the statement is developed in this section. First, however, we need to discuss the definition of funds, cash flow through the firm, and the classification of sources and uses.

Definition of Funds: Cash or Net Working Capital?

funds Either cash or net working capital.

net working capital The numerical difference between total current assets and total current liabilities.

Funds can be defined as either cash or net working capital. **Net working capital** is the numerical difference between total current assets and total current liabilities (net working capital = total current assets − total current liabilities). Both forms of funds are necessary for the firm to function effectively. Cash is needed to pay current bills. Net working capital—especially in a seasonal business—is needed to provide a cushion for the payment of bills due in the near future.

Current corporate practice reflects a preference for the *net-working-capital-based* form of the statement of changes in financial position. However, the accounting profession has lately been urging the required inclusion of a *cash-based* form of this statement in the annual stockholders' report. Due to its greater detail, the cash-based statement is more informative and thus is emphasized here.

Cash Flow through the Firm

operating flows Cash flows relating to the firm's production cycle.

Figure 3.2 illustrates the overall flow of cash through the firm. For convenience the cash flows are divided into (1) operating flows and (2) financial and legal flows. The **operating flows** are cash outlays and inflows that relate to the firm's production cycle. In carrying out this cycle a firm must utilize, and pay for, raw materials, labor, and fixed assets while also paying sales expenses and operating and administrative expenses and salaries. In turn the firm produces and sells its finished goods. As Figure 3.2 shows, not all expenses are made for cash; many are made on credit through an account payable or an accrual. Similarly, not all sales are made for cash; many are made on credit through accounts receivable.

financial and legal flows Cash flows that include payment and receipt of interest, payment and refund of taxes, incurrence and repayment of debt, payment of dividends and stock repurchases, and cash inflow from sale of stock.

The **financial and legal flows** depicted in Figure 3.2 include the payment and receipt of interest; the payment and refund of taxes; the incurrence and repayment of debt; the effect of distributions of equity through payment of dividends and stock repurchases; and cash inflow from the sale of stock.

Classifying Sources and Uses of Cash

The cash-based statement of changes in financial position summarizes the sources and uses of cash during a given period. (Table 3.7 classifies the basic sources and uses.) For example, if a firm's accounts payable increased by $1,000 during the year, this change would be a *source of*

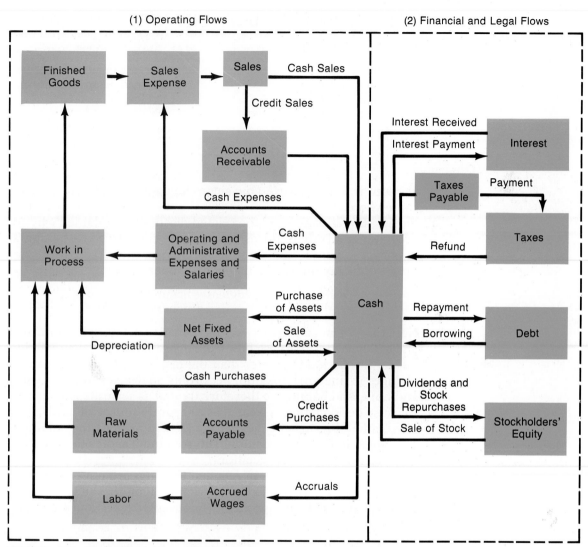

FIGURE 3.2 Cash Flow Through the Firm
The firm's cash flows can be broken into (1) operating flows, which relate directly to the
production and sale of the firm's products, and (2) financial and legal flows, which are
concerned with the firm's debt and equity financing activities as well as taxes.

cash. If the firm's inventory increased by $2,500 the change would be a
use of cash, meaning that $2,500 was tied up in goods available for sale.

A few additional points should be clarified with respect to the classification scheme in Table 3.7:

1 A *decrease* in an asset, such as the firm's cash balance, is a *source of
   cash flow* because cash is released for some purpose, such as adding
   to inventory. On the other hand, an *increase* in the firm's bank

TABLE 3.7 The Sources and Uses of Cash

Sources	Uses
Decrease in any asset	Increase in any asset
Increase in any liability	Decrease in any liability
Net profits after taxes	Net loss
Depreciation and other noncash charges	Dividends paid
Sale of stock	Repurchase or retirement of stock

account is a *use of cash flow* since the cash must be drawn from somewhere.

2 Earlier, Equation 3.1 and the related discussion explained why depreciation and other noncash charges are considered cash inflows, or sources of cash. Adding noncash charges back to the firm's net profits after taxes gives cash flow from operations:

$$\text{Cash flow from operations} = \text{net profits after taxes} + \text{noncash charges}$$

Note that a firm can have a *net loss* (negative net profits after taxes) and still have positive cash flow from operations when depreciation during the period is greater than the net loss. In the statement of changes in financial position, net profits after taxes (or net losses) and noncash charges are therefore treated as separate entries.

3 Because depreciation is treated as a separate source of funds, only *gross* rather than *net* changes in fixed assets appear on the statement of changes in financial position. This treatment avoids the potential double counting of depreciation.

4 Direct entries of changes in retained earnings are not classified as sources or uses of cash; instead, entries for items that affect retained earnings appear as net profits or losses after taxes and cash dividends.

Developing the Statement of Changes in Financial Position

The statement of changes in financial position can be developed in two steps: (1) prepare a preliminary statement and (2) adjust the preliminary statement to obtain the final statement. Using this two-step procedure, the financial statements for Elton Corporation presented in Tables 3.1 and 3.2 can be used to demonstrate the preparation of its 1987 cash statement of changes in financial position.

THE PRELIMINARY STATEMENT   A three-step procedure can be used to prepare a preliminary statement of changes in financial position.

Step 1: Calculate the balance sheet changes in assets, liabilities, and stockholders' equity over the period of concern. (*Note:* Calculate only the *net* fixed asset change for the fixed asset account.)

Step 2: Using the classification scheme in Table 3.7, classify each change calculated in Step 1 as either a source (S) or a use (U). (*Note:* Changes in stockholders' equity accounts are classified in the same way as changes in liabilities—increases are sources and decreases are uses.)

Step 3: List and sum all sources found in Steps 1 and 2 on the left and all uses found in Steps 1 and 2 on the right to create a preliminary statement of changes in financial position. If this statement is prepared correctly, *total sources should equal total uses*.

Application of the three-step procedure to prepare a preliminary statement of changes in financial position is demonstrated in the following example.

EXAMPLE

The Elton Corporation's balance sheets in Table 3.2 can be used to develop its 1987 preliminary statement of changes in financial position.

Step 1: The key balance sheet entries from Elton Corporation's balance sheet in Table 3.2 are listed in a stacked format in Table 3.8. Column (1) lists the account name and columns (2) and (3) give the 1987 and 1986 values, respectively, for each account. In column (4) the change in the balance sheet account between 1986 and 1987 is calculated. Note that for fixed assets only the net fixed asset change of +$200,000 is calculated.

Step 2: Using the classification scheme from Table 3.7 and recognizing that changes in stockholders' equity are classified in the same way as changes in liabilities, the changes in column (4) of Table 3.8 are classified in column (5).

Step 3: The sources (S) and uses (U) from Table 3.8 are listed and totaled in Table 3.9 to create the preliminary statement of changes in financial position. Note: (1) all sources are listed on the left and all uses are listed on the right; (2) accounts for which no change (N) occurred are excluded from the statement; and (3) total sources ($900,000) equal total uses ($900,000). ■

TABLE 3.8 Balance Sheet Changes and Classification of Elton Corporation's Key Accounts ($000) between 1986 and 1987

Account (1)	ACCOUNT BALANCE (FROM TABLE 3.2) 1987 (2)	1986 (3)	Change [(2) − (3)] (4)	Classification source (S); use (U); no change (N) (5)
Assets				
Cash	$ 400	$ 300	+$100	U
Marketable securities	600	200	+ 400	U
Accounts receivable	400	500	− 100	S
Inventories	600	900	− 300	S
Net fixed assets	1,200	1,000	+ 200	U
Liabilities				
Accounts payable	700	500	+ 200	S
Notes payable	600	700	− 100	U
Accruals	100	200	− 100	U
Long-term debts	600	400	+ 200	S
Stockholders' equity				
Preferred stock	100	100	0	N
Common stock at par	120	120	0	N
Paid-in capital in excess of par	380	380	0	N
Retained earnings	600	500	+ 100	S

ADJUSTMENTS TO GET FINAL STATEMENT While the preliminary statement of changes in financial position in Table 3.9 is in balance, it lacks important income statement information. Two of the entries in the statement — (1) the increase in retained earnings and (2) the increase in net fixed assets — contain important cash flow information. The two adjustments needed to convert the preliminary to the final statement involve these entries.

TABLE 3.9 Preliminary Statement of Changes in Financial Position for Elton Corporation ($000) for the Year Ended December 31, 1987

Sources (S)[a]		Uses (U)[a]	
Decrease in accounts receivable	$100	Increase in cash	$100
Decrease in inventories	300	Increase in marketable securities	400
Increase in accounts payable	200	Increase in net fixed assets	200
Increase in long-term debts	200	Decrease in notes payable	100
Increase in retained earnings	100	Decrease in accruals	100
Total sources	$900	Total Uses	$900

[a] Data from columns (4) and (5) of Table 3.8.

CASH FLOW: THE NEW GOSPEL

On Wall Street today, it seems that everyone is following the money. Cash flow is the new gospel, and financial analysts, investors and takeover specialists praise its revelatory power. The cash generated by a company's operations is being hailed as a far more reliable barometer of financial health than the more traditional earnings yardstick, which, critics contend, can be skewed by accounting conventions. "Cash flow is a real measure of a company's ability to finance itself and pay its obligations," says John Crosby, a managing director at Merrill Lynch.

Businessmen have always understood that solvency and strength are more a function of cash flow than of reported earnings. Wall Street began to grasp this distinction largely in the wake of numerous leveraged buyouts — the feasibility of which are a function of cash flow projections as well as of the collateral value of assets. The fixation on cash flow was reinforced by the coincident adoption of the accelerated cost recovery system (ACRS) in the 1981 Economic Recovery Tax Act, which unleashed a torrential flow of corporate cash.

Wall Street's enthusiasm seems to vindicate a small group of gadfly analysts who for years have maintained that cash flow measures provide a more penetrating glimpse into a company's financial condition than reported earnings. But the new cash flow cultists have adapted — some would say subverted — the discipline for radically different ends than its pioneers, who generally used the numbers as a critical gloss on sometimes hyperbolic earnings reports. By contrast, Wall Street's new breed of practitioners exploit the discrepancy between strong cash flow and lackluster earnings as the lever for acquisition bids. These takeover specialists, critics claim, are all too eager to mortgage the company's future to accomplish their goals.

The pursuit of cash flow numbers is certainly fraught with danger, accounting professionals and some analysts warn. To begin with, there is little consensus about what the term actually means. "It's a Tower of Babel situation," says Halsey Bullen of the Financial Accounting Standards Board, the accounting profession's rulemaking body. "People are using the same words but not the same definitions." FASB's concern over the lack of comparability among cash flow statements prompted it to launch a study of the issue in the hope of developing some standards for reporting cash flow. . . .

Source: Elizabeth Kaplan, "Wall Street Zeros in on Cash Flow," pp. 40–41. Reprinted with the permission of *DUN'S BUSINESS MONTH*, July 1985. Copyright 1985, Dun & Bradstreet Publications Corporation.

Retained Earnings Adjustment. The change in retained earnings reflects the *difference* between net profits and dividend payments during the period:

> Net profits after taxes
> Less: Dividends paid
> Change in retained earnings

Therefore in order to provide more useful information in the final statement of changes in financial position, net profits after taxes and dividends are substituted for the change in retained earnings on the preliminary statement.

EXAMPLE

The Elton Corporation's change in retained earnings of +$100,000 during 1987 resulted from the following:

Net profits after taxes (from 1987 income statement in Table 3.2)	$180,000
Less: Dividends paid (from 1987 statement of retained earnings in Table 3.3)	80,000
Change in retained earnings	+$100,000

Note that the amount of dividends paid was obtained from the statement of retained earnings. If such a statement is not available, this value can be found by subtracting the change in retained earnings from net profits after taxes (dividends = $180,000 − $100,000 = $80,000).

In the final statement of changes in financial position in Table 3.10 the following two entries:

Net profits after taxes	$180,000 (Source)
Dividends paid	$ 80,000 (Use)

are substituted for:

Increase in retained earnings	$100,000 (Source)

It can be seen that the net effect of the net profit and dividend entries is a $100,000 source ($180,000 source − $80,000 use), which is the amount of the retained earnings change eliminated. ■

Net Fixed Assets Adjustment. The change in net fixed assets reflects the *difference* between any change in gross fixed assets and depreciation expense. The depreciation expense from the income statement is generally equal to the change in accumulated depreciation during the period.[6]

---

[6] When the firm retires or sells fixed assets, the change in accumulated depreciation during the period will not equal the depreciation expense on the income statement. In this case special adjustments to gross fixed assets are required. To simplify, we will use depreciation expense, which is assumed equal to the change in accumulated depreciation.

> Change in gross fixed assets
> Less: Depreciation expense
> Change in net fixed assets

In order to provide more useful information on the statement of changes in financial position, the change in gross fixed assets and depreciation expense are substituted for the change in net fixed assets on the preliminary statement.

EXAMPLE

The Elton Corporation's change in net fixed assets of $+\$200,000$ during 1987 resulted from the following:

Change in gross fixed assets (from 1987 and 1986 balance sheets in Table 3.2; $2,500,000 in 1987 − $2,200,000 in 1986)	+$300,000
Less: Depreciation expense (from 1987 income statement in Table 3.1)	100,000
Change in net fixed assets	+$200,000

Thus in the final statement of changes in financial position in Table 3.10, the following two entries:

Increase in gross fixed assets	$300,000 (Use)
Depreciation expense	$100,000 (Source)

are substituted for:

Increase in net fixed assets	$200,000 (Use)

The net effect of the gross fixed asset and depreciation entries is a $200,000 use ($300,000 use − $100,000 source), which is the amount of the net fixed asset entry eliminated. ■

The Final Statement. A number of important points relative to the statement of changes in financial position are to be noted in Table 3.10:

1 "Total sources" and "total uses" should be equal. If they are not, an error has been made somewhere. The amount of total sources and uses ($1,080,000) is not an important value.
2 Net profits after taxes are normally the first source listed, and dividends are normally the first use. Ordering items this way makes it easy to calculate the change in retained earnings.
3 Depreciation expense and increases in gross fixed assets are listed

TABLE 3.10 Final Cash Statement of Changes in Financial Position for Elton Corporation ($000) for the Year Ended December 31, 1987

Sources (S)		Uses (U)	
Net profits after taxes	$ 180	Dividends paid	$ 80
Depreciation expense	100	Increase in gross fixed	
Decrease in accounts		assets	300
receivable	100	Increase in cash	100
Decrease in		Increase in marketable	
inventories	300	securities	400
Increase in accounts		Decrease in notes payable	100
payable		Decrease in accruals	100
Increase in long-		Total uses	$1,080
term debts	200		
Total sources	$1,080		

second to make it easy to compare them. Placing depreciation just below net profits after taxes also makes the firm's cash flow from operations easily calculable (see Equation 3.1).

4 The order of the remaining sources and uses does not matter; the only requirement is that sources appear on the left and uses on the right.

NET WORKING CAPITAL STATEMENT The statement of changes in financial position in Table 3.10 is a cash statement summarizing the changes in all accounts during the period of concern. A more compact statement of changes is one in which *net working capital* rather than cash is the pivital element. In this statement, instead of individual current asset and current liability changes, a summary entry—the change in net working capital—is made. (*Net working capital,* as noted earlier, is the difference between total current assets and total current liabilities.) Changes in net working capital are classified in a fashion similar to changes in assets:

Decrease in net working capital (Source)
Increase in net working capital (Use)

To prepare the statement of changes in financial position on a net working capital basis, all noncurrent account entries are the same as for the cash statement.

EXAMPLE

The first step in preparing the statement of changes in net working capital for Elton Corporation is to calculate the actual change in

TABLE 3.11 Calculation of Elton Corporation's Change in Net Working Capital ($000), 1986 to 1987

	1987	1986
Total current assets	$2,000	$1,900
Less: Total current liabilities	1,400	1,400
Net working capital	$ 600	$ 500
Change in net working capital	+$100 (Use)	

net working capital. Using the balance sheets in Table 3.2, the change in net working capital between 1986 and 1987 is calculated as shown in Table 3.11. Net working capital increased from $500,000 in 1986 to $600,000 in 1987, resulting in an increase of $100,000. As noted in Table 3.11, this change is a use of funds. Substituting the $100,000 increase in net working capital for all current account entries in the cash statement in Table 3.10 and retaining all other (noncurrent) entries results in the statement shown in Table 3.12. ■

Comparing the cash and net working capital statements for Elton Corporation in Tables 3.10 and 3.12, respectively, the more detailed nature of the cash statement is apparent. Due to the useful cash flow information provided by the more detailed cash statement, most financial analysts prefer it. An understanding of the cash statement is therefore of prime importance to the financial manager.

INTERPRETING THE STATEMENT The statement of changes in financial position allows the financial manager and other interested parties to analyze the firm's past and possibly future funds flow. The manager should pay special attention to the major sources and uses of funds in order to determine whether any developments have occurred that are contrary to the company's financial policies. In addition, the fulfillment of projected goals can be evaluated using the statement. Specific links between sources and uses cannot be made using this statement, but it

TABLE 3.12 Net Working Capital Statement of Changes in Financial Position for Elton Corporation ($000) for the Year Ended December 31, 1987

Sources (S)		Uses (U)	
Net profits after taxes	$180	Dividends paid	$ 80
Depreciation expense	100	Increase in gross fixed assets	300
Increase in long-term debts	200	Increase in net working capital	100
Total sources	$480	Total uses	$480

can be used to isolate inefficiencies. For example, increases in accounts receivable and inventories resulting in major uses of funds may respectively signal credit or inventory problems.

In addition, the financial manager can prepare and analyze a statement of changes in financial position developed from projected, or pro forma, financial statements. This approach can be used to determine whether planned actions are desirable in view of the resulting cash flows.

EXAMPLE

Analysis of Elton Corporation's cash statement of changes in financial position in Table 3.10 does not seem to indicate the existence of any major problems for the company. The sources and uses of funds seem to be distributed in a fashion consistent with prudent financial management. The firm seems to be growing since (1) less than half of its earnings ($80,000 out of $180,000) were paid to owners as dividends and (2) gross fixed assets increased by three times the amount of historic cost written off through depreciation expense ($300,000 increase in gross fixed assets versus $100,000 in depreciation expense). Major sources of funds were obtained by decreasing inventories and increasing accounts payable. The major use of funds — an increase in marketable securities — reflects improved liquidity. Other sources and uses by Elton Corporation tend to support the fact that the firm was well managed financially during the period. *An understanding of the basic financial principles presented throughout this text is a prerequisite to the effective interpretation of the statement of changes in financial position.* ■

SUMMARY

● The stockholders' annual report of a publicly traded corporation includes, in addition to the president's letter and various subjective and factual information, four key financial statements: (1) the income statement, (2) the balance sheet, (3) the statement of retained earnings, and (4) the statement of changes in financial position (covering at least the two most recent years of operations.)
● The income statement summarizes operating results during the period of concern. The balance sheet summarizes the firm's financial position at a

given point in time. The statement of retained earnings reconciles income and cash dividends with retained earnings for the period. The statement of changes in financial position provides a summary of funds flow over the period.

● Depreciation, or the allocation of historic cost, is the most common type of corporate noncash expenditure. To estimate cash flow from operations, depreciation and any other noncash charges are added back to net profits after taxes.

● The depreciable value of an asset and its depreciable life are determined using the Accelerated Cost Recovery System (ACRS) standards set out in the federal tax codes. ACRS groups assets (excluding real estate) into six property classes based on length of recovery period—3, 5, 7, 10, 15, and 20 years—and can be applied over the appropriate period using a schedule of yearly depreciation percentages for each period.

● The funds flow of a firm can be measured either by cash or by net working capital. Sources of funds increase the firm's cash flow, and uses of funds result in a decrease in cash flow.

● A preliminary statement of changes in financial position can be developed by finding, classifying as sources or uses, and totaling changes in balance sheet accounts over the period. The final statement of changes is developed from the preliminary by replacing the change in retained earnings with net profits after taxes and dividends, and by replacing the change in net fixed assets with the change in gross fixed assets and depreciation expense.

● Interpretation of the statement of changes in financial position involves evaluation of the level of and relationship between various sources and uses of funds. An understanding of basic financial principles is a prerequisite to the effective interpretation of the statement.

QUESTIONS

3-1 What are *generally accepted accounting principles (GAAP)*? Who authorizes GAAP? What role does the *Securities and Exchange Commission (SEC)* play in the financial reporting activities of corporations?

3-2 Describe the basic contents, including the key financial statements, included in the stockholders' reports of publicly held corporations.

3-3 What basic information is contained in each of the following financial statements? Briefly describe each.
   a Income statement
   b Balance sheet
   c Statement of retained earnings

3-4 In what sense does depreciation act as cash inflow? How can a firm's after-tax profits be adjusted to determine cash flow from operations?

3-5 Briefly describe the first four Accelerated Cost Recovery System (ACRS) property classes and recovery periods. Explain how the depreciation percentages are determined using the ACRS recovery periods.

3-6 Define *net working capital* and discuss its use as a measure of funds flow. What is the alternative and more popular definition of *funds flow?*

3-7 Describe the overall cash flow through the firm in terms of (a) operating flows and (b) financial and legal flows.

3-8 List and describe *sources of cash* and *uses of cash*. Discuss why a decrease in cash is a source and an increase in cash is a use.

3-9 Describe the three-step procedure used to develop a *preliminary* statement of changes in financial position. What two adjustments are required in order to obtain the *final* statement?

3-10 Describe the statement of changes in financial position, and explain the difference between the cash and the net working capital statement.

3-11 How is the statement of changes in financial position interpreted and used by the financial manager and other interested parties?

PROBLEMS

3-1 **(Reviewing Basic Financial Statements)**   The income statement for the year ended December 31, 1987, the balance sheets for December 31, 1987 and 1986, and the statement of retained earnings for the year ended December 31, 1987, for Gold Equipment Company are given below. Briefly discuss the form and informational content of each of these statements.

Income Statement
Gold Equipment Company
for the Year Ended December 31, 1987

Sales revenue		$600,000
Less: Cost of goods sold		460,000
Gross profit		$140,000
Less: Operating expenses		
General and administrative expense	$30,000	
Depreciation expense	30,000	
Total operating expense		60,000
Operating profit		$ 80,000
Less: Interest expense		10,000
Net profits before taxes		$ 70,000
Less: Taxes		27,100
Earnings available for common stockholders		$ 42,900
Earnings per share (EPS)		$2.15

Balance Sheets
Gold Equipment Company

	DECEMBER 31,	
Assets	1987	1986
Cash	$ 15,000	$ 16,000
Marketable securities	7,200	8,000
Accounts receivable	34,100	42,200
Inventories	82,000	50,000
Total current assets	$138,300	$116,200
Land and buildings	$150,000	$150,000
Machinery and equipment	200,000	190,000
Furniture and fixtures	54,000	50,000
Other	11,000	10,000
Total gross fixed assets	$415,000	$400,000
Less: Accumulated depreciation	145,000	115,000
Net fixed assets	$270,000	$285,000
Total assets	$408,300	$401,200

Liabilities and stockholders' equity

Accounts payable	$ 57,000	$ 49,000
Notes payable	13,000	16,000
Accruals	5,000	6,000
Total current liabilities	$ 75,000	$ 71,000
Long-term debt	$150,000	$160,000
Stockholders' equity		
Common stock equity (20,000 shares outstanding)	$110,200	$120,000
Retained earnings	73,100	50,200
Total stockholders' equity	$183,300	$170,200
Total liabilities and stockholders' equity	$408,300	$401,200

Statement of Retained Earnings
Gold Equipment Company
for the Year Ended December 31, 1987

Retained earnings balance (January 1, 1987)	$50,200
Plus: Net profits after taxes (for 1987)	42,900
Less: Cash dividends (paid during 1987)	(20,000)
Retained earnings balance (December 31, 1987)	$73,100

3-2 **(Financial Statement Account Identification)** For each of the accounts listed at the top of page 70:
   a In column (1) indicate in which statement—income statement (IS) or
   balance sheet (BS)—the account belongs.
   b In column (2) indicate whether the account is a current asset (CA),
   current liability (CL), expense (E), fixed asset (FA), long-term debt
   (LTD), revenue (R), or stockholders' equity (SE).

Account name	(1) Statement	(2) Type of account
Accounts payable	————	————
Accounts receivable	————	————
Accruals	————	————
Accumulated depreciation	————	————
Administrative expense	————	————
Buildings	————	————
Cash	————	————
Common stock (at par)	————	————
Cost of goods sold	————	————
Depreciation	————	————
Equipment	————	————
General expense	————	————
Interest expense	————	————
Inventories	————	————
Land	————	————
Long-term debts	————	————
Machinery	————	————
Marketable securities	————	————
Notes payable	————	————
Operating expense	————	————
Paid-in capital in excess of par	————	————
Preferred stock	————	————
Preferred stock dividends	————	————
Retained earnings	————	————
Sales revenue	————	————
Selling expense	————	————
Taxes	————	————
Vehicles	————	————

3-3 **(Income Statement Preparation)** Use the *appropriate items* from those listed below to prepare in good form Driscoll Corporation's income statement for the year ended December 31, 1987.

Item	Values ($000) at or for year ended December 31, 1987
Accounts receivable	$350
Accumulated depreciation	205
Cost of goods sold	285
Depreciation expense	55
General and administrative expense	60
Interest expense	25
Preferred stock dividends	10
Sales revenue	525
Selling expense	35
Stockholders' equity	265
Taxes	rate = 40%

3-4 **(Income Statement Preparation)** Mary Hernandez, a self-employed Certified Public Accountant (CPA), on December 31, 1987, completed her first full year in business. During the year she billed $135,000 in business. She had two employees, a bookkeeper and a clerical assistant. In addition to her *monthly* salary of $2,750, she paid annual salaries of $18,000 and $14,000, respectively, to the bookkeeper and the clerical assistant. Employment taxes and benefit costs for health insurance, etc., for Ms. Hernandez and her employees totaled $12,800 for the year. Expenses for office supplies, including postage, totaled $3,800 for the year. In addition, Ms. Hernandez spent $6,500 during the year on travel and entertainment associated with client visits and new business development. Lease payments (a tax-deductible expense) for the office space rented were $1,000 *per month*. Depreciation expense on the office furniture and fixtures was $6,200 for the year. During the year Ms. Hernandez paid interest of $6,900 on the $50,000 borrowed to start the business. She paid an average tax rate of 30 percent during 1987.

a Prepare an income statement for Mary Hernandez, CPA for the year ended December 31, 1987.

b How much operating cash flow did Mary realize during 1987?

c Evaluate her 1987 financial performance.

3-5 **(Calculation of EPS and Retained Earnings)** Zach Inc. ended 1987 with net profit *before* taxes of $218,000. The company is subject to a 40 percent tax rate and must pay $32,000 in preferred stock dividends prior to distributing any earnings on the 85,000 shares of common stock currently outstanding.

a Calculate Zach, Inc.'s 1987 earnings per share (EPS).

b If the firm paid common stock dividends of $.80 per share, how many dollars would go to retained earnings?

3-6 **(Balance Sheet Preparation)** Use the *appropriate items* from those listed below to prepare in good form Kowalski Corporation's balance sheet at December 31, 1987.

Item	Values ($000) at year ended December 31, 1987
Accounts payable	$ 220
Accounts receivable	450
Accruals	55
Accumulated depreciation	265
Buildings	225
Cash	215
Common stock (at par)	90
Cost of goods sold	2,500
Depreciation expense	45
Equipment	140
Furniture and fixtures	170
General expense	320
Inventories	375
Land	100
Long-term debts	420

(Continued)

(*Continued*)

Machinery	420
Marketable securities	75
Notes payable	475
Paid-in capital in excess of par	360
Preferred stock	100
Retained earnings	210
Sales revenue	3,600
Vehicles	25

3-7 (Initial Sale Price of Common Stock)   OK Industries has one issue of preferred stock and one issue of common stock outstanding. Given OK's stockholders' equity account below, determine the original price per share at which the firm sold its single issue of common stock.

Stockholders' Equity ($000)

Preferred stock	$ 125
Common stock ($.75 par, 300,000 shares outstanding)	225
Paid-in capital in excess of par on common stock	2,625
Retained earnings	900
Total stockholders' equity	$3,875

3-8 (Financial Statement Preparation)   The balance sheet for Todd Enterprises for December 31, 1986 is given below. Following the statement is information relevant to Todd's 1987 operations. Using the data presented:
  a Prepare in good form an income statement for Todd Enterprises for the year ended December 31, 1987. Be sure to show earnings per share (EPS).
  b Prepare in good form a balance sheet for Todd Enterprises for December 31, 1987.

Balance Sheet ($000)
Todd Enterprises
December 31, 1986

Assets		Liabilities and stockholders' equity	
Cash	$ 40	Accounts payable	$ 50
Marketable securities	10	Notes payable	80
Accounts receivable	80	Accruals	10
Inventories	100	Total current liabilities	$140
Total current assets	$230	Long-term debt	$270
Gross fixed assets	$890	Preferred stock	40
Less: Accumulated		Common stock ($.75 par,	
depreciation	240	80,000 shares)	60
Net fixed assets	$650	Paid-in capital in excess of par	260
Total assets	$880	Retained earnings	110
		Total stockholders' equity	$470
		Total liabilities and stockholders' equity	$880

Relevant Information
Todd Enterprises

1. Sales in 1987 were $1,200,000.
2. Cost of goods sold equals 60 percent of sales.
3. Operating expenses equals 15 percent of sales.
4. Interest expense is 10 percent of the total beginning balance of notes payable and long-term debts.
5. The firm pays 40 percent taxes on ordinary income.
6. Preferred stock dividends of $4,000 were paid in 1987.
7. Cash and marketable securities are unchanged.
8. Accounts receivable equal 8 percent of sales.
9. Inventory equals 10 percent of sales.
10. The firm acquired $30,000 of additional fixed assets in 1987.
11. Total depreciation expense in 1987 was $20,000.
12. Accounts payable equals 5 percent of sales.
13. Notes payable, long-term debt, preferred stock, common stock, and paid-in capital in excess of par remain unchanged.
14. Accruals are unchanged.
15. Cash dividends of $119,000 were paid to common stockholders in 1987.

3-9 **(Statement of Retained Earnings)** Colton Cosmetics began 1987 with a retained earnings balance of $928,000. During 1987 the firm earned $377,000 after taxes. From this amount preferred stockholders were paid $47,000 in dividends. At year-end 1987 the firm's retained earnings totaled $1,048,000. The firm had 140,000 shares of common stock outstanding during 1987.

  a Prepare a statement of retained earnings for the year ended December 31, 1987 for Colton Cosmetics.

  b Calculate the firm's 1987 earnings per share (EPS).

  c How large a per share cash dividend did the firm pay on common stock during 1987?

3-10 **(Cash Flow)** A firm had earnings after taxes of $50,000 in 1987. Depreciation charges were $28,000, and a $2,000 charge for amortization on a bond discount was incurred. What was the actual cash flow from operations?

3-11 **(Depreciation)** On January 1, 1987, Antex Corporation acquired two new assets. Asset A was research equipment costing $17,000 and having a three-year recovery period. Asset B was duplicating equipment having an installed cost of $45,000 and a five-year recovery period. Using the ACRS depreciation percentages in Table 3.6, prepare a depreciation schedule for each of these assets.

3-12 **(Depreciation and Cash Flows)** A firm expects to have earnings before depreciation and taxes of $160,000 in each of the next six years. It is considering the purchase of an asset costing $140,000, requiring $10,000 in installation costs, and having a recovery period of five years.

  a Calculate the annual depreciation for the asset purchase using the ACRS depreciation percentages in Table 3.6.

b Calculate the annual operating cash flows for each of the six years. Assume a 40 percent ordinary tax rate.

c Compare and discuss your findings in **a** and **b**.

3-13 **(Depreciation and Cash Flow)** A firm in the third year of depreciating its only asset, originally costing $180,000 and having a five-year ACRS recovery period, has gathered the following data relative to the given year's operations.

Accruals	$ 15,000
Current assets	120,000
Interest expense	15,000
Sales revenue	400,000
Inventory	70,000
Total costs before depreciation, interest, and taxes	290,000
Tax rate on ordinary income	40%

a Use the *relevant data* above to determine the *cash flow from operations* for the current year.

b Explain the impact that depreciation, as well as any other noncash charges, has on a firm's cash flows.

3-14 **(Classifying Sources and Uses)** Classify each of the following items as a source (S) or a use (U) of funds, or as neither (N).

Item	Change ($)	Item	Change ($)
Cash	+100	Accounts receivable	−700
Accounts payable	−1,000	Net profits	+600
Notes payable	+500	Depreciation	+100
Long-term debt	−2,000	Repurchase of stock	+600
Inventory	+200	Cash dividends	+800
Fixed assets	+400	Sale of stock	+1,000

3-15 **(Finding Dividends Paid)** Vent Manufacturing's net profits after taxes in 1987 totaled $186,000. The firm's year-end 1987 and 1986 retained earnings on its balance sheet totaled $812,000 and $736,000, respectively. How many dollars, if any, in dividends did Vent pay in 1987?

3-16 **(Preparing Statements of Changes in Financial Position)** Given the balance sheets and selected data from the income statement of Raney Russell Company at the top of page 75:

a Prepare the firm's statement of changes in financial position on a *cash basis* for the year ended December 31, 1987.

b Interpret the statement prepared in **a**.

c Prepare the firm's statement of changes in financial position on a *net working capital basis* for the year ended December 31, 1987.

d Compare and discuss the net working capital statement developed in **c** with the cash statement in **a**.

Balance Sheets
Raney Russell Company

	DECEMBER 31	
Assets	**1987**	**1986**
Cash	$ 1,500	$ 1,000
Marketable securities	1,800	1,200
Accounts receivable	2,000	1,800
Inventories	2,900	2,800
Total current assets	$ 8,200	$ 6,800
Gross fixed assets	$29,500	$28,100
Less: Accumulated depreciation	14,700	13,100
Net fixed assets	$14,800	$15,000
Total assets	$23,000	$21,800

Liabilities and stockholders' equity

Accounts payable	$ 1,600	$ 1,500
Notes payable	2,800	2,200
Accruals	200	300
Total current assets	$ 4,600	$ 4,000
Long-term debt	$ 5,000	$ 5,000
Common stock	$10,000	$10,000
Retained earnings	3,400	2,800
Total stockholders' equity	$13,400	$12,800
Total liabilities and stockholders' equity	$23,000	$21,800

Additional data

Depreciation expense	$ 1,600
Net profits after taxes	1,400

3-17 **(Preparing Statements of Changes in Financial Position)** Using the 1987 income statement and the 1987 and 1986 balance sheets for Gold Equipment Company given in Problem 3-1, do the following:
  a Prepare the firm's statement of changes in financial position on a *cash basis* for the year ended December 31, 1987.
  b Interpret the statement prepared in **a**.
  c Prepare the firm's statement of changes in financial position on a *net working capital basis* for the year ended December 31, 1987.
  d Compare and discuss the net working capital statement developed in **c** with the cash statement in **a**.

Part Two

FINANCIAL ANALYSIS AND PLANNING

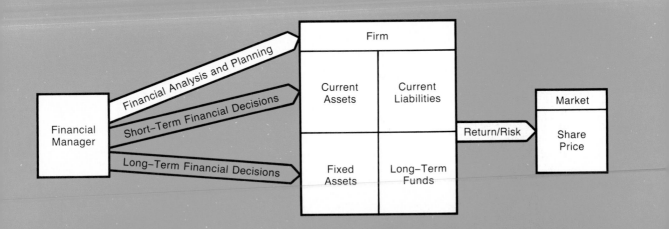

4

FINANCIAL STATEMENT ANALYSIS

After studying this chapter, you should be able to:

- Understand the parties interested in performing financial ratio analysis and the common types of ratio comparisons.

- Use popular ratios to analyze a firm's liquidity and the activity of inventory, accounts receivable, accounts payable, fixed assets, and total assets.

- Assess the firm's debt position as well as its ability to meet the payments associated with debt.

- Evaluate a firm's profitability relative to sales, asset investment, owners' equity investment, and share value.

- Use the DuPont system and a complete ratio analysis to evaluate a firm's financial status and make appropriate recommendations.

In the preceding chapter we studied the format, components, and basic purpose of each of the firm's four basic financial statements. The information contained in these statements is of major significance to shareholders, creditors, and managers, all of whom regularly need to have relative measures of the company's operating efficiency and condition. *Relative* is the key word here since the analysis of financial statements is based on the knowledge and use of *ratios* or *relative values*.

THE USE OF FINANCIAL RATIOS

ratio analysis Involves the methods of calculating and interpreting financial ratios to assess the firm's performance and status.

Ratio analysis involves the methods of calculating and interpreting financial ratios in order to assess the firm's performance and status. The basic inputs to ratio analysis are the firm's income statement and balance sheet for the periods to be examined. However, before proceeding further we need to describe the various parties and the types of comparisons made using ratio analysis.

Interested Parties

Ratio analysis of a firm's financial statements is of interest to shareholders, creditors, and the firm's own management. Both the present and prospective shareholders are interested in the firm's current and future level of risk (liquidity, activity, and debt) and return (profitability). As will be explained in Chapter 12, these two dimensions directly affect share price. The firm's creditors are primarily interested in the short-term liquidity of the company and in its ability to make interest and principal payments. A secondary concern of creditors is the firm's profitability; they want assurance that the business is healthy and will continue to be successful. Management, like stockholders, must be concerned with all aspects of the firm's financial situation. Thus it attempts to operate in a manner that will result in financial ratios that will be considered favorable by both owners and creditors. In addition, management uses ratios to monitor the firm's performance from period to period. Any unexpected changes are examined in order to isolate developing problems.

Types of Comparisons

Ratio analysis does not merely involve the application of a formula to financial data in order to calculate a given ratio. More important is the *interpretation* of the ratio value. To answer such questions as, Is it too high or too low? Is it good or bad?, a meaningful standard or basis for comparison is needed. Two types of ratio comparisons can be made: cross-sectional and time-series.

CROSS-SECTIONAL ANALYSIS **Cross-sectional analysis** involves the comparison of different firms' financial ratios at the same point in time. The typical business is interested in how well it has performed in relation to its competitors. (If the competitors are also corporations, their reported financial statements should be available for analysis.) Often the firm's performance will be compared to that of the industry leader; and the firm may uncover major operating differences, which, if changed, will increase efficiency. Another popular type of comparison is to industry averages. These figures can be found in the *Almanac of Business and Industrial Financial Ratios, Dun & Bradstreet's Key Business Ratios, Dun's Business Month, FTC Quarterly Reports, Robert Morris Associates Statement Studies,* and other sources such as industry association publications. A sample from one available source of industry averages is given in Table 4.1.

> **cross-sectional analysis**
> The comparison of different firms' financial ratios at the same point in time.

The comparison of a particular ratio to the standard is made in order to isolate any *deviations from the norm*. Many people mistakenly believe that in the case of ratios for which higher values are preferred, as long as the firm being analyzed has a value in excess of the industry average, it can be viewed favorably. However, this "bigger is better" viewpoint can be misleading. Quite often a ratio value that has a large but positive deviation from the norm can be indicative of problems that may, upon more careful analysis, be more severe than had the ratio been below the industry average.[1] It is therefore important to look for *large deviations to either side* of the industry standard.

The analyst must also recognize that ratio comparisons resulting in large deviations from the norm reflect only the *symptoms* of a problem. Further analysis of the financial statements coupled with discussions with key managers is typically required to isolate the *causes* of the problem. Once this is accomplished, the financial manager must develop prescriptive actions for eliminating such causes. The fundamental point is that *ratio analysis merely directs the analyst to potential areas of concern; it does not provide conclusive evidence as to the existence of a problem.*

EXAMPLE

In early 1988 the chief financial analyst at Dwiggins Manufacturing gathered data on the firm's financial performance during 1987, the year just ended. The analyst calculated a variety of ratios and obtained industry averages for use in making comparisons.

---

[1] Similarly, in the case of ratios for which "smaller is better," one must be as concerned with calculated values that deviate significantly *below* the norm, or industry average, as with values that fall above it. Significant deviations, regardless of the side of the norm, require further investigation by the analyst.

TABLE 4.1 Industry Average Ratios for Selected Lines of Business[a]

Line of business (number of concerns reporting)	Quick ratio (X)	Current ratio (X)	Current liabilities to net worth (%)	Current liabilities to inventory (%)	Total liabilities to net worth (%)	Fixed assets to net worth (%)	Collection period (days)	Net sales to inventory (X)	Total assets to net sales (%)	Net sales to net working capital (X)	Accounts payable to net sales (%)	Return on net sales (%)	Return on total assets (%)	Return on net worth (%)
Computer-related services (785)	2.9	3.9	17.6	66.7	24.4	22.3	23.8	51.2	24.1	17.7	1.2	21.6	27.8	73.0
	1.3	**1.8**	**58.6**	**161.2**	**80.3**	**49.6**	**45.2**	**17.3**	**40.4**	**8.1**	**3.3**	**9.3**	**12.7**	**31.7**
	0.7	1.1	138.9	336.1	178.6	98.6	75.9	6.0	80.8	3.8	8.9	2.9	4.7	14.4
Crude oil and natural gas (1192)	2.0	3.5	8.9	169.6	14.3	21.0	32.4	41.2	109.2	10.9	5.1	23.1	10.2	21.1
	0.9	**1.4**	**27.0**	**400.8**	**60.1**	**64.1**	**64.4**	**20.1**	**222.5**	**4.1**	**12.1**	**9.7**	**4.0**	**9.2**
	0.5	0.8	73.4	710.4	152.7	136.7	130.5	10.4	396.7	1.6	35.2	0.4	(0.9)	(1.4)
Grocery stores (2096)	1.3	4.5	15.2	36.4	27.4	28.2	1.0	23.9	12.3	32.4	1.1	4.0	15.8	32.1
	0.5	**2.2**	**44.6**	**73.8**	**73.1**	**59.3**	**2.5**	**17.2**	**18.3**	**17.5**	**2.1**	**1.7**	**7.6**	**15.2**
	0.2	1.4	103.6	118.4	182.9	113.3	6.2	11.8	29.9	9.8	3.6	0.5	2.2	5.1
Metal-working machinery (67)	1.9	5.4	14.3	65.1	22.8	18.3	29.8	7.4	47.1	7.0	2.1	11.9	15.8	40.9
	0.9	**2.5**	**43.6**	**104.3**	**84.7**	**44.2**	**52.5**	**5.3**	**64.1**	**3.9**	**5.0**	**4.0**	**7.1**	**13.3**
	0.5	1.2	130.9	198.3	255.6	73.1	70.0	4.5	95.1	2.7	7.9	(0.1)	0.5	1.3
Petroleum products (1498)	1.9	2.9	26.6	110.5	35.4	23.2	12.0	54.3	13.3	37.0	2.2	2.5	9.1	21.6
	1.1	**1.7**	**66.8**	**198.3**	**87.4**	**50.3**	**20.8**	**32.5**	**19.3**	**17.4**	**3.6**	**1.1**	**4.5**	**10.6**
	0.7	1.2	148.9	347.1	202.1	94.5	34.3	18.0	31.4	8.7	5.7	0.3	1.4	3.4
Petroleum refining (59)	0.9	1.8	49.3	180.4	103.8	106.4	22.5	27.7	32.1	37.3	6.0	4.7	4.7	13.5
	0.7	**1.2**	**80.8**	**246.5**	**184.7**	**147.3**	**29.0**	**17.4**	**46.0**	**17.4**	**8.4**	**1.3**	**2.5**	**8.4**
	0.5	1.0	133.5	401.4	299.7	203.8	49.0	10.8	79.5	6.2	12.7	0.2	0.7	1.8
Variety stores (827)	1.1	6.7	12.8	18.7	18.0	8.2	1.4	5.3	33.4	7.5	2.3	9.6	16.4	32.9
	0.5	**3.6**	**33.2**	**35.0**	**43.5**	**18.9**	**4.0**	**3.5**	**45.2**	**4.2**	**4.1**	**4.5**	**8.6**	**15.9**
	0.2	2.0	77.9	63.8	125.8	45.5	8.9	2.5	70.0	2.6	7.2	1.7	4.4	7.5

[a] These values are given for each ratio for each line of business. The center value is the median, and the values immediately above and below it are the upper and lower quartiles, respectively.

SOURCE: Extracted from *Industry Norms and Key Business Ratios*, 1984–85 edition, Dun & Bradstreet, Inc., New York, 1985.

One ratio she was especially interested in was inventory turnover, which reflects the speed with which the firm moves its inventory from raw materials through production into finished goods and to the customer as a completed sale. Generally, higher values of this ratio are preferred, since they indicate a quicker turnover of inventory. Dwiggins Manufacturing's calculated inventory turnover for 1987 and the industry average inventory turnover were, respectively:

	Inventory turnover, 1987
Dwiggins Manufacturing	14.8
Industry average	9.7

The analyst's initial reaction to these data was that the firm had managed its inventory significantly better than the average firm in the industry. The turnover was in fact nearly 53 percent faster than the industry average. Upon reflection, however, the analyst felt there could be a problem, since a very high inventory turnover could also mean very low levels of inventory. In turn, the consequence of low inventory could be excessive stockouts (insufficient inventory). The analyst's review of other ratios and discussions with persons in the manufacturing and marketing departments did in fact uncover such a problem: The firm's inventories during the year were extremely low as a result of numerous production delays that hindered its ability to meet demand and resulted in lost sales. What had initially appeared to reflect extremely efficient inventory management was actually the symptom of a major problem. ■

TIME-SERIES ANALYSIS **Time-series analysis** is applied when a financial analyst evaluates performance over time. Comparison of current to past performance utilizing ratio analysis allows the firm to determine whether it is progressing as planned. Developing trends can be seen by using multiyear comparisons, and knowledge of these trends should assist the firm in planning future operations. As in cross-sectional analysis, any significant year-to-year changes can be evaluated to assess whether they are symptomatic of a major problem. The theory behind time-series analysis is that the company must be evaluated in relation to its past performance, developing trends must be isolated, and appropriate action taken to direct the firm toward immediate and long-run goals. Time-series analysis is often helpful in checking the reasonableness of a firm's projected (pro forma) financial statements. A comparison of *current* and *past* ratios to those resulting from an analysis of *projected* statements may reveal discrepancies or overoptimism.

time-series analysis
Evaluation of the firm's financial performance over time by financial ratio analysis.

COMBINED ANALYSIS   The most informative approach to ratio analysis is one that combines cross-sectional and time-series analyses. A combined view permits assessment of the trend in the behavior of the ratio in relation to the trend for the industry. Figure 4.1 depicts this type of approach using Alcott Oil Company's average collection period ratio in the years 1984–1987. Generally, lower values of this ratio, which reflects the average amount of time it takes the firm to collect bills, are preferred. A look at the figure quickly discloses that (1) Alcott Oil's effectiveness in collecting its receivables is poor in comparison to the industry and (2) there is a trend toward longer collection periods. Clearly Alcott Oil needs to shorten its collection period.

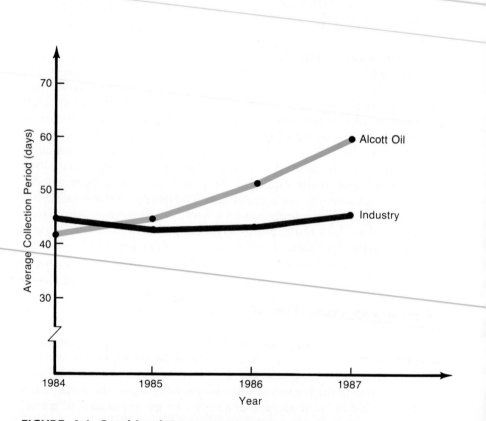

**FIGURE 4.1 Combined Cross-sectional and Time-series
View of Alcott Oil Company's Average
Collection Period, 1984–1987**

Combining cross-sectional and time-series analysis permits assessment of the trend in the behavior of the ratio in relation to the trend for the industry. Alcott Oil's collection of receivables is poor both in comparison to the industry and in its trend.

WHO'S NUMBER 8 OF THE "BIG EIGHT"?

Accountants are masters at juggling numbers. So is it any wonder that two major accounting firms claim to be the seventh biggest in the U.S.?

Touche Ross & Co. and Deloitte, Haskins & Sells both say they are No. 7; neither wants to be the last among the Big Eight.

"It's a fight down to the last decimal place," says Arthur W. Bowman, editor of Public Accounting Report, a newsletter that keeps tabs on accounting firms' size.

"In the game for big clients, being eighth means you're a loser," says Bruce Marcus, who has written a book on marketing professional services.

Edward A. Kangas, Touche's managing partner, notes that Touche's U.S. revenues in the last fiscal year ended Aug. 31 rose to $513 million, $13 million more than Deloitte reported for its fiscal year ended last June 1. "Until we hear differently, we're definitely seventh," says Mr. Kangas.

But J. Michael Cook, Deloitte's chairman, says that Deloitte has just changed its fiscal year to Sept. 30 from June 1. "Based on our new fiscal year, we're No. 7 with $528 million in U.S. revenues," says Mr. Cook. "I'd prefer to stay out of this size race, but the truth is the truth. We're not eighth."

Mr. Cook says Deloitte changed its fiscal year to be more compatible with the other big accounting firms whose fiscal years end late in the year. "Because of the effects of inflation and hiring during the year, the later we issue our figures, the higher the revenues," he adds.

Touche's Mr. Kangas insists that his firm won't change its accounting period just to stay out of last place. "Deloitte sent its (June 1) financial report all over the place," he notes. "Now it's changing the rules."

The managing partner of another big accounting firm, who requests anonymity, says the argument is "ludicrous." He notes that the eight major accounting firms use different methods, and some have claimed revenues from the same jointly shared foreign affiliate. "I don't put much stock in either of their figures," he adds.

Some Words of Caution

Before discussing specific ratios, the following cautions are in order:

1. A single ratio does not generally provide sufficient information from which to judge the overall performance of the firm. Only when a group of ratios is used can reasonable judgments be made. If an

analysis is concerned only with certain specific aspects of a firm's financial position, one or two ratios may be sufficient.

2. Be sure that the dates of the financial statements being compared are the same. If not, the effects of seasonality may produce erroneous conclusions and decisions.

3. It is preferable to use audited financial statements for ratio analysis. If the statements have not been audited, there may be no reason to believe that the data contained in them reflect the firm's true financial condition.

4. Be certain that the data being compared have all been developed in the same way. The use of differing accounting treatments—especially relative to depreciation and inventory—can distort the results of ratio analysis, regardless of whether cross-sectional or time-series analysis is used.

TABLE 4.2 Alcott Oil Company Income Statements ($000)

	FOR THE YEARS ENDED DECEMBER 31	
	1987	1986
Sales revenue	$3074	$2567
Less: Cost of goods sold	2088	1711
Gross profits	$ 986	$ 856
Less: Operating expenses		
Selling expense	$ 100	$ 108
General and administrative expenses	229	222
Depreciation expense	239	223
Total operating expense	$ 568	$ 553
Operating profits	$ 418	$ 303
Less: Interest expense[a]	93	91
Net profits before taxes	$ 325	$ 212
Less: Taxes (rate = 29%)[b]	94	64
Net profits after taxes	$ 231	$ 148
Less: Preferred stock dividends	10	10
Earnings available for common stockholders	$ 221	$ 138
Earnings per share (EPS)[c]	$ 2.90	$ 1.81

[a] Interest expense includes the interest component of the annual financial lease payment as specified by the Financial Accounting Standards Board (FASB).

[b] The 29 percent tax rate for 1987 results from the fact that the firm has certain special tax write-offs that do not show up directly on its income statement.

[c] Calculated by dividing the earnings available for common stockholders by the number of shares of common stock outstanding—76,262 in 1987 and 76,244 in 1986. Earnings per share in 1987: ($221,000 ÷ 76,262 = $2.90); in 1986: ($138,000 ÷ 76,244 = $1.81).

TABLE 4.3 Alcott Oil Company Balance Sheets ($000)

	DECEMBER 31	
Assets	**1987**	**1986**
Current assets		
Cash	$ 363	$ 288
Marketable securities	68	51
Accounts receivable	503	365
Inventories	289	300
Total current assets	$1,223	$1,004
Gross fixed assets (at cost)[a]		
Land and buildings	$2,072	$1,903
Machinery and equipment	1,866	1,693
Furniture and fixtures	358	316
Vehicles	275	314
Other (includes financial leases)	98	96
Total gross fixed assets (at cost)	$4,669	$4,322
Less: Accumulated depreciation	2,295	2,056
Net fixed assets	$2,374	$2,266
Total assets	$3,597	$3,270

Liabilities and stockholders' equity		
Current liabilities		
Accounts payable	$ 382	$ 270
Notes payable	79	99
Accruals	159	114
Total current liabilities	$ 620	$ 483
Long-term debts (includes financial leases)[b]	$1,023	$ 967
Total liabilities	$1,643	$1,450
Stockholders' equity		
Preferred stock—cumulative 5%, $100 par, 2,000 shares authorized and issued	$ 200	$ 200
Common stock—$2.50 par, 100,000 shares authorized, shares issued and outstanding in 1987: 76,262; in 1986: 76,244	191	190
Paid-in capital in excess of par on common stock	428	418
Retained earnings	1,135	1,012
Total stockholders' equity	$1,954	$1,820
Total liabilities and stockholders' equity	$3,597	$3,270

[a] In 1987, the firm has a six-year financial lease requiring annual beginning-of-year payments of $42,000. Four years of the lease have yet to run.

[b] Annual principal repayments on a portion of the firm's total outstanding debt amount to $71,000.

Groups of Financial Ratios

Financial ratios can be divided into four basic groups or categories: liquidity ratios, activity ratios, debt ratios, and profitability ratios. The important near-term elements are liquidity, activity, and profitability, since these provide the information critical to the short-run operation of the firm. (If a firm cannot survive in the short run, we need not be concerned with its longer-term prospects.) Debt ratios are useful primarily when the analyst is sure the firm will successfully weather the short run.

As a rule, the necessary inputs to an effective financial analysis include, at minimum, the income statement and the balance sheet. The 1987 and 1986 income statements and balance sheets for Alcott Oil Company are presented in Tables 4.2 and 4.3, respectively, to demonstrate calculation of the ratios presented in the remainder of this chapter.

■ ANALYZING LIQUIDITY

liquidity A firm's ability to satisfy its short-term obligations as they come due.

The **liquidity** of a business firm is measured by its ability to satisfy its short-term obligations *as they come due*. Liquidity refers to the solvency of the firm's *overall* financial position. The three basic measures of liquidity are (1) net working capital, (2) the current ratio, and (3) the quick (acid-test) ratio.

Net Working Capital

The firm's *net working capital*, as noted in Chapter 3, is calculated by subtracting current liabilities from current assets. The net working capital for Alcott Oil in 1987 was as follows:

$$\text{Net working capital} = \$1,223,000 - \$620,000 = \$603,000$$

The figure for net working capital is *not* useful for comparing the performance of different firms, but is quite useful for internal control.[2] A time-series comparison of the firm's net working capital is often helpful in evaluating its operations.

---

[2] To make cross-sectional as well as better time-series comparisons, *net working capital as a percent of sales* can be calculated. For Alcott Oil in 1987 this ratio would be 19.6 percent ($603,000 ÷ $3,074,000). In general, the larger this value, the greater the firm's liquidity, and vice versa. Because of the relative nature of this measure, it is frequently used to make liquidity comparisons.

Current Ratio

The **current ratio,** one of the most commonly cited financial ratios, is expressed as follows:

$$\text{Current ratio} = \frac{\text{current assets}}{\text{current liabilities}}$$

The current ratio for Alcott Oil in 1987 is

$$\frac{\$1,223,000}{\$620,000} = 1.97$$

A current ratio of 2.0 is occasionally cited as acceptable, but acceptability of the value depends on the industry in which a firm operates. For example, a current ratio of 1.0 would be considered acceptable for a utility but might be unacceptable for a manufacturing firm. The more predictable a firm's cash flows, the lower the acceptable current ratio. Since Alcott Oil is in a business with a relatively predictable annual cash flow, its current ratio of 1.97 should be quite acceptable.

current ratio A measure of liquidity calculated by dividing the firm's current assets by its current liabilities.

Quick (Acid-Test) Ratio

The **quick (acid-test) ratio** is similar to the current ratio except that it excludes inventory (generally the least liquid current asset). The quick ratio is calculated as follows:

$$\text{Quick ratio} = \frac{\text{current assets} - \text{inventory}}{\text{current liabilities}}$$

The quick ratio for Alcott Oil in 1987 is

$$\frac{\$1,223,000 - \$289,000}{\$620,000} = \frac{\$934,000}{\$620,000} = 1.51$$

A quick ratio of 1.0 or greater is occasionally recommended, but, as with the current ratio, an acceptable value depends largely on the industry. The quick ratio provides a better measure of overall liquidity only when a firm's inventory cannot easily be converted into cash. If inventory is liquid, the current ratio is a preferred measure of overall liquidity.

quick (acid-test ratio) A measure of liquidity calculated by dividing the firm's current assets minus inventory by current liabilities.

ANALYZING ACTIVITY

Activity ratios are used to measure the speed with which various accounts are converted into sales or cash. Measures of liquidity are generally inadequate because differences in the composition of a firm's cur-

activity ratios Used to measure the speed with which various accounts are converted into sales or cash.

rent assets and liabilities can significantly affect the firm's "true" liquidity. For example, consider the current portion of the balance sheets for firms A and B in the following table:

Firm A

Cash	$ 0	Accounts payable	$ 0
Marketable securities	0	Notes payable	10,000
Accounts receivable	0	Accruals	0
Inventories	20,000	Total current liabilities	$10,000
Total current assets	$20,000		

Firm B

Cash	$ 5,000	Accounts payable	$ 5,000
Marketable securities	5,000	Notes payable	3,000
Accounts receivable	5,000	Accruals	2,000
Inventories	5,000	Total current liabilities	$10,000
Total current assets	$20,000		

Although both firms appear to be equally liquid since their current ratios are both 2.0 ($20,000 ÷ $10,000), a closer look at the differences in the composition of current assets and liabilities suggests that *firm B is more liquid than firm A.* This results for two reasons: (1) firm B has more liquid assets in the form of cash and marketable securities than firm A, which has only a single and relatively illiquid asset in the form of inventories, and (2) firm B's current liabilities are in general more flexible than the single current liability—notes payable—of firm A.

It is therefore important to look beyond measures of overall liquidity to assess the activity (or liquidity) of specific current accounts. A number of ratios are available for measuring the activity of the most important current accounts, which include inventory, accounts receivable, and accounts payable. The activity of fixed and total assets can also be assessed.

Inventory Turnover

inventory turnover
Measures the activity, or liquidity, of a firm's inventory.

Inventory turnover commonly measures the activity, or liquidity, of a firm's inventory. It is calculated as follows:

$$\text{Inventory turnover} = \frac{\text{cost of goods sold}}{\text{inventory}}$$

Applying this relationship to Alcott Oil in 1987 yields

$$\text{Inventory turnover} = \frac{\$2,088,000}{\$289,000} = 7.2$$

The resulting turnover is meaningful only when compared with that of other firms in the same industry or to the firm's past inventory turnover. An inventory turnover of 20.0 would not be unusual for a grocery store, whereas a common inventory turnover for an aircraft manufacturer would be 4.0.

Inventory turnover can easily be converted into an **average age of inventory** by dividing it into 360 — the number of days in a year.[3] For Alcott Oil, the average age of inventory would be 50.0 days (360 ÷ 7.2). This value can also be viewed as the average number of days' sales in inventory.

average age of inventory Average length of time inventory is held by the firm; calculated by dividing inventory turnover into 360, the number of days in a year.

Average Collection Period

The **average collection period,** or average age of accounts receivable, is useful in evaluating credit and collection policies.[4] It is arrived at by dividing the average daily sales[5] into the accounts receivable balance:

average collection period The average amount of time needed to collect accounts receivable.

$$\text{Average collection period} = \frac{\text{accounts receivable}}{\text{average sales per day}} = \frac{\text{accounts receivable}}{\dfrac{\text{annual sales}}{360}}$$

The average collection period for Alcott Oil in 1987 is

$$\frac{\$503,000}{\dfrac{\$3,074,000}{360}} = \frac{\$503,000}{\$8,539} = 58.9 \text{ days}$$

On the average it takes the firm 58.9 days to collect an account receivable.

The average collection period is meaningful only in relation to the firm's credit terms. If, for instance, Alcott Oil extends 30-day credit terms to customers, an average collection period of 58.9 days would indicate a poorly managed credit or collection department, or both. If it extended 60-day credit terms, the 58.9-day average collection period would be acceptable.

---

[3] Unless otherwise specified, a 360-day year consisting of twelve 30-day months is assumed throughout this text. This assumption allows some simplification of the calculations used to illustrate key concepts.

[4] A discussion of the evaluation and establishment of credit and collection policies is presented in Chapter 9.

[5] The formula as presented assumes, for simplicity, that all sales are made on a credit basis. If such is not the case, *average credit sales per day* should be substituted for average sales per day.

Average Payment Period

average payment period
The average amount of time needed to pay accounts payable.

The **average payment period,** or average age of accounts payable, is calculated in the same manner as the average collection period:

$$\text{Average payment period} = \frac{\text{accounts payable}}{\text{average purchases per day}} = \frac{\text{accounts payable}}{\dfrac{\text{annual purchases}}{360}}$$

The difficulty in calculating this ratio stems from the need to find annual purchases—a value not available in published financial statements. Ordinarily, purchases are estimated as a given percentage of cost of goods sold. If we assume that Alcott Oil's purchases equaled 70 percent of its cost of goods sold in 1987, its average payment period is

$$\frac{\$382,000}{\dfrac{.70(\$2,088,000)}{360}} = \frac{\$382,000}{\$4,060} = 94.1 \text{ days}$$

The above figure is meaningful only in relation to the average credit terms extended to the firm. If Alcott Oil's suppliers, on the average, have extended 30-day credit terms, an analyst would give it a low credit rating. If the firm has been generally extended 90-day credit terms, its credit would certainly be acceptable.

Fixed Asset Turnover

fixed asset turnover
Ratio used to measure the efficiency with which the firm has been using its *fixed*, or earning, assets to generate sales.

The **fixed asset turnover** is used to measure the efficiency with which the firm has been using its *fixed*, or earning, assets to generate sales. It is calculated by dividing the firm's sales by its net fixed assets:

$$\text{Fixed asset turnover} = \frac{\text{sales}}{\text{net fixed assets}}$$

The fixed asset turnover for Alcott Oil in 1987 is

$$\frac{\$3,074,000}{\$2,374,000} = 1.29$$

This means the company turns over its net fixed assets 1.29 times a year. Generally, higher fixed asset turnovers are preferred.

Total Asset Turnover

total asset turnover
Indicates the efficiency with which the firm uses all assets in generating sales.

The **total asset turnover** indicates the efficiency with which the firm is able to use all its assets to generate sales dollars. Generally, the higher a firm's total asset turnover, the more efficiently its assets have been used. Total asset turnover is calculated as follows:

$$\text{Total asset turnover} = \frac{\text{sales}}{\text{total assets}}$$

The value of Alcott Oil's total asset turnover in 1987 is

$$\frac{\$3,074,000}{\$3,597,000} = 0.85$$

The company therefore turns its assets over .85 times a year.

◼ ANALYZING DEBT

The *debt position* of the firm indicates the amount of other people's money being used in attempting to generate profits. In general, the financial analyst is most concerned with long-term debts, since these commit the firm to paying interest over the long run as well as eventually repaying the principal borrowed. In general, the more debt a firm uses, the greater its **financial leverage,** a term used to describe the magnification of risk and return introduced through the use of fixed-cost financing such as debt and preferred stock. In other words, the more debt, or financial leverage, a firm uses, the greater will be its risk and return. The concept of financial leverage is developed in Chapter 5. Attention is given here to the use of financial debt ratios as a measure of the degree of corporate indebtedness and the ability to meet the fixed payments associated with debt.

financial leverage
Describes the magnification of risk and return introduced by the use of fixed-cost financing, such as debt and preferred stock.

Debt Ratio

The **debt ratio** measures the proportion of total assets provided by the firm's creditors. The higher this ratio, the greater the amount of other people's money being used in an attempt to generate profits. The ratio is calculated as follows:

debt ratio Measures the proportion of total assets provided by the firm's creditors.

$$\text{Debt ratio} = \frac{\text{total liabilities}}{\text{total assets}}$$

The debt ratio for Alcott Oil in 1987 is

$$\frac{\$1,643,000}{\$3,597,000} = .457 = 45.7\%$$

This indicates that the company has financed 45.7 percent of its assets with debt. The higher this ratio, the more financial leverage a firm has.

Times Interest Earned Ratio

The **times interest earned ratio** measures the ability to pay contractual interest payments. The higher the value of this ratio, the better able the firm is to fulfill its interest obligations. Times interest earned is calculated as follows:

times interest earned ratio Measures the firm's ability to pay contractual interest payments.

$$\text{Times interest earned} = \frac{\text{earnings before interest and taxes}}{\text{interest}}$$

Applying this ratio to Alcott Oil yields the following 1987 value:

$$\text{Times interest earned} = \frac{\$418,000}{\$93,000} = 4.5$$

The value of earnings before interest and taxes is the same as the figure for operating profits shown in the income statements given in Table 4.2. The times interest earned ratio for Alcott Oil seems acceptable; as a rule, a value of at least 3.0—and preferably closer to 5.0—is suggested.

Fixed-Payment Coverage Ratio

fixed-payment coverage ratio Measures the firm's ability to meet all fixed-payment obligations.

The **fixed-payment coverage ratio** measures the firm's ability to meet all fixed-payment obligations, such as loan interest and principal and preferred stock dividends. Like the times interest earned ratio, the higher this value, the better. Principal payments on debt, scheduled lease payments, and preferred stock dividends[6] are commonly included in this ratio. Since financial (long-term) lease payments are written off in a fashion similar to owned assets, they do not require itemization. The formula for fixed-payment coverage ratio is as follows:

$$\text{Fixed-payment coverage ratio} =$$

$$\frac{\text{earnings before interest and taxes}}{\text{interest} + [(\text{principal payments} + \text{preferred stock dividends}) \times [1/(1-t)]]}$$

where t is the corporate tax rate applicable to the firm's income. The term $1/(1-t)$ is included to adjust the after-tax principal and preferred stock dividend payments back to a before-tax equivalent consistent with the before-tax value in the numerator. Applying the formula to Alcott Oil's 1987 data yields

Fixed-payment coverage ratio

$$= \frac{\$418,000}{\$93,000 + [(\$71,000 + \$10,000) \times [1/(1-.29)]]}$$

$$= \frac{\$418,000}{\$207,000} = 2.0$$

Since the earnings available are twice as large as its fixed-payment obligations, the firm appears able to safely meet the latter.

---

[6] Although preferred stock dividends, which are stated at the time of issue, can be "passed" (not paid) at the option of the firm's directors, it is generally believed that the payment of such dividends is necessary. This text therefore treats the preferred stock dividend as if it were a contractual obligation, not only to be paid as a fixed amount, but also to be paid as scheduled.

ANALYZING PROFITABILITY

There are many measures of profitability. Each relates the returns of the firm to its sales, assets, equity, or share value. As a group, these measures allow the analyst to evaluate the firm's earnings with respect to a given level of sales, a certain level of assets, the owners' investment, or share value. Without profits a firm could not attract outside capital; moreover, present owners and creditors would become concerned about the company's future and attempt to recover their funds.

Common-Size Income Statements

A popular tool for evaluating profitability in relation to sales is the **common-size income statement.** On this statement each item is expressed as a percentage of sales, thus enabling the relationship between sales and specific revenues and expenses to be easily evaluated. Common-size income statements are especially useful in comparing the performance for one year with that for another year. Two frequently cited ratios of profitability that can be read directly from the common-size income statement are: (a) the gross profit margin and (b) the net profit margin. (These are both discussed below.)

Common-size income statements for 1987 and 1986 for Alcott Oil are presented in Table 4.4. An evaluation of these statements reveals that the firm's cost of goods sold increased from 66.7 percent of sales in 1986 to 67.9 percent in 1987, resulting in a decrease in the gross profit margin

common-size income statement Used in evaluating profitability in relation to sales.

TABLE 4.4 Alcott Oil Company Common-Size Income Statements

	FOR THE YEARS ENDED DECEMBER 31	
	1987	1986
Sales revenue	100.0%	100.0%
Less: Cost of goods sold	67.9	66.7
(a) Gross profit margin	32.1%	33.3%
Less: Operating expenses		
Selling expense	3.3%	4.2%
General and administrative expenses	7.4	8.6
Depreciation expense	7.8	8.7
Total operating expense	18.5%	21.5%
Operating profit margin	13.6%	11.8%
Less: Interest expense	3.0	3.5
Net profits before taxes	10.6%	8.3%
Less: Taxes	3.1	2.5
(b) Net profit margin	7.5%	5.8%

from 33.3 to 32.1 percent. However, thanks to a decrease in operating expenses from 21.5 percent in 1986 to 18.5 percent in 1987, the firm's net profit margin rose from 5.8 percent of sales in 1986 to 7.5 percent in 1987. The decrease in expenses in 1987 more than compensated for the increase in the cost of goods sold. A decrease in the firm's 1987 interest expense (3.0 percent of sales versus 3.5 percent in 1986) added to the increase in 1987 profits.

Gross Profit Margin

gross profit margin
Indicates the percentage of each sales dollar left after the firm has paid for its goods.

The **gross profit margin** indicates the percentage of each sales dollar remaining after the firm has paid for its goods. The higher the gross profit margin the better, and the lower the relative cost of merchandise sold. Of course, the opposite case is also true, as the Alcott Oil example shows. The gross profit margin is calculated as follows:

$$\text{Gross profit margin} = \frac{\text{sales} - \text{cost of goods sold}}{\text{sales}} = \frac{\text{gross profits}}{\text{sales}}$$

The value for Alcott Oil's gross profit margin for 1987 is

$$\frac{\$3,074,000 - \$2,088,000}{\$3,074,000} = \frac{\$986,000}{\$3,074,000} = 32.1\%$$

This value is shown on line (a) of the common-size income statement in Table 4.4.

Net Profit Margin

net profit margin
Measures the percentage of each sales dollar left after all expenses, including taxes, have been deducted.

The **net profit margin** measures the percentage of each sales dollar remaining after all expenses, including taxes, have been deducted. The higher the firm's net profit margin, the better. The net profit margin is a commonly cited measure of the corporation's success with respect to earnings on sales. The net profit margin is calculated as follows:

$$\text{Net profit margin} = \frac{\text{net profits after taxes}}{\text{sales}}$$

Alcott Oil's net profit margin for 1987 is

$$\frac{\$231,000}{\$3,074,000} = 7.5\%$$

This value is shown on line (b) of the common-size income statement in Table 4.4.

return on investment (ROI) Measures the overall effectiveness of management in producing profits from available assets.

Return on Investment (ROI)

The **return on investment (ROI)**, which is often called the firm's *return on total assets*, measures the overall effectiveness of management in generating profits with its available assets. The higher the firm's return on investment, the better. The return on investment is calculated as follows:

$$\text{Return on investment} = \frac{\text{net profits after taxes}}{\text{total assets}}$$

Alcott Oil's return on investment in 1987 is

$$\frac{\$231,000}{\$3,597,000} = 6.4\%$$

This value, which seems acceptable, could have been derived using the DuPont system of analysis, which will be described in a subsequent section.

Return on Equity *(ROE)*

The **return on equity *(ROE)*** measures the return earned on the owners' (both preferred and common stockholders') investment. Generally, the higher this return, the better off the owners. Return on equity is calculated as follows:

$$\text{Return on equity} = \frac{\text{net profits after taxes}}{\text{stockholders' equity}}$$

This ratio for Alcott Oil in 1987 is

$$\frac{\$231,000}{\$1,954,000} = 11.8\%$$

The above value, which seems to be quite good, could also have been derived using the DuPont system of analysis, to be described shortly.

return on equity *(ROE)* Measures the return on the owners' (preferred and common stockholders') investment in the firm.

Price/Earnings (P/E) Ratio

Though not a true measure of profitability, the **price/earnings (P/E) ratio** is commonly used to assess the owners' appraisal of share value.[7] The P/E ratio represents the amount investors are willing to pay for each dollar of the firm's earnings. The level of the price/earnings ratio indicates the degree of confidence (or certainty) that investors have in the firm's future performance. The higher the P/E ratio, the greater investor confidence in the firm's future. The P/E ratio is calculated as follows:

price/earnings (P/E) ratio Represents the amount investors are willing to pay for each dollar of the firm's earnings.

$$\text{Price/earnings (P/E) ratio} = \frac{\text{market price per share of common stock}}{\text{earnings per share}}$$

[7] Use of the price/earnings ratio to estimate the value of the firm is included as part of the discussion of popular approaches to common stock valuation in Chapter 12.

STRATEGIES FOR STRENGTHENING FINANCIAL RATIOS

Ratio analysis is a common way lenders analyze balance sheets. Most familiar is the current ratio, computed by dividing current assets — cash, accounts receivable, inventory — by current liabilities, or debt due within a year.

A company can strengthen this ratio by paying off current debt. If a business has, say, $40,000 cash (its only current asset) and $20,000 of current liabilities, its current ratio is 2:1. If $10,000 of the cash is used to reduce debt, however, the ratio improves significantly to 3:1.

A financial statement can be enhanced by borrowing long term to pay off short-term debt. "If you can get debt out of short term into long term, it cleans up the balance sheet," says Edward H. Pendergast, chairman of Kennedy & Lehan CPAs Inc., North Quincy, Mass. But this isn't mere window dressing, he says. "The company is much stronger because it is more liquid. Current demands on the business have been reduced considerably."

Bankers look carefully at the equity a small business has in relationship to debt. "There's nothing like equity," says the executive vice president of a $7 billion bank. "It's your cushion in the event something comes up that could damage the company." In the past, nothing less than a one-to-one debt-equity ratio would satisfy most banks. Nowadays, debt one and a half times greater than equity is usually acceptable. And some banks won't balk if it exceeds this, says David F. Nasman, president of Bellingham National Bank, Tacoma, Wash.

High debt-equity ratios could be acceptable, Mr. Nasman says, for a young company "that is strong and operating and growing well." But, he says, a bank would view with alarm "a company in business for 25 years whose debt-equity ratio starts to slide." The difference, he says, is that the young profitable company probably can "increase its equity along the way."

Profits left in the business become retained earnings and increase equity. However, small-business owners usually try to minimize profits for income tax purposes, and often do this by paying themselves year-end bonuses. One way to satisfy tax considerations and bolster the financial statement is for the owner to take the bonus, providing the company a tax deduction, and then loan the money back to the company.

"If you indicate that the company doesn't have to pay the owner back for a year," says Herbert C. Speiser, a partner at Touche Ross & Co., CPAs, "a banker will consider it equity."

Such a solution isn't always possible, however. "Sometimes tax planning goes against the financial statement," says Irwin Math, a partner in the CPA firm of Laventhol & Horwath. "Sometimes I tell a client to pay taxes and strengthen your statement." In some small companies this means valuing year-end inventory as high as possible to maximize profits, and thus incur higher taxes.

If Alcott Oil's common stock at the end of 1987 was selling at 32¼, using the earnings per share *(EPS)* of $2.90 from the income statement in Table 4.2, the P/E ratio at year-end 1987 is

$$\frac{\$32.25}{\$2.90} = 11.1$$

This figure indicates that investors were paying $11.10 for each $1.00 of earnings.

A COMPLETE RATIO ANALYSIS

As indicated earlier in the chapter, no single ratio is adequate for assessing all aspects of the firm's financial condition. Two popular approaches to a complete ratio analysis are (1) the DuPont system of analysis and (2) the summary analysis of a large number of ratios. Each of these approaches has merit. The DuPont system acts as a *search technique* aimed at finding the key areas responsible for the firm's financial performance. The summary analysis approach tends to view *all aspects* of the firm's financial activities in order to isolate key areas of responsibility.

DuPont System of Analysis

The **DuPont system of analysis** has for many years been used by financial managers as a structure for dissecting the firm's financial statements in order to assess its financial condition. The DuPont system merges the income statement and balance sheet into two summary measures of profitability: return on investment *(ROI)* and return on equity *(ROE)*. Figure 4.2 depicts the basic DuPont system. The upper portion of the chart summarizes the income statement ratios; the lower portion summarizes the balance sheet ratios.

The DuPont system first brings together the *net profit margin,* which measures the firm's profitability on sales, with its *total asset turnover,* which indicates how efficiently the firm has used its assets to generate sales. In the **DuPont formula,** the product of these two ratios results in the *return on investment (ROI):*

$$ROI = \text{net profit margin} \times \text{total asset turnover}$$

Substituting the appropriate formulas into the equation and simplifying results in the formula given earlier,

$$ROI = \frac{\text{net profits after taxes}}{\text{sales}} \times \frac{\text{sales}}{\text{total assets}} = \frac{\text{net profits after taxes}}{\text{total assets}}$$

DuPont system of analysis System used by management as a framework for dissecting the firm's financial statements and assessing its financial condition.

DuPont formula Relates the firm's net profit margin and total asset turnover to its return on investment *(ROI)*. The *ROI* is the product at the net profit margin and the total asset turnover.

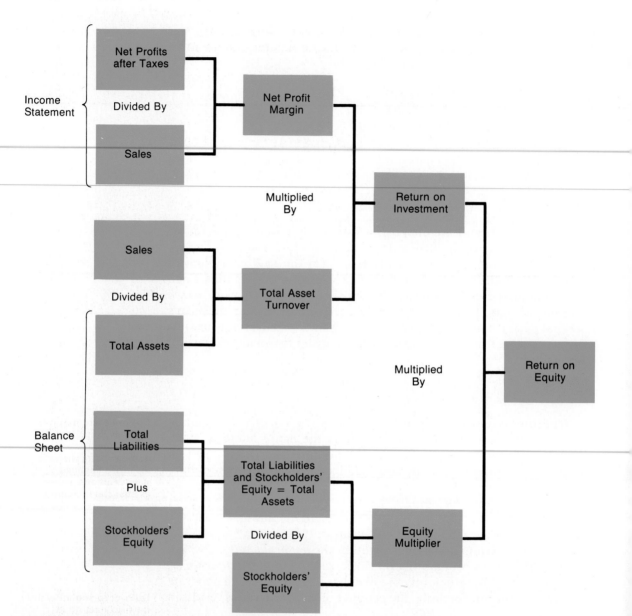

FIGURE 4.2 The DuPont System of Analysis

The DuPont system of analysis creates a structure used to dissect the firm's income statement and balance sheet in order to assess its financial condition. The system focuses on return on investment and return on equity.

If the 1987 values of the net profit margin and total asset turnover for Alcott Oil, calculated earlier, are substituted into the DuPont formula, the result is

$$ROI = 7.5\% \times 0.85 = 6.4\%$$

As expected, this value is the same as that calculated directly in an earlier section. The DuPont formula allows the firm to break down its return into a profit-on-sales and an efficiency-of-asset-use component. Typically, a firm with a low net profit margin has a high total asset turnover, which results in a reasonably good return on investment. Often, the opposite situation exists.

The second step in the DuPont system employs the **modified Du-Pont formula.** This formula relates the firm's return on investment *(ROI)* to the return on equity *(ROE)*. The latter is calculated by multiplying the return on investment by the **equity multiplier,** which is the ratio of total assets to stockholders' equity:

modified DuPont formula Relates the firm's return on investment *(ROI)* to its return on equity *(ROE)* using the equity multiplier.

$$ROE = ROI \times \text{equity multiplier}$$

Substituting the appropriate formulas into the equation and simplifying results in the formula given earlier,

equity multiplier The ratio of the firm's total assets to stockholders' equity.

$$ROE = \frac{\text{net profits after taxes}}{\text{total assets}} \times \frac{\text{total assets}}{\text{stockholders' equity}} = \frac{\text{net profits after taxes}}{\text{stockholders' equity}}$$

Use of the equity multiplier to convert the *ROI* to the *ROE* reflects the impact of leverage (use of debt) on owners' return. Substituting the values for Alcott Oil's *ROI* of 6.4%, calculated earlier, and Alcott's equity multiplier of 1.84 ($3,597,000 total assets ÷ $1,954,000 stockholders' equity) into the modified DuPont formula yields

$$ROE = 6.4\% \times 1.84 = 11.8\%$$

The 11.8 percent *ROE* calculated using the modified DuPont formula is the same as that calculated directly.

The considerable advantage of the DuPont system is that it allows the firm to break its return on equity into a profit-on-sales component (net profit margin), an efficiency-of-asset-use component (total asset turnover), and a use-of-leverage component (equity multiplier). The total return to the owners can therefore be analyzed in light of these important dimensions. As an illustration, let's look ahead to the ratio values summarized in Table 4.5. Alcott Oil's net profit margin and total asset turnover increased between 1986 and 1987 to levels above the industry average. In combination, improved profit on sales and better asset utilization resulted in an improved return on investment *(ROI)*. Increased investment return coupled with the increased use of debt reflected in the increased equity multiplier (not shown) caused the

TABLE 4.5 Summary of Alcott Oil Company Ratios (1985 – 1987, including 1987 industry averages)

Ratio	Formula	YEAR 1985[a]	YEAR 1986[b]	YEAR 1987[b]	Industry average 1987[c]	EVALUATION[d] Cross-sectional 1987	EVALUATION[d] Time-series 1985–1987	EVALUATION[d] Overall
Liquidity								
Net working capital	current assets − current liabilities	$583,000	$521,000	$603,000	$427,000	good	good	good
Current ratio	$\dfrac{\text{current assets}}{\text{current liabilities}}$	2.04	2.08	1.97	2.05	OK	OK	OK
Quick (acid-test) ratio	$\dfrac{\text{current assets} - \text{inventory}}{\text{current liabilities}}$	1.32	1.46	1.51	1.43	OK	good	good
Activity								
Inventory turnover	$\dfrac{\text{cost of goods sold}}{\text{inventory}}$	5.1	5.7	7.2	6.6	good	good	good
Average collection period	$\dfrac{\text{accounts receivable}}{\text{average sales per day}}$	46.9 days	51.2 days	58.9 days	44.3 days	poor	poor	poor
Average payment period	$\dfrac{\text{accounts payable}}{\text{average purchases per day}}$	75.8 days	81.2 days	94.1 days	66.5 days	poor	poor	poor
Fixed asset turnover	$\dfrac{\text{sales}}{\text{net fixed assets}}$	1.50	1.13	1.29	1.35	OK	OK	OK
Total asset turnover	$\dfrac{\text{sales}}{\text{total assets}}$	0.94	0.79	0.85	0.75	OK	OK	OK

Debt

	Formula					Evaluation[b]			
Debt ratio	$\dfrac{\text{total liabilities}}{\text{total assets}}$	36.8%	44.3%	45.7%	40.0%	OK	OK	OK	OK
Times interest earned ratio	$\dfrac{\text{earnings before interest and taxes}}{\text{interest}}$	5.6	3.3	4.5	4.3	good	OK	OK	OK
Fixed-payment coverage ratio	$\dfrac{\text{earnings before interest and taxes}}{\text{int.} + [(\text{prin.} + \text{pref. div}) \times [1/(1-t)]]}$	2.7	1.5	2.0	1.5	good	good	OK	good

Profitability

	Formula					Evaluation[b]			
Gross profit margin	$\dfrac{\text{gross profit}}{\text{sales}}$	31.4%	33.3%	32.1%	30.0%	OK	OK	OK	OK
Net profit margin	$\dfrac{\text{net profits after taxes}}{\text{sales}}$	8.8%	5.8%	7.5%	6.4%	good	good	OK	good
Return on investment (ROI)	$\dfrac{\text{net profits after taxes}}{\text{total assets}}$	8.3%	4.5%	6.4%	4.8%	good	good	OK	good
Return on equity (ROE)	$\dfrac{\text{net profits after taxes}}{\text{stockholders' equity}}$	13.1%	8.1%	11.8%	8.0%	good	good	OK	good
Price/earnings (P/E) ratio	$\dfrac{\text{market price per share of common stock}}{\text{earnings per share}}$	10.5	10.0	11.1	12.5	OK	OK	OK	OK

[a] Calculated from data not included in the chapter.

[b] Calculated using the financial statements presented in Tables 4.2 and 4.3.

[c] Obtained from data from sources not included in this chapter.

[d] Represent subjective assessments based on data provided.

owners' return *(ROE)* to increase. Simply stated, it is clear from the DuPont system of analysis that the improvement in Alcott Oil's 1987 *ROE* resulted from greater profit on sales, better asset utilization, and the increased use of leverage.

■ Summarizing All Ratios

The 1987 ratio values calculated earlier and the ratio values calculated for 1985 and 1986 for Alcott Oil, along with the industry average ratios for 1987, are summarized in Table 4.5. The table shows the formula used to calculate each ratio. Using these data, we can discuss the four key aspects of Alcott's performance — (1) liquidity, (2) activity, (3) debt, and (4) profitability — on a cross-sectional and time-series basis.

LIQUIDITY   The overall liquidity of the firm seems to exhibit a reasonably stable trend, having been maintained at a level that is relatively consistent with the industry average in 1987. The firm's liquidity seems to be good.

ACTIVITY   Alcott Oil's inventory appears to be in good shape. Its inventory management seems to have improved, and in 1987 it performed at a level above that of the industry. The firm may be experiencing some problems with accounts receivable. The average collection period seems to have crept up to a level above that of the industry. Alcott also appears to be slow in paying its bills; it is paying nearly 30 days later than the industry average. Payment procedures should be examined to make sure that the company's credit standing is not adversely affected. While overall liquidity appears to be good, some attention should be given to the management of accounts receivable and payable. Alcott's fixed asset turnover and total asset turnover reflect sizable declines in the efficiency of fixed and total asset utilization between 1985 and 1986. Although in 1987 the total asset turnover rose to a level considerably above the industry average, it appears that the pre-1986 level of efficiency has not yet been achieved.

DEBT   Alcott Oil's indebtedness increased over the 1985–1987 period and is currently at a level above the industry average. Although the increase in the debt ratio could be cause for alarm, the firm's ability to meet interest and fixed-payment obligations improved from 1986 to 1987 to a level that outperforms the industry. The firm's increased indebtedness in 1986 apparently caused a deterioration in its ability to pay debt adequately. However, Alcott has evidently improved its income in 1987 so that it is able to meet its interest and fixed-payment obligations in a fashion consistent with the average firm in the industry. In summary, it appears that although 1986 was an off year, the company's ability to pay debts in 1987 adequately compensates for the increased degree of indebtedness.

PROFITABILITY Alcott's profitability relative to sales in 1987 was better than that of the average company in the industry, although it did not match the firm's 1985 performance. While the *gross profit margin* in 1986 and 1987 was better than in 1985, it appears that higher levels of operating and interest expenses in 1986 and 1987 caused the 1987 *net profit margin* to fall below that of 1985. However, Alcott's 1987 net profit margin is quite favorable when compared to the industry average. The firm's return on investment and return on equity behaved in a fashion similar to its net profit margin over the 1985–1987 period. Alcott appears to have experienced either a sizable drop in sales between 1985 and 1986 or a rapid expansion in assets during that period. The owners' return, as evidenced by the exceptionally high 1987 level of return on equity, seems to suggest that the firm is performing quite well. In addition, although the firm's shares are selling at a price/earnings (P/E) multiple below that of the industry, some improvement occurred between 1986 and 1987. The firm's above-average returns—net profit margin, *ROI*, and *ROE*—may be attributable to its above-average risk as reflected in its below-industry-average P/E ratio.

In summary, it appears that the firm is growing and has recently undergone an expansion in assets, this expansion being financed primarily through the use of debt. The 1986–1987 period seems to reflect a phase of adjustment and recovery from the rapid growth in assets. Alcott's sales, profits, and other performance factors seem to be growing with the increase in the size of the operation. In short, the firm appears to have done quite well in 1987.

SUMMARY

- Ratio analysis allows present and prospective stockholders and lenders and the firm's management to evaluate the firm's performance and status. It can be performed on a cross-sectional or a time-series basis. Cross-sectional analysis involves comparison of different firms' ratios at the same point in time. Time-series analysis measures a firm's performance over time.
- Cautions in ratio analysis include: (1) a single ratio does not generally provide sufficient information; (2) ratios should be compared for similar time periods; (3) audited financial statements should be used; and (4) data should be checked for consistency of accounting treatment
- The most common ratios can be divided into four basic groups: liquidity ratios; activity ratios; debt ratios; and profitability ratios.
- The liquidity, or ability of the firm to pay its bills as they come due, can be measured by the firm's net working capital, its current ratio, or its quick (acid-test) ratio.
- Activity ratios measure the speed with which various accounts are converted into sales or cash. The activity of inventory can be measured by its turnover, that of accounts receivable by the average collection period, and that of accounts payable by the average payment period. Fixed and total asset turn-

overs can be used to measure the efficiency with which the firm has used its fixed and total assets to generate sales.

● Financial debt ratios measure both degree of corporate indebtedness and the ability to pay debts. A commonly used measure of debt position is the debt ratio. The ability to pay contractual obligations such as interest, principal, and preferred stock dividends can be measured by times interest earned and fixed-payment coverage ratios.

● Measures of profitability can be made in various ways. The common-size income statement, which shows all items as a percentage of sales, can be used to determine gross profit margin and net profit margin. Other measures of profitability include return on investment, return on equity, and the price/earnings ratio.

● The DuPont system of analysis is a search technique aimed at finding the key areas responsible for the firm's financial performance. It allows the firm to break the return on equity into a profit-on-sales component, an efficiency-of-asset-use component, and a use-of-leverage component.

● By summarizing a large number of ratios, all aspects of the firm's activities can be assessed in order to isolate key areas of responsibility.

QUESTIONS

4-1 With regard to financial ratio analyses of a firm, how do the viewpoints held by the firm's present and prospective shareholders, creditors, and management differ? How can these viewpoints be related to the firm's fund-raising ability?

4-2 How can ratio analysis be used for *cross-sectional* and *time-series* comparisons? Which type of comparison would be most common for internal analysis? Why?

4-3 When performing cross-sectional ratio analysis, to what types of deviations from the norm should the analyst devote primary attention? Explain why.

4-4 Financial ratio analysis is often divided into four areas: liquidity ratios, activity ratios, debt ratios, and profitability ratios. Describe and differentiate each of these areas of analysis from the others. Which is of the greatest relative concern to present and prospective creditors?

4-5 Why is net working capital useful only in time-series comparisons of overall liquidity while the current and quick ratios can be used for both cross-sectional and time-series analysis?

4-6 In order to assess the reasonableness of the firm's average collection period and average payment period ratios, what additional information is needed in each instance? Explain.

4-7 What is *financial leverage?* What ratio can be used to measure the degree of indebtedness? What ratios are used to assess the ability of the firm to meet fixed payments associated with debt?

4-8 What is a *common-size income statement?* Which two ratios of profitability are found on this statement? How is the statement used?

4-9 How can a firm's having a high gross profit margin and a low net profit margin be explained? To what must this situation be attributable?

4-10 Define and differentiate between return on investment *(ROI)* and return on equity *(ROE)?* Which measure is probably of greatest interest to owners? Why?

4-11 What is the *price/earnings (P/E) ratio?* How does its level relate to the degree of confidence (or certainty) of investors in the firm's future performance? Is the P/E ratio a true measure of profitability?

4-12 Three areas of analysis or concern are combined in the *DuPont system of analysis.* What are these concerns, and how are they combined to explain the firm's return on equity *(ROE)?* Can this formula yield useful information through cross-sectional or time-series analysis?

4-13 Describe how you would approach a complete ratio analysis of the firm on both a cross-sectional and a time-series basis by summarizing a large number of ratios.

PROBLEMS

4-1 ◼ **(Liquidity Management)** The Bently Corporation's total current assets, net working capital, and inventory for each of the past four years are given below.

Item	1984	1985	1986	1987
Total current assets	$16,950	$21,900	$22,500	$27,000
Net working capital	7,950	9,300	9,900	9,600
Inventory	6,000	6,900	6,900	7,200

a Calculate the firm's current and quick ratios for each year. Compare the resulting time series of each measure of liquidity (i.e., net working capital, the current ratio, and the quick ratio).

b Comment on the firm's liquidity over the 1984–1987 period.

c If you were told that the Bently Corporation's inventory turnover for each year in the 1984–1987 period and the industry averages were as follows, would this support or conflict with your evaluation in b? Why?

Inventory turnover	1984	1985	1986	1987
Bently Corporation	6.3	6.8	7.0	6.4
Industry average	10.6	11.2	10.8	11.0

4-2 ◼ **(Inventory Management)** The Pearson Company has sales of $4 million and a gross profit margin of 40 percent. Its *end-of-quarter inventories* are as follows:

Quarter	Inventory
1	$ 400,000
2	800,000
3	1,200,000
4	200,000

a Find the average quarterly inventory and use it to calculate the firm's inventory turnover and the average age of inventory.

b Assuming the company is in an industry with an average inventory turnover of 2.0, how would you evaluate the activity of Pearson's inventory?

4-3 ■ (Accounts Receivable Management) An evaluation of the books of Bowman Supply Company shows the following end-of-year accounts receivable balance, which is believed to consist of amounts originating in the months indicated. The company had annual sales of $2.4 million. The firm extends 30-day credit terms.

Month of origin	Amounts receivable
July	$ 3,875
August	2,000
September	34,025
October	15,100
November	52,000
December	193,000
Year-end accounts receivable	$300,000

a Use the year-end total to evaluate the firm's collection system.

b If the firm's peak season is from July to December, how would this affect the validity of your conclusion above? Explain.

4-4 ■ (Debt Analysis) The Center City Bank is evaluating the Tiley Corporation, which has requested a $4,000,000 loan, in order to assess its financial leverage and financial risk. Based on the debt ratios for Tiley, along with the industry averages and Tiley's recent financial statements (presented below), evaluate and recommend appropriate action on the Tiley request.

Income Statement
Tiley Corporation
For the Year Ended December 31, 1987

Sales revenue		$30,000,000
Less: Cost of goods sold		21,000,000
Gross profits		$ 9,000,000
Less: Operating expenses		
Selling expense	$3,000,000	
General and administrative expenses	2,000,000	
Depreciation expense	1,000,000	
Total operating expense		6,000,000
Operating profits		$ 3,000,000
Less: Interest expense		1,000,000
Net profits before taxes		$ 2,000,000
Less: Taxes (rate = 40%)		800,000
Net profits after taxes		$ 1,200,000

Balance Sheet
Tiley Corporation
December 31, 1987

Assets

Current assets	
Cash	$ 1,000,000
Marketable securities	3,000,000
Accounts receivable	12,000,000
Inventories	7,500,000
Total current assets	$23,500,000
Gross fixed assets (at cost)	
Land and buildings	$11,000,000
Machinery and equipment	20,500,000
Furniture and fixtures	8,000,000
Gross fixed assets	$39,500,000
Less: Accumulated depreciation	13,000,000
Net fixed assets	$26,500,000
Total assets	$50,000,000

Liabilities and stockholders' equity

Current liabilities	
Accounts payable	$ 8,000,000
Notes payable	8,000,000
Accruals	500,000
Total current liabilities	$16,500,000
Long-term debt[a]	$20,000,000
Stockholders' equity	
Preferred stock[b]	$ 2,500,000
Common stock (1 million shares at $5 par)	5,000,000
Paid-in capital in excess of par value	4,000,000
Retained earnings	2,000,000
Total stockholders' equity	$13,500,000
Total liabilities and stockholders' equity	$50,000,000

[a] Required annual principal payments are $800,000.

[b] 25,000 shares of $4.00 preferred stock is outstanding.

Industry averages

Debt ratio	0.51
Times interest earned ratio	7.30
Fixed-payment coverage ratio	1.85

4-5 **(Common-Size Statement Analysis)** A common-size income statement for the Tiley Corporation's 1986 operations is presented at the top of page 110. Using the firm's 1987 income statement presented in Problem 4-4, develop the 1987 common-size income statement and compare it to the 1986 statement. Which areas require further analysis and investigation?

Common-Size Income Statement
Tiley Corporation
For the Year Ended December 31, 1986

Sales revenue ($35,000,000)		100.0%
Less: Cost of goods sold		65.9
Gross profits		34.1%
Less: Operating expenses		
Selling expense	12.7%	
General and administrative expenses	6.9	
Depreciation expense	3.6	
Total operating expense		23.2%
Operating profits		10.9%
Less: Interest expense		1.5
Net profits before taxes		9.4%
Less: Taxes (rate = 40%)		3.8
Net profits after taxes		5.6%

4-6 **(DuPont System of Analysis)** Use the following ratio information for Boswell Industries and the industry averages for Boswell's line of business to

a Construct the DuPont system for both Boswell and the industry.
b Evaluate Boswell (and the industry) over the three-year period.
c Determine which areas of Boswell Industries require further analysis.

Boswell	1985	1986	1987
Equity multiplier	1.75	1.75	1.85
Net profit margin	.059	.058	.049
Total asset turnover	2.11	2.18	2.34

Industry averages			
Equity multiplier	1.67	1.69	1.64
Net profit margin	.054	.047	.041
Total asset turnover	2.11	2.18	2.34

4-7 **(Ratio Interpretation)** Without referring to the text, indicate for each of the following ratios the formula for its calculation and the kinds of problems, if any, the firm is likely to be having if these ratios are too high relative to the industry average. What if they are too low relative to the industry? Create a table similar to that shown below and fill in the empty blocks.

Ratio	Too high	Too low
Current ratio =		
Inventory turnover =		
Times interest earned =	✕	
Gross profit margin =		
Return on investment =	✕	

4-8 **(Ratio Manipulation)** Complete the 1987 balance sheet for Piedmont Enterprises using the information that follows it.

Balance Sheet
Piedmont Enterprises
December 31, 1987

Cash	$30,000	Accounts payable	$120,000
Marketable securities	25,000	Notes payable	
Accounts receivable	_____	Accruals	20,000
Inventories	_____	Total current liabilities	_____
Total current assets	_____	Long-term debt	_____
Net fixed assets	_____	Stockholders' equity	600,000
Total assets	_____	Total liabilities and stockholders' equity	_____

Information (1987 values):
(1) Sales totaled $1,800,000
(2) The gross profit margin was 25 percent.
(3) Inventory turnover was 6.0
(4) There are 360 days in the year.
(5) The average collection period was 40 days.
(6) The current ratio was 1.60.
(7) The total asset turnover ratio was 1.20.
(8) The debt ratio was 60 percent.

4-9 **(Cross-Sectional Ratio Analysis)** Use the financial statements provided below for Delta Equipment Company for the year ended December 31, 1987, along with the industry average ratios, to:
  a Prepare and interpret a ratio analysis of the firm's 1987 operations.
  b Summarize your findings and make recommendations.

Income Statement
Delta Equipment Company
For the Year Ended December 31, 1987

Sales revenue		$600,000
Less: Cost of goods sold		460,000
Gross profits		$140,000
Less: Operating expenses		
General and administrative expense	$30,000	
Depreciation expense	30,000	
Total operating expense		60,000
Operating profits		$ 80,000
Less: Interest expense		10,000
Net profits before taxes		$ 70,000
Less: Taxes		27,100
Net profits after taxes (Earnings available for common stockholders)		$ 42,900
Earnings per share (EPS)		$ 2.15

Balance Sheet
Delta Equipment Company
December 31, 1987

Assets

Cash	$ 15,000
Marketable securities	7,200
Accounts receivable	34,100
Inventories	82,000
Total current assets	$138,300
Net fixed assets	$270,000
Total assets	$408,300

Liabilities and stockholders' equity

Accounts payable	$ 57,000
Notes payable	13,000
Accruals	5,000
Total current liabilities	$ 75,000
Long-term debt	$150,000
Stockholders' equity	
Common stock equity (20,000 shares outstanding)	$110,200
Retained earnings	73,100
Total stockholders' equity	$183,300
Total liabilities and stockholders' equity	$408,300

Ratio	Industry average, 1987
Net working capital	$125,000
Current ratio	2.35
Quick ratio	.87
Inventory turnover	4.55
Average collection period	35.3 days
Fixed asset turnover	1.97
Total asset turnover	1.09
Debt ratio	.300
Times interest earned ratio	12.3
Gross profit margin	.202
Net profit margin	.091
Return on investment (ROI)	.099
Return on equity (ROE)	.167

4-10 ■ (Financial Statement Analysis) The financial statements of the Robin Manufacturing Company for the year ended December 31, 1987, are given on page 113.

Robin Manufacturing Company
Balance Sheet
December 31, 1987

Assets

Cash	$ 500
Marketable securities	1,000
Accounts receivable	25,000
Inventories	45,500
Total current assets	$ 72,000
Land	$ 26,000
Buildings and equipment	90,000
Less: Accumulated depreciation	38,000
Net fixed assets	$ 78,000
Total assets	$150,000

Liabilities and stockholders' equity

Accounts payable	$ 22,000
Notes payable	47,000
Total current liabilities	$ 69,000
Long-term debt	$ 22,950
Common stock	31,500
Retained earnings	26,550
Total liabilities and stockholders' equity	$150,000

Robin Manufacturing Company
Income Statement
For the Year Ended December 31, 1987

Sales revenue	$160,000
Less: Cost of goods sold	106,000
Gross profits	$ 54,000
Less: Operating expenses	
Selling expense	$ 16,000
General and administrative expense	11,000
Depreciation expense	10,000
Total operating expense	$ 37,000
Operating profits	$ 17,000
Less: Interest expense	6,100
Net profits before taxes	$ 10,900
Less: Taxes	4,360
Net profits after taxes	$ 6,540

a Use the preceding financial statements to complete the table at the top of page 114. Assume that the industry averages given in the table are applicable for both 1986 and 1987.

Robin Manufacturing Company Ratio Analysis

Ratio	Industry average	Actual 1986	Actual 1987
Current ratio	1.80	1.84	_____
Quick ratio	.70	.78	_____
Average collection period[a]	37 days	36 days	_____
Inventory turnover[a]	2.50	2.59	_____
Debt ratio	65%	67%	_____
Times interest earned ratio	3.8	4.0	_____
Gross profit margin	38%	40%	_____
Net profit margin	3.5%	3.6%	_____
Return on investment	4.0%	4.0%	_____
Return on equity	9.5%	8.0%	_____

[a] Based on a 360-day year and on end-of-year figures.

b Analyze Robin Manufacturing Company's financial condition as it relates to (1) liquidity, (2) activity, (3) debt, and (4) profitability. Summarize the company's overall financial condition.

4-11 **(Integrative—Complete Ratio Analysis)** Given the following financial statements, historical ratios, and industry averages, calculate the Reid Company's financial ratios for the most recent year. Analyze
its overall financial situation from both a cross-sectional and a time-series
viewpoint. Break your analysis into an evaluation of the firm's liquidity,
activity, debt, and profitability.

Income Statement
Reid Company
For the Year Ended December 31, 1987

Sales revenue		$10,000,000
Less: Cost of goods sold		7,500,000
Gross profits		$ 2,500,000
Less: Operating expenses		
Selling expense	$300,000	
General and administrative expense	700,000	
Depreciation expense	200,000	1,200,000
Operating profits		$ 1,300,000
Less: Interest expense[a]		200,000
Net profits before taxes		$ 1,100,000
Less: Taxes (rate = 40%)		440,000
Net profits after taxes		$ 660,000
Less: Preferred stock dividends		50,000
Earnings available for common stockholders		$ 610,000
Earnings per share (EPS)		$ 3.01

[a] Interest expense includes the interest component of the annual financial lease
payment as specified by the Financial Accounting Standards Board (FASB).

Balance Sheet
Reid Company
December 31, 1987

Assets

Current assets		
Cash		$ 200,000
Marketable securities		50,000
Accounts receivable		800,000
Inventories		950,000
Total current assets		$ 2,000,000
Gross fixed assets (includes financial leases)[a]	$12,000,000	
Less: Accumulated depreciation	3,000,000	
Net fixed assets		$ 9,000,000
Other assets		$ 1,000,000
Total assets		$12,000,000

Liabilities and stockholders' equity

Current liabilities		
Accounts payable[b]		$ 900,000
Notes payable		200,000
Accruals		100,000
Total current liabilities		$ 1,200,000
Long-term debts (includes financial leases)[c]		$ 3,000,000
Stockholders' equity		
Preferred stock (25,000 shares, $2 dividend)		$ 1,000,000
Common stock (200,000 shares at $3 par)[d]		600,000
Paid-in capital in excess of par value		5,200,000
Retained earnings		1,000,000
Total stockholders' equity		$ 7,800,000
Total liabilities and stockholders' equity		$12,000,000

[a] The firm has an eight-year financial lease requiring annual beginning-of-year payments. Five years of the lease have yet to run.

[b] Annual credit purchases of $6,200,000 were made during the year.

[c] The annual principal payment on the long-term debt is $100,000.

[d] On December 31, 1987, the firm's common stock closed at $27½.

Historical and Industry-Average Ratios
Reid Company

Ratio	1985	1986	Industry average, 1987
Net working capital	$760,000	$720,000	$1,600,000
Current ratio	1.40	1.55	1.85
Quick ratio	1.00	.92	1.05
Inventory turnover	9.52	9.21	8.60
Average collection period	45.0 days	36.4 days	35.0 days
Average payment period	58.5 days	60.8 days	45.8 days
Fixed asset turnover	1.08	1.05	1.07
Total asset turnover	0.74	0.80	0.74
Debt ratio	0.20	0.20	0.30
Times interest earned ratio	8.2	7.3	8.0
Fixed-payment coverage ratio	4.8	4.5	4.5
Gross profit margin	0.30	0.27	0.25
Net profit margin	0.067	0.067	0.058
Return on investment (ROI)	0.049	0.054	0.043
Return on equity (ROE)	0.066	0.073	0.072
Price/earnings (P/E) ratio	12.0	10.5	11.2

5

BREAKEVEN ANALYSIS AND LEVERAGE

After studying this chapter, you should be able to:

- Relate operating leverage, financial leverage, and total leverage to the firm's income statement.

- Discuss the calculation and graphic depiction of the operating breakeven point in terms of units, dollars, and cash, and describe its limitations.

- Measure the degree of operating leverage and discuss its relationship to fixed costs and business risk.

- Calculate the degree of financial leverage, graphically compare financing plans, and discuss financial risk.

- Discuss the degree of total leverage and describe its relationship to operating leverage, financial leverage, and total risk.

leverage The use of fixed-cost assets or funds to magnify returns to the firm's owners.

Breakeven analysis and leverage are two closely related concepts that can be used to evaluate various aspects of the firm's return and risk. *Breakeven analysis* is a popular technique used to measure the firm's returns (profits) against various cost structures and levels of sales. **Leverage** results from the use of fixed-cost assets or funds to magnify returns to the firm's owners. Generally, increases in leverage result in both increased return and increased risk, while decreases in leverage result in decreased return and risk.

TYPES OF LEVERAGE

The three basic types of leverage can best be defined with reference to the firm's income statement. In the general income statement format in Table 5.1, the portions related to the firm's operating leverage, financial leverage, and total leverage are clearly labeled. *Operating leverage* is concerned with the relationship between the firm's sales revenue and its earnings before interest and taxes. *Financial leverage* is concerned with the relationship between the firm's earnings before interest and taxes and its earnings per share of common stock. *Total leverage* is concerned with the relationship between the firm's sales revenue and the earnings per share of common stock. In subsequent sections we will develop the three leverage concepts separately in detail, but first it is important to understand various aspects of breakeven analysis.

◼ BREAKEVEN ANALYSIS

breakeven analysis (cost-volume-profit analysis) Used (1) to determine the level of operations necessary to cover all operating costs and (2) to evaluate the profitability associated with various levels of sales.

Breakeven analysis, which is sometimes called **cost-volume-profit analysis,** is used by the firm (1) to determine the level of operations it

TABLE 5.1 General Income Statement Format and Types of Leverage

Operating leverage	⎧ Sales revenue	⎫
	Less: Cost of goods sold	
	Gross profits	
	Less: Operating expenses	
	Earnings before interest and taxes *(EBIT)*	
	Less: Interest	Total leverage
	Earnings before taxes	
Financial leverage	Less: Taxes	
	Earnings after taxes	
	Less: Preferred stock dividends	
	Earnings available for common stockholders	
	⎩ Earnings per share *(EPS)*	⎭

must maintain to cover all operating costs and (2) to evaluate the profitability associated with various levels of sales. To understand breakeven analysis, it is necessary to analyze further the firm's costs.

Types of Costs

The three types of costs are depicted graphically in Figure 5.1. **Fixed costs** are a function of time, not sales, and are typically contractual. These costs require the payment of a specified amount in each accounting period. Rent, for example, is a fixed cost. **Variable costs** vary directly with sales and are a function of volume rather than time. Production and delivery costs are variable costs. **Semivariable costs** are partly fixed and partly variable. One example of semivariable costs might be sales commissions, which may be fixed for a certain volume of sales and then increase to higher levels for higher volumes.

fixed costs Expenses to the firm that are a function of time, not sales, and that are typically contractual.

variable costs Costs that vary directly with sales, and that are a function of volume, not time.

semivariable costs Costs that are partly fixed and partly variable.

Finding the Operating Breakeven Point

The firm's **operating breakeven point** is the level of sales necessary to cover all operating costs. At the operating breakeven point, earnings

operating breakeven point The level of sales necessary to cover all operating costs.

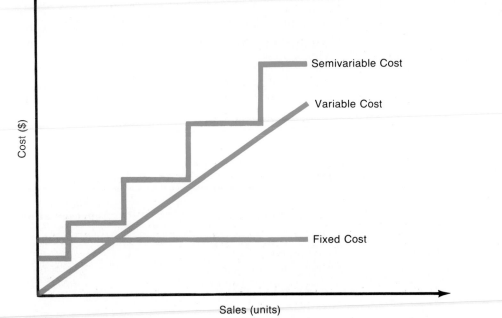

FIGURE 5.1 Types of Costs
Costs may be fixed, variable, or semivariable. Fixed costs are a function of time, not sales; variable costs vary with sales; and semivariable costs are partly fixed and partly variable.

before interest and taxes, or *EBIT*, equals zero.[1] (*EBIT* is a descriptive label for *operating profits*.) The first step in finding the operating breakeven point involves dividing the cost of goods sold and operating expenses into fixed and variable operating costs. The top portion of Table 5.1 can then be recast as shown in the left-hand side of Table 5.2. Using this framework, the firm's operating breakeven point can be developed and evaluated.

THE ALGEBRAIC APPROACH Using the following variables, the operating portion of the firm's income statement can be represented as shown in the right-hand portion of Table 5.2.

$$Q = \text{sales quantity in units}$$
$$P = \text{sale price per unit}$$
$$FC = \text{fixed operating cost per period}$$
$$VC = \text{variable operating cost per unit}$$

Rewriting the algebraic calculations in Table 5.2 as a formula for earnings before interest and taxes yields Equation 5.1:

$$EBIT = (P \times Q) - FC - (VC \times Q) \tag{5.1}$$

Simplifying Equation 5.1 yields

$$EBIT = Q \times (P - VC) - FC \tag{5.2}$$

As noted above, the operating breakeven point is the level of sales at which all fixed and variable operating costs are covered—that is, the level at which *EBIT* equals zero. Setting *EBIT* equal to zero and solving Equation 5.2 for *Q* yields

$$Q = \frac{FC}{P - VC} \tag{5.3}$$

Q is the firm's operating breakeven volume. Let us look at an example.

TABLE 5.2 Operating Leverage, Costs, and Breakeven Analysis

	Item	Algebraic representation
Operating leverage	Sales revenue	$P \times Q$
	Less: Fixed operating costs	$- \quad FC$
	Less: Variable operating costs	$-(VC \times Q)$
	Earnings before interest and taxes	$EBIT$

[1] Quite often the breakeven point is calculated so that it represents the point where *all operating and financial costs* are covered. Our concern in this chapter is not with this overall breakeven point.

EXAMPLE

Assume that a firm has fixed operating costs of $2,500, the sale price per unit of its product is $10, and its variable operating cost per unit is $5. Applying Equation 5.3 to these data yields

$$Q = \frac{\$2,500}{\$10 - \$5} = \frac{\$2,500}{\$5} = 500 \text{ units}$$

At sales of 500 units the firm's *EBIT* should just equal zero. ■

In the example, the firm will have positive *EBIT* for sales greater than 500 units and negative *EBIT*, or a loss, for sales less than 500 units. We can confirm this by substituting values above and below 500 units, along with the other values given, into Equation 5.1.

THE GRAPHIC APPROACH Figure 5.2 presents in graph form the breakeven analysis of the data in the example above. The firm's operating breakeven point is the point at which its *total operating cost,* or the sum of its fixed and variable operating costs, equals sales revenue. At this point *EBIT* equals zero. The figure shows that a loss occurs when the

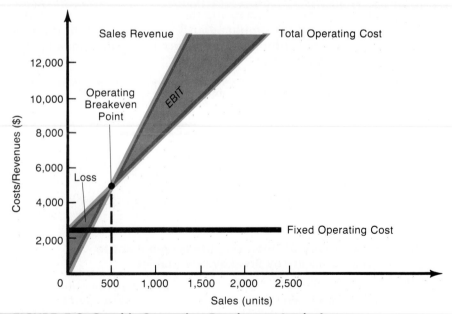

FIGURE 5.2 Graphic Operating Breakeven Analysis
The operating breakeven point of 500 units is the level of sales at which total operating cost, which is the sum of fixed and variable operating costs, equals sales revenue. *EBIT* is positive above the operating breakeven point, and a loss occurs below it.

firm's sales are *below* the operating breakeven point. In other words, for sales of less than 500 units total operating costs exceed sales revenue and *EBIT* is less than zero. For sales levels *greater than* the breakeven point of 500 units, sales revenue exceeds total operating costs and *EBIT* is greater than zero.

Changing Costs and the Operating Breakeven Point

A firm's operating breakeven point is sensitive to a number of variables: fixed operating costs (*FC*), the sale price per unit (*P*), and the variable operating cost per unit (*VC*). The effects of increases or decreases in each of these variables can be readily assessed by referring to Equation 5.3. The sensitivity of the breakeven sales volume (*Q*) to an *increase* in each of these variables is summarized in Table 5.3. As might be expected, the table indicates that an increase in cost (*FC* or *VC*) tends to increase the operating breakeven point, while an increase in price per unit (*P*) will decrease the operating breakeven point.

EXAMPLE

Assume that the firm wishes to evaluate the impact of (1) increasing fixed operating costs to $3,000, (2) increasing the sale price per unit to $12.50, (3) increasing the variable operating cost per unit to $7.50, and (4) simultaneously implementing all three of these changes. Substituting the appropriate data into Equation 5.3 yields the following:

(1) Operating breakeven point $= \dfrac{\$3,000}{\$10 - \$5} = 600$ units

(2) Operating breakeven point $= \dfrac{\$2,500}{\$12.50 - \$5} = 333\frac{1}{3}$ units

(3) Operating breakeven point $= \dfrac{\$2,500}{\$10 - \$7.50} = 1,000$ units

(4) Operating breakeven point $= \dfrac{\$3,000}{\$12.50 - \$7.50} = 600$ units

TABLE 5.3 Sensitivity of Operating Breakeven Point to Increases in Key Breakeven Variables

Increase in variable	Effect on operating breakeven point
Fixed operating cost (*FC*)	Increase
Sale price per unit (*P*)	Decrease
Variable operating cost per unit (*VC*)	Increase

NOTE: Decreases in each of the variables shown would have the opposite effect from that indicated on the breakeven point.

USING BREAKEVEN ANALYSIS TO GET RESULTS

It was back in the 1982 recession, and the numbers at Bayer A.G.'s Mobay Chemical Corp. subsidiary were bad — sales down by nearly 10%, to $1.1 billion, net income plunging from $57.7 million to a loss of $8.3 million. Howard Martin, Mobay's manager of strategic planning, wanted better information — some historical perspective to see if profits were really keeping up with costs.

"Accountants tend to be interested in comparisons against this year's budget or last year's actual, but they're not interested in much more history than that," Martin says. He wanted to know things like: How much had so-called fixed costs actually changed over time? How had the company's break-even point changed? How did the 1982 earnings compare with the last time Mobay had a comparable level of capacity utilization? What level of profitability could Mobay expect at full capacity? . . .

Not an easy job. It's one thing to figure specific break-even points on individual products — in Mobay's case as disparate as soybean herbicides and polyurethane components. Putting those together into aggregate numbers for the whole company plotted over time is more complex.

Armed with a hand-held Texas Instruments calculator, Martin spent several months developing what he calls "profit geometry" analysis of the entire company's break-even history. . . .

First he developed two maximum performance curves representing break-even gross margins and operating results at various levels of capacity utilization. Then he plotted Mobay's actual results for the previous ten years against those curves. He could compare current performance with prior years' records and conceivably the projected performance of competitors.

Result: 1982 results as adjusted by Martin turned out to be higher than "historical" break-even at the 50% capacity level where the firm was running. "In fact we were doing no worse than we might have expected, given our prior record," says Martin. "Without that historical perspective, we might have taken much more dramatic action than we needed to. We might have laid off a lot of people or sold off businesses or closed down capacity."

Martin's analysis indicated that the company was well poised for a recovery, once capacity utilization picked up. "That convinced us to reverse a 5% salary cutback on Apr. 1, 1983, when the rest of the economy was only beginning to recognize the recovery," he says. "And we approved our annual salary raises early." Martin's optimism proved to be justified. Since 1982, Mobay's gross margins and operating results have been well above break-even.

Source: Jill Andresky, "Break-Dancing in the Dark," *Forbes*, August 12, 1985, p. 68. Reprinted by permission of *Forbes* Magazine. © Forbes, Inc. 1985.

Comparing the resulting operating breakeven points to the initial value of 500 units, we can see that, as noted in Table 5.3, the cost increases (1 and 3) raise the breakeven point (600 units and 1,000 units, respectively), while the revenue increase (2) lowers the breakeven point to $333\frac{1}{3}$ units. The combined effect of increasing all three variables (4) results in an increased breakeven point of 600 units. ■

Other Approaches to Breakeven Analysis

Two other popular approaches to breakeven analysis are (1) measuring the breakeven point in terms of dollars and (2) determining the cash breakeven point. Each of these approaches is briefly described below.

BREAKEVEN IN DOLLARS When a firm has more than one product, it is useful to calculate the breakeven point in terms of dollars rather than units. The use of a dollar breakeven point is especially important for firms that have a variety of products, each selling at a different price. Assuming that the firm's product mix remains relatively constant, the breakeven point can be calculated in terms of dollars by using a contribution margin approach. The **contribution margin** in this case will be defined as the percent of each sales dollar that remains after satisfying variable operating costs. Utilizing the following variable terms, the firm's dollar operating breakeven point can be defined:

contribution margin
The percent of each sales dollar remaining after variable operating costs are satisfied.

TR = total sales revenue in dollars
TVC = total variable operating costs paid to achieve TR dollars of sales
FC = total fixed operating costs paid during the period in which TR dollars of sales are achieved

In the case of a single-product firm, using the notation presented earlier, $TR = P \times Q$ and $TVC = VC \times Q$.

The variable operating cost per dollar of sales can be represented as $TVC \div TR$. Subtracting $TVC \div TR$ from 1 will yield the contribution margin, which reflects the per-dollar contribution toward fixed operating costs and profits provided by each dollar of sales:

$$\text{Contribution margin} = 1 - \frac{TVC}{TR} \qquad (5.4)$$

Dividing the contribution margin into the fixed operating costs, FC, yields the dollar breakeven point for any level of sales, D.

$$D = \frac{FC}{\left(1 - \dfrac{TVC}{TR}\right)} \qquad (5.5)$$

Let us look at the following example.

EXAMPLE

Assume that during a period a firm has fixed operating costs of
$100,000, total sales of $800,000, and total variable operating
costs of $600,000. Applying Equation 5.5 to these data yields

$$D = \frac{\$100,000}{\left(1 - \dfrac{\$600,000}{\$800,000}\right)} = \frac{\$100,000}{.25} = \$400,000$$

Assuming the firm's product mix does not change, at a $400,000
sales level the firm will break even on its operation. At that point
its *EBIT* will equal zero. ■

CASH BREAKEVEN ANALYSIS   Under certain conditions it is sometimes
useful to perform a **cash breakeven analysis.** This technique is used to
find the operating breakeven point when certain noncash charges, such
as depreciation, constitute an important portion of the firm's fixed
operating costs. Any charges of this type that are included as part of the
firm's fixed costs must be adjusted in preparing the cash analysis because the presence of such charges tends to overstate the firm's breakeven point. Assuming that the firm has certain noncash charges, *NC*,
included in its fixed operating costs, Equation 5.3 can be rewritten for
the cash operating breakeven point as shown in Equation 5.6:

$$\text{Cash operating breakeven point} = \frac{FC - NC}{P - VC} \qquad (5.6)$$

cash breakeven analysis
A technique used to find
the operating breakeven
point when certain
noncash charges, such as
depreciation, constitute
an important portion of
the firm's fixed operating
costs.

EXAMPLE

Assume that the firm in the example on page 121 had included in
its fixed operating costs of $2,500, $1,500 of depreciation. Substituting this information along with the firm's $10 per unit sale price
and $5 per unit variable operating cost into Equation 5.6 yields the
following:

$$\text{Cash operating breakeven point} = \frac{\$2,500 - \$1,500}{\$10 - \$5} = \frac{\$1,000}{\$5} = 200 \text{ units}$$

The firm's cash operating breakeven point is therefore 200 units,
which is considerably below the 500-unit operating breakeven
point calculated earlier using accounting data. ■

Although the cash breakeven analysis provides a convenient mechanism for assessing the level of sales necessary to meet cash operating
costs, it is not a substitute for detailed cash plans. Chapter 6 provides a

discussion of more formal techniques for analyzing and budgeting cash flows.

Limitations of Breakeven Analysis

Although breakeven analysis is widely used by business, it has a number of inherent limitations. First it assumes that the firm faces linear, or nonvarying, total revenue and total operating cost functions. Generally, however, this is not the case because neither the firm's sale price per unit nor its variable cost per unit is independent of sales volume. The sale price per unit generally decreases with volume, while the cost per unit generally increases with volume, thereby resulting in *curved*, rather than straight (linear), revenue and cost functions. Figure 5.3 shows a graphic operating breakeven analysis using nonlinear sales revenue and operating cost functions. Recognition of these curved functions may complicate the analysis and result in solutions different from those obtained using linear revenue and cost functions.

A second limitation of breakeven analysis is the difficulty of breaking semivariable costs into fixed and variable components. And still an-

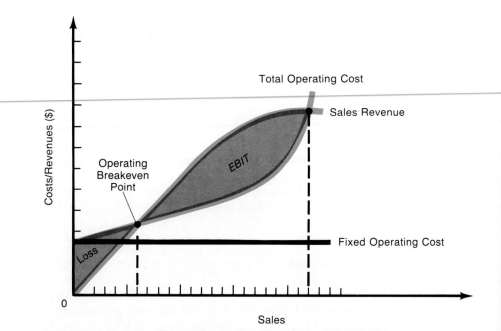

FIGURE 5.3 A Nonlinear Operating Breakeven Analysis
Nonlinear (curved) breakeven analysis reflects the fact that the firm faces varying sales revenue and total operating cost functions. This occurs since the sale price generally decreases with sales volume and cost per unit generally increases with sales volume.

other limitation occurs in the application of breakeven analysis to multiproduct firms. Due to the difficulty of allocating costs to products, special and more sophisticated multiproduct breakeven models must be used to determine breakeven points for each product line.

Finally, the short-term — typically one year — time horizon of breakeven analysis often limits its use. A large outlay in the current financial period could significantly raise the firm's breakeven point, while the benefits may occur over a period of years. Expenses for advertising and research and development (R and D) are examples of such outlays. Clearly, all of these potential limitations must be considered when applying breakeven analysis.

OPERATING LEVERAGE

Operating leverage results from the existence of *fixed operating costs* in the firm's income stream. Using the structure presented in Table 5.2, **operating leverage** can be defined as the potential use of fixed operating costs to magnify the effects of changes in sales on earnings before interest and taxes *(EBIT)*. The following example illustrates how operating leverage works.

operating leverage The potential use of fixed operating costs to magnify the effects of changes in sales on earnings before interest and taxes *(EBIT)*.

EXAMPLE

Using the data presented earlier (sale price, $P = \$10$ per unit; variable operating costs, $VC = \$5$ per unit; fixed operating costs, $FC = \$2,500$), Figure 5.4 presents the operating breakeven chart originally shown in Figure 5.2. It can be seen from the additional notations on the chart that as the firm's sales increase from 1,000

TABLE 5.4 The *EBIT* for Various Sales Levels

	Case 2		Case 1
	−50%		+50%
Sales (in units)	500	1,000	1,500
Sales revenue[a]	$5,000	$10,000	$15,000
Less: Variable operating costs[b]	2,500	5,000	7,500
Less: Fixed operating costs	2,500	2,500	2,500
Earnings before interest and taxes *(EBIT)*	$ 0	$ 2,500	$ 5,000
	−100%		+100%

[a] Sales revenue = $10/unit × sales in units.

[b] Variable operating costs = $5/unit × sales in units.

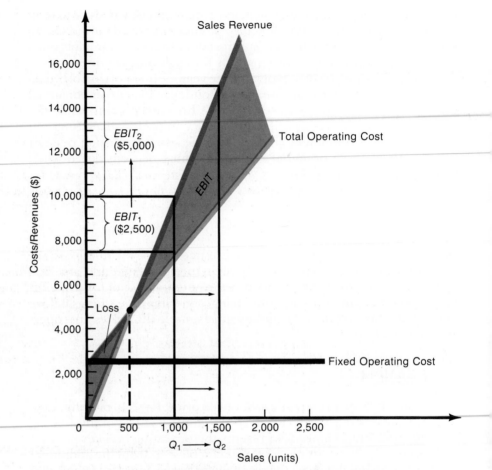

FIGURE 5.4 Breakeven Analysis and Operating Leverage
The breakeven chart can be used to demonstrate operating leverage. As sales increase by 50 percent from 1,000 units (Q_1) to 1,500 units (Q_2), EBIT increases by 100 percent from $2,500 (EBIT$_1$) to $5,000 (EBIT$_2$).

to 1,500 units (Q_1 to Q_2), its *EBIT* increases from $2,500 to $5,000 (*EBIT*$_1$ to *EBIT*$_2$). In other words, a 50 percent increase in sales (1,000 to 1,500 units) results in a 100 percent increase in *EBIT*. Table 5.4 includes the data for Figure 5.4 as well as relevant data for a 500-unit sales level. Using the 1,000-unit sales level as a reference point, two cases can be illustrated.

Case 1 A 50 percent *increase* in sales (from 1,000 to 1,500 units) results in a 100 percent *increase* in earnings before interest and taxes (from $2,500 to $5,000).

Case 2 A 50 percent *decrease* in sales (from 1,000 to 500 units) results in a 100 percent *decrease* in earnings before interest and taxes (from $2,500 to zero). ▪

From the above example we see that operating leverage works in both directions. When a firm has fixed operating costs, operating leverage is present. An increase in sales results in a more than proportional increase in earnings before interest and taxes; a decrease in sales results in a more than proportional decrease in earnings before interest and taxes.

Measuring the Degree of Operating Leverage *(DOL)*

The **degree of operating leverage *(DOL)*** is the numerical measure of the firm's operating leverage. It can be derived using the following equation:[2]

degree of operating leverage *(DOL)* The numerical measure of the firm's operating leverage.

$$DOL = \frac{\text{percentage change in } EBIT}{\text{percentage change in sales}} \qquad (5.7)$$

Whenever the percentage change in *EBIT* resulting from a given percentage change in sales is greater than the percentage change in sales, operating leverage exists. This means that as long as *DOL* is greater than 1, there is operating leverage.

EXAMPLE

Applying Equation 5.7 to Cases 1 and 2 in Table 5.4 yields the following results:[3]

$$\text{Case 1: } \frac{+100\%}{+50\%} = 2.0$$

$$\text{Case 2: } \frac{-100\%}{-50\%} = 2.0$$

Since the result is greater than 1, operating leverage exists. For a given base level of sales, the higher the value resulting from applying Equation 5.7, the greater the degree of operating leverage. ▪

[2] The degree of operating leverage also depends on the base level of sales used as a point of reference. The closer the base sales level used is to the operating breakeven level, the greater the operating leverage. *Comparison of the degree of operating leverage of two firms is valid only when the base level of sales used for each firm is the same.*

[3] Because the concept of leverage is *linear*, positive and negative changes of equal magnitude will always result in equal degrees of leverage when the same base sales level is used as a point of reference. This relationship holds for all types of leverage discussed in this chapter.

A more direct formula for calculating the degree of operating leverage at a base sales level, Q, is shown in Equation 5.8, using the symbols given on page 120.

$$DOL \text{ at base sales level } Q = \frac{Q \times (P - VC)}{Q \times (P - VC) - FC} \qquad (5.8)$$

EXAMPLE

Substituting $Q = 1,000$, $P = \$10$, $VC = \$5$, and $FC = \$2,500$ into Equation 5.8 yields the following result:

$$DOL \text{ at } 1,000 \text{ units} = \frac{1,000 \times (\$10 - \$5)}{1,000 \times (\$10 - \$5) - \$2,500} = \frac{\$5,000}{\$2,500} = 2.0$$

It should be clear that the use of the formula results in the same value for DOL (2.0) as that found using Table 5.4 and Equation 5.7.[4] ■

Fixed Costs and Operating Leverage

Changes in fixed operating costs affect operating leverage significantly. This effect can be best illustrated by continuing our example.

EXAMPLE

Assume that the firm discussed earlier is able to exchange a portion of its variable operating costs for fixed operating costs. This exchange results in a reduction in the variable operating cost per unit from $5 to $4.50 and an increase in the fixed operating costs from $2,500 to $3,000. Table 5.5 presents an analysis similar to that given in Table 5.4 using these new costs. Although the *EBIT* of $2,500 at the 1,000-unit sales level is the same as before the shift in operating cost structure, it should be clear from Table 5.5 that by shifting to greater fixed operating costs, the firm has increased its operating leverage.

---

[4]When total sales in dollars — instead of unit sales — are available, the following equation in which TR = dollar level of base sales and TVC = total variable operating costs in dollars can be used:

$$DOL \text{ at base dollar sales } TR = \frac{TR - TVC}{TR - TVC - FC}$$

This formula is especially useful for finding the *DOL* for multiproduct firms. It should be clear that since in the case of a single-product firm $TR = P \times Q$ and $TVC = VC \times Q$, substitution of these values into Equation 5.8 results in the equation given here.

TABLE 5.5 Operating Leverage and Increased Fixed Costs

		Case 2		Case 1
		−50%		+50%
Sales (in units)		500	1,000	1,500
Sales revenue[a]		$5,000	$10,000	$15,000
Less: Variable operating costs[b]		2,250	4,500	6,750
Less: Fixed operating costs		3,000	3,000	3,000
Earnings before interest and taxes (EBIT)		−$250	$ 2,500	$ 5,250
			−110%	+110%

[a] Sales revenue was calculated as indicated in Table 5.4.

[b] Variable operating costs = $4.50/unit × sales in units.

With the substitution of the appropriate values into Equation 5.8, the degree of operating leverage at the 1,000-unit base level of sales becomes

$$DOL \text{ at } 1,000 \text{ units} = \frac{1,000 \times (\$10 - \$4.50)}{1,000 \times (\$10 - \$4.50) - \$3,000} = \frac{\$5,500}{\$2,500} = 2.2$$

Comparing this value to the *DOL* of 2.0 before the shift to more fixed costs, it is clear that the higher the firm's fixed operating costs relative to variable operating costs, the greater the degree of operating leverage. ■

Business Risk

Because leverage works in two ways, a shift toward more fixed costs increases business risk. Stated simply, **business risk** is the risk of being unable to cover operating costs. In the foregoing examples the increase in business risk can be demonstrated by comparing the operating breakeven points before and after the shift. Before the shift, the firm's operating breakeven point is 500 units [$2,500 ÷ ($10 − $5)]; after the shift the operating breakeven point is 545 units [($3,000 ÷ ($10 − $4.50)]. Clearly the firm must achieve a higher level of sales in order to meet increased fixed operating costs. On the positive side, however, higher operating leverage causes *EBIT* to increase more for a given increase in sales. When considering fixed operating cost increases, the financial manager must weigh the increased business risk associated with greater operating leverage against the expected increase in returns.

business risk The risk to the firm of being unable to cover operating costs.

FINANCIAL LEVERAGE

financial leverage The potential use of fixed financial charges to magnify the effects of changes in earnings before interest and taxes *(EBIT)* on earnings per share *(EPS)*.

Financial leverage results from the presence of fixed *financial charges* in the firm's income stream. Using the framework in Table 5.1, **financial leverage** can be defined as the potential use of fixed financial charges to magnify the effects of changes in earnings before interest and taxes *(EBIT)* on the firm's earnings per share *(EPS)*. The two fixed financial charges normally found on the firm's income statement are (1) interest on debt and (2) preferred stock dividends. These charges must be paid regardless of the amount of *EBIT* available to pay them. The following example illustrates how financial leverage works.

EXAMPLE

A firm expects earnings before interest and taxes of $10,000 in the current year. It has a $20,000 bond with a 10 percent stated annual interest rate and an issue of 600 shares of $4 (annual dividend per share) preferred stock outstanding. It also has 1,000 shares of common stock outstanding. The annual interest on the bond issue is $2,000 (.10 × $20,000). The annual dividends on the preferred stock are $2,400 ($4.00/share × 600 shares). Table 5.6 presents the levels of earnings per share resulting from levels of earnings before interest and taxes of $6,000, $10,000, and $14,000 assuming

TABLE 5.6 The *EPS* for Various *EBIT* Levels

		Case 2		Case 1
		−40%		+40%
EBIT	$6,000		$10,000	$14,000
Less: Interest *(I)*	2,000		2,000	2,000
Earnings before taxes (*EBT*)	$4,000		$ 8,000	$12,000
Less: Taxes *(T)(t* = .40)	1,600		3,200	4,800
Earnings after taxes (*EAT*)	$2,400		$ 4,800	$ 7,200
Less: Preferred stock dividends *(PD)*	2,400		2,400	2,400
Earnings available for common *(EAC)*	$ 0		$ 2,400	$ 4,800
Earnings per share *(EPS)*	$\dfrac{\$0}{1,000} = \$0$		$\dfrac{\$2,400}{1,000} = \$2.40$	$\dfrac{\$4,800}{1,000} = \$4.80$
		−100%		+100%

the firm is in the 40 percent tax bracket. Two situations are illustrated in the table.

Case 1 A 40 percent *increase* in *EBIT* (from $10,000 to $14,000) results in a 100 percent *increase* in earnings per share (from $2.40 to $4.80).

Case 2 A 40 percent *decrease* in *EBIT* (from $10,000 to $6,000) results in a 100 percent *decrease* in earnings per share (from $2.40 to $0). ■

The effect of financial leverage is such that an increase in the firm's *EBIT* results in a greater than proportional increase in the firm's earnings per share, while a decrease in the firm's *EBIT* results in a more than proportional decrease in *EPS*.

Measuring the Degree of Financial Leverage *(DFL)*

The **degree of financial leverage *(DFL)*** is the numerical measure of the firm's financial leverage. It can be computed in a fashion similar to that used to measure the degree of operating leverage. The following equation presents one approach for obtaining *DFL*.[5]

degree of financial leverage *(DFL)* The numerical measure of the firm's financial leverage.

$$DFL = \frac{\text{percentage change in } EPS}{\text{percentage change in } EBIT} \qquad (5.9)$$

Whenever the percentage change in *EPS* resulting from a given percentage change in *EBIT* is greater than the percentage change in *EBIT*, financial leverage exists. This means that whenever *DFL* is greater than 1, there is financial leverage.

EXAMPLE

Applying Equation 5.9 to cases 1 and 2 in Table 5.6 yields

$$\text{Case 1:} \frac{+100\%}{+40\%} = 2.5$$

$$\text{Case 2:} \frac{-100\%}{-40\%} = 2.5$$

In both cases, the quotient is greater than 1, and financial leverage exists. The higher this value, the greater the degree of financial leverage. ■

---

[5] This approach is valid only when the base level of *EBIT* used to calculate and compare these values is the same. In other words, *the base level of EBIT must be held constant to compare the financial leverage associated with different levels of fixed financial costs.*

A more direct formula for calculating the degree of financial leverage at a base level of *EBIT* is given by Equation 5.10, using the notation from Table 5.6.

$$DFL \text{ at base level } EBIT = \frac{EBIT}{EBIT - I - \left(PD \times \frac{1}{1 - t}\right)} \quad (5.10)$$

EXAMPLE

Substituting $EBIT = \$10,000$, $I = \$2,000$, $PD = \$2,400$, and the tax rate ($t = .40$) into Equation 5.10 yields the following result:

$$DFL \text{ at } \$10,000 \ EBIT = \frac{\$10,000}{\$10,000 - \$2,000 - \left(\$2,400 \times \frac{1}{1 - .40}\right)}$$

$$= \frac{\$10,000}{\$4,000} = 2.5$$

It should be apparent that the formula given in Equation 5.10 provides a more direct method for calculating the degree of financial leverage than the approach illustrated using Table 5.6 and Equation 5.9. ■

Graphic Comparison of Financing Plans

Financing plans can be compared graphically by plotting them on a set of *EBIT-EPS* axes. This approach can be illustrated with an example.

EXAMPLE

The key characteristics of the financing plan presented earlier, referred to as plan A, and a new financing plan, plan B, are summarized below:

Type of financing	Plan A	Plan B
Debt Annual interest	$20,000 of 10% debt .10 × $20,000 = $2,000	$10,000 of 10% debt .10 × $10,000 = $1,000
Preferred stock Annual dividend	600 shares of $4 600 × $4 = $2,400	300 shares of $4 300 × $4 = $1,200
Common stock Number of shares	1,000	1,750

THE FINANCIAL MANAGEMENT ASSOCIATION (FMA)

The Financial Management Association was established in 1970 in order to develop a continuing relationship between successful financial practitioners and leading academicians and to encourage the free exchange of ideas, techniques, and advances in the field of financial management and business finance. . . .

Financial Management

The quarterly journal of the Association, *Financial Management,* is dedicated to the common interests of financial managers and academicians. Articles report on and refine the most advanced academic research and review developments made by practitioners in many financially oriented fields. The journal's scope includes major business concerns operating in a variety of areas, regulated industries, nonprofit organizations, financial institutions, and a variety of other public and private sector concerns. . . .

Student Chapters Program

FMA sponsors student finance clubs throughout the U.S. and Canada in order to provide students of finance, banking, and investments an association which will encourage their professional development and increase the interaction between business executives, faculty, and students. FMA student chapters are a valuable link for students to a successful future as professionals in finance. . . .

National Honor Society

The purpose of the National Honor Society is to encourage and reward scholarship and accomplishment in business and nonbusiness finance and banking among undergraduate and graduate students, to provide an association for college students actively interested in these fields, and to encourage an interaction between business executives and students of finance and banking. The National Honor Society is the *only* national honorary [organization] for students of finance. . . .

Source: *Careers in Finance* (Tampa, Fl.: Financial Management Association, 1983), pp. 51–52.

These two plans can be illustrated graphically. Like all plans of this type, they can be plotted as a *straight line* on a set of *EBIT-EPS* axes. Two *EBIT-EPS* coordinates, or plotting points, are needed for each plan. These coordinates can be drawn from Table 5.6 for plan A, but we need to calculate two coordinates for plan B. The *EPS* associated with *EBIT* values of $10,000 and $14,000, respectively, are calculated for plan B in Table 5.7. It can be seen that for plan B

TABLE 5.7 Calculation of Plan B's *EBIT-EPS* Coordinates

		+40%	
EBIT	$10,000		$14,000
−*I*	1,000		1,000
EBT	$ 9,000		$13,000
−*T*(*t* = .40)	3,600		5,200
EAT	$ 5,400		7,800
−*PD*	1,200		1,200
EAC	$ 4,200		$ 6,600

$$EPS \quad \frac{\$4,200}{1,750} = \$2.40/share \qquad \frac{\$6,600}{1,750} = \$3.77/share$$

+57%

a 40 percent increase in the firm's *EBIT* will result in a 57 percent increase in *EPS*. Applying Equation 5.10 to these values yields

$$DFL \text{ at } \$10,000 \ EBIT = \frac{\$10,000}{\$10,000 - \$1,000 - \$1,200 \times \left(\dfrac{1}{1-.40}\right)}$$

$$= \frac{\$10,000}{\$7,000} = 1.4$$

The degree of financial leverage of 1.4, when compared to the *DFL* of 2.5 calculated earlier for plan A, indicates that plan B has a lower degree of financial leverage than plan A.

The three *EBIT-EPS* coordinates from Table 5.6 for plan A and the two coordinates derived in Table 5.7 for plan B are summarized below:

	COORDINATES	
Plan	***EBIT***	***EPS***
A	$ 6,000	$0.00
	10,000	2.40
	14,000	4.80
B	$10,000	$2.40
	14,000	3.77

Using these coordinates, the two financing plans are presented graphically in Figure 5.5.

As figure 5.5 illustrates, the slope of plan A is steeper than that of plan B. This indicates that plan A has more financial leverage than

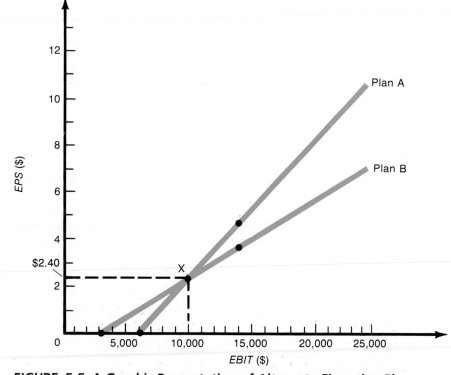

FIGURE 5.5 A Graphic Presentation of Alternate Financing Plans
Because the slope of Plan A is steeper than that of Plan B, Plan A has more
financial leverage. In addition, Plan A has a higher financial breakeven point
($6,000) than Plan B ($3,000). At *EBIT* below the $10,000 indifference point
Plan B is preferred; above $10,000 *EBIT* Plan A is preferred.

plan B. This result is as expected, since the degree of financial
leverage *(DFL)* is 2.5 for plan A and 1.4 for plan B. The higher the
DFL, the greater the leverage a plan has, and the steeper its slope
when plotted on *EBIT-EPS* axes. ■

FINANCIAL BREAKEVEN POINT   In our example, the point of intersec-
tion of each plan with the *EBIT* axis represents the amount of earnings
before interest and taxes necessary for the firm to cover its fixed financial charges — that is, the point at which *EPS* = $0. This point of inter-
section can be thought of as a **financial breakeven point**, since it
represents the level of *EBIT* necessary for the firm to cover its fixed
financial charges. The breakeven *EBIT* for plan A is $6,000, and for plan
B it is $3,000. In other words, earnings before interest and taxes of less
than $6,000 with plan A or less than $3,000 with plan B will result in a
loss, or negative *EPS*.

**financial breakeven
point** The level of *EBIT*
necessary for the firm to
cover its fixed financial
charges.

indifference point On a graphed comparison of two financial plans, the point at which, for a given *EBIT*, *EPS* is the same for each plan respectively.

INDIFFERENCE POINT The point labeled X in Figure 5.5 represents the **indifference point** between plan A and plan B. It indicates that at a level of *EBIT* of $10,000, *EPS* of $2.40 would result under either plan. At levels of *EBIT* below $10,000, plan B results in higher levels of *EPS*. At levels of *EBIT* above $10,000, plan A results in higher levels of *EPS*. The usefulness of this type of analysis is discussed in Chapter 16.

Financial Risk

financial risk The risk to the firm of being unable to cover financial costs.

Increasing financial leverage results in increasing risk, since increased financial payments require the firm to maintain a higher level of *EBIT* in order to break even. **Financial risk** is the risk of being unable to cover financial costs. If the firm cannot cover these financial payments, it can be forced out of business by creditors whose claims remain unsettled.[6] On the positive side, higher financial leverage causes *EPS* to increase more for a given increase in *EBIT*. Financial leverage is often measured using various debt ratios (Chapter 4). These ratios indicate the relationship between the funds on which fixed financial charges must be paid and the total funds invested in the firm. When considering the increased use of debt or preferred stock financing, the financial manager must weigh the increased financial risk associated with greater financial leverage against the expected increase in returns.

TOTAL LEVERAGE: THE COMBINED EFFECT

total leverage The potential use of fixed costs, both operating and financial, to magnify the effect of changes in sales on the firm's earnings per share *(EPS)*.

The combined effect of operating and financial leverage on the firm's risk can be assessed using a framework similar to that used to develop the individual concepts of leverage. This combined effect, or **total leverage,** can be defined as the potential use of fixed costs, both operating and financial, to magnify the effect of changes in sales on the firm's earnings per share *(EPS)*. Total leverage can therefore be viewed as the total impact of the fixed costs in the firm's operating and financial structure.

EXAMPLE

A firm expects sales of 20,000 units at $5 per unit in the coming year and must meet the following: variable operating costs at $2 per unit, fixed operating costs of $10,000, interest of $20,000, and

[6] Preferred stockholders do not have the power to force liquidation if their claims remain unpaid. The problem with not paying preferred stock dividends is that then the common stockholders can receive no dividends.

TABLE 5.8 The Total Leverage Effect

	+50%		
Sales (in units)	20,000	30,000	$DOL =$
Sales revenue[a]	$100,000	$150,000	$+60\%$
Less: Variable operating costs[b]	40,000	60,000	$\dfrac{+60\%}{+50\%} = 1.2$
Less: Fixed operating costs	10,000	10,000	
Earnings before interest and taxes (EBIT)	$ 50,000	$ 80,000	
	+60%		$DTL =$
Less: Interest	20,000	20,000	$\dfrac{+300\%}{+50\%} = 6.0$
Earnings before taxes	$30,000	$60,000	
Less: Taxes (40%)	12,000	24,000	
Earnings after taxes	$18,000	$36,000	$DFL =$
Less: Preferred stock dividends	12,000	12,000	$\dfrac{+300\%}{+60\%} = 5.0$
Earnings available for common	$ 6,000	$24,000	
Earnings per share (EPS)	$\dfrac{\$6,000}{5,000} = \$1.20$	$\dfrac{\$24,000}{5,000} = \$4.80$	
	+300%		

a Sales revenue = $5/unit × sales in units.

b Variable operating costs = $2/unit × sales in units.

preferred stock dividends of $12,000. The firm is in the 40 percent tax bracket and has 5,000 shares of common stock outstanding. Table 5.8 presents the levels of earnings per share (EPS) associated with the expected sales of 20,000 units and with sales of 30,000 units.

The table illustrates that as a result of a 50 percent increase in sales (20,000 to 30,000 units), the firm would experience a 300 percent increase in earnings per share (from $1.20 to $4.80). Although not shown in the table, a 50 percent decrease in sales would, conversely, result in a 300 percent decrease in earnings per share. The linear nature of the leverage relationship accounts for the fact that sales changes of equal magnitude in opposite directions result in earnings per share changes of equal magnitude in the corresponding direction. At this point it should be clear that whenever a firm has fixed costs—operating or financial—in its structure, total leverage will exist. ■

Measuring the Degree of Total Leverage (DTL)

The **degree of total leverage (DTL)** is the numerical measure of total leverage. It can be obtained in a fashion similar to that used to measure

degree of total leverage (DTL) The numerical measure of the firm's total leverage.

operating and financial leverage. The following equation presents one approach for measuring DTL.[7]

$$DTL = \frac{\text{percentage change in } EPS}{\text{percentage change in sales}} \qquad (5.11)$$

Whenever the percentage change in EPS resulting from a given percentage change in sales is greater than the percentage change in sales, total leverage exists. This means that as long as the DTL is greater than 1, there is total leverage.

EXAMPLE

Applying Equation 5.11 to the data in Table 5.8 yields

$$DTL = \frac{+300\%}{+50\%} = 6.0$$

Since this result is greater than 1, total leverage exists. The higher the value, the greater the degree of total leverage. ■

A more direct formula for calculating the degree of total leverage at a given base level of sales, Q, is given by Equation 5.12, which uses the same notation presented earlier:

$$DTL \text{ at base sales level } Q = \frac{Q \times (P - VC)}{Q \times (P - VC) - FC - I - \left(PD \times \dfrac{1}{1-t}\right)} \qquad (5.12)$$

EXAMPLE

Substituting $Q = 20{,}000$, $P = \$5$, $VC = \$2$, $FC = \$10{,}000$, $I = \$20{,}000$, $PD = \$12{,}000$, and the tax rate ($t = .40$) into Equation 5.12 yields the following result:

DTL at 20,000 units

$$= \frac{20{,}000 \times (\$5 - \$2)}{20{,}000 \times (\$5 - \$2) - \$10{,}000 - \$20{,}000 - \left(\$12{,}000 \times \dfrac{1}{1 - .40}\right)}$$

$$= \frac{\$60{,}000}{\$10{,}000} = 6.0$$

Clearly, the formula used in Equation 5.12 provides a more direct method for calculating the degree of total leverage than the approach illustrated using Table 5.8 and Equation 5.11. ■

[7] This approach is valid only when the base level of sales used to calculate and compare these values is the same. In other words, *the base level of sales must be held constant in order to compare the total leverage associated with different levels of fixed costs.*

The Relationship of Operating, Financial, and Total Leverage

Total leverage reflects the combined impact of operating and financial leverage on the firm. High operating and high financial leverage will cause total leverage to be high. The opposite will also be true. The relationship between operating and financial leverage is *multiplicative* rather than *additive*. The relationship between the degree of total leverage *(DTL)* and the degrees of operating *(DOL)* and financial *(DFL)* leverage is given by Equation 5.13.

$$DTL = DOL \times DFL \qquad (5.13)$$

EXAMPLE

Substituting the values calculated for *DOL* and *DFL*, shown on the right-hand side of Table 5.8, into Equation 5.13 yields

$$DTL = 1.2 \times 5.0 = 6.0$$

The resulting degree of total leverage (6.0) is the same value as was calculated directly in the preceding section. ■

Total Risk

In a relationship similar to operating leverage = business risk and financial leverage = financial risk, total leverage reflects the total risk of the firm. The firm's **total risk** is therefore the firm's risk of being unable to cover both operating and financial costs. With increasing costs—especially fixed operating and financial costs—comes increasing risk, since the firm will have to achieve a higher level of sales just to break even. If a firm is unable to meet these costs, it could be forced out of business by its creditors. On the positive side, higher total leverage causes *EPS* to increase more for a given increase in sales. When considering fixed operating or financial cost increases, the financial manager must weigh the increased risk associated with greater leverage against the expected increase in returns.

total risk The risk to the firm of being unable to cover both operating and financial costs.

SUMMARY

- Breakeven analysis is used both to determine the level of sales necessary to cover all operating costs and to evaluate profitability. Below the operating breakeven point, the firm experiences a loss; above the operating breakeven point, the firm's earnings before interest and taxes *(EBIT)* are positive. Cost increases raise the breakeven point and sales price increases lower it, and vice versa.
- The breakeven point can be found in terms of units of sales, dollars of sales, or on a cash basis.

● Breakeven analysis suffers from a number of limitations, chief among which are the assumption of linearity, the difficulty of classifying costs, problems caused by multiproduct situations, and the short-term nature of the typical time horizon.

● Operating leverage is the potential use of fixed operating costs by the firm to magnify the effects of changes in sales on earnings before interest and taxes *(EBIT)*. The higher the fixed operating costs, the greater the operating leverage.

● The degree of operating leverage at a specified level of sales can be calculated using a tabular approach or by formula. The firm's business risk is directly related to its degree of operating leverage.

● Financial leverage is the potential use of fixed financial costs by the firm to magnify the effects of changes in earnings before interest and taxes *(EBIT)* on earnings per share *(EPS)*. The higher the fixed financial costs—typically interest on debt and preferred stock dividends—the greater the financial leverage.

● The degree of financial leverage at a specified level of earnings before interest and taxes can be calculated using a tabular approach or by formula. The firm's financial risk is directly related to its degree of financial leverage.

● Financing plans can be graphed on a set of *EBIT-EPS* axes. The steeper the slope of a financing plan, the higher its degree of financial leverage. The level of *EBIT* at which *EPS* just equals zero is the financial breakeven point.

● The total leverage of the firm is the potential use of fixed costs—both operating and financial—to magnify the effects of changes in sales on earnings per share. Total leverage reflects the combined effect of operating and financial leverage.

● The degree of total leverage at a specified level of sales can be measured using a tabular approach or by formula. It can also be found by multiplying the degree of operating leverage by the degree of financial leverage. The firm's total risk is directly related to its degree of total leverage.

QUESTIONS

5-1 What is meant by the term *leverage*? How do the operating leverage, financial leverage, and total leverage relate to the income statement?

5-2 Define and differentiate between fixed costs, variable costs, and semivariable costs. Which of these costs is the key element creating leverage?

5-3 Define and differentiate between each of the following operating breakeven points:
a Breakeven in *units*
b Breakeven in *dollars*
c *Cash* breakeven

5-4 How do changes in fixed operating costs, the selling price per unit, and the variable operating cost per unit affect the firm's *operating breakeven point*?

5-5 One of the key limitations of breakeven analysis is the assumption of linear total revenue and total operating cost functions. Why might these functions actually be curved? What are some other limitations of break-even analysis?

5-6 What is meant by *operating leverage?* What causes it? How is the *degree of operating leverage (DOL)* measured?

5-7 What is the relationship between operating leverage and business risk? How is each of these related to the operating breakeven point and risk-return trade-off?

5-8 What is meant by *financial leverage?* What causes it?

5-9 What is the *degree of financial leverage (DFL)?* What two methods can be used to calculate the *DFL?*

5-10 Why must financial managers assess the firm's degree of financial leverage? Why is this measure important in evaluating various financing plans?

5-11 What is the relationship between financial leverage and financial risk? How is each of these related to the financial breakeven point and risk-return trade-off?

5-12 What is the general relationship among operating leverage, financial leverage, and the total leverage of the firm? Do these types of leverage complement each other? Why, or why not?

PROBLEMS

5-1 **(Breakeven Point – Algebraic)** Marilyn Cosgrove wishes to estimate the number of pairs of shoes she must sell at $24.95 per pair in order to break even. She has estimated fixed operating costs of $12,350 per year and variable operating costs of $15.45 per pair. How many pairs of shoes must Marilyn sell in order to break even on operating costs?

5-2 **(Breakeven Point – Algebraic and Graphic)** Sting Industries sells its single product for $129.00 per unit. The firm's fixed operating costs are $473,000 annually and its variable operating costs are $86.00 per unit.

a Find the firm's operating breakeven point.

b Label the *x*-axis "Sales (units)" and the *y*-axis "Costs/Revenues ($)" and then graph the firm's sales revenue, total operating cost, and fixed operating cost functions on these axes. In addition, label the operating breakeven point and the areas of loss and profit *(EBIT)*.

5-3 **(Breakeven Analysis)** Doug Mills is considering opening a record store. He wants to estimate the number of records he must sell in order to break even. The records will be sold for $6.98 each, variable operating costs are $5.23 per record, and fixed operating costs are $36,750.

a Find the operating breakeven point.

b Calculate the total operating costs at the breakeven volume found in a.

c If Doug estimates that at a minimum he can sell 2,000 records *per month*, should he go into the record business?

d How much *EBIT* would Doug realize if he sells the minimum 2,000 records per month noted in **c**?

5-4 **(Breakeven Point – Changing Costs/Revenues)** Hi-Tek Press publishes the *Video Yearbook.* Last year the book sold for $10 with variable operating cost per book of $8 and fixed operating costs of $40,000. How many books must be sold this year to achieve the breakeven point for the stated operating costs given the following different circumstances?

a All figures remain the same as last year.

b Fixed operating costs increase to $44,000; all other figures remain the same as last year.

c The selling price increases to $10.50; all costs remain the same as last year.

d Variable operating cost per book increases to $8.50; all other figures remain the same.

e What conclusions about the operating breakeven point can be drawn from your answers?

5-5 **(Breakeven Comparisons)** Given the following price and cost data for each of the three firms M, N, and O, answer the questions below.

	M	N	O
Sale price per unit	$ 18.00	$ 21.00	$ 30.00
Variable operating cost per unit	6.75	13.50	12.00
Fixed operating cost	45,000	30,000	90,000

a What is the operating breakeven point in units for each firm?

b Compute the dollar operating breakeven point.

c Assuming $10,000 of each firm's fixed operating costs are depreciation, compute the cash operating breakeven point for each firm.

d How would you rank these firms in terms of their risk?

5-6 **(EBIT Sensitivity)** The Harlow Company sells its finished product for $9 per unit. Its fixed operating costs are $20,000 and the variable operating cost per unit is $5.

a Calculate the firm's earnings before interest and taxes *(EBIT)* for sales of 10,000 units.

b Calculate the firm's *EBIT* for sales of 8,000 and 12,000 units, respectively.

c Calculate the percentage change in sales (from the 10,000-unit base level) and associated percentage changes in *EBIT* for the shifts in sales indicated in **b**.

5-7 **(Degree of Operating Leverage)** The Withers Design Group has fixed operating costs of $380,000, variable operating costs per unit of $16, and a selling price of $63.50 per unit.

a Calculate the operating breakeven point in units and sales dollars.

b Calculate the firm's *EBIT* at 9,000, 10,000, and 11,000 units, respectively.

c Using 10,000 units as a base, what are the percentage changes in units sold and *EBIT* as sales move from the base to the other sales levels used in **b**?

d Use the percentages computed in **c** to determine the degree of operating leverage *(DOL)*.

    e Use the degree of operating leverage formula to determine the *DOL* at 10,000 units.

5-8 **(Breakeven — Graphical)** Zandy, Inc. has fixed operating costs of $72,000, variable operating costs of $6.75 per unit, and a selling price of $9.75 per unit.

    a Calculate the operating breakeven point in units.

    b Compute the degree of operating leverage *(DOL)* for the following unit sales levels: 25,000, 30,000, 40,000. Use the formula given in the chapter.

    c Graph the *DOL* figures you computed in **b** (on the *y*-axis) against sales levels (on the *x*-axis).

    d Compute the degree of operating leverage at 24,000 units; add this point to your graph.

    e What principle is illustrated by your graph and figures?

5-9 **(*EPS* Calculations)** Fleet Corporation has $60,000 of 16-percent (annual interest) bonds outstanding, 1,500 shares of preferred stock paying an annual dividend of $5 per share, and 4,000 shares of common stock outstanding. Assuming the firm has a 40 percent tax rate, compute earnings per share *(EPS)* for the following levels of *EBIT:*

    a $24,600

    b $30,600

    c $35,000

5-10 **(Degree of Financial Leverage)** Central Canning Company has *EBIT* of $67,500. Interest costs are $22,500 and the firm has 15,000 shares of common stock outstanding. Assume a 40 percent tax rate.

    a Use the degree of financial leverage *(DFL)* formula to calculate the *DFL* for the firm.

    b Using a set of *EBIT-EPS* axes, plot Central Canning's financing plan.

    c Assuming the firm also has 1,000 shares of preferred stock paying a $6.00 annual dividend per share, what is the *DFL*?

    d Plot the financing plan including the 1,000 shares of $6.00 preferred stock on the axes used in **b**.

    e Briefly discuss the graphs of the two financing plans.

5-11 **(*DFL* and Graphic Display of Financing Plans)** Western Oil Corporation has a current capital structure consisting of $250,000 of 16 percent (annual interest) debt and 2,000 shares of common stock. The firm pays taxes at the rate of 40 percent on ordinary income.

    a Using *EBIT* values of $80,000 and $120,000, determine the associated earnings per share *(EPS)*.

    b Using $80,000 of *EBIT* as a base, calculate the degree of financial leverage *(DFL)*.

    c Graph the firm's current financing plan on a set of *EBIT-EPS* axes.

    d Rework parts **a** and **b** assuming the firm has $100,000 of 16 percent (annual interest) debt and 3,000 shares of common stock.

    e Graph the financing plan in **d** on the same axes used in **c**, and discuss the relationship between financial leverage and the graphic display of the two financing plans.

5-12 **(Financing Plan Comparisons)** Newlin Electronics is considering additional financing of $10,000. They currently have $50,000 of 12 percent (annual interest) bonds and 10,000 shares of common stock outstanding. The firm can obtain the financing through a 12 percent (annual interest) bond issue or the sale of 1,000 shares of common stock. If the firm expects *EBIT* to be $30,000 and has a 40 percent tax rate,

a What would the degree of financial leverage *(DFL)* be under each financing plan?

b Plot the two financing plans on a set of *EBIT-EPS* axes.

c Based on your graph in **b**, at what level of *EBIT* does the bond plan become superior to the stock plan?

5-13 **(Total Breakeven)** Magowan Manufacturing produces small motors. Their fixed operating costs are $20,000, variable operating costs are $18 per unit, and the motors sell for $23 each. Magowan has $50,000 in 10 percent (annual interest) bonds and 20,000 shares of common stock outstanding. The firm is in the 40 percent tax bracket.

a What is Magowan's operating breakeven point in units?

b What is Magowan's financial breakeven point?

c What is Magowan's total (i.e., both operating and financial costs) breakeven point?

5-14 **(Integrative — Multiple Leverage Measures)** Musk Oil Cosmetics produces skin-care products, selling 400,000 bottles a year. Each bottle produced has a variable operating cost of $.84 and sells for $1.00. Fixed operating costs are $28,000. The firm has annual interest charges of $6,000, preferred dividends of $2,000, and a 40 percent tax rate.

a Calculate (1) the operating breakeven point in units and (2) the total (including both operating and financial costs) breakeven point in units.

b Use the degree of operating leverage *(DOL)* formula to calculate *DOL*.

c Use the degree of financial leverage *(DFL)* formula to calculate *DFL*.

d Use the degree of total leverage *(DTL)* formula to calculate *DTL*. Compare this to the product of *DOL* and *DFL* calculated in **b** and **c**.

5-15 **(Integrative — Leverage and Risk)** Firm J has sales of 100,000 units at $2.00 per unit, variable operating costs of $1.70 per unit, and fixed operating costs of $6,000. Interest is $10,000 per year. Firm R has sales of 100,000 units at $2.50, variable operating costs of $1.00 per unit, and fixed operating costs of $62,500. Interest is $17,500 per year. Assume that both firms are in the 40 percent tax bracket.

a Compute the degree of operating, financial, and total leverage for firm J.

b Compute the degree of operating, financial, and total leverage for firm R.

c Compare the relative risks of the two firms.

d Discuss the principles of leverage illustrated in your answers.

5-16 **(Integrative — Leverage)** TOR's most recent sales were $750,000, its variable operating costs represent 40 percent of sales, and its fixed operating costs are $250,000. Annual interest charges total $80,000, and the firm has 8,000 shares of $5 (annual dividend) preferred stock outstanding. It currently has 20,000 shares of common stock oustanding. Assume that the firm has a 40 percent tax rate.

a At what level of sales would the firm break even on operations (i.e., *EBIT* = 0)?

b Calculate the firm's earnings per share *(EPS)* in tabular form at (1) the current level of sales and (2) at a $900,000 sales level.

c Using the *$750,000 level of sales as a base,* calculate the firm's degree of operating leverage *(DOL).*

d Using the *EBIT associated with the $750,000 level of sales as a base,* calculate the firm's degree of financial leverage *(DFL).*

e Use the degree of total leverage *(DTL)* concept to determine the effect (in percentage terms) of a 50 percent increase in TOR's sales from the $750,000 base level on its earnings per share.

6

FINANCIAL PLANNING

After studying this chapter, you should be able to:

● Understand the financial planning process, including the role of and interrelationship between long-run (strategic) financial plans, and short-run (operating) plans.

● Discuss the cash planning process, the role of sales forecasts, and the procedures for preparing and evaluating the cash budget.

● Develop, prepare, and evaluate a pro forma income statement using the percent-of-sales method.

● Develop, prepare, and evaluate a pro forma balance sheet using the judgmental approach.

● Describe the weaknesses of the simplified approaches to pro forma preparation, and describe the common uses of pro forma financial statements.

Financial planning is an important aspect of the firm's operation and livelihood since it provides road maps for guiding, coordinating, and controlling the firm's actions in order to achieve its objectives. Two key aspects of the financial planning process are *cash planning* and *profit planning*. Cash planning involves the preparation of the firm's cash budget. Without adequate cash—regardless of the level of profits—any firm could fail. Profit planning is usually done by means of pro forma financial statements, which show anticipated levels of profits, assets, liabilities, and equity. Cash budgets and pro forma statements are useful not only for internal financial planning but are also routinely required by present and prospective lenders. Before studying the preparation and use of these statements, let us first examine the relationship between long-run and short-run financial plans.

THE FINANCIAL PLANNING PROCESS

The **financial planning process** begins with long-run, or strategic, financial plans that in turn guide the formulation of short-run operating plans and budgets. Generally, the short-run plans and budgets operationalize, or implement, the firm's long-run strategic objectives. While the major emphasis in this chapter is on short-run financial plans and budgets, a few comments on the long-run plans are appropriate here.

financial planning process Long-run (strategic) financial planning used as a guide to the formulation of short-run plans and budgets.

Long-Run (Strategic) Financial Plans

Long-run (strategic) financial plans are planned long-term financial actions and the anticipated financial impact of those actions. Such plans tend to cover periods ranging from two to ten years. The use of five-year strategic plans, which are periodically revised as significant new information becomes available, is common. Generally, firms subject to high degrees of operating uncertainty, relatively short production cycles, or both tend to use shorter planning horizons. Long-run financial plans consider proposed fixed-asset outlays, research and development activities, marketing and product development actions, and major sources of financing. Also included would be termination of existing projects, product lines, or lines of business; repayment or retirement of outstanding debts; and any planned acquisitions. Such plans tend to be supported by a series of annual budgets and profit plans.

long-run (strategic) financial plans Planned long-term financial actions and the anticipated financial impact of those actions.

Short-Run (Operating) Financial Plans

Short-run (operating) financial plans are planned short-term financial actions and the anticipated financial impact of those actions. These

short-run (operating) financial plans Planned short-term financial actions and the anticipated financial impact of those actions.

plans most often cover a one- to two-year period. Key inputs include the sales forecast and various forms of operating and financial data. Key outputs include a number of operating budgets, the cash budget, and pro forma financial statements. The short-run financial planning process, from the initial sales forecast through the development of the cash budget and pro forma income statement and balance sheet, is presented in the flow diagram in Figure 6.1.

From the sales forecast are developed production plans that take into account lead (preparation) times and include estimates of the required types and quantities of raw materials. Based on the production plans, direct labor requirements, factory overhead outlays, and operating expenses can also be estimated. Once these estimates have been made, the firm's pro forma income statement and cash budget can be prepared. With the pro forma income statement, cash budget, fixed-asset outlay

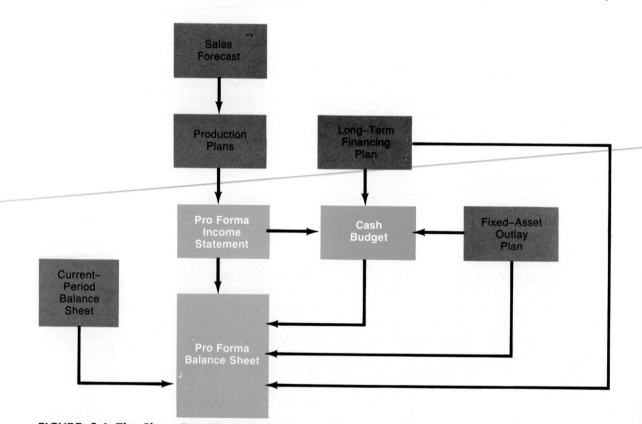

FIGURE 6.1 The Short-Run (Operating) Financial Planning Process
The key input to the short-run (operating) financial planning process is the sales forecast, from which production plans, schedules, and costs can be estimated. These estimates are input to the pro forma income statement and cash budget, which with additional data are used to prepare the pro forma balance sheet.

plan, long-term financing plan, and current-period balance sheet as basic inputs, the pro forma balance sheet can finally be developed. Throughout the remainder of this chapter we will concentrate on the key outputs of the short-run financial planning process: the cash budget, the pro forma income statement, and the pro forma balance sheet.

CASH PLANNING: CASH BUDGETS

The **cash budget,** or **cash forecast,** allows the firm to plan its short-term cash needs. Attention is given to planning for surplus cash and for cash shortages. A firm expecting a cash surplus can plan short-term investments (marketable securities), whereas a firm expecting shortages in cash must arrange for short-term (notes payable) financing. The cash budget gives the financial manager a clear view of the timing of the firm's expected cash inflows and outflows over a given period.

Typically, the cash budget is designed to cover a one-year period, although any time period is acceptable. The period covered is normally divided into smaller time intervals. The number and type of intervals depend on the nature of the business. The more seasonal and uncertain a firm's cash flows, the greater the number of intervals. Since many firms are confronted with a seasonal cash flow pattern, the cash budget is quite often presented on a monthly basis. Firms with stable patterns of cash flow may use quarterly or annual time intervals. If a cash budget is developed for a period greater than one year, fewer time intervals may be warranted due to the difficulty and uncertainty of forecasting sales and other related cash items.

> **cash budget (cash forecast)** Financial projection of the firm's short-term cash surpluses or shortages.

The Sales Forecast

The key input to the short-run financial planning process and therefore any cash budget is the firm's **sales forecast.** This is the prediction of the firm's sales over a given period and is ordinarily furnished to the financial manager by the marketing department. On the basis of this forecast, the financial manager estimates the monthly cash flows that will result from projected sales receipts and from production-related, inventory-related, and sales-related outlays. The manager also determines the level of fixed assets required and the amount of financing, if any, needed to support the forecast level of production and sales. The sales forecast may be based on an analysis of external or internal data or on a combination of the two.

> **sales forecast** The prediction of the firm's sales over a given period, based on internal and/or external data, and used as the key input to the short-run financial planning process.

EXTERNAL FORECASTS An **external forecast** is based on the relationships that can be observed between the firm's sales and certain key external economic indicators such as the gross national product (GNP),

> **external forecast** A sales forecast based on the relationships observed between the firm's sales and certain key external economic indicators.

new housing starts, and disposable personal income. Forecasts containing these indicators are readily available. The rationale for this approach is that since the firm's sales are often closely related to some aspect of overall national economic activity, a forecast of economic activity should provide insight into future sales.

internal forecast A sales forecast based on a buildup, or consensus, of forecasts through the firm's own sales channels.

INTERNAL FORECASTS Internal forecasts are based on a buildup, or consensus, of sales forecasts through the firm's own sales channels. Typically, the firm's salespeople in the field are asked to estimate the number of units of each type of product they expect to sell in the coming year. These forecasts are collected and totaled by the sales manager, who may adjust the figures using his or her own knowledge of specific markets or of the salesperson's forecasting ability. Finally, adjustments may be made for additional internal factors, such as production capabilities.

COMBINED FORECASTS Firms generally use a combination of external and internal forecast data in making the final sales forecast. The internal data provide insight into sales expectations, while the external data provide a means of adjusting these expectations to take into account general economic factors. The nature of the firm's product also often affects the mix and types of forecasting methods used.

Preparing the Cash Budget

The general format of the cash budget is presented in Table 6.1. We will discuss each of its components individually.

cash receipts All items from which the firm receives cash inflows during a given financial period.

CASH RECEIPTS Cash receipts includes all items from which cash inflows result in any given financial period. The most common components of cash receipts are cash sales, collections of accounts receivable, and other cash receipts.

TABLE 6.1 The General Format of the Cash Budget

	Jan.	Feb.	. . .	Nov.	Dec.
Cash receipts					
Less: Cash disbursements					
Net cash flow	___	___	. . .	___	___
Add: Beginning cash	___ ↗ ___	↗ . . . ↗ ___	↗ ___		
Ending cash					
Less: Minimum cash balance	___	___	. . .	___	___
Required total financing					
Excess cash balance			. . .		

EXAMPLE

The Halley Company is developing a cash budget for October, November, and December. Halley's sales in August and September were $100,000 and $200,000, respectively. Sales of $400,000, $300,000, and $200,000 have been forecast for October, November, and December, respectively. Historically, 20 percent of the firm's sales have been for cash, 50 percent have generated accounts receivable collected after one month, and the remaining 30 percent have generated accounts receivable collected after two months. Bad-debt expenses (uncollectible accounts) have been negligible.[1] In December, the firm will receive a $30,000 dividend from stock in a subsidiary. The schedule of expected cash receipts for the company is presented in Table 6.2. It contains the following items.

Forecast sales This initial entry is *merely informational*. It is provided as an aid in calculating other sales-related items.

Cash sales The cash sales shown for each month represent 20 percent of the total sales forecast for that month.

Collections of A/R These entries represent the collection of accounts receivable resulting from sales in earlier months.

Lagged one month These figures represent sales made in the preceding month that generated accounts receivable collected in the current month. Since 50 percent of the current month's sales are collected one month later, the collections of accounts receivable with a one-month lag shown for September,

TABLE 6.2 A Schedule of Projected Cash Receipts for the Halley Company ($000)

	Aug.	Sept.	Oct.	Nov.	Dec.
Forecast sales	$100	$200	$400	$300	$200
Cash sales (.20)	$ 20	$ 40	$ 80	$ 60	$ 40
Collections of A/R:					
Lagged one month (.50)		50	100	200	150
Lagged two months (.30)			30	60	120
Other cash receipts					30
Total cash receipts			$210	$320	$340

[1] Normally it would be expected that the collection percentages would total slightly less than 100 percent to reflect the fact that some of the accounts receivable would be uncollectible. In this example the sum of the collection percentages is 100 percent (20% + 50% + 30%), which reflects the fact that all sales are assumed to be collected since bad debts are said to be negligible.

October, November, and December represent 50 percent of the sales in August, September, October, and November, respectively.

Lagged two months These figures represent sales made two months earlier that generated accounts receivable collected in the current month. Since 30 percent of sales are collected two months later, the collections with a two-month lag shown for October, November, and December represent 30 percent of the sales in August, September, and October, respectively.

Other cash receipts These are cash receipts expected to result from sources other than sales. Items such as dividends received, interest received, proceeds from the sale of equipment, stock and bond sale proceeds, and lease receipts may show up here. For the Halley Company, the only other cash receipt is the $30,000 dividend due in December.

Total cash receipts This figure represents the total of all the cash receipt items listed for each month in the cash receipt schedule. In the case of the Halley Company, we are concerned only with October, November, and December; the total cash receipts for these months are shown in Table 6.2. ■

cash disbursements All cash outlays by the firm during a given financial period.

CASH DISBURSEMENTS **Cash disbursements** include all outlays of cash in the period covered. The most common cash disbursements are

Cash purchases
Payments of accounts payable
Payments of cash dividends
Rent expense
Wages and salaries
Tax payments
Fixed-asset outlays
Interest payments
Principal payments (loans)
Repurchases or retirements of stock

It is important to recognize that *depreciation and other noncash charges are NOT included in the cash budget* because they merely represent a scheduled write-off of an earlier cash outflow. The impact of depreciation, as noted in Chapter 3, is reflected in the level of cash outflow represented by the tax payments.

EXAMPLE

The Halley Company has gathered the following data needed for the preparation of a cash disbursements schedule for the months of October, November, and December.

Purchases The firm's purchases represent 70 percent of

sales. Ten percent of this amount is paid in cash, 70 percent is paid in the month immediately following the month of purchase, and the remaining 20 percent is paid two months following the month of purchase.[2]

Cash dividends   Cash dividends of $20,000 will be paid in October.

Rent expense   Rent of $5,000 will be paid each month.

Wages and salaries   The firm's wages and salaries can be estimated by adding 10 percent of its monthly sales to the $8,000 fixed-cost figure.

Tax payments   Taxes of $25,000 must be paid in December.

Fixed-asset outlays   New machinery costing $130,000 will be purchased and paid for in November.

Interest payments   An interest payment of $10,000 is due in December.

Principal payments (loans)   A $20,000 principal payment is also due in December.

Repurchases or retirements of stock   No repurchase or retirement of stock is expected during the October–December period.

The firm's cash disbursement schedule, based on the data above, is presented in Table 6.3. Some items in Table 6.3 are explained in greater detail below.

TABLE 6.3 A Schedule of Projected Cash Disbursements for the Halley Company ($000)

	Aug.	Sept.	Oct.	Nov.	Dec.
Purchases (.70 × sales)	$70	$140	$280	$210	$140
Cash purchases (.10)	$ 7	$ 14	$ 28	$ 21	$ 14
Payments of A/P:					
Lagged one month (.70)		49	98	196	147
Lagged two months (.20)			14	28	56
Cash dividends			20		
Rent expense			5	5	5
Wages and salaries			48	38	28
Tax payments					25
Fixed-asset outlays				130	
Interest payments					10
Principal payments					20
Total cash disbursements			$213	$418	$305

[2] Unlike the collection percentages for sales, the total of the payment percentages should equal 100 percent since it is expected that the firm will pay off all of its accounts payable. In line with this expectation, the Halley Company's percentages total 100 percent (10% + 70% + 20%).

Purchases This entry is *merely informational*. The figures represent 70 percent of the forecast sales for each month. They have been included to facilitate the calculation of the cash purchases and related payments.

Cash purchases The cash purchases for each month represent 10 percent of the month's purchases.

Payments of A/P These entries represent the payment of accounts payable resulting from purchases in earlier months.

Lagged one month These figures represent purchases made in the preceding month that are paid for in the current month. Since 70 percent of the firm's purchases are paid for one month later, the payments lagged one month shown for September, October, November, and December represent 70 percent of the August, September, October, and November purchases, respectively.

Lagged two months These figures represent purchases made two months earlier that are paid for in the current month. Since 20 percent of the firm's purchases are paid for two months later, the payments lagged two months for October, November, and December represent 20 percent of the August, September, and October purchases, respectively.

Wages and salaries These values were obtained by adding $8,000 to 10 percent of the *sales* in each month. The $8,000 represents the salary component; the rest represents wages.

The remaining items on the cash disbursements schedule are self-explanatory. ■

net cash flow The mathematical difference between the firm's cash receipts and its cash disbursements in each period.

ending cash The sum of the firm's beginning cash and its net cash flow for the period.

required total financing Amount of funds needed by the firm if the ending cash for the period is less than the minimum cash balance.

excess cash balance The (excess) amount available for investment by the firm if the period's ending cash is greater than the minimum cash balance.

NET CASH FLOW, ENDING CASH, FINANCING, AND EXCESS CASH A firm's **net cash flow** is found by subtracting the cash disbursements from cash receipts in each period. By adding beginning cash to the firm's net cash flow, the **ending cash** for each period can be found. Finally, subtracting the minimum cash balance from ending cash yields the **required total financing** or the **excess cash balance.** If the ending cash is less than the minimum cash balance, *financing* is required. If the ending cash is greater than the minimum cash balance, *excess cash* exists.

EXAMPLE

Table 6.4 presents the Halley Company's cash budget, based on the cash receipt and cash disbursement data already developed for the firm. Halley's end-of-September cash balance was $50,000, and the company wishes to maintain a minimum cash balance of $25,000.

For the Halley Company to maintain its required $25,000 ending cash balance, it will need to have borrowed $76,000 in No-

WHY MAKE CASH FLOW PROJECTIONS?

Cash flow projections make a lot of sense for a lot of reasons. For example, they force companies to address operational issues in a timely fashion: Will fringe benefits be changed this year? When will a new product be introduced? How much more will be spent on advertising? Will overall debt be slashed?

Cash flow forecasts also compel corporations to decide — in a proven, systematic way — how much inventory to maintain and when additional people must be hired. Royal Silk Ltd., of Clifton, N.J., is a case in point. The $21-million company, which sells blouses and other silk garments by mail order, has installed a sophisticated cash forecasting system to track the number of items it sells per advertisement and per mailing list. That information enables it to estimate accurately how many blouses it must have in its warehouse when, for example, it takes out an ad in the July issue of *Cosmopolitan* magazine. It also knows how many people it must hire to take telephone orders.

Cash flow projections also can be used to motivate employees. For example, Sillerman-Morrow Broadcasting Co., of Middletown, N.Y., shares its monthly sales estimates with employees of its eight radio stations. The stations then use these figures as their sales goals. If a station exceeds its stated goal, its salespeople share a bonus that equals 4% of the revenues in excess of the amount projected.

Even more importantly, cash flow projections are key to long-term fiscal prosperity. Done right, a cash forecast can predict a company's cash crises months, even years, in advance, so that a business owner doesn't wake up one morning and discover that his corporation can't pay its current bills. A cash flow projection buys chief executive officers the time they need to raise capital. And it enhances their credibility with lenders by demonstrating that the company has a handle on its day-to-day finances.

"I don't care if the projections are done on a computer or with a pencil," says Frank J. Pipp, an assistant vice-president of First Wisconsin National Bank of Milwaukee, which has some $3.5 billion in assets. But the numbers must be on target and based on hard facts, such as a small company's sales and purchasing history. In addition, the corporation's CEO must possess a solid working knowledge of the documents.

"The worst thing," Pipp notes, "is when the business owner doesn't understand the numbers himself. If I ask a few simple questions, and, right off the bat, he hesitates, that's a clue that there's a problem — a serious problem. And that makes me . . . hesitant [to make the loan]."

Another red flag, in Pipp's opinion, is a business owner's inability to explain how a change in one number (the time it takes to collect accounts receivable, for example) affects the rest of the forecast. "What happens if inventory isn't selling as fast as you thought?" he asks. "What does that imply on the liability side? Are you asking me for too much or too little?"

Source: Donna Sammons Carpenter, "Going with the Flow," *INC.*, March 1985, pp. 145–146. Reprinted with permission of INC. Magazine, March 1985. Copyright © 1985 by INC. Publishing Company, 38 Commercial Wharf, Boston, MA 02110.

vember and $41,000 in December. In the month of October the firm will have an excess cash balance of $22,000, which can be placed in some interest-earning form. The required total financing figures in the cash budget refer to *how much will have to be owed at the end of the month;* they do *not* show the monthly changes in borrowing.

The monthly changes in borrowing as well as excess cash can be found by further analyzing the cash budget in Table 6.4. It can be seen that in October the $50,000 beginning cash, which becomes $47,000 after the $3,000 net cash outflow is deducted, results in a $22,000 excess cash balance once the $25,000 minimum cash is deducted. In November the $76,000 of required total financing resulted from the $98,000 net cash outflow less the $22,000 of excess cash from October. The $41,000 of total required financing in December resulted from reducing November's $76,000 of required total financing by the $35,000 of net cash inflow during December. Summarizing, the activities for each month would be as follows:

October: Invest $22,000 of excess cash.
November: Liquidate $22,000 of excess cash and borrow $76,000.
December: Repay $35,000 of amount borrowed. ■

Evaluating the Cash Budget

The cash budget provides the firm with figures indicating the expected ending cash balance, which can be analyzed to determine whether a cash shortage or surplus is expected to result in each of the months

TABLE 6.4 A Cash Budget for the Halley Company ($000)

	Oct.	Nov.	Dec.
Total cash receipts[a]	$210	$320	$340
Less: Total cash disbursements[b]	213	418	305
Net cash flow	$ (3)	$ (98)	$ 35
Add: Beginning cash	50	47	(51)
Ending cash	$ 47	$ (51)	$ (16)
Less: Minimum cash balance	25	25	25
Required total financing[c]	—	$ 76	$ 41
Excess cash balance[d]	$ 22	—	—

[a] From Table 6.2.
[b] From Table 6.3.
[c] Values are placed in this line when the ending cash is less than the minimum cash balance since in this instance financing is required.
[d] Values are placed in this line when the ending cash is greater than the minimum cash balance since in this instance an excess cash balance exists.

covered by the forecast. The Halley Company can expect a surplus of $22,000 in October, a deficit of $76,000 in November, and a deficit of $41,000 in December. Each of these figures is based on the internally imposed requirement of a $25,000 minimum cash balance and represents the total balance at the end of the month.

The excess cash balance in October can be invested in marketable securities. The deficits in November and December will have to be financed, typically, by short-term borrowing (notes payable). Since it may be necessary for the firm to borrow up to $76,000 for the three-month period evaluated, the financial manager should be sure that a line of credit is established or some other arrangement made to assure the availability of these funds. The manager will usually request or arrange to borrow more than the maximum financing indicated in the cash budget. This is necessary due to the uncertainty of the ending cash values, which are based on the sales forecast and other forecast values.

PROFIT PLANNING: PRO FORMA STATEMENT FUNDAMENTALS

The profit-planning process centers on the preparation of **pro forma statements,** which are projected, or forecast, financial statements— income statements and balance sheets. The preparation of these statements requires a careful blending of a number of procedures to account for the revenues, costs, expenses, assets, liabilities, and equity resulting from the firm's anticipated level of operations. The basic steps in this process were shown in the flow diagram presented in Figure 6.1. The financial manager frequently uses one of a number of simplified approaches to estimate the pro forma statements. The most popular are based on the belief that the financial relationships reflected in the firm's historical (past) financial statements will not change in the coming period. The commonly used approaches are presented in subsequent discussions.

pro forma statements Projected, or forecast, financial statements: income statements and balance sheets.

The inputs required for preparing pro forma statements using the simplified approaches are financial statements for the preceding year and the sales forecast for the coming year. A variety of assumptions must also be made when using simplified approaches. The company we will use to illustrate the simplified approaches to pro forma preparation is the Metcalfe Manufacturing Company, which manufactures and sells one product. It has two basic models — model X and model Y. Although each model is produced by the same process, each requires different amounts of raw material and labor.

Past Year's Financial Statements

The income statement for the firm's 1987 operations is given in Table 6.5. It indicates that Metcalfe had sales of $101,000, total cost of goods

TABLE 6.5 An Income Statement for the Metcalfe Manufacturing Company for the Year Ended December 31, 1987

Sales revenue		
Model X (1,000 units at $20/unit)	$20,000	
Model Y (3,000 units at $27/unit)	81,000	
Total sales		$101,000
Less: Cost of goods sold		
Labor	$28,500	
Material A	8,000	
Material B	5,500	
Overhead	38,000	
Total cost of goods sold		80,000
Gross profits		$ 21,000
Less: Operating expenses		10,000
Operating profits		$ 11,000
Less: Interest expense		1,000
Net profits before taxes		$ 10,000
Less: Taxes (.15 × $10,000)		1,500
Net profits after taxes		$ 8,500
Less: Common stock dividends		4,000
To retained earnings		$ 4,500

sold of $80,000, and net profits after taxes of $8,500. The firm paid $4,000 in cash dividends, leaving $4,500 to be transferred to retained earnings. The firm's balance sheet at the end of 1987 is given in Table 6.6.

Sales Forecast

Like the cash budget, the key input for the development of pro forma statements is the sales forecast. The sales forecast by model for the coming year, 1988, for the Metcalfe Company is given in Table 6.7. This forecast is based on both external and internal data. The unit sale prices of the product reflect an increase from $20 to $25 for model X and from $27 to $35 for model Y. These increases are required to cover the firm's anticipated increases in the cost of labor, material, overhead, and operating expenses.

percent-of-sales method
A method for developing the pro forma income statement that expresses the cost of goods sold, operating expenses, and interest expense as a percentage of projected sales.

■ PREPARING THE PRO FORMA INCOME STATEMENT

A simple method for developing a pro forma income statement is to use the **percent-of-sales method,** which forecasts sales and then expresses the cost of goods sold, operating expenses, and interest expense as a

**TABLE 6.6 A Balance Sheet for the Metcalfe Manufacturing Company
(December 31, 1987)**

Assets		Liabilities and equities	
Cash	$ 6,000	Accounts payable	$ 7,000
Marketable securities	4,016	Taxes payable	375
Accounts receivable	13,000	Notes payable	8,260
Inventories	15,984	Other current liabilities	3,365
Total current assets	$39,000	Total current liabilities	$19,000
Net fixed assets	51,000	Long-term debts	$18,000
Total assets	$90,000	Stockholders' equity	
		Common stock	$30,000
		Retained earnings	$23,000
		Total liabilities and stockholders' equity	$90,000

percentage of projected sales. The percentages used are likely to be the percentage of sales for these items in the immediately preceding year. For the Metcalfe Manufacturing Company, these percentages are as follows:

$$\frac{\text{Cost of goods sold}}{\text{Sales}} = \frac{\$80,000}{\$101,000} = 79.2\%$$

$$\frac{\text{Operating expenses}}{\text{Sales}} = \frac{\$10,000}{\$101,000} = 9.9\%$$

$$\frac{\text{Interest expense}}{\text{Sales}} = \frac{\$1,000}{\$101,000} = 1.0\%$$

The dollar values used are taken from the 1987 income statement (Table 6.5).

Applying these percentages to the firm's forecast level of sales of $135,500, developed in Table 6.7, and assuming that the firm will pay $4,000 in cash dividends in 1988, results in the pro forma income state-

**TABLE 6.7 1988 Sales Forecast for
the Metcalfe
Manufacturing Company**

Unit sales	
Model X	1,500
Model Y	2,800
Dollar sales	
Model X ($25/unit)	$ 37,500
Model Y ($35/unit)	98,000
Total	$135,500

ment in Table 6.8. The expected contribution to retained earnings is $7,402, which represents a considerable increase over $4,500 in the preceding year.

Considering Types of Costs and Expenses

The technique used to prepare the pro forma income statement in Table 6.8 assumes that all the firm's costs are *variable*. This means that the use of the historical (1987) ratios of cost of goods sold, operating expenses, and interest expense to sales assumes that for a given percentage increase in sales, the same percentage increase in each of these expense components will result. For example, as Metcalfe's sales increased by 34.2 percent (from $101,000 in 1987 to $135,500 projected for 1988), its cost of goods sold also increased by 34.2 percent (from $80,000 in 1987 to $107,316 projected for 1988). Based on this assumption, the firm's net profits before taxes also increased by 34.2 percent (from $10,000 in 1987 to $13,414 projected for 1988).

In the approach just illustrated, the broader implication is that since the firm has no fixed costs, it will not receive the benefits often resulting from them.[3] Therefore, the use of past cost and expense ratios generally tends to understate profits, since the firm is in fact likely to have certain beneficial fixed operating and financial costs. The best way to adjust for the presence of fixed costs when using a simplified approach for pro

TABLE 6.8 A Pro Forma Income Statement, Using the Percent-of-Sales Method, for the Metcalfe Manufacturing Company for the Year Ended December 31, 1988

Sales revenue	$135,500
Less: Cost of goods sold (79.2%)	107,316
Gross profits	$ 28,184
Less: Operating expenses (9.9%)	13,415
Operating profits	$ 14,769
Less: Interest expense (1.0%)	1,355
Net profits before taxes	$ 13,414
Less: Taxes (.15 × $13,414)	2,012
Net profits after taxes	$ 11,402
Less: Common stock dividends	4,000
To retained earnings	$ 7,402

[3] The potential returns as well as risks resulting from use of fixed (operating and financial) costs to create "leverage" are discussed in Chapter 5. The key point to recognize here is that when the firm's revenue is *increasing*, fixed costs can magnify returns.

forma income statement preparation is to break the firm's historical costs into *fixed* and *variable components* and make the forecast using this relationship.

EXAMPLE

The RST Company's last-year and pro forma income statements, which are broken into fixed- and variable-cost components, are given below.

RST Company Income Statements

	Last year	Pro forma
Sales revenue	$100,000	$120,000
Less: Cost of goods sold		
Fixed cost	20,000	20,000
Variable cost (.40 × sales)	40,000	48,000
Gross profits	$ 40,000	$ 52,000
Less: Operating expense		
Fixed expense	5,000	5,000
Variable expense (.15 × sales)	15,000	18,000
Operating profits	$ 20,000	$ 29,000
Less: Interest expense (all fixed)	8,000	8,000
Net profits before taxes	$ 12,000	$ 21,000
Less: Taxes (.40 × net profits before taxes)	4,800	8,400
Net profits after taxes	$ 7,200	$ 12,600

By breaking its costs and expenses into fixed and variable components, the RST Company's pro forma profit is expected to provide a more accurate projection. Had the firm treated all costs as variable, its pro forma net profits before taxes would equal 12 percent of sales, just as was the case in the last year ($12,000 profits before taxes ÷ $100,000 sales). The net profits before taxes would therefore have been $14,400 (12% × $120,000 projected sales) instead of the $21,000 of net profits before taxes obtained by using the firm's fixed-cost–variable-cost breakdown. ■

The preceding example should make it clear that when using a simplified approach to pro forma income statement preparation, it is advisable to consider first breaking down costs and expenses into fixed and variable components. Due to a lack of available data, the pro forma income statement prepared for Metcalfe Manufacturing Company in Table 6.8 was based on the assumption that all costs were variable—which is likely *not* to be the case. Therefore, Metcalfe's projected profits were probably understated.

◼ PREPARING THE PRO FORMA BALANCE SHEET

judgmental approach
A method of developing the pro forma balance sheet in which the values of certain accounts are estimated while others are calculated, using the firm's external financing as a balancing, or "plug," figure.

A number of simplified approaches are available for preparing the pro forma balance sheet. Probably the best and most popular is the judgmental approach.[4] Under the **judgmental approach** for developing the pro forma balance sheet, the values of certain balance sheet accounts are estimated while others are calculated. When this approach is applied, the firm's external financing is used as a balancing, or "plug," figure. To apply the judgmental approach to Metcalfe Manufacturing Company's balance sheet, a number of assumptions must be made:

1. A minimum cash balance of $6,000 is desired.
2. Marketable securities are assumed to remain unchanged from their current level of $4,016.
3. Accounts receivable will on average represent 45 days of sales. Since Metcalfe's annual sales are projected to be $135,500, the accounts receivable should average $16,938 ($\frac{1}{8} \times$ $135,500). (Forty-five days expressed fractionally is one-eighth of a year: $45/360 = \frac{1}{8}$).
4. The ending inventory should remain at a level of about $16,000, of which 25 percent (approximately $4,000) should be raw materials, while the remaining 75 percent (approximately $12,000) should consist of finished goods.
5. A new machine costing $20,000 will be purchased. Total depreciation for the year will be $8,000. Adding the $20,000 acquisition to the existing net fixed assets of $51,000 and subtracting the depreciation of $8,000 will yield net fixed assets of $63,000.
6. Purchases are expected to represent approximately 30 percent of annual sales, which in this case would be approximately $40,650 (.30 $\times$ $135,500). The firm estimates it can take 72 days on average to satisfy its accounts payable. Thus accounts payable should equal one-fifth (72 days ÷ 360 days) of the firm's purchases, or $8,130 ($\frac{1}{5} \times$ $40,650).
7. Taxes payable are expected to equal one-fourth of the current year's tax liability, which would equal $503 (one-fourth of the tax liability of $2,012 shown in the pro forma income statement presented in Table 6.8).
8. Notes payable are assumed to remain unchanged from their current level of $8,260.

---

[4] The judgmental approach represents an improved version of the often discussed *percent-of-sales approach* to pro forma balance sheet preparation. Because the judgmental approach requires only slightly more information and should yield better estimates than the somewhat naive percent-of-sales approach, it is presented here.

FINANCIAL PLANNING AND BUDGETING WITH PERSONAL COMPUTERS: THE ELECTRONIC SPREADSHEET

The wide distribution of personal computers has greatly simplified the process of financial planning and budgeting. Prior to this time, a financial planner was required to work laboriously through several separate spreadsheets, but now one can accomplish the same results much faster by entering the information on what is called an "electronic spreadsheet." After the data are entered, the user is free to manipulate the data in several ways in response to computer-generated questions. The user may merge or blend separate data sets; reformat existing data sets into an entirely new form; develop complex financial statements rapidly; provide pro forma financial forecasts by simply altering key financial variables such as sales, cost of goods sold, or similar entries; and perform other equally easy program functions.

Some software packages have critical financial calculations embedded within the main body of the program; others require that a separate "electronic template," or subsidiary program, be employed. Almost all software packages also allow the user to create special calculations while running the program to fit unique and temporary needs. Many major corporations employ personal computers in the finance activity for firm-specific financial planning and budgeting and alter commercially available software packages to fit their specific needs.

Many software packages are designed to accomplish specific tasks, but some currently available general-purpose software packages are Microsoft's Multiplan, Sorcim's Supercalc, VisiCorp's VisiCalc, and Lotus's 1-2-3.

Source: Courtesy of Charles E. Maxwell, Hempstead, New York.

9. No change in other current liabilities is expected. They will remain at the level of the previous year: $3,365.

10. The firm's long-term debts and its common stock are expected to remain unchanged, at $18,000 and $30,000, respectively, since no issues, retirements, or repurchases of bonds or stocks are planned.

11. Retained earnings will increase from the beginning level of $23,000 (from the balance sheet dated December 31, 1987, in Table 6.6) to $30,402. The increase of $7,402 represents the amount of retained earnings calculated in the year-end 1988 pro forma income statement in Table 6.8.

external funds required ("plug" figure) Under the judgmental approach for developing a pro forma balance sheet, the amount of external financing needed to bring the statement into balance.

A 1988 pro forma balance sheet for the Metcalfe Manufacturing Company based on these assumptions is presented in Table 6.9. It can be seen that a **"plug" figure** — called the **external funds required** — of $7,294 is needed in order to bring the statement into balance. This means that the firm will have to obtain about $7,294 of additional external financing to support the increased sales level of $135,500 for 1988. When this approach is used, under certain circumstances a negative external funds requirement might result. This would indicate that the firm's financing is in excess of its needs and that funds would therefore be available for repaying debt, repurchasing stock, or increasing the dividend to stockholders. Analysts sometimes use the judgmental approach to pro forma preparation as a technique for estimating financing needs, but for our purposes the approach is used to prepare the pro forma balance sheet.

EVALUATION OF PRO FORMA STATEMENTS

It is difficult to forecast the many variables involved in pro forma statement preparation. As a result, analysts — including lenders, investors, and managers — frequently use the techniques presented here in order to make rough estimates of pro forma financial statements. While the growing availability and acceptance of electronic spreadsheets and personal computers is streamlining the financial planning process,

TABLE 6.9 A Pro Forma Balance Sheet, Using the Judgmental Approach, for the Metcalfe Manufacturing Company (December 31, 1988)

Assets			Liabilities and equities	
Cash		$ 6,000	Accounts payable	$ 8,130
Marketable securities		4,016	Taxes payable	503
Accounts receivable		16,938	Notes payable	8,260
Inventories			Other current liabilities	3,365
Raw materials	$ 4,000		Total current liabilities	$ 20,258
Finished goods	12,000		Long-term debts	$ 18,000
Total inventory		16,000	Stockholders' equity	
Total current assets		$ 42,954	Common stock	$ 30,000
Net fixed assets		63,000	Retained earnings	$ 30,402
Total assets		$105,954	Total	$ 98,660
			External funds required[a]	$ 7,294
			Total liabilities and stockholders' equity	$105,954

[a] The amount of external funds needed to force the firm's balance sheet to balance. Due to the nature of the judgmental approach to preparing the pro forma balance sheet, the balance sheet is not expected to balance without some type of adjustment.

simplified approaches to pro forma preparation are expected to remain popular. An understanding of the basic weaknesses of these simplified approaches is therefore important. Equally important is the ability to effectively use pro forma statements to make financial decisions.

Weaknesses of Simplified Approaches

The basic weaknesses of the simplified pro forma approaches demonstrated lie in (1) the assumption that the firm's past financial condition is an accurate indicator of its future and (2) the assumption that the values of certain variables such as cash, accounts receivable, and inventory can be forced to take on certain "desired" values. These assumptions are questionable, but due to the ease of the calculations involved, the use of these approaches is quite common.

Other simplified approaches exist. Most are based on the assumption that certain relationships among income, costs and expenses, assets, liabilities, and equity will prevail in the future. For example, in preparing the pro forma balance sheet, all assets, liabilities, *and* equity are often increased by the percentage increase expected in sales. The financial analyst must know the techniques that have been used in preparing pro forma statements so that he or she can judge the quality of the estimated values and thus the degree of confidence he or she can have in them.

Using Pro Forma Statements

In addition to estimating the amount, if any, of external financing required to support a given level of sales, pro forma statements provide a basis for analyzing in advance the level of profitability and overall financial performance of the firm in the coming year. Using pro forma statements, the financial manager, as well as lenders, can analyze the firm's sources and uses of funds as well as various aspects of performance, such as liquidity, activity, debt, and profitability. Sources and uses can be evaluated by preparing a pro forma statement of changes in financial position. Various ratios can be calculated from the pro forma income statement and balance sheet to evaluate performance.

After analyzing the pro forma statements, the financial manager can take steps to adjust planned operations to achieve short-run financial goals. For example, if profits on the pro forma income statement are too low, a variety of pricing or cost-cutting actions, or both, might be initiated. If the projected level of accounts receivable shown on the pro forma balance sheet is too high, changes in credit policy may avoid this outcome. Pro forma statements are therefore of key importance in solidifying the firm's financial plans for the coming year.

SUMMARY

- The two key aspects of the financial planning process are cash planning, which involves preparation of the cash budget or cash forecast, and profit planning, which relies on preparation of the pro forma income statement and balance sheet.
- Long-run (strategic) financial plans act as a guide for preparing short-run (operating) financial plans. Long-run plans tend to cover periods ranging from two to ten years and are updated periodically.
- Key inputs to short-run (operating) plans are the sales forecast and various forms of operating and financial data; key outputs include operating budgets, the cash budget, and the pro forma financial statements.
- The cash budget is typically prepared for a one-year period divided into months. It nets cash receipts and disbursements for each period in order to indicate net cash flow. Ending cash is estimated by adding beginning cash to the net cash flow. By subtracting the minimum cash balance from the ending cash, the required total financing or excess cash balance (whichever is the case) can be determined.
- A pro forma income statement can be developed by calculating past percentage relationships between certain cost and expense items and the firm's sales and then applying these percentages to forecasts.
- A pro forma balance sheet can be estimated using the judgmental approach. Under this simplified technique, an entry for external funds required acts as a balancing, or "plug," figure.
- The use of simplified approaches for pro forma statement preparation, while quite popular, can be criticized for assuming the firm's past condition is an accurate predictor of the future and for assuming that certain variables can be forced to take on desired values.
- Pro forma statements are commonly used by financial managers and lenders to analyze in advance the firm's level of profitability and overall financial performance. Based on their analysis, financial managers adjust planned operations in order to achieve short-run financial goals.

QUESTIONS

6-1 What is the *financial planning process?* Define, compare, and contrast *long-run (strategic) financial plans* and *short-run (operating) financial plans.*

6-2 Which three statements result as part of the short-run (operating) financial planning process? Describe the flow of information from the sales forecast through the preparation of these statements.

6-3 What is the purpose of the *cash budget?* The key input to the cash budget is the sales forecast. What is the difference between *external* and *internal* forecast data?

6-4 Briefly describe the basic format of the cash budget, beginning with the sales forecast and ending with required total financing or excess cash balance.

6-5 How can the two bottom lines of the cash budget be used to determine the firm's short-term borrowing and investment requirements?

6-6 What is the purpose of *pro forma financial statements?* Which of the pro forma statements must be developed first? Why?

6-7 Briefly describe the pro forma income statement preparation process using the percent-of-sales method. What are the strengths and weaknesses of this simplified approach?

6-8 Describe the judgmental approach for simplified preparation of the pro forma balance sheet. Contrast this with the more detailed approach shown in Figure 6.1.

6-9 What is the significance of the balancing ("plug") figure, *external funds required,* used with the judgmental approach for preparing the pro forma balance sheet?

6-10 What are the two key weaknesses of the simplified approaches to pro forma statement preparation? In spite of these weaknesses, why do these approaches remain popular?

6-11 How may the financial manager wish to evaluate pro forma statements? What is his or her objective in evaluating these statements?

PROBLEMS

6-1 **(Cash Receipts)** A firm has actual sales of $65,000 in April and $60,000 in May. It expects sales of $70,000 in June and $100,000 in July and in August. Assuming that sales are the only source of cash inflows and that half of these are for cash and the remainder are collected evenly over the following two months, what are the firm's expected cash receipts for June, July, and August?

6-2 ■ **(Cash Budget — Basic)** Beth Davis, a financial analyst for INK, Inc., has prepared the following sales and cash disbursement estimates for the period February–June of the current year.

Month	Sales	Cash disbursements
February	$500	$400
March	600	300
April	400	600
May	200	500
June	200	200

Ms. Davis notes that historically 30 percent of sales have been for *cash.* Of *credit sales,* 70 percent are collected one month after the sale, and the remaining 30 percent are collected two months after the sale. The firm wishes to maintain a minimum ending balance in its cash account of $25. Balances above this amount would be invested in short-term government securities, while any deficits would be financed through short-term bank borrowing. The beginning cash balance at April 1 is $115.

a Prepare a cash budget for April, May, and June.

b How much financing, if any, at a maximum would INK, Inc., need to meet its obligations during this three-month period?

c If a pro forma balance sheet dated at the end of June were prepared from the information presented, give the size of each of the following: cash, notes payable, and marketable securities.

6-3 **(Cash Budget — Basic)** The Quick Digital Company had sales of $50,000 in March and $60,000 in April. Forecast sales for May, June, and July are $70,000, $80,000, and $100,000, respectively. The firm has a cash balance of $5,000 on May 1 and wishes to maintain a minimum cash balance of $5,000. Given the following data, prepare and interpret a cash budget for the months of May, June, and July.

(1) Twenty percent of the firm's sales are for cash, 60 percent are collected in the next month, the remaining 20 percent are collected in the second month following sale.

(2) The firm receives other income of $2,000 per month.

(3) The firm's actual or expected purchases, all made for cash, are $50,000, $70,000, and $80,000 for the months of May through July, respectively.

(4) Rent is $3,000 per month.

(5) Wages and salaries are 10 percent of the previous month's sales.

(6) Cash dividends of $3,000 will be paid in June.

(7) Payment of principal and interest of $4,000 is due in June.

(8) A cash purchase of equipment costing $6,000 is scheduled in July.

(9) Taxes of $6,000 are due in June.

6-4 **(Cash budget — Advanced)** Advanced Appliance Company's actual sales and purchases for September and October 1987, along with its forecast sales and purchases for the period November 1987 through April 1988, follow.

Year	Month	Sales	Purchases
1987	September	$210,000	$120,000
1987	October	250,000	150,000
1987	November	170,000	140,000
1987	December	160,000	100,000
1988	January	140,000	80,000
1988	February	180,000	110,000
1988	March	200,000	100,000
1988	April	250,000	90,000

The firm makes 20 percent of all sales for cash and collects on 40 percent of its sales in each of the two months following the sale. Other cash inflows are expected to be $12,000 in September and April, $15,000 in January and March, and $27,000 in February. The firm pays cash for 10 percent of its purchases. It pays for 50 percent of its purchases in the following month and for 40 percent of its purchases two months later.

Wages and salaries amount to 20 percent of the preceding month's sales. Rent of $20,000 per month must be paid. Interest payments of $10,000 are due in January and April. A principal payment of $30,000 is also due in April. The firm expects to pay cash dividends of $20,000 in January and April. Taxes of $80,000 are due in April. The firm also intends to make a $25,000 cash purchase of fixed assets in December.

a Assuming that the firm has a cash balance of $22,000 at the beginning of November, determine the end-of-month cash balances for each month, November through April.

b Assuming that the firm wishes to maintain a $15,000 minimum cash balance, determine the monthly total financing requirements or excess cash balances.

c If the firm were requesting a line of credit to cover needed financing for the period November to April, how large would this line have to be? Explain your answer.

6-5 **(Cash Flow Concepts)**   The following represent financial transactions that the Ballou Company will be undertaking in the next planning period. For each transaction check the statement or statements that will be affected immediately.

STATEMENT

Transaction	Cash budget	Pro forma income statement	Pro forma balance sheet
Cash sale			
Credit sale			
Accounts receivable are collected			
Asset with five-year life is purchased			
Depreciation is taken			
Amortization of goodwill is taken			
Sale of common stock			
Retirement of outstanding bonds			
Fire insurance premium is paid for the next three years			

6-6 **(Multiple Cash Budgets)** Patterson's Parts Store expects to sell $100,000 in parts during each of the next three months. It will make monthly purchases of $60,000 during this time. Wages and salaries are $10,000 per month plus 5 percent of sales. Patterson's expects to make a tax payment of $20,000 in the next month, a $15,000 purchase of fixed assets in the second month, and receive $8,000 in cash from the sale of an asset in the third month. All sales and purchases are for cash. Beginning cash and the minimum cash balance are assumed to be zero.

a Construct a cash budget for the next three months.

b Patterson's is unsure of the sales levels, but all other figures are certain. If the most pessimistic sales figure is $80,000 per month and the most optimistic is $120,000 per month, what are the monthly minimum and maximum ending cash balances the firm can expect for each of the one-month periods?

c Briefly discuss how the data in **a** and **b** can be used by the financial manager to plan for his or her financing needs.

6-7 **(Pro Forma Income Statement — Basic)** Charles Oleg Corporation expects sales during 1988 to rise from the 1987 level of $3.5 million to $3.9 million. Due to a scheduled large loan payment, the interest expense in 1988 is expected to drop to $325,000. The firm plans to increase its cash dividend payments during 1988 to $320,000. The company's year-end 1987 income statement is given below.

Income Statement
Charles Oleg Corporation
for the Year Ended December 31, 1987

Sales revenue	$3,500,000
Less: Cost of goods sold	1,925,000
Gross profits	$1,575,000
Less: Operating expenses	420,000
Operating profits	$1,155,000
Less: Interest expense	400,000
Net profits before taxes	$ 755,000
Less: Taxes (40%)	302,000
Net profits after taxes	$ 453,000
Less: Cash dividends	250,000
To retained earnings	$ 203,000

a Use the percent-of-sales method to prepare Charles Oleg Corporation's 1988 pro forma income statement.

b Explain why the statement may underestimate the company's actual 1988 pro forma income.

6-8 **(Pro Forma Income Statement)** The marketing department of Hartman Manufacturing estimates that its sales in 1988 will be $1.5 million. Interest expense is expected to remain unchanged at $35,000, and the firm plans to pay $70,000 in cash dividends during 1988. Hartman Manufacturing's income statement for the year ended December 31, 1987 is given at the top of page 173, followed by a breakdown of the firm's cost of goods sold and operating expenses into its fixed- and variable-cost components.

a Use the *percent-of-sales method* to prepare a pro forma income statement for the year ended December 31, 1988 for Hartman Manufacturing.

b Use the *fixed- and variable-cost data* to develop a pro forma income statement for the year ended December 31, 1988 for Hartman Manufacturing.

c Compare and contrast the statements developed in **a** and **b**. Which statement will likely provide the better estimates of 1988 income? Explain why.

Income Statement
Hartman Manufacturing Company
for the Year Ended December 31, 1987

Sales revenue	$1,400,000
Less: Cost of goods sold	910,000
Gross profits	$ 490,000
Less: Operating expenses	120,000
Operating profits	$ 370,000
Less: Interest expense	35,000
Net profits before taxes	$ 335,000
Less: Taxes (40%)	134,000
Net profits after taxes	$ 201,000
Less: Cash dividends	66,000
To retained earnings	$ 135,000

Fixed- and Variable-Cost Breakdown
Hartman Manufacturing Company
for the Year Ended December 31, 1987

Cost of goods sold	
Fixed cost	$210,000
Variable cost	700,000
Total cost	$910,000
Operating expenses	
Fixed expenses	$ 36,000
Variable expenses	84,000
Total expenses	$120,000

6-9 ■ **(Pro Forma Balance Sheet — Basic)** May Cosmetics wishes to prepare a pro forma balance sheet for December 31, 1988. The firm expects 1988 sales to total $3,000,000. The following information has been gathered.

(1) A minimum cash balance of $50,000 is desired.
(2) Marketable securities are expected to remain unchanged.
(3) Accounts receivable represent 10 percent of sales.
(4) Inventories represent 12 percent of sales.
(5) A new machine costing $90,000 will be acquired during 1988. Total depreciation for the year will be $32,000.
(6) Accounts payable represent 14 percent of sales.
(7) Accruals, other current liabilities, long-term debt, and common stock are expected to remain unchanged.
(8) The firm's net profit margin is 4 percent and it expects to pay out $70,000 in cash dividends during 1988.
(9) The December 31, 1987 balance sheet is given at the top of page 174.

May Cosmetics
Balance Sheet
December 31, 1987

Assets		Liabilities and equities	
Cash	$ 45,000	Accounts payable	$ 395,000
Marketable securities	15,000	Accruals	60,000
Accounts receivable	255,000	Other current liabilities	30,000
Inventories	340,000	Total current liabilities	$ 485,000
Total current assets	$ 655,000	Long-term debt	350,000
Net fixed assets	600,000	Common Stock	200,000
Total assets	$1,255,000	Retained Earnings	220,000
		Total liabilities and stockholders' equity	$1,255,000

a Use the judgmental approach to prepare a pro forma balance sheet dated December 31, 1988 for May Cosmetics.

b How much, if any, additional financing will be required by May Cosmetics in 1988? Discuss.

c Could May Cosmetics adjust its planned 1988 dividend in order to avoid the situation described in **b**? Explain how.

6-10 **(Pro Forma Balance Sheet)** Widget Tool has 1987 sales of $10 million. It wishes to analyze expected performance and financing needs for 1989—two years ahead. Given the following information, answer questions **a** and **b**.

(1) The percent of sales for items that vary directly with sales are as follows:
Receivables, 12 percent
Inventory, 18 percent
Accounts payable, 14 percent
Net profit margin, 3 percent

(2) Marketable securities and other current liabilities are expected to remain unchanged.

(3) A minimum cash balance of $480,000 is desired.

(4) A new machine costing $650,000 will be acquired in 1988 and equipment costing $850,000 will be purchased in 1989. Total depreciation in 1988 is forecast as $290,000 and in 1989 $390,000 of depreciation will be taken.

(5) Accruals are expected to rise to $500,000 by the end of 1989.

(6) No sale or retirement of long-term debt is expected.

(7) No sale or repurchase of common stock is expected.

(8) The dividend payout of 50 percent of net profits is expected to continue.

(9) Sales are expected to be $11 million in 1988 and $12 million in 1989.

(10) The December 31, 1987, balance sheet appears below.

Widget Tool
Balance Sheet
December 31, 1987
($000)

Assets		Liabilities and equities	
Cash	$ 400	Accounts payable	$1,400
Marketable securities	200	Accruals	400
Accounts receivable	1,200	Other current liabilities	80
Inventories	1,800	Total current liabilities	$1,880
Total current assets	$3,600	Long-term debt	$2,000
Net fixed assets	$4,000	Common equity	$3,720
Total assets	$7,600	Total liabilities and	
		stockholders' equity	$7,600

a Prepare a pro forma balance sheet dated December 31, 1989.

b Discuss the financing changes suggested by the statement prepared in **a**.

6-11 ■ **(Integrative — Pro Forma Statements)** The Clancey Daughters Corporation wishes to prepare financial plans. Using the financial statements below and the other information provided,

a Prepare a pro forma income statement using the percent-of-sales method.

b Prepare a pro forma balance sheet using the judgmental approach.

c Analyze these statements and discuss the resulting external funds required.

Income Statement
Clancey Daughters Corporation
for the Year Ended December 31, 1987

Sales revenue	$800,000
Less: Cost of goods sold	600,000
Gross profits	$200,000
Less: Operating expenses	100,000
Net profits before taxes	$100,000
Less: Taxes (40%)	40,000
Net profits after taxes	$ 60,000
Less: Cash dividends	20,000
To retained earnings	$ 40,000

Balance Sheet
Clancey Daughters Corporation
December 31, 1987

Assets		Liabilities and equities	
Cash	$ 32,000	Accounts payable	$100,000
Marketable securities	18,000	Taxes payable	20,000
Accounts receivable	150,000	Other current liabilities	5,000
Inventories	100,000	Total current liabilities	$125,000
Total current assets	$300,000	Long-term debt	$200,000
Net fixed assets	$350,000	Common stock	$150,000
Total assets	$650,000	Retained earnings	$175,000
		Total liabilities and stockholders' equity	$650,000

The following financial data are also available:

(1) The firm has estimated that its sales for 1988 will be $900,000.

(2) The firm expects to pay $35,000 in cash dividends in 1988.

(3) The firm wishes to maintain a minimum cash balance of $30,000.

(4) Accounts receivable represent approximately 18 percent of annual sales.

(5) The firm's ending inventory will change directly with changes in sales in 1988.

(6) A new machine costing $42,000 will be purchased in 1988. Total depreciation for 1988 will be $17,000.

(7) Accounts payable will change directly in response to changes in sales in 1988.

(8) Taxes payable will equal one-fourth of the tax liability on the pro forma income statement.

(9) Marketable securities, other current liabilities, long-term debt, and common stock will remain unchanged.

Part Three

SHORT-TERM FINANCIAL DECISIONS

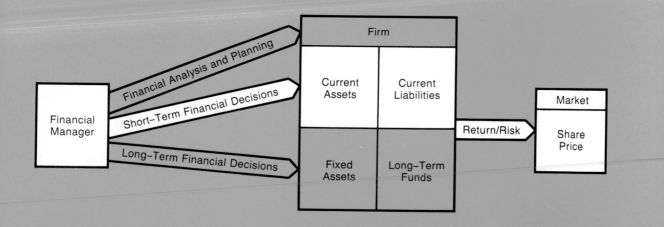

7

WORKING CAPITAL FUNDAMENTALS

After studying this chapter, you should be able to:

● Define net working capital, profitability, and risk as they relate to managing the firm's current accounts.

● Use changes in the asset mix and changes in the financing mix to demonstrate the trade-off between profitability and risk.

● Explain how the firm's funds requirements, when viewed over time, can be broken into a permanent component and a seasonal component.

● Describe, in terms of profitability and risk, the aggressive strategy and the conservative strategy for determining the firm's financing mix.

● Discuss financing strategies that trade-off the high profitability and risk effects of aggressive strategies and the lower profitability and risk effects of conservative strategies.

working capital management Management of the firm's current accounts, which include current assets and current liabilities.

An important responsibility of the financial manager is overseeing the firm's day-to-day financial activities. This area of finance, known as **working capital management,** is concerned with management of the firm's current accounts, which include current assets and current liabilities. In U.S. manufacturing firms, current assets account for nearly 38 percent of the total assets and current liabilities represent nearly 27 percent of total financing. It is therefore not surprising that managing working capital is one of the most important and time-consuming activities of the financial manager. The goal is to manage each of the firm's current assets (cash, marketable securities, accounts receivable, and inventory) and current liabilities (accounts payable, notes payable, and accruals) in order to achieve a balance between profit and risk that maximizes the firm's value. In this chapter attention is given to the basic relationship between current assets and current liabilities rather than to the individual current accounts, which will be considered later in the book.

NET WORKING CAPITAL

Net working capital was introduced in Chapter 4 as a ratio measure whose primary use is to evaluate the firm's liquidity over time. The *current ratio* and *quick ratio* are more appropriately used for cross-sectional liquidity comparisons. Since our concern here is the single firm, we will review the commonly used definition of net working capital and present an alternative definition.

The Common Definition and Its Implications

net working capital The difference between the firm's current assets and current liabilities. Alternatively, the portion of current assets financed with long-term funds.

Most commonly, **net working capital** is defined as the difference between the firm's current assets and its current liabilities. As long as current assets exceed current liabilities, the firm has *positive net working capital*. In general, the greater the margin by which a firm's current assets cover its short-term obligations (current liabilities), the better able it will be to pay its bills as they come due. This relationship results from the fact that current assets are sources of *cash inflow*, while current liabilities are sources of *cash outflow*.

The cash outflows resulting from payment of current liabilities are relatively predictable. When an obligation is incurred, the firm generally learns when the corresponding bills will be due. For instance, when merchandise is purchased on credit, the terms extended to the firm require payment by a known point in time. What is difficult to predict are the cash inflows. The more predictable its cash inflows, the less net working capital a firm may require. Because most firms are unable to match cash inflows to outflows, sources of inflow (current assets) that more than cover outflows (current liabilities) are necessary. Let us look at an example.

EXAMPLE

For the Berenson Company, which has the current position given in Table 7.1, the following situation may exist. All $600 of the firm's accounts payable, plus $200 of its notes payable and $100 of accruals, are due at the end of the current period. The $900 in outflows is certain; how the firm will cover these outflows is not certain. The firm can be sure that $700 will be available since it has $500 in cash and $200 in marketable securities, which can easily be converted into cash. The remaining $200 must come from the collection of accounts receivable, the sale of inventory for cash, or both.[1] However, the firm cannot be sure when either the collection of an account receivable or a cash sale will occur. Generally, the more accounts receivable and inventories on hand, the greater the probability that some of these items will be converted into cash.[2] Thus a certain level of net working capital is often recommended to ensure the firm's ability to pay bills. The Berenson Company has $1,100 of net working capital (current assets minus current liabilities, or $2,700 − $1,600), which will most likely be sufficient to cover its bills. Its current ratio of 1.69 (current assets divided by current liabilities, or $2,700 ÷ $1,600) should provide sufficient liquidity as long as its accounts receivable and inventories remain relatively active. ■

TABLE 7.1 The Current Position of the Berenson Company

Current assets		Current liabilities	
Cash	$ 500	Accounts payable	$ 600
Marketable securities	200	Notes payable	800
Accounts receivable	800	Accruals	200
Inventories	1,200	Total	$1,600
Total	$2,700		

[1] A sale of inventory for credit would show up as a new account receivable, which could not be easily converted into cash. Only a *cash sale* will guarantee the firm that its bill-paying ability during the period of the sale has been enhanced.

[2] It should be recognized that levels of accounts receivable or inventory can be too high, reflecting certain management inefficiencies. Acceptable levels for any firm can be calculated. The efficient management of accounts receivable and inventory is discussed in Chapter 9.

An Alternate Definition of Net Working Capital

net working capital The portion of the firm's current assets financed with long-term funds. Alternatively, the difference between the firm's current assets and current liabilities.

Alternatively to its earlier definition, **net working capital** can be defined as the portion of the firm's current assets financed with long-term funds. This definition can best be illustrated by a special type of balance sheet like that for the Berenson Company presented in Figure 7.1. The vertical axis of this special balance sheet is a dollar scale on which all the major items on the firm's regular balance sheet are indicated. The Berenson Company has current assets of $2,700, fixed assets of $4,300, total assets of $7,000, current liabilities of $1,600, long-term debts of $2,400 ($4,000 − $1,600), and stockholders' equity of $3,000 ($7,000 − $4,000). The firm's **long-term funds** — the sum of long-term debt and stockholders' equity — equal $5,400. The portion of Berenson's current assets that have been financed with long-term funds equals $1,100. It is labeled "net working capital" in Figure 7.1. Since current liabilities represent the firm's sources of short-term funds, as long as current assets exceed current liabilities, the amount of the excess must be financed with longer-term funds. The usefulness of this alternate concept of net working capital will become more apparent later in this chapter.

long-term funds The sum of the firm's long-term debt and stockholders' equity.

THE TRADE-OFF BETWEEN PROFITABILITY AND RISK

profitability The relationship between revenues and costs.

A trade-off exists between a firm's profitability and its risk. **Profitability**, in this context, is the relationship between revenues and costs. A

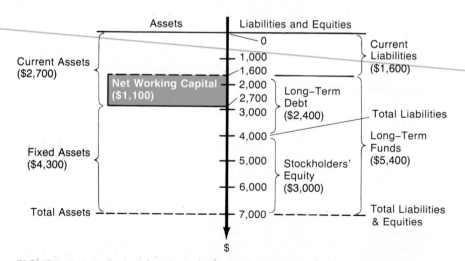

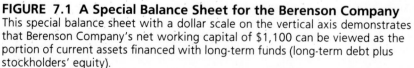

FIGURE 7.1 A Special Balance Sheet for the Berenson Company
This special balance sheet with a dollar scale on the vertical axis demonstrates that Berenson Company's net working capital of $1,100 can be viewed as the portion of current assets financed with long-term funds (long-term debt plus stockholders' equity).

THE IMPORTANCE OF WORKING CAPITAL MANAGEMENT

The responses of 238 chief financial officers to a mail questionnaire sent to firms in the *Fortune's* 1000 offer strong support for the importance of the working capital management activity. The table shows the *importance* of working capital management relative to three other major financial activities and the amount of *time spent* on working capital management relative to them. These data clearly indicate that working capital management is an important and time-consuming financial activity.

Financial Activity Considered of Greatest Importance

Financial activity	Percent selecting as most important	Percent of time spent on activity
Financial planning and budgeting	59%	35%
Managing working capital	27	32
Managing capital expenditures	9	19
Raising long-term funds	5	14
Total	100%	100%

Source: Lawrence J. Gitman and Charles E. Maxwell, "Financial Activities of Major U.S. Firms: Survey and Analysis of *Fortune's* 1000," *Financial Management*, Winter 1985, pp. 57–65.

firm's profits can be increased in two ways: (1) by increasing revenues or (2) by decreasing costs. **Risk** is the probability that the firm will be unable to pay its bills as they come due. A firm that cannot pay its bills is said to be **technically insolvent**. The risk of becoming technically insolvent is commonly measured using either the current ratio or the amount of net working capital. In this chapter the latter measure will be used. It is assumed that the *greater the amount of net working capital a firm has, the less at risk the firm is*. In other words, the more net working capital, the more liquid the firm, and therefore the less likely it is to become technically insolvent.

risk The probability that a firm will be unable to pay its bills as they come due.

technically insolvent When a firm is unable to pay bills as they are due.

Some Basic Assumptions

In evaluating the profitability-risk trade-off, three basic assumptions must be made:

1 The type of firm under consideration is a *manufacturing firm*.
2 The firm is expected, on average, to *earn more from its fixed, or earning, assets than from its current assets*. Current assets are vitally necessary for the effective operation of the firm. However, without

fixed assets to generate finished goods inventories that can be converted into cash, marketable securities, and accounts receivable, the firm could not function.

3   The firm can obtain financing from two sources: current liabilities and long-term funds. Current liabilities generally consist of accounts payable, notes payable, and accruals (amounts owed for services for which a bill is not generally received). Only notes payable, which represent about 20 percent of the current liabilities of manufacturers, have a stated cost. The other current liabilities (accounts payable and accruals) are basically debts on which the firm pays no charge or interest. Therefore *current liabilities are a cheaper form of financing than long-term funds,* which are costly.

The Nature of the Trade-Off

A firm can increase or decrease its profitability through the manipulation of its net working capital. The consequence of this manipulation will be a corresponding increase or decrease in risk as measured by the level of net working capital. We will now discuss the effects of changing current assets and liabilities on the firm's profitability-risk trade-off separately prior to combining them.

CURRENT ASSETS   The effects of changing the level of the firm's current assets on its profitability-risk trade-off can be demonstrated using the ratio of current assets to total assets. This ratio indicates the *percentage of total assets* that is current. Assuming that the level of total assets remains unchanged,[3] the effects on both profitability and risk of an increase or decrease in this ratio are summarized at the top of Table 7.2. When the ratio increases, profitability decreases because current assets are less profitable than fixed assets. In turn, however, the risk of techni-

TABLE 7.2 Effects of Changing Ratios on Profits and Risk

Ratio	Change in ratio	Effect on profit	Effect on risk
Current assets / Total assets	Increase Decrease	Decrease Increase	Decrease Increase
Current liabilities / Total assets	Increase Decrease	Increase Decrease	Increase Decrease

[3] The level of total assets is assumed *constant* in this and the following discussions in order to isolate the effect of changing asset and financing mixes on the firm's profitability and risk.

cal insolvency decreases because the increase in current assets increases net working capital. The opposite effects on profit and risk result from a decrease in the ratio.

EXAMPLE

The balance sheet for the Berenson Company presented in Figure 7.1 is shown with the initial as well as a second asset mix in Table 7.3. Assume the firm earns 2 percent annually on its current assets and 15 percent annually on its fixed assets. As noted in the evaluation in Table 7.3, the initial asset mix results in a ratio of current to total assets of .386, an annual profit on total assets of $699, and net working capital of $1,100. If the firm shifts its asset mix by investing $300 more in fixed assets (and thus $300 less in current assets), current and fixed assets will be as shown in Table 7.3. After the shift the ratio of current to total assets drops to .343, annual profits on total assets increase by $39 to $738, and net working capital drops by $300 to $800. Clearly, a decrease in the ratio resulted in higher profits ($39 increase) and higher risk (liquidity is reduced by $300 from net working capital of $1,100 to $800). These shifts support our earlier conclusions concerning the profitability-risk trade-off as related to current assets. ■

TABLE 7.3 Evaluation of a Shift in Berenson's Current Assets

Balance sheet

ASSETS				
	Initial	After shift	LIABILITIES AND EQUITY	
Current assets	$2,700	$2,400	Current liabilities	$1,600
Fixed assets	4,300	4,600	Long-term funds	5,400
Total	$7,000	$7,000	Total	$7,000

Evaluation

Initial assets

Ratio of current to total assets = $2,700 ÷ $7,000   =   .386

Profit on total assets = (2% × $2,700) + (15% × $4,300) = $699

Net working capital = $2,700 − $1,600   = $1,100

After shift in assets

Ratio of current to total assets = $2,400 ÷ $7,000   =   .343

Profit on total assets = (2% × $2,400) + (15% × $4,600) = $738

Net working capital = $2,400 − $1,600   = $800

Effect of shift on profit = $738 − $699   = +$39

Change in net working capital = $800 − $1,100   = −$300

CURRENT LIABILITIES The effects of changing the level of the firm's current liabilities on its profitability-risk trade-off can be demonstrated using the ratio of current liabilities to total assets. This ratio indicates the percentage of total assets that has been financed with current liabilities. Assuming that total assets remain unchanged, the effects on both profitability and risk of an increase or decrease in the ratio are summarized at the bottom of Table 7.2. When the ratio increases, profitability increases due to the decreased cost associated with using more of the less expensive current-liability financing and less long-term financing. The risk of technical insolvency also increases because the increase in current liabilities in turn decreases net working capital. The opposite effects on profit and risk result from a decrease in the ratio.

EXAMPLE

The balance sheet for the Berenson Company is shown with the initial as well as a second financing mix in Table 7.4. Assume that the firm's current liabilities cost 3 percent annually to maintain and that the average cost of long-term funds is 11 percent. As noted in the evaluation in Table 7.4, the initial financing mix results in a

TABLE 7.4 Evaluation of a Shift in Berenson's Current Liabilities

Balance sheet

	ASSETS		LIABILITIES AND EQUITY	Initial	After shift
Current assets	$2,700	Current liabilities		$1,600	$1,900
Fixed assets	4,300	Long-term funds		5,400	5,100
Total	$7,000	Total		$7,000	$7,000

Evaluation

Initial financing
Ratio of current liabilities to total assets = $1,600 ÷ $7,000 =   .229
Cost of total financing = (3% × $1,600) + (11% × $5,400)   = $642
Net working capital = $2,700 − $1,600   = $1,100

After shift in liabilities
Ratio of current liabilities to total assets = $1,900 ÷ $7,000 =   .271
Cost of total financing = (3% × $1,900) + (11% × $5,100)   = $618
Net working capital = $2,700 − $1,900   = $800

Effect of shift on profit[a] = −$618 − (−$642)   = +$24
Change in net working capital $800 − $1,100   = −$300

[a] The minus sign preceding the $618 and $642 values reflects the fact that they are costs.

ratio of current liabilities to total assets of .229, an annual cost of total financing of $642, and net working capital of $1,100. If the firm shifts its financing mix by using $300 more current-liability financing (and thus $300 less in long-term financing), current liabilities and long-term funds will be as shown in Table 7.4. After the shift the ratio of current liabilities to total assets rises to .271, the annual cost of total financing decreases by $24 to $618, and net working capital drops to $800. Clearly, an increase in the ratio resulted in higher profits ($24 increase due to a decrease in financing cost) and higher risk (liquidity reduced from net working capital of $1,100 to $800). This supports our earlier conclusions concerning the profitability-risk trade-off as related to current liabilities. ■

COMBINED EFFECTS In the preceding examples, the effects of a decrease in the ratio of current assets to total assets and the effects of an increase in the ratio of current liabilities to total assets were illustrated. Both changes were shown to increase the firm's profits and, correspondingly, risk. Logically, then, the *combined effect* of these actions should also increase profits and increase risk (decrease net working capital).

EXAMPLE

Table 7.5 illustrates the results of combining the changes in current assets and current liabilities demonstrated in Tables 7.3 and 7.4. The values in Table 7.5 show that the combined effect of the two shifts illustrated earlier is an increase in annual profits of $63 and a decrease in net working capital (liquidity) of $600. The trade-off here is obvious; the firm has increased its profitability by increasing its risk. ■

TABLE 7.5 The Combined Effects of Changes in Berenson's Current Assets and Current Liabilities

Change	Change in profits	Change in net working capital
Decrease in ratio of current to total assets	+$39	−$300
Increase in ratio of current liabilities to total assets	+$24	−$300
Combined effect	+$63	−$600

DETERMINING THE FIRM'S FINANCING MIX

One of the most important decisions that must be made with respect to current assets and liabilities is how current liabilities will be used to finance current assets. The amount of current liabilities available is limited by the dollar amount of purchases in the case of accounts payable, by the dollar amount of accrued liabilities in the case of accruals, and by the amount of seasonal borrowing considered acceptable by lenders in the case of notes payable. Lenders make short-term loans to allow a firm to finance seasonal buildups of accounts receivable or inventory. *They generally do not lend short-term money for long-term uses.*[4]

The firm's financing requirements can be separated into a permanent and a seasonal need. The **permanent need**, which consists of fixed assets plus the permanent portion of the firm's current assets, remains unchanged over the year, while the **seasonal need**, which is attributable to the existence of certain temporary current assets, varies over the year. The relationship between current and fixed assets and permanent and seasonal funds requirements can be illustrated graphically with the aid of a simple example.

permanent need Financing requirements for the firm's fixed assets plus the permanent portion of the firm's current assets. These requirements remain unchanged over the year.

seasonal need Financing requirements for temporary current assets, which vary throughout the year.

EXAMPLE

The Berenson Company's estimate of current, fixed, and total asset requirements on a monthly basis for the coming year is given in columns 1, 2, and 3 of Table 7.6. Note that the relatively stable level of total assets over the year reflects, for convenience, an absence of growth by the firm. Columns 4 and 5 present a breakdown of the total requirement into its permanent and seasonal components. The permanent component (column 4) is the lowest level of total funds required during the period, while the seasonal portion is the difference between the total funds requirement (i.e., total assets) for each month and the permanent funds requirement.

By comparing the firm's fixed assets (column 2) to its permanent funds requirement (column 4), it can be seen that the permanent funds requirement exceeds the firm's level of fixed assets. This result occurs because a portion of the firm's current assets are permanent, since they are apparently always being replaced. The size of the permanent component of current assets is $800 for

[4] The rationale for, techniques of, and parties to short-term business loans are discussed in detail in Chapter 10. The primary sources of short-term loans to businesses, commercial banks, make these loans *only for seasonal or self-liquidating purposes* such as temporary buildups of accounts receivable or inventory.

TABLE 7.6 Estimated Funds Requirements for the Berenson Company

Month	Current assets (1)	Fixed assets (2)	Total assets[a] [(1) + (2)] (3)	Permanent funds requirement (4)	Seasonal funds requirement [(3) − (4)] (5)
January	$4,000	$13,000	$17,000	$13,800	$3,200
February	3,000	13,000	16,000	13,800	2,200
March	2,000	13,000	15,000	13,800	1,200
April	1,000	13,000	14,000	13,800	200
May	800	13,000	13,800	13,800	0
June	1,500	13,000	14,500	13,800	700
July	3,000	13,000	16,000	13,800	2,200
August	3,700	13,000	16,700	13,800	2,900
September	4,000	13,000	17,000	13,800	3,200
October	5,000	13,000	18,000	13,800	4,200
November	3,000	13,000	16,000	13,800	2,200
December	2,000	13,000	15,000	13,800	1,200
Monthly Average[b]				$13,800	$1,950

[a] This represents the firm's total funds requirement.

[b] Found by summing the monthly amounts for 12 months and dividing the resulting totals by 12.

the Berenson Company. This value represents the base level of current assets that remains on the firm's books throughout the entire year. This value can also be found by subtracting the level of fixed assets from the permanent funds requirement ($13,800 − $13,000 = $800). The relationships presented in Table 7.6 are depicted graphically in Figure 7.2. ▇

There are a number of strategies for determining an appropriate financing mix. The three basic strategies — (1) the aggressive strategy, (2) the conservative strategy, and (3) a trade-off between the two — are discussed below in terms of both cost and risk considerations. In these discussions the alternate definition that defines *net working capital* as *the portion of current assets financed with long-term funds* is applied.

AN AGGRESSIVE FINANCING STRATEGY

The **aggressive financing strategy** requires that the firm finance its seasonal needs with short-term funds and its permanent needs with long-term funds. Short-term borrowing is geared to the actual need for funds. In other words, the aggressive strategy involves a process of *matching* maturities of debt with the duration of each of the firm's financial needs. This approach can be illustrated graphically.

aggressive financing strategy Plan by which the firm finances its seasonal needs with short-term funds and its permanent needs with long-term funds.

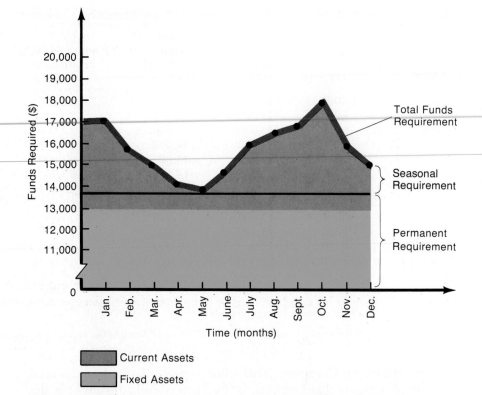

FIGURE 7.2 The Berenson Company's Estimated Funds Requirements
The Berenson Company's total funds requirement varies over the year. It consists of a permanent component, which includes fixed assets and the permanent portion of current assets, and a seasonal component attributable to temporary current assets.

EXAMPLE

The Berenson Company's estimate of its total funds requirements (i.e., total assets) on a monthly basis for the coming year is given in Table 7.6, column 3. Columns 4 and 5 divide this requirement into permanent and seasonal components.

The aggressive strategy requires that the permanent portion of the firm's funds requirement ($13,800) be financed with long-term funds and that the seasonal portion (ranging from $0 in May to $4,200 in October) be financed with short-term funds. The application of this financing strategy to the firm's total funds requirement is illustrated graphically in Figure 7.3. ■

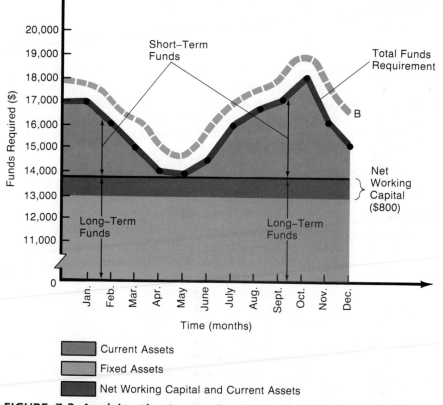

FIGURE 7.3 Applying the Aggressive Strategy to the Berenson Company's Funds Requirements

Under the aggressive financing strategy Berenson Company would finance its permanent need of $13,800 with long-term funds and finance its seasonal needs with short-term funds. This strategy results in $800 of net working capital ($13,800 long-term financing − $13,000 fixed assets).

Cost Considerations

From columns 4 and 5 of Table 7.6, it can be seen that under the aggressive strategy Berenson's average short-term borrowing (seasonal funds requirement) is $1,950 and average long-term borrowing (permanent funds requirement) is $13,800. If the annual cost of short-term funds needed by Berenson is 3 percent and the annual cost of long-term financing is 11 percent, the total cost of the financing strategy is estimated as follows:

$$
\begin{aligned}
\text{Cost of short-term financing} &= 3\% \times \$1,950 = \$\quad 58.50 \\
\text{Cost of long-term financing} &= 11\% \times 13,800 = \underline{\quad 1,518.00} \\
\text{Total cost} &\qquad\qquad\qquad\qquad\quad \underline{\underline{\$1,576.50}}
\end{aligned}
$$

The total annual cost of $1,576.50 will become more meaningful when compared to the cost of various other strategies.

Risk Considerations

The aggressive strategy operates with minimum net working capital since only the permanent portion of the firm's current assets is being financed with long-term funds. For the Berenson Company, as noted in Figure 7.3, the level of net working capital is $800, which is the amount of permanent current assets ($13,800 permanent funds requirement − $13,000 fixed assets = $800).

The aggressive financing strategy is risky not only from the standpoint of low net working capital but also because the firm must draw as heavily as possible on its short-term sources of funds to meet seasonal fluctuations in its requirements. If its total requirement turns out to be, say, the level represented by dashed curve, B, in Figure 7.3, the firm may find it difficult to obtain longer-term funds quickly enough to satisfy short-term needs. This aspect of risk associated with the aggressive strategy results from the fact that a firm has only a limited amount of short-term borrowing capacity. If it draws too heavily on this capacity, unexpected needs for funds may become difficult to satisfy.

A final aspect of risk associated with the aggressive strategy's maximum use of short-term financing is the fact that changing short-term interest rates can result in significantly higher borrowing costs as the short-term debt is refinanced. With long-term financing, a more stable rate and less frequent refinancing needs result in greater certainty and less risk.

A CONSERVATIVE FINANCING STRATEGY

conservative financing strategy Plan by which the firm finances all projected funds needs with long-term funds and uses short-term financing only for emergencies or unexpected outflows.

The most **conservative financing strategy** should be to finance all projected funds requirements with long-term funds and use short-term financing in the event of an emergency or an unexpected outflow of funds. It is difficult to imagine how this strategy could actually be implemented, since the use of short-term financing tools, such as accounts payable and accruals, is virtually unavoidable. In illustrating this approach, the spontaneous short-term financing provided by payables and accruals will be ignored.

EXAMPLE

Figure 7.4 shows graphically the application of the conservative strategy to the estimated funds requirements for the Berenson Company given in Table 7.6. Long-term financing of $18,000,

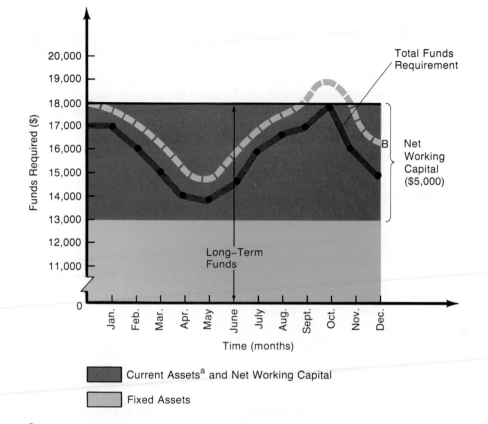

Current Assets[a] **and Net Working Capital**

Fixed Assets

[a]The current assets above the total funds requirement line and below the long-term funds line are excess current assets created by investment of the excess long-term funds in marketable securities.

FIGURE 7.4 Applying the Conservative Strategy to the Berenson Company's Funds Requirements

Under the conservative financing strategy Berenson Company would finance all projected funds requirements, including the entire $18,000 forecast for October, with long-term funds. This strategy results in $5,000 of net working capital ($18,000 long-term financing − $13,000 fixed assets).

which equals the firm's peak need (during October) is used under this strategy. Therefore all the funds required over the one-year period, including the entire $18,000 forecast for October, are financed with long-term funds. ◼

Cost Considerations

In the preceding example the annual cost of long-term funds was 11 percent per year. Since the average long-term financing balance under the conservative financing strategy is $18,000, the total cost of this plan

ASSISTANT TREASURER — CASH CONTROL: A JOB DESCRIPTION

Basic Function

Responsible for operations of the Treasury Department involving cash management operations with specific attention to the effective direction and control of corporate funds internally and through the company's various bank accounts.

Primary Responsibilities and Duties

Manage, in conjunction with lock box banks retained by company, the processing of over 120,000 customer payments daily.

Disbursement of all company funds, including payrolls, pensions, and vendor payments.

Direct the management staff to assure compliance with our stated objectives and planning in order to assure the effectiveness of the organization.

Sign checks and review and approve various documents such as wire transfer confirmations and investment letters.

Meet with banks and their representatives.

Perform various assignments for senior management.

Also responsible for the risk management/insurance function.

Education and Experience

Minimum B. A.

Formerly held positions as Director of Auditing, General Manager — Administration, and Division Manager — Customer Service.

Source: *Careers in Finance* (Tampa, Fla.: Financial Management Association, 1983), pp. 21–22.

is $1,980 or (11% × $18,000). Comparing this figure to the total cost of $1,576.50 using the aggressive strategy indicates the greater expense of the conservative strategy. The reason for this higher expense is apparent if we examine Figure 7.4. The area above the Total Funds Requirement curve and below the long-term funds, or borrowing, line represents the level of funds not actually needed but on which the firm is paying interest. In spite of the fact that the financial manager will invest these excess available funds in some type of marketable security so as partially to offset their cost, it is highly unlikely that the firm can earn more on such funds than their interest cost.

Risk Considerations

The $5,000 of net working capital ($18,000 long-term financing − $13,000 fixed assets) associated with the conservative strategy should mean a very low level of risk for the firm.[5] The firm's risk should also be lowered by the fact that the plan does not require the firm to use any of its limited short-term borrowing capacity. In other words, if total required financing actually turns out to be the level represented by the dashed line B in Figure 7.4, sufficient short-term borrowing capacity should be available to cover the unexpected needs and avoid technical insolvency. In addition, the need to frequently refinance high levels of short-term financing, possibly at high rates, is avoided, thereby further lowering financial risk.

Conservative versus Aggressive Strategy

Unlike the aggressive strategy, the conservative strategy requires the firm to pay interest on unneeded funds. The lower cost of the aggressive strategy therefore makes it more profitable than the conservative strategy; however, the aggressive strategy involves much more risk. For most firms a trade-off between the extremes represented by these two strategies should result in an acceptable financing strategy.

TRADE-OFF FINANCING STRATEGY

Most businesses employ a **trade-off financing strategy,** a compromise between the high-profit, high-risk aggressive strategy and the low-profit, low-risk conservative strategy. One of the many possible trade-offs in the Berenson Company's case is described in the following example.

trade-off financing strategy A compromise strategy between the high-profit, high-risk aggressive strategy and the low-profit, low-risk conservative strategy.

EXAMPLE

After careful analysis, the Berenson Company has decided on a financing plan based on an amount of permanent financing equal to the midpoint of the minimum and maximum monthly funds requirements for the period. An examination of column 3 of Table 7.6 reveals that the minimum monthly funds requirement is $13,800 (in May) and the maximum monthly funds requirement is $18,000 (in October). The midpoint between these two values is $15,900 [($13,800 + $18,000) ÷ 2]. Thus the firm will use $15,900 in long-term funds each month and will raise any additional funds required from short-term sources. The breakdown of long- and short-term funds under this plan is given in Table 7.7.

---

[5] The level of net working capital is constant throughout the year since the firm has $5,000 in current assets that will be fully financed with long-term funds. Because the portion of the $5,000 in excess of the scheduled level of current assets is assumed to be held as marketable securities, the firm's current asset balance will increase to this level.

TABLE 7.7 A Financing Plan Based on a Trade-off Between Profitability and Risk for the Berenson Company

Month	Total assets[a] (1)	Long-term funds (2)	Short-term funds (3)
January	$17,000	$15,900	$1,100
February	16,000	15,900	100
March	15,000	15,900	0
April	14,000	15,900	0
May	13,800	15,900	0
June	14,500	15,900	0
July	16,000	15,900	100
August	16,700	15,900	800
September	17,000	15,900	1,100
October	18,000	15,900	2,100
November	16,000	15,900	100
December	15,000	15,900	0
Monthly Average[b]		$15,900	$ 450

[a] This represents the firm's total funds requirement from column 3 of Table 7.6.

[b] Found by summing the monthly amounts for the 12 months and dividing the resulting totals by 12.

Column 3 in Table 7.7 shows the amount of short-term funds required each month. These values were found by subtracting $15,900 from the total funds required each month, given in column 1. For March, April, May, June, and December, the level of total funds required is less than the level of long-term funds available; therefore, no short-term funds are needed. Figure 7.5 presents graphically the trade-off strategy (line 3) described in Table 7.7 along with the plans based on the aggressive (line 1) and the conservative (line 2) strategies, respectively. Line 3 represents the $15,900 financed with long-term funds; the seasonal needs above that amount are financed with short-term funds. ■

Cost Considerations

From columns 2 and 3 of Table 7.7 it can be seen that under the trade-off strategy Berenson's average short-term borrowing is $450 and average long-term borrowing is $15,900. Applying the cost of short-term financing at 3 percent and the cost of long-term financing at 11 percent, the total cost of this financing strategy is estimated as follows:

$$\text{Cost of short-term financing} = 3\% \times \$450 \quad = \$ \quad 13.50$$
$$\text{Cost of long-term financing} = 11\% \times 15,900 = \underline{\quad 1,749.00}$$
$$\text{Total cost} \qquad\qquad \underline{\underline{\$1,762.50}}$$

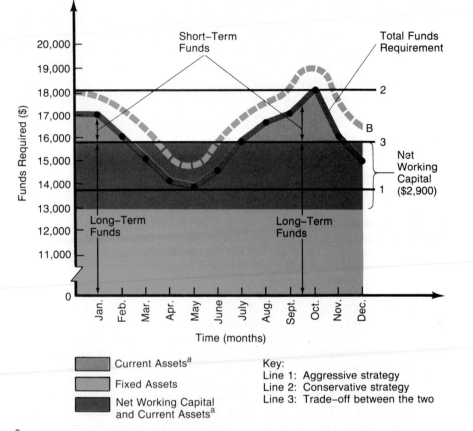

FIGURE 7.5 Three Alternative Financing Strategies for the Berenson Company

Under the trade-off financing strategy, represented by Line 3, Berenson would finance $15,900 of its funds need with long-term funds and the remaining seasonal needs with short-term funds. This strategy results in $2,900 of net working capital ($15,900 long-term financing − $13,000 fixed assets).

The total financing cost under the trade-off strategy is therefore $1,762.50.

Risk Considerations

As Figure 7.5 shows, the trade-off plan results in $2,900 of net working capital ($15,900 long-term financing − $13,000 fixed assets). This is less risky than the aggressive strategy but more risky than the conservative strategy. Under the trade-off plan, if the total funds requirement is actually at the level represented by dashed line B in Figure 7.5, the likelihood that the firm will be able to obtain additional short-term financing is good, since a portion of its short-term financial requirements is actually being financed with long-term funds. Under this plan the risk of having to refinance frequently at possibly higher interest rates falls between the aggressive and conservative strategies.

SUMMARY

- Net working capital is defined either as the difference between current assets and current liabilities or as the portion of a firm's current assets financed with long-term funds. Firms maintain net working capital to provide a cushion between cash outflows and inflows.
- Net working capital is often used as a measure of the risk of technical insolvency by the firm. The more liquid a firm is, the more net working capital it has and the less likely that it will be unable to satisfy its current obligations as they come due.
- The higher a firm's ratio of current assets to total assets, the less profitable the firm, and the less risky it is. The converse is also true. The higher a firm's ratio of current liabilities to total assets, the more profitable and more risky the firm is. The converse of this statement is also true. These trade-offs between profitability and risk must be considered in managing the net working capital position.
- Financing requirements can be forecast and broken down into seasonal and permanent needs. The permanent need is attributable to fixed assets and the permanent portion of current assets, whereas the seasonal need is attributable to the existence of certain temporary current assets.
- The aggressive strategy for determining an appropriate financing mix is a high-profit, high-risk financing strategy whereby seasonal needs are financed with short-term funds and permanent needs are financed with long-term funds. The maturity of debt is matched with the duration of each of the firm's financial needs.
- The conservative strategy is a low-profit, low-risk financing strategy. All funds requirements—both seasonal and permanent—are financed with long-term funds. Short-term funds are saved for emergencies.
- Most firms use a trade-off strategy whereby some seasonal needs are financed with long-term funds; this strategy falls between the high-profit, high-risk aggressive strategy and the low-profit, low-risk conservative strategy.

QUESTIONS

7-1 Why is working capital management considered so important by stockholders, creditors, and the firm's financial manager? What is the definition of *net working capital?*

7-2 What relationship would you expect to exist between the predictability of a firm's cash flows and its required level of net working capital?

7-3 How are net working capital, liquidity, technical insolvency, and risk related?

7-4 Why is an increase in the ratio of current to total assets expected to decrease both profits and risk as measured by net working capital?

7-5 How can changes in the ratio of current liabilities to total assets affect profitability and risk?

7-6 How would you expect an increase in a firm's ratio of current assets to total assets and a decrease in its ratio of current liabilities to total assets to affect profit and risk? Why?

7-7 What is the basic premise of the *aggressive strategy* for meeting a firm's funds requirements? What are the effects of this strategy on the firm's profitability and risk?

7-8 What is the *conservative strategy* for financing funds requirements? What kind of profitability-risk trade-off is involved?

7-9 If a firm has a constant funds requirement throughout the year, which, if any, of the three financing plans is preferable? Why?

7-10 As the difference between the cost of short-term and long-term financing becomes smaller, which financing strategy — aggressive or conservative — becomes more attractive? Would the aggressive or the conservative strategy be preferable if the costs were equal? Why?

PROBLEMS

7-1 **(Changing Level of Current Assets)** Bonnie Bowl Products had the following levels of assets, liabilities, and equity:

Assets		Liabilities and equity	
Current assets	$ 5,000	Current liabilities	$ 3,000
Fixed assets	12,000	Long-term debt	6,000
Total	$17,000	Equity	8,000
		Total	$17,000

The company annually earns approximately 4 percent on its current assets and 14 percent on its fixed assets.

a Calculate the firm's initial values of (1) the ratio of current to total assets, (2) annual profits on total assets, and (3) net working capital.

b If the firm were to *shift $2,000 of current assets to fixed assets,* find the values of (1) the ratio of current to total assets, (2) annual profits on total assets, and (3) net working capital.

c If the firm were to *shift $2,000 of fixed assets to current assets,* find the values of (1) the ratio of current to total assets, (2) annual profits on total assets, and (3) net working capital.

d Summarize your findings in **a**, **b**, and **c** in tabular form and discuss the impact of shifts in the asset mix on profits and risk.

7-2 **(Changing Level of Current Liabilities)** Mullhollan Smelting had the following levels of assets, liabilities, and equity:

Assets		Liabilities and equity	
Current assets	$18,000	Current liabilities	$ 9,000
Fixed assets	32,000	Long-term debt	22,000
Total	$50,000	Equity	19,000
		Total	$50,000

The firm's current liabilities cost approximately 5 percent annually to maintain, and the average annual cost of its long-term funds is 16 percent.
a Calculate the firm's initial values of (1) the ratio of current liabilities to total assets, (2) the annual cost of financing, and (3) net working capital.
b If the firm were to *shift $5,000 of current liabilities to long-term funds*, find the value of (1) the ratio of current liabilities to total assets, (2) the annual cost of financing, and (3) net working capital.
c If the firm were to *shift $5,000 of long-term funds to current liabilities*, find the value of (1) the ratio of current liabilities to total assets, (2) the annual cost of financing, and (3) net working capital.
d Summarize your findings in a, b, and c in tabular form and discuss the impact of shifts in the asset mix on profits and risk.

7-3 **(Liquidity, Risk, and Return — Basic)** Last year, the NRC Corporation had the following balance sheet:

Assets		Liabilities and equity	
Current assets	$ 6,000	Current liabilities	$ 2,000
Fixed assets	14,000	Long-term funds	18,000
Total	$20,000	Total	$20,000

The firm estimated it earned 10 percent annually on current assets, current liabilities cost 14 percent annually, fixed assets earned 25 percent annually, and long-term funds cost 16 percent annually.

For the coming year, calculate the expected annual profits on total assets, annual financing costs, and net working capital under the following different circumstances:
a There are no changes.
b The firm shifts $1,000 from current assets to fixed assets and $500 from long-term funds to current liabilities.
c Discuss the changes in annual profits and risk illustrated by a and b.

7-4 **(Liquidity, Risk, and Return — Advanced)** The Badger Company had the following balance sheet at the end of 1987:

Assets		Liabilities and equity	
Current assets	$ 30,000	Current liabilities	$ 15,000
Fixed assets	90,000	Long-term funds	105,000
Total	$120,000	Total	$120,000

a Calculate the annual profits on total assets, annual financing costs, and net working capital if the firm (1) expects to earn annually 8 percent on current assets and 20 percent on fixed assets, current liabilities cost 12 percent annually, and long-term funds cost 16 percent annually; and (2) expects to earn annually 10 percent on current assets and 20 percent on fixed assets, current liabilities cost 11 percent annually, and long-term funds cost 15 percent annually.

b The firm wishes to decrease net working capital by $10,000. This could be accomplished by either decreasing current assets or by increasing current liabilities. Under each circumstance above — a(1) and a(2) — would this goal be most profitably accomplished by decreasing current assets or by increasing current liabilities? Explain.

7-5 **(Permanent versus Seasonal Funds Requirements)** Mintex Corporation's current, fixed, and total assets for each month of the coming year are summarized in the table below:

Month	Current assets (1)	Fixed assets (2)	Total assets [(1) + (2)] (3)
January	$15,000	$30,000	$45,000
February	22,000	30,000	52,000
March	30,000	30,000	60,000
April	18,000	30,000	48,000
May	10,000	30,000	40,000
June	6,000	30,000	36,000
July	9,000	30,000	39,000
August	9,000	30,000	39,000
September	15,000	30,000	45,000
October	20,000	30,000	50,000
November	22,000	30,000	52,000
December	20,000	30,000	50,000

a Divide the firm's monthly total funds requirements (total assets) into a permanent and a seasonal component.

b Find the monthly average (1) permanent and (2) seasonal funds requirements using your findings in a.

7-6 **(Annual Loan Cost)** What is the average loan balance and the annual loan cost, given an annual interest rate on loans of 15 percent, for a firm with total monthly borrowings as follows?

Month	Amount	Month	Amount
Jan.	$12,000	July	$6,000
Feb.	13,000	Aug.	5,000
Mar.	9,000	Sept.	6,000
Apr.	8,000	Oct.	5,000
May	9,000	Nov.	7,000
June	7,000	Dec.	9,000

7-7 **(Aggressive versus Conservative)** Dynabase Tool has forecast its total funds requirements for the coming year as follows:

Month	Amount	Month	Amount
Jan.	$2,000,000	July	$12,000,000
Feb.	2,000,000	Aug.	14,000,000
Mar.	2,000,000	Sept.	9,000,000
Apr.	4,000,000	Oct.	5,000,000
May	6,000,000	Nov.	4,000,000
June	9,000,000	Dec.	3,000,000

a Calculate the total annual financing costs of the aggressive strategy and the conservative strategy if (1) the cost of short-term funds is 12 percent and the cost of long-term funds is 17 percent; and (2) the cost of short-term funds is 11 percent and the cost of long-term funds is 12 percent. (*Note:* Use the average annual loan balance when appropriate.)

b Discuss the profitability-risk trade-offs associated with the aggressive strategy and the conservative strategy.

c Which strategy would more closely approximate your choice in **a**(1) and **a**(2)? Why?

7-8 **(Aggressive versus Conservative)** Santo Gas has forecast its seasonal financing needs for the next year as follows:

Month	Seasonal requirement	Month	Seasonal requirement
Jan.	$2,400,000	July	$ 800,000
Feb.	500,000	Aug.	400,000
Mar.	0	Sept.	0
Apr.	300,000	Oct.	300,000
May	1,200,000	Nov.	1,000,000
June	1,000,000	Dec.	1,800,000

Assuming that the firm's permanent funds requirement is $5 million, calculate the total annual financing costs using the aggressive strategy and the conservative strategy, respectively. Recommend one of the strategies under the following conditions:

a Short-term funds cost 10 percent annually and long-term funds cost 16 percent annually.

b Short-term funds cost 11 percent annually and long-term funds cost 14 percent annually.

c Both short-term and long-term funds cost 12 percent annually.

7-9 **(Testing Assumptions)** LSB, Inc. has seasonal financing needs that vary from zero to $2 million. For each separate condition in **a** through **f**, would the condition tend to move the firm toward an aggressive financing strategy or toward a conservative financing strategy?

a The difference between short-term and long-term financing costs has decreased.

b The average seasonal financing need is $400,000.

c The average seasonal financing need is $1.8 million.

d The long-term financing cost is much higher than the short-term cost.

e The firm has a high proportion of its assets in current assets.

f Sales are very difficult to predict.

7-10 **(Aggressive, Conservative, and Trade-off)** Ideas Enterprises expects to need the following amounts of funds next year:

Month	Amount	Month	Amount
Jan.	$10,000	July	$10,000
Feb.	10,000	Aug.	9,000
Mar.	11,000	Sept.	8,000
Apr.	12,000	Oct.	8,000
May	13,000	Nov.	9,000
June	11,000	Dec.	9,000

a What is the average amount of funding needed during the year?

b If annual short-term financing costs 8 percent and long-term financing costs 20 percent, what will be the total financing costs for the aggressive and conservative financing strategies, respectively?

c If the firm finances $10,000 with long-term financing, what will be the total financing cost?

7-11 **(Aggressive versus Conservative — No Seasonality)** Snyder Supply has financing needs of $250,000 per month forecast for every month of the coming year. The annual cost of short-term financing is 12 percent and the annual cost of long-term financing is 14 percent.

a What are the total annual costs of the aggressive and conservative financing strategies, respectively?

b Which strategy is preferable? Why?

8

CASH AND MARKETABLE SECURITIES

After studying this chapter, you should be able to:

- Discuss the three basic cash management strategies and demonstrate their impact on the firm's minimum operating cash, using the cash cycle model.

- Define *float*, including its three basic components, and explain the firm's major objective with respect to the levels of collection float and disbursement float.

- Describe the basic cash management techniques, including popular collection procedures and disbursement procedures.

- Understand marketable security fundamentals, including the basic motives for holding these securities, their key characteristics, and the trade-off in purchase decisions.

- List and briefly describe the basic features of the popular marketable securities, including government issues and nongovernment issues.

Cash and marketable securities are the most liquid of the firm's assets. Together they act as a pool of funds that can be used to pay bills as they come due and to meet any unexpected outlays. **Cash** is the ready currency to which all liquid assets can be reduced. **Marketable securities** are short-term interest-earning instruments used by the firm to obtain a return on temporarily idle funds. Because the rate of interest applied by banks to checking accounts is relatively low, firms tend to move excess bank balances into other instruments. A number of marketable securities allow the firm to profit on its idle cash without sacrificing much liquidity.

cash The ready currency to which all liquid assets can be reduced.

marketable securities Short-term interest-earning instruments used to obtain a return on temporarily idle funds.

THE EFFICIENT MANAGEMENT OF CASH

The basic strategies that should be employed by the business firm in managing cash are as follows:

1. Pay accounts payable as late as possible without damaging the firm's credit rating, but take advantage of any favorable cash discounts.
2. Turn over inventory as quickly as possible, avoiding depletions of stock (stockouts) that might result in a loss of sales.
3. Collect accounts receivable as quickly as possible without losing future sales due to high-pressure collection techniques. Cash discounts, if they are economically justifiable, may be used to accomplish this objective.

The overall implications of these strategies for the firm can be demonstrated by looking at cash cycles and cash turnovers.

The Cash Cycle and Cash Turnover

The **cash cycle** of a firm is defined as the amount of time that elapses from the point when the firm makes an outlay to purchase raw materials to the point when cash is collected from the sale of the finished product using the raw material. **Cash turnover** refers to the number of times each year the firm's cash is actually turned into a marketable product and then back into cash. The concept of the cash cycle and cash turnover can be illustrated using a simple example.

cash cycle The amount of time elapsed from the point when an outlay is made to purchase raw materials to the point when cash is collected from the sale of the finished product using the raw material.

cash turnover The number of times per year the firm's cash is turned into a marketable product and then back into cash.

EXAMPLE

The RIF Company currently purchases all its raw materials on a credit basis and sells all its merchandise on credit. The credit terms extended the firm currently require payment within 30 days

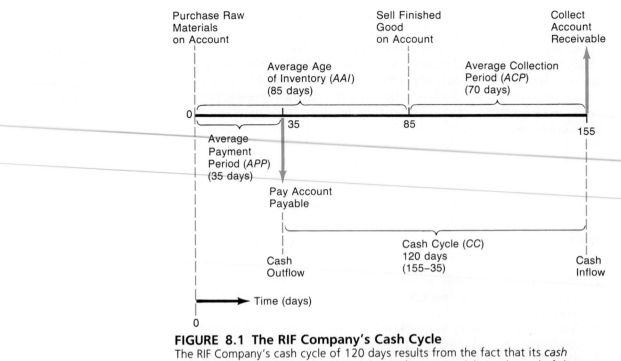

FIGURE 8.1 The RIF Company's Cash Cycle
The RIF Company's cash cycle of 120 days results from the fact that its *cash outflow* occurs 35 days after the purchase of raw materials (at the end of the average payment period) while, due to an 85 day average age of inventory and a 70 day average collection period, *cash inflow* occurs 155 days after the purchase.

of a purchase, while the firm currently requires its customers to pay within 60 days of a sale. The firm's calculations of the average payment period and average collection period indicate that it is taking, on the average, 35 days to pay its accounts payable and 70 days to collect its accounts receivable. Further calculations reveal that, on the average, 85 days elapse between the purchase of a raw material and the sale of a finished good. In other words, the average age of the firm's inventory is 85 days.

The firm's cash cycle can be shown by a simple graph, as in Figure 8.1. There are 120 days between the *cash outflow* to pay the account payable (on day 35) and the *cash inflow* from the collection of the account receivable (on day 155). During this period the firm's money is tied up. The firm's cash cycle is calculated by finding the average number of days that elapse between the cash outflows associated with paying accounts payable and the cash inflows associated with collecting accounts receivable. Stated as an equation, the cash cycle (*CC*) is

$$CC = AAI + ACP - APP \qquad (8.1)$$

where

$$AAI = \text{average age of inventory}$$
$$ACP = \text{average collection period}$$
$$APP = \text{average payment period}$$

Substituting $AAI = 85$ days, $ACP = 70$ days, and $APP = 35$ days into Equation 8.1, RIF's cash cycle is found to be 120 days or (85 days + 70 days − 35 days). This result can be seen in Figure 8.1.

A firm's cash turnover (CT) is calculated by dividing the cash cycle into 360:

$$CT = \frac{360}{CC} \qquad (8.2)$$

The RIF Company's cash turnover is currently 3 (360 days ÷ 120 days). The higher a firm's cash turnover, the less cash the firm requires. Cash turnover, like inventory turnover, should be maximized. ■

Determining Minimum Operating Cash

A primary objective of corporate cash management should be to operate the firm *in a fashion that requires minimum cash*. This will in turn allow the availability of surplus cash funds for various investments and for repayment of debts. On the other hand, the more cash required for the firm's operation, the more investment opportunities (and potential returns) the firm must forgo. In other words, the fewer interest-earning assets a company can acquire, due to cash needed elsewhere, the higher the **opportunity cost** of the failure to make such investments.

Establishing an optimal minimum cash level depends on both expected and unexpected receipts and disbursements. One simple approach is to set the minimum level as a *percentage of sales*. For example, a firm that wishes to maintain a cash balance equal to 8 percent of $2 million annual sales would set a balance of $160,000 or (.08 × $2,000,000).

Using another simple technique, the minimum operating cash (*MOC*) needed by a firm can be estimated by *dividing the firm's total annual outlays (TAO)* by its *cash turnover (CT)*:

$$MOC = \frac{TAO}{CT} \qquad (8.3)$$

opportunity cost The cost to the firm of foregone returns due to the failure to make short-term investments.

The minimum operating cash can be multiplied by the opportunity cost in order to estimate the cost of these funds. The following example demonstrates this process.

THE USE AND ABUSE OF FLOAT

Float is money in transit. For example, a taxpayer enjoyed a two-week float, during which he drew interest on the funds, when his check, mailed to the Internal Revenue Service on April 15, was not charged to his account until April 29. Similarly, an American charged a meal on a credit card in Ghent, Belgium, in September, 1984, and was billed in April, 1985. In a more common case, a husband deposits a paycheck in the bank and his wife immediately mails a check against it to pay a charge-account bill, counting on the paycheck to clear before her check for the charge account reaches the bank for payment.

Since 40 billion checks are written each year, the float is enormous. It is widely used in the form of interest-free "loans" by companies.

As an example of illegal use, a large firm has accounts with hundreds of banks, many in remote areas with no access to the automated check-clearing system. The company might deposit in a Virginia bank a check for $300,000 drawn on a small bank in Nebraska. The firm does not have $300,000 in this bank but knows that its check will take five business days to clear. So, in three or four days, it deposits by courier or wire $500,000 in the Nebraska bank, drawing on a remote Oregon bank in which the firm does not have $500,000 but in which, just before five business days are up, it will deposit $800,000 drawn on another remote bank and so on.

Banks and individuals also use float. A sore point with individuals is that many banks create float by putting an automatic "hold" on deposited checks. As an example, when a customer of First American Bank in Washington, D.C., deposits a check drawn on an Illinois bank, the money will not be credited to his or her account for eight business days. The bank, however, usually will receive the funds in one or two days, the time it takes 90 percent of checks to clear.

First American's hold or "delayed availability" schedule lists 80 areas, showing hold days for each. Many banks list only three types of holds: For local checks, for other in-state checks and for out-of-state checks.

The banks' explanation for holds is that a deposited check might bounce, although the Federal Reserve Board says that only 1 percent do.

Source: John W. Hazard, "Playing the 'Float' for Legal Profits," *U.S. News & World Report,* May 27, 1985, p. 75.

EXAMPLE

If the RIF Company spends approximately $12 million annually on operating outlays *(TAO)* and has a cash turnover, *CT*, of 3, its minimum operating cash *(MOC)* is $4 million or ($12,000,000 ÷

3.00). This means that if it begins the year with $4 million in cash, it should have sufficient cash to pay bills as they come due. If the firm could earn at best 10 percent on investments or loan repayments, its opportunity cost of holding cash is 10 percent. Using this value, the cost of maintaining a $4 million cash balance will be $400,000 or (.10 × $4,000,000) per year. ■

It is important to note that while the corporate cash budget (discussed in Chapter 6) is a useful tool in cash planning, it does not deal with establishing the appropriate cash balance.

Cash Management Strategies

The effects of implementing each of the cash management strategies mentioned earlier are described in the following paragraphs, using the RIF Company data. The costs of implementing each proposed strategy are ignored, whereas in practice these costs would be measured against the calculated savings in order to make the appropriate strategy decision.

STRETCHING ACCOUNTS PAYABLE   One strategy available to RIF is to **stretch accounts payable**—that is, for RIF to pay its bills as late as possible without damaging its credit rating. Although this approach is financially attractive, its raises an important ethical issue since clearly a supplier would not look favorably on a customer who purposely postponed payments.

stretch accounts payable To pay the firm's bills as late as possible without damaging its credit rating.

EXAMPLE

If RIF Company can stretch the payment period from the current average of 35 days to an average of 45 days, its cash cycle will be reduced to 110 days ($CC = 85$ days $+ 70$ days $- 45$ days $= 110$ days). By stretching its accounts payable 10 additional days, the firm increases its cash turnover rate from 3.00 to 3.27 ($CT = 360$ days $\div 110$ days $= 3.27$). This increased cash turnover rate results in a decrease in the firm's minimum operating cash requirement from $4,000,000 to approximately $3,670,000 ($MOC = $12,000,000 \div 3.27 = $3,670,000$). The reduction in required operating cash of approximately $330,000 ($4,000,000 − $3,670,000) represents an *annual savings* to the firm of $33,000 (.10 × $330,000), which is the opportunity cost of tying up that amount of funds. This savings clearly demonstrates the potential benefits of stretching accounts payable. ■

EFFICIENT INVENTORY-PRODUCTION MANAGEMENT Another means of minimizing required cash is to increase inventory turnover. This can be achieved by increasing raw materials turnover, shortening the production cycle, or increasing finished goods turnover. Regardless of which of these approaches is used, the result will be a reduction in the amount of operating cash required.

EXAMPLE

If RIF manages to increase inventory turnover by reducing the average age of inventory from the current level of 85 days to 70 days—a reduction of 15 days—the effects on its minimum operating cash will be as follows: There will be a reduction of 15 days in the cash cycle, from 120 days to 105 days ($CC = 70$ days $+$ 70 days $-$ 35 days $= 105$ days). The decreased average age of inventory for RIF increases the annual cash turnover rate from the initial level of 3.00 to 3.43 ($CT = 360$ days $\div$ 105 days $= 3.43$). The increased cash turnover rate in turn results in a decrease in the firm's minimum operating cash requirement from \$4 million to approximately \$3.5 million ($MOC = \$12,000,000 \div 3.43 = \$3,500,000$). The reduction in required operating cash of approximately \$500,000 (\$4,000,000 $-$ \$3,500,000) represents an *annual savings* to the firm of \$50,000 (.10 $\times$ \$500,000). This savings clearly indicates the importance of efficiency in inventory and production management. ∎

ACCELERATING THE COLLECTION OF ACCOUNTS RECEIVABLE A third means of reducing the operating cash requirement is to speed up, or accelerate, the collection of accounts receivable. This is desirable because accounts receivable, like inventory, tie up dollars that could otherwise be invested in earning assets. Let us consider the following example.

EXAMPLE

If the RIF Company, by changing its credit terms, is able to reduce the average collection period from the current level of 70 days to 50 days, this will reduce its cash cycle by 20 days (70 days $-$ 50 days) to 100 days ($CC = 120$ days $-$ 20 days $= 100$ days). The decrease in the collection period from 70 to 50 days raises the annual cash turnover rate from the initial level of 3.00 to 3.60 ($CT = 360$ days $\div$ 100 days $= 3.60$). The increased cash turnover results in a decrease in the firm's minimum operating cash requirement from \$4,000,000 to approximately \$3,330,000 ($MOC = \$12,000,000 \div$

3.60 = $3,330,000). The reduction in required operating cash of approximately $670,000 ($4,000,000 − $3,330,000) represents an *annual savings* to the firm of approximately $67,000 (.10 × $670,000). The $67,000 annual earnings represents the amount the firm can earn at its 10 percent opportunity cost on the $670,000 reduction in operating cash. ■

CASH MANAGEMENT TECHNIQUES

Financial managers have at their disposal a variety of cash management techniques that can provide additional savings. These techniques are aimed at minimizing the firm's cash requirements by taking advantage of certain imperfections in the collection and payment systems. Assuming that the firm has done all it can to stimulate customers to pay promptly and to select vendors offering the most attractive and flexible credit terms, certain techniques can further speed collections and slow disbursements. These procedures take advantage of the "float" existing in the collection and payment systems.

Float

In the broadest sense, **float** refers to funds that have been dispatched by a payer (the firm or individual *making* payment) but are not yet in a form that can be spent by the payee (the firm or individual *receiving* payment). Float also exists when a payee has received funds in a spendable form but these funds have not been withdrawn from the account of the payer. Delays in the collection-payment system resulting from the transportation and processing of checks are responsible for float. With electronic payments systems as well as deliberate action by the Federal Reserve system, it seems clear that in the foreseeable future float will virtually disappear. Until that time, however, financial managers must continue to understand and take advantage of float.

TYPES OF FLOAT   Currently business firms and individuals can experience both collection and disbursement float as part of the process of making financial transactions. **Collection float** results from the delay between the time when a payer or customer deducts a payment from the checking account ledger and the time when the payee or vendor actually receives these funds in a spendable form. Thus collection float is experienced by the payee and is a delay in the receipt of funds. **Disbursement float** results from the lapse between the time when a firm deducts a payment from its checking account ledger (disburses it) and the time when funds are actually withdrawn from its account. Disbursement float is experienced by the payer and results in a delay in the actual withdrawal of funds.

float Refers to funds dispatched by a payer that are not yet in a form that can be spent by the payee.

collection float The delay between the time when a payer or customer deducts a payment from the checking account ledger and the time when the payee or vendor actually receives the funds in a spendable form.

disbursement float The lapse between the time when a firm deducts a payment from its checking account ledger (disburses it) and the time when funds are actually withdrawn from its account.

COMPONENTS OF FLOAT Both collection float and disbursement float have the same three basic components:

mail float The delay between the time when a payer mails a payment and the time when the payee receives it.

1. **Mail float:** the delay between the time when a payer places payment in the mail and the time when it is received by the payee.
2. **Processing float:** the delay between the receipt of a check by the payee and the actual deposit of it in the firm's account.
3. **Clearing float:** The delay between the deposit of a check by the payee and the actual availability of the funds. This component of float is attributable to the time required for a check to clear the banking system.

processing float The delay between the receipt of a check by the payee and its actual deposit in the firm's account.

clearing float The delay between the deposit of a check by the payee and the actual availability of the funds.

Figure 8.2 illustrates the key components of float resulting from the issuance and mailing of a check by the payer company to the payee company on day zero. It can be seen that the entire process required a total of nine days: three days' mail float; two days' processing float; and four days' clearing float. To the payer company, the delay is disbursement float; to the payee company, the delay is collection float.

Collection Techniques

The firm's objective is not only to stimulate customers to pay their accounts as promptly as possible but also to convert their payments into a spendable form as quickly as possible — in other words, to *minimize*

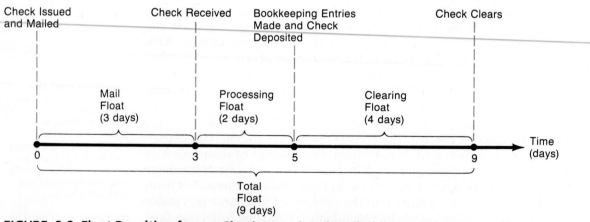

FIGURE 8.2 Float Resulting from a Check Issued and Mailed by the Payer Company to the Payee Company
On a check issued by the payer company to the payee company it takes 3 days (mail float) to reach the payee who then takes 2 days (processing float) to process the check and deposit it in its account where it takes 4 days (clearing float) to clear the banking system and become spendable funds. A total of 9 days (total float) therefore results from this transaction.

collection float. A variety of techniques aimed at *speeding up collections,* and thereby reducing collection float, are available.

CONCENTRATION BANKING Firms with numerous sales outlets throughout the country often designate certain offices as collection centers for given geographic areas. Customers in these areas remit their payments to these sales offices, which in turn deposit the receipts in local banks. At certain times, or on a when-needed basis, funds are transferred by wire from these regional banks to a concentration, or disbursing, bank, from which bill payments are dispatched.

Concentration banking is used to reduce collection float by shortening the mail and clearing float components. Mail float is reduced because regionally dispersed collection centers bring the collection point closer to the point from which the check is sent. Clearing float should also be reduced, since the payee's regional bank is likely to be in the same Federal Reserve district or the same city as the bank on which the check is drawn; it may even be the same bank. A reduction in clearing float will, of course, make funds available to the firm more quickly.

> **concentration banking** Reduces collection float by shortening mail and clearing float. Payments are made to regionally dispersed collection centers, then deposited in local banks for quick clearing.

LOCKBOXES Another method used to reduce collection float is the **lockbox system,** which differs from concentration banking in several important ways. Instead of mailing payment to a collection center, the payer sends it to a post office box that is emptied by the firm's bank one or more times each business day. The bank opens the payment envelopes, deposits the checks in the firm's account, and sends a deposit slip (or, under certain arrangements, a computer tape) indicating the payments received, along with any enclosures, to the collecting firm. Lockboxes are normally geographically dispersed, and the funds, when collected, are wired from each lockbox bank to the firm's disbursing bank.

> **lockbox system** Reduces collection float by having the payer send the payment to a nearby post office box that is emptied by the firm's bank several times daily, thus accelerating the deposit process.

The lockbox system is superior to concentration banking because it reduces processing float as well as mail and clearing float. The receipts are immediately deposited in the firm's account by the bank so that processing occurs after, rather than before, funds are deposited in the firm's account. This allows the firm to use the funds almost immediately for disbursing payments. Additional reductions in mail float may also result since payments do not have to be delivered but are picked up by the bank at the post office.

DIRECT SENDS To reduce clearing float, firms that have received large checks drawn on distant banks, or a large number of checks drawn on banks in a given city, may arrange to present these checks directly for payment to the bank on which they are drawn. Such a procedure is called a **direct send.** Rather than depositing these checks in its collec-

> **direct send** Reduces clearing float by allowing the payee to present payment checks directly to the banks on which they are drawn, thus avoiding the delay of the clearing process.

tion account, the firm arranges to present the checks to the bank on which they are drawn and receive immediate payment. The firm can use Express Mail or private express services to get the checks into a bank in the same city or to a sales office where an employee can take the checks to the bank and present them for payment. In most cases the funds will be transferred via wire into the firm's disbursement account.

Deciding whether or not to use direct sends is relatively straightforward. If the benefits from the reduced clearing time are greater than the cost, the checks should be sent directly for payment rather than cleared through normal banking channels.

EXAMPLE

If a firm with an opportunity to earn 10 percent on its idle balances can, through a direct send, make available $1.2 million three days earlier than otherwise would be the case, the benefit of this direct send would be $1,000 [.10 × (3 days ÷ 360 days) × $1,200,000]. If the cost of achieving this three-day reduction in float is less than $1,000, the direct send would be recommended. ■

preauthorized check
A check written by the payee against a customer's checking account for a previously agreed-upon amount. Due to prior legal authorization, the check does not require the customer's signature.

OTHER TECHNIQUES A number of other techniques can be used to reduce collection float. One method commonly used by firms, such as insurance companies, that collect a fixed amount from customers on a regular basis is the preauthorized check. A **preauthorized check (PAC)** is a check written against a customer's checking account for a previously agreed-upon amount by the firm to which it is payable. Because the check has been legally authorized by the customer, it does not require their signature. The payee merely issues and then deposits the PAC in its account. The check then clears through the banking system just as though written by the customer and received and deposited by the firm.

depository transfer check (DTC) An unsigned check drawn on one of the firm's bank accounts and deposited into its account at a concentration or major disbursement bank, thereby avoiding clearance delays.

A method used by firms with multiple collection points to move funds is the depository transfer check. A **depository transfer check (DTC)** is an unsigned check drawn on one of the firm's bank accounts and deposited into its account at another bank—typically a concentration or major disbursing bank. Once the DTC has cleared the bank on which it is drawn, the actual transfer of funds is completed. Most firms currently transmit deposit information via telephone rather than by mail to their concentration banks, which then prepare and deposit DTCs into the firm's accounts.

wire transfers Telegraphic communications that, via bookkeeping entries, remove funds from the payer's bank and deposit them in the payee's bank, thereby reducing collection float.

Firms frequently use wire transfers to reduce collection float by quickly transferring funds from one bank account to another. **Wire transfers** are telegraphic communications that, via bookkeeping entries, remove funds from the payer's bank and deposit them into the payee's bank. Wire transfers can eliminate mail and clearing float and may provide processing float reductions as well. They are sometimes used instead of DTCs to move funds into key disbursing accounts.

Disbursement Techniques

The firm's objective relative to accounts payable is not only to pay its accounts as late as possible but also to slow down the availability of funds to suppliers and employees once the payment has been dispatched—in other words, to *maximize disbursement float*. A variety of techniques aimed at *slowing down disbursements,* and thereby increasing disbursement float, are available.

CONTROLLED DISBURSING   **Controlled disbursing** involves the strategic use of mailing points and bank accounts to lengthen mail float and clearing float, respectively. When the date of postmark is considered the effective date of payment by the supplier, the firm may be able to lengthen the mail time associated with disbursements. This is done by placing payments in the mail at locations from which it is known they will take a considerable amount of time to reach the supplier. Typically, small towns not close to major highways and cities provide excellent opportunities to increase mail float.

controlled disbursing
The strategic use of mailing points and bank accounts to lengthen mail float and clearing float respectively.

The widespread availability of computers and data on check clearing times allows firms to develop disbursement schemes that maximize clearing float on their payments. These methods involve assigning payments going to vendors in certain geographic areas to be drawn on specific banks from which maximum clearing float will result.

PLAYING THE FLOAT   **Playing the float** is a method of consciously anticipating the resulting float, or delay, associated with the payment process. Firms often play the float by writing checks against funds not currently in their checking accounts. They are able to do this because they know a delay will occur between the receipt and the deposit of checks by suppliers and the actual withdrawal of funds from their checking accounts. It is likely that the firm's bank account will not be drawn down by the amount of the payments for a few additional days. Although the ineffective use of this practice could result in problems associated with "bounced checks," many firms use float to stretch out their accounts payable.

playing the float
A method of consciously anticipating the resulting float, or delay, associated with the payment process.

Firms play the float in a variety of ways—all of which are aimed at keeping funds in an interest-earning form for as long as possible. For example, one way of playing the float is to deposit a certain proportion of a payroll or payment into the firm's checking account on several successive days *following* the actual issuance of a group of checks. If the firm can determine from historic data that only 25 percent of its payroll checks are cashed on the day immediately following the issuance of the checks, then only 25 percent of the value of the payroll needs to be in its checking account one day later. The amount of checks cashed on each of several succeeding days can also be estimated, until the entire payroll is accounted for. Normally, however, to protect itself against any irregularities a firm will place slightly more money in its account than is needed to cover the expected withdrawals.

OVERDRAFT SYSTEMS AND ZERO-BALANCE ACCOUNTS   Firms that aggressively manage cash disbursements will often arrange for some type of overdraft system or zero-balance account. Under an **overdraft system,** if the firm's checking account balance is insufficient to cover all checks presented against the account, the bank will automatically lend the firm enough money to cover the amount of the overdraft. The bank, of course, will charge the firm interest on the funds lent and will limit the amount of overdraft coverage. Such an arrangement is important for a business that actively plays the float.

overdraft system
Automatic coverage by the bank of all checks presented against the firm's account, regardless of the account balance.

Firms can also establish **zero-balance accounts**—checking accounts in which zero balances are maintained. Under this arrangement, each day the bank will notify the firm of the total amount of checks presented against the account. The firm then transfers only that amount—typically from a master account or through liquidation of a portion of its marketable securities—into the account. Once the corresponding checks have been paid, the account balance reverts to zero. The bank, of course, must be compensated for this service.

zero-balance account
A checking account in which a zero balance is maintained and the bank requires the firm to deposit funds to cover checks drawn on the account only as they are presented.

MARKETABLE SECURITIES FUNDAMENTALS

marketable securities
Short-term money market instruments that can easily be converted into cash.

Marketable securities are short-term money market instruments that can easily be converted into cash.[1] Marketable securities are classified as part of the firm's liquid assets.

Motives for Holding Marketable Securities

There are three motives for holding marketable securities, which act as a storehouse of liquidity. Each motive is based on the premise that the firm should attempt to earn a return on temporarily idle funds. The type of marketable security purchased will depend on the motive for its purchase.

[1]As explained in Chapter 2, the *money market* results from a financial relationship between the suppliers and demanders of short-term funds, that is, marketable securities.

TRANSACTIONS MOTIVE A firm that must make various planned payments in the near future may already have the cash with which to make these payments. In order to earn some return on these funds, the firm invests them in a marketable security that matures or can be easily liquidated on or just before the required payment date. These marketable securities are held for **transactions motives.**

SAFETY MOTIVE Marketable securities held for **safety motives** are used to service the firm's cash account. These securities must be very liquid, since they are bought with funds that will be needed at some unknown future time. Such securities protect the firm against being unable to satisfy unexpected demands for cash.

SPECULATIVE MOTIVE Marketable securities held because the firm currently has no other use for certain funds are said to be held for **speculative motives.** Although this motive is the least common, some firms occasionally have excess cash. Until the firm finds a suitable use for this money, it invests it in marketable securities as well as in long-term instruments.

Characteristics of Marketable Securities

The basic characteristics of marketable securities affect the degree of their salability. To be truly marketable, a security must have two basic characteristics: (1) a ready market and (2) safety of principal (no likelihood of a loss in value).

A READY MARKET The market for a security should have both breadth and depth in order to minimize the amount of time required to convert it into cash. The **breadth of a market** is determined by the number of participants (buyers). A broad market is one that has many participants. The **depth of a market** is determined by its ability to absorb the purchase or sale of a large dollar amount of a particular security. It is therefore possible to have a broad market that has no depth. Thus 100,000 participants each willing to purchase 1 share of a security is less desirable than 1,000 participants each willing to purchase 2,000 shares. Although both breadth and depth are desirable, it is much more important for a market to have depth for a security to be salable.

SAFETY OF PRINCIPAL (NO LIKELIHOOD OF LOSS IN VALUE) There should be little or no loss in the value of a marketable security over time. Consider a security recently purchased for $1,000. If it can be sold quickly for $500, does that make it marketable? No. According to the definition of marketability, the security must not only be salable quickly but must also be salable for close to the $1,000 initially invested. This

transactions motives Reasons for which marketable securities are held to earn a temporary return and then liquidated in order to make various planned payments.

safety motives Reasons for which marketable securities are held to earn returns and liquidated as needed in order to service the firm's cash account.

speculative motives Reasons for which marketable securities are held to earn returns until the firm finds a suitable use for the excess cash.

breadth of a market Determined by the number of participants (buyers).

depth of a market Determined by its ability to absorb the purchase or sale of a large dollar amount of a particular security.

INVESTING IDLE CASH IN BANK DEPOSITS

The recent wave of bank failures has led many companies to take a closer look at how, and where, they invest their idle cash. After all, nobody wants to wake up one morning and find that the corporate treasure is now sunken treasure, lost aboard a ship that turned out to be leaky.

One way to minimize the risks of rate-chasing is to diversity. That is the strategy of A. R. Eberhardt, chief financial officer at NetAir International Corp., a Denver-based national air charter network. Eberhardt keeps eight separate $100,000 accounts in banks and savings institutions located in Texas, Arizona, and California. Every month, Eberhardt takes the interest earned on the accounts and puts it in another institution. That's because the Federal Deposit Insurance Corp. and the Federal Savings & Loan Insurance Corp. protect deposits only up to $100,000 per account, including principal and interest.

Of course, this approach only spreads the risk; it doesn't eliminate it altogether. One of the institutions may still go under, taking with it a portion of your corporate cash. Even if the money is insured, it can take months to collect on your losses.

Investors can guard against this possibility by conducting a thorough check of a bank's or S&L's four most recent quarterly statements. "If you or your comptroller don't understand the fine print and footnotes, call in your accountant to do it," advises John Wolfarth, manager of financial services consulting in Arthur Young & Co.'s Dallas office.

NetAir goes one step further, using an outside adviser to help pick appropriate banks. Meanwhile, Eberhardt himself has developed his own rules of thumb: The institution must be profitable for a full year and carry a 3% ratio of net worth to assets. Robert Heady, publisher of *100 Highest Yields,* a financial newsletter in North Palm Beach, Fla., suggests, in addition, that potential investors speak only to the person in charge of national consumer money-market accounts (or whoever would be in charge of handling your business) and "find out how, why, and with whom the bank is loaning money."

In the end, however, it still comes down to a judgment call. Yes, you may pick up two or three percentage points with a bank account in, say, Slidell, La., or Vernon, Tex. (to cite but two places where banks are currently [December 1985] offering interest rates above the national average). But there are trade-offs. "The function of a treasurer is not only to maximize earnings, but to protect funds," notes Paul Garfinkle, an audit partner at Seidman & Seidman's in New York City. "Is it worth a couple of points in interest to give up an eyeball-to-eyeball relationship with your banker?"

Source: Richard Kreisman, "New Twists in the Interest Rate Game," *INC.*, December 1985, p. 154. Reprinted with permission, INC. magazine, December 1985. Copyright © 1985 by INC. Publishing Company, 38 Commercial Wharf, Boston, MA 02110.

aspect of marketability is referred to as **safety of principal.** Only securities that can be easily converted into cash without experiencing any appreciable reduction in principal are candidates for short-term investment.

safety of principal The ease of salability of a security for close to its initial value.

Making Purchase Decisions

A major decision confronting the business firm is when to purchase marketable securities. This decision is difficult because it involves a trade-off between the opportunity to earn a return on idle funds during the holding period and the brokerage costs associated with the purchase and sale of marketable securities.

EXAMPLE

Assume that a firm must pay $35 in brokerage costs to purchase and sell $4,500 worth of marketable securities yielding an annual return of 8 percent that will be held for one month. Since the securities are to be held for $\frac{1}{12}$ of a year, the firm will earn interest of .67 percent ($\frac{1}{12} \times 8\%$) or $30 (.0067 $\times$ $4,500). Since this is less than the $35 cost of the transaction, the firm should not make the investment. This trade-off between interest returns and brokerage costs is a key factor in determining when and whether to purchase marketable securities. ■

THE POPULAR MARKETABLE SECURITIES

The securities most commonly held as part of the firm's marketable securities portfolio are divided into two groups: (1) government issues and (2) nongovernment issues. Table 8.1 presents the February 28, 1986, yields for the marketable securities described in the sections that follow.

Government Issues

The short-term obligations issued by the federal government and available as marketable security investments are Treasury bills, Treasury notes, and federal agency issues.

TREASURY BILLS **Treasury bills** are obligations of the U.S. Treasury that are issued weekly on an auction basis. The most common maturities are 91 and 182 days, although bills with one-year maturities are occasionally sold. Treasury bills are sold by competitive bidding. Be-

Treasury bills U.S. Treasury obligations issued weekly on an auction basis, having varying maturities, generally under a year, and virtually no risk.

SHORT-TERM FINANCIAL DECISIONS

TABLE 8.1 Yields on Popular Marketable Securities for the Week Ending February 28, 1986

Security	Maturity period	Yield
Banker's acceptances	3 months	7.50%
Certificates of deposit	3 months	7.62
Commercial paper	3 months	7.59
Eurodollar deposits	3 months	7.86
Federal agency issues[a]	3 months	7.29
Money market mutual funds[b]	approx. 30 days	7.23
Treasury bills	3 months	7.04
Treasury notes	1 year	7.52

[a] A Federal Home Loan Bank (FHLB) issue maturing in June 1986 is used here in the absence of any average-yield data.

[b] A Paine Webber Cash Fund with an average maturity of 29 days is used here in the absence of any average-yield data.

SOURCE: All data, except for that of federal agency issues and money market mutual funds, were obtained from *Federal Reserve Bulletin*, May 1986 (Washington, D.C.: Board of Governors of the Federal Reserve System, 1986), p. A24. Data for federal agency issues and money market mutual funds were obtained from *The Wall Street Journal*, March 6, 1986, pp. 25, 29.

cause they are issued in bearer form, there is a strong *secondary (resale) market*. The bills are sold at a discount from their face value, the face value being received at maturity. The smallest denomination of a Treasury bill currently available is $10,000. Since Treasury bills are issues of the United States government, they are considered to be virtually risk-free. For this reason, and because of the strong secondary market for them, Treasury bills are one of the most popular marketable securities. The yields on Treasury bills are generally lower than those on any other marketable securities due to their virtually risk-free nature.

Treasury notes U.S. Treasury obligations with initial maturities of between one and seven years, paying interest at a stated rate semiannually, and having virtually no risk.

TREASURY NOTES **Treasury notes** have initial maturities of between one and seven years, but due to the existence of a strong secondary market, they are quite attractive marketable security investments. They are generally issued in minimum denominations of $5,000, carry a stated interest rate, and pay interest semiannually. A firm that purchases a Treasury note that has less than one year left to maturity is in the same position as if it had purchased a marketable security with an initial maturity of less than one year. Due to their virtually risk-free nature, Treasury notes generally have a relatively low yield.

federal agency issues Low-risk securities not guaranteed by the U.S. Treasury but issued by government agencies, having generally short maturities and offering slightly higher yields than comparable Treasury issues.

FEDERAL AGENCY ISSUES Certain agencies of the federal government issue their own debt. These **federal agency issues** are not part of the public debt, are not a legal obligation of the U.S. Treasury, and are not guaranteed by the U.S. Treasury. Regardless of their lack of direct government backing, the issues of government agencies are readily accepted as low-risk securities, since most purchasers feel they are implicitly guaranteed by the federal government. Agency issues generally have minimum denominations of $5,000 and are issued either with a stated interest rate or at a discount. Agencies commonly issuing short-term instruments include the Bank for Cooperatives (BC), the Federal Home Loan Banks (FHLB), the Federal Intermediate Credit Banks (FICB), the Federal Land Banks (FLB), and the Federal National Mortgage Association (FNMA). Most agency issues have short maturities and offer slightly higher yields than Treasury issues having similar maturities. Agency issues have a strong secondary market, which is most easily reached through government security dealers.

Nongovernment Issues

A number of additional marketable securities are issued by banks or businesses. These nongovernment issues typically have slightly higher yields than government issues due to the slightly higher risks associated with them. The principal nongovernment marketable securities are negotiable certificates of deposit, commercial paper, banker's acceptances, Eurodollar deposits, money market mutual funds, and repurchase agreements.

NEGOTIABLE CERTIFICATES OF DEPOSIT (CDs) **Negotiable certificates of deposit (CDs)** are negotiable instruments evidencing the deposit of a certain number of dollars in a commercial bank. The amounts and maturities are normally tailored to the investor's needs. Average maturities of 30 days are quite common. A good secondary market for CDs exists. Normally the smallest denomination for a negotiable CD is $100,000. The yields on CDs are initially set on the basis of size, maturity, and prevailing money market conditions. They are typically above those on Treasury bills and slightly above the yield on commercial paper.

negotiable certificates of deposit (CDs)
Negotiable instruments representing specific cash deposits in commercial banks, having varying maturities and yields based on size, maturity, and prevailing money market conditions.

COMMERCIAL PAPER **Commercial paper** is a short-term, unsecured promissory note issued by a corporation with a very high credit standing.[2] These notes are issued, generally in multiples of $100,000, by all types of firms and have initial maturities of anywhere from 3 to 270 days.

commercial paper
A short-term, unsecured promissory note issued by a corporation with a very high credit standing, having a yield slightly below that of negotiable CDs but above that of comparable government issues.

---

[2] Discussion of commercial paper from the point of view of the issuer is deferred until Chapter 10, which is devoted to the various sources of short-term financing available to business.

They can be sold directly by the issuer or through dealers. The yield on commercial paper typically is slightly below that available on negotiable CDs but above that paid on government issues with similar maturities.

banker's acceptances
Short-term, low-risk marketable securities arising from bank guarantees of business transactions; they are sold by banks at a discount from their maturity value and provide yields competitive with negotiable CDs and commercial paper.

BANKER'S ACCEPTANCES **Banker's acceptances** arise from a short-term credit arrangement used by businesses to finance transactions, especially those involving firms in foreign countries or firms with unknown credit capacities. The purchaser, to assure payment to the seller, requests its bank to issue a *letter of credit* on its behalf, authorizing the seller to draw a *time draft*—an order to pay a specified amount at a specified time—on the bank in payment for the goods. Once the goods are shipped, the seller presents a time draft along with proof of shipment to its bank. The seller's bank then forwards the draft with appropriate shipping documents to the buyer's bank for acceptance and receives payment for the transaction. The buyer's bank may either hold the acceptance to maturity or sell it at a discount in the money market. If sold, the size of the discount from the acceptance's maturity value and the amount of time until the acceptance is paid determine the purchaser's yield.

As a result of its sale, the banker's acceptance becomes a marketable security that can be traded in the marketplace. The initial maturities of banker's acceptances are typically between 30 and 180 days, 90 days being most common. A banker's acceptance is a low-risk security because at least two, and sometimes three, parties may be liable for its payment at maturity. The yields on banker's acceptances are similar to those on negotiable CDs and commercial paper.

Eurodollar deposits
Deposits denominated in U.S. dollars and deposited in banks outside the United States, having varying maturities, and having yields above nearly all other marketable securities.

EURODOLLAR DEPOSITS **Eurodollar deposits** are deposits denominated in U.S. dollars and deposited in banks located outside the United States. The nationality of the bank makes no difference. It might be a foreign bank or the foreign branch of an American bank. The deposit is always a time deposit or negotiable CDs in large denominations, typically in units of $1 million. London is the center of the Eurodollar market. Other important centers are Paris, Frankfurt, Zürich, Nassau (Bahamas), Singapore, and Hong Kong. The maturities of Eurodollar deposits range from overnight to several years, with most of the money held in the one-week to six-month maturity range. Because of the added foreign exchange risks, Eurodollar deposits tend to provide yields above nearly all other marketable securities, government or nongovernment. An active secondary market allows Eurodollar deposits to be used to meet both transactions and safety motives.

money market mutual funds Portfolios (groups) of various popular marketable securities, having instant liquidity, competitive yields, and low transactions costs.

MONEY MARKET MUTUAL FUNDS **Money market mutual funds,** often called "money funds," are portfolios of marketable securities such as those described earlier. Shares or interests in these funds can be easily acquired — often without paying any brokerage commissions. A minimum initial investment of as low as $500, but generally $1,000 or more, is required. Money funds provide instant liquidity in much the same fashion as a checking or savings account. In exchange for investing in these funds, investors earn returns that — especially during periods of high interest rates — are higher than those obtainable from most other marketable securities. Due to the high liquidity, competitive yields, and often low transactions costs, these funds have achieved significant growth in size and popularity in recent years.

REPURCHASE AGREEMENTS A **repurchase agreement** is not a specific security. It is an arrangement whereby a bank or security dealer sells specific marketable securities to a firm and agrees to repurchase the securities at a specific price at a specified point in time. In exchange for the tailor-made maturity date provided by this arrangement, the bank or security dealer provides the purchaser with a return slightly below that obtainable through outright purchase of similar marketable securities. The benefit to the purchaser is the guaranteed repurchase, and the tailor-made maturity date ensures that the purchaser will have cash at a specified point in time. The actual securities involved may be government or nongovernment issues. Repurchase agreements are ideal for marketable securities investments made to satisfy the transactions motive.

repurchase agreement
An agreement whereby a bank or security dealer sells a firm specific securities and agrees to repurchase them at a specific price and time.

SUMMARY

- Cash and marketable securities act as a pool of liquid assets, providing the firm with funds for paying bills as they come due and for meeting any unexpected outlays.
- The efficient management of cash is based on three basic strategies: (1) paying accounts payable as late as possible; (2) managing the inventory-production cycle efficiently; and (3) collecting accounts receivable as quickly as possible.
- Although the cash budget is useful for cash planning, decisions on the appropriate cash balance for the firm depend on the magnitude of both expected and unexpected cash receipts and cash disbursements.
- Financial managers can use a variety of techniques to manipulate certain imperfections in the collection and payment system to take advantage of float in order to minimize the firm's cash requirements.
- Popular collection techniques include concentration banking, lockboxes, direct sends, preauthorized checks (PACs), depository transfer checks (DTCs), and wire transfers.
- Disbursement techniques include controlled disbursing, playing the float, overdraft systems, and zero-balance accounts.

● Marketable securities allow the firm to earn a return on temporarily idle funds. They are held for three primary reasons: the transactions motive, the safety motive, and the speculative motive.

● For a security to be considered marketable, it must have a ready market that has both breadth and depth. Furthermore, the risks associated with the safety of the principal must be quite low.

● The decision to purchase marketable securities depends on the trade-off between the return earned during the holding period and the brokerage costs associated with purchasing and selling the securities.

● The most popular marketable securities are government and nongovernment issues. Government issues include Treasury bills, Treasury notes, and federal agency issues.

● The most common nongovernment issues are negotiable certificates of deposit, commercial paper, banker's acceptances, Eurodollar deposits, money market mutual funds, and repurchase agreements.

QUESTIONS

8-1 What is the objective of the financial manager in cash management? What conditions must be satisfied in meeting this objective?

8-2 What are the *key strategies* with respect to accounts payable, inventory, and accounts receivable for the firm that wants to manage its cash efficiently?

8-3 What is a firm's "cash cycle"? How are the cash cycle and cash turnover of a firm related? What should a firm's objective with respect to cash cycle and cash turnover be?

8-4 If a firm reduces the average age of its inventories, what effect might this action have on the cash cycle? On the firm's total sales? Is there a trade-off between average inventory and sales? Give reasons for your answer.

8-5 Define *float* and describe its three basic components. Compare and contrast collection and disbursement float and cite the financial manager's goal with respect to each of these types of float.

8-6 Briefly describe the key features of each of the following collection techniques.
  a Concentration banking   **d** Preauthorized checks (PACs)
  b Lockboxes   **e** Depository transfer checks (DTCs)
  c Direct sends   **f** Wire transfers

8-7 Briefly describe the key features of each of the following disbursement techniques.
  a Controlled disbursing   **c** Overdraft systems
  b Playing the float   **d** Zero-balance accounts

8-8 What are the possible motives for holding marketable securities? What two characteristics are essential for a security to be deemed "marketable"?

8-9 For each of the following government-based marketable securities, give a brief description emphasizing maturity, liquidity, risk, and return.

    a Treasury bill
    b Treasury note
    c Federal agency issue

8-10 Describe the basic features—including maturity, liquidity, risk, and return—of each of the following nongovernment marketable securities.
    a Negotiable certificate of deposit (CD)   **c** Banker's acceptance
    b Commercial paper   **d** Eurodollar deposit

8-11 Briefly describe the basic features of the following marketable securities and explain how they both involve other marketable securities.
    a Money market mutual funds
    b Repurchase agreements

PROBLEMS

8-1   **(Cash Cycle and Minimum Operating Cash)** Basic Supply is concerned about managing cash in an efficient manner. On the average, accounts receivable are collected in 60 days, and inventories have an average age of 90 days. Accounts payable are paid approximately 30 days after they arise. The firm spends $30 million each year, at a constant rate. Assuming a 360-day year,
    a Calculate the firm's cash cycle.
    b Calculate the firm's cash turnover.
    c Calculate the minimum operating cash balance the firm must maintain to meet its obligations.

8-2   **(Cash Cycle and Minimum Operating Cash)** The Melton Company has an inventory turnover of 12, an average collection period of 45 days, and an average payment period of 40 days. The firm spends $1 million per year. Assuming a 360-day year,
    a Calculate the firm's cash cycle.
    b Calculate the firm's cash turnover.
    c Calculate the minimum operating cash balance the firm must maintain to meet its obligations.

8-3   **(Comparison of Cash Cycles)** A firm collects accounts receivable, on the average, after 75 days. Inventory has an average age of 105 days, and accounts payable are paid an average of 60 days after they arise. Assuming a 360-day year, what changes will occur in the cash cycle and cash turnover with each of the following circumstances?
    a The average collection period changes to 60 days.
    b The average age of inventory changes to 90 days.
    c The average payment period changes to 105 days.
    d The circumstances in **a**, **b**, and **c** occur simultaneously.

8-4   **(Changes in Cash Cycles)** A firm is considering several plans that affect working capital accounts. Given the five plans and their probable results in the table at the top of next page, which one would you favor? Explain.

| | | CHANGE | |
Plan	Average age of inventory	Average collection period	Average payment period
A	+30 days	+20 days	+5 days
B	+20 days	−10 days	+15 days
C	−10 days	0 days	−5 days
D	−15 days	+15 days	+10 days
E	+5 days	−10 days	+15 days

8-5 **(Annual Savings and the Cash Cycle)** The Hurkin Manufacturing Company pays accounts payable on the tenth day after purchase. The average collection period is 30 days, and the average age of inventory is 40 days. Annual cash outlays are approximately $18 million. The firm is considering a plan that would stretch its accounts payable by 20 days. If the firm can earn 12 percent on equal-risk investments, what annual savings can it realize by this plan? Assume no discount for early payment of trade credit and a 360-day year.

8-6 **(Changing Cash Cycle)** Barnstead Industries turns its inventory eight times each year, has an average payment period of 35 days, and has an average collection period of 60 days. The firm's total annual outlays are $3.5 million.

a Calculate the firm's minimum operating cash, assuming a 360-day year.

b Assuming that the firm can earn 14 percent on its short-term investments, how much would the firm earn annually if it could *favorably change* its current cash cycle by 20 days?

8-7 **(Multiple Changes in Cash Cycle)** Hubbard Corporation turns its inventory six times each year, has an average payment period of 30 days, and has an average collection period of 45 days. The firm's total annual outlays are $3 million.

a Calculate the firm's minimum operating cash, assuming a 360-day year.

b Find the firm's minimum operating cash in the event that it makes the following changes simultaneously.

(1) Extends average payment period by 10 days.

(2) Shortens the average age of inventory by five days.

(3) Speeds the collection of accounts receivable by an average of 10 days.

c If the firm can earn 13 percent on its short-term investments, how much, if anything, could it earn annually as a result of the changes in **b**?

d If the annual cost of achieving the savings in **c** is $35,000, what action would you recommend to the firm? Why?

8-8 **(Float)** Breeland Industries has daily cash recipts of $65,000. A recent analysis of its collections indicated that customers' payments were in the mail an average of 2½ days. Once received the firm spends 1½ days processing payments, and once deposited, it takes an average of three days for these receipts to clear the banking system.

a How much collection float (in days) does the firm currently have?

b If the firm's opportunity cost is 11 percent, would it be economically advisable for the firm to pay an annual fee of $16,500 in order to reduce collection float by three days? Explain why or why not.

8-9 **(Concentration Banking)** Tal-Off Corporation sells to a national market and bills all credit customers from the New York City office. Using a continuous billing system, the firm has collections of $1.2 million per day. Under consideration is a concentration banking system that would require customers to mail payments to the nearest regional office to be deposited in local banks.

Tal-Off estimates that the collection period for accounts will be shortened an average of $2\frac{1}{2}$ days under this system. The firm also estimates that *annual* service charges and administrative costs of $300,000 will result from the proposed system. The firm can earn 14 percent on equal-risk investments.

a How much cash will be made available for other uses if the firm accepts the proposed concentration banking system?

b What savings will the firm realize on the $2\frac{1}{2}$-day reduction in the collection period?

c Would you recommend the change? Explain your answer.

8-10 **(Lockbox System)** A firm that has an opportunity cost of 9 percent is contemplating installation of a lockbox system at an annual cost of $90,000. The system is expected to reduce mailing time by $2\frac{1}{2}$ days and reduce check clearing time by $1\frac{1}{2}$ days. If the firm collects $300,000 per day, would you recommend the system? Explain.

8-11 **(Lockbox System)** Orient Oil feels a lockbox system can shorten its accounts receivable collection period by three days. Credit sales are $3,240,000 per year, billed on a continuous basis. The firm has other equally risky investments with a return of 15 percent. The cost of the lockbox system is $9,000 per year.

a What amount of cash will be made available for other uses under the lockbox system?

b What net benefit (cost) will the firm receive if it adopts the lockbox system?

8-12 **(Direct Send—Single)** Lorca Industries of San Diego, California, just received a check in the amount of $800,000 from a customer in Bangor, Maine. If the firm processes the check in the normal manner, the funds will become available in six days. To speed up this process, the firm could send an employee to the bank in Bangor on which the check is drawn to present it for payment. Such action will cause the funds to become available after two days. If the cost of the direct send is $650 and the firm can earn 11 percent on these funds, what recommendation would you give them? Explain.

8-13 **(Direct Sends—Multiple)** Ricor Enterprises just received four sizable checks drawn on various distant banks throughout the United States. The data on these checks is summarized in the table on page 230. The firm, which has a 12 percent opportunity cost, can lease a small business jet with pilot to fly the checks to the cities of the banks on which they are drawn and present them for immediate payment. This task can be accomplished in a single day—thereby reducing to one day the funds availability from each of the four checks. The total cost of leasing the jet with pilot and other incidental expenditures is $4,500. Analyze the proposal and make a recommendation as to the proposed action.

Check	Amount	Number of days until funds are available
1	$ 600,000	7 days
2	2,000,000	5 days
3	1,300,000	4 days
4	400,000	6 days

8-14 **(Controlled Disbursing)** A large Midwestern firm has annual cash disbursements of $360 million made continuously over the year. Although annual service and administrative costs would increase by $100,000, the firm is considering writing all disbursement checks on a small bank in Alabama. The firm estimates this will allow an additional $1\frac{1}{2}$ days of cash usage. If the firm earns a return on other equally risky investments of 12 percent, should it change to the distant bank? Why, or why not?

8-15 **(Playing the Float)** Tollfree Enterprises routinely funds its checking account to cover all checks when written. A thorough analysis of its checking account discloses that the firm could maintain an average account balance 25 percent below the current level and adequately cover all checks presented. The average account balance is currently $900,000. If the firm can earn 10 percent on short-term investments, what, if any, annual savings would result from maintaining the lower average account balance?

8-16 **(Payroll Account Management)** Clearview Window has a weekly payroll of $250,000. The payroll checks are issued on Friday afternoon each week. In examining the check-cashing behavior of its employees, it has found the following pattern:

Number of business days[a] since issue of check	Percentage of checks cleared
1	20
2	40
3	30
4	10

[a] Excludes Saturday and Sunday.

Given this information, what recommendation would you give the firm with respect to managing its payroll account? Explain.

8-17 **(Zero-Balance Account)** Danzig Industries is considering establishment of a zero-balance account. The firm currently maintains an average

In order to keep current customers and attract new ones, most manufacturing concerns must extend credit and maintain inventories. *Accounts receivable* represents the extension of credit by the firm to its customers. *Inventory,* or goods on hand, is a necessary current asset that permits the production-sale process to operate with a minimum of disturbances. Accounts receivable and inventory are the dominant current assets held by most firms. For the average manufacturer, together they account for over 80 percent of *current assets* and just over 33 percent of *total assets.* The firm's financial manager generally has direct control over accounts receivable, and must act as a "watchdog" and adviser in matters concerning inventory, which is generally under the direct control of the firm's manufacturing department.

CREDIT POLICY

A firm's **credit policy** provides guidelines for determining whether to extend credit to a customer, and how much credit to extend. The firm must establish *credit standards* to use in making these decisions. Appropriate *sources of credit information* and *methods of credit analysis* must be developed. Each of these aspects of credit policy is important to the successful management of accounts receivable. A brief look at credit scoring will help place credit policy in proper perspective.

> **credit policy** A set of guidelines used to determine whether to extend credit and how much credit to extend.

Credit Scoring

Consumer credit decisions, because they involve a large group of similar applicants, each representing a small part of the firm's total business, can be handled using impersonal, computer-based credit decision techniques. One popular technique is **credit scoring**—a procedure resulting in a score reflecting an applicant's overall credit strength, derived as a weighted average of the scores obtained on a variety of key financial and credit characteristics. Credit scoring is often used by large credit card operations such as oil companies and department stores. This technique can best be illustrated by an example.

> **credit scoring** The ranking of an applicant's overall credit strength, derived as a weighted average of scores on key financial and credit characteristics.

EXAMPLE

Paula's Petroleum Company uses a credit scoring model to make its consumer credit decisions. Each credit applicant fills out and submits a credit application to the company. The application is reviewed and scored by one of the company's credit analysts and then entered into the computer; the rest of the process, including making the credit decision, generating a letter of acceptance or

TABLE 9.1 Credit Scoring of Herb Consumer by Paula's Petroleum Company

Financial and credit characteristics	Score (0 to 100) (1)	Predetermined weight (2)	Weighted score [(1) × (2)] (3)
Credit references	80	.15	12.00
Home ownership	100	.15	15.00
Income range	70	.25	17.50
Payment history	75	.25	18.75
Years at address	90	.10	9.00
Years on job	80	.10	8.00
Total		1.00	Credit score	80.25

KEY: Column 1: Scores assigned by analyst and computer using company guidelines on the basis of data presented in credit application. Scores range from 0 (lowest) to 100 (highest). Column 2: Weights based on the company's analysis of the relative importance of each financial and credit characteristic in predicting whether or not a customer will pay an account. These weights must sum to 1.00.

rejection to the applicant, and dispatching the preparation and mailing of a credit card, is automated.

Table 9.1 demonstrates the calculation of Herb Consumer's credit score. The firm's predetermined credit standards are summarized in Table 9.2. The cutoff credit scores were developed to accept the group of credit applicants that will result in a positive contribution to the firm's share value. In evaluating Herb Consumer's credit score of 80.25 in light of the firm's credit standards, the decision would be to *extend standard credit terms* to him (80.25 > 75). ■

The attractiveness of credit scoring should be clear from the above example. Unfortunately, most manufacturers sell to a diversified group of different-sized businesses, not individuals. The statistical characteristics necessary for applying credit scoring to decisions regarding *mercantile credit*—credit extended by business firms to other business firms—rarely exist. In the following discussion we concentrate on the basic concepts of mercantile credit decisions, which cannot easily be expressed in quantifiable terms.

TABLE 9.2 Credit Standards for Paula's Petroleum Company

Credit score	Action
Greater than 75	Extend standard credit terms.
65 to 75	Extend limited credit; if account is properly maintained, convert to standard credit terms after one year.
Less than 65	Reject application.

Credit Standards

The firm's **credit standards** are the minimum criteria for the extension of credit to a customer. Our concern here is with the restrictiveness or nonrestrictiveness of a firm's overall policy. Understanding the key variables that must be considered when a firm is contemplating relaxing or tightening its credit standards will give a general idea of the kinds of decisions involved.

credit standards The minimum criteria for the extension of credit to a customer.

KEY VARIABLES The major variables that should be considered in evaluating proposed changes in credit standards are (1) sales volume, (2) the investment in accounts receivable, and (3) bad debt expenses. Let us examine each in more detail.

Sales Volume. Changing credit standards can be expected to change the volume of sales. If credit standards are relaxed, sales are expected to increase; if credit standards are tightened, sales are expected to decrease. Generally, increases in sales affect profits positively, while decreases in sales affect profits negatively.

Investment in Accounts Receivable. Carrying, or maintaining, accounts receivable involves a cost to the firm. This cost is attributable to the forgone earnings opportunities resulting from the necessity to tie up funds in accounts receivable. Therefore, the higher the firm's investment in accounts receivable, the greater the carrying cost, and vice versa. If the firm relaxes its credit standards, the volume of accounts receivable increases and so does the firm's carrying cost (investment). This results from increased sales and longer collection periods due to slower payment on average by credit customers. The opposite occurs if credit standards are tightened. Thus a relaxation of credit standards is expected to affect profits negatively due to higher carrying costs, whereas tightening credit standards would affect profits positively as a result of lower carrying costs.

Bad Debt Expenses. The probability, or risk, of acquiring a bad debt increases as credit standards are relaxed. The increase in bad debts associated with relaxation of credit standards raises bad debt expenses and impacts profits negatively. The opposite effects on bad debt expenses and profits result from a tightening of credit standards.

The basic changes and effects on profits expected to result from the *relaxation* of credit standards are tabulated as follows:

Variable	Direction of change	Effect on profits
Sales volume	Increase	Positive
Investment in accounts receivable	Increase	Negative
Bad debt expenses	Increase	Negative

If credit standards were tightened, the opposite effects would be expected.

DETERMINING VALUES OF KEY VARIABLES The way in which the key credit standard variables are determined can be illustrated by the following example.

EXAMPLE

The Binz Company is currently selling a product for $10 per unit. Sales (all on credit) for last year were 60,000 units. The variable cost per unit is $6, and the average cost per unit, given a sales volume of 60,000 units, is $8. The difference of $2 between the average cost per unit and the variable cost per unit represents the contribution of each of the 60,000 units toward the firm's fixed costs. Working backward, since each of the 60,000 units sold contributes $2 to fixed costs, the firm's total fixed costs must be $120,000.

The firm is currently contemplating a *relaxation of credit standards* that is expected to result in a 5 percent increase in unit sales to 63,000 units, an increase in the average collection period from its current level of 30 days to 45 days, and an increase in bad debt expenses from the current level of 1 percent of sales to 2 percent. The firm's required return on equal-risk investments, which is the opportunity cost of tying funds up in accounts receivable, is 15 percent.

To determine whether the Binz Company should implement the proposed relaxation in credit standards, the effect on the firm's additional profit contribution from sales, the cost of the marginal investment in accounts receivable, and the cost of marginal bad debts must be calculated.

Additional profit contribution from sales The additional profit contribution from sales expected to result from the relaxation of credit standards can be calculated easily. Because fixed costs are "sunk" and thereby unaffected by a change in the sales level, the only cost relevant to a change in sales would be out-of-pocket or variable costs. Sales are expected to increase by 5 percent, or 3,000 units. The profit contribution per unit will equal the difference between the sale price per unit ($10) and the variable cost per unit ($6). The profit contribution per unit would therefore be $4. Thus the total additional profit contribution from sales will be $12,000 (3,000 units $\times$ $4 per unit).

Cost of the marginal investment in accounts receivable The cost of the marginal investment in accounts receivable can be calculated by finding the difference between the cost of carrying receivables before and after the introduction of the relaxed credit standards. The average investment in accounts receivable can be calculated using the following formula:

Average investment in accounts receivable

$$= \frac{\text{cost of annual sales}}{\text{turnover of accounts receivable}} \quad (9.1)$$

where

$$\text{Turnover of accounts receivable}^1 = \frac{360}{\text{average collection period}}$$

The cost of annual sales under the proposed and present plans can be found as noted below.

Cost of annual sales:

Under proposed plan: ($8)(60,000 units) + ($6)(3,000 units)
$480,000 + $18,000 = $498,000
Under present plan: ($8)(60,000 units) = $480,000

The calculation of the sales cost for the present plan involves the straightforward use of the average cost per unit of $8. The cost under the proposed plan is found by adding to the total cost of producing 60,000 units the marginal cost of producing an additional 3,000 units at $6 per unit. It can be seen that with implementation of the proposed plan, the cost of annual sales will increase from $480,000 to $498,000.

The turnover of accounts receivable refers to the number of times each year the firm's accounts receivable are actually turned into cash. In each case it is found by dividing the average collection period into 360—the number of days in a year.

Turnover of accounts receivable:

$$\text{Under proposed plan: } \frac{360}{45} = 8$$

$$\text{Under present plan: } \frac{360}{30} = 12$$

It can be seen that with implementation of the proposed plan, the accounts receivable turnover would drop from 12 to 8.

Substituting the cost and turnover data just calculated into Equation 9.1 for each case, the following average investments in accounts receivable result:

---

[1] The turnover of accounts receivable can also be calculated by *dividing annual sales by accounts receivable*. For the purposes of this chapter, only the formula transforming the average collection period to a turnover of accounts receivable is emphasized.

Average investment in accounts receivable:

$$\text{Under proposed plan: } \frac{\$498,000}{8} = \$62,250$$

$$\text{Under present plan: } \frac{\$480,000}{12} = \$40,000$$

The marginal investment in accounts receivable as well as its cost are calculated as follows:

Cost of marginal investment in accounts receivable:

Average investment under proposed plan	$62,250
− Average investment under present plan	40,000
Marginal investment in accounts receivable	$22,250
× Required return on investment	.15
Cost of marginal investment in A/R[2]	$ 3,338

It should be clear that the cost of investing an additional $22,250 in accounts receivable was found by multiplying it by 15 percent (the firm's required return on investment). The resulting value of $3,338 is considered a cost because it represents the maximum amount that could have been earned on the $22,250 had it been placed in the best equal-risk investment alternative available.

Cost of marginal bad debts The cost of marginal bad debts is found by taking the difference between the level of bad debts before and after the relaxation of credit standards, as shown here.

Cost of marginal bad debts:

Under proposed plan: (.02)($10/unit)(63,000 units) =	$12,600
Under present plan: (.01)($10/unit)(60,000 units) =	6,000
Cost of marginal bad debts	$ 6,600

Thus the resulting cost of marginal bad debts is $6,600. ■

MAKING THE CREDIT STANDARD DECISION To decide whether the firm should relax its credit standards, the additional profit contribution from sales must be compared to the sum of the cost of the marginal investment in accounts receivable and the cost of marginal bad debts. If the additional profit contribution is greater than marginal costs, credit standards should be relaxed; otherwise, current standards should remain unchanged. Let us look at an example.

---

[2] Throughout the text, *A/R* will frequently be used interchangeably with *accounts receivable*.

ACCOUNTS RECEIVABLE AND INVENTORY MANAGEMENT: IMPORTANT WORKING CAPITAL ACTIVITIES

A recent survey yielding 238 responses from chief financial officers of the respondent firms in the *Fortune* 1000 listing provides some interesting insights into the relative importance of various working capital activities. As can be seen in the table below, based on the responses, accounts receivable management is the most time consuming activity. Together accounts receivable and inventory management account for 30 percent of working capital time. While "time spent" and "importance" may not necessarily coincide, these data tend to suggest that accounts receivable and inventory management are very important working capital activities.

Time Spent on Individual Working Capital Activities

Working capital activity	Percent of working capital time
Accounts receivable management	16%
Cash management	15
Short-term financial planning and budgeting	15
Inventory management	14
Banking relationships	11
Accounts payable management	10
Short-term investment management	10
Short-term borrowing	9
Total	100%

Source: Lawrence J. Gitman and Charles E. Maxwell, "Financial Activities of Major U.S. Firms: Survey and Analysis of *Fortune's* 1000," *Financial Management*, Winter 1985, pp. 57–65.

EXAMPLE

The results and key calculations relative to the Binz Company's decision to relax its credit standards are summarized in Table 9.3. It can be seen that since the additional profit contribution from the increased sales would be $12,000, which exceeds the sum of the cost of the marginal investment in accounts receivable and the cost of marginal bad debts, the firm *should* relax its credit standards as proposed. The net addition to total profits resulting from such an action will be $2,062 per year. ∎

TABLE 9.3 The Effects of a Relaxation of Credit Standards on the Binz Company

Additional profit contribution from sales [(3,000 units)($10 − $6)]		$12,000
Cost of marginal investment in A/R[a]		
Average investment under proposed plan:		
$$\frac{(\$8)(60,000) + (\$6)(3,000)}{8} = \frac{\$498,000}{8}$$	$62,250	
Average investment under present plan:		
$$\frac{(\$8)(60,000)}{12} = \frac{\$480,000}{12}$$	40,000	
Marginal investment in A/R	$22,250	
Cost of marginal investment in A/R [(.15)($22,250)]		($3,338)
Cost of marginal bad debts		
Bad debts under proposed plan [(.02)($10)(63,000)]	$12,600	
Bad debts under present plan [(.01)($10)(60,000)]	6,000	
Cost of marginal bad debts		($6,600)
Net profit from implementation of proposed plan		$2,062

[a] The denominators 8 and 12 in the calculation of the average investment in accounts receivable under the proposed and present plans are the accounts receivable turnovers for each of these plans (360/45 = 8 and 360/30 = 12).

The technique described here for making a credit standard decision is commonly used for evaluating other types of changes in the management of accounts receivable as well. If the firm in the preceding example had been contemplating more restrictive credit standards, the cost would have been a reduction in the profit contribution from sales, and the return would have been reductions in the cost of the marginal investment in accounts receivable and in bad debts. Another application of this analytical technique is described later in the chapter.

Credit Analysis

credit analysis The evaluation of a credit applicant to estimate creditworthiness and the maximum amount of credit to extend.

Once the firm has established its credit standards, it must develop procedures for **credit analysis**—the evaluation of credit applicants. Often the firm must not only determine the creditworthiness of a customer but it must also estimate the maximum amount of credit the customer is capable of supporting. Once this is done, the firm can establish a **line of credit**, the maximum amount the customer can owe the firm at any time. Lines of credit are established to eliminate the necessity of checking a major customer's credit each time a purchase is made.

line of credit The maximum amount a customer can owe the firm at any time.

OBTAINING CREDIT INFORMATION When a business is approached by a customer desiring credit terms, the credit department typically begins the evaluation process by requiring the applicant to fill out various forms requesting financial and credit information and references.

Working from the application, the firm obtains additional information from other sources. If the firm has previously extended credit to the applicant, it will have its own information on the applicant's payment history. The major external sources of credit information are as follows:

Financial Statements. By requiring the credit applicant to provide financial statements for the past few years, the firm can analyze the applicant firm's liquidity, activity, debt, and profitability positions.

Dun & Bradstreet, Inc. **Dun & Bradstreet** is the largest mercantile credit-reporting agency in the U.S. It provides subscribers with a copy of a reference book containing credit ratings and keyed estimates of overall financial strength for approximately 3 million U.S. and Canadian firms. The key to the D & B ratings is shown in Figure 9.1. For example, a firm rated 2A3 would have estimated financial strength (net worth) in the range of $750,000 to $999,999 and would have a FAIR credit rating. For an additional charge subscribers can obtain detailed reports on specific companies.

Dun & Bradstreet The largest mercantile credit-reporting agency in the U.S.

Credit Interchange Bureaus. Firms can obtain credit information through the National Credit Interchange System, a national network of

Key to Ratings						
Estimated Financial Strength			**Composite Credit Appraisal**			
			High	Good	Fair	Limited
5A	$50,000,000	and over	1	2	3	4
4A	$10,000,000 to	49,999,999	1	2	3	4
3A	1,000,000 to	9,999,999	1	2	3	4
2A	750,000 to	999,999	1	2	3	4
1A	500,000 to	749,999	1	2	3	4
BA	300,000 to	499,999	1	2	3	4
BB	200,000 to	299,999	1	2	3	4
CB	125,000 to	199,999	1	2	3	4
CC	75,000 to	124,999	1	2	3	4
DC	50,000 to	74,999	1	2	3	4
DD	35,000 to	49,999	1	2	3	4
EE	20,000 to	34,999	1	2	3	4
FF	10,000 to	19,999	1	2	3	4
GG	5,000 to	9,999	1	2	3	4
HH	Up to	4,999	1	2	3	4

**Dun & Bradstreet
Credit Services**

DB a company of
The Dun & Bradstreet Corporation

FIGURE 9.1 The Key to Dun & Bradstreet's Ratings
The rating key used in the *Dun and Bradstreet Reference Book* indicates both the estimated financial strength and a composite credit appraisal for each rated firm. A rating of 2A3 would indicate an estimated financial strength between $750,000 and $999,999 and a "Fair" credit appraisal.

local credit bureaus that exchange information on a reciprocal basis. The reports obtained through these exchanges contain factual data rather than analyses. A fee is usually levied for each inquiry.

Direct Credit Information Exchanges. Another means of obtaining credit information is through local, regional, or national credit associations. Often, an industry association maintains certain credit information that is available to members. Another method is to contact other suppliers selling to the applicant and ask what its payment patterns are like.

Bank Checking. It may be possible for the firm's bank to obtain credit information from the applicant's bank. However, the type of information obtained will most likely be vague, unless the applicant aids the firm in obtaining it. Typically an estimate of the firm's cash balance is provided. For instance, it may be found that a firm maintains a "high five-figure" balance.

ANALYZING CREDIT INFORMATION   A credit applicant's financial statements and accounts payable ledger can be used to calculate its "average payment period." This value can then be compared to the credit terms currently extended the firm. For customers requesting large amounts of credit or lines of credit, a thorough ratio analysis of the firm's liquidity, activity, debt, and profitability should be performed using the relevant financial statements. A time-series comparison (discussed in Chapter 4) of similar ratios for various years should uncover any developing trends. The *Dun & Bradstreet Reference Book* can be used for estimating the maximum line of credit to extend. Dun & Bradstreet itself suggests 10 percent of a customer's "estimated financial strength" (see Figure 9.1).

One of the key inputs to the final credit decision is the credit analyst's *subjective judgment* of a firm's creditworthiness. Experience provides a "feel" for the nonquantifiable aspects of the quality of a firm's operations. The analyst will add his or her knowledge of the character of the applicant's management, references from other suppliers, and the firm's historic payment patterns to any quantitative figures developed to determine creditworthiness. The analyst will then make the final decision as to whether to extend credit to the applicant, and possibly what amount of credit to extend. Often these decisions are made not by one individual but by a credit review committee.

CREDIT TERMS

credit terms Specification of the repayment terms required of a firm's credit customers.

A firm's **credit terms** specify the repayment terms required of all its credit customers.[3] Typically a type of shorthand is used. For example,

[3] An in-depth discussion of credit terms as viewed by the customer is presented in Chapter 10. In this chapter our concern is with credit terms from the point of view of the seller.

credit terms may be stated as *2/10 net 30*, which means that the purchaser receives a 2 percent cash discount if the bill is paid within 10 days after the beginning of the credit period; if the customer does not take the cash discount, the full amount must be paid within 30 days after the beginning of the credit period. Credit terms cover three things: (1) the cash discount, if any (in this case 2 percent), (2) the cash discount period (in this case 10 days), and (3) the credit period (in this case 30 days). Changes in any aspect of the firm's credit terms may have an effect on its overall profitability. The positive and negative factors associated with such changes, and quantitative procedures for evaluating them, are presented in this section.

Cash Discounts

When a firm initiates or *increases* a cash discount, the following changes and effects on profits can be expected:

Variable	Direction of change	Effect on profits
Sales volume	Increase	Positive
Investment in accounts receivable	Decrease	Positive
Bad debt expenses	Decrease	Positive
Profit per unit	Decrease	Negative

As shown in the table above, the sales volume should increase because if a firm is willing to pay by day 10, the unit price decreases. The decreased accounts receivable investment results from the fact that some customers who did not previously take the cash discount will now take it. The bad debt expense should decline since, as customers on the average will pay earlier, the probability of their not paying at all will decrease. Both the decrease in the receivables investment and the decrease in the bad debt expense should result in increased profits. The negative aspect of an increased cash discount is a decreased profit per unit as more customers take the discount and pay the reduced price.

Decreasing or eliminating a cash discount would have opposite effects. The quantitative effects of changes in cash discounts can be evaluated by a method similar to that used to evaluate changes in credit standards.

EXAMPLE

Assume that the Binz Company is contemplating initiating a cash discount of 2 percent for payment prior to day 10 after a purchase. The firm's current average collection period is 30 days [turnover = (360/30) = 12], credit sales of 60,000 units are made, the variable cost per unit is $6, and the average cost per unit is currently $8. The firm expects that if the cash discount is initiated, 60 percent of its sales will be on discount, and sales will increase by 5 percent to 63,000 units. The average collection period is expected to drop to 15 days [turnover = (360/15) = 24]. Bad debt expenses are expected to drop from the current level of 1 percent of sales to .5 percent of sales. The firm's required return on equal-risk investments remains at 15 percent.

The analysis of this decision is presented in Table 9.4. It can be seen that the calculations are quite similar to those presented for the credit standard decision in Table 9.3 except for the final entry, "Cost of cash discount." This cost of $7,560 reflects the fact that *profits will be reduced* as a result of a 2 percent cash discount being taken on 60 percent of the new level of sales. The Binz Company can increase profit by $10,178 by initiating the proposed cash discount. Such an action therefore seems advisable. This type of analysis can also be applied to decisions concerning the elimination or reduction of cash discounts. ■

Cash Discount Period

The net effect of changes in the cash discount period is quite difficult to analyze due to the nature of the forces involved. For example, if the cash

TABLE 9.4 The Effects of Initiating a Cash Discount on the Binz Company

Additional profit contribution from sales [(3,000 units)($10 − $6)]		$12,000
Cost of marginal investment in A/R		
Average investment under proposed plan:		
$\dfrac{(\$8)(60,000) + (\$6)(3,000)}{24} = \dfrac{\$498,000}{24}$	$20,750	
Average investment under present plan:		
$\dfrac{(\$8)(60,000)}{12} = \dfrac{\$480,000}{12}$	40,000	
Marginal investment in A/R	($19,250)	
Cost of marginal investment in A/R [(.15)($19,250)]		$2,888[a]
Cost of marginal bad debts		
Bad debts under proposed plan [(.005)($10)(63,000)]	$ 3,150	
Bad debts under present plan [(.01)($10)(60,000)]	6,000	
Cost of marginal bad debts		$2,850[a]
Cost of cash discount[b] [(.02)(.60)($10)(63,000)]		($7,560)
Net profit from implementation of proposed plan		$10,178

[a] This value is positive since it represents a savings rather than a cost.

[b] This calculation reflects the fact that a 2 percent cash discount will be taken on 60 percent of the new level of sales—63,000 units at $10 each.

discount period were *increased*, the following changes could be expected:

Variable	Direction of change	Effect on profits
Sales volume	Increase	Positive
Investment in accounts receivable due to nondiscount takers now paying earlier	Decrease	Positive
Investment in accounts receivable due to discount takers still getting cash discount but paying later	Increase	Negative
Bad debt expenses	Decrease	Positive
Profit per unit	Decrease	Negative

The problems in determining the exact results of changes in the cash discount period are directly attributable to the two forces affecting the firm's *investment in accounts receivable*. If the firm were to shorten the cash discount period, the effects would be the opposite of those described above.

Credit Period

Changes in the credit period also affect the firm's profitability. The following effects on profits can be expected from an *increase* in the credit period:

Variable	Direction of change	Effect on profits
Sales volume	Increase	Positive
Investment in accounts receivable	Increase	Negative
Bad debt expenses	Increase	Negative

Increasing the credit period should increase sales, but both the investment in accounts receivable and bad debt expenses are likely to increase as well. Thus the net effect on profits of the sales increase is positive, while the increases in accounts receivable investment and bad debt expenses will negatively affect profits. A decrease in the credit period is likely to have the opposite effect. The credit period decision is analyzed in the same ways as the credit standard decision illustrated earlier in Table 9.3.

COLLECTION POLICIES

The firm's **collection policies** are the procedures for collecting accounts receivable when they are due. The effectiveness of these policies

collection policies The procedures for collecting a firm's accounts receivable when they are due.

can be partly evaluated by looking at the level of bad debt expenses. This level depends not only on collection policies, but also on the policies on which the extension of credit is based. If one assumes that the level of bad debts attributable to credit policies is relatively constant, increasing collection expenditures can be expected to reduce bad debts. This relationship is depicted in Figure 9.2. As the figure indicates, beyond point A, additional collection expenditures will not reduce bad debt losses sufficiently to justify the outlay of funds. Popular approaches used to evaluate credit and collection policies include the *average collection period ratio* (presented in Chapter 4) and *aging accounts receivable*.

Aging Accounts Receivable

aging A technique for providing information concerning the proportion of the accounts receivable balance that has been outstanding for a specified period of time.

Aging is a technique that provides the analyst with information concerning the proportion of the accounts receivable balance that has been outstanding for a specified period of time. By highlighting irregularities, it allows the analyst to pinpoint the cause of credit and/or

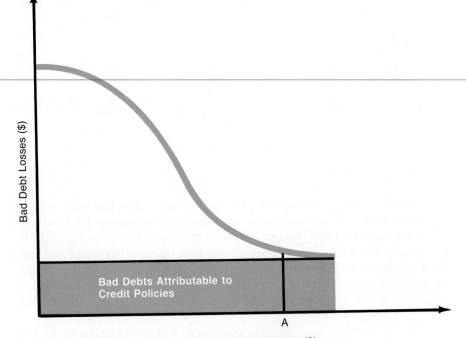

FIGURE 9.2 Collection Expenditures and Bad Debt Losses
By increasing collection expenditures the firm can decrease bad debt losses up to a point (A), beyond which bad debts cannot be economically reduced. These inescapable bad debts are attributed to the firm's credit policies.

collection problems. Aging requires that the firm's accounts receivable be broken down into groups based on the time of origin. This break-down is typically made on a month-by-month basis, going back three or four months. Let us look at an example.

EXAMPLE

Assume that the Binz Company extends 30-day credit terms to its customers. The firm's December 31, 1987, balance sheet shows $503,000 of accounts receivable. An evaluation of the $503,000 of accounts receivable results in the following breakdown:

DAYS	CURRENT	0–30	31–60	61–90	OVER 90	
Month	December	November	October	September	August	Total
Accounts receivable	$151,000	$101,000	$166,000	$65,000	$20,000	$503,000
Percentage of total	30	20	33	13	4	100

Since it is assumed that the Binz Company gives its customers 30 days after the end of the month in which the sale is made to pay off their accounts, any December receivables still on the firm's books are considered current. November receivables are between zero and 30 days overdue, while October receivables still unpaid are 31 to 60 days overdue, and so on.

The table shows that 30 percent of the firm's receivables are current, 20 percent are one month late, 33 percent are two months late, 13 percent are three months late, and 4 percent are more than three months late. While payment seems generally slow, a notice-able irregularity in these data is the high percentage represented by October receivables. This indicates that some problem may have occurred in October. Investigation may find that the prob-lem can be attributed to the hiring of a new credit manager, the acceptance of a new account that has made a large credit purchase it has not yet paid for, or ineffective collection policies. When accounts are aged and such a discrepancy is found, the analyst should determine its cause. ■

Basic Trade-Offs

The basic trade-offs expected to result from an *increase* in collection efforts are as follows:

Variable	Direction of change	Effect on profits
Sales volume	None or decrease	None or negative
Investment in accounts receivable	Decrease	Positive
Bad debt expenses	Decrease	Positive
Collection expenditures	Increase	Negative

Increased collection expenditures should reduce the investment in accounts receivable and bad debt expenses, increasing profits. The costs of this strategy may include lost sales in addition to increased collection expenditures if the level of collection effort is too intense. In other words, if the firm pushes its customers too hard to pay their accounts, they may be angered and may take their business elsewhere. The firm should therefore be careful not to be overly aggressive. The basic collection policy trade-offs can be evaluated quantitatively in a manner similar to that used to evaluate the trade-offs for credit standards and cash discounts.

Types of Collection Techniques

A number of collection techniques are employed. As an account becomes more and more overdue, the collection effort becomes more personal and more strict. The basic techniques are presented in the order typically followed in the collection process.

LETTERS   After an account receivable becomes overdue a certain number of days, the firm normally sends a polite letter reminding the customer of its obligation. If the account is not paid within a certain period of time after the letter has been sent, a second, more demanding letter is sent. This letter may be followed by yet another letter, if necessary. Collection letters are the first step in the collection process for overdue accounts.

TELEPHONE CALLS   If letters prove unsuccessful, a telephone call may be made to the customer to personally request immediate payment. If the customer has a reasonable excuse, arrangements may be made to extend the payment period. A call from the seller's attorney may be used if all other discussions seem to fail.

PERSONAL VISITS   This technique is much more common at the consumer credit level, but it may be effectively employed by industrial suppliers. Sending a local salesperson, or a collection person, to confront the customer can be a very effective collection procedure. Payment may be made on the spot.

USING COLLECTION AGENCIES   A firm can turn uncollectible accounts over to a collection agency or an attorney for collection. The fees for this service are typically quite high; the firm may receive less than 50 cents on the dollar from accounts collected in this way.

EFFECTIVE USE OF SALESPEOPLE AS COLLECTORS

Any company that says it has never had an accounts-receivable problem either isn't looking very hard or isn't selling very hard. Meanwhile, those thousands of companies that do suffer from bad debt might consider a strategy that Macke Business Products Inc., in Buffalo and Rochester, N.Y., has been using for 15 years: tying salespeople's commissions to the collection of receivables.

At Macke, a $13-million office furniture and supply company, a salesperson's commission is reduced by 5% if an account is 60 days past due; at 90 days past due, it is reduced by 10%; at 120 days, the commission is lost altogether. "It depends on how you define a sale," says Larry Romano, head of the company's Buffalo office. "It's not just a matter of going out and getting [it], but also of getting paid. If a customer drags us out, it costs us money."

The theory behind Macke's approach is that a call to a delinquent customer from the company's credit department is probably less effective, and more alienating, than a reminder from the salesperson in charge of the account. As for the sales force itself, the system encourages greater awareness of customers' financial stability. Jack Lumadue, for example, goes on every sales call with a binder that includes not just a weekly sales printout and an inventory sheet, but also a monthly aging report on that particular account's payment history. "When an order is placed, I can make sure we have the product. And if I see from the aging report that something has gone into the 60-day column, I can talk to [the customer's] purchasing department or someone else to see why [the bill] hasn't been paid. . . ."

A system like this, says John Gordana, president of Equitable Adjustment Service Inc., "enlists the sales force in the service of the credit department. If a connection is made between commissions and bad debts, salespeople are less likely to go overboard . . . It makes them more accountable."

It doesn't always make them happy: When Macke first introduced the system in the mid-1960s, it wasn't a popular move among the company's 15 salespeople, who were used to getting paid up front. "So we told them we would pay a cash advance to anyone who needed it during the swing period," says Macke president Edward H. Fischer. The result was a smooth transition. Nor does the system make it difficult for Macke to retain top salespeople, says Romano: Turnover among the company's sales force is very low.

Source: "Collection Duty for Salespeople" *INC.*, December 1985, p. 16. Reprinted with permission, INC. magazine, December 1985. Copyright © 1985 by INC. Publishing Company, 38 Commercial Wharf, Boston, MA 02110.

LEGAL ACTION   This is the most stringent step in the collection process. It is an alternative to the use of a collection agency. Not only is direct legal action expensive, but it may force the debtor into bankruptcy, thereby reducing the possibility of future business without guaranteeing the ultimate receipt of the overdue amount.

INVENTORY MANAGEMENT

As noted earlier, inventory, like accounts receivable, represents a significant monetary investment on the part of most firms. In Chapter 8 the importance of turning over inventory quickly in order to minimize this investment was illustrated. The financial manager generally does not have direct control over inventory, but does provide input into the inventory management process.

Inventory Fundamentals

Two aspects of inventory require some elaboration. One aspect is the *types of inventory;* the other concerns differing viewpoints as to the *appropriate level of inventory.*

raw materials inventory Items purchased by the firm for use in the manufacture of a finished product.

TYPES OF INVENTORY   The three basic types of inventory are raw materials, work in process, and finished goods. **Raw materials inventory** consists of items purchased by the firm — usually basic materials such as screws, plastic, raw steel, or rivets — for use in the manufacture of a finished product. If a firm manufactures complex products with numerous parts, its raw materials inventory may consist of manufactured items that have been purchased from another company or from another division of the same firm. **Work-in-process inventory** consists of all items currently in production. These are normally partially finished goods at some intermediate stage of completion. **Finished goods inventory** consists of items that have been produced but not yet sold.

work-in-process inventory All items currently in production.

finished goods inventory Items that have been produced but not yet sold.

DIFFERING VIEWPOINTS ABOUT INVENTORY LEVEL   Differing viewpoints concerning appropriate inventory levels commonly exist between the finance, marketing, manufacturing, and purchasing activities of a company. Each sector views inventory levels in light of its own objectives. The *financial manager's* general disposition toward inventory levels is to keep them low. The financial manager must police the inventories, making sure that the firm's money is not being unwisely invested in excess resources. The *marketing manager,* on the other hand, would like to have large inventories of each of the firm's finished products. This would ensure that all orders could be filled quickly, thus eliminating the need for backorders due to stockouts.

The *manufacturing manager's* major responsibility is to make sure that the production plan is correctly implemented and that it results in the desired amount of finished goods. In fulfilling this role, the manufacturing manager would keep raw materials inventories high to avoid production delays, and would favor high finished goods inventories by making large production runs for the sake of lower unit production costs. The *purchasing manager* is concerned solely with the raw materials inventories. He or she is responsible for seeing that whatever raw materials are required by production are available in the correct quantities at the desired times and at a favorable price. Without proper control, the purchasing manager may purchase larger quantities of resources than are actually needed in order to get quantity discounts or in anticipation of rising prices or a shortage of certain materials.

Inventory as an Investment

Inventory is an investment in the sense that it requires that the firm tie up its money, thereby forgoing certain other earnings opportunities. In general, the higher a firm's average inventories, the larger the dollar investment and cost required, and vice versa. In evaluating planned changes in inventory levels, the financial manager should consider such changes from a benefit-versus-cost standpoint.

EXAMPLE

A firm is contemplating making larger production runs in order to reduce the high setup costs associated with the production of its only product. The total *annual* reduction in setup costs that can be obtained has been estimated at $20,000. As a result of the larger production runs, the average inventory investment is expected to increase from $200,000 to $300,000. If the firm can earn 25 percent per year on equal-risk investments, the *annual* cost of the additional $100,000 ($300,000 − $200,000) inventory investment will be $25,000 (.25 × $100,000). Comparing the annual $25,000 cost of the system with the annual savings of $20,000 shows that the proposal should be rejected since it results in a net annual *loss* of $5,000. ■

TECHNIQUES FOR MANAGING INVENTORY

Techniques commonly used in managing inventory are (1) the ABC system, (2) the basic economic order quantity (EOQ) model, and (3) the reorder point. Although these techniques are not strictly financial, it is helpful for the financial manager to understand them.

The ABC System

A firm using the **ABC system** divides its inventory into three groups: A, B, and C. The *A group* includes those items that require the largest dollar investment. In the typical distribution of inventory items, this

ABC system Divides inventory into three categories of descending importance, based on the dollar investment in each.

group consists of the 20 percent of inventory items that account for 80 percent of the firm's dollar investment. The *B group* consists of the items accounting for the next largest investment. The *C group* typically consists of a large number of items accounting for a relatively small dollar investment. Dividing its inventory into A, B, and C items allows the firm to determine the level and types of inventory control procedures needed. Control of the A items should be most intensive due to the high dollar investment involved, while the B and C items would be subject to correspondingly less sophisticated control procedures.

The Basic Economic Order Quantity (EOQ) Model

economic order quantity (EOQ) model A technique for determining the optimal quantity of an inventory item, based on the trade-off between various operating and financial inventory costs.

One of the most commonly cited sophisticated tools for determining the optimal order quantity for an item of inventory is the **economic order quantity (EOQ) model.** This model could well be used to control the firm's A items. It takes into account various operating and financial costs and determines the order quantity that minimizes total inventory costs.

BASIC COSTS   Excluding the actual cost of the merchandise, the costs associated with inventory can be divided into three broad groups: order costs, carrying costs, and total cost. Each has certain key components and characteristics.

order costs The fixed clerical costs of placing and receiving an inventory order.

Order Costs.   **Order costs** include the fixed clerical costs of placing and receiving an order—the cost of writing a purchase order, of processing the resulting paperwork, and of receiving an order and checking it against the invoice. Order costs are normally stated as dollars per order.

carrying costs The variable costs per unit of holding an item in inventory for a specified time period.

Carrying Costs.   **Carrying costs** are the variable costs per unit of holding an item in inventory for a specified time period. These costs are typically stated as dollars per unit per period. Carrying costs include storage costs, insurance costs, the cost of deterioration and obsolescence, and most important, the opportunity, or financial, cost of tying up funds in inventory. A commonly cited rule of thumb suggests that the cost of carrying an item in inventory for one year is between 20 and 30 percent of the cost (value) of the item.

total cost The sum of the order and carrying costs of inventory.

Total Cost.   The **total cost** of inventory is defined as the sum of the order and carrying costs. Total cost is important in the EOQ model, since the model's objective is to determine the order quantity that minimizes it.

A GRAPHIC APPROACH   The stated objective of the EOQ approach is to find the order quantity that minimizes the firm's total inventory cost.

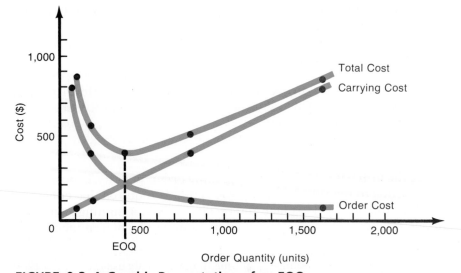

FIGURE 9.3 A Graphic Presentation of an EOQ
The total cost line represents the sum of the order costs and carrying costs for each order quantity. The EOQ, which is the order quantity that minimizes total inventory costs, occurs where the order cost line and carrying cost line intersect.

The economic order quantity can be found graphically by plotting order quantities on the *x*, or horizontal, axis and costs on the *y*, or vertical, axis. Figure 9.3 shows the general behavior of these costs. The total cost line represents the sum of the order costs and carrying costs for each order quantity. The minimum total cost occurs at the point labeled EOQ, where the order cost line and the carrying cost line intersect.

A MATHEMATICAL APPROACH   The formula given in Equation 9.2 can be used to determine the firm's EOQ for a given inventory item:

$$EOQ = \sqrt{\frac{2 \times S \times O}{C}} \qquad (9.2)$$

where

S = usage in units per period
O = order cost per order
C = carrying cost per unit per period

EXAMPLE

Assume that a firm uses 1,600 units of an item annually and that its order costs are $50 per order and carrying costs are $1 per unit per year. Substituting $S = 1,600$, $O = \$50$, and $C = \$1$ into Equation 9.2 yields an EOQ of 400 units:

$$EOQ = \sqrt{\frac{2 \times 1,600 \times \$50}{\$1}} = \sqrt{160,000} = \underline{400 \text{ units}}$$

If the firm orders in quantities of 400 units, it will minimize its total inventory cost. This solution is depicted in Figure 9.3. ■

The Reorder Point

Once the firm has calculated its economic order quantity, it must determine when to place orders. A reorder point is required that considers the lead time needed to place and receive orders. Assuming a constant usage rate for inventory, the **reorder point** can be determined by the following equation:

reorder point The point at which to reorder inventory, expressed equationally as: lead time in days × daily usage.

$$\text{Reorder point} = \text{lead time in days} \times \text{daily usage} \tag{9.3}$$

For example, if a firm knows that it requires 10 days to receive an order once the order is placed, and if it uses five units of inventory daily, the reorder point would be 50 units (10 days × 5 units per day). Thus as soon as the firm's inventory level reaches 50 units, an order will be placed for an amount equal to the economic order quantity. If the estimates of lead time and daily usage are correct, the order will be received exactly when the inventory level reaches zero.

SUMMARY

- Accounts receivable and inventory represent sizable investments by the firm. The management of accounts receivable centers on credit policies, credit terms, and collection policies. Inventory management is generally not the direct responsibility of the financial manager.
- Credit policies involve establishing credit standards and performing credit analysis in order to make credit decisions. Consumer credit decisions are often made using impersonal techniques, such as credit scoring.
- At the mercantile level, credit standards must be set by considering the trade-offs between the profit contribution from sales, the cost of investment in accounts receivable, and the cost of bad debts.
- Credit analysis is devoted to the collection and evaluation of credit information on credit applicants in order to determine whether they can meet the firm's standards. The subjective judgment of the credit analyst is an important input to the credit decision.
- Credit terms have three components: (1) the cash discount, (2) the cash discount period, (3) and the credit period. Changes in each of these variables

affect the firm's sales, investment in accounts receivable, bad debt expenses, and profit per unit.

● Collection policies determine the type and degree of effort exercised to collect overdue accounts. In addition to looking at the average collection period ratio, accounts receivable are often aged to evaluate the effectiveness of the firm's credit and collection policies. The procedures used to evaluate changes in collection policy are similar to those used to evaluate credit policies and credit terms.

● The basic collection techniques include letters, telephone calls, personal visits, the use of collection agencies, and, as a last resort, legal action.

● The respective viewpoints held by marketing, manufacturing, and purchasing managers relative to the appropriate levels of various types of inventory (raw materials, work in process, and finished goods) tend to conflict with that of the financial manager. The financial manager views inventory as an investment that should be kept at a low level.

● Several techniques are used to manage inventory. The ABC system determines which inventories require the most attention according to dollar investment. One of the most common techniques for determining optimal order quantities is the economic order quantity (EOQ) model. Once the optimal order quantity has been determined, the firm can set a reorder point, the level of inventory at which an order will be placed.

QUESTIONS

9-1   What do the *accounts receivable* of a firm typically represent? What is meant by a firm's *credit policy?*

9-2   Describe *credit scoring* and explain why this technique is typically applied to consumer credit decisions rather than to mercantile credit decisions.

9-3   What key variables should be considered in evaluating possible changes in a firm's credit standards? What are the basic trade-offs in a *tightening* of credit standards?

9-4   What is *credit analysis?* Describe the two basic steps in the credit investigation process and summarize the basic sources of credit information.

9-5   Discuss what is meant by *credit terms.* What are the three components of credit terms? How do credit terms affect the firm's accounts receivable?

9-6   What are the expected effects of a *decrease* in the firm's cash discount on sales volume, investment in accounts receivable, bad debt expenses, and per-unit profits, respectively?

9-7   What are the expected effects of a *decrease* in the firm's credit period? What is likely to happen to sales volume, investment in accounts receivable, and bad debt expenses, respectively?

9-8   What is meant by a firm's *collection policy?* Explain how *aging accounts receivable* can be used to evaluate the effectiveness of both the credit policy and the collection policy.

9-9   Describe the basic trade-offs involved in collection policy decisions, and describe the popular types of collection techniques.

9-10 What is the financial manager's role with respect to the management of

inventory? What are likely to be the viewpoints of each of the following managers, respectively, about the levels of the various types of inventory?
a Finance
b Marketing
c Manufacturing
d Purchasing

9-11 What is the *ABC system* of inventory control? On what key premise is this system based?

9-12 What is the *EOQ model?* To which group of inventory items is it most applicable? What costs does it consider? What financial cost is involved?

9-13 Describe the *reorder point* and explain its use and the elements of uncertainty affecting its accuracy.

PROBLEMS

9-1 **(Credit Scoring)** Dooley Department Store uses credit scoring to evaluate retail credit applications. The financial and credit characteristics considered and weights indicating their relative importance in the credit decision are as follows:

Financial and credit characteristics	Predetermined weight
Credit references	.25
Education	.15
Home ownership	.10
Income range	.10
Payment history	.30
Years on job	.10

The firm's credit standards are to accept all applicants with credit scores of 80 or more, to extend limited credit on a probationary basis to applicants with scores of greater than 70 and less than 80, and to reject all applicants with scores below 70.

The firm currently needs to process three applications recently received and scored by one of its credit analysts. The scores for each of the applicants on each of the financial and credit characteristics are summarized in the following table:

	APPLICANT		
Financial and credit characteristics	A	B	C
	Score (0 to 100)		
Credit references	60	90	80
Education	70	70	80
Home ownership	100	90	60
Income range	75	80	80
Payment history	60	85	70
Years on job	50	60	90

    a Use the data presented to find the credit score for each of the applicants.

    b Recommend the appropriate action for each of the three applicants.

9-2 **(Accounts Receivable and Costs)** Wicklow Products currently has an average collection period of 45 days and annual credit sales of $1 million. Assume a 360-day year.

    a What is the firm's average accounts receivable balance?

    b If the average cost of each product is 60 percent of sales, what is the average investment in accounts receivable?

    c If the equal-risk opportunity cost of the investment in accounts receivable is 12 percent, what is the total opportunity cost of the investment in accounts receivable?

9-3 **(Changes in Credit Policy Without Bad Debts)** Wholehouse Appliance currently has credit sales of $600 million per year and an average collection period of 60 days. Assume that the price of Wholehouse's products is $100 per unit, the variable costs are $55 per unit, and the average costs are $85 per unit at the current level of sales. The firm is considering changing its credit policy. This will result in a 20 percent increase in sales and an equal 20 percent increase in the average collection period. No change in bad debts is expected. The firm's equal-risk opportunity cost on its investment in accounts receivable is 14 percent.

    a What are the firm's total fixed costs with and without the policy change?

    b Calculate the additional profits from new sales the firm will realize if it changes its credit policy.

    c What marginal investment in accounts receivable will result?

    d Calculate the cost of the marginal investment in accounts receivable.

    e Should the firm change its credit policy? What other information would be helpful in your analysis?

9-4 **(Bad Debt Policy)** A firm is evaluating a credit policy change that would increase bad debts from 2 to 4 percent of sales. Sales are currently 50,000 units, the selling price is $20 per unit, variable cost per unit is $9, and average cost per unit is $11 at the current level of sales. As a result of the change in accounts receivable policy, sales are forecast to increase to 60,000 units.

    a What are bad debts in dollars under the present and proposed plans?

    b Calculate the cost of the marginal bad debts to the firm.

    c Ignoring the profitability from increased sales, if the policy saves $3,500 and causes no change in the average investment in accounts receivable, would you recommend the policy change? Explain.

    d Considering *all* changes in costs and benefits, would you recommend this policy change? Explain.

    e Compare and discuss your answers in **c** and **d**.

9-5 **(Tightening Credit Standards — Bad Debt Losses)** Cheryl's Menswear feels its credit costs are too high. By tightening its credit standards, bad debts will fall from 5 percent of sales to 2 percent. However, sales will fall from $100,000 to $90,000 per year. If the variable cost per unit is 50 percent of the sale price, fixed costs are $10,000, and the average investment in receivables does not change,

    a What cost will the firm face in a reduced contribution to profits from sales?

    b Should the firm tighten its credit standards? Explain your answer.

9-6 **(Relaxation of Credit Standards)** Adair Industries is considering relaxing its credit standards in order to increase its currently sagging sales. As a result of the proposed relaxation, sales are expected to increase by 10 percent from 10,000 to 11,000 units during the coming year, the average collection period is expected to increase from 45 to 60 days, and bad debts are expected to increase from 1 percent to 3 percent of sales. The sale price per unit is $40, the variable cost per unit is $31, and the average cost per unit at the current 10,000-unit sales volume is $36. If the firm's required return on equal-risk investments is 25 percent, evaluate the proposed relaxation and make a recommendation to the firm.

9-7 **(Initiating a Cash Discount)** Pritchard Products currently makes all sales on credit and offers no cash discount. The firm is considering a 2 percent cash discount for payment within 15 days. The firm's current average collection period is 60 days, sales are 40,000 units, selling price is $45 per unit, variable cost per unit is $36, and average cost per unit is $40 at the current sales volume. The firm expects that the change in credit terms will result in an increase in sales to 42,000 units, that 70 percent of the sales will take the discount, and that the average collection period will fall to 30 days. If the firm's required rate of return on equal-risk investments is 25 percent, should the proposed discount be offered?

9-8 **(Credit Term Change — Shortening the Credit Period)** A firm is contemplating *shortening* its credit period from 40 to 30 days and believes that as a result of this change its average collection period will decline from 45 to 36 days. Bad debt expenses are expected to decrease from 1.5 percent to 1 percent of sales. The firm is currently selling 12,000 units but believes that as a result of the proposed change, sales will decline to 10,000 units. The sale price per unit is $56, its variable cost per unit is $45, and the average cost per unit at the 12,000-unit volume is $53. The firm has a required return on equal-risk investments of 25 percent. Evaluate this decision and make a recommendation to the firm.

9-9 **(Credit Term Change — Lengthening the Credit Period)** The Heaton Equipment Company is considering lengthening its credit period from 30 to 60 days. All customers will continue to pay on the net date. The firm currently bills $450,000 for sales, has $345,000 in variable costs, and has $45,000 in fixed costs. The change in credit terms is expected to increase sales to $510,000. Bad debt expense will increase from 1 percent to 1.5 percent of sales. The firm has a required rate of return on equal-risk investments of 20 percent. (*Hint:* Calculate the contribution margin $\left[1 - \dfrac{\text{variable costs}}{\text{sales revenue}}\right]$ and use it along with the total fixed costs to find the additional profit contribution and the marginal investment in accounts receivable.)

a What additional profit contribution from sales will be realized from the change?

b What changes in the cost of financing the investment in accounts receivable and bad debts will the firm face?

c Do you recommend this change in credit terms? Why?

9-10 **(Aging Accounts Receivable)** Cellular Corporation's accounts receivable totaled $874,000 on August 31, 1987. A breakdown of these outstanding accounts on the basis of the month in which the credit sale was initially made is given below. The firm extends 30-day credit terms to its credit customers.

Month of credit sale	Accounts receivable
August 1987	$320,000
July 1987	250,000
June 1987	81,000
May 1987	195,000
April 1987 or before	28,000
Total (August 31, 1987)	$874,000

a Prepare an aging schedule for Cellular Corporation's August 31, 1987, accounts receivable balance.

b Using your findings in **a**, evaluate the firm's credit and collection activities.

c What are some probable causes of the situation discussed in **b**?

9-11 **(Inventory — The ABC System)** Zap Supply has 16 different items in its inventory. The average number of units held in inventory and the average unit cost are listed below for each item. The firm wishes to introduce the ABC system of inventory control. Suggest a breakdown of the items into classifications of A, B, and C. Justify your selection and point out items that could be considered borderline cases.

Item	Average number of units in inventory	Average cost per unit
1	1,800	$ 0.54
2	1,000	8.20
3	100	6.00
4	250	1.20
5	8	94.50
6	400	3.00
7	80	45.00
8	1,600	1.45
9	600	0.95
10	3,000	0.18
11	900	15.00
12	65	1.35
13	2,200	4.75
14	1,800	1.30
15	60	18.00
16	200	17.50

9-12 **(Easing Collection Efforts)** The Regency Rug Repair Company is attempting to evaluate whether it should ease collection efforts. The firm repairs 72,000 rugs per year at an average price of $32 each. Bad debt expenses are 1 percent of sales, and collection expenditures are $60,000. The average collection period is 40 days, the average cost per unit is $29 at the current sales level, and the variable cost per unit is $28. By easing the collection efforts, Regency expects to save $40,000 per year in collection expense. Bad debts will increase to 2 percent of sales, and the average collection period will increase to 58 days. Sales will increase by 1,000 repairs per year. If the firm has a required rate of return on equal-risk investments of 24 percent, what recommendation would you give the firm? Use your analysis to justify your answer.

9-13 **(Inventory Investment)** Winblad, Inc., is considering leasing a computerized inventory control system in order to reduce its average inventories. The annual cost of the system is $46,000. It is expected that with the system the firm's average inventory will decline by 50 percent from its current level of $980,000. The level of stockouts is expected to be unaffected by this system. The firm can earn 20 percent per year on equal-risk investments.

a How much of a reduction in average inventory will result from the proposed installation of the computerized inventory control system?

b How much, if any, annual savings will the firm realize on the reduced level of average inventory?

c Should the firm lease the computerized inventory control system? Explain why or why not.

9-14 **(EOQ Analysis)** Lyons Electronics purchases 1,200,000 units per year of one component. Annual carrying costs of the item are 27 percent of the item's $2 cost. Fixed costs per order are $25.

a Determine the EOQ under the following conditions: (1) no changes, (2) carrying cost of zero, (3) order cost of zero.

b What do your answers illustrate about the EOQ model? Explain.

9-15 **(Reorder Point)** Ticho Gas and Electric (TG&E) is required to carry a minimum of 20 days' average coal usage, which is 100 tons of coal. It takes ten days between order and delivery. At what level of coal would TG&E reorder?

9-16 **(EOQ and Reorder Point)** The Gaffney Paint Company uses 60,000 gallons of pigment per year. The cost of carrying the pigment in inventory is $1 per gallon per year, and the cost of ordering pigment is $200 per order. The firm uses pigment at a constant rate throughout the year.

a Calculate the EOQ.

b Assuming that it takes 20 days to receive an order once it has been placed, determine the reorder point in terms of gallons of pigment. (*Note:* Assume a 360-day year to calculate daily usage.)

9-17 **(EOQ and Reorder Point)** A firm uses 800 units of a product per year on a continuous basis. The product has carrying costs of $2 per unit per year and fixed costs of $50 per order. It takes five days to receive a shipment after an order is placed.

a Calculate the EOQ.

b Determine the reorder point. (*Note:* Assume a 360-day year to calculate daily usage.)

10

SOURCES OF SHORT-TERM FINANCING

After studying this chapter, you should be able to:

● Describe the basic features of the major sources of spontaneous short-term financing.

● Analyze credit terms and decide, in view of a borrowing alternative, whether to take or forgo cash discounts and whether to stretch accounts payable.

● Discuss the basic forms and key features of unsecured bank sources of short-term loans, and define commercial paper and explain its role in short-term financing.

● Describe the characteristics, acceptable collateral, and terms of secured short-term loans, and identify the key institutions extending these loans.

● Explain how accounts receivable and inventory can be used as collateral to secure short-term loans.

secured short-term financing Financing that matures in one year or less and has specific assets pledged as collateral.

unsecured short-term financing Financing that matures in one year or less and has no assets pledged as collateral.

Short-term financing is debt that matures in one year or less and is used to fulfill seasonal and current asset needs. **Secured short-term financing** has specific assets pledged as collateral, whereas **unsecured short-term financing** does not. Both these forms of financing appear on the balance sheet as *current liabilities*—accounts payable, accruals, and notes payable. *Accounts payable* and *accruals* are spontaneous unsecured sources of short-term financing that arise from the normal operations of the firm. *Notes payable* can be either secured or unsecured financing and result from some type of negotiated borrowing. For convenience, a summary table of the key features of the common sources of short-term financing is included as Table 10.3 in the chapter summary.

SPONTANEOUS SOURCES

The two major spontaneous sources of short-term financing are accounts payable and accruals. Each of these sources is unsecured and results from normal business operations. As the firm's sales increase, accounts payable increases in response to the increased purchases required to produce at higher levels. Also in response to increasing sales, the firm's accruals increase as wages and taxes rise as a result of greater labor requirements and the increased taxes on the firm's increased earnings. There is normally no explicit cost attached to either of these current liabilities, although they do have certain implicit costs. The firm should take advantage of these often "interest-free" sources of short-term financing whenever possible.

Accounts Payable

Accounts payable is the major source of unsecured short-term financing for business firms. They result from transactions in which merchandise is purchased but no formal note is signed evidencing the purchaser's liability to the seller. The purchaser, by accepting merchandise, in effect agrees to pay the supplier the amount required in accordance with the terms of sale. The credit terms extended in such transactions are normally stated on the supplier's invoice. The discussion of accounts payable here is presented from the viewpoint of the purchaser rather than the supplier of "trade credit."[1]

CREDIT TERMS The supplier's credit terms state the credit period, the size of the cash discount offered (if any), the cash discount period, and

---

[1] An account payable of a purchaser is an account receivable on the supplier's books. Chapter 9 highlighted the key strategies and considerations involved in extending credit to customers.

the date the credit period begins. Each of these aspects of a firm's credit terms is concisely stated in such expressions as "2/10 net 30 EOM." These expressions are a kind of shorthand containing the key information about the length of the credit period (30 days), the cash discount (2 percent), the cash discount period (10 days), and the time the credit period begins, which is the end of each month (EOM).

Credit Period. The **credit period** of an account payable is the number of days until payment in full is required. Regardless of whether a cash discount is offered, the credit period associated with any transaction must always be indicated. Credit periods usually range from zero to 120 days, although in certain instances longer times are provided. Most credit terms refer to the credit period as the "net period." The word *net* indicates that the full amount of the purchase must be paid within the number of days indicated from the beginning of the credit period. For example, "net 30 days" indicates that the firm must make *full payment* within 30 days of the beginning of the credit period.

credit period The number of days until full payment of an account payable is required.

Cash Discount. A **cash discount,** if offered as part of the firm's credit terms, is a percentage deduction from the purchase price if the buyer pays within a specified time shorter than the credit period. Cash discounts normally range from between 1 and 5 percent. A 2 percent cash discount indicates that the purchaser of $100 of merchandise need pay only $98 if payment is made within the specified earlier interval. The purchaser, whose objective is to stretch accounts payable by paying as late as possible, must determine whether it is more advantageous to take the cash discount or to pay at the end of the full credit period. Techniques for analyzing the benefits of each alternative will be discussed in a later section.

cash discount A percentage deduction from the purchase price of an item offered if the buyer pays within a specified time interval that is shorter than the credit period.

Cash Discount Period. The **cash discount period** is the number of days after the beginning of the credit period during which the cash discount is available. Typically the cash discount period is between 5 and 20 days. Often large customers of smaller firms use their position as key customers as a form of leverage, enabling them to take cash discounts far beyond the end of the cash discount period. This strategy, although ethically questionable, is common practice.

cash discount period The number of days after the beginning of the credit period during which the cash discount is available.

Beginning of the Credit Period. The beginning of the credit period is stated as part of the supplier's credit terms. One of the most common designations for the beginning of the credit period is the **date of invoice.** Both the cash discount period and the net period are then measured from the invoice data. **End of month (EOM)** indicates that the credit period for all purchases made within a given month begins on the first day of the month immediately following. These terms simplify record keeping on the part of the firm extending credit. The following example may help to clarify the differences between credit period beginnings.

date of invoice Indicates that the beginning of the credit period is the date on the invoice for the purchase.

end of month (EOM) Indicates that the credit period for any purchase made within a given month begins on the first day of the month immediately following.

EXAMPLE

The McKinley Company made two purchases from a certain supplier offering credit terms of 2/10 net 30. One purchase was made on September 10 and the other on September 20. The payment dates for each purchase, based on date of invoice and end of month (EOM) credit period beginnings are given in Table 10.1. The payment dates if the firm takes the cash discount and if it pays the net amount are shown. It can be seen that from the point of view of the recipient of trade credit, a credit period beginning at the end of the month is preferable in both cases since purchases can be paid for at a later date than otherwise would have been possible. ∎

In order to maintain their competitive position, firms within an industry generally offer the same terms. In many cases, stated credit terms are not the terms actually given to a customer. Special arrangements, or "deals," are made to provide certain customers with more favorable terms. The prospective purchaser is wise to look closely at the credit terms of suppliers when making a purchase decision. In many instances concessions may be available.

ANALYZING CREDIT TERMS   The credit terms offered a firm by its suppliers allow it to delay payments for its purchases. Since the supplier's cost of having its money tied up in merchandise after it is sold is probably reflected in the purchase price, the purchaser is already indirectly paying for this benefit. The purchaser should therefore carefully analyze credit terms in order to determine the best trade credit strategy.

Taking the Cash Discount.   If a firm is extended credit terms that include a cash discount, it has two options. Its first option is to *take the cash discount*. If a firm intends to take a cash discount, it should pay on the last day of the discount period. There is no cost associated with taking a cash discount.

TABLE 10.1 Payment Dates for the McKinley Company Given Various Assumptions

Beginning of credit period	SEPTEMBER 10 PURCHASE		SEPTEMBER 20 PURCHASE	
	Discount taken	Net amount paid	Discount taken	Net amount paid
Date of invoice	Sept. 20	Oct. 10	Sept. 30	Oct. 20
End of month (EOM)	Oct. 10	Oct. 30	Oct. 10	Oct. 30

SMALL BUSINESS LINES OF CREDIT

Most major lending institutions are more eager to service the megaborrowing needs of big corporations and foreign governments than they are to take care of the working-capital needs of the small businesses in their own backyards. But over the past few months [late 1984/early 1985], one commercial institution, Wells Fargo Bank, headquartered in San Francisco, has begun taking the interests of smaller companies more to heart. The nation's 11th largest bank has recently introduced a new, unsecured line of credit available to solid businesses with sales from $200,000 to $3 million. In effect, this puts them on equal footing with the best of the bank's big customers.

Before the new credit-line program was unveiled last September [1984], Wells Fargo, like most commercial banks, required many of its smaller, unsecured customers to obtain approvals from their lending officers each time they needed to borrow money. Not surprisingly, many small business owners found this to be a major source of migraines. Some complained about the inconvenience of having to review detailed bank documents every few months. Others sounded off about the frustrations of tracking down their loan officers when they needed approval for small loans. For still others, the approval process was destructively slow. There were the times, for example, when they missed important discount opportunities offered by suppliers. . . .

Before granting an unsecured line of credit, Wells Fargo conducts a thorough financial analysis of the company's credit, just as it does for any loan. Among other things, the bank likes to see several years of operating profits, a stable management team, and no more than moderate leverage. If a business passes the test, it is offered a credit line from $10,000 to $250,000, depending on its circumstances. In fact, the bank has set up a special toll-free number that customers can use to request credit advances to their checking accounts. Unlike most other types of working capital loans, moreover, the only payment that is mandatory at the end of each month is interest — and only on the portion of the line that has been used.

Source: Bruce G. Posner, "Another Line," *INC.*, February 1985, p. 122. Reprinted with permission, INC. magazine, February 1985. Copyright © 1985 by INC. Publishing Company, 38 Commercial Wharf, Boston, MA 02110.

EXAMPLE

The Presti Corporation purchased $1,000 worth of merchandise on February 27 from a supplier extending terms of 2/10 net 30 EOM. If the corporation takes the cash discount, it will have to pay $980 [$1,000 − .02($1,000)] on March 10, thereby saving $20. ■

Forgoing the Cash Discount. The second option open to the firm is to *forgo the cash discount* and pay on the final day of the credit period.

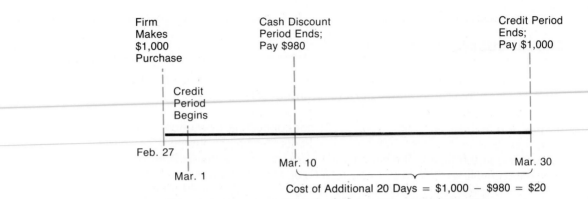

FIGURE 10.1 Payment Options for the Presti Corporation
As a result of its February 27 $1,000 purchase under credit terms of 2/10 net 30 EOM, the Presti Corporation can either take the $20 discount and pay $980 on March 10 or forgo the discount and pay the full $1,000 twenty days later on March 30.

cost of forgoing a cash discount The implied rate of interest paid in order to delay payment of an account payable for an additional number of days.

Although there is no direct cost associated with forgoing a cash discount, there is an implicit cost. The **cost of forgoing a cash discount** is the implied rate of interest paid in order to delay payment for an additional number of days. This cost can be illustrated by a simple example. The example assumes that if the firm takes a cash discount, payment will be made on the final day of the cash discount period, and if the cash discount is forgone, payment will be made on the final day of the credit period.

EXAMPLE

As in the preceding example, the Presti Corporation has been extended credit terms of 2/10 net 30 EOM on $1,000 worth of merchandise. If it takes the cash discount on its February 27 purchase, payment will be required on March 10. If the cash discount is forgone, payment can be made on March 30. To keep its money for an extra 20 days (from March 10 to March 30), the firm must forgo an opportunity to pay $980 for its $1,000 purchase. In other words, it will cost the firm $20 to delay payment for 20 days. Figure 10.1 shows the payment options open to the corporation.

To calculate the cost of forgoing the cash discount, the *true purchase price* must be viewed as the discounted cost of the merchandise. For the Presti Corporation, this discounted cost would be $980. To delay paying the $980 for an extra 20 days, the firm must pay $20 ($1,000 − $980). The annual percentage cost of forgoing the cash discount can be calculated using Equation 10.1.

$$\text{Cost of forgoing cash discount} = \frac{CD}{100\% - CD} \times \frac{360}{N} \qquad (10.1)$$

where

CD = the stated cash discount in percentage terms
N = the number of days payment can be delayed by forgoing the cash discount

Substituting the values for CD (2%) and N (20 days) into equation 10.1 results in a cost of forgoing the cash discount of 36.73 percent [(2% ÷ 98%) × (360 ÷ 20)]. A 360-day year is assumed.

A simple way to *approximate* the cost of a forgone discount is to use the stated cash discount percentage, CD, in place of the first term of Equation 10.1.

$$\text{Approximate cost of forgoing cash discount} = CD \times \frac{360}{N} \qquad (10.2)$$

The smaller the cash discount, the closer the approximation to the actual cost of forgoing the cash discount. Using this approximation, the cost of forgoing the cash discount for the Presti Corporation is 36 percent [(2% × (360 ÷ 20)]. ■

Using the Cost of Forgoing a Cash Discount in Decision Making. The financial manager must determine whether it is advisable to take a cash discount.

EXAMPLE

The Omst Company has four possible suppliers, each offering different credit terms. Except for the differences in credit terms, their products and services are identical. Table 10.2 presents the credit terms offered by suppliers, A, B, C, and D, respectively, and the cost of forgoing the cash discounts in each transaction. The approximation method of calculating the cost of forgoing a cash

TABLE 10.2 Cash Discounts and Associated Costs for the Omst Company

Supplier	Credit terms	Approximate cost of forgoing cash discount
A	2/10 net 30 EOM	36.0%
B	1/10 net 55 EOM	8.0
C	3/20 net 70 EOM	21.6
D	4/10 net 60 EOM	28.8

discount has been used to simplify the analysis. The cost of forgoing the cash discount from supplier A is 36 percent; from supplier B, 8 percent; from supplier C, 21.6 percent; and from supplier D, 28.8 percent.

If the firm needs short-term funds, which are currently available from its bank at an interest rate of 13 percent, and if each of the suppliers (A, B, C, and D) is viewed *separately*, which (if any) of the suppliers' cash discount will the firm forgo? To answer this question, each supplier's terms must be evaluated as they would be if it were the firm's sole supplier. In dealing with supplier A, the firm will take the cash discount since the cost of forgoing it is 36 percent. The firm will then borrow the funds it requires from its commercial bank at 13 percent interest. In dealing with supplier B, the firm will do better to forgo the cash discount since the cost of this action is less than the cost of borrowing money from the bank (8 percent as opposed to 13 percent). In dealing with either supplier C or supplier D, the firm should take the cash discount since in both cases the cost of forgoing the discount is greater than the 13 percent cost of borrowing from the bank. ∎

The example shows that the cost of forgoing a cash discount is relevant when evaluating a single supplier's credit terms in light of certain *bank borrowing costs*. In comparing various suppliers' credit terms, the cost of forgoing the cash discount may not be the most important factor in the decision process. Other factors relative to payment strategies may also need to be considered.

EFFECTS OF STRETCHING ACCOUNTS PAYABLE If a firm anticipates stretching accounts payable, the cost of forgoing a cash discount is reduced. Stretching accounts payable is sometimes suggested as a reasonable strategy for a firm as long as it does not damage its credit rating. As noted in Chapter 8, although this strategy is financially attractive, it raises an important ethical issue: It may cause the firm to violate the agreement it entered into with its supplier when it purchased merchandise. Clearly, a supplier would not look kindly on a customer who purposely postponed paying for purchases.

EXAMPLE

The Presti Corporation was extended credit terms of 2/10 net 30 EOM. The cost of forgoing the cash discount, assuming payment on the last day of the credit period, was found to be approximately 36 percent [2% × (360 ÷ 20)]. If the firm were able to stretch its account payable to 70 days without damaging its credit rating, the cost of forgoing the cash discount would be only 12 percent [2% × (360 ÷ 60)]. Stretching accounts payable reduces the implicit cost of forgoing a cash discount. ■

Accruals

The second spontaneous source of short-term financing for a business is accruals. **Accruals** are liabilities for services received for which payment has yet to be made. The most common items accrued by a firm are wages and taxes. Since taxes are payments to the government, their accrual cannot be manipulated by the firm. However, the accrual of wages can be manipulated to some extent. This is accomplished by delaying payment of wages, thereby receiving an interest-free loan from employees who are paid sometime after they have performed the work. The pay period for employees who earn an hourly rate is often governed by union regulations or by state or federal law. However, in other cases the frequency of payment is at the discretion of the company's manager.

accruals Liabilities for services received for which payment has not yet been made.

EXAMPLE

The Chan Company currently pays its employees at the end of each work week. The weekly payroll totals $400,000. If the firm were to extend the pay period so as to pay its employees one week later throughout an entire year, then the employees would in effect be loaning the firm $400,000 for a year. If the firm could earn 10 percent annually on invested funds, such a strategy would be worth $40,000 per year (.10 × $400,000). By increasing accruals in this way the firm can save this amount of money. ■

UNSECURED BANK SOURCES

Banks are a major source of unsecured short-term loans to businesses. Unlike the spontaneous sources of unsecured short-term financing, bank loans are negotiated and result from deliberate actions taken by the financial manager. The major type of loan made by banks to businesses is the **short-term self-liquidating loan.** Self-liquidating loans are intended merely to carry the firm through seasonal peaks in financing needs attributable primarily to buildups of accounts receivable and inventory. It is expected that as receivables and inventories are converted into cash, the funds needed to retire these loans will automatically be generated. In other words, the use to which the borrowed money is put provides the mechanism through which the loan is repaid

short-term self-liquidating loan An unsecured short-term loan in which the borrowed funds provide the mechanism through which the loan itself is repaid.

(hence the term *self-liquidating*). Banks lend unsecured short-term funds in three basic ways: through single-payment notes, lines of credit, and revolving credit agreements.

Single-Payment Notes

single-payment note
A short-term, one-time loan payable as a single amount at its maturity.

A **single-payment note** can be obtained from a commercial bank by a creditworthy business borrower. This type of loan is usually a "one-shot" deal made when a borrower needs additional funds for a short period but does not believe this need will continue. The resulting instrument is a *note*, which must be signed by the borrower. The note states the terms of the loan, which include the length of the loan (the maturity date) and the interest rate charged. This type of short-term note generally has a maturity of 30 days to 9 months or more. The interest charged on the note is generally tied in some fashion to the prime rate of interest.

prime rate of interest (prime rate) The lowest interest rate charged by leading banks for business loans to their most important and reliable business borrowers.

PRIME RATE OF INTEREST The **prime rate of interest (prime rate)** is the lowest rate of interest charged by the nation's leading banks on business loans to the most important and reliable business borrowers. The prime rate fluctuates with changing supply-and-demand relationships for short-term funds.[2] Banks generally determine the rate charged on loans to various borrowers by adding some type of premium to the prime rate to adjust it for the borrower's "riskiness." The premium may amount to 4 percent or more, although most unsecured short-term notes carry premiums of less than 2 percent. In general, commercial banks do not make short-term unsecured loans to businesses that are believed to be questionable risks.

fixed-rate note A note whose rate of interest is determined as a set increment above the prime rate and remains unvarying at that rate until maturity.

floating-rate note A note whose rate of interest is established as an increment above the prime rate and is allowed to "float," or vary, above prime *as the prime rate varies* until maturity.

FIXED- AND FLOATING-RATE NOTES Notes can have either fixed or floating interest rates. On a **fixed-rate note** the rate of interest is determined as a set increment above the prime rate and remains unvarying at that rate until maturity. On a **floating-rate note** the increment above the prime rate is initially established and the rate of interest is allowed to "float," or vary, above prime *as the prime rate varies* until maturity. Generally the increment above the prime rate on a floating-rate note will be *lower* than on a fixed-rate note of equivalent risk because the lender bears less risk with a floating-rate note. The highly volatile nature of the prime rate in recent years, coupled with the widespread use

[2] From 1975 through the third quarter of 1978 the prime rate was generally below 9 percent. From the end of 1978 until June of 1985 the prime rate remained above 9.5 percent. In late December 1980 the prime rate reached a record high, 21.5 percent. The prime rate slowly dropped from 9.5 percent in June 1985 to 7.5 percent in late August 1986. At that time the general expectation was a gradual increase in the prime rate.

of computers by banks to monitor and calculate loan interest, has been responsible for the current dominance of floating-rate notes and loans. Let us look at an example.

EXAMPLE

The MAC Company recently borrowed $100,000 from each of two banks—bank A and bank B. The loans were incurred on the same day, when the prime rate of interest was 12 percent. Each loan involved a 90-day note. The interest rate was set at $1\frac{1}{2}$ percent above the prime rate on bank A's fixed-rate note. This means that over the 90-day period the rate of interest will remain at $13\frac{1}{2}$ percent (12 percent prime rate + $1\frac{1}{2}$ percent increment) regardless of fluctuations in the prime rate. The interest rate was set at 1 percent above the prime rate on bank B's floating-rate note. This means that the rate charged over the 90 days will vary directly *with* the prime rate. Initially the rate will be 13 percent (12 percent + 1 percent), but when the prime rate changes, so will the rate of interest on the note. For instance, if after 30 days the prime rate rises to 12.5 percent and after another 30 days drops to 12.25 percent, the firm would be paying 13 percent interest for the first 30 days, 13.5 percent for the next 30 days, and 13.25 percent for the last 30 days. It should be clear that depending upon fluctuations in the prime rate over the 90 days, the MAC Company could pay more or less interest on the floating-rate loan from bank B than on the fixed-rate loan from bank A. ■

Lines of Credit

A **line of credit** is an agreement between a commercial bank and a business that states the amount of unsecured short-term borrowing the bank will make available to the firm over a given period of time. A line of credit agreement is typically made for a period of one year and often places certain constraints on the borrower. A line of credit agreement is *not a guaranteed loan* but indicates that if the bank has sufficient funds available, it will allow the borrower to owe it up to a certain amount of money. The amount of a line of credit is *the maximum amount the firm can owe the bank* at any point in time.

In applying for a line of credit the borrower may be required to submit such documents as its cash budget, its pro forma income statement, its pro forma balance sheet, and its recent financial statements. If the bank finds the customer acceptable, the line of credit will be extended. The major attraction of a line of credit from the bank's point of view is that it eliminates the need to examine the creditworthiness of a

line of credit An agreement between a commercial bank and a business specifying the amount of unsecured short-term borrowing the bank will make available to the firm over a given period.

customer each time it borrows money. A few characteristics of lines of credit require further explanation.

INTEREST RATES   As with single-payment notes, the interest charge on a line of credit is normally stated as a floating rate — the *prime rate plus a percent*. If the prime rate changes, the interest rate charged on new *as well as outstanding* borrowing will automatically change. The amount a borrower is charged in excess of the prime rate depends on its creditworthiness. The more creditworthy the borrower, the lower the interest increment above prime, and vice versa.

effective rate of interest
The actual rate of interest paid on a loan as opposed to the stated rate.

METHOD OF COMPUTING INTEREST   Once the rate of interest charged a given customer has been established, the method of computing interest should be determined. Interest can be paid either when a loan matures or in advance. If interest is paid at maturity, the **effective rate of interest** — the actual rate of interest paid — is equal to the stated interest rate. The effective rate of interest is found by dividing the dollar interest paid by the amount of loan proceeds available to the borrower. When interest is paid in advance, it is deducted from the loan so that the borrower actually receives less money than it requested. Paying interest in advance therefore raises the effective rate of interest above the stated rate. Let us look at an example.

EXAMPLE

The Cray Company wants to borrow $10,000 at a stated rate of 12 percent interest for one year. If the interest on the loan is paid at maturity, the firm will pay $1,200 (.12 × $10,000) for the use of the $10,000 for the year. The effective rate of interest will therefore be

$$\frac{\$1,200}{\$10,000} = 12.0 \text{ percent}$$

If the money is borrowed at the same *stated* rate but interest is paid in advance, the firm will still pay $1,200 in interest, but it will receive only $8,800 ($10,000 − $1,200). Thus the effective rate of interest in this case is

$$\frac{\$1,200}{\$8,800} = 13.6 \text{ percent}$$

discount loans Loans on which interest is paid in advance.

Paying interest in advance thus makes the effective rate of interest greater than the stated rate. Loans on which interest is paid in advance are often called **discount loans.** Most commercial bank loans to businesses require the interest payment at maturity. ■

OPERATING CHANGE RESTRICTIONS In a line of credit agreement, a bank may impose **operating change restrictions,** thereby retaining the right to revoke the line if any major changes occur in the firm's financial condition or operations. The firm is usually required to submit for review periodically—quarterly or semiannually—up-to-date and, preferably, audited financial statements. In addition, the bank typically needs to be informed of shifts in key managerial personnel or in the firm's operations prior to changes taking place because such changes may affect the future success and debt-paying ability of the firm and thus could alter its credit status. If the bank does not agree with the proposed changes and the firm makes them anyway, the bank has the right to revoke the line of credit agreement.

operating change restrictions Contractual restrictions that a bank may impose on a firm as part of a line of credit agreement.

COMPENSATING BALANCES To ensure that the borrower will be a good customer, most short-term unsecured bank loans—single-payment notes and lines of credit—often require the borrower to maintain a **compensating balance** in a demand deposit account (checking account) equal to a certain percentage of the amount borrowed. Compensating balances of 10 to 20 percent are normally required. A compensating balance not only forces the borrower to be a good customer of the bank but may also raise the interest cost to the borrower, thereby increasing the bank's earnings. An example will illustrate.

compensating balance A required checking account balance equal to a certain percentage of the borrower's short-term unsecured loan.

EXAMPLE

A company has borrowed $1 million under a line of credit agreement. It must pay a stated interest charge of 12 percent and maintain a compensating balance of 20 percent of the funds borrowed, or $200,000, in its checking account. Thus it actually receives the use of only $800,000. To use the $800,000 for a year, the firm pays $120,000 (.12 × $1,000,000). The effective rate of interest on the funds is therefore 15 percent ($120,000 ÷ $800,000), 3 percent more than the stated rate of 12 percent.

If the firm normally maintains a balance of $200,000 or more in its checking account, the effective interest cost will equal the stated interest rate of 12 percent because none of the $1 million borrowed is needed to satisfy the compensating balance requirement. If the firm normally maintains a $100,000 balance in its checking account, only an additional $100,000 will have to be tied up, leaving it with $900,000 ($1,000,000 − $100,000) of usable funds. The effective interest cost in this case would be 13.3 percent ($120,000 ÷ $900,000). Thus a compensating balance raises the cost of borrowing *only* if it is larger than the firm's normal cash balance. ■

annual cleanup The requirement that for a certain number of days annually borrowers under a line of credit carry a zero loan balance (i.e., owe the bank nothing).

ANNUAL CLEANUPS To ensure that money lent under a line of credit agreement is actually being used to finance seasonal needs, many banks require an **annual cleanup.** This means that the borrower must have a loan balance of zero—that is, owe the bank nothing—for a certain number of days during the year. Forcing the borrower to carry a zero loan balance for a certain period of time ensures that short-term loans do not turn into long-term loans.

All the characteristics of a line of credit agreement are negotiable to some extent. Today, banks bid competitively to attract large, well-known firms. A prospective borrower should attempt to negotiate a line of credit with the most favorable interest rate, for an optimal amount of funds, and with a minimum of restrictions. Lenders will often accept fees instead of deposit balances, and vice versa, as compensation for loans and other services rendered to their commercial customers. The lender will attempt to get a good return with maximum safety. These negotiations should produce a line of credit suitable to both borrower and lender.

Revolving Credit Agreements

revolving credit agreement A line of credit guaranteed to the borrower by the bank for a stated time period and regardless of the scarcity of money.

A **revolving credit agreement** is nothing more than a *guaranteed line of credit.* It is guaranteed in the sense that the commercial bank making the arrangement assures the borrower that a specified amount of funds will be made available regardless of the scarcity of money. The interest rate and other requirements for a revolving credit agreement are similar to those for a line of credit. It is not uncommon for a revolving credit agreement to be for a period greater than one year. Since the bank guarantees the availability of funds to the borrower, a **commitment fee** is normally charged on a revolving credit agreement. This fee often applies to the average unused balance of the line of credit. It is normally about .5 percent of the *average unused portion* of the funds. An example may clarify the nature of the commitment fees.

commitment fee The fee normally charged on a revolving credit agreement, often based on the average unused balance of the borrower's credit line.

EXAMPLE

The Blount Company has a $2 million revolving credit agreement with its bank. Its average borrowing under the agreement for the past year was $1.5 million. The bank charges a commitment fee of .5 percent. Since the average unused portion of the committed funds was $500,000 ($2 million − $1.5 million), the commitment fee for the year was $2,500 (.005 × $500,000). Of course, Blount also had to pay interest on the actual $1.5 million borrowed under the agreement. Although more expensive than a line of credit, a revolving credit agreement can be less risky from the borrower's viewpoint, since the availability of funds is guaranteed by the bank. ■

COMMERCIAL PAPER

Commercial paper is a form of financing that consists of short-term, unsecured promissory notes issued by firms with a high credit standing. Generally, only quite large firms of unquestionable financial soundness and reputation are able to issue commercial paper. Most commercial paper has maturities ranging from 3 to 270 days. Although there is no set denomination, it is generally issued in multiples of $100,000 or more. A large portion of the commercial paper today is issued by finance companies; manufacturing firms account for a smaller portion of this type of financing. As was indicated in Chapter 8, businesses often purchase commercial paper, which they hold as marketable securities, to provide an interest-earning reserve of liquidity.

commercial paper
A form of financing consisting of short-term, unsecured promissory notes issued by firms with a high credit standing.

Interest on Commercial Paper

The interest paid by the issuer of commercial paper is determined by the size of the discount and the length of time to maturity. Commercial paper is sold at a discount from its *par*, or *face, value*, and the actual interest earned by the purchaser is determined by certain calculations. These can be illustrated by the following example.

EXAMPLE

The Deems Corporation has just issued $1 million worth of commercial paper that has a 90-day maturity and sells for $970,000. At the end of 90 days the purchaser of this paper will receive $1 million for its $970,000 investment. The interest paid on the financing is therefore $30,000 on a principal of $970,000. This is equivalent to an annual interest rate for the Deems Corporation commercial paper of 12.4 percent [($30,000 ÷ $970,000) × (360 days ÷ 90 days)]. ■

An interesting characteristic of commercial paper is that it *normally* has a yield of 1 to 2 percent below the prime bank lending rate. In other words, firms are able to raise funds through the sale of commercial paper more cheaply than by borrowing from a commercial bank. This is because many suppliers of short-term funds do not have the option of making low-risk business loans at the prime rate. They can invest only in marketable securities such as Treasury bills and commercial paper.

Although the cost of borrowing through the sale of commercial paper is usually lower than the prime bank loan rate, it must be remembered that a firm needs to maintain a good working relationship with its bank. Therefore even if it is slightly more expensive to borrow from a commercial bank, it may at times be advisable to do so in order to establish the necessary rapport with a particular institution. This strategy ensures that when money is tight, funds can be obtained promptly and at a reasonable interest rate.

Sale of Commercial Paper

Commercial paper is *directly placed with investors* by the issuer or is *sold by commercial paper dealers*. For performing the marketing function, the commercial paper dealer is paid a fee. Regardless of the method of sale, most commercial paper is purchased from a firm by other businesses, banks, life insurance companies, pension funds, and money market mutual funds.

SECURED SOURCES

secured loan A loan for which the lender requires collateral.

collateral The security offered the lender by the borrower, usually in the form of an asset such as accounts receivable or inventory.

security agreement The agreement between the borrower and the lender that specifies the collateral held against a secured loan.

Once a firm has exhausted its unsecured sources of short-term financing, it may be able to obtain additional short-term financing on a secured basis. A **secured loan** is a loan for which the lender requires collateral. The **collateral** commonly takes the form of an asset, such as accounts receivable or inventory. The lender obtains a security interest in the collateral through the execution of a contract (security agreement) with the borrower. The **security agreement** specifies the collateral held against the loan. In addition, the terms of the loan against which the security is held are attached to, or form part of, the security agreement. They specify the conditions required for the security interest to be removed, along with the interest rate on the loan, repayment dates, and other loan provisions. A copy of the security agreement is filed in a public office within the state — typically a county or state court. Filing provides subsequent lenders with information about which assets of a prospective borrower are free to be used as collateral. The filing requirement protects the lender by legally establishing the lender's security interest.

Characteristics of Secured Short-Term Loans

Although many people believe that holding collateral as security reduces the risk of the loan, lenders do not usually view loans in this way. Lenders recognize that by having an interest in collateral they can reduce losses if the borrower defaults, but *as far as changing the risk of default, the presence of collateral has no impact.* A lender requires

HE CAN'T GET A LOAN?

Bankers won't give Ron Berger a loan. His hometown newspaper in Portland, Ore. won't sell him an ad unless it is paid for in advance. But all the same, Berger is riding high on the home video boom as founder and chairman of National Video, the largest chain of franchised video specialty stores in North America, with 515 locations.

Berger's bad credit rating stems from the collapse only six years ago of another franchising business he founded, the 57-store Photo Factory. That bankruptcy, caused by a bank error, high leverage and rising interest rates, "is frequently used against us by competitors," says Berger. "But it has also forced us to build this business without owing anybody a dime."

A few months after the failure of Photo Factory, Berger hired some former employees who were still out of work to do market research on video. He then sold the results through classified ads in the *Wall Street Journal* to raise money and to measure interest in video franchises. "We were deluged," recalls Berger, 37, a college dropout who was born in Tel Aviv and raised in New York City.

His research contained some surprising results. Most video stores were then situated in downtown areas, prime territory for X-rated cassettes. But Berger saw that the business would move to family-oriented suburbia. Men decide which VCR to buy, he learned, but women usually choose which programs to buy or rent. Middle- and lower-middle-class VCR owners would be better customers than the wealthy because they had fewer leisure choices.

Berger and his wife, Carol, sold their first franchises for $10 each out of a Las Vegas hotel room during the 1981 Consumer Electronics Show. Today, with VCRs in about 25% of all U.S. TV homes, Berger is selling an average of 30 new franchises a month for just under $20,000 each, plus a 4.9% royalty on sales. Each franchisee, who needs at least $80,000 more for fixtures and inventory, also contributes 7% of sales for advertising. During the 1985 fiscal year that ended Mar. 31, National Video earned $341,000 on revenues of $6.4 million, about doubling 1984 results.

Source: Alex Ben Block, "First Rewind, Then Fast Forward," *Forbes*, August 12, 1985, pp. 112–113. Reprinted with permission of *Forbes* Magazine. © Forbes, Inc. 1985.

collateral to ensure recovery of some portion of the loan in the event of default. What the lender wants above all, however, is to be repaid as scheduled. In general lenders prefer to make less risky loans at lower rates of interest than to be in a position in which they are forced to liquidate collateral.

COLLATERAL AND TERMS   A number of factors must be highlighted relative to the characteristics desirable in collateral and the basic terms of secured short-term loans.

Collateral. Lenders of secured short-term funds prefer collateral that has a life, or duration, closely matched to the term of the loan. This assures the lender that the collateral can be used to satisfy the loan in the event of a default. Current assets—accounts receivable and inventories—are the most desirable short-term loan collateral since they normally convert into cash much sooner than do fixed assets. Thus the short-term lender of secured funds generally accepts only liquid current assets as collateral.

percentage advance The percent of the book value of the collateral that constitutes the principal of a secured loan.

Terms. Typically, the lender determines the desirable **percentage advance** to make against the collateral. This percentage advance constitutes the principal of the secured loan and is normally between 30 and 100 percent of the book value of the collateral. It varies not only according to the type and activity of collateral but also according to the type of security interest being taken.

The interest rate charged on secured short-term loans is typically *higher* than the rate on unsecured short-term loans. Commercial banks and other institutions do not normally consider secured loans less risky than unsecured loans and therefore require higher interest rates on them. In addition, negotiating and administering secured loans is more troublesome for the lender than negotiating and administering unsecured loans. The lender therefore normally requires added compensation in the form of a service charge, a higher interest rate, or both. The higher cost of secured as opposed to unsecured borrowing is attributable to the greater risk of default and to the increased administration costs involved.

INSTITUTIONS EXTENDING SECURED SHORT-TERM LOANS The primary sources of secured short-term loans to businesses are commercial banks and commercial finance companies. Both institutions deal in short-term loans secured primarily by accounts receivable and inventory. The operations of commercial banks have already been described. **Commercial finance companies** are lending institutions that make *only* secured—both short-term and long-term—loans to businesses. Unlike banks, finance companies are not permitted to hold deposits.

commercial finance companies Lending institutions that make *only* secured loans—both short- and long-term—to businesses.

Only when its unsecured and secured short-term borrowing power from the commercial bank is exhausted will a borrower turn to the commercial finance company for additional secured borrowing. Because the finance company generally ends up with higher-risk borrowers, its interest charges on secured short-term loans are usually higher than those of commercial banks. The leading U.S. commercial finance companies include the Commercial Investors Trust (CIT) Corporation and Westinghouse Credit Corporation, Industrial Division.

The Use of Accounts Receivable as Collateral

Two commonly used means of obtaining short-term financing with accounts receivable are pledging accounts receivable and factoring accounts receivable. Actually, only a pledge of accounts receivable creates a secured short-term loan; factoring really entails the *sale* of accounts receivable at a discount. Although factoring is not actually a form of secured short-term borrowing, it does involve the use of accounts receivable to obtain needed short-term funds.

PLEDGING ACCOUNTS RECEIVABLE   A **pledge of accounts receivable** is often used to secure a short-term loan. Because accounts receivable are normally quite liquid, they are an attractive form of short-term collateral. Both commercial banks and commercial finance companies extend loans against pledges of accounts receivable.

When a firm approaches a prospective lender for a loan against accounts receivable, the lender will first evaluate the receivables to assess their desirability as collateral. Next, the dollar value of the acceptable accounts is adjusted by the lender for expected returns on sales and other allowances. Then, the percentage advanced against the adjusted collateral is determined by the lender based on its evaluation of the quality of the acceptable receivables and the expected cost of their liquidation. This percentage represents the principal of the loan and typically ranges between 50 and 90 percent of the face value of acceptable accounts receivable. Finally, to protect its interest in the collateral the lender will file a *lien*, which is a publicly disclosed legal claim on the collateral.

Pledges of accounts receivable are normally made on a **nonnotification basis.** This means that a customer whose account has been pledged as collateral is not notified of this action. Under the nonnotification arrangement the borrower still collects the pledged account receivable and the lender trusts that the borrower will remit these payments as they are received. If a pledge of accounts receivable is made on a **notification basis,** the customer is notified to remit payments, directly to the lender.

The stated cost of a pledge of accounts receivable is normally 2 to 5 percent above the prime interest rate offered by banks. In addition to the stated interest rate, a service charge of up to 3 percent may be levied. Although the interest payment is expected to compensate the lender for making the loan, the service charge is needed to cover the administrative costs incurred by the lender.

FACTORING ACCOUNTS RECEIVABLE   **Factoring accounts receivable** involves their outright sale to a factor or other financial institution. A **factor** is a financial institution that purchases accounts receivable from businesses. There are 15 to 20 firms currently operating in the United States that deal solely in factoring accounts receivable. Some commercial banks and commercial finance companies also factor accounts receivable. While not actually the same as obtaining a short-term loan, factoring accounts receivable is similar to borrowing with accounts

---

pledge of accounts receivable The use of a firm's accounts receivable as security, or collateral, to obtain a short-term loan.

nonnotification basis The basis on which a borrower, having pledged an account receivable, continues to collect the account payments without notifying the account customer.

notification basis The basis on which an account customer whose account has been pledged or factored is notified to remit payments directly to the lender or factor rather than to the borrower.

factoring accounts receivable The outright sale of accounts receivable at a discount to a factor or other financial institution in order to obtain funds.

factor A financial institution that specializes in purchasing accounts receivable from businesses.

receivable as collateral. Factoring constitutes approximately one-third of the total financing secured by accounts receivable (including factoring) and inventory in the United States currently.

A factoring agreement normally states the exact conditions, charges, and procedures for the purchase of an account. The factor, like a lender against a pledge of accounts receivable, chooses accounts for purchase, selecting only those that appear to be acceptable credit risks. Where factoring is to be on a continuing basis, the factor will actually make the firm's credit decisions, since this will guarantee the acceptability of accounts. Factoring is normally done on a *notification basis*, and the factor receives payment of the account directly from the customer. In addition, most sales of accounts receivable to a factor are made on a **nonrecourse** basis. This means that the factor agrees to accept all credit risks. Thus if a purchased account turns out to be uncollectible, the factor must absorb the loss.

nonrecourse basis The basis on which accounts receivable are sold to a factor with the understanding that the factor accepts all credit risks on the purchased accounts.

Typically the factor is not required to pay the firm until the account is collected or until the last day of the credit period, whichever occurs first. The factor sets up an account similar to a bank deposit account for each customer. As payment is received or as due dates arrive, the factor deposits money into the seller's account, from which the seller is free to make withdrawals as needed. In many cases, if the firm leaves the money in the account, a *surplus* will exist on which the factor will pay interest. In other instances, the factor may make *advances* to the firm against uncollected accounts that are not yet due. These advances represent a negative balance in the firm's account, on which interest is charged.

Factoring costs include commissions, interest levied on advances, and interest earned on surpluses. The face value of the accounts purchased by the factor less the commissions is deposited, when due, by the factor in the firm's account. The commissions are typically stated as a 1 to 3 percent discount from the face value of factored accounts receivable. The *interest levied on advances* is generally 2 to 4 percent above the prime rate. It is levied on the actual amount advanced. The interest paid on surpluses or positive account balances left with a factor is generally around .5 percent per month. While the cost of factoring may seem high, factoring has certain advantages that make it quite attractive to many firms. One is the ability it gives the firm to *turn accounts receivable immediately into cash* without having to worry about repayment. Another advantage of factoring is that it ensures a *known pattern of cash flows*. In addition, if factoring is undertaken on a continuous basis, the firm *can eliminate its credit and collection departments*.

The Use of Inventory as Collateral

Inventory is generally second to accounts receivable in desirability as short-term loan collateral. Inventory is attractive as collateral since it normally has a market value greater than its book value, which is used to establish its value as collateral. A lender securing a loan with inventory will probably be able to sell it for at least book value if the borrower defaults on its obligations.

DESIRABLE CHARACTERISTICS   Raw materials, work in process, or finished goods may all be offered as collateral for a short-term loan, but usually only raw materials or finished goods inventories are considered acceptable. The most important characteristic of inventory being evaluated as loan collateral is *marketability,* which must be considered in light of its physical properties. A warehouse of *perishable* items, such as fresh peaches, may be quite marketable, but if the cost of storing and selling the peaches is high, they may not be desirable collateral. *Specialized items* such as moon-roving vehicles are not desirable collateral either, since finding a buyer for them could be difficult. The lender, in evaluating inventory as possible loan collateral, looks for items with very stable market prices that have ready markets and that lack undesirable physical properties.

FLOATING INVENTORY LIENS   A lender may be willing to secure a loan under a **floating inventory lien,** which is a claim on inventory in general. This arrangement is most attractive when the firm has a stable level of inventory that consists of a diversified group of relatively inexpensive merchandise. Since it is difficult for a lender to verify the presence of the inventory, the lender will generally advance less than 50 percent of the book value of the average inventory. Inventories of items such as auto tires, screws and bolts, and shoes are candidates for floating-lien loans. The interest charge on a floating lien is 3 to 5 percent above the prime rate. Floating liens are often required by commercial banks as extra security on what would otherwise be an unsecured loan. A floating-lien inventory loan may also be available from commercial finance companies.

floating inventory lien
A lender's claim on the borrower's general inventory as collateral for a secured loan.

TRUST RECEIPT INVENTORY LOANS   A **trust receipt inventory loan** can often be made against relatively expensive automotive, consumer-durable, and industrial equipment that can be identified by serial number. Under this agreement, the borrower receives the inventory and the lender may advance 80 to 100 percent of its cost. The lender files a lien on all the items financed. The borrower is free to sell the merchandise but is trusted to remit the amount lent against each item along with accrued interest to the lender immediately after the sale. The lender then releases the lien on the appropriate item. The lender makes periodic checks of the borrower's inventory to make sure that the required amount of collateral remaining is still in the hands of the borrower. The interest charge to the borrower is normally 2 percent or more above the prime rate.

trust receipt inventory loan An agreement under which the lender advances 80 to 100 percent of the cost of the borrower's salable inventory items in exchange for the borrower's promise to immediately repay the loan, with accrued interest, upon the sale of each item.

TABLE 10.3 Summary of Key Features of Common Sources of Short-Term Financing

Type of financing	Source	Cost or conditions	Characteristics
I. Spontaneous sources			
Accounts payable	Suppliers of merchandise	No stated cost except when a cash discount is offered for early payment.	Credit extended on open account for 0 to 120 days. The largest source of short-term financing.
Accruals	Employees and government	Free.	Result from the fact that wages (employees) and taxes (government) are paid at discrete points in time after the service has been rendered. Hard to manipulate this source of financing.
II. Unsecured bank sources			
Single-payment note	Commercial banks	Prime plus 0% to 4% risk premium—fixed or floating rate.	A single-payment loan used to meet a funds shortage expected to last only a short period of time.
Lines of credit	Commercial banks	Prime plus 0% to 4% risk premium—fixed or floating rate. Often must maintain 10% to 20% compensating balance and clean up the line.	A prearranged borrowing limit under which funds, if available, will be lent to allow the borrower to meet seasonal needs.
Revolving credit agreements	Commercial banks	Prime plus 0% to 4% risk premium—fixed or floating rate. Often must maintain 10% to 20% compensating balance and pay a commitment fee of approximately .5% of the average unused balance.	A line of credit agreement under which the availability of funds is guaranteed. Often for a period greater than one year.
III. Commercial paper	Other businesses, banks, life insurance companies, pension funds, and money market mutual funds	Generally 1 to 2 percent below the prime rate of interest.	An unsecured short-term promissory note issued by the most financially sound firms. May be placed directly or sold through commercial paper dealers.

IV. Secured sources

Accounts receivable collateral

Source of short-term financing	Source	Cost or conditions	Characteristics
Pledging	Commercial banks and commercial finance companies	2% to 5% above prime plus up to 3% in fees. Advance 50% to 90% of collateral value.	Selected accounts receivable are used as collateral. The borrower is trusted to remit to the lender upon collection of pledged accounts. Done on a nonnotification basis.
Factoring	Factors, commercial banks, and commercial finance companies	1% to 3% discount from face value of factored accounts. Interest levied on advances of 2% to 4% above prime. Interest earned on surplus balances left with factor of about .5% per month.	Selected accounts are sold—generally without recourse—at a discount. All credit risks go with the accounts. Factor will loan (make advances) against uncollected accounts that are not yet due. Factor will also pay interest on surplus balances. Typically done on a notification basis.

Inventory collateral

Source of short-term financing	Source	Cost or conditions	Characteristics
Floating liens	Commercial banks and commercial finance companies	3% to 5% above prime. Advance less than 50% of collateral value.	A loan against inventory in general. Made when firm has stable inventory of a variety of inexpensive items.
Trust receipts	Manufacturers' captive financing subsidiaries, commercial banks, and commercial finance companies	2% or more above prime. Advance 80% to 100% of cost of collateral.	Loan against relatively expensive automotive, consumer-durable, and industrial equipment that can be identified by serial number. Collateral remains in possession of borrower, who is trusted to remit proceeds to lender upon its sale.
Warehouse receipts	Commercial banks and commercial finance companies	3% to 5% above prime plus a 1% to 3% warehouse fee. Advance 75% to 90% of collateral value.	Inventory used as collateral is placed under control of the lender by putting it in a terminal warehouse or through a field warehouse. A third party—a warehousing company—guards the inventory for the lender. Inventory is released only upon written approval of the lender.

Trust receipt loans are often made by manufacturers' wholly owned financing subsidiaries, known as *captive finance companies,* to their customers. *Floor planning* of automobile or equipment retailers is done under this arrangement. For example, General Motors Acceptance Corporation (GMAC), the financing subsidiary of General Motors, grants these types of loans to its dealers. Trust receipt loans are also available through commercial banks and commercial finance companies.

warehouse receipt loan
An arrangement in which the lender receives control of the pledged collateral, which is warehoused by a designated agent in the lender's behalf.

WAREHOUSE RECEIPT LOANS A **warehouse receipt loan** is an arrangement whereby the lender, who may be a commercial bank or commercial finance company, receives control of the pledged collateral, which is stored, or warehoused, in the lender's possession. After selecting acceptable collateral, the lender hires a warehousing company to act as its agent and take possession of the inventory. Two types of warehousing arrangements are possible: terminal warehouses and field warehouses. A *terminal warehouse* is a central warehouse used to store the merchandise of various customers. A terminal warehouse is normally used by the lender when the inventory is easily transported and can be delivered to the warehouse relatively inexpensively. Under a *field warehouse* arrangement, the lender hires a field warehousing company to set up a warehouse on the borrower's premises or to lease part of the borrower's warehouse as a repository for the pledged collateral. Regardless of whether a terminal or field warehouse is established, the warehousing company places a guard over the inventory. Only upon written approval of the lender can any portion of the secured inventory be released.

The actual lending agreement specifically states the requirements for the release of inventory. As in the case of other secured loans, the lender accepts only collateral believed to be readily marketable and advances only a portion — generally 75 to 90 percent — of the collateral's value. The specific costs of warehouse receipt loans are generally higher than those of any other secured lending arrangements due to the need to hire and pay a third party (the warehousing company) to guard and supervise the collateral. The basic interest charged on warehouse receipt loans is higher than that charged on unsecured loans, generally ranging from 3 to 5 percent above the prime rate. In addition to the interest charge, the borrower must absorb the costs of warehousing by paying the warehouse fee, which is generally between 1 and 3 percent of the amount of the loan. The borrower is normally also required to pay the insurance costs on the warehoused merchandise.

SUMMARY

● The key features of the most common sources of short-term financing for businesses are summarized in Table 10.3.

● Spontaneous sources of short-term financing include accounts payable and accruals. Accounts payable result from credit purchases of merchandise and are the primary source of short-term funds. Accruals result primarily from wage and tax obligations.

● Credit terms may differ with respect to the credit period, cash discount, cash discount period, and beginning of the credit period. The cost of forgoing cash discounts is a factor in deciding whether to take or forgo a cash discount. Stretching accounts payable can lower the cost of forgoing a cash discount.

● Banks are the major source of unsecured short-term loans to businesses. The interest rate on these loans may be fixed or may float and is tied to the prime rate of interest by a risk premium. Bank loans may take the form of a single-payment note, a line of credit, or a revolving credit agreement.

● The line of credit and revolving credit agreement often require compensating balances. The line of credit normally has an annual cleanup feature, while the revolving credit agreement normally requires that a commitment fee be paid on unused funds.

● Commercial paper can be issued only by large, financially strong firms. Commercial paper is directly placed with investors by the issuer or sold by commercial paper dealers.

● Secured short-term loans are those for which the lender requires collateral —typically current assets such as accounts receivable or inventory. Only a certain percentage of the book value of acceptable collateral is advanced by the lender. Both commercial banks and commercial finance companies make secured short-term loans.

● Accounts receivable is the most common type of collateral for short-term secured loans. A pledge of accounts receivable is an arrangement whereby the lender advances a certain percentage of the face value of the accounts found to be acceptable. Factoring involves the outright sale of accounts receivable at a discount from their face value to a factor who accepts all credit risk.

● Inventory can be used as collateral under a floating lien, a trust receipt arrangement, or a warehouse receipt loan. A floating inventory lien is a claim on inventory in general. Under the trust receipt arrangement, specific items are designated as collateral and the lender trusts that upon their sale the borrower will remit the portion owed. In a warehouse receipt loan, the lender gains control of the collateral through a third-party warehousing company.

QUESTIONS

10-1   What are the two key sources of spontaneous short-term financing for a firm? Why are these sources considered spontaneous, and how are they related to the firm's sales? Do they normally have a stated cost?

10-2   Is there a cost associated with taking a cash discount? Is there any cost associated with forgoing a cash discount? How is the decision to take a cash discount affected by the firm's cost of borrowing short-term funds?

10-3   What are *accruals?* What items are most commonly accrued by the firm? How attractive are accruals as a source of financing to the firm?

10-4 What is the primary source of *unsecured* short-term loans to business? When are loans considered short-term self-liquidating loans?

10-5 What are the basic terms and characteristics of a single-payment note? How is the prime interest rate relevant to the cost of short-term bank borrowing? What is a *floating-rate note?*

10-6 What is a *line of credit?* Describe each of the following features often included in these agreements.
   a Operating change restrictions
   b Compensating balance
   c Annual cleanup

10-7 What is meant by a *revolving credit agreement?* How does this arrangement differ from the line of credit agreement? What is a *commitment fee?*

10-8 How is commercial paper used to raise short-term funds? Who can issue commercial paper? Who buys commercial paper? How is it sold?

10-9 What are the key differences between unsecured and secured forms of short-term borrowing? In what circumstances do firms borrow short-term money on a secured basis?

10-10 In general, what kind of interest rates and fees are levied on secured short-term loans? Why are these rates generally *higher* than the rates on unsecured short-term loans?

10-11 Compare, contrast, and describe the basic features of
   a Pledging accounts receivable
   b Factoring accounts receivable
   Be sure to mention the institutions offering each of them.

10-12 Describe the basic features and compare each of the following methods of using *inventory* as short-term loan collateral.
   a Floating lien
   b Trust receipt loan
   c Warehouse receipt loan

PROBLEMS

10-1 **(Payment Dates)**   Determine when a firm must make payment for purchases made and invoices dated on November 25 under each of the following credit terms.
   a net 30   c net 45 date of invoice
   b net 30 EOM   d net 60 EOM

10-2 **(Cost of Forgoing Cash Discounts)**   Determine the cost of forgoing cash discounts under each of the following terms of sale.
   a 2/10 net 30   e 1/10 net 60
   b 1/10 net 30   f 3/10 net 30
   c 2/10 net 45   g 4/10 net 180
   d 3/10 net 45

10-3 **(Cash Discount versus Loan)**   Ann Daniels works in the accounts payable department of Penrod Industries. She has attempted to convince her boss to take the discount on the 3/10 net 45 credit terms most suppliers offer, but her boss argues that forgoing the 3 percent discount is less costly than a short-term loan at 14 percent. Prove that either Ann or her boss is incorrect.

10-4 **(Cash Discount Decisions)** The credit terms for each of three suppliers are as follows:

Supplier	Credit terms
X	1/10 net 55 EOM
Y	2/10 net 30 EOM
Z	2/20 net 60 EOM

a Determine the *approximate* cost of forgoing the cash discount from each supplier.

b Assuming that the firm needs short-term financing, recommend whether or not it would be better to forgo the cash discount or borrow from the bank at 15 percent annual interest. Evaluate each supplier separately.

c What impact, if any, would the fact that the firm could stretch its accounts payable (net period only) by 20 days from supplier Z have on your answer in **b** relative to this supplier?

10-5 **(Cash Discount Decisions)** Lenly Manufacturing has four possible suppliers, each offering different credit terms. Except for the differences in credit terms, their products and services are virtually identical. The credit terms offered by each supplier are as follows:

Supplier	Credit terms
Q	1/10 net 30 EOM
R	2/20 net 80 EOM
S	1/20 net 60 EOM
T	3/10 net 55 EOM

a Calculate the *approximate* cost of forgoing the cash discount from each supplier.

b If the firm needs short-term funds, which are currently available from its commercial bank at 16 percent, and if each of the suppliers is viewed *separately*, which, if any, of the suppliers' cash discounts should the firm forgo? Explain why.

c What impact, if any, would the fact that the firm could stretch its accounts payable (net period only) by 30 days from supplier T have on your answer in **b** relative to this supplier?

10-6 **(Changing Payment Cycle)** Upon accepting the position of chief executive officer and chairman of Ringup Cash Register, David Stanley changed the firm's weekly payday from Monday afternoon to the following Friday afternoon. The firm's weekly payroll was $10 million, and the cost of short-term funds was 13 percent. If the effect of this change was to delay check clearing by one week, what *annual* savings, if any, were realized?

10-7 **(Cost of Bank Loan)** Quick Enterprises has obtained a 90-day bank loan at an annual interest rate of 15 percent. If the loan is for $10,000, how much interest (in dollars) will the firm pay?

10-8 **(Effective Rate of Interest)** A financial institution lends a firm $10,000 for one year at 10 percent on a discounted basis and requires compensating balances of 20 percent of the face value of the loan. Determine the effective annual rate of interest associated with this loan.

10-9 **(Integrative — Comparison of Loan Terms)** Baldwin Can wishes to establish a prearranged borrowing agreement with its local commercial bank. The bank's terms for a line of credit are 3.30 percent over the prime rate, and the borrowing must be reduced to zero for a 30-day period. For an equivalent revolving credit agreement, the rate is 2.80 percent over prime with a commitment fee of .50 percent on the average unused balance. With both loans, the compensating balance is 20 percent of the amount borrowed. The prime rate is currently 8 percent. The revolving credit agreement is for $1 million. Baldwin Can expects on average to borrow $500,000 during the year no matter which loan agreement it decides to use.

  a What is the effective annual rate of interest under the line of credit?

  b What is the effective annual rate of interest under the revolving credit agreement? (*Hint:* Compute the ratio of the dollars the firm will pay in interest and commitment fees to the dollars the firm will effectively have use of.)

  c If the firm does expect to borrow an average of half the prearranged funds, which arrangement would you recommend for the borrower? Explain why.

10-10 **(Cost of Commercial Paper)** Commercial paper is usually sold at a discount. PULP has just sold an issue of 90-day commercial paper with a face value of $1 million. The firm has received $978,000.

  a What effective *annual* interest rate will the firm pay for financing with commercial paper?

  b If a brokerage fee of $9,612 was paid from the initial proceeds to an investment banker for selling the issue, what effective annual interest rate will the firm pay?

10-11 **(Accounts Receivable as Collateral)** Vosburgh Plate and Glass wishes to borrow $80,000 from the Vosburgh National Bank using its accounts receivable to secure the loan. The bank's policy is to accept as collateral any accounts that are normally paid within 30 days of the end of the credit period so long as the average age of the account is not greater than the customer's average payment period. Vosburgh Plate's accounts receivable, their average ages, and the average payment period for each customer are given in the table at the top of the next page. The company extends terms of net 30 days.

  a Calculate the dollar amount of acceptable accounts receivable collateral held by Vosburgh Plate and Glass.

  b The bank reduces collateral by 10 percent for returns and allowances. What is the level of acceptable collateral under this condition?

  c The bank will advance 75 percent against the firm's acceptable collateral (after adjusting for returns and allowances). What amount can Vosburgh Plate and Glass borrow against these accounts?

Customer	Account receivable	Average age of account	Average payment period of customer
A	$20,000	10 days	40 days
B	6,000	40 days	35 days
C	22,000	62 days	50 days
D	11,000	68 days	65 days
E	2,000	14 days	30 days
F	12,000	38 days	50 days
G	27,000	55 days	60 days
H	19,000	20 days	35 days

10-12 **(Factoring)** Freeflow Finance factors the accounts of the Mooring Company. All eight factored accounts are listed, with the amount factored, the date due, and the status as of May 30. Indicate the amounts Freeflow should have remitted to Mooring as of May 30 and the dates of those remittances. Assume that the factor's commission of 2 percent is deducted as part of determining the amount of the remittance.

Account	Amount	Date due	Status on May 30
A	$200,000	May 30	Collected May 15
B	90,000	May 30	Uncollected
C	110,000	May 30	Uncollected
D	85,000	June 15	Collected May 30
E	120,000	May 30	Collected May 27
F	180,000	June 15	Collected May 30
G	90,000	May 15	Uncollected
H	30,000	June 30	Collected May 30

10-13 **(Inventory Financing)** Lake Turbine Company faces a liquidity crisis — it needs a loan of $100,000 for 30 days. Having no source of additional unsecured borrowing, the firm must find a secured short-term lender. The firm's accounts receivable are quite low, but its inventory is considered liquid and reasonably good collateral. The book value of the inventory is $300,000, of which $120,000 is finished goods.

(1) Center City Bank will make a $100,000 trust receipt loan against the finished goods inventory. The annual interest rate on the loan is 12 percent on the outstanding loan balance plus a .25 percent administration fee levied against the $100,000 initial loan amount. Because it will be liquidated as inventory is sold, the average amount owed over the month is expected to be $75,000.

(2) First Local Bank is willing to lend $100,000 against a floating lien on the book value of inventory for the 30-day period at an annual interest rate of 13 percent.

(3) North Mall Bank and Trust will loan $100,000 against a warehouse receipt on the finished goods inventory and charge 15 percent annual interest on the outstanding loan balance. A .5 percent ware-

housing fee will be levied against the average amount borrowed. Because the loan will be liquidated as inventory is sold, the average loan balance is expected to be $60,000.

a Calculate the cost of each of the proposed plans for obtaining an initial loan amount of $100,000.

b Which plan do you recommend? Why?

c If the firm had made a purchase of $100,000 for which it had been given terms of 2/10 net 30, would it increase the firm's profitability to forgo the discount and borrow as recommended in **b**? Why or why not?

Part Four

BASIC LONG-TERM FINANCIAL CONCEPTS

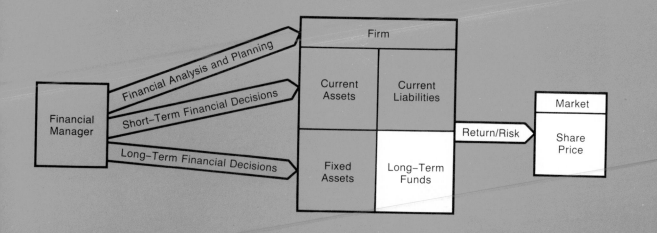

11

TIME
VALUE
OF MONEY

After studying this chapter, you should be able to:

● Understand the concept of future value, its calculation, the use of future-value interest tables, and the compounding of interest more frequently than annually.

● Determine the future value of an annuity using future-value interest tables for an annuity.

● Discuss the concept of present value, its calculation, the use of present-value interest tables, and the relationship of present to future value.

● Find the present value of a mixed stream of cash flows and an annuity, and use present-value interest tables for an annuity.

● Describe the procedures involved in (1) determining deposits to accumulate a future sum, (2) loan amortization, (3) finding interest or growth rates, and (4) evaluating perpetuities.

Imagine that at age 25 you begin making annual cash deposits of $2,000 into a savings account that pays 5 percent annual interest. At the end of 40 years, at age 65, you would have made deposits totaling $80,000 (40 years × $2,000 per year). Assuming you have made no withdrawals, what do you think your account balance would be then? $100,000?, $150,000?, $200,000? No, your $80,000 would have grown to $242,000! Why? Because the time value of money allowed the deposits to earn interest that was compounded over the 40 years. Because opportunities to earn interest on funds are readily available, the time value of money affects everyone — individuals, businesses, and government.

Financial managers use time-value concepts primarily when making long-term decisions, since costs and benefits occur over a period of future years. The key concepts of *time value* are *future value* and *present value*. Future-value techniques are used to determine the future worth of current investments; and present-value techniques are used to find the current worth of future benefits expected to result from a given action. Time-value methods are used to calculate the payments required to accumulate a future sum, to amortize loans by calculating loan payment schedules, to determine interest or growth rates of money streams, and to evaluate perpetuities. In addition, time-value techniques are used to find the internal rate of return — an important concept discussed in Chapter 15.

◼ FUTURE VALUE OF A SINGLE SUM

future value The value of a present sum at a future date found by applying compound interest over a specified period of time.

The **future value** of a present sum is found by applying compound interest for a specified period of time. Savings institutions advertise compound interest returns at a rate of *x* percent or *x* percent interest compounded annually, semiannually, quarterly, monthly, weekly, daily, or even continuously. The principles of future value are quite simple, regardless of the period of time involved.

The Concept of Future Value

compounded interest When the amount earned on a given deposit has become part of the principal at the end of a specified period.

principal The amount of money on which interest is paid.

We speak of **compounded interest** when we wish to indicate that the amount earned on a given deposit has become part of the principal at the end of a specified period. The term **principal** refers to the amount of

NOTE: Many of the computations introduced in this chapter and applied throughout the text can be streamlined using a calculator or personal computer. Procedures for making routine financial calculations using a simple calculator having only the four standard math functions are described in Appendix E. The reader is strongly urged to learn these procedures once the basic underlying financial concepts are understood. With a little practice, both the speed and accuracy of financial computations using a calculator can be enhanced with application of the procedures presented.

money on which the interest is paid. Annual compounding is the most common type. The concept of future value with annual compounding can be illustrated by a simple example.

EXAMPLE

If Rich Saver placed $100 in a savings account paying 8 percent interest compounded annually, at the end of one year he will have $108 in the account. This $108 represents the initial principal of $100 plus 8 percent ($8) in interest. The future value at the end of the first year is calculated using Equation 11.1:

$$\text{Future value at end of year 1} = \$100 \times (1 + .08) = \$108 \quad (11.1)$$

If Rich were to leave this money in the account for another year, he would be paid interest at the rate of 8 percent on the new principal of $108. At the end of this second year, there would be $116.64 in the account. This $116.64 would represent the principal at the beginning of year 2 ($108) plus 8 percent of the $108 ($8.64) in interest. The future value at the end of the second year is calculated using Equation 11.2:

$$\text{Future value at end of year 2} = \$108 \times (1 + .08) = \$116.64 \quad (11.2) \quad \blacksquare$$

Substituting the expression between the equal signs in Equation 11.1 for the $108 figure in Equation 11.2 gives us Equation 11.3.

$$\begin{aligned} \text{Future value at end of year 2} &= \$100 \times (1 + .08) \times (1 + .08) \quad (11.3) \\ &= \$100 \times (1.08)^2 \\ &= \$116.64 \end{aligned}$$

The Calculation of Future Value

The basic relationship in Equation 11.3 can be generalized to find the future value after any number of periods. Let

F_n = the future value at the end of period n
P = the initial principal, or present value
k = the annual rate of interest paid
n = the number of periods—typically years—the money is left on deposit

Using this notation, a general equation for the future value at the end of period n can be formulated:

$$F_n = P \times (1 + k)^n \quad (11.4)$$

The usefulness of Equation 11.4 for finding the future value, F_n, in an account paying k percent interest compounded annually for n periods if P dollars were deposited initially can be illustrated by a simple example.

THE MAGIC OF COMPOUND INTEREST

John Maynard Keynes supposedly called it magic. One of the Rothschilds is said to have proclaimed it the eighth wonder of the world. Today people continue to extol its wonder and its glory.

The object of their affection: compound interest, a subject that bores or confuses as many people as it impresses.

Yet understanding compound interest can help people calculate the return on savings and investments, as well as the cost of borrowing. These calculations apply to almost any financial decision, from the reinvestment of dividends to the purchase of a zero-coupon bond for an individual retirement account.

Simply stated, compound interest is "interest on interest." Interest earned after a given period, for example, a year, is added to the principal amount and included in the next period's interest calculation. . . .

The power of compound interest has intrigued people for years. Early in the last century, an English astronomer, Francis Baily, figured that a British penny invested at an annual compound interest of 5% at the birth of Christ would have yielded enough gold by 1810 to fill 357 million earths. Benjamin Franklin was more practical. At his death in 1790, he left 1,000 pounds each to the cities of Boston and Philadelphia on the condition they wouldn't touch the money for 100 years. Boston's bequest, which was equivalent to about $4,600, ballooned to $332,000 by 1890.

But savers and investors don't have to live to 100 to reap its benefits.

Consider an investment with a current value of $10,000 earning annual interest of 8%. After a year the investment grows to $10,800 (1.08 times $10,000). After the second year it's worth $11,664 (1.08 times $10,800). After three more years, the investment grows to $14,693.

The same concept applies to consumer borrowing. A $10,000 loan, with an 8% interest charge compounded annually, would cost $14,693 to repay in a lump sum after five years. . . .

Investors and savers can also take a rule-of-thumb shortcut to determine how long it would take to double a sum of money at a given interest rate with annual compounding: Divide 72 by the rate. For example, the $10,000 investment yielding 8% a year would double in about nine years (72 divided by eight).

But people should be aware that inflation compounds, too. Unless inflation disappears, that projected $20,000 investment nine years from now will be worth something less than that in today's dollars.

Source: Robert L. Rose, "Compounding: It's Boring But a Wonder," *The Wall Street Journal*, June 17, 1985, p. 21. Reprinted by permission of *The Wall Street Journal*. © 1985 Dow Jones & Company, Inc. All rights reserved.

EXAMPLE

Jane Frugal has placed $800 in a savings account paying 6 percent interest compounded annually. She wishes to determine how much money will be in the account at the end of five years. Substituting $P = \$800$, $k = .06$, and $n = 5$ into Equation 11.4 gives the amount at the end of year 5.

$$F_5 = \$800 \times (1 + .06)^5 = \$800 \times (1.338) = \$1,070.40$$

Jane will have $1,070.40 in the account at the end of the fifth year. This analysis can be depicted diagramatically on a time line as shown in Figure 11.1. ■

Future-Value Interest Tables

Solving the preceding equation is quite time-consuming, since one must raise 1.06 to the fifth power. To simplify the calculations, future-value interest tables have been compiled. A table for the amount generated by the payment of compound interest on an initial principal of $1 is given as Appendix Table D-1. The table provides values for $(1 + k)^n$ in Equation 11.4. This portion of Equation 11.4 is called the **future-value interest factor.** This factor is the multiplier used to calculate at a specified interest rate the future value as of a given time of a present amount. The future-value interest factor for an initial principal of $1 compounded at k percent for n periods is referred to as $FVIF_{k,n}$:

future-value interest factor The muliplier used to calculate at a specified interest rate the future value as of a given time of a present amount.

$$\text{Future-value interest factor} = FVIF_{k,n} = (1 + k)^n \qquad (11.5)$$

By accessing the table with respect to the annual interest rate, k, and the appropriate periods,[1] n, the factor relevant to a particular problem can be found.

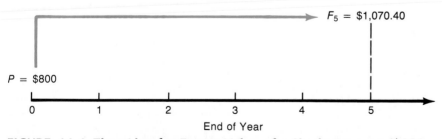

FIGURE 11.1 Time Line for Future Value of a Single Amount ($800 Initial Principal, Earning 6 Percent Annual Interest, at End of 5 Years)
An initial principal, P, of $800 deposited into an account paying 6 percent annual interest, k, will have a future value at the end of 5 years, F_5, of $1,070.40.

[1] Although we commonly deal with years rather than periods, financial tables are frequently presented in terms of periods to provide maximum flexibility.

A sample portion of Table D-1 is shown in Table 11.1. Because the factors in Table D-1 give the value for the expression $(1 + k)^n$ for various k and n combinations, by letting $FVIF_{k,n}$ represent the appropriate factor from Table D-1 we can rewrite Equation 11.4 as follows:

$$F_n = P \times (FVIF_{k,n}) \qquad (11.6)$$

The expression indicates that to find the future value, F_n, at the end of period n of an initial deposit, we have merely to multiply the initial deposit, P, by the appropriate future-value interest factor from Table D-1. An example will illustrate the use of this table.

EXAMPLE

Jane Frugal has placed $800 in her savings account at 6 percent interest compounded annually. She wishes to find out how much would be in the account at the end of five years and does so by the cumbersome process of raising $(1 + .06)$ to the fifth power. Using the table for the future value of one dollar (Table 11.1 or Table D-1), she could find the future-value interest factor for an initial principal of $1 on deposit for five years at 6 percent interest compounded annually without performing any calculations. The appropriate factor for 6 percent and 5 years, $FVIF_{6\%,5yrs}$, is 1.338. Multiplying this factor by her actual initial principal of $800 would then give her the future value at the end of year 5, which is $1,070.40. ■

Four important observations should be made about the table for the future value of one dollar:

TABLE 11.1 The Future-Value Interest Factors for One Dollar, $FVIF_{k,n}$

Period	5%	6%	7%	8%	9%	10%
1	1.050	1.060	1.070	1.080	1.090	1.100
2	1.102	1.124	1.145	1.166	1.188	1.210
3	1.158	1.191	1.225	1.260	1.295	1.331
4	1.216	1.262	1.311	1.360	1.412	1.464
5	1.276	1.338	1.403	1.469	1.539	1.611
6	1.340	1.419	1.501	1.587	1.677	1.772
7	1.407	1.504	1.606	1.714	1.828	1.949
8	1.477	1.594	1.718	1.851	1.993	2.144
9	1.551	1.689	1.838	1.999	2.172	2.358
10	1.629	1.791	1.967	2.159	2.367	2.594

NOTE: All table values have been rounded to the nearest thousandth. Thus the calculated values may differ slightly from the table values.

1. The factors in the table are those for determining the future value of one dollar *at the end of the given period.*
2. *The future-value interest factor for a single amount is always greater than 1.* Only if the interest rate were 0 would this factor equal 1.
3. *As the interest rate increases for any given period, the future-value interest factor also increases.* Thus the higher the interest rate, the greater the future value.
4. *For a given interest rate, the future value of a dollar increases with the passage of time.* Thus the longer the period of time, the greater the future value.

The relationship between various interest rates, the numbers of periods interest is earned, and future-value interest factors is illustrated in Figure 11.2. The fact that the higher the interest rate the higher the future-value interest factor is, and the longer the period of time the higher the future-value interest factor is, should be clear. Note that for an interest rate of 0 percent, the future-value interest factor always equals 1.00, and the future value therefore always equals the initial principal.

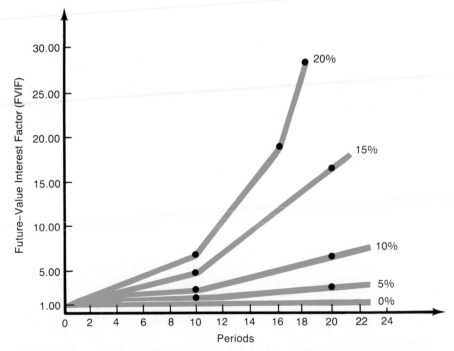

FIGURE 11.2 Interest Rates, Time Periods, and Future-Value Interest Factors Used to Find the Future Value of One Dollar
The future-value interest factor increases with increases in the interest rate or the period of time funds are left on deposit. At zero percent interest, the future-value interest factor equals 1.00 and for interest rates greater than zero the factor is always greater than 1.00.

Compounding More Frequently than Annually

Interest is often compounded more frequently than once a year. Savings institutions compound interest semiannually, quarterly, monthly, weekly, daily, or even continuously. This section discusses semiannual and quarterly compounding and explains how to use future-value interest tables in these situations.

semiannual compounding Compounding of interest over two periods within the year.

SEMIANNUAL COMPOUNDING **Semiannual compounding** of interest involves two compounding periods within the year. Instead of the stated interest rate being paid once a year, one-half of the stated interest rate is paid twice a year.

EXAMPLE

Rich Saver has decided to invest $100 in a savings account paying 8 percent interest *compounded semiannually*. If he leaves his money in the account for two years, he will be paid 4 percent interest compounded over four periods, each of which is six months long. Table 11.2 shows that at the end of one year, when the 8 percent interest is compounded semiannually, Rich will have $108.16; at the end of two years, he will have $116.99. ■

quarterly compounding Compounding of interest over four periods within the year.

QUARTERLY COMPOUNDING **Quarterly compounding** of interest involves four compounding periods within the year. One-fourth of the stated interest rate is paid four times a year.

EXAMPLE

Rich Saver, after further investigation of his savings opportunities, has found an institution that will pay him 8 percent *compounded quarterly*. If he leaves his money in this account for two years, he

TABLE 11.2 The Future Value from Investing $100 at 8 Percent Interest Compounded Semiannually over Two Years

Period	Beginning principal (1)	Future-value interest factor (2)	Future value at end of period [(1) × (2)] (3)
6 months	$100.00	1.04	$104.00
1 year	104.00	1.04	108.16
18 months	108.16	1.04	112.49
2 years	112.49	1.04	116.99

TABLE 11.3 The Future Value from Investing $100 at 8 Percent Interest Compounded Quarterly over Two Years

Period	Beginning principal (1)	Future-value interest factor (2)	Future value at end of period [(1) × (2)] (3)
3 months	$100.00	1.02	$102.00
6 months	102.00	1.02	104.04
9 months	104.04	1.02	106.12
1 year	106.12	1.02	108.24
15 months	108.24	1.02	110.40
18 months	110.40	1.02	112.61
21 months	112.61	1.02	114.86
2 years	114.86	1.02	117.16

will be paid 2 percent interest compounded over eight periods, each of which is three months long. Table 11.3 presents the calculations required to determine the amount Rich will have at the end of two years. As the table shows, at the end of one year, when the 8 percent interest is compounded quarterly, Rich will have $108.24; at the end of two years, he will have $117.16.

Table 11.4 presents comparative values for Rich Saver's $100 at the end of years 1 and 2 given annual, semiannual, and quarterly compounding at the 8 percent rate. As the table shows, the *more frequently interest is compounded, the greater the amount of money accumulated.* This is true for any interest rate for any period of time. ■

USING TABLE D-1 Table D-1, the table of future-value interest factors for one dollar, can be used to find the future value when interest is compounded *m* times each year. Instead of indexing the table for *k* percent and *n* years, as we do when interest is compounded annually, we index it for $(k \div m)$ percent and $(m \times n)$ periods. The usefulness of the table is usually somewhat limited, since only selected rates for a limited number of periods can be found. The table can commonly be

TABLE 11.4 The Future Value from Investing $100 at 8 Percent for Years 1 and 2 Given Various Compounding Periods

End of year	COMPOUNDING PERIOD		
	Annual	Semiannual	Quarterly
1	$108.00	$108.16	$108.24
2	116.64	116.99	117.16

used to calculate the results of semiannual ($m = 2$) and quarterly ($m = 4$) compounding, but when more frequent compounding is done, the aid of a financial calculator or computer may be necessary. The following example will clarify the use of the future-value interest factor table in situations where interest is compounded more frequently than annually.

EXAMPLE

In the earlier examples, Rich Saver wished to find the future value of $100 invested at 8 percent compounded both semiannually and quarterly for two years. The number of compounding periods, m, was 2 and 4, respectively, in these cases. The values by which the table for the future value of one dollar is accessed, along with the future-value interest factor in each case, are given below.

Compounding period	m	Percentage interest rate $(k \div m)$	Periods $(m \times n)$	Future-value interest factor from Table D-1
Semiannual	2	$.08 \div 2 = .04$	$2 \times 2 = 4$	1.170
Quarterly	4	$.08 \div 4 = .02$	$4 \times 2 = 8$	1.172

The factor for 4 percent and four periods is used for the semiannual compounding, while the factor for 2 percent and eight periods is used for quarterly compounding. Multiplying each of the factors by the initial $100 deposit results in a value of $117.00 ($1.170 \times 100) for semiannual compounding and a value of $117.20 ($1.172 \times 100) for quarterly compounding. The corresponding values found by the long method are $116.99 and $117.16, respectively. The discrepancy can be attributed to the rounding of values in the table. ■

FUTURE VALUE OF AN ANNUITY

annuity A stream of equal annual cash flows. These cash flows can be *inflows* of returns earned on investments or *outflows* of funds invested in order to earn future returns.

An **annuity** is a stream of equal annual cash flows. These cash flows can be *inflows* of returns earned on investments or *outflows* of funds invested in order to earn future returns. The calculations required to find the future value of an annuity on which interest is paid at a specified rate compounded annually can be illustrated by the following example.

EXAMPLE

Mollie Carr wishes to determine how much money she will have at the end of five years if she deposits $1,000 annually in a savings

TABLE 11.5 The Future Value of a $1,000 Five-Year Annuity Compounded at 7 Percent

End of year	Amount deposited (1)	Number of years compounded (2)	Future-value interest factors from Table D-1 (3)	Future value at end of year [(1) × (3)] (4)
1	$1,000	4	1.311	$1,311
2	1,000	3	1.225	1,225
3	1,000	2	1.145	1,145
4	1,000	1	1.070	1,070
5	1,000	0	1.000	1,000
Future value of annuity at end of year 5				$5,751

account paying 7 percent annual interest. The deposits will be made at the end of each of the next five years. Table 11.5 presents the calculations required. This situation is depicted diagramatically on a time line in Figure 11.3. As the table and figure show, at the end of year 5 Mollie will have $5,751 in her account. Column 2 of the table indicates that since the deposits are made at the end of the year, the first deposit will earn interest for four years, the second for three years, and so on. The future-value interest factors in column 3 correspond to these interest-earning periods and the 7 percent rate of interest. ■

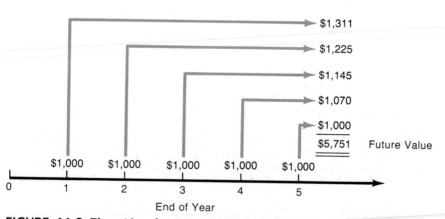

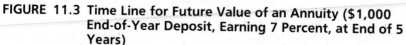

FIGURE 11.3 Time Line for Future Value of an Annuity ($1,000 End-of-Year Deposit, Earning 7 Percent, at End of 5 Years)
Annual end-of-year deposits, A, of $1,000 into an account paying 7 percent annual interest, k, will have a future value at the end of 5 years, S_5, of $5,751.

Using a Future Value of an Annuity Table

future-value interest factor for an annuity
The multiplier used to calculate the future value of an annuity at a specified interest rate over a given period of time.

Annuity calculations can be simplified using a **future-value interest factor for an annuity.** This factor is the multiplier used to calculate the future value of an annuity at a specified interest rate over a given period of time. A portion of Appendix Table D-2, which contains future-value interest factors for an annuity, is shown in Table 11.6. The factors included in the table are based on the assumption that every deposit is made at the *end of the period*.[2] The formula for the future-value interest factor for an n-year annuity with end-of-year cash flows when interest is compounded annually at k percent, $FVIFA_{k,n}$, is[3]

$$FVIFA_{k,n} = \sum_{t=1}^{n} (1+k)^{t-1} \tag{11.7}$$

Letting S_n equal the future value of an n-year annuity, A equal the amount to be deposited annually at the end of each year, and $FVIFA_{k,n}$ represent the appropriate *future-value interest factor for an n-year annuity compounded at k percent,* the relationship among these variables can be expressed as follows:

$$S_n = A \times (FVIFA_{k,n}) \tag{11.8}$$

TABLE 11.6 The Future-Value Interest Factors for a One-Dollar Annuity, $FVIFA_{k,n}$

Period	5%	6%	7%	8%	9%	10%
1	1.000	1.000	1.000	1.000	1.000	1.000
2	2.050	2.060	2.070	2.080	2.090	2.100
3	3.152	3.184	3.215	3.246	3.278	3.310
4	4.310	4.375	4.440	4.506	4.573	4.641
5	5.526	5.637	5.751	5.867	5.985	6.105
6	6.802	6.975	7.153	7.336	7.523	7.716
7	8.142	8.394	8.654	8.923	9.200	9.487
8	9.549	9.897	10.260	10.637	11.028	11.436
9	11.027	11.491	11.978	12.488	13.021	13.579
10	12.578	13.181	13.816	14.487	15.193	15.937

[2] The discussions of annuities throughout this text concentrate on the more common form of annuity—the *ordinary annuity,* which is an annuity that occurs at the *end* of each period. An annuity that occurs at the *beginning* of each period is called an *annuity due.* The financial tables for annuities included in this book are prepared for use with ordinary annuities.

[3] This formula merely states that the future-value interest factor for an n-year annuity is found by adding the sum of the first $n-1$ future-value interest factors to 1.000 $\left(\text{i.e., } FVIFA_{k,n} = 1.000 + \sum_{t=1}^{n-1} FVIF_{k,t} \right)$.

Equation 11.8 along with Table D-2 can be conveniently used to find the future value of an annuity. In Mollie Carr's case, the $1,000 deposit (A) can be multiplied by the interest factor for the future value of a one-dollar annuity at 7 percent for a five-year life ($FVIFA_{7\%,5}$) obtained from Table D-2. Multiplying the $1,000 by the table value, 5.751, results in a future value for the annuity of $5,751. The following example further illustrates the usefulness of Table D-2.

EXAMPLE

Randy Middleton wishes to determine the sum of money he will have in his savings account, which pays 6 percent annual interest, at the end of ten years if he deposits $600 at the end of each year for the next ten years. The appropriate interest factor for the future value at 6 percent for a ten-year annuity, $FVIFA_{6\%,10yrs}$, is given in Table D-2 as 13.181. Multiplying this factor by the $600 deposit results in a future value of $7,908.60. The simple calculations required to find the future value of an annuity using Table D-2 should be clear from this example. ■

PRESENT VALUE OF A SINGLE SUM

It is often useful to determine the "present value" of a future sum of money. **Present value** is the current dollar value of a future sum — the amount of money that would have to be invested today at a given interest rate over a specified period in order to equal the future sum. Present value, like future value, is based on the belief that a dollar today is worth more than a dollar that will be received at some future date. The actual present value of a dollar depends largely on the investment opportunities of the recipient and the point in time at which the earned return is to be received. This section explores the present value of a single sum.

present value The current dollar value of a future sum. The amount that would have to be invested today at a given interest rate over the period in order to equal the future sum.

The Concept of Present Value

The process of finding present values, is often referred to as **discounting cash flows.** This process is actually the inverse of compounding. It is concerned with answering the question "If I can earn k percent on my money, what is the most I would be willing to pay for an opportunity to receive F_n dollars n periods from today?" Instead of finding the future value of present dollars invested at a given rate, discounting determines the present value of a future amount, assuming that the decision maker has an opportunity to earn a certain return, k, on the money. This return is often referred to as the *discount rate, required return, cost of capital,*

discounting cash flows The process of finding present values; the inverse of compounding interest.

or *opportunity cost*. These terms will be used interchangeably in this text. The discounting process can be illustrated by a simple example.

EXAMPLE

Mr. Cotter has been given an opportunity to receive $300 one year from now. If he can earn 6 percent on his investments in the normal course of events, what is the most he should pay for this opportunity? To answer this question, we must determine how many dollars must be invested at 6 percent today to have $300 one year from now. Letting P equal this unknown amount, and using the same notation as in the compounding discussion, the situation can be expressed as follows:

$$P \times (1 + .06) = \$300 \tag{11.9}$$

Solving Equation 11.9 for P gives us Equation 11.10

$$P = \frac{\$300}{1.06} \tag{11.10}$$
$$= \$283.02$$

which results in a value of $283.02 for P. In other words, the "present value" of $300 received one year from today, given an opportunity cost of 6 percent, is $283.02. Mr. Cotter should be indifferent to whether he receives $283.02 today or $300.00 one year from now. If he can receive either by paying less than $283.02 today, he should, of course, do so. ■

A Mathematical Expression for Present Value

The present value of a future amount can be found mathematically by solving Equation 11.4 for P. In other words, one merely wants to obtain the present value, P, of some future amount, F_n, to be received n periods from now, assuming an opportunity cost of k. Solving Equation 11.4 for P gives us Equation 11.11, which is the general equation for the present value of a future amount.

$$P = \frac{F_n}{(1 + k)^n} = F_n \times \left[\frac{1}{(1 + k)^n} \right] \tag{11.11}$$

The similarity between this general equation for present value and the equation in the preceding example (Equation 11.10) should be clear. The use of this equation in finding the present value of a future amount can be illustrated by a simple example.

EXAMPLE

Bob Lambert wishes to find the present value of $1,700 that will be received eight years from now. Bob's opportunity cost is 8 percent. Substituting $F_8 = \$1,700$, $n = 8$, and $k = .08$ into Equation 11.11 yields Equation 11.12.

$$P = \frac{\$1700}{(1 + .08)^8} \tag{11.12}$$

To solve Equation 11.12, the term $(1 + .08)$ must be raised to the eighth power. The value resulting from this time-consuming calculation is 1.851. Dividing this value into $1,700 yields a present value for the $1,700 of $918.42. This analysis can be depicted diagramatically on a time line as shown in Figure 11.4. ■

Present-Value Interest Tables

The present-value calculation can be simplified using a **present-value interest factor.** This factor is the multiplier used to calculate at a specified discount rate the present value of an amount to be received in a future period. To further facilitate present-value operations, tables of present-value interest factors are available. The table for the present-value interest factor, $PVIF_{k,n}$, gives values for the expression $1/(1 + k)^n$ where k is the discount rate and n is the number of periods—typically years—involved.

present-value interest factor The multiplier used to calculate at a specified discount rate the present value of an amount to be received in a future period.

$$\text{Present-value interest factor} = PVIF_{k,n} = \frac{1}{(1 + k)^n} \tag{11.13}$$

Table D-3 in the Appendix presents present-value interest factors for various discount rates and periods. A portion of Table D-3 is shown in Table 11.7. Since the factors in Table D-3 give the value for the expres-

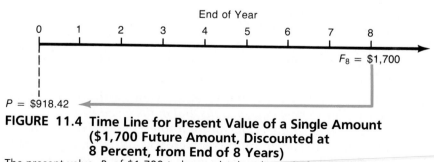

FIGURE 11.4 Time Line for Present Value of a Single Amount ($1,700 Future Amount, Discounted at 8 Percent, from End of 8 Years)

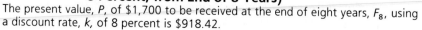

The present value, P, of $1,700 to be received at the end of eight years, F_8, using a discount rate, k, of 8 percent is $918.42.

TABLE 11.7 The Present-Value Interest Factors for One Dollar, $PVIF_{k,n}$

Period	5%	6%	7%	8%	9%	10%
1	.952	.943	.935	.926	.917	.909
2	.907	.890	.873	.857	.842	.826
3	.864	.840	.816	.794	.772	.751
4	.823	.792	.763	.735	.708	.683
5	.784	.747	.713	.681	.650	.621
6	.746	.705	.666	.630	.596	.564
7	.711	.665	.623	.583	.547	.513
8	.677	.627	.582	.540	.502	.467
9	.645	.592	.544	.500	.460	.424
10	.614	.558	.508	.463	.422	.386

sion $1/(1 + k)^n$ for various k and n combinations, we can, by letting $PVIF_{k,n}$ represent the appropriate factor from Table D-3, rewrite Equation 11.11 as follows:

$$P = F_n \times (PVIF_{k,n}) \tag{11.14}$$

This expression indicates that to find the present value, P, of an amount to be received in a future period, n, we have merely to multiply the future amount, F_n, by the appropriate present-value interest factor from Table D-3. An example should help clarify the use of Equation 11.14.

EXAMPLE

Bob Lambert wishes to find the present value of $1,700 to be received eight years from now, assuming an 8 percent opportunity cost. Table D-3 gives us a present-value interest factor for 8 percent and eight years, $PVIF_{8\%, 8\,yrs}$, of .540. Multiplying this factor by the $1,700 yields a present value of $918. This value is 42 cents less than the value obtained using the long method. This difference is attributable to the fact that the table values have been rounded to the nearest thousandth. ■

Four additional points with respect to present-value tables are also important:

1. The factors in the table are those for determining the present value of one dollar to be *received at the end of the given period.*
2. *The present-value interest factor for a single amount is always less than 1.* Only if the opportunity cost were 0 would this factor equal 1.
3. *The higher the discount rate for a given year, the smaller the present-value interest factor.* Thus the greater the potential return on an

investment, the less an amount to be received in a specified future year is worth today.

4. *For a given discount rate, the present value of a dollar decreases with the passage of time.* Thus the longer the period of time, the smaller the present value.

The relationship among various discount rates, discount periods, and present-value interest factors is illustrated in Figure 11.5. Everything else being equal, the higher the discount rate, the lower the present-value interest factor; and the longer the period of time, the lower the present-value interest factor. The reader should also note that given a

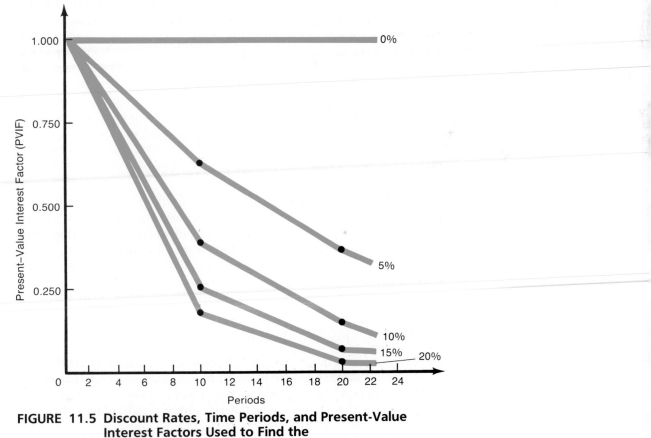

FIGURE 11.5 Discount Rates, Time Periods, and Present-Value Interest Factors Used to Find the Present Value of One Dollar

The present-value interest factor decreases with increases in the interest rate or the period of time until the future funds are received. At zero percent interest the present-value interest factor equals 1.00 and for discount rates greater than zero the factor is always less than 1.00.

discount rate of 0 percent, the present-value interest factor always equals 1.00, and the future value of the funds therefore equals their present value.

Comparing Present Value and Future Value

A few important observations must be made with respect to present values. One is that the expression for the present-value interest factor for k percent and n periods, $1/(1 + k)^n$, is the inverse of the future-value interest factor for k percent and n periods, $(1 + k)^n$. This observation can be confirmed by dividing a present-value interest factor for k percent and n periods, $PVIF_{k,n}$, into 1 and comparing the resulting value to the future-value interest factor given in Table D-1 for k percent and n periods, $FVIF_{k,n}$. The two values should be equivalent. Because of the relationship between present-value interest factors and future-value interest factors, we can find the present-value interest factors given a table of future-value interest factors, and vice versa. For example, the future-value interest factor from Table D-1 for 10 percent and five periods is 1.611. Dividing this value into 1 yields .621, which is the present-value interest factor given in Table D-3 for 10 percent and five periods.

■ PRESENT VALUE OF CASH FLOW STREAMS

Quite often in finance there is a need to find the present value of a stream of cash flows to be received in various future years. Two basic types of cash-flow streams are possible: the mixed stream and the annuity. A **mixed stream** of cash flows reflects no particular pattern, while, as stated earlier, an *annuity* is a pattern of equal annual cash flows. Since certain shortcuts are possible in finding the present value of an annuity, mixed streams and annuities will be discussed separately.

mixed stream A group of cash flows that reflects no particular pattern.

Present Value of a Mixed Stream

To find the present value of a mixed stream of cash flows, determine the present value of each future amount in the manner described in the preceding section, then add all the individual present values to find the total present value of the stream. An example should clarify this process.

EXAMPLE

The QTD Company has been offered an opportunity to receive the following mixed stream of cash flows over the next five years:

Year	Cash flow
1	$400
2	800
3	500
4	400
5	300

If the firm must earn 9 percent, at minimum, on its investments, what is the most it should pay for this opportunity?

To solve this problem, the present value of each cash flow discounted at 9 percent for the appropriate number of years is determined. The sum of all these individual values is then calculated to get the present value of the total stream. The present-value interest factors required are obtained from Table D-3. Table 11.8 presents the calculations needed to find the present value of the cash flow stream, which turns out to be $1,904.60.

QTD should not pay more than $1,904.60 for the opportunity to receive these cash flows, since paying $1,904.60 would provide exactly a 9 percent return. This situation is depicted diagramatically on a time line in Figure 11.6. ■

Present Value of an Annuity

The present value of an annuity can be found in a manner similar to that used for a mixed stream, but a shortcut is possible.

EXAMPLE

The Labco Company is attempting to determine the most it should pay to purchase a particular annuity. The firm requires a mini-

TABLE 11.8 The Present Value of a Mixed Stream of Cash Flows

Year (n)	Cash flow (1)	$PVIF^a_{9\%,n}$ (2)	Present value [(1) × (2)] (3)
1	$400	.917	$ 366.80
2	800	.842	673.60
3	500	.772	386.00
4	400	.708	283.20
5	300	.650	195.00
Present value of mixed stream			$1,904.60

[a] Present-value interest factors at 9 percent are from Table D-3.

TIME VALUE OF MONEY: A PERSONAL INVESTMENT PERSPECTIVE

Lauren — a publishing executive who "dabbles" in the market — bought stock at a total cost, including commissions, of $4,000. After two years she sold the stock, which paid no dividends, for $4,600.

How well did Lauren do? In her own estimation, the answer is "very." What was her reason for that judgment? "Well," she said, "I spent $4,000. And I got back $4,600. That's a $600 gain on a $4,000 investment. Not bad."

Is she right? Suppose she had invested the $4,000 in a one-year money market instrument that earned her 9% per annum, the interest to be paid in a lump sum at maturity. Ignoring tax considerations for a moment, suppose she then repeated the process. Investing the $4,000 + $360 = $4,360 at 9% would have brought her $392. At the second maturity date, Lauren would have had $4,752.

She held the stock for approximately two years. She in fact did no better than she'd have done had her $4,000 remained in a money market fund. In essence she wasn't rewarded for the added risk she took in buying stocks instead of CDs or T-bills.

Lauren's view of stock market profits is entirely typical. What she omits from her calculations, the majority of investors also overlook. Namely, the *time value of money*. A dollar you own today differs from the one you owned yesterday, and a dollar you receive tomorrow is not the same as one you receive today. There is a date attached to every investment you make, and the longer your money is invested, the more it has to earn just for you to break even.

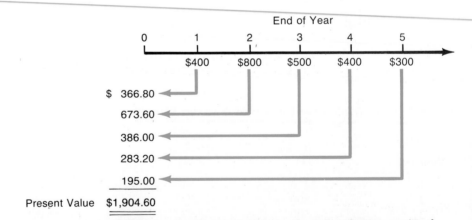

FIGURE 11.6 Time Line for Present Value of a Mixed Stream (End-of-Year Cash Flows, Discounted at 9 Percent, over Corresponding Number of Years)

The $1,904.60 present value of the mixed stream of cash flows occurring at the end of each of the next five years is calculated by finding the sum of the present values of the individual cash flows using the 9 percent discount rate.

TABLE 11.9 The Long Method for Finding the Present Value of an Annuity

Year (n)	Cash flow (1)	$PVIF^{a}_{8\%,n}$ (2)	Present value [(1) × (2)] (3)
1	$700	.926	$ 648.20
2	700	.857	599.90
3	700	.794	555.80
4	700	.735	514.50
5	700	.681	476.70
Present value of annuity			$2,795.10

a Present-value interest factors at 8 percent are from Table D-3.

mum return of 8 percent on all investments, and the annuity consists of cash flows of $700 per year for five years. Table 11.9 shows the long way of finding the present value of the annuity, which is the same as the method used for mixed streams. This procedure yields a present value of $2,795.10, which can be interpreted in the same manner as for the mixed cash flow stream in the preceding example. Similarly, this situation is depicted graphically on a time line in Figure 11.7. ■

Using a Present Value of an Annuity Table

Annuity calculations can be simplified by using a **present-value interest factor for an annuity.** This factor is the multiplier used to calculate

present-value interest factor for an annuity The multiplier used to calculate the present value of an annuity at a specified discount rate over a given period of time.

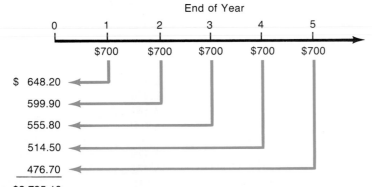

Present Value $2,795.10

FIGURE 11.7 Time Line for Present Value of an Annuity ($700 End-of-Year Cash Flows, Discounted at 8 Percent, over 5 Years)

The $2,795.10 present value of the annuity cash flow of $700 occurring at the end of each of the next five years is calculated by finding the sum of the present values of the individual cash flows using the 8 percent discount rate.

the present value of an annuity at a specified discount rate over a given period of time. A portion of Appendix Table D-4, which contains present-value interest factors for an annuity, is shown in Table 11.10. The interest factors in Table D-4 actually represent the sum of the first n present-value interest factors in Table D-3 for a given discount rate. The formula for the present-value interest factor for an n-year annuity with end-of-year cash flows that are discounted at k percent, $PVIFA_{k,n}$, is[4]

$$PVIFA_{k,n} = \sum_{t=1}^{n} \frac{1}{(1+k)^t} \qquad (11.15)$$

Letting P_n equal the present value of an n-year annuity, A equal the amount to be received annually at the end of each year, and $PVIFA_{k,n}$ represent the appropriate value for the *present-value interest factor for a one-dollar annuity discounted at* k *percent for* n *years,* the relationship among these variables can be expressed as follows:

$$P_n = A \times (PVIFA_{k,n}) \qquad (11.16)$$

The problem presented earlier involving the calculation of the present value of a five-year annuity of $700 assuming an 8 percent opportunity cost can be easily worked out with the aid of Table D-4 and Equation 11.16. The present-value interest factor for a one-dollar annuity in Table D-4 for 8 percent and five years, $PVIFA_{8\%,5}$, is 3.993. Multiplying the $700 annuity by this factor provides a present value for the annuity of $2,795.10. A simple example may help clarify the usefulness of Table D-4 in finding the present value of an annuity.

TABLE 11.10 The Present-Value Interest Factors for a One-Dollar Annuity, $PVIFA_{k,n}$

Period	5%	6%	7%	8%	9%	10%
1	.952	.943	.935	.926	.917	.909
2	1.859	1.833	1.808	1.783	1.759	1.736
3	2.723	2.673	2.624	2.577	2.531	2.487
4	3.546	3.465	3.387	3.312	3.240	3.170
5	4.329	4.212	4.100	3.993	3.890	3.791
6	5.076	4.917	4.767	4.623	4.486	4.355
7	5.786	5.582	5.389	5.206	5.033	4.868
8	6.463	6.210	5.971	5.747	5.535	5.335
9	7.108	6.802	6.515	6.247	5.995	5.759
10	7.722	7.360	7.024	6.710	6.418	6.145

[4] This formula merely states that the present-value interest factor for an n-year annuity is found by summing the first n present-value interest factors at the given rate $\left(\text{i.e., } PVIFA_{k,n} = \sum_{t=1}^{n} PVIF_{k,t} \right).$

EXAMPLE

The Birmingham Company expects to receive $160,000 per year at the end of each of the next 20 years. If the firm's opportunity cost of funds is 10 percent, how much is the present value of this annuity? The appropriate interest factor for the present value at 10 percent for a 20-year annuity, $PVIFA_{10\%,20\,\text{yrs}}$, is found in Table D-4 to be 8.514. Multiplying this factor by the $160,000 cash flow results in a present value of $1,362,240. ■

■ SPECIAL APPLICATIONS OF TIME VALUE

Future-value and present-value techniques have a number of important applications. Four will be presented in this section: (1) the calculation of the deposits needed to accumulate a future sum, (2) the calculation of amortization on loans, (3) the determination of interest or growth rates, and (4) the calculation of the present value of perpetuities.

Deposits to Accumulate a Future Sum

Often an individual may wish to determine the annual deposit necessary to accumulate a certain amount of money so many years hence. Suppose a person wishes to purchase a house five years from now and recognizes that an initial down payment of $20,000 will be required at that time. She wishes to make equal annual end-of-year deposits in an account paying annual interest of 6 percent, so she must determine what size annuity will result in a lump sum equal to $20,000 at the end of year 5. The solution to this problem is closely related to the process of finding the future value of an annuity.

In an earlier section of this chapter, the future value of an n-year annuity, S_n, was found by multiplying the annual deposit, A, by the appropriate interest factor from Table D-2, $FVIFA_{k,n}$. The relationship of the three variables has been defined by Equation 11.8, which is rewritten here as Equation 11.17.

$$S_n = A \times (FVIFA_{k,n}) \tag{11.17}$$

We can find the annual deposit required to accumulate S_n dollars, given a specified interest rate, k, and a certain number of years, n, by solving Equation 11.17 for A. Isolating A on the left side of the equation gives us

$$A = \frac{S_n}{FVIFA_{k,n}} \tag{11.18}$$

Once this is done, we have only to substitute the known values of S_n and $FVIFA_{k,n}$ into the right side of the equation to find the annual deposit required.

EXAMPLE

In the problem just stated, a person wished to determine the equal annual end-of-year deposits required to accumulate $20,000 at the end of five years given an interest rate of 6 percent. Table D-2 indicates that the future-value interest factor for an annuity at 6 percent for five years, $FVIFA_{6\%,5\,yrs}$, is 5.637. Substituting $S_5 = $20,000$ and $FVIFA_{6\%,5\,yrs} = 5.637$ into Equation 11.18 yields an annual required deposit, A, of $3,547.99 ($20,000 ÷ 5.637). If $3,547.99 is deposited at the end of each year for five years at 6 percent, at the end of the five years there will be $20,000 in the account. ■

Loan Amortization

loan amortization The determination of the equal annual loan payments necessary to provide a lender with a specified interest return and repay the loan principal over a specified period.

loan amortization schedule A schedule of equal payments to repay a loan. It shows the allocation of each loan payment to interest and principal.

The term **loan amortization** refers to the determination of the equal annual loan payments necessary to provide a lender with a specified interest return and repay the loan principal over a specified period. The loan amortization process involves finding the future payments (over the term of the loan) whose present value at the loan interest rate equals the amount of initial principal borrowed. Lenders use a **loan amortization schedule** to determine these payment amounts. In the case of home mortgages, these tables are used to find the equal *monthly* payments necessary to amortize or pay off the mortgage at a specified interest rate over a 15- to 30-year period.

Amortizing a loan actually involves creating an annuity out of a present amount. For example, an individual may borrow $6,000 at 10 percent and agree to make equal annual end-of-year payments over four years. To determine the size of the payments, the four-year annuity discounted at 10 percent that has a present value of $6,000 must be determined. This process is actually the inverse of finding the present value of an annuity.

Earlier in this chapter the present value, P_n, of an n-year annuity of A dollars was found by multiplying the annual amount, A, by the present-value interest factor for an annuity from Table D-4, $PVIFA_{k,n}$. This relationship, which was originally expressed as Equation 11.16, is rewritten here as Equation 11.19:

$$P_n = A \times (PVIFA_{k,n}) \qquad (11.19)$$

To find the equal annual payment, A, required to pay off, or amortize, the loan, P_n, over a certain number of years at a specified interest rate, we need to solve Equation 11.19 for A. Isolating A on the left side of the equation gives us

$$A = \frac{P_n}{PVIFA_{k,n}} \qquad (11.20)$$

Once this is done, we have only to substitute the known values of P_n and $PVIFA_{k,n}$ into the right side of the equation to find the annual payment required.

EXAMPLE

In the problem stated at the beginning of this section, a person wished to determine the equal annual end-of-year payments necessary to amortize fully a $6,000, 10 percent loan over four years. Table D-4 indicates that the present-value interest factor for an annuity corresponding to 10 percent and four years, $PVIFA_{10\%,4\,yrs}$, is 3.170. Substituting $P_4 = \$6,000$ and $PVIFA_{10\%,4\,yrs} = 3.170$ in Equation 11.20 and solving for A yields an annual loan payment of $1,892.74 ($6,000 ÷ 3.170). Thus to repay the principal and interest on a $6,000, 10 percent, four-year loan, equal annual end-of-year payments of $1,892.74 are necessary.

The allocation of each loan payment to interest and principal in order to repay the loan fully can be seen in columns 3 and 4 of the *loan amortization schedule* given in Table 11.11. The portion of each payment representing interest (column 3) declines, and the portion going to principal repayment (column 4) increases over the repayment period. This is typical of amortized loans because with level payments, as the principal is reduced, the interest component declines, leaving a larger portion of each subsequent payment to repay principal. ∎

Interest or Growth Rates

It is often necessary to calculate the compound annual interest or growth rate associated with a stream of cash flows. In doing this, either

TABLE 11.11 Loan Amortization Schedule ($6,000 principal, 10 percent interest, 4-year repayment period)

End of year	Loan payment (1)	Beginning-of-year principal (2)	PAYMENTS Interest $[.10 \times (2)]$ (3)	PAYMENTS Principal $[(1) - (3)]$ (4)	End-of-year principal $[(2) - (4)]$ (5)
1	$1,892.74	$6,000.00	$600.00	$1,292.74	$4,707.26
2	1,892.74	4,707.26	470.73	1,422.01	3,285.25
3	1,892.74	3,285.25	328.53	1,564.21	1,721.04
4	1,892.74	1,721.04	172.10	1,720.64	—[a]

[a] Due to rounding, a slight difference ($.40) exists between the beginning-of-year-4 principal (in column 2) and the year-4 principal payment (in column 4).

future-value or present-value interest factors can be used. The approach using present-value interest tables is described in this section. The simplest situation is where one wishes to find the rate of interest or growth in a cash flow stream.[5] This can be illustrated by the following example.

EXAMPLE

Al Taylor wishes to find the rate of interest or growth of the following stream of cash flows.

Year	Cash flow	
1987	$1,520	4
1986	$1,440	3
1985	$1,370	2
1984	$1,300	1
1983	$1,250	

Using the first year (1983) as a base year, it can be seen that interest has been earned (or growth experienced) for four years. To find the rate at which this has occurred, the amount received in the earliest year is divided by the amount received in the latest year. This gives the present-value interest factor for four years, $PVIF_{k,4\,yrs}$, which is 0.822 ($1,250 ÷ $1,520). The interest rate in Table D-3 associated with the factor closest to 0.822 for four years is the rate of interest or growth rate associated with the cash flows. Looking across year 4 of Table D-3 shows that the factor for 5 percent is 0.823 — almost exactly the 0.822 value. Therefore, the rate of interest or growth rate associated with the cash flows given is approximately (to the nearest whole percent)[6] 5 percent. ■

Sometimes one wishes to determine the interest rate associated with an equal-payment loan. For instance, if a person were to borrow $2,000 to be repaid in equal annual end-of-year amounts of $514.14 for the next five years, he or she might wish to determine the rate of interest being paid on the loan. Referring to Equation 11.19 shows that $P_5 = $2,000 and $A = $514.14. Rearranging the equation and substituting these

---

[5] Since the calculations required for finding interest rates and growth rates, given certain cash flow or principal flow streams, are the same, this section refers to the calculations as those required to find interest *or* growth rates.

[6] Rounding of interest and growth rate estimates to the nearest whole percent is assumed throughout this text. To obtain more precise estimates, interpolation would be required.

Present-Value Interest Factors for One Dollar Discounted at k Percent for n Periods: $PVIF_{k,n} = \dfrac{1}{(1+k)^n}$

Period	1%	2%	3%	4%	5%	6%	7%	8%	9%	10%	11%	12%	13%	14%	15%	16%	17%
1	.990	.980	.971	.962	.952	.943	.935	.926	.917	.909	.901	.893	.885	.877	.870	.862	.855
2	.980	.961	.943	.925	.907	.890	.873	.857	.842	.826	.812	.797	.783	.769	.756	.743	.731
3	.971	.942	.915	.889	.864	.840	.816	.794	.772	.751	.731	.712	.693	.675	.658	.641	.624
4	.961	.924	.888	.855	.823	.792	.763	.735	.708	.683	.659	.636	.613	.592	.572	.552	.534
5	.951	.906	.863	.822	.784	.747	.713	.681	.650	.621	.593	.567	.543	.519	.497	.476	.456
6	.942	.888	.837	.790	.746	.705	.666	.630	.596	.564	.535	.507	.480	.456	.432	.410	.390
7	.933	.871	.813	.760	.711	.665	.623	.583	.547	.513	.482	.452	.425	.400	.376	.354	.333
8	.923	.853	.789	.731	.677	.627	.582	.540	.502	.467	.434	.404	.376	.351	.327	.305	.285
9	.914	.837	.766	.703	.645	.592	.544	.500	.460	.424	.391	.361	.333	.308	.284	.263	.243
10	.905	.820	.744	.676	.614	.558	.508	.463	.422	.386	.352	.322	.295	.270	.247	.227	.208
11	.896	.804	.722	.650	.585	.527	.475	.429	.388	.350	.317	.287	.261	.237	.215	.195	.178
12	.887	.789	.701	.625	.557	.497	.444	.397	.356	.319	.286	.257	.231	.208	.187	.168	.152
13	.879	.773	.681	.601	.530	.469	.415	.368	.326	.290	.258	.229	.204	.182	.163	.145	.130
14	.870	.758	.661	.577	.505	.442	.388	.340	.299	.263	.232	.205	.181	.160	.141	.125	.111
15	.861	.743	.642	.555	.481	.417	.362	.315	.275	.239	.209	.183	.160	.140	.123	.108	.095
16	.853	.728	.623	.534	.458	.394	.339	.292	.252	.218	.188	.163	.141	.123	.107	.093	.081
17	.844	.714	.605	.513	.436	.371	.317	.270	.231	.198	.170	.146	.125	.108	.093	.080	.069
18	.836	.700	.587	.494	.416	.350	.296	.250	.212	.180	.153	.130	.111	.095	.081	.069	.059
19	.828	.686	.570	.475	.396	.331	.277	.232	.194	.164	.138	.116	.098	.083	.070	.060	.051
20	.820	.673	.554	.456	.377	.312	.258	.215	.178	.149	.124	.104	.087	.073	.061	.051	.043
21	.811	.660	.538	.439	.359	.294	.242	.199	.164	.135	.112	.093	.077	.064	.053	.044	.037
22	.803	.647	.522	.422	.342	.278	.226	.184	.150	.123	.101	.083	.068	.056	.046	.038	.032
23	.795	.634	.507	.406	.326	.262	.211	.170	.138	.112	.091	.074	.060	.049	.040	.033	.027
24	.788	.622	.492	.390	.310	.247	.197	.158	.126	.102	.082	.066	.053	.043	.035	.028	.023
25	.780	.610	.478	.375	.295	.233	.184	.146	.116	.092	.074	.059	.047	.038	.030	.024	.020
30	.742	.552	.412	.308	.231	.174	.131	.099	.075	.057	.044	.033	.026	.020	.015	.012	.009
35	.706	.500	.355	.253	.181	.130	.094	.068	.049	.036	.026	.019	.014	.010	.008	.006	.004
40	.672	.453	.307	.208	.142	.097	.067	.046	.032	.022	.015	.011	.008	.005	.004	.003	.002
45	.639	.410	.264	.171	.111	.073	.048	.031	.021	.014	.009	.006	.004	.003	.002	.001	.001
50	.608	.372	.228	.141	.087	.054	.034	.021	.013	.009	.005	.003	.002	.001	.001	.001	*

Period	18%	19%	20%	21%	22%	23%	24%	25%	26%	27%	28%	29%	30%	35%	40%	45%	50%
1	.847	.840	.833	.826	.820	.813	.806	.800	.794	.787	.781	.775	.769	.741	.714	.690	.667
2	.718	.706	.694	.683	.672	.661	.650	.640	.630	.620	.610	.601	.592	.549	.510	.476	.444
3	.609	.593	.579	.564	.551	.537	.524	.512	.500	.488	.477	.466	.455	.406	.364	.328	.296
4	.516	.499	.482	.467	.451	.437	.423	.410	.397	.384	.373	.361	.350	.301	.260	.226	.198
5	.437	.419	.402	.386	.370	.355	.341	.328	.315	.303	.291	.280	.269	.223	.186	.156	.132
6	.370	.352	.335	.319	.303	.289	.275	.262	.250	.238	.227	.217	.207	.165	.133	.108	.088
7	.314	.296	.279	.263	.249	.235	.222	.210	.198	.188	.178	.168	.159	.122	.095	.074	.059
8	.266	.249	.233	.218	.204	.191	.179	.168	.157	.148	.139	.130	.123	.091	.068	.051	.039
9	.225	.209	.194	.180	.167	.155	.144	.134	.125	.116	.108	.101	.094	.067	.048	.035	.026
10	.191	.176	.162	.149	.137	.126	.116	.107	.099	.092	.085	.078	.073	.050	.035	.024	.017
11	.162	.148	.135	.123	.112	.103	.094	.086	.079	.072	.066	.061	.056	.037	.025	.017	.012
12	.137	.124	.112	.102	.092	.083	.076	.069	.062	.057	.052	.047	.043	.027	.018	.012	.008
13	.116	.104	.093	.084	.075	.068	.061	.055	.050	.045	.040	.037	.033	.020	.013	.008	.005
14	.099	.088	.078	.069	.062	.055	.049	.044	.039	.035	.032	.028	.025	.015	.009	.006	.003
15	.084	.074	.065	.057	.051	.045	.040	.035	.031	.028	.025	.022	.020	.011	.006	.004	.002
16	.071	.062	.054	.047	.042	.036	.032	.028	.025	.022	.019	.017	.015	.008	.005	.003	.002
17	.060	.052	.045	.039	.034	.030	.026	.023	.020	.017	.015	.013	.012	.006	.003	.002	.001
18	.051	.044	.038	.032	.028	.024	.021	.018	.016	.014	.012	.010	.009	.005	.002	.001	.001
19	.043	.037	.031	.027	.023	.020	.017	.014	.012	.011	.009	.008	.007	.003	.002	.001	*
20	.037	.031	.026	.022	.019	.016	.014	.012	.010	.008	.007	.006	.005	.002	.001	.001	*
21	.031	.026	.022	.018	.015	.013	.011	.009	.008	.007	.006	.005	.004	.002	.001	*	*
22	.026	.022	.018	.015	.013	.011	.009	.007	.006	.006	.005	.004	.003	.001	.001	*	*
23	.022	.018	.015	.012	.010	.009	.007	.006	.005	.004	.004	.003	.002	.001	*	*	*
24	.019	.015	.013	.010	.008	.007	.006	.005	.004	.003	.003	.002	.002	.001	*	*	*
25	.016	.013	.010	.009	.007	.006	.005	.004	.003	.003	.002	.002	.001	.001	*	*	*
30	.007	.005	.004	.003	.003	.002	.002	.001	.001	.001	.001	*	*	*	*	*	*
35	.003	.002	.002	.001	.001	.001	.001	*	*	*	*	*	*	*	*	*	*
40	.001	.001	.001	*	*	*	*	*	*	*	*	*	*	*	*	*	*
45	.001	*	*	*	*	*	*	*	*	*	*	*	*	*	*	*	*
50	*	*	*	*	*	*	*	*	*	*	*	*	*	*	*	*	*

*PVIF is zero to three decimal places.

Present-Value Interest Factors for a One-Dollar Annuity Discounted at k Percent for n Periods: $PVIFA_{k,n} = \sum_{t=1}^{n} \dfrac{1}{(1+k)^t}$

Period	1%	2%	3%	4%	5%	6%	7%	8%	9%	10%	11%	12%	13%	14%	15%	16%	17%
1	.990	.980	.971	.962	.952	.943	.935	.926	.917	.909	.901	.893	.885	.877	.870	.862	.855
2	1.970	1.942	1.913	1.886	1.859	1.833	1.808	1.783	1.759	1.736	1.713	1.690	1.668	1.647	1.626	1.605	1.585
3	2.941	2.884	2.829	2.775	2.723	2.673	2.624	2.577	2.531	2.487	2.444	2.402	2.361	2.322	2.283	2.246	2.210
4	3.902	3.808	3.717	3.630	3.546	3.465	3.387	3.312	3.240	3.170	3.102	3.037	2.974	2.914	2.855	2.798	2.743
5	4.853	4.713	4.580	4.452	4.329	4.212	4.100	3.993	3.890	3.791	3.696	3.605	3.517	3.433	3.352	3.274	3.199
6	5.795	5.601	5.417	5.242	5.076	4.917	4.767	4.623	4.486	4.355	4.231	4.111	3.998	3.889	3.784	3.685	3.589
7	6.728	6.472	6.230	6.002	5.786	5.582	5.389	5.206	5.033	4.868	4.712	4.564	4.423	4.288	4.160	4.039	3.922
8	7.652	7.326	7.020	6.733	6.463	6.210	5.971	5.747	5.535	5.335	5.146	4.968	4.799	4.639	4.487	4.344	4.207
9	8.566	8.162	7.786	7.435	7.108	6.802	6.515	6.247	5.995	5.759	5.537	5.328	5.132	4.946	4.772	4.607	4.451
10	9.471	8.983	8.530	8.111	7.722	7.360	7.024	6.710	6.418	6.145	5.889	5.650	5.426	5.216	5.019	4.833	4.659
11	10.368	9.787	9.253	8.760	8.306	7.887	7.499	7.139	6.805	6.495	6.207	5.938	5.687	5.453	5.234	5.029	4.836
12	11.255	10.575	9.954	9.385	8.863	8.384	7.943	7.536	7.161	6.814	6.492	6.194	5.918	5.660	5.421	5.197	4.988
13	12.134	11.348	10.635	9.986	9.394	8.853	8.358	7.904	7.487	7.013	6.750	6.424	6.122	5.842	5.583	5.342	5.118
14	13.004	12.106	11.296	10.563	9.899	9.295	8.745	8.244	7.786	7.367	6.982	6.628	6.302	6.002	5.724	5.468	5.229
15	13.865	12.849	11.938	11.118	10.380	9.712	9.108	8.560	8.061	7.606	7.191	6.811	6.462	6.142	5.847	5.575	5.324
16	14.718	13.578	12.561	11.652	10.838	10.106	9.447	8.851	8.313	7.824	7.379	6.974	6.604	6.265	5.954	5.668	5.405
17	15.562	14.292	13.166	12.166	11.274	10.477	9.763	9.122	8.544	8.022	7.549	7.120	6.729	6.373	6.047	5.749	5.475
18	16.398	14.992	13.754	12.659	11.690	10.828	10.059	9.372	8.756	8.201	7.702	7.250	6.840	6.467	6.128	5.818	5.534
19	17.226	15.679	14.324	13.134	12.085	11.158	10.336	9.604	8.950	8.365	7.839	7.366	6.938	6.550	6.198	5.877	5.584
20	18.046	16.352	14.878	13.590	12.462	11.470	10.594	9.818	9.129	8.514	7.963	7.469	7.025	6.623	6.259	5.929	5.628
21	18.857	17.011	15.415	14.029	12.821	11.764	10.836	10.017	9.292	8.649	8.075	7.562	7.102	6.687	6.312	5.973	5.665
22	19.661	17.658	15.937	14.451	13.163	12.042	11.061	10.201	9.442	8.772	8.176	7.645	7.170	6.743	6.359	6.011	5.696
23	20.456	18.292	16.444	14.857	13.489	12.303	11.272	10.371	9.580	8.883	8.266	7.718	7.230	6.792	6.399	6.044	5.723
24	21.244	18.914	16.936	15.247	13.799	12.550	11.469	10.529	9.707	8.985	8.348	7.784	7.283	6.835	6.434	6.073	5.746
25	22.023	19.524	17.413	15.622	14.094	12.783	11.654	10.675	9.823	9.077	8.422	7.843	7.330	6.873	6.464	6.097	5.766
30	25.808	22.396	19.601	17.292	15.373	13.765	12.409	11.258	10.274	9.427	8.694	8.055	7.496	7.003	6.566	6.177	5.829
35	29.409	24.999	21.487	18.665	16.374	14.498	12.948	11.655	10.567	9.644	8.855	8.176	7.586	7.070	6.617	6.215	5.858
40	32.835	27.356	23.115	19.793	17.159	15.046	13.332	11.925	10.757	9.779	8.951	8.244	7.634	7.105	6.642	6.233	5.871
45	36.095	29.490	24.519	20.720	17.774	15.456	13.606	12.108	10.881	9.863	9.008	8.283	7.661	7.123	6.654	6.242	5.877
50	39.196	31.424	25.730	21.482	18.256	15.762	13.801	12.233	10.962	9.915	9.042	8.304	7.675	7.133	6.661	6.246	5.880

Period	18%	19%	20%	21%	22%	23%	24%	25%	26%	27%	28%	29%	30%	35%	40%	45%	50%
1	.847	.840	.833	.826	.820	.813	.806	.800	.794	.787	.781	.775	.769	.741	.714	.690	.667
2	1.566	1.547	1.528	1.509	1.492	1.474	1.457	1.440	1.424	1.407	1.392	1.376	1.361	1.289	1.224	1.165	1.111
3	2.174	2.140	2.106	2.074	2.042	2.011	1.981	1.952	1.923	1.896	1.868	1.842	1.816	1.696	1.589	1.493	1.407
4	2.690	2.639	2.589	2.540	2.494	2.448	2.404	2.362	2.320	2.280	2.241	2.203	2.166	1.997	1.849	1.720	1.605
5	3.127	3.058	2.991	2.926	2.864	2.803	2.745	2.689	2.635	2.583	2.532	2.483	2.436	2.220	2.035	1.876	1.737
6	3.498	3.410	3.326	3.245	3.167	3.092	3.020	2.951	2.885	2.821	2.759	2.700	2.643	2.385	2.168	1.983	1.824
7	3.812	3.706	3.605	3.508	3.416	3.327	3.242	3.161	3.083	3.009	2.937	2.868	2.802	2.508	2.263	2.057	1.883
8	4.078	3.954	3.837	3.726	3.619	3.518	3.421	3.329	3.241	3.156	3.076	2.999	2.925	2.598	2.331	2.109	1.922
9	4.303	4.163	4.031	3.905	3.786	3.673	3.566	3.463	3.366	3.273	3.184	3.100	3.019	2.665	2.379	2.144	1.948
10	4.494	4.339	4.192	4.054	3.923	3.799	3.682	3.570	3.465	3.364	3.269	3.178	3.092	2.715	2.414	2.168	1.965
11	4.656	4.486	4.327	4.177	4.035	3.902	3.776	3.656	3.544	3.437	3.335	3.239	3.147	2.752	2.438	2.185	1.977
12	4.793	4.611	4.439	4.278	4.127	3.985	3.851	3.725	3.606	3.493	3.387	3.286	3.190	2.779	2.456	2.196	1.985
13	4.910	4.715	4.533	4.362	4.203	4.053	3.912	3.780	3.656	3.538	3.427	3.322	3.223	2.799	2.469	2.204	1.990
14	5.008	4.802	4.611	4.432	4.265	4.108	3.962	3.824	3.695	3.573	3.459	3.351	3.249	2.814	2.478	2.210	1.993
15	5.092	4.876	4.675	4.489	4.315	4.153	4.001	3.859	3.726	3.601	3.483	3.373	3.268	2.825	2.484	2.214	1.995
16	5.162	4.938	4.730	4.536	4.357	4.189	4.033	3.887	3.751	3.623	3.503	3.390	3.283	2.834	2.489	2.216	1.997
17	5.222	4.990	4.775	4.576	4.391	4.219	4.059	3.910	3.771	3.640	3.518	3.403	3.295	2.840	2.492	2.218	1.998
18	5.273	5.033	4.812	4.608	4.419	4.243	4.080	3.928	3.786	3.654	3.529	3.413	3.304	2.844	2.494	2.219	1.999
19	5.316	5.070	4.843	4.635	4.442	4.263	4.097	3.942	3.799	3.664	3.539	3.421	3.311	2.848	2.496	2.220	1.999
20	5.353	5.101	4.870	4.657	4.460	4.279	4.110	3.954	3.808	3.673	3.546	3.427	3.316	2.850	2.497	2.221	1.999
21	5.384	5.127	4.891	4.675	4.476	4.292	4.121	3.963	3.816	3.679	3.551	3.432	3.320	2.852	2.498	2.221	2.000
22	5.410	5.149	4.909	4.690	4.488	4.302	4.130	3.970	3.822	3.684	3.556	3.436	3.323	2.853	2.498	2.222	2.000
23	5.432	5.167	4.925	4.703	4.499	4.311	4.137	3.976	3.827	3.689	3.559	3.438	3.325	2.854	2.499	2.222	2.000
24	5.451	5.182	4.937	4.713	4.507	4.318	4.143	3.981	3.831	3.692	3.562	3.441	3.327	2.855	2.499	2.222	2.000
25	5.467	5.195	4.948	4.721	4.514	4.323	4.147	3.985	3.834	3.694	3.564	3.442	3.329	2.856	2.499	2.222	2.000
30	5.517	5.235	4.979	4.746	4.534	4.339	4.160	3.995	3.842	3.701	3.569	3.447	3.332	2.857	2.500	2.222	2.000
35	5.539	5.251	4.992	4.756	4.541	4.345	4.164	3.998	3.845	3.703	3.571	3.448	3.333	2.857	2.500	2.222	2.000
40	5.548	5.258	4.997	4.760	4.544	4.347	4.166	3.999	3.846	3.703	3.571	3.448	3.333	2.857	2.500	2.222	2.000
45	5.552	5.261	4.999	4.761	4.545	4.347	4.166	4.000	3.846	3.704	3.571	3.448	3.333	2.857	2.500	2.222	2.000
50	5.554	5.262	4.999	4.762	4.545	4.348	4.167	4.000	3.846	3.704	3.571	3.448	3.333	2.857	2.500	2.222	2.000

values results in a present-value interest factor for a five-year annuity, $PVIFA_{k,5\,yrs}$, of 3.890:

$$PVIFA_{k,5\,yrs} = \frac{P_5}{A} = \frac{\$2{,}000}{\$514.14} = 3.890 \qquad (11.21)$$

The interest rate for five years associated with a factor of 3.890 in Table D-4 is 9 percent; therefore, the interest rate on the loan is approximately (to the nearest whole percent) 9 percent.

Perpetuities

A **perpetuity** is an annuity with an infinite life—in other words, an annuity that never stops providing its holder with A dollars at the end of each year. It is sometimes necessary to find the present value of a perpetuity. The present value of an A-dollar perpetuity discounted at the rate k is defined by Equation 11.22.

perpetuity An annuity with an infinite life, making continual annual payments.

Present value of an A-dollar perpetuity discounted at k percent

$$= A \times (PVIFA_{k,\infty}) = A \times \left(\frac{1}{k}\right) \qquad (11.22)$$

As noted in the equation, the appropriate factor, $PVIFA_{k,\infty}$, is found merely by dividing the discount rate, k (stated as a decimal), into 1. The validity of this method can be seen by looking at the factors in Table D-4 for 8 percent, 10 percent, and 20 percent. As the number of years approaches 50, the value of these factors approaches 12.500, 10.000, and 5.000, respectively. Dividing .08, .10, and .20 (for k) into 1 gives factors for finding the present value of perpetuities at these rates of 12.500, 10.000, and 5.000. An example will help clarify the application of Equation 11.22.

EXAMPLE

A person wishes to determine the present value of a $1,000 perpetuity discounted at 10 percent. The appropriate present-value interest factor can be found by dividing 1 by .10. As prescribed by Equation 11.22, the resulting factor, 10, is then multiplied by the annual perpetuity cash inflow of $1,000 to get the present value of the perpetuity, which is $10,000. In other words, the receipt of $1,000 every year for an indefinite period is worth only $10,000 today if a person can earn 10 percent on investments. This is because, if the person had $10,000 and earned 10 percent interest on it each year, $1,000 a year could be withdrawn indefinitely without affecting the initial $10,000, which would never be drawn upon. ■

SUMMARY

- The key concepts related to the time value of money are future value and present value. The key time-value definitions, formulas, and equations are given in Table 11.12.
- Future value relies on compound interest to measure the value of future sums. When interest is compounded, the initial principal or deposit in one period, along with the interest earned on it, becomes the beginning principal of the following period, and so on.
- Interest can be compounded annually, semiannually, quarterly, monthly, weekly, daily, or even continuously. The more frequently interest is compounded, the larger the future amount that will be accumulated.

TABLE 11.12 Summary of Key Definitions, Formulas, and Equations for Time Value of Money

Variable definitions

F_n = future value or amount at the end of period n
P = initial principal, or present value
k = annual rate of interest
n = number of periods—typically years—over which money earns a return
t = period number index
S_n = future value of an n-year annuity
A = amount deposited or received annually at the end of each year
P_n = present value of an n-year annuity

Interest factor formulas
Future value of a single sum

$$FVIF_{k,n} = (1 + k)^n \qquad \text{[Factors in Table D-1]}$$

Future value of an (ordinary) annuity

$$FVIFA_{k,n} = \sum_{t=1}^{n} (1 + k)^{t-1} \qquad \text{[Factors in Table D-2]}$$

Present value of a single sum

$$PVIF_{k,n} = \frac{1}{(1 + k)^n} \qquad \text{[Factors in Table D-3]}$$

Present value of an annuity

$$PVIFA_{k,n} = \sum_{t=1}^{n} \frac{1}{(1 + k)^t} \qquad \text{[Factors in Table D-4]}$$

Basic equations
Future value (single sum): $F_n = P \times (FVIF_{k,n})$
Future value (annuity): $\quad S_n = A \times (FVIFA_{k,n})$
Present value (single sum): $P = F_n \times (PVIF_{k,n})$
Present value (annuity): $\quad P_n = A \times (PVIFA_{k,n})$

● The future value of an annuity, which is a pattern of equal annual cash flows, can be found using the future-value interest factor for an annuity.
● Present value represents the inverse of future value. In finding the present value of a future sum, we determine what amount of money today would be equivalent to the given future amount, considering the fact that we can earn a certain return on the current money.
● Occasionally it is necessary to find the present value of a stream of cash flows. For mixed streams, the individual present values must be found and summed. In the case of an annuity, the present value can be found by using the present-value interest factor for an annuity.
● By manipulating the equations for the future value and present value of single sums and annuities, the deposits needed to accumulate a future sum, loan amortization payments, interest or growth rates, and the present value of perpetuities can be calculated.

QUESTIONS

11-1 How is the *compounding process* related to the payment of interest on savings? What is the general equation for the future value, F_n, in period n if P dollars are deposited in an account paying k percent annual interest?

11-2 What effect would (a) a *decrease* in the interest rate or (b) an *increase* in the holding period of a deposit have on its future value? Why?

11-3 What effect does compounding interest more frequently than annually have on the future value generated by a beginning principal? Why?

11-4 Explain how one can conveniently determine the future value of an annuity that provides a stream of end-of-period cash inflows.

11-5 What is meant by the phrase "the present value of a future sum"? How are present-value and future-value calculations related?

11-6 What is the equation for the present value of a future amount, F_n, to be received in period n assuming that the firm requires a minimum return of k percent? How is this equation different from the equation for the future value of one dollar?

11-7 What effect do *increasing* (a) required return and (b) time periods have on the present value of a future amount? Why?

11-8 How can present-value tables be used to find the present value of a mixed stream of cash flows? How can the calculations required to find the present value of an annuity be simplified?

11-9 How can the size of the equal annual end-of-year deposits necessary to accumulate a certain future sum in a specified future period be determined? How might one of the financial tables discussed in this chapter aid in this calculation?

11-10 Describe the procedure used to amortize a loan into a series of equal annual payments. What is a *loan amortization schedule?*

11-11 Which financial table(s) would be used to find (a) the growth rate associated with a stream of cash flows and (b) the interest rate associated with an equal-payment loan? How would each of these be calculated?

11-12 What is a *perpetuity?* How might the present-value interest factor for such a stream of cash flows be determined?

PROBLEMS

11-1 **(Future-Value Calculation)** *Without tables,* use the basic formula for future value along with the given interest rate, k, and number of periods, n, to calculate the future-value interest factor in each of the following cases. Compare the calculated value to the table value in Appendix Table D-1.

Case	Interest rate, k (%)	Number of periods, n
A	12	2
B	6	3
C	9	2
D	3	4

11-2 **(Future-Value Tables)** Use the future-value interest factors in Appendix Table D-1 in each of the following cases to estimate, to the nearest year, how long it would take an initial deposit assuming no withdrawals
   a To double.
   b To quadruple.

Case	Interest rate (%)
A	7
B	40
C	20
D	10

11-3 **(Future Values)** For each of the following cases, calculate the future value of the single cash flow deposited today that will be available at the end of the deposit period if the interest is compounded annually at the rate specified for the given period.

Case	Single cash flow ($)	Interest rate (%)	Deposit period (years)
A	200	5	20
B	4,500	8	7
C	10,000	9	10
D	25,000	10	12
E	37,000	11	5
F	40,000	12	9

11-4 **(Single-Payment Loan Repayment)** A person borrows $200 to be repaid in eight years with 14 percent annually compounded interest. The loan may be repaid at the end of any earlier year with no prepayment penalty.

a What amount would be due if the loan is repaid at the end of year 1?

b What is the repayment at the end of year 4?

c What amount is due at the end of the eighth year?

11-5 ■ **(Changing Compounding Frequency)** Using annual, semiannual, and quarterly compounding periods, calculate the future value if $5,000 is deposited

a At 12 percent for five years.

b At 16 percent for six years.

c At 20 percent for ten years.

11-6 ■ **(Compounding Frequency and Bank Choice)** Delia Martin has $10,000 that she can deposit in any of three savings accounts for a three-year period. Bank A pays interest on an annual basis, bank B pays interest twice each year, and bank C pays interest each quarter. If all banks have a stated annual interest rate of 8 percent but follow the different payment practices above,

a Which bank should Ms. Martin deal with? Why?

b What amount would Ms. Martin have at the end of the third year, leaving all interest paid on deposit, in each bank?

11-7 ■ **(Future Value of an Annuity)** For each of the following cases, calculate the future value of the annuity at the end of the deposit period, assuming that the annuity cash flows occur at the end of each year.

Case	Amount of annuity ($)	Interest rate (%)	Deposit period (years)
A	2,500	8	10
B	500	12	6
C	30,000	20	5
D	11,500	9	8
E	6,000	14	30

11-8 ■ **(Future Value of a Mixed Stream)** For each of the following mixed streams of cash flows, determine the future value at the end of the final year if deposits are made at the *beginning of each year* into an account paying annual interest of 12 percent, assuming no withdrawals are made during the period.

CASH FLOW STREAM

Year	A	B	C
1	$ 900	$30,000	$1,200
2	1,000	25,000	1,200
3	1,200	20,000	1,000
4		10,000	1,900
5		5,000	

11-9 (Present-Value Calculation) *Without tables,* use the basic formula for present value along with the given opportunity cost, k, and number of periods, n, to calculate the present-value interest factor in each of the following cases. Compare the calculated value to the table value.

Case	Opportunity cost, k (%)	Number of periods, n
A	2	4
B	10	2
C	5	3
D	13	2

11-10 ◨ **(Present Values)** For each of the following cases, calculate the present value of the cash flow, discounting at the rate given and assuming that the cash flow will be received at the end of the period noted.

Case	Single cash flow ($)	Discount rate (%)	End of period (years)
A	7,000	12	4
B	28,000	8	20
C	10,000	14	12
D	150,000	11	6
E	45,000	20	8

11-11 (Present Value) Terry Murphy has been offered a future payment of $500 three years from today. If his opportunity cost is 7 percent compounded annually, what value would he place on this opportunity?

11-12 (Present Value) An Ohio state savings bond can be converted to $100 at maturity six years from purchase. If the state bonds are to be competitive with U.S. Savings Bonds, which pay 8 percent annual interest (compounded annually), at what price will the state sell its bonds? Assume no cash payments on savings bonds prior to redemption.

11-13 ◨ **(Present Value—Mixed Streams)** Given the following mixed streams of cash flows:

	CASH FLOW STREAM	
Year	A	B
1	$ 50,000	$ 10,000
2	40,000	20,000
3	30,000	30,000
4	20,000	40,000
5	10,000	50,000
Totals	$150,000	$150,000

a Find the present value of each stream using a 15 percent discount rate.

b Compare the calculated present values and discuss them in light of the fact that the undiscounted total cash flows amount to $150,000 in each case.

11-14 ■ **(Present Value — Mixed Streams)** Find the present value of the following streams of cash flows. Assume that the firm's opportunity cost is 12 percent.

A		B		C	
Year	Amount	Year	Amount	Year	Amount
1	− $2,000	1	$10,000	1–5	$10,000/yr.
2	3,000	2–5	5,000/yr.	6–10	8,000/yr.
3	4,000	6	7,000		
4	6,000				
5	8,000				

11-15 (Relationship Between Future Value and Present Value) Using *only* the following information:

Year (*t*)	Cash flow ($)	Future-value interest factor at 5 percent ($FVIF_{5\%,t}$)
1	800	1.050
2	900	1.102
3	1,000	1.158
4	1,500	1.216
5	2,000	1.276

a Determine the *present value* of the mixed stream of cash flows using a 5 percent discount rate.

b How much would you be willing to pay for an opportunity to buy this stream, assuming that you can at best earn 5 percent on your investments.

c What effect, if any, would a 7 percent rather than 5 percent opportunity cost have on your analysis? (Explain verbally.)

11-16 ■ **(Present Value of an Annuity)** For each of the following cases, calculate the present value of the annuity, assuming that the annuity cash flows occur at the end of each year.

Case	Amount of annuity ($)	Interest rate (%)	Period (years)
A	12,000	7	3
B	55,000	12	15
C	700	20	9
D	140,000	5	7
E	22,500	10	5

11-17 ◼ (**Cash Flow Investment Decision**)   Jerry Carney has an opportunity to purchase any of the following investments. The purchase
price, amount of the single cash inflow, and its year of receipt are given
below for each investment. Which purchase recommendations would
you make, assuming that Mr. Carney can earn 10 percent on his investments?

Investment	Price ($)	Single cash inflow ($)	Year of receipt
A	18,000	30,000	5
B	600	3,000	20
C	3,500	10,000	10
D	1,000	15,000	40

11-18 ◼ (**Investment Decision**)   You have a choice of accepting either of
two 5-year cash flow streams or lump-sum amounts. One cash flow
stream is an annuity and the other is a mixed stream. You may accept
alternative A or B—either as a cash flow stream or as a lump sum. Given
the cash flow and lump-sum amounts associated with each, and assuming a 9 percent opportunity cost, which alternative (A or B) and in which
form (cash flow stream or lump sum amount) would you prefer?

End of Year	ALTERNATIVE	
	A	B
Cash flow stream		
1	$ 700	$1,100
2	700	900
3	700	700
4	700	500
5	700	300
Lump-sum amount		
At time zero	$2,800	$2,850

11-19 ◼ (**Accumulating a Future Sum**)   Judi Jordan wishes to accumulate $8,000 by the end of five years by making equal annual end-of-
year deposits over the next five years. If Judi can earn 9 percent on her
investments, how much must she deposit at the *end of each year* to meet
this goal?

11-20 (**Accumulating a Growing Future Sum**)   A retirement home at Ma-
rineworld Estates now costs $85,000. Inflation is expected to cause this
price to increase at 6 percent per year over the 20 years before J. R.
Rogers retires. How large an equal annual end-of-year deposit must be
made each year into an account paying an annual rate of 10 percent in
order for Rogers to have the cash to purchase his home at retirement?

11-21 (**Loan Amortization**) Determine the equal annual end-of-year payment required each year over the life of the following loans in order to repay them fully during the stated term of the loan.

Loan	Principal ($)	Interest rate (%)	Term of loan (years)
A	12,000	8	3
B	60,000	12	10
C	75,000	10	30
D	4,000	15	5

11-22 (**Loan Amortization Schedule**) Val Hawkins borrowed $15,000 at a 14 percent annual rate of interest to be repaid over three years. The loan is amortized into three equal annual end-of-year payments.
  a Calculate the annual end-of-year loan payment.
  b Prepare a loan amortization schedule showing the interest and principal breakdown of each of the three loan payments.
  c Explain why the interest portion of each payment declines with the passage of time.

11-23 (**Growth Rates**) You are given the following series of cash flows:

CASH FLOWS

Year	A	B	C
1	$500	$1,500	$2,500
2	560	1,550	2,600
3	640	1,610	2,650
4	720	1,680	2,650
5	800	1,760	2,800
6		1,850	2,850
7		1,950	2,900
8		2,060	
9		2,170	
10		2,280	

  a Calculate the compound growth rate associated with each cash flow stream.
  b If year 1 values represent initial deposits in a savings account paying annual interest, what is the rate of interest earned on each account?
  c Compare and discuss the growth rates and interest rates found in **a** and **b**, respectively.

11-24 (**Rate of Return**) Carlos Cordero has $1,500 to invest. His investment counselor suggests an investment that pays no explicit interest but will return $2,000 at the end of three years.
  a What annual rate of return will Mr. Cordero earn with this investment?

b Mr. Cordero is considering another investment, of equal risk, which earns a return of 8 percent. Which investment should he take, and why?

11-25 **(Rate of Return — Annuity)** What is the rate of return on an investment of $10,606 if the company expects to receive $2,000 each year for the next ten years?

11-26 **(Loan Rates of Interest)** David Pearson has been shopping for a loan to finance the purchase of his new car. He has found three possibilities that seem attractive and wishes to select the one having the lowest interest rate. The information available with respect to each of the three $5,000 loans follows.

Loan	Principal ($)	Annual payment ($)	Term (years)
A	5,000	1,352.81	5
B	5,000	1,543.21	4
C	5,000	2,010.45	3

a Determine the interest rate that would be associated with each of the loans.
b Which loan should Mr. Pearson take?

11-27 **(Perpetuities)** Given the following data, determine for each of the following perpetuities:

Perpetuity	Annual amount ($)	Discount rate (%)
A	20,000	8
B	100,000	10
C	3,000	6
D	60,000	5

a The appropriate present-value interest factor.
b The present value.

11-28 **(Annuity and Perpetuity)** You have decided to endow your favorite university with a scholarship in honor of your successful completion of managerial finance. It is expected that it will cost $6,000 per year to attend the university into perpetuity. You expect to give the university the endowment in 10 years and will accumulate it by making annual (end-of-year) deposits into an account. The rate of interest is expected to be 10 percent for all future time periods.
a How large must the endowment be?
b How much must you deposit at the end of each of the next ten years to accumulate the required amount?

11-29 **(Integrative — Future and Present Value)** A major corporation wishes to accumulate funds to provide a retirement annuity for a key executive. The executive by contract will retire at the end of exactly

12 years. Upon retirement the executive is entitled to receive an annual end-of-year payment of $42,000 for exactly 20 years. In the event the executive dies prior to the end of the 20-year period, the annual payments will pass to his heirs. During the 12-year "accumulation period," the corporation wishes to fund the annuity by making equal annual end-of-year deposits into an account earning 9 percent interest. Once the 20-year "distribution period" begins, the corporation plans to move the accumulated monies into an account earning a guaranteed 12 percent per year. At the end of the distribution period, the account balance will equal zero. How large must the equal annual end-of-year deposits into the account be over the 12-year accumulation period in order to allow the $42,000 annual end-of-year distributions to be made over the 20-year period? Note that the first deposit will occur at the end of year 1 and the first distribution payment at the end of year 13. (*Hint:* It may be helpful to draw a time line of cash flows before solving this problem.)

12

RISK, RETURN, AND VALUATION

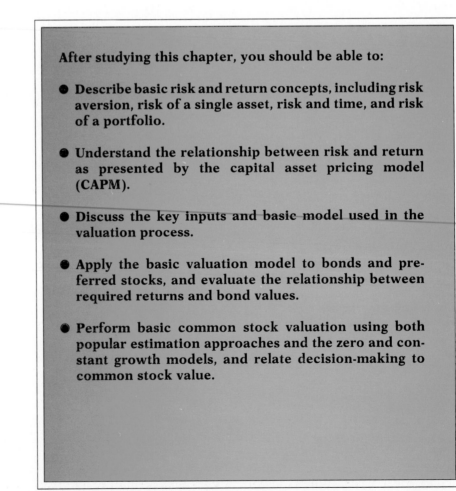

After studying this chapter, you should be able to:

● Describe basic risk and return concepts, including risk aversion, risk of a single asset, risk and time, and risk of a portfolio.

● Understand the relationship between risk and return as presented by the capital asset pricing model (CAPM).

● Discuss the key inputs and basic model used in the valuation process.

● Apply the basic valuation model to bonds and preferred stocks, and evaluate the relationship between required returns and bond values.

● Perform basic common stock valuation using both popular estimation approaches and the zero and constant growth models, and relate decision-making to common stock value.

In Chapter 1 the goal of the firm, and therefore of its financial manager, was specified as owner wealth maximization. For the publicly traded corporation, the financial manager's primary mission is therefore to maximize the price of the firm's common stock. To do this the manager must learn to assess the two key determinants of share price: risk and return. **Valuation** is the process that links risk and return in order to determine the worth of any asset — bonds, preferred stocks, common stocks, and fixed assets. Valuation relies on the use of the time value techniques presented in Chapter 11. Like investors, financial managers must understand how to value assets in order to determine whether or not they are a "good buy." Each financial decision presents certain risk and return characteristics, and all major financial decisions must be viewed in terms of expected risk, expected return, and their combined impact on share value.

valuation The process of determining the value of any asset.

BASIC RISK AND RETURN CONCEPTS

Risk and return concepts can be viewed as they relate to a single asset or to a **portfolio,** or collection, of assets. Although the portfolio risk concept is probably of greatest importance to the financial manager, the general concept of risk can be most readily viewed in terms of a single asset.

portfolio A collection, or group, of assets.

Fundamentals

Before developing risk and return concepts, we must define risk, return, and risk aversion.

RISK DEFINED   In the most basic sense, **risk** can be defined as the chance of financial loss. Assets having greater chances of loss are viewed as more risky than those with lesser chances of loss. More formally, the term *risk* is used interchangeably with the term *uncertainty* to refer to the *variability of returns associated with a given asset.* For instance, a government bond that guarantees its holder $100 interest after 30 days has no risk, since there is no variability associated with the return. An equivalent investment in a firm's common stock that may earn over the same period anywhere from $0 to $200 is very risky due to the high variability of the return. The more certain the return from an asset, the less variability and therefore the less risk.

risk The chance of financial loss or, more formally, the variability of returns associated with a given asset.

RETURN DEFINED   As noted in Chapter 2 (see Equation 2.1), the **return** on an asset is the change in value plus any cash distribution expressed as a percentage of the initial value. The return on common stock is calculated by dividing the sum of any increase (or decrease) in share price

return The change in value of an asset plus any cash distribution expressed as a percentage of the initial value.

and any cash dividends earned by the initial share price. For example, assume you purchased a share of stock one year ago for $20. If the stock is now selling for $22 per share and during the year you received a $1 cash dividend, your return would be 15 percent ([$2 increase in price ($22 − $20) + $1 cash dividend] ÷ $20 initial price).

RISK AVERSION   Financial managers generally seek to avoid risk. This behavior is known as **risk aversion.** For example, if a given risk is expected to increase from say 4 to 6, the risk-averse manager would require more than a proportional increase in return, say from 5 to 10. In this case, in order to take 50 percent more risk ([6 − 4] ÷ 4 = 2 ÷ 4 = 0.50 = 50%), the financial manager would require a 100 percent increase in return ([10 − 5] ÷ 5 = 5 ÷ 5 = 1.00 = 100%). *Most managers are risk averse, since for a given increase in risk they require as compensation a greater-than-proportional increase in return.* Accordingly, a risk-averse financial manager requiring higher returns for greater risk is assumed throughout this text.

risk aversion The tendency of financial managers to avoid risk.

Risk of a Single Asset

Although the risk of a single asset is measured in much the same way as the risk of an entire portfolio of assets, it is important to differentiate between these two entities, since certain benefits accrue to holders of portfolios. It is also useful to assess risk from both a behavioral and a quantitative point of view.

SENSITIVITY ANALYSIS   **Sensitivity analysis** is an approach that uses a number of possible return estimates to obtain a sense of the variability among outcomes. One common method involves the estimation of the pessimistic (worst), the most likely (expected), and the optimistic (best) return associated with a given asset. In this case the asset's risk can be measured by the **range,** which is found by subtracting the pessimistic (worst) outcome from the optimistic (best) outcome. The greater the range for a given asset, the more variability, or risk, it is said to have.

sensitivity analysis An approach in assessing risk that uses a number of possible return estimates to obtain a sense of the variability among outcomes.

range The extent of an asset's risk, which is found by subtracting the pessimistic (worst) outcome from the optimistic (best) outcome.

EXAMPLE

Alfred Company is attempting to choose the best of two alternative investments, A and B, each requiring an initial outlay of $10,000 and each having a *most likely* annual rate of return of 15 percent. To evaluate the riskiness of these assets, management has made *pessimistic* and *optimistic* estimates of the returns associated with each. The three estimates for each asset, along with its range, are given in Table 12.1. It can be seen that asset A appears to be less

TABLE 12.1 Assets A and B

	Asset A	Asset B
Initial investment	$10,000	$10,000
Annual rate of return		
Pessimistic	13%	7%
Most likely	15%	15%
Optimistic	17%	23%
Range	4%	16%

risky than asset B since its range of 4 percent (17 − 13 percent) is less than the range of 16 percent (23 − 7 percent) for asset B. The risk-averse financial decision maker would prefer asset A over asset B since A offers the same most likely return as B (15%) but with lower risk (smaller range). ■

PROBABILITIES   Probabilities can be used to assess more precisely the risk involved in an asset. The **probability** of an event occurring is the *percentage chance* of a given outcome. If an outcome has an 80 percent probability of occurrence, the given outcome would be expected to occur eight out of ten times. If an outcome has a probability of 100 percent, it is certain to occur. Outcomes having a probability of zero will never occur.

probability The *percentage chance* that a given outcome will occur.

EXAMPLE

An evaluation of the Alfred Company's past estimates indicates that the probabilities of the pessimistic, most likely, and optimistic outcomes' occurring are 25 percent, 50 percent, and 25 percent, respectively. The sum of these probabilities must equal 100 percent; that is, they must be based on all the alternatives considered. ■

PROBABILITY DISTRIBUTIONS   A **probability distribution** is a model that relates probabilities to the associated outcomes. The simplest type of probability distribution is the **bar chart,** which shows only a limited number of outcome-probability coordinates. The bar charts for Alfred Company's assets A and B are shown in Figure 12.1. Although both assets have the same most likely return, the range of return is much more dispersed for asset B than for asset A — 16 percent versus 4 percent. If we knew all the possible outcomes and associated probabilities, **a continuous probability distribution** could be developed. This type of distribution can be thought of as a bar chart for a very large number of outcomes. Figure 12.2 presents continuous probability distributions

probability distribution A model that relates probabilities to the associated outcomes.

bar chart The simplest type of probability distribution showing only a limited number of outcomes and associated probabilities for a given event.

continuous probability distribution A probability distribution showing all the possible outcomes and associated probabilities for a given event.

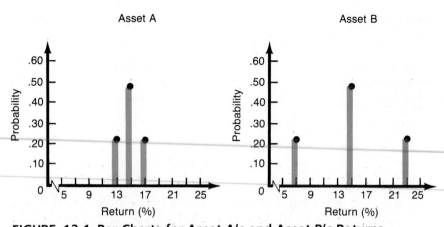

FIGURE 12.1 Bar Charts for Asset A's and Asset B's Returns
The bar charts show that although Assets A and B have the same most likely
return of 15 percent, the range of returns for Asset B has much greater dispersion
than that of Asset A. Asset B is therefore more risky.

for assets A and B. Note in Figure 12.2 that although assets A and B have
the same most likely return (15 percent), the distribution of returns for
asset B has much greater *dispersion* than the distribution for asset A.
Clearly asset B is more risky than asset A.

STANDARD DEVIATION The most common statistical indicator of an
asset's risk is the **standard deviation, σ_k,** which measures the disper-

standard deviation (σ_k)
The most common
statistical indicator of an
asset's risk, which
measures the dispersion
around the *expected*
value.

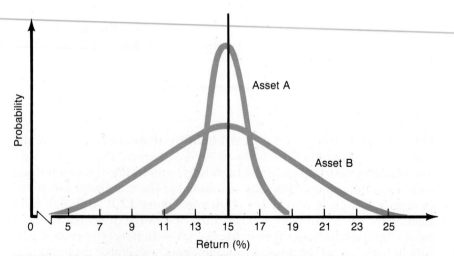

**FIGURE 12.2 Continuous Probability Distributions for Asset A's and
Asset B's Returns**
The continuous distribution of returns for Asset B has much greater dispersion
than that of Asset A, although both assets have the same most likely return of 15
percent. Asset B is therefore more risky.

ONE PROFESSOR'S ATTEMPT TO DEFINE RISK

In the business world, we casually discuss this poor word as if just the mere verbalization of the concept relieves us of the responsibility to do anything about it. . . .

Huge sums are spent in reducing, measuring, compensating for, averting, and insuring against risk, usually without much success. The risk is always there. And, of course, the next question becomes, "Whose risk is it?" The task of handling risk has created a legion of business parasites, i.e., lawyers, accountants, regulators, consultants, insurance persons, and a host of staff functions. What an incredible overhead burden to protect one's ASSets against RISK. Are we really getting our money's worth for such a huge cost? I think not. And still risk remains, in spite of the sums we spend at the altar. . . .

Being true to my academic bent, I asked several colleagues to define what risk meant to them. The following random sample of six (with a confidence level of zero) led to these responses:

Finance type: variation about an expected return.
Accountant: errors and irregularities.
Management: making decisions in the face of unknown conditions.
Quantitative type: decision-making in which at least one decision variable is random.
Economist: uncertainty about the outcome.
Lawyer: not a legal concept (I loved this one).

Some consistency appears from these samples, but not enough for me to feel comfortable with real, live businessmen. Is this what we're really teaching? No wonder businessmen hold us in such low esteem — we're too parochial.

Now after all of this, you expect me to define what risk really is? No way . . . I'm a risk averter. But we might form a committee to . . .

Source: Daniel L. Schneid, "Risk: Four-Letter Word," *Financial Executive*, January 1984, pp. 16–17. Reprinted by permission from *Financial Executive*, January 1984, copyright 1984 by Financial Executives Institute.

---

sion around the *expected* value. The **expected value of a return**, $\bar{k}$, is the most likely return on an asset. This can be calculated using Equation 12.1:

expected value of a return ($\bar{k}$) The most likely return on a given asset.

$$\bar{k} = \sum_{i=1}^{n} k_i \times Pr_i \qquad (12.1)$$

where

k_i = return for the ith outcome
Pr_i = probability of occurrence of ith return
n = number of outcomes considered

EXAMPLE

The calculation of the expected values for Alfred Company's assets A and B are presented in Table 12.2. Column 1 gives the Pr_i's and column 2 gives the k_i's, n equaling 3 in each case. The expected value for each asset's return is 15 percent. ■

The expression for the *standard deviation of returns*, σ_k, is given in Equation 12.2:

$$\sigma_k = \sqrt{\sum_{i=1}^{n} (k_i - \bar{k})^2 \times Pr_i} \qquad (12.2)$$

In general, the higher the standard deviation, the greater the risk.

EXAMPLE

Table 12.3 presents the calculation of standard deviations for Alfred Company's assets A and B, based on the data presented earlier. The standard deviation for asset A is 1.41 percent, and the standard deviation for asset B is 5.66 percent. The higher risk of asset B is clearly reflected in its higher standard deviation. ■

coefficient of variation (CV) A measure of relative dispersion used in comparing the risk of assets with differing expected returns.

COEFFICIENT OF VARIATION   The **coefficient of variation**, *CV*, is a measure of relative dispersion that is useful in comparing the risk of assets with differing expected returns. Equation 12.3 gives the expression for the coefficient of variation:

$$CV = \frac{\sigma_k}{\bar{k}} \qquad (12.3)$$

The higher the coefficient of variation, the greater the risk.

TABLE 12.2 Expected Values of Returns for Assets A and B

Possible outcomes	Probability (1)	Returns (%) (2)	Weighted value (%) [(1) × (2)] (3)
Asset A			
Pessimistic	.25	13	3.25
Most likely	.50	15	7.50
Optimistic	.25	17	4.25
Total	1.00	Expected return	15.00
Asset B			
Pessimistic	.25	7	1.75
Most likely	.50	15	7.50
Optimistic	.25	23	5.75
Total	1.00	Expected return	15.00

TABLE 12.3 The Calculation of the Standard Deviation of the Returns for Assets A and B

ASSET A

i	k_i	$\bar{k}$	$k_i - \bar{k}$	$(k_i - \bar{k})^2$	Pr_i	$(k_i - \bar{k})^2 \times Pr_i$
1	13%	15%	−2%	4%	.25	1%
2	15	15	0	0	.50	0
3	17	15	2	4	.25	1

$$\sum_{i=1}^{3} (k_i - \bar{k})^2 \times Pr_i = 2\%$$

$$\sigma_{k_A} = \sqrt{\sum_{i=1}^{3} (k_i - \bar{k})^2 \times Pr_i} = \sqrt{2\%} = \underline{\underline{1.41\%}}$$

ASSET B

i	k_i	$\bar{k}$	$k_i - \bar{k}$	$(k_i - \bar{k})^2$	Pr_i	$(k_i - \bar{k})^2 \times Pr_i$
1	7%	15%	−8%	64%	.25	16%
2	15	15	0	0	.50	0
3	23	15	8	64	.25	16

$$\sum_{i=1}^{3} (k_i - \bar{k})^2 \times Pr_i = 32\%$$

$$\sigma_{k_B} = \sqrt{\sum_{i=1}^{3} (k_i - \bar{k})^2 \times Pr_i} = \sqrt{32\%} = \underline{\underline{5.66\%}}$$

EXAMPLE

Substituting the standard deviation values (from Table 12.3) and the expected returns (from Table 12.2) for assets A and B into Equation 12.3, the coefficients of variation for A and B, respectively, are .094 (1.41% ÷ 15%) and .377 (5.66% ÷ 15%). Asset B has the higher coefficient of variation and is therefore more risky than asset A. Since both assets have the same expected return, the coefficient of variation has not provided any more information than the standard deviation. ■

The real utility of the coefficient of variation is in comparing assets that have *different* expected returns. A simple example will illustrate this point.

EXAMPLE

A firm is attempting to select the least risky of two alternative assets—X and Y. The expected return, standard deviation, and coefficient of variation for each of these assets' returns is given below.

Statistics	Asset X	Asset Y
(1) Expected return	12%	20%
(2) Standard deviation	9%[a]	10%
(3) Coefficient of variation [(2) ÷ (1)]	.75	.50[a]

[a] Preferred asset using the given risk measure.

If the firm were to compare the assets solely on the basis of their standard deviations, it would prefer asset X, since asset X has a lower standard deviation than asset Y (9 percent versus 10 percent). However, comparing the coefficients of variation of the assets shows that management would be making a serious error in accepting asset X in preference to asset Y, since the relative dispersion, or risk, of the assets as reflected in the coefficient of variation is lower for Y than for X (.50 versus .75). Clearly the use of the coefficient of variation to compare asset risk is effective because it also considers the relative size, or expected return, of the assets. ■

Risk and Time

Risk can be viewed not only with respect to the current time period but also as an *increasing function of time*. Figure 12.3 depicts probability distributions of returns for a 1-year, 10-year, 15-year, and 20-year forecast, assuming each year's expected returns are equal. A band representing ± 1 standard deviation, σ, from the expected return, $\bar{k}$, is indicated in the figure. It can be seen that the *variability of the returns, and therefore the risk, increases with the passage of time*. Generally, the longer-lived an asset investment, the greater its risk due to increasing variability of returns resulting from increased forecasting errors for distant years.

Risk of a Portfolio

efficient portfolio
A portfolio that maximizes return for a given level of risk or minimizes risk for a given level of return.

The risk of any single proposed asset investment should not be viewed independently of other assets. New investments must be considered in light of their impact on the risk and return of the *portfolio* of assets. The financial manager's goal for the firm is to create an **efficient portfolio,** which is one that maximizes return for a given level of risk or minimizes risk for a given level of return. The statistical concept of correlation underlies the process of diversification that is used to develop an efficient portfolio of assets.

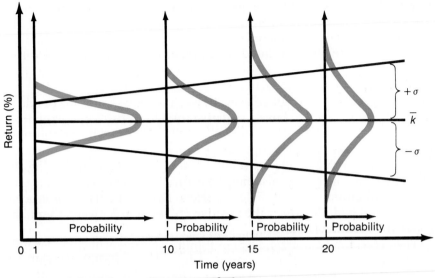

FIGURE 12.3 Risk as a Function of Time
The probability distributions of returns for a 1-year, 10-year, 15-year, and 20-year forecast, assuming each year's expected returns ($\bar{k}$) are equal, show that the variability of returns (σ), and therefore the risk, increases with the passage of time.

CORRELATION Correlation is a statistical measure of the relationship, if any, between series of numbers representing any data from returns to test scores. If two series move in the same direction, they are **positively correlated**; if the series move in opposite directions, they are **negatively correlated**. The degree of correlation is measured by the **correlation coefficient**, which has a range of $+1$ for **perfectly positively**

correlation A statistical measure of the relationship, if any, between series of numbers representing data of any kind.

positively correlated Descriptive of two series that move in the same direction.

negatively correlated Descriptive of two series that move in opposite directions.

correlation coefficient A measure of the degree of correlation between two series.

perfectly positively correlated Describes two positively correlated series having a correlation coefficient of $+1$.

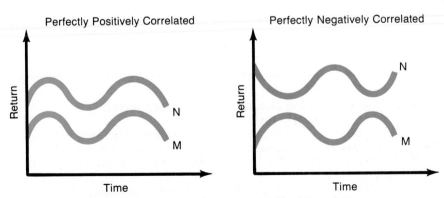

FIGURE 12.4 The Correlation Between Series M and N
The perfectly positively correlated series M and N in the left graph move exactly together, while the perfectly negatively correlated series M and N in the right graph move in exactly opposite directions.

BASIC LONG-TERM FINANCIAL CONCEPTS

perfectly negatively correlated Describes two negatively correlated series having a correlation coefficient of −1.

correlated series and −1 for **perfectly negatively correlated** series. These two extremes are depicted for series M and N in Figure 12.4. The perfectly positively correlated series move exactly together, while the perfectly negatively correlated series move in exactly opposite directions.

DIVERSIFICATION   To reduce overall risk, it is best to combine or add to the portfolio assets that have a negative (or a low positive) correlation. By combining negatively correlated assets, the overall variability of returns, or risk, can be reduced. Figure 12.5 shows that a portfolio containing the negatively correlated assets F and G, both having the same expected return, $\bar{k}$, also has the return, $\bar{k}$, but has less risk (variability) than either of the individual assets. Even if assets are not negatively correlated, the lower the positive correlation between them, the lower the resulting risk.[1]

The creation of a portfolio by combining two assets having perfectly positively correlated returns *cannot* reduce the portfolio's overall risk below the risk of the least risky asset, whereas a portfolio combining two assets with less than perfectly positive correlation *can* reduce total risk to a level below that of either of the components. For example, assume you are in the machine-tool manufacturing business which is very *cyclical*, having high sales when the economy is expanding and low

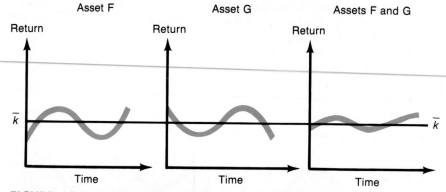

FIGURE 12.5 Combining Negatively Correlated Assets to Diversify Risk
The risk, or variability of returns, resulting from combining negatively correlated Assets F and G, both having the same expected return, $\bar{k}$, results in a portfolio (shown in the graph at right) with the same level of expected return but less risk.

[1] Some assets are *uncorrelated*, that is, they are completely unrelated in the sense that there is no interaction between their returns. Combining uncorrelated assets can reduce risk—not as effectively as combining negatively correlated assets, but more effectively than combining positively correlated assets. The correlation coefficient for uncorrelated assets is close to zero and acts as the midpoint between perfect positive and perfect negative correlation.

sales during a recession. If you acquired another machine-tool company, which would have sales positively correlated with those of your firm, the combined sales would continue to be cyclical. As a result risk would remain the same. As an alternative, however, you could acquire a sewing machine manufacturer which is *countercyclical*, having low sales during economic expansion and high sales during recession (since consumers are more likely to make their own clothes at such a time). Combination with the sewing machine manufacturer, which has negatively correlated sales, should reduce risk since the low machine tool sales during a recession would be balanced out by high sewing machine sales, and vice versa. A numeric example will provide a better understanding of the role of correlation in the diversification process.

EXAMPLE

Table 12.4 presents the anticipated returns from three different assets—X, Y, and Z—over the next five years, along with their

TABLE 12.4 Returns, Expected Values, and Standard Deviations for Assets X, Y, and Z and Portfolios XY and XZ

	ASSETS			PORTFOLIOS	
Year	X	Y	Z	XY[a] (50%X + 50%Y)	XZ[b] (50%X + 50%Z)
1988	8%	16%	8%	12%	8%
1989	10	14	10	12	10
1990	12	12	12	12	12
1991	14	10	14	12	14
1992	16	8	16	12	16
Statistics:					
Expected value	12%	12%	12%	12%	12%
Standard deviation[c]	2.83%	2.83%	2.83%	0%	2.83%

[a] Portfolio XY, which consists of 50 percent of asset X and 50 percent of asset Y, illustrates *perfect negative correlation*, since these two return streams behave in completely opposite fashion over the five-year period.

[b] Portfolio XZ, which consists of 50 percent of asset X and 50 percent of asset Z, illustrates *perfect positive correlation*, since these two return streams behave identically over the five-year period.

[c] Since the probabilities associated with the returns are not given, the formula given earlier in Equation 12.2 could not be used to calculate the standard deviations, σ_k. Instead the general formula

$$\sigma_k = \sqrt{\frac{\sum_{i=1}^{n} (k_i - \bar{k})^2}{n}}$$

where k_i = return i, $\bar{k}$ = expected value of return, and n = the number of outcomes considered, was used.

expected values and standard deviations. It can be seen that each of the assets has an expected value of return of 12 percent and a standard deviation of 2.83 percent. The assets therefore have equal return and equal risk, although their return patterns are not necessarily identical. A comparison of the return patterns of assets X and Y shows that they are perfectly negatively correlated, since they move in exactly opposite directions over time. A comparison of assets X and Z shows that they are perfectly positively correlated, since they move in precisely the same direction. (Note that the returns for X and Z are identical.)

Portfolio XY By combining equal portions of assets X and Y—the perfectly negatively correlated assets—portfolio XY (shown in Table 12.4) is created. The risk in the portfolio created by this combination, as reflected in the standard deviation, is reduced to 0 percent, while the expected return value remains at 12 percent. Since both assets had the same expected return values, are combined in equal parts, and are perfectly negatively correlated, the combination results in the complete elimination of risk. Whenever assets are perfectly negatively correlated, an optimum combination (similar to the 50-50 mix in the case of assets X and Y) exists for which the resulting standard deviation will equal 0.

Portfolio XZ By combining equal portions of assets X and Z—the perfectly positively correlated assets—portfolio XZ (shown in Table 12.4) is created. The risk in this portfolio, as reflected by its standard deviation, which remains at 2.83 percent, is unaffected by this combination, and the expected return value remains at 12 percent. Whenever perfectly positively correlated assets such as X and Z are combined, the standard deviation of the resulting portfolio cannot be reduced below that of the least risky asset; the maximum portfolio standard deviation will also be that of the riskiest asset. Since assets X and Z have the same standard deviation (2.83 percent), the minimum and maximum standard deviations are both 2.83 percent, which is the only value that could be taken on by a combination of these assets. This result can be attributed to the unlikely situation that X and Z are identical assets. ∎

Although detailed statistical explanations can be given for the behaviors illustrated in Table 12.4, the important point is that assets can be combined so that the resulting portfolio has less risk than that of either of the assets independently. And this can be achieved without any loss of return. Portfolio XY in the preceding example illustrated such behavior. The more negative (or less positive) the correlation between asset returns, the greater the risk-reducing benefits of diversification. In no case will creating portfolios of assets result in greater risk than that of the riskiest asset included in the portfolio. It is important to recognize that these relationships apply when considering the addition of an asset to an existing portfolio.

RISK AND RETURN: THE CAPITAL ASSET PRICING MODEL (CAPM)

The most important aspect of risk is the *overall risk* of the firm as viewed by investors in the marketplace. Overall risk significantly affects investment opportunities — and even more important, the owners' wealth. The basic theory that links together risk and return for all assets is commonly called the **capital asset pricing model (CAPM).** Here we will use CAPM to understand the basic risk-return trade-offs involved in all types of financial decisions.

capital asset pricing model (CAPM) The basic theory that links together risk and return for all assets.

Types of Risk

To understand the basic types of risk, consider what happens when we begin with a single security (asset) in a portfolio. Then we expand the portfolio by randomly selecting additional securities from, say, the population of all actively traded securities. Using the standard deviation, σ, to measure the total portfolio risk, Figure 12.6 depicts the behavior of the total portfolio risk (y-axis) as more securities are added (x-axis). With the addition of securities, the total portfolio risk declines, due to the effects of diversification (as explained in the previous section), and tends to approach a limit. Research has shown that virtually all the benefits of diversification, in terms of risk reduction, can be gained by forming portfolios containing 10 to 20 randomly selected securities. Figure 12.6 depicts this general behavior.

The **total risk** of a security can be viewed as consisting of two parts:

$$\text{Total security risk} = \text{nondiversifiable risk} + \text{diversifiable risk} \quad (12.4)$$

total risk The combination of a security's nondiversifiable risk and diversifiable risk.

Diversifiable risk represents the portion of an asset's risk that can be eliminated through diversification. It is attributable to firm-specific events, such as strikes, lawsuits, regulatory actions, loss of a key account, and so forth. **Nondiversifiable risk** is attributable to factors that affect all firms. Factors such as war, inflation, international incidents, and political events account for nondiversifiable risk.

diversifiable risk The portion of an asset's risk attributable to firm-specific events that can be eliminated through diversification.

Because, as illustrated in Figure 12.6, any investor can create a portfolio of assets that will eliminate all, or virtually all, diversifiable risk, the *only relevant risk is nondiversifiable risk.* Any investor (or firm) must therefore be concerned solely with nondiversifiable risk, which reflects the contribution of an asset to the risk, or standard deviation, of the portfolio. The measurement of nondiversifiable risk is thus of primary

nondiversifiable risk The relevant portion of an asset's risk attributable to factors that affect all firms; it cannot be eliminated through diversification.

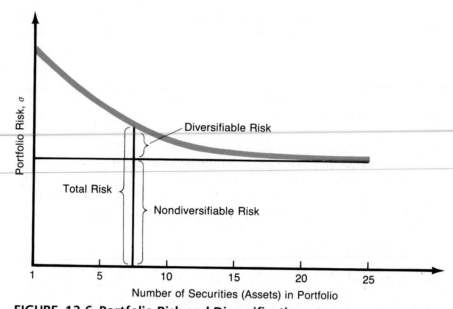

FIGURE 12.6 Portfolio Risk and Diversification
As randomly selected securities (assets) are combined to create a portfolio, the *total risk* of the portfolio declines until 10 to 20 securities are included. The portion of the risk eliminated is *diversifiable risk,* while that remaining is *nondiversifiable risk.*

importance in selecting those assets possessing the most desired risk-return characteristics.

The Model: CAPM

The capital asset pricing model (CAPM) links together nondiversifiable risk and return for all assets. We will discuss the model in three parts. The first part defines and describes the beta coefficient, which is a measure of nondiversifiable risk. The second part presents an equation of the model itself, and the final part graphically describes the relationship between risk and return.

beta coefficient (b)
A measure of nondiversifiable risk. The *index* of the degree of movement of an asset's return in response to a change in the market return.

market return The return on the market portfolio of all traded securities.

BETA COEFFICIENT   The **beta coefficient, b**, is used to measure nondiversifiable risk. It is an *index* of the degree of movement of an asset's return in response to a change in the market return. The **market return** is the return on the market portfolio of all traded securities. The return on a portfolio of the stocks in *Standard & Poor's 500 Stock Composite Index* or some similar stock index is commonly used to measure the market return. Beta coefficients can be obtained for actively traded stocks from published sources, such as *Value Line Investment Survey,* or through brokerage firms. Betas for selected stocks are given in Table

TABLE 12.5 Beta Coefficients for Selected Stocks (May 16, 1986)

Stock	Beta
Apple Computer	1.60
Avon Products	1.00
Briggs & Stratton	.70
CBS Inc.	1.05
Cascade Natural Gas	.60
Delta Air Lines	1.15
Exxon Corporation	.80
General Motors	1.15
Gerber Scientific	1.80
International Business Machines	1.05
Merrill Lynch & Company	1.85
NCR Corporation	1.25
Paine Webber Group	1.90
Reynolds & Reynolds	1.05
Seagram Company	1.10
Standard Register	.80
Tandy Corporation	1.25
Union Electric	.70
U.S. Steel	1.05
Xerox Corporation	1.05

SOURCE: *Value Line Investment Survey* (New York: Value Line, Inc., May 16, 1986).

12.5. The beta coefficient for the market is equal to 1.0; all other betas are viewed in relation to this value. Asset betas may take on values that are either positive or negative, but positive betas are the norm. The majority of beta coefficients fall between .5 and 2.0. Table 12.6 provides some selected beta values and their associated interpretations.

TABLE 12.6 Selected Beta Coefficients and Their Interpretations

Beta	Comment	Interpretation[a]
2.0		Twice as responsive, or risky, as the market
1.0	Move in same direction as market	Same response or risk as the market (i.e., average risk)
.5		Only half as responsive as the market
0		Unaffected by market movement
− .5		Only half as responsive as the market
−1.0	Move in opposite direction to market	Same response or risk as the market
−2.0		Twice as responsive as the market

[a] A stock that is twice as responsive as the market will experience a 2 percent change in its return for each 1 percent change in the return of the market portfolio, whereas the return of a stock that is half as responsive as the market will change by $\frac{1}{2}$ of 1 percent for each 1 percent change in the return of the market portfolio.

THE EQUATION Using the beta coefficient, b, to measure nondiversifiable risk, the *capital asset pricing model (CAPM)* is given in Equation 12.5:

$$k_j = R_F + [b_j \times (k_m - R_F)] \tag{12.5}$$

where

k_j = required return on asset j
R_F = risk-free rate of return, commonly measured by the return
on a U.S. Treasury bill
b_j = beta coefficient or index of nondiversifiable risk for asset j
k_m = market return; the return on the market portfolio of assets

The required return on an asset, k_j, is an increasing function of beta, b_j, which measures nondiversifiable risk. In other words, *the higher the risk, the higher the required return, and vice versa.* The model can be broken into two parts: (1) the *risk-free rate*, R_F; and (2) the *risk premium*, $b_j \times (k_m - R_F)$. The $(k_m - R_F)$ portion of the risk premium is called the *market risk premium,* since it represents the premium the investor must receive for taking the average amount of risk associated with holding the market portfolio of assets. Let us look at an example.

EXAMPLE

Herbst Corporation wishes to determine the required return on an asset—asset Z—that has a beta, b_z, of 1.5. The risk-free rate of return is found to be 7 percent, while the return on the market portfolio of assets is 11 percent. Substituting $b_z = 1.5$, $R_F = 7$ percent, and $k_m = 11$ percent into the capital asset pricing model given in Equation 12.5 yields a required return:

$$k_z = 7\% + [1.5 \times (11\% - 7\%)] = 7\% + 6\% = \underline{\underline{13\%}}$$

It can be seen that the market risk premium of 4 percent (11 percent − 7 percent), when adjusted for the assets index of risk (beta) of 1.5, results in a risk premium of 6 percent (1.5 × 4%), which when added to the 7 percent risk-free rate, results in a 13 percent required return. It should be clear that other things being equal, the higher the beta, the greater the required return, and vice versa. ■

THE GRAPH: THE SECURITY MARKET LINE (SML) When the capital asset pricing model (Equation 12.5) is depicted graphically, it is called the **security market line (SML).** It should be clear from Equation 12.5 that the SML will, in fact, be a straight line. It reflects for each level of nondiversifiable risk (beta) the required return in the marketplace. In the graph, risk as measured by beta, b, is plotted on the x-axis, and

security market line (SML) The depiction of the capital asset pricing model (CAPM) as a graph.

required returns, k, are plotted on the y-axis. The risk-return trade-off is clearly represented by the SML. Let us look at an illustration.

EXAMPLE

In the preceding example for the Herbst Corporation, the risk-free rate, R_F, was 7 percent, and the market return, k_m, was 11 percent. Since the betas associated with R_F and k_m, b_{R_F} and b_m, are by definition 0^2 and 1, respectively, the SML can be plotted using these two sets of coordinates (i.e., $b_{R_F} = 0$, $R_F = 7\%$, and $b_m = 1$, $k_m = 11\%$). Figure 12.7 presents the security market line that results from plotting the coordinates given. As traditionally shown, the security market line in Figure 12.7 presents the required return associated with all positive betas. The market risk premium of 4 percent (k_m of 11 percent minus R_F of 7 percent) has been highlighted. Using the beta for asset Z, b_z, of 1.5, its corresponding required return, k_z, is 13 percent. Also shown in the figure is asset Z's risk premium of 6 percent (k_z of 13% minus R_F of 7%). It should be clear that for assets with betas greater than 1, the risk premium is greater than that for the market; for assets with betas less than 1, the risk premium is less than that for the market. ■

VALUATION FUNDAMENTALS

As stated at the beginning of this chapter, *valuation* is the process of determining the worth of an asset. It can be applied to expected streams of benefits from bonds, stocks, income properties, oil wells, and so on in order to determine their worth at a given point in time. To do this the manager uses the time value of money techniques presented in Chapter 11 and the concepts of risk and return developed earlier in this chapter.

Key Inputs

The key inputs to the valuation process include cash flows (returns), timing, and the discount rate (risk). Each is described briefly below.

CASH FLOWS (RETURNS)   The value of any asset depends on the cash flow(s) it is expected to provide over the ownership period. To have value an asset does not have to provide an annual cash flow; it can

---

[2] Since R_F is the rate of return on a risk-free asset, the beta associated with the risk-free asset, b_{R_F}, would equal 0. The 0 beta on the risk-free asset reflects not only its absence of risk but also that the asset's return is unaffected by movements in the market return.

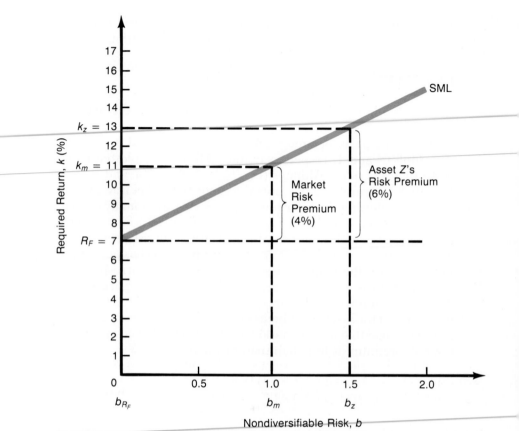

FIGURE 12.7 The Security Market Line (SML) with Herbst Corporation's Asset Z Data Shown

At a beta of 0, the required return is the risk-free rate of 7 percent, and at a beta of 1.0, the required return is 11 percent (the 7 percent risk-free rate plus a 4 percent market risk premium). The required return for Asset Z, which has a beta of 1.5, is 13 percent (the 7 percent risk-free rate plus a 6 percent risk premium).

provide an intermittent cash flow or even a single cash flow over the period.

EXAMPLE

Nancy Dorr, the financial analyst for Kent Industries, wishes to estimate the value of three assets—common stock in Wortz United, an interest in an oil well, and an original painting by a well-known artist. Her cash flow estimates for each were:

Stock in Wortz United: Expect to receive cash dividends of $300 per year indefinitely.

Oil well: Expect to receive cash flow of $2,000 at the end of one year, $4,000 at the end of two years, and $10,000 at the end of four years, when the well is to be sold.

Original painting: Expect to be able to sell the painting in five years for $85,000.

Having developed these cash flow estimates, Nancy has taken the first step toward placing a value on each of these assets. ■

TIMING   In addition to making cash flow estimates, the timing of the cash flows must be specified.[3] It is customary to specify the timing along with the amounts of cash flow. For example, the cash flows of $2,000, $4,000, and $10,000 for the oil well in the example were scheduled to occur at the end of years 1, 2, and 4, respectively. In combination, the cash flow and its timing fully define the return expected from the asset.

DISCOUNT RATE (RISK)   Risk, as noted earlier, describes the chance that an expected outcome will not be realized. The level of risk associated with a given cash flow can significantly affect its value. In general, the greater the risk of (or the less certain) a cash flow, the lower its value. In terms of present value (see Chapter 11), greater risk can be incorporated into an analysis by using a higher discount rate or required return. Recall that in the capital asset pricing model (CAPM) (see Equation 12.5), the greater the risk as measured by beta, b, the higher the required return, k. In the valuation process, too, the discount rate is used to incorporate risk into the analysis—the higher the risk, the greater the discount rate (required return), and vice versa.

EXAMPLE

Let's return to Nancy Dorr's job of placing a value on Kent Industries' original painting, which is expected to provide a single cash flow of $85,000 from its sale at the end of five years, and consider two scenarios.

Scenario 1—Certainty: A major art gallery has contracted to buy the painting for $85,000 at the end of five years. Because this is considered a certain situation, Nancy views this as "money in the bank" and would use the prevailing risk-free rate, R_F, of 9 percent as the discount rate when calculating the value of the painting.

---

[3] Although cash flows can occur at any time during a year, for computational convenience as well as custom, they will be assumed to occur at the *end* of the year unless otherwise noted.

BUSINESS VALUATION USING AN APPRAISER

"Business valuation has made quantum leaps in the past few years," says Allan Lannom, director of operations at Lloyd-Thomas/Coats & Burchard, a 90-year-old general appraisal firm based in Calabasas Park, Calif. Patrick Hurley, in his seventh year at Howard & Co., a Philadelphia firm engaged in corporate financing, publication, and valuation, agrees. Hurley, mincing no words, says, "We've seen a lot more potential, and decided consciously to market directly instead of waiting for referrals. Now, instead of waiting for an attorney to call up and say, 'You do valuations, right?' I tell everyone I see, 'We do valuations.'"

. . .

Voluntary transfers of equity, however, are not the only transactions that call for the appraiser's stamp. Divorce — which more and more often features a closely held business as one of the most hotly contested properties — requires his-and-hers stock valuations. And the Internal Revenue Service, long an inadvertent fee generator for lawyers and accountants, is now performing the same service for valuation experts. "About 75% of our business is tax-litigation related," says John E. Bakken, who heads up his own business valuation firm in Denver. The hefty proportion of litigation-bound clients explains why the agenda of the ASA's [American Society of Appraisers's] fourth annual business valuation seminar this past November [1985] featured a session on "The Business Appraiser as Expert Witness."

Finally, there's the trickle-down effect of the media's current love affair with entrepreneurship to be considered. Small-business owners are eager to explore the dimensions of their starring roles in the age of the entrepreneur. "A number of my clients don't have a transaction at hand when they bring us in," says Napier. "They want to know the value of their companies, for whatever might arise in the future. They know they've got something of value, and they want to know what that value is."

Whether or not they find out will have a lot to do with which of the current crop of valuation "experts" they end up picking. The appraiser's art — recent gains in respectability notwithstanding — remains, as Patrick Hurley puts it, "a judgment call based on knowledge of how a company really works." And uncovering that information is no easy task for even the best of appraisers. Detailed and sophisticated examination of the books is necessary, but hardly sufficient. The conscientious value expert will also have to assess a barrage of information ranging from personal, financial, and legal relations among founding/owning families to game plans of prospective successors to whatever local, national, and worldwide conditions exist affect the company.

Scenario 2—High Risk: The value of original paintings by this artist has fluctuated widely over the past 10 years, and although Nancy expects to be able to get $85,000 for the painting, she realizes its sale price in five years could range between $30,000 and $140,000. Due to the high uncertainty surrounding the painting's value, Nancy believes a 15 percent discount rate is appropriate. ■

The preceding example and the associated estimates of the appropriate discount rate illustrate the role this rate plays in capturing risk. The often subjective nature of such estimates is also clear.

The Basic Valuation Model

Simply stated, the value of any asset is *the present value of all future cash flows it is expected to provide over the relevant time period.* The time period can be as short as one year or as long as infinity. The value of an asset is therefore determined by discounting the expected cash flows back to their present value, using a discount rate commensurate with the asset's risk. Utilizing the present-value techniques presented in Chapter 11, the value of any asset at time zero, V_0, can be expressed as

$$V_0 = \frac{CF_1}{(1+k)^1} + \frac{CF_2}{(1+k)^2} + \cdots + \frac{CF_n}{(1+k)^n} \qquad (12.6)$$

where

V_0 = value of the asset at time zero
CF_t = cash flow expected at the end of year t
k = appropriate discount rate
n = relevant time period

Using present-value interest factor notation, $PVIF_{k,n}$ from Chapter 11, Equation 12.6 can be rewritten as

$$V_0 = CF_1 \times (PVIF_{k,1}) + CF_2 \times (PVIF_{k,2}) + \cdots + CF_n \times (PVIF_{k,n}) \quad (12.7)$$

Substituting the expected cash flows, CF_t, over the relevant time period, n, and the appropriate discount rate, k, into Equation 12.7, we can determine the value of any asset.

EXAMPLE

Nancy Dorr, with the addition of appropriate discount rates, calculated the value of each asset as shown in Table 12.7 using Equation 12.7. The Wortz United stock has a value of $2,500, the oil well's value is $9,262, and the original painting has a value of $42,245. It should be clear that regardless of the pattern of the

TABLE 12.7 Valuation of Kent Industries' Assets by Nancy Dorr

ASSET	CASH FLOW, CF	APPROPRIATE DISCOUNT RATE (%)	VALUATION
Wortz United stock[a]	$300/year indefinitely	12	$V_0 = \$300 \times (PVIFA_{12\%,\infty})$ $= \dfrac{\$300}{.12} = \underline{\$2,500}$
Oil well[b]	Year (t) $\quad CF_t$ 1 $\quad$ \$ 2,000 2 $\quad$ 4,000 3 $\quad$ 0 4 $\quad$ 10,000	20	$V_0 = \$2,000 \times (PVIF_{20\%,1})$ $\quad + \$4,000 \times (PVIF_{20\%,2})$ $\quad + \$0 \times (PVIF_{20\%,3})$ $\quad + \$10,000 \times (PVIF_{20\%,4})$ $= \$2,000 \times (.833)$ $\quad + \$4,000 \times (.694)$ $\quad + \$0 \times (.579)$ $\quad + \$10,000 \times (.482)$ $= \$1,666 + \$2,776$ $\quad + \$0 + \$4,820$ $= \underline{\$9,262}$
Original painting[c]	$85,000 at end of year 5	15	$V_0 = \$85,000 \times (PVIF_{15\%,5})$ $= \$85,000 \times (.497)$ $= \underline{\$42,245}$

[a] This is a perpetuity (infinite-lived annuity), and therefore Equation 11.22 is applied.

[b] This is a mixed stream of cash flows and therefore requires finding and summing the individual *PVIF*s noted.

[c] This is a lump-sum cash flow and therefore requires finding a single *PVIF*.

expected cash flow from an asset, the basic valuation equation can be used to determine value.

BOND AND PREFERRED STOCK VALUES

The basic valuation equation can be customized for use in valuing specific securities—bonds, preferred stock, and common stock. Bonds and preferred stocks are similar since they have stated contractual interest and dividend cash flows. The dividends on common stock, on the other hand, are not known in advance. Bond and preferred stock valuation is described in this section, while common stock valuation is discussed in the following section.

■ Bond Valuation

Bonds, which are discussed in detail in Chapter 18, are long-term debt instruments used by business and government to raise large sums of money, typically from a diverse group of lenders. As noted in Chapter 2, most corporate bonds pay interest *semiannually* (every six months), have an initial *maturity* of 10 to 30 years, and have a *par*, or *face*, *value* of $1,000 that must be repaid at maturity. An example will illustrate the point.

EXAMPLE

The ABC Company on January 1, 1988, issued a 10 percent, 10-year bond with a $1,000 par value that pays interest semiannually. Investors who buy this bond receive the contractual right to (1) $100 annual interest (10 percent × $1,000 par value) distributed as $50 ($\frac{1}{2}$ × $100) at the end of each six months and (2) the $1,000 par value at the end of the tenth year. ■

BASIC BOND VALUATION The value of a bond is the present value of the contractual payments its issuer is obligated to make from the current time until it matures. The appropriate discount rate would be the required return, k_d, which depends on prevailing interest rates and risk. The basic equation for the value, B_0, of a bond that pays *annual* interest of I dollars[4], has n years to maturity, has an M dollar par value, and for which the required return is k_d, is given by Equation 12.8:

$$B_0 = I \times \left[\sum_{t=1}^{n} \frac{1}{(1 + k_d)^t} \right] + M \times \left[\frac{1}{(1 + k_d)^n} \right] \qquad (12.8)$$

$$= I \times (PVIFA_{k_d,n}) + M \times (PVIF_{k_d,n}) \qquad (12.8a)$$

EXAMPLE

Using the ABC Company data for the January 1, 1988, new issue and *assuming that interest is paid annually* and that the required return is equal to the bond's stated interest rate, $I = 100, $k_d = 10$ percent, $M = $1,000$, and $n = 10$ years. Substituting these values in Equation 12.8a yields

$$B_0 = $100 \times (PVIFA_{10\%,10\,\text{yrs}}) + $1,000 \times (PVIF_{10\%,10\,\text{yrs}})$$
$$= $100 \times (6.145) + $1,000 \times (.386)$$
$$= $614.50 + $386.00 = \underline{$1,000.50}$$

The bond therefore has a value of approximately $1,000.[5] *Note that the value calculated above is equal to par value; this will always be*

---

[4] The payment of annual rather than semiannual bond interest is assumed throughout the following discussion. This assumption simplifies the calculations involved while maintaining the conceptual accuracy of the valuation procedures presented.

[5] Note that a slight rounding error ($.50) results here due to the use of the table factors rounded to the nearest thousandth.

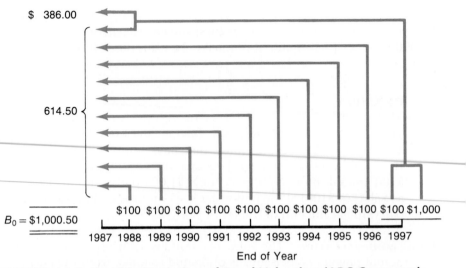

FIGURE 12.8 Graphic Depiction of Bond Valuation (ABC Company's 10-Percent Interest, 10-Year Maturity, $1,000 Par, January 1, 1988, Issue Paying Annual Interest; Required Return = 10 Percent)

The $1,000.50 value of the ABC Company bond is found by adding the $614.50 present value (found using the 10 percent required return) of the ten annual $100 interest payments to the $386.00 present value (also at 10 percent) of the $1,000 par value to be received in ten years at maturity.

the case when the required return is equal to the stated rate of interest. The computations involved in finding the bond value are depicted graphically on the time line in Figure 12.8. ■

REQUIRED RETURNS AND BOND VALUES Whenever the required return on a bond differs from the bond's stated interest rate, the bond's value will differ from its par, or face, value. The required return on the bond is likely to differ from the stated interest rate either (1) because economic conditions have changed, causing a shift in the basic cost of long-term funds, or (2) the firm's risk has changed. Increases in the basic cost of long-term funds or in risk will raise the required return, and vice versa.

Regardless of the exact cause, the important point is that when the required return is greater than the stated rate of interest, the bond value, B_0, will be less than its par value, M. In this case the bond is said to sell at a **discount**, which will equal $M - B_0$. On the other hand, when the required rate of return falls below the stated rate of interest, the bond value will be greater than par. In this situation the bond is said to sell at a **premium**, which will equal $B_0 - M$. An example will illustrate.

discount The amount by which a bond sells at a value that is less than its par, or face, value.

premium The amount by which a bond sells at a value greater than its par, or face, value.

EXAMPLE

In the preceding example it was shown that when the required return equaled the stated rate of interest, the bond's value equaled its $1,000 par value. If for the same bond the required return were to rise to 12 percent, its value would be

$$B_0 = \$100 \times (PVIFA_{12\%, 10\,yrs}) + \$1,000 \times (PVIF_{12\%, 10\,yrs})$$
$$= \$100 \times (5.650) + \$1,000 \times (.322) = \underline{\$887.00}$$

The bond would therefore sell at a *discount* of $113.00 ($1,000 par value — $887.00 value).

If, on the other hand, the required return fell to, say, 8 percent, the bond's value would be

$$B_0 = \$100 \times (PVIFA_{8\%, 10\,yrs}) + \$1,000 \times (PVIF_{8\%, 10\,yrs})$$
$$= \$100 \times (6.710) + \$1,000 \times (.463) = \underline{\$1,134.00}$$

The bond would therefore sell at a *premium* of $134.00 ($1,134.00 value — $1,000 par value). These results are summarized in Table 12.8. ■

Preferred Stock Valuation

As noted in Chapter 2, preferred stock pays a fixed periodic dividend. Since preferred stock never matures, its dividend payments can be viewed as a perpetuity. Assuming that preferred stock dividends, D_p, are paid *annually*,[6] and the required return is k_p, the value of preferred stock, PS_0, can be given by Equation 12.9:

$$PS_0 = D_P \times \left(\frac{1}{k_p}\right) = \frac{D_p}{k_p} \qquad (12.9)$$

TABLE 12.8 Bond Values for Various Required Returns (10-Percent Stated Interest Rate, 10-Year Maturity, $1,000 Par, Interest Paid Annually)

Required return, k_d (%)	Bond value, B_0	Status
12	$ 887.00	Discount
10	1,000.00	Par value
8	1,134.00	Premium

[6] The payment of annual rather than quarterly dividends is assumed for simplicity. Preferred stock is discussed in detail in Chapter 19.

Recall from Chapter 11 that in the case of a perpetuity, the present-value interest factor, $PVIFA_{k_p,\infty} = 1/k_p$, must be used. The application of this factor to find the value of preferred stock can be noted in the first term to the right in Equation 12.9. An example will show how this is done.

EXAMPLE

The ABC Company has an issue of preferred stock outstanding that has a stated annual dividend of $5. The required return on the preferred stock has been estimated to be 13 percent. Substituting $D_p = \$5$ and $k_p = 13\%$ into Equation 12.9 yields a preferred stock value of $38.46 ($5 ÷ .13). Equation 12.9 can be used in this manner to find the value of any perpetuity. ■

◼ COMMON STOCK VALUATION

Common stockholders expect to be rewarded through the receipt of periodic cash dividends and an increasing — or at least nondeclining — share value. Like current owners, prospective owners and security analysts frequently estimate the firm's value. They choose to purchase the stock when they believe it to be *undervalued* (i.e., that its true value is greater than its market price) and to sell when they feel it is *overvalued* (i.e., that its market price is greater than its true value).

Popular Approaches

Many popular approaches for measuring value exist, but only one is widely accepted. The popular approaches to valuation include the use of book value, liquidation value, or some type of a price/earnings multiple.

book value per share
The amount per share of common stock to be received if all assets are liquidated for their book value, and if the proceeds remaining after paying all liabilities (including preferred stock) are divided among the common stockholders.

BOOK VALUE **Book value per share** is simply the amount per share of common stock to be received if all assets are liquidated for their exact book (accounting) value and if the proceeds remaining after paying all liabilities (including preferred stock) are divided among the common stockholders. This method lacks sophistication and can be criticized on the basis of its reliance on historical balance sheet data. It ignores the firm's expected earnings potential and generally lacks any true relationship with the firm's value in the marketplace. Let us look at an example.

EXAMPLE

The Honee Company currently (December 31, 1987) has total assets of $6 million, total liabilities including preferred stock of $4.5 million, and 100,000 shares of common stock outstanding. Its book value per share would therefore be

$$\frac{\$6,000,000 - \$4,500,000}{100,000 \text{ shares}} = \underline{\$15 \text{ per share}}$$

Since this value assumes that assets are liquidated for their book value, it may not represent the minimum share value. As a matter of fact, although most stocks sell above book value, it is not unusual to find stocks selling below book value. ■

LIQUIDATION VALUE   **Liquidation value per share** is the *actual* amount per share of common stock to be received if all the firm's assets are sold, liabilities (including preferred stock) are paid, and any remaining money is divided among the common stockholders.[7] This measure is more realistic than book value, but it still fails to consider the earning power of the firm's assets. An example will illustrate.

liquidation value per share The *actual* amount per share of common stock to be received if all the firm's assets are sold, liabilities (including preferred stock) are paid, and the remaining proceeds divided among the common stock-holders.

EXAMPLE

The Honee Company found upon investigation that it would obtain only $5.25 million if it liquidated its assets today. The firm's liquidation value per share would therefore be

$$\frac{\$5,250,000 - \$4,500,000}{100,000 \text{ shares}} = \underline{\$7.50 \text{ per share}}$$

Ignoring any expenses of liquidation, this would be the firm's minimum value. ■

PRICE/EARNINGS MULTIPLES   Price/earnings (P/E) ratios were introduced in Chapter 4. The average P/E ratio in a particular industry can be used as the guide to a firm's value if it is assumed that investors value the earnings of a given firm in the same manner as they do the "average" firm in that industry. **The price/earnings multiple approach** to value is a popular technique whereby the firm's expected earnings per share (EPS) are multiplied by the average price/earnings (P/E) ratio for the industry to estimate the firm's share value. The average P/E ratio for

price/earnings multiple approach A technique whereby the firm's expected earnings per share (EPS) are multiplied by the average price/earnings (P/E) ratio for the industry to estimate the firm's share value.

[7] In the event of liquidation, creditors' claims must be satisfied first, then those of the preferred stockholders. Anything left goes to common stockholders. A more detailed discussion of liquidation procedures is presented in Chapter 17.

an industry can be obtained from a source such as *Standard & Poor's Industrial Ratios*.

The use of P/E multiples is especially helpful in valuing firms that are not publicly traded, whereas the use of market price may be preferable in the case of a publicly traded firm. In any case, the price/earnings multiple approach is considered superior to the use of book or liquidation values since it considers *expected* earnings. Before we discuss the most widely accepted approach, let us consider an example of price/earnings multiples.

EXAMPLE

The Honee Company is expected to earn $2.60 per share next year (1988). This expectation is based on an analysis of the firm's historical earnings trend and expected industry and economic conditions. The average price/earnings ratio for firms in the same industry is 7. Multiplying Honee's expected earnings per share (EPS) of $2.60 by this ratio gives us a value for the firm's shares of $18.20, assuming that investors will continue to measure the value of the average firm at 7 times its earnings. ■

The Basic Equation

Like bonds and preferred stock, the value of a share of common stock is equal to the present value of all future benefits it is expected to provide. Simply stated, *the value of a share of common stock is equal to the present value of all future dividends it is expected to provide over an infinite time horizon.* Although by selling stock at a price above that originally paid, a stockholder can earn capital gains in addition to dividends, what is really sold is the right to all future dividends. Therefore, from a valuation viewpoint only dividends are relevant. Redefining terms, the basic valuation model in Equation 12.6 can be specified for common stock as given in Equation 12.10:

$$P_0 = \frac{D_1}{(1 + k_s)^1} + \frac{D_2}{(1 + k_s)^2} + \cdots + \frac{D_\infty}{(1 + k_s)^\infty} \tag{12.10}$$

where

P_0 = value of common stock
D_t = per-share dividend expected at the end of year t
k_s = required return on common stock

The equation can be simplified somewhat by redefining each year's dividend, D_t, in terms of anticipated growth. Two cases are considered here — zero growth and constant growth.

zero growth model An approach to dividend valuation that assumes a constant, nongrowing dividend stream.

ZERO GROWTH The simplest approach to dividend valuation, the **zero growth model**, is one that assumes a constant, nongrowing dividend stream. In terms of the notation already introduced,

$$D_1 = D_2 = \cdots = D_\infty$$

Letting D_1 represent the amount of the annual dividend, Equation 12.10 under zero growth would reduce to

$$P_0 = D_1 \sum_{t=1}^{\infty} \frac{1}{(1 + k_s)^t} = D_1 \times (PVIFA_{k_s, \infty}) = \frac{D_1}{k_s} \qquad (12.11)$$

The equation shows that with zero growth, the value of a share of stock would equal the present value of a perpetuity of D_1 dollars discounted at a rate k_s. Let us look at an example.

EXAMPLE

The Addison Company's dividend is expected to remain constant at $3 per share indefinitely. If the required return on its stock is 15 percent, the stock's value is $20 ($3 ÷ .15). ■

CONSTANT GROWTH The most widely cited dividend valuation approach, the **constant growth model,** assumes that dividends will grow at a constant rate, g, that is less than the required return, $k_s(g < k_s)$. Letting D_0 represent the most recent dividend, Equation 12.10 can be rewritten as follows:

constant growth model
A widely cited dividend valuation approach that assumes dividends will grow at a constant rate that is less than the required return.

$$P_0 = \frac{D_0 \times (1 + g)^1}{(1 + k_s)^1} + \frac{D_0 \times (1 + g)^2}{(1 + k_s)^2} + \cdots + \frac{D_0 \times (1 + g)^\infty}{(1 + k_s)^\infty} \qquad (12.12)$$

If we simplify Equation 12.12, it can be rewritten as follows

$$P_0 = \frac{D_1}{k_s - g} \qquad (12.13)$$

The constant growth model in Equation 12.13 is commonly called the **Gordon model.** An example will show how it works.

Gordon model
A common name for the *constant growth model* widely used in dividend valuation.

EXAMPLE

The Honee Company from 1982 through 1987 paid the per-share dividends shown below.

Year	Dividend ($)
1987	1.40
1986	1.29
1985	1.20
1984	1.12
1983	1.05
1982	1.00

Using Appendix Table D-3 for the present-value interest factor, *PVIF,* in conjunction with the technique described for finding growth rates in Chapter 11, the annual growth rate of dividends, which is assumed to equal the expected constant rate of dividend growth, *g*, is found to equal 7 percent.[8] The company estimates that its dividend in 1988, D_1, will equal $1.50. The required return, k_s, is assumed to be 15 percent. Substituting these values into Equation 12.13, the value of the stock is

$$P_0 = \frac{\$1.50}{.15 - .07} = \frac{\$1.50}{.08} = \underline{\$18.75 \text{ per share}}$$

Assuming that the values of D_1, k_s, and *g* are accurately estimated, the Honee Company's stock value is $18.75. ◼

Decision Making and Common Stock Value

Valuation equations measure the stock value at a point in time based on expected return (D_1, *g*) and risk (k_s) data. The decisions of the financial manager, through their effect on these variables, can cause the value of the firm, P_0, to change.

CHANGES IN EXPECTED RETURN   Assuming that economic conditions remain stable, any management action that would cause current and prospective stockholders to raise their dividend expectations should increase the firm's value. In Equation 12.13 we can see that P_0 will increase for any increase in D_1 or *g*. Any action the financial manager can take that will increase the level of expected returns without changing risk (the required return) should be undertaken, since it will positively affect owners' wealth. An example will illustrate this.

EXAMPLE

Imagine that the Honee Company, which was found to have a share value of $18.75 in the preceding example, on the following

---

[8] The technique involves solving the following equation for *g*:

$$D_{1987} = D_{1982} \times (1 + g)^5$$

$$\frac{D_{1982}}{D_{1987}} = \frac{1}{(1 + g)^5} = PVIF_{g,5}$$

Two basic steps can be followed. First, dividing the earliest dividend ($D_{1982} = \$1.00$) by the most recent dividend ($D_{1987} = \$1.40$), a factor for the present value of one dollar, *PVIF*, of .714 ($1.00 ÷ $1.40) results. Although six dividends are shown, they reflect only five years of growth. Looking across the table at the present-value interest factors, *PVIF*, for five years, the factor closest to .714 occurs at 7 percent (.713). Therefore, the growth rate of the dividends, rounded to the nearest whole percentage, is 7 percent.

day announced a major technological breakthrough that would revolutionize its industry. Current and prospective shareholders are not expected to adjust their required return of 15 percent, but they do expect that future dividends will be increased. Specifically, they feel that although the dividend next year, D_1, will remain at $1.50, the expected rate of growth will increase from 7 to 9 percent. Substituting $D_1 = \$1.50$, $k_s = .15$, and $g = .09$ into Equation 12.13, the resulting value is found to equal $25 [i.e., $1.50 ÷ (.15 − .09)]. The increased value therefore resulted from the higher expected future dividends reflected in the increase in the growth rate, g. ■

CHANGES IN RISK   Although k_s is defined as the required return, it is, as pointed out earlier in this chapter, directly related to the nondiversifiable risk, which can be measured by the beta coefficient. The capital asset pricing model (CAPM) in Equation 12.5 shows this relationship. Reviewing the model with the risk-free rate, R_F, and the market return, k_m, held constant, the required return, k_s, depends directly on beta. In other words, any action taken by the financial manager that increases risk will also increase the required return. In Equation 12.13 it can be seen that with all else constant, an increase in the required return, k_s, will reduce share value, P_0, and vice versa. Thus any action by the financial manager that increases risk contributes toward a reduction in value, and vice versa. An example will illustrate.

EXAMPLE

Assume that the Honee Company's 15 percent required return resulted from a risk-free rate, R_F, of 9 percent, a market return, k_m, of 13 percent, and a beta, b, of 1.50. Substituting into the capital asset pricing model, Equation 12.5, the 15 percent required return, k_s, results

$$k_s = 9\% + [1.50 \times (13\% − 9\%)] = \underline{15\%}$$

Using this return, the value of the firm, P_0, was calculated to be $18.75 in the earlier example.

Now imagine that the financial manager makes a decision that, without changing expected dividends, increases the firm's beta to 1.75. Assuming that R_F and k_m remain at 9 and 13 percent, respectively, the required return will increase to 16 percent (i.e., 9% + [1.75 × (13% − 9%)]) to compensate stockholders for the increased risk. Substituting $D_1 = \$1.50$, $k_s = .16$, and $g = .07$ into the valuation equation, Equation 12.13, results in a share value of $16.67 [i.e., $1.50 ÷ (.16 − .07)]. As expected, the owners, by raising the required return (without any corresponding increase in expected return), cause the firm's share value to decline. Clearly the financial manager's action was not in the owners' best interest. ■

COMBINED EFFECT   A financial decision rarely affects return and risk independently; most decisions affect both factors. In terms of the measures presented, with an increase in risk (beta, b) one would expect an increase in return (D_1 or g, or both), assuming that R_F and k_m remain unchanged. Depending on the relative magnitude of the changes in these variables, the net effect on value can be assessed.

EXAMPLE

If we assume that the two changes illustrated for the Honee Company in the preceding examples occur simultaneously as a result of an action of the financial decision maker, key variable values would be $D_1 = \$1.50$, $k_s = .16$, and $g = .09$. Substituting into the valuation model, a share price of $21.43 [i.e., $1.50 ÷ (.16 − .09)] is obtained. The net result of the decision, which increased return (g from 7 to 9 percent) as well as risk (b from 1.50 to 1.75 and therefore k_s from 15 to 16 percent), is positive, since the share price increased from $18.75 to $21.43. Assuming that the key variables are accurately measured, the decision appears to be in the best interest of the firm's owners, since it increases their wealth. ■

SUMMARY

● The key risk and return and valuation definitions and formulas are given in Table 12.9.
● *Risk* is the chance of loss, or, more formally, refers to the variability of returns. *Return* is the change in value plus any cash distributions expressed as a percentage of the initial value. Most financial decision-makers are risk averse.
● Two approaches commonly used to get a sense of asset risk are sensitivity analysis and the use of probabilities. Probability distributions can be used to examine risk. Two statistics that provide a measure of an asset's risk are the standard deviation and the coefficient of variation. Risk is an increasing function of time.
● New investments must be considered in light of their impact on the portfolio of assets. The correlation of asset returns affects the diversification process.
● The only relevant risk is nondiversifiable risk, since diversifiable risk can be easily eliminated through diversification. Nondiversifiable risk can be measured by the beta coefficient.

TABLE 12.9 Summary of Key Definitions and Formulas for Risk, Return, and Valuation

Variable definitions

$\bar{k}$ = expected value of a return

k_i = return on the ith outcome

Pr_i = probability of occurrence of the ith return

n = number of outcomes considered

σ_k = standard deviation of returns

CV = coefficient of variation

k_j = required return on asset j

R_F = risk-free rate of return

b_j = beta coefficient or index of nondiversifiable risk for asset j

k_m = market return; the return on the market portfolio of assets

k_d = required return on a bond

B_0 = bond value

I = annual interest on a bond

M = par value of a bond

PS_0 = value of preferred stock

k_p = required return on preferred stock

D_p = annual preferred stock dividend

P_0 = value of common stock

D_t = per-share dividend expected at the end of year t

k_s = required return on common stock

g = constant rate of growth in dividends

Risk and return formulas

Expected Value of a Return

$$\bar{k} = \sum_{t=1}^{n} k_i \times Pr_i$$

Standard Deviation of Returns

$$\sigma_k = \sqrt{\sum_{i=1}^{n} (k_i - \bar{k})^2 \times Pr_i}$$

Coefficient of Variation

$$CV = \frac{\sigma_k}{\bar{k}}$$

Capital Asset Pricing Model (CAPM)

$$k_j = R_F + [b_j \times (k_m - R_F)]$$

Valuation formulas

Bond Value

$$B_0 = I \times \left[\sum_{t=1}^{n} \frac{1}{(1 + k_d)^t} \right] + M \times \left[\frac{1}{(1 + k_d)^n} \right]$$
$$= I \times (PVIFA_{k_d,n}) + M \times (PVIF_{k_d,n})$$

Preferred Stock Value

$$PS_0 = \frac{D_p}{k_p}$$

Common Stock Value

Zero Growth: $P_0 = \dfrac{D_1}{k_s}$

Constant Growth: $P_0 = \dfrac{D_1}{k_s - g}$

● The capital asset pricing model (**CAPM**) uses beta to relate an asset's risk relative to the market to the asset's required return. The graphic depiction of the CAPM is the security market line (**SML**).

● The value of any asset is equal to the present value of all future cash flows it is expected to provide over the relevant time period. Key inputs to the valuation process include cash flows (returns), timing, and the discount rate (risk).

- The value of a bond is the present value of interest payments plus the present value of its par, or face, value. The discount rate used to determine bond value is the required return. A bond can sell at a discount, at par, or at a premium, depending upon whether the required return is respectively greater than, equal to, or less than its stated interest rate.

- The value of preferred stock is determined by applying the appropriate present-value interest factor for a perpetuity to its annual dividend.

- Popular approaches for estimating common stock value include book value, liquidation value, and price/earnings (P/E) multiples. The value of common stock is the present value of all future dividends expected to be received over an infinite time horizon. Of the two cases of dividend growth, zero and constant, the most widely cited is the constant growth model.

- Because most financial decisions affect both return and risk, an assessment of their combined effect on value must be part of the financial decision-making process.

QUESTIONS

12-1 Define *risk* as it relates to financial decision making. How can the return on common stock be calculated? Why are financial managers commonly viewed as *risk averse?*

12-2 How can *sensitivity analysis* be used to assess asset risk? What is one of the most common approaches to sensitivity analysis? Define and describe the role of the *range* as an aid in sensitivity analysis.

12-3 How does a plot of the distribution of outcomes allow the decision maker to get a sense of asset risk? What is the difference between a bar chart and a continuous probability distribution?

12-4 What does the *standard deviation* of a distribution of asset returns indicate? What is the *coefficient of variation?* When is the coefficient of variation preferred over the standard deviation for comparing asset risk?

12-5 Why must assets be evaluated in a portfolio context? What is an *efficient portfolio?* What is *correlation*, and how is it related to the process of diversification?

12-6 What is the relationship of total risk, nondiversifiable risk, and diversifiable risk? Which risk is measured by *beta?* Why would someone argue that nondiversifiable risk is the only relevant risk?

12-7 What is the equation for the *capital asset pricing model (CAPM)?* Explain the meaning of each variable. Assuming a risk-free rate of 8 percent and a market return of 12 percent, graph the risk-return trade-off as defined by the CAPM.

12-8 What are the three key inputs to the valuation process? Define and specify the general equation for the value of any asset, V_0, in terms of its expected cash flow, CF_t, in each year t, and the appropriate discount rate, k.

12-9   In terms of the required return and the stated interest rate, what relationship between them will cause a bond to sell (a) at a discount? (b) at a
premium? (c) at its par value? Explain.

12-10   Describe the procedure used to estimate the value of preferred stock.
Why are preferred stock dividends treated as a perpetuity?

12-11   Explain each of the three popular approaches — (a) book value, (b) liquidation value, and (c) price/earnings multiples — for estimating common
stock value. Which of these is best? Why?

12-12   Describe, compare, and contrast the zero growth and constant growth
cases for estimating the value of common stock.

12-13   Explain the linkages among financial decisions, return, risk, and share
value. How does the capital asset pricing model (CAPM) fit into this basic
framework? Explain.

PROBLEMS

12-1   **(Risk Preference)**   Oren Wells, the financial manager for Winston Enterprises, wishes to evaluate three prospective investments — X, Y, and
Z. Currently the firm earns 12 percent on its investments, which have a
risk index of 6 percent. The three investments under consideration are
profiled below in terms of expected return and expected risk. If Oren
Wells were risk averse, which investment, if any, would he select? Explain why.

Investment	Expected return (%)	Expected risk index (%)
X	14	8
Y	19	9
Z	20	10

12-2   **(Risk Analysis)**   Babb Products is considering an investment in an expanded product line. Two possible types of expansion are being considered. After investigating the possible outcomes, the following estimates
were made:

	Expansion A	Expansion B
Initial investment	$12,000	$12,000
Annual rate of return		
Pessimistic	16%	10%
Most likely	20	20
Optimistic	24	30

a Determine the range of the rates of return for each of the two projects.
b Which project is less risky? Why?

    c If you were making the investment decision which one would you choose? Why? What does this imply about your feelings toward risk?

    d Assume that expansion B's most likely outcome was 21 percent per year and all other facts remained the same. Does this change your answer to part **c**? Why?

12-3 **(Risk and Probability)** Micro-Pub, Inc., is considering the purchase of one of two microfilm cameras—R or S. Both should provide benefits over a 10-year period, and each requires an initial investment of $4,000. Management has constructed the following table of estimates of probabilities and rates of return for pessimistic, most likely, and optimistic results:

	CAMERA R		CAMERA S	
	Amount	Probability	Amount	Probability
Initial investment	$4,000	1.00	$4,000	1.00
Annual rate of return				
Pessimistic	20%	.25	15%	.20
Most likely	25	.50	25	.55
Optimistic	30	.25	35	.25

    a Determine the range for the rate of return for each of the two cameras.

    b Determine the expected value of return for each camera.

    c Which camera is more risky? Why?

12-4 **(Bar Charts and Risk)** David's Sportswear is considering bringing out a line of designer jeans. Currently it is negotiating with two different well-known designers. Because of the highly competitive nature of the industry, the two designs have been given code names. After market research, the firm has established the following expectations about the annual rates of return:

		ANNUAL RATE OF RETURN	
Market acceptance	Probability	Line J	Line K
Very poor	.05	.0075	.010
Poor	.15	.0125	.025
Average	.60	.0850	.080
Good	.15	.1475	.135
Excellent	.05	.1625	.150

Use the table to:

    a Construct a bar chart for each line's annual rate of return.

    b Calculate the expected value of return for each line.

    c Evaluate the relative riskiness for each jean line's rate of return using the bar charts.

12-5 **(Assessing Return and Risk)** Newby Tool must choose between two asset purchases. The annual rate of return and the related probabilities given below summarize the firm's analysis to this point.

PROJECT 257		PROJECT 432	
Rate of return	Probability	Rate of return	Probability
−10%	.01	10%	.05
10	.04	15	.10
20	.05	20	.10
30	.10	25	.15
40	.15	30	.20
45	.30	35	.15
50	.15	40	.10
60	.10	45	.10
70	.05	50	.05
80	.04		
100	.01		

a For each project, compute:
   (1) The range of possible rates of return.
   (2) The expected value of return.
   (3) The standard deviation of the returns.
   (4) The coefficient of variation for each project.
b Construct a bar chart of each distribution of rates of return.
c Which project would you consider the less risky? Why?

12-6 **(Integrative — Expected Return, Standard Deviation, and Coefficient of Variation)** Three assets — F, G, and H — are currently being considered by Bix Manufacturing. The following probability distributions of returns for these assets have been developed.

	ASSET F		ASSET G		ASSET H	
i	Pr_i	Return, k_i	Pr_i	Return, k_i	Pr_i	Return, k_i
1	.10	40%	.40	35%	.10	40%
2	.20	10	.30	10	.20	20
3	.40	0	.30	−20	.40	10
4	.20	−5			.20	0
5	.10	−10			.10	−20

a Calculate the expected value of return, $\bar{k}$, for each of the three assets. Which provides the largest expected return?
b Calculate the standard deviation, σ_k, for each of the three assets' returns. Which appears to have the greatest risk?
c Calculate the coefficient of variation, CV, for each of the three assets. Which appears to have the largest *relative* risk?

12-7 **(Portfolio Selection)** You have been asked for your advice in selecting a portfolio of assets. You have been supplied with the following data:

	EXPECTED RETURN (%)		
Year	Asset A	Asset B	Asset C
1988	12	16	12
1989	14	14	14
1990	16	12	16

No probabilities have been supplied. You have been told that you must create portfolios by investing equal proportions (i.e., 50 percent), in each of two different assets.

a What is the expected return for each asset over the three-year period?
b What is the standard deviation for each asset's return?
c What is the expected return for each possible portfolio? (There are three possible portfolios.)
d How would you characterize the correlations of returns of the two assets making up each of the three portfolios identified in **c**?
e What is the standard deviation for each portfolio?
f Which portfolio do you recommend? Why?

12-8 **(Total, Nondiversifiable, and Diversifiable Risk)** Allen Ferris randomly selected securities from all those listed on the New York Stock Exchange to be included in a portfolio. He began with one security and added securities one by one until a total of 20 securities were held in the portfolio. After each security was added, Allen calculated the portfolio standard deviation, σ; the calculated values are given below:

Number of securities	Portfolio risk, σ (%)	Number of securities	Portfolio risk, σ (%)
1	14.50	11	7.00
2	13.30	12	6.80
3	12.20	13	6.70
4	11.20	14	6.65
5	10.30	15	6.60
6	9.50	16	6.56
7	8.80	17	6.52
8	8.20	18	6.50
9	7.70	19	6.48
10	7.30	20	6.47

a On a set of number of securities in portfolio (x-axis)–portfolio risk (y-axis) axes, plot the portfolio risk data given in the preceding table.
b Divide the total portfolio risk in the graph into its *nondiversifiable* and *diversifiable* risk components and label each of these on the graph.
c Describe which of the two risk components is the "relevant risk" and explain why it is relevant. How much of this risk exists in Allen Ferris's portfolio?

12-9 **(Interpreting Beta)** A firm wishes to assess the impact of changes in the market return on one of its assets that has a beta of 1.20.

a If the market return increased by 15 percent, what impact would this have on the asset's return?

b If the market return decreased by 8 percent, what impact would this have on the asset's return?

c If the market return did not change, what impact, if any, would this have on the asset's return?

d Would this asset be considered more or less risky than the market? Explain.

12-10 (Betas) Answer the questions below for each of the following assets.

Asset	Beta
A	0.50
B	1.60
C	−0.20
D	0.90

a What impact would a *10 percent increase* in the market return have on each asset's return?

b What impact would a *10 percent decrease* in the market return have on each asset's return?

c If you were certain that the market return would *increase* in the near future, which asset would you prefer? Why?

d If you were certain that the market return would *decrease* in the near future, which asset would you prefer? Why?

12-11 (Betas and Risk Rankings) Stock A has a beta of 0.80, stock B has a beta of 1.40, and stock C has a beta of −0.30.

a Rank these stocks from the most risky to the least risky.

b If the return on the market portfolio increases by 12 percent, what change in the return for each of the stocks would you expect?

c If the return on the market portfolio declines by 5 percent, what change in the return for each of the stocks would you expect?

d If you felt the stock market was just ready to experience a significant decline, which stock would you likely add to your portfolio? Why?

e If you anticipated a major stock market rally, which stock would you add to your portfolio? Why?

12-12 (Capital Asset Pricing Model — CAPM) For each of the following cases, use the capital asset pricing model to find the required return.

Case	Risk-free rate, R_F (%)	Market return, k_m (%)	Beta, b
A	5	8	1.30
B	8	13	.90
C	9	12	−.20
D	10	15	1.00
E	6	10	.60

12-13 **(Manipulating CAPM)** Use the basic equation for the capital asset pricing model (CAPM) to work each of the following:
  a Find the *required return* for an asset with beta of 0.90 when the risk-free rate and market return are 8 percent and 12 percent, respectively.
  b Find the *risk-free rate* for a firm with a required return of 15 percent and a beta of 1.25 when the market return is 14 percent.
  c Find the *market return* for an asset with a required return of 16 percent and a beta of 1.10 when the risk-free rate is 9 percent.
  d Find the *beta* for an asset with a required return of 15 percent when the risk-free rate and market return are 10 percent and 12.5 percent, respectively.

12-14 **(Security Market Line — SML)** Assume that the risk-free rate, R_F, is currently 9 percent and that the market return, k_m, is currently 13 percent.
  a Draw the security market line (SML) on a set of nondiversifiable risk (*x*-axis) – required return (*y*-axis) axes.
  b Calculate and label on the axes in **a** the *market risk premium*.
  c Given the data above, calculate the required return on asset A having a beta of 0.80 and asset B having a beta of 1.30.
  d Draw in the betas and required returns from **c** for assets A and B on the axes in **a**. Label the *risk premium* associated with each of these assets and discuss them.

12-15 **(Integrative — Risk, Return, and CAPM)** The Jessup Box Company must consider several investment projects, A through E, using the capital asset pricing model (CAPM) and its graphic representation, the security market line (SML). Using the table below,

Item	Rate of return (%)	Beta (b) value
Risk-free asset	9	0
Market portfolio	14	1.00
Project A	—	1.50
Project B	—	.75
Project C	—	2.00
Project D	—	0
Project E	—	− .50

  a Calculate the required return and risk premium for each project given its level of nondiversifiable risk.
  b Graph the security market line (required return relative to nondiversifiable risk) for all projects listed in the table.
  c Discuss the relative nondiversifiable risk of projects A through E.

12-16 **(Valuation Fundamentals)** Imagine that you are trying to evaluate the economics of purchasing an automobile. Assume that you expect the car to provide annual after-tax cash benefits of $1,200 and that you can sell the car for after-tax proceeds of $5,000 at the end of the planned five-year ownership period. All funds for purchasing the car will be drawn from your savings, which are currently earning 6 percent after taxes.

a Identify the cash flows, their timing, and the discount rate applicable to valuing the car.

b What is the maximum price you would be willing to pay to acquire the car? Explain why.

12-17 **(Valuation of Assets)** Using the information provided, find the value of each of the following assets.

	CASH FLOW		
Asset	End of year	Amount ($)	Appropriate discount rate (%)
A	1	5,000	18
	2	5,000	
	3	5,000	
B	1 through ∞	300	15
C	1	0	16
	2	0	
	3	0	
	4	0	
	5	35,000	
D	1 through 5	1,500	12
	6	8,500	
E	1	2,000	14
	2	3,000	
	3	5,000	
	4	7,000	
	5	4,000	
	6	1,000	

12-18 **(Asset Valuation and Risk)** Dora Hayes wishes to estimate the value of an asset expected to provide cash inflows of $3,000 per year at the end of years 1 through 4 and $15,000 at the end of year 5. Her research indicates that she must earn 10 percent on low-risk assets, 15 percent on average-risk assets, and 22 percent on high-risk assets.

a What is the most Dora should pay for the asset if it is classified as (1) low risk? (2) average risk? or (3) high risk?

b If Dora is unable to assess the risk of the asset and wants to be certain she makes a good deal, based on your findings in **a**, what is the most she should pay? Why?

c All else being the same, what effect does increasing risk have on the value of an asset? Explain in light of your findings in **a**.

12-19 **(Basic Bond Valuation)** Redenour Supply has an issue of $1,000-par-value bonds with a 12 percent stated interest rate outstanding. The issue pays interest annually and has 16 years remaining to its maturity date.

a If bonds of similar risk are currently earning a 10 percent rate of return, how much will the Redenour Supply bond sell for today?

b Describe the *two* possible reasons that similar-risk bonds are currently earning a return below the stated rate on the Redenour Supply bond.

c If the required return were at 12 percent instead of 10 percent, what would the current value of Redenour's bond be? Contrast this finding with **a** and discuss.

12-20 **(Bond Valuation — Annual Interest)** Calculate the value of each of the following bonds, all of which pay interest *annually*.

Bond	Par value ($)	Stated interest rate (%)	Years to maturity	Required return (%)
A	1,000	14	20	12
B	1,000	8	16	8
C	100	10	8	13
D	500	16	13	18
E	1,000	12	10	10

12-21 **(Bond Value and Changing Required Returns)** National Telephone has outstanding a bond issue that will mature to its $1,000 par value in 12 years. The bond has a stated rate of 11 percent and pays interest *annually*.

a Find the value of the bond if the required return is
  (1) 11 percent
  (2) 15 percent
  (3) 8 percent

b What two reasons cause the required return to differ from the stated rate?

12-22 **(Preferred Stock Valuation)** Poltak Stamping wishes to estimate the value of its outstanding preferred stock. The preferred issue has an $80 par value and pays an annual dividend of 8 percent (of par). Similar-risk preferred stocks are currently earning a 9.3 percent annual rate of return.

a What is the market value of the outstanding preferred stock?

b If an investor purchases the preferred stock at the value calculated in **a**, how much would she gain or lose per share if she sells the stock when the required return is 10.5 percent? Explain.

12-23 **(Book and Liquidation Value)** The balance sheet for the Grannis Mill Company appears at the top of page 375.

The following additional information with respect to the firm is available:

(1) Preferred stock can be liquidated for its book value.

(2) Accounts receivable and inventory can be liquidated at 90 percent of book value.

(3) The firm has 5,000 shares of common stock outstanding.

(4) All interest and dividends are currently paid up.

(5) Fixed assets can be liquidated at 70 percent of book value.

(6) Cash and marketable securities can be liquidated at book value.

Given this information, answer the following:

Balance Sheet
Grannis Mill Company
Ending December 31

Assets		Liabilities and stockholders' equity	
Cash	$ 40,000	Accounts payable	$100,000
Marketable securities	60,000	Notes payable	30,000
Accounts receivable	120,000	Accrued wages	30,000
Inventory	160,000	Total current liabilities	$160,000
Total current assets	$380,000	Long-term debt	$180,000
Fixed assets	$400,000	Preferred stock	$ 80,000
Total assets	$780,000	Common stock (5,000 shares)	360,000
		Total liabilities and stock-	
		holders' equity	$780,000

a What is Grannis Mill's book value per share?
b What is their liquidation value per share?
c Compare, contrast, and discuss the values found in **a** and **b**.

12-24 ■ (**Valuation with Price/Earnings Multiples**) For each of the following firms, use the data given to estimate their common stock value employing price/earnings multiples.

Firm	Expected EPS ($)	Price/earnings multiple
A	3.00	6.2
B	4.50	10.0
C	1.80	12.6
D	2.40	8.9
E	5.10	15.0

12-25 ■ (**Common Stock Valuation—Zero Growth**) Cable Enterprises is a mature firm in the machine tool component industry. The firm's most recent common stock dividend was $2.40 per share. Due to its maturity as well as stable sales and earnings, the firm's management feels that their dividends will remain at the current level for the foreseeable future.
a If the required return is 12 percent, what is the value of Cable Enterprises' common stock?
b If the firm's risk as perceived by market participants suddenly increases, causing the required return to rise to 20 percent, what will be the common stock value?
c Based on your findings in **a** and **b**, what impact does risk have on value? Explain.

12-26 ■ (**Common Stock Value—Constant Growth**) Use the constant growth valuation model (Gordon model) to find the value of each of the firms described in the table at the top of the next page.

Firm	Dividend expected next year ($)	Dividend growth rate (%)	Required return (%)
A	1.20	8	13
B	4.00	5	15
C	.65	10	14
D	6.00	8	9
E	2.25	8	20

12-27 **(Common Stock Value — Constant Growth)** The Moody Boiler Company has paid the following dividends over the past six years:

Year	Dividend ($)
1987	2.87
1986	2.76
1985	2.60
1984	2.46
1983	2.37
1982	2.25

The firm's dividend next year is expected to be $3.02.

a If you can earn 13 percent on similar-risk investments, what is the most you would pay per share for this firm?

b If you can earn only 10 percent on similar-risk investments, what is the most you would be willing to pay per share?

c Compare and contrast your findings in **a** and **b** and discuss the impact of changing risk on share value.

12-28 **(Common Stock Value — Both Growth Models)** You are evaluating the potential purchase of a small business currently generating $42,500 of after-tax cash flow ($D_0 = \$42,500$). Based on a review of similar-risk investment opportunities, your required return is 18 percent on the proposed purchase. Since you are relatively uncertain as to future cash flows, you have decided to estimate the firm's value using two possible cash flow growth rate assumptions.

a What is the firm's value if dividends are expected to grow at 0 percent to infinity?

b What is the firm's value if dividends are expected to grow at a constant annual rate of 7 percent to infinity?

12-29 **(Management Action and Stock Value)** Blanding Enterprises' most recent dividend was $3 per share, its expected annual rate of dividend growth is 5 percent, and the required return is now 15 percent. A variety of proposals are currently being considered by management in order to redirect the firm's activities. For each of the proposed actions below, determine the resulting impact on share price and indicate the best alternative.

a Do nothing, which will leave the key financial variables unchanged.

b Invest in a new machine that will increase the dividend growth rate to 6 percent and lower the required return to 14 percent.

c Eliminate an unprofitable product line, which will increase the dividend growth rate to 7 percent and raise the required return to 17 percent.

d Merge with another firm, which will reduce the growth rate to 4 percent and raise the required return to 16 percent.

e Acquire a subsidiary operation from another manufacturer. The acquisition should increase the dividend growth rate to 8 percent and increase the required return to 17 percent.

12-30 (**Integrative — Risk and Valuation**) RPM Enterprises has a beta of 1.20, the risk-free rate of interest is currently 10 percent, and the market return is 14 percent. The company, which plans to pay a dividend of $2.60 per share in the coming year, anticipates that its future dividends will increase at an annual rate consistent with that experienced over the 1981 to 1987 period, when the following dividends were paid:

Year	Dividend ($)	Year	Dividend ($)
1987	2.45	1983	1.82
1986	2.28	1982	1.80
1985	2.10	1981	1.73
1984	1.95		

a Use the capital asset pricing model (CAPM) to determine the required return on RPM Enterprises' stock.

b Using the constant growth dividend valuation model and your finding in **a**, estimate the value of RPM Enterprises' stock.

c Explain what effect, if any, a decrease in beta would have on the value of RPM's stock.

12-31 (**Integrative — Valuation and CAPM**) Pinckney Steel Company wishes to determine the value of Acme Foundry, a firm that it is considering acquiring for cash. Pinckney wishes to use the capital asset pricing model (CAPM) to determine the applicable discount rate to use as an input to the constant growth valuation model. Because Acme's stock is not publicly traded, Pinckney, after studying the betas of similar firms to Acme that are publicly traded, believes that an appropriate beta for Acme's stock would be 1.25. The risk-free rate is currently 9 percent, and the market return is 13 percent. Acme's dividends for each of the past six years are given below:

Year	Dividend ($)
1987	3.44
1986	3.28
1985	3.15
1984	2.90
1983	2.75
1982	2.75

    a Given that Acme is expected to pay a dividend of $3.68 next year, determine the maximum cash price Pinckney should pay for each share of Acme.

    b Discuss the use of the CAPM for estimating the value of common stock, and describe the effect on the resulting value of Acme of:

        (1) A decrease in the dividend growth rate of 2 percent from that exhibited over the 1982–1987 period.

        (2) A decrease in the beta to 1.

13

THE COST OF CAPITAL

After studying this chapter, you should be able to:

● Understand the basic concept of cost of capital and the reasons why a weighted average is the appropriate cost measurement.

● Calculate both the cost of long-term debt (bonds), using popular approximation techniques, and the cost of preferred stock.

● Find the cost of common stock equity and convert it into the cost of new issues of common stock and the cost of retained earnings.

● Discuss the various weighting schemes and use them to calculate the weighted average cost of capital *(WACC)*.

● Describe the weighted marginal cost of capital *(WMCC)* and its use with the investment opportunities schedule *(IOS)* to make financing/investment decisions.

The cost of capital is an extremely important financial concept. It acts as a major link between the firm's long-term financial decisions (discussed in Part Five) and the wealth of the owners as determined by investors in the marketplace. It is in effect the "magic number" used to decide whether a proposed corporate investment will increase or decrease the firm's stock price. Clearly only those investments expected to increase stock price would be recommended. Due to its key role in financial decision making, the importance of the cost of capital cannot be overemphasized.

AN OVERVIEW OF THE COST OF CAPITAL

cost of capital The rate of return a firm must earn on its investments in projects in order to maintain the market value of its stock. Also, the rate of return required by the market suppliers of capital in order to attract their funds to the firm.

The **cost of capital** is the rate of return a firm must earn on its investments in projects in order to maintain the market value of its stock. It can also be thought of as the rate of return required by the market suppliers of capital in order to attract their funds to the firm. Holding risk constant, the implementation of projects with a rate of return below the cost of capital will decrease the value of the firm, and vice versa.

The Basic Concept

The cost of capital is measured at a given point in time. It reflects the cost of funds over the long run, based on the best information available. This view is consistent with the use of the cost of capital to make long-term financial investment decisions. Although firms typically raise money in lumps, the cost of capital should reflect the interrelatedness of financing activities. For example, if a firm raises funds with debt (borrowing) today, it is likely that some form of equity, such as common stock, will have to be used next time. Most firms maintain a deliberate, optimal mix of debt and equity financing. This mix is commonly called a

target capital structure The desired optimal mix of debt and equity financing that most firms attempt to achieve and maintain.

target capital structure — a topic that will be discussed in greater detail in Chapter 16. It is sufficient here to say that although firms raise money in lumps, they tend toward some desired *mix of financing* in order to maximize owner wealth.

To capture the interrelatedness of financing assuming the presence of a target capital structure, we need to look at the *overall cost of capital* rather than the cost of the specific source of funds used to finance a given expenditure. The importance of such a view can be illustrated by a simple example.

EXAMPLE

A firm is *currently* faced with an opportunity. Assume the following:

Best project available
        Cost = $100,000
        Life = 20 years
        Return = 7 percent
Cost of least-cost financing source available
        Debt = 6 percent

Since it can earn 7 percent on the investment of funds costing only 6 percent, the firm undertakes the opportunity. Imagine that *one week later* a new opportunity is available:

Best project available
        Cost = $100,000
        Life = 20 years
        Return = 12 percent
Cost of least-cost financing source available
        Equity = 14 percent

In this instance the firm rejects the opportunity, since the 14 percent financing cost is greater than the 12 percent return expected.

The firm's actions were not in the best interests of its owners. It accepted a project yielding a 7 percent return and rejected one with a 12 percent return. Clearly, there is a better way. Due to the interrelatedness of financing decisions, the firm must use a combined cost, which over the long run would provide for better decisions. By weighting the cost of each source of financing by its target proportion in the firm's capital structure, a *weighted average cost* that reflects the interrelationship of financing decisions can be obtained. Assuming that a 50-50 mix of debt and equity is desired, the weighted average cost above would be 10 percent [$(.50 \times 6\% \text{ debt}) + (.50 \times 14\% \text{ equity})$]. Using this cost, the first opportunity would have been rejected (7% return < 10% weighted average cost), while the second one would have been accepted (12% return > 10% weighted average cost). Such an outcome would clearly be more desirable. ■

The Cost of Specific Sources of Capital

The ultimate objective of this chapter is to analyze specific sources to show the basic inputs for determining the weighted average cost of capital. Our concern is only with the long-term sources of funds available to a business firm, since these sources supply the permanent financing. Long-term financing supports the firm's fixed-asset investments[1], which, we assume, are selected using appropriate techniques.

There are four basic sources of long-term funds for the business firm:

[1] The role of both long-term and short-term financing in supporting both fixed and current asset investments was addressed in Chapter 7. Suffice it to say that long-term funds are at minimum used to finance fixed assets.

long-term debt, preferred stock, common stock, and retained earnings.
The right-hand side of a balance sheet can be used to illustrate these
sources.

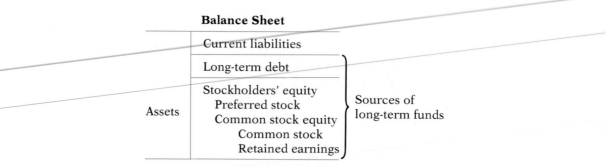

Although all firms will not necessarily use each of these methods of
financing, each firm is expected to have funds from some of these
sources in its capital structure. The *specific cost* of each source of
financing is the *after-tax* cost of obtaining the financing *today*, not the
historically based cost reflected by the existing financing on the firm's
books. Techniques for determining the specific costs of each source of
long-term funds are presented on the following pages. Although these
techniques tend to develop precisely calculated values of specific as
well as weighted average costs, the resulting values are at best *rough
approximations* due to the numerous assumptions and forecasts that
underlie them.

■ THE COST OF LONG-TERM DEBT (BONDS)

**cost of long-term debt
(bonds), k_i** The after-tax
cost today of raising
long-term funds through
borrowing.

The **cost of long-term debt (bonds), k_i**, is the after-tax cost today of
raising long-term funds through borrowing. For convenience we typically assume that the funds are raised through issuance and sale of
bonds. In addition, consistent with Chapter 12, we assume that the
bonds pay *annual*—rather than *semiannual*—interest.

Net Proceeds

net proceeds Funds
actually received from
the sale of a security.

flotation costs The total
costs of issuing and
selling a security.

Most corporate long-term debts are incurred through the sale of bonds.
The **net proceeds** from the sale of a bond are the funds actually received from the sale. **Flotation costs**—the total costs of issuing and
selling a security—reduce the net proceeds from the sale of a bond at a
premium, at a discount, or at its par (face) value.

EXAMPLE

The Debbo Company is contemplating selling $10 million worth of 20-year, 9 percent (stated *annual* interest rate) bonds, each with a par value of $1,000. Since similar-risk bonds earn returns greater than 9 percent, the firm must sell the bonds for $980 to compensate for the lower stated interest rate. The flotation costs paid the investment banker are 2 percent of the par value of the bond (2% × $1,000), or $20. The net proceeds to the firm from the sale of each bond are therefore $960 ($980 − $20). ■

Before-Tax Cost of Debt

The before-tax cost of debt, k_d, for a bond with a $1,000 par value can be approximated using the following equation:

$$k_d = \frac{I + \dfrac{\$1,000 - N_d}{n}}{\dfrac{N_d + \$1,000}{2}} \qquad (13.1)$$

where

$$I = \text{annual interest in dollars}$$
$$N_d = \text{net proceeds from the sale of debt (bond)}$$
$$n = \text{number of years to the bond's maturity}$$

EXAMPLE

Substituting the appropriate values from the Debbo Company example into Equation 13.1 results in an approximate before-tax debt cost, k_d, of 9.39 percent. Note that the annual interest, I, is $90 (9% stated rate × $1,000 par value).

$$k_d = \frac{\$90 + \dfrac{\$1,000 - \$960}{20}}{\dfrac{\$960 + \$1,000}{2}} = \frac{\$90 + \$2}{\$980}$$

$$= \frac{\$92}{\$980} = 9.39\% \ ■$$

After-Tax Cost of Debt

As indicated earlier, the *specific cost* of financing must be stated on an after-tax basis. Since interest on debt is tax-deductible, a tax adjustment

COST OF CAPITAL WEIGHTING SCHEMES

The 177 responses relative to weighting schemes used to calculate the weighted average cost of capital for a sample of *Fortune's* 1000 firms is summarized in the table below. It can be seen that the majority of respondents used some type of weighted average when determining their cost of capital. Somewhat surprising is the fact that nearly 16 percent of the respondents used the cost of the specific source of funds employed as a cutoff rate for making financial decisions. Such an approach clearly runs counter to theory. Of the firms using a weighted average, the majority appear to use target capital structure weights. Second most popular are market value weights, followed by book value weighting schemes.

General Approach and Weighting Schemes

Approach or weighting scheme	Percentage of 177 respondents
Use the cost of the specific source of financing planned for funding the alternative	16%
Use a weighted average cost of capital based on:	
Book value weights	16
Target capital structure weights	40
Market value weights	27
Other weighting scheme	1
Total	100%

Source: Adapted from Lawrence J. Gitman and Vincent A. Mercurio, "Cost of Capital Techniques Used by Major U.S. Firms: Survey and Analysis of *Fortune's* 1000," *Financial Management,* Winter 1982, pp. 22–23.

is required. The before-tax debt cost, k_d, can be converted to an after-tax debt cost, k_i, by the following equation:

$$k_i = k_d \times (1 - t) \tag{13.2}$$

The t represents the firm's tax rate.

EXAMPLE

The before-tax debt cost for the Debbo Company, which has a 40 percent tax rate, is 9.39 percent. Applying Equation 13.2 results in an after-tax cost of debt of 5.63 percent [i.e., 9.39% × (1 − .40)]. Typically, the cost of long-term debt is less than the cost of any of the alternative forms of long-term financing. This is primarily due to the tax-deductibility of interest. ■

■ THE COST OF PREFERRED STOCK

Preferred stock represents a special type of ownership interest in the firm. Preferred shareholders must receive their *stated* dividends prior to the distribution of any earnings to common shareholders. Since preferred stock is a form of ownership, the proceeds from the sale of preferred stock are expected to be held for an infinite period of time. A complete discussion of the various characteristics of preferred stock is presented in Chapter 19. However, the one aspect of preferred stock that requires clarification at this point is dividends.

Preferred Stock Dividends

The amount of preferred stock dividends that must be paid each year before earnings can be distributed to common stockholders may be stated in dollars or as a percentage of the stock's par, or face, value.

DOLLAR AMOUNTS Most preferred stock dividends are stated as "*x* dollars per year." When dividends are stated this way, the stock is often referred to as "*x* dollar preferred stock." Thus a $4 preferred stock is expected to pay preferred shareholders $4 in dividends each year on each share of preferred stock owned.

PERCENTAGE AMOUNTS Sometimes preferred stock dividends are stated as an annual percentage rate. This rate represents the percentage of the stock's par, or face, value that equals the annual dividend. For instance, an 8 percent preferred stock with a $50 par value would be expected to pay an annual dividend of $4 a share (.08 × $50 par = $4). Before calculating the cost of preferred stock, any dividends stated as percentages should be converted to annual dollar dividends.

Calculating the Cost of Preferred Stock

The **cost of preferred stock, k_p,** is found by dividing the annual preferred stock dividend, D_p, by the net proceeds from the sale of the preferred stock, N_p. The net proceeds represent the amount of money to be received net of any flotation costs required to issue and sell the stock. For example, if a preferred stock is sold for $100 per share but $3 per share flotation costs are incurred, the net proceeds from the sale are $97. Equation 13.3 gives the cost of preferred stock, k_p, in terms of the

cost of preferred stock, k_p The annual preferred stock dividend, D_p, divided by the net proceeds from the sale of the preferred stock, N_p.

annual dollar dividend, D_p, and the net proceeds from the sale of the stock, N_p:

$$k_p = \frac{D_p}{N_p} \tag{13.3}$$

Since preferred stock dividends are paid out of the firm's *after-tax* cash flows, a tax adjustment is not required.

EXAMPLE

The Debbo Company is contemplating issuance of a 9 percent preferred stock expected to sell for its $85 per share par value. The cost of issuing and selling the stock is expected to be $3 per share. The firm would like to determine the cost of the stock. The first step in finding this cost is to calculate the dollar amount of preferred dividends, since the dividend is stated as a percentage of the stock's $85 par value. The annual dollar dividend is $7.65 (9% × $85). The net proceeds from the proposed sale of stock can be found by subtracting the flotation costs from the sale price. This gives a value of $82 per share. Substituting the annual dividend, D_p, of $7.65 and the net proceeds, N_p, of $82 into Equation 13.3 gives the cost of preferred stock, 9.33 percent ($7.65 ÷ $82). ■

Comparing the 9.33 percent cost of preferred stock to the 5.63 percent cost of long-term debt (bonds) shows that the preferred stock is more expensive. This difference results primarily because the cost of long-term debt (interest) is tax deductible.

◼ THE COST OF COMMON STOCK

The *cost of common stock* is the return required on the stock by investors in the marketplace. There are two forms of common stock financing: (1) new issues of common stock and (2) retained earnings. As a first step in finding each of these costs we must estimate the cost of common stock equity.

Finding the Cost of Common Stock Equity

cost of common stock equity, k_s The rate at which investors discount the expected dividends of the firm in order to determine its share value.

The **cost of common stock equity, k_s**, is the rate at which investors discount the expected dividends of the firm in order to determine its share value. Two techniques for measuring the cost of common stock equity capital are available. One uses the constant growth valuation model; and the other relies on the capital asset pricing model (CAPM).

USING THE CONSTANT GROWTH VALUATION (GORDON) MODEL The constant growth valuation model—the **Gordon model**—was presented in Chapter 12. It is based on the widely accepted premise that the value of a share of the stock is equal to the present value of all future dividends it is expected to provide over an infinite time horizon. The key expression derived in Chapter 12 and presented as Equation 12.13 is restated in Equation 13.4:

$$P_0 = \frac{D_1}{k_s - g} \qquad (13.4)$$

where

P_0 = value of common stock
D_1 = per-share dividend expected at the end of year 1
k_s = required return on common stock
g = constant rate of growth in dividends

Solving Equation 13.4 for k_s results in the following expression for the *cost of common stock equity:*

$$k_s = \frac{D_1}{P_0} + g \qquad (13.5)$$

Equation 13.5 indicates that the cost of common stock equity can be found by dividing the dividend expected at the end of year 1 by the current price of the stock and adding the expected growth rate. Since common stock dividends are paid from after-tax income, no tax adjustment is required.

constant growth valuation (Gordon) model Assumes that the value of a share of stock equals the present value of all future dividends it will provide over an infinite time horizon.

EXAMPLE

The Debbo Company wishes to determine its cost of common stock equity capital, k_s. The market price, P_0, of its common stock is $50 per share. The firm expects to pay a dividend, D_1, of $4 at the end of the coming year, 1988. The dividends paid on the outstanding stock over the past six years (1982–1987) are as follows:

Year	Dividend
1987	$3.80
1986	3.62
1985	3.47
1984	3.33
1983	3.12
1982	2.97

Using the table for the present-value interest factors, *PVIF* (Table D-3), in conjunction with the technique described for finding growth rates in Chapter 11, the annual growth rate of dividends, g, can be calculated. It turns out to be approximately 5 percent. Substituting $D_1 = \$4$, $P_0 = \$50$, and $g = 5$ percent into Equation 13.5 results in the cost of common stock equity:

$$k_s = \frac{\$4}{\$50} + .05 = .08 + .05 = .13 = \underline{13\%}$$

The 13 percent cost of common stock equity capital represents the return required by *existing* shareholders on their investment in order to leave the market price of the firm's outstanding shares unchanged. ■

capital asset pricing model *(CAPM)* Describes the relationship between the required return, or cost of common stock equity capital, k_s, and the nondiversifiable risk of the firm as measured by the beta coefficient, b.

USING THE CAPITAL ASSET PRICING MODEL *(CAPM)* The **capital asset pricing model *(CAPM)*** was developed and discussed in Chapter 12. It describes the relationship between the required return, or cost of common stock equity capital, k_s, and the nondiversifiable risk of the firm as measured by the beta coefficient, b. The basic *CAPM* is given in Equation 13.6:

$$k_s = R_F + [b \times (k_m - R_F)] \tag{13.6}$$

where

R_F = risk-free rate of return, commonly measured by the return on a U.S. Treasury bill

k_m = market return — the return on the market portfolio of assets

Using *CAPM*, the cost of common stock equity is the return required by investors as compensation for the firm's nondiversifiable risk, which is measured by beta, b.

EXAMPLE

The Debbo Company, which calculated its cost of common stock equity capital, k_s, using the constant growth valuation model in the preceding example, also wishes to calculate this cost using the capital asset pricing model. From information provided by the firm's investment advisers and its own analyses, it is found that the risk-free rate, R_F, equals 7 percent; the firm's beta, b, equals 1.50; and the market return, k_m, equals 11 percent. Substituting these values into the *CAPM* (Equation 13.6), it estimates the cost of common stock equity capital, k_s, as follows:

$$k_s = 7\% + [1.50 \times (11\% - 7\%)] = 7\% + 6\% = \underline{13\%}$$

The 13 percent cost of common stock equity capital, which is the same as that previously found using the constant growth valuation model, represents the required return of investors in Debbo Company common stock. ■

The Cost of New Issues of Common Stock

Our purpose in finding the firm's overall cost of capital is to determine the after-tax cost of *new* funds required for financing projects. Attention must therefore be given to the **cost of a new issue of common stock,** k_n. This cost is determined by calculating the cost of common stock after considering both the amount of underpricing and the associated flotation costs. Normally, in order to sell a new issue it will have to be **underpriced**—sold at a price below the current market price, P_0. In addition, flotation costs paid for issuing and selling the new issue will reduce proceeds.

The cost of new issues can be calculated by determining the net proceeds after underpricing and flotation costs, using the constant growth valuation model expression for the cost of existing common stock, k_s, as a starting point. If we let N_n represent the net proceeds from the sale of new common stock after allowing for underpricing and flotation costs, the cost of the new issue, k_n, can be expressed as follows:

$$k_n = \frac{D_1}{N_n} + g \qquad (13.7)$$

Since the net proceeds from sale of new common stock, N_n, will be less than the current market price, P_0, the cost of new issues, k_n, will always be greater than the cost of existing issues, k_s. The cost of new common stock is normally greater than any other long-term financing cost. Since common stock dividends are paid from after-tax cash flows, no tax adjustment is required.

cost of a new issue of common stock, k_n Determined by calculating the cost of common stock after considering both the amount of underpricing and the associated flotation costs.

underpriced Stock sold at a price below its current market price, P_0.

EXAMPLE

In the example using the constant growth valuation model, an expected dividend, D_1, of $4, a current market price, P_0, of $50, and an expected growth rate of dividends, g, of 5 percent were used to calculate Debbo Company's cost of common stock equity capital, k_s, which was found to be 13 percent. To determine its cost of *new* common stock, k_n, the Debbo Company, with the aid of its advisers, has estimated that on average, new shares can be sold for $49. The $1 per share underpricing is necessary due to the competitive nature of the market. A second cost associated with a new issue is an underwriting fee of $.80 per share that would have to be paid to cover the costs of issuing and selling the new issue. The total underpricing and flotation costs per share are therefore expected to be $1.80 ($1.00 per share underpricing plus $.80 per share flotation).

Subtracting the $1.80 per share underpricing and flotation cost from the current $50 share price, P_0, results in expected net proceeds, N_n, of $48.20 per share ($50.00 − $1.80). Substituting $D_1 = $4, $N_n = $48.20, and $g = 5$ percent into Equation 13.7 results in a cost of new common stock, k_n, as follows:

$$k_n = \frac{\$4.00}{\$48.20} + .0500 = .0830 + .0500 = .1330 = \underline{13.30\%}$$

Debbo Company's cost of new common stock, k_n, is therefore 13.30 percent. This is the value to be used in the subsequent calculation of the firm's overall cost of capital. ■

The Cost of Retained Earnings

cost of retained earnings, k_r The same as the cost of an equivalent fully subscribed issue of additional common stock, which is measured by the cost of common stock equity, k_s.

If earnings were not retained, they would be paid out to the common stockholders as dividends. Thus the **cost of retained earnings, k_r**, to the firm is the same as the cost of an *equivalent fully subscribed issue of additional common stock*. This means that retained earnings increase the stockholders' equity in the same way as a new issue of common stock. Stockholders find the firm's retention of earnings acceptable only if they expect it will earn at least their required return on the reinvested funds.

Viewing retained earnings as a fully subscribed issue of additional common stock, the firm's cost of retained earnings, k_r, can be set equal to the cost of common stock equity as given by Equations 13.5 and 13.6.[2]

$$k_r = k_s \qquad (13.8)$$

It is not necessary to adjust the cost of retained earnings for either underpricing or flotation costs. By retaining earnings, the firm bypasses these costs and still raises the equity capital.

EXAMPLE

The cost of retained earnings for the Debbo Company was actually calculated in the preceding examples, since it is equal to the cost of common stock equity when underpricing and flotation costs

[2] Technically, if a stockholder received dividends and wished to invest them in additional shares of the firm's stock, he or she would have to pay personal taxes on the dividends prior to acquiring additional shares. Using pt as the average stockholder's personal tax rate, the cost of retained earnings, k_r, can be specified as: $k_r = k_s \times (1 - pt)$. Due to the difficulty in estimating pt, only the simpler definition of k_r given in Equation 13.8 is used here.

are ignored. Thus k_r equals 13 percent. The cost of retained earnings is always lower than the cost of a new issue of common stock, which in this case is 13.30 percent. This is due to the absence of underpricing and flotation costs in financing projects with retained earnings. ■

■ THE WEIGHTED AVERAGE COST OF CAPITAL *(WACC)*

Now that methods for calculating the cost of specific sources of financing have been reviewed, we can present techniques for determining the overall cost of capital. As noted earlier, the **weighted average cost of capital (WACC), k_a**, is found by weighting the cost of each specific type of capital by its proportion in the firm's capital structure. Let us look at the common weighting schemes and the procedures and considerations involved.

Weighting Schemes

Weights can be calculated as *book value* or *market value* and as *historic* or *target*.

BOOK VALUE VERSUS MARKET VALUE   **Book value weights** are based on the use of accounting values to measure the proportion of each type of capital in the firm's financial structure. **Market value weights** measure the proportion of each type of capital at its market value. Market value weights are appealing, since the market values of securities closely approximate the actual dollars to be received from their sale. Moreover, since the costs of the various types of capital are calculated using prevailing market prices, it seems only reasonable to use market value weights. *Market value weights are clearly preferred over book value weights.*

HISTORIC VERSUS TARGET   **Historic weights** can be either book or market weights based on *actual data*. For example, past as well as current book proportions would constitute a form of historic weighting. Likewise, past or current market proportions would represent a historic weighting scheme. Such a weighting scheme would therefore be based on real — rather than desired — proportions. **Target weights,** which can also be based on either book or market values, reflect the firm's *desired* capital structure proportions. Firms using target weights establish such proportions on the basis of the "optimal" capital structure they wish to achieve. When one considers the somewhat approximate nature of the calculations, the choice of weights may not be critical. However, from a strictly theoretical point of view the *preferred*

weighted average cost of capital (WACC), k_a
Determined by weighting the cost of each specific type of capital by its proportion in the firm's capital structure.

book value weights
Based on the use of accounting values to measure the proportion of each type of capital in the firm's structure; used in calculation of the firm's *weighted average cost of capital.*

market value weights
Based on the use of market values to measure the proportion of each type of capital in the firm's structure; used in calculation of the firm's *weighted average cost of capital.*

historic weights Either book or market value weights based on *actual* capital structure proportions and used in calculation of the firm's *weighted average cost of capital.*

target weights Either book or market value weights based on *desired* capital structure proportions and used in calculation of the firm's *weighted average cost of capital.*

weighting scheme is target market value proportions, and these will be used throughout this chapter.

Calculating the Weighted Average Cost of Capital

Once the cost of the specific sources of financing and the appropriate weighting scheme have been determined, the weighted average cost of capital *(WACC)* can be calculated. This calculation is performed by multiplying the specific cost of each form of financing by its proportion in the firm's capital structure and summing the weighted values. As an equation, the weighted average cost of capital, k_a, can be specified as follows:

$$k_a = w_i \times k_i + w_p \times k_p + w_s \times k_{rorn} \tag{13.9}$$

where

w_i = proportion of long-term debt in capital structure
w_p = proportion of preferred stock in capital structure
w_s = proportion of common stock equity in capital structure
$w_i + w_p + w_s = 1$

Two important points should be noted in Equation 13.9:

1. *The sum of weights must equal 1.* Simply stated, all capital structure components must be accounted for.
2. The firm's common stock equity weight, w_s, is multiplied by either the cost of retained earnings, k_r, or the cost of new common stock, k_n. The specific cost used in the common stock equity term depends on whether the firm's common stock equity financing will be obtained using retained earnings, k_r, or new common stock, k_n.

EXAMPLE

Earlier in the chapter, the costs of the various types of capital for the Debbo Company were found to be as follows:

Cost of debt, k_i = 5.63 percent
Cost of preferred stock, k_p = 9.33 percent
Cost of new common stock, k_n = 13.30 percent
Cost of retained earnings, k_r = 13.00 percent

The company has determined what it believes to be the optimal capital structure for it to achieve. Debbo Company uses this target capital structure, which is based on market values, to calculate the weighted average cost of capital. The target market value proportions are as follows:

Source of capital	Target market value proportions
Long-term debt	40%
Preferred stock	10
Common stock equity	50
Total	100%

Because the firm expects to have a sizable amount ($300,000) of retained earnings available, it plans to use its cost of retained earnings, k_r, as the cost of common stock equity. Using this value along with the other data presented, Debbo Company's weighted average cost of capital is calculated in Table 13.1. The resulting weighted average cost of capital for Debbo is 9.685 percent. In view of this cost of capital and assuming an unchanged risk level, the firm should accept all projects that earn a return greater than or equal to 9.685 percent. ■

■ THE MARGINAL COST AND INVESTMENT DECISIONS

The firm's weighted average cost of capital is a key input to the investment decision-making process. As demonstrated earlier in the chapter, the firm should make only those investments for which the expected return is greater than the weighted average cost of capital. Of course at any given time the firm's financing costs and investment returns will be affected by the volume of financing/investment undertaken. The concepts of a *weighted marginal cost of capital* and an *investment opportunities schedule* provide the mechanisms whereby financing and investment decisions can be made simultaneously at a given point in time.

TABLE 13.1 Calculation of the Weighted Average Cost of Capital for the Debbo Company

Source of capital	Target proportion (1)	Cost (2)	Weighted cost [(1) × (2)] (3)
Long-term debt	40%	5.63%	2.252%
Preferred stock	10	9.33	.933
Common stock equity	50	13.00	6.500
Totals	100%		9.685%
Weighted average cost of capital = 9.685%			

The Weighted Marginal Cost of Capital (WMCC)

The weighted average cost of capital may vary at any time depending on the volume of financing the firm plans to raise. As the volume of financing increases, the costs of the various types of financing will increase, raising the firm's weighted average cost of capital. A schedule or graph relating the firm's weighted average cost of capital to the level of new financing is called the **weighted marginal cost of capital (WMCC).** These increasing costs are attributable to the fact that suppliers of capital will require greater returns in the form of interest, dividends, or growth to compensate for the increased risk introduced as larger volumes of *new* financing are incurred.

weighted marginal cost of capital (WMCC) A schedule or graph relating the firm's weighted average cost of capital to the level of new financing.

A second factor relates to the use of common stock equity financing. The portion of new financing provided by common stock equity will be taken from available retained earnings until exhausted and then obtained through new common stock financing. Since retained earnings are a less expensive form of common stock equity financing than the actual sale of new common stock, it should be clear that once retained earnings have been exhausted, the weighted average cost of capital will rise with the addition of more expensive new common stock.

EXAMPLE

In the preceding example the weighted average cost of capital (WACC) for the Debbo Company was calculated in Table 13.1 using the 13.00 percent cost of retained earnings, k_r, as the cost of common stock equity. Once the $300,000 of available retained earnings is exhausted, the firm must use the more expensive new common stock financing ($k_n = 13.30\%$) to meet its common stock equity needs. Since the target capital structure dictates that common stock equity represent 50 percent of total capital, the $300,000 of retained earnings will support only $600,000 of *total new financing*. This value is found by dividing the available retained earnings of $300,000 by the common equity target proportion of 50 percent ($300,000 ÷ .50 = $600,000). Therefore, when the firm's total new financing increases beyond $600,000 the weighted average cost of capital will rise since the cost of common stock equity increases from the 13.00 percent cost of retained earnings to the 13.30 percent cost of new common stock. Table 13.1 demonstrated the WACC calculation for the first $600,000 of total new financing. The WACC calculation for greater than $600,000 of total new financing is given in Table 13.2.

When the total new financing exceeds $600,000, the WACC rises from 9.685 percent (Table 13.1) to 9.835 percent (Table 13.2). Of course the firm may face other increases in the WACC due to

TABLE 13.2 Calculation of the *WACC* for the Debbo Company for Greater than $600,000 of Total New Financing

Source of capital	Target proportion (1)	Cost (2)	Weighted cost [(1) × (2)] (3)
Long-term debt	40%	5.63%	2.252%
Preferred stock	10	9.33	.933
Common stock equity	50	13.30	6.650
Totals	100%		9.835%
Weighted average cost of capital = 9.835%			

increases in debt, preferred stock, and common equity costs as additional new funds are raised. Using calculations similar to those demonstrated above, the Debbo Company developed a complete schedule of the weighted average cost of capital associated with the ranges of total new financing shown in Table 13.3. This schedule represents the weighted marginal cost of capital (*WMCC*). Figure 13.1 presents the same data graphically. Graph *a* shows a plot of the actual data, while graph *b* presents a smoothed function that more realistically depicts the firm's *WMCC*. It is quite clear from both the tabular and graphic data that the *WMCC* is an *increasing* function of the amount of total new financing raised. ■

The Investment Opportunities Schedule (IOS)

At any given time a firm has certain investment opportunities available to it. These opportunities differ with respect to the size of investment anticipated, risk, and return. (For convenience, we assume all opportunities have equal risk similar to the firm's risk.) The firm's **investment opportunities schedule (IOS)** is a ranking of investment possibilities

investment opportunities schedule (IOS)
A ranking of investment possibilities from best (highest returns) to worst (lowest returns).

TABLE 13.3 Weighted Marginal Cost of Capital for the Debbo Company

Range of total new financing	Weighted average cost of capital
$0 to $600,000	9.685%
$600,000 to $1,000,000	9.835
$1,000,000 to $1,500,000	10.310
$1,500,000 to $2,000,000	11.410
$2,000,000 and above	11.650

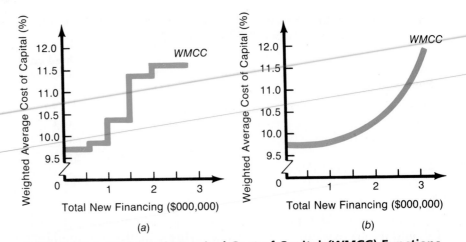

FIGURE 13.1 Weighted Marginal Cost of Capital *(WMCC)* Functions for the Debbo Company

Graph *a* is a plot of the actual data showing Debbo Company's *WMCC* function, while graph *b* presents a smoothed form of the firm's *WMCC*. The increasing nature of this function is clearly depicted by both graphs.

from best (highest returns) to worst (lowest returns). As the cumulative amount of money invested in a firm's capital projects increases, its return on the projects will decrease, since generally the first project selected will have the highest return, the next project the second highest, and so on. In other words, the return on investments will *decrease* as the firm accepts additional projects.

EXAMPLE

The Debbo Company's current investment opportunities schedule *(IOS)* lists the best (highest return) to the worst (lowest return) investment possibilities in column 1 of Table 13.4. In column 2 of the table, the initial investment required by each project is shown, and in column 3 the cumulative total invested funds required to finance all projects better than and including the corresponding investment opportunity are given. Plotting the project returns against the cumulative investment (column 1 against column 3 in Table 13.4) on a set of total new financing or investment-weighted average cost of capital and return axes, the firm's investment opportunities schedule *(IOS)* results. A graph of the *IOS* for Debbo Company is given in Figure 13.2. ∎

Making Financing/Investment Decisions

As long as a project's rate of return is greater than the weighted marginal cost of new financing, the project should be accepted by the firm.

TABLE 13.4 Investment Opportunities Schedule *(IOS)* for the Debbo Company

Investment opportunity	Rate of return (1)	Initial investment (2)	Cumulative investment[a] (3)
A	16%	$ 200,000	$ 200,000
B	15	400,000	600,000
C	14	1,000,000	1,600,000
D	13	100,000	1,700,000
E	12	300,000	2,000,000
F	11	500,000	2,500,000
G	10	200,000	2,700,000
H	9	400,000	3,100,000
I	8	100,000	3,200,000
J	7	300,000	3,500,000

[a] The cumulative investment represents the total amount invested in projects with higher returns plus the investment required for the given investment opportunity.

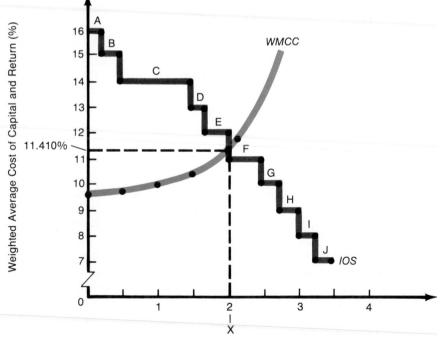

Total New Financing or Investment ($000,000)

FIGURE 13.2 Using the *IOS* and *WMCC* to Select Projects

Debbo Company's investment opportunities schedule *(IOS)* depicts in descending order its investment possibilities. A total of $2 million should be raised and invested in projects A, B, C, D, and E since their marginal returns are in excess of the associated weighted marginal cost of capital *(WMCC)*.

OVERALL COST OF CAPITAL: SOME SURVEY DATA

In a relatively recent survey, firms in the *Fortune's* 1000 were asked to indicate the approximate level of their cost of capital on October 15, 1980. The table summarizes the responses. The mean cost of capital for the respondents was 14.3 percent.

Actual Cost of Capital (October 15, 1980)

Range of overall cost of capital	Percentage of 177 respondents
Less than 5%	1.7%
5% to 7%	0.6
7% to 9%	3.4
9% to 11%	10.1
11% to 13%	20.9 ⎤
13% to 15%	21.5 ⎬ 65%
15% to 17%	22.6 ⎦
17% to 19%	12.3
19% to 21%	4.0
21% to 23%	0.6
23% to 25%	0.6
Greater than 25%	1.7
Total	100.0%

Source: Adapted from Lawrence J. Gitman and Vincent A. Mercurio, "Cost of Capital Techniques Used by Major U.S. Firms: Survey and Analysis of *Fortune's* 1000," *Financial Management*, Winter 1982, p. 24.

While the return will decrease with the acceptance of more projects, the weighted marginal cost of capital will increase because greater amounts of financing will be required. The firm would therefore *accept projects up to the point where the marginal return on its investment equals its weighted marginal cost of capital.* Beyond that point its investment return will be less than its capital cost. This approach is consistent with achievement of the goal of owner wealth maximization. Returning to the Debbo Company example, we can demonstrate the application of this procedure.

EXAMPLE

Figure 13.2 shows Debbo Company's *WMCC* and *IOS* on the same set of axes. Using these two functions in combination, the firm's optimal capital budget ("X" in Figure 13.2) is determined. By raising $2 million of new financing and investing these funds in projects A, B, C, D, and E, the wealth of the firm's owners should be maximized, since the 12 percent return on the last dollar invested (in project E) *exceeds* its 11.410 percent weighted average cost. Investment in project F is not feasible because its 11 percent return is *less* than the 11.650 percent cost of funds available for investment. The importance of the *WMCC* and *IOS* for investment decision making should now be quite clear. ■

SUMMARY

● The key cost of capital definitions and formulas are given in Table 13.5.
● The cost of capital is the rate of return a firm must earn on its investments in order to maintain its market value and attract needed funds. To capture the interrelatedness of financing, an overall or weighted average cost of capital should be used.
● The specific costs of the basic sources of capital (long-term debt, preferred

**TABLE 13.5 Summary of Key Definitions and Formulas
for Cost of Capital**

Variable definitions
k_d = before-tax cost of debt
I = annual interest in dollars
N_d = net proceeds from the sale of debt (bond)
n = number of years to the bond's maturity
k_i = after-tax cost of debt
t = firm's tax rate
k_p = cost of preferred stock
D_p = annual preferred stock dividend
N_p = net proceeds from the sale of preferred stock
k_s = required return on common stock
D_1 = per-share dividend expected at the end of year 1
P_0 = value of common stock
g = constant rate of growth in dividends
R_F = risk-free rate of return
b = beta coefficient or measure of nondiversifiable risk
k_m = the market return — return on the market portfolio of assets
k_n = cost of a new issue of common stock
N_n = net proceeds from sale of new common stock
k_r = cost of retained earnings
k_a = weighted average cost of capital
w_i = proportion of long-term debt in capital structure
w_p = proportion of preferred stock in capital structure
w_s = proportion of common stock equity in capital structure

(Continued)

TABLE 13.5 *(Continued)*

Cost of Capital Formulas

Before-Tax Cost of Debt

$$k_d = \frac{I + \dfrac{\$1{,}000 - N_d}{n}}{\dfrac{N_d + \$1{,}000}{2}}$$

After-Tax Cost of Debt

$$k_i = k_d \times (1 - t)$$

Cost of Preferred Stock

$$k_p = \frac{D_p}{N_p}$$

Cost of Common Stock Equity

Using constant growth valuation model: $k_s = \dfrac{D_1}{P_0} + g$

Using capital asset pricing model *(CAPM)*: $k_s = R_F + [b \times (k_m - R_F)]$

Cost of New Issues of Common Stock

$$k_n = \frac{D_1}{N_n} + g$$

Cost of Retained Earnings

$$k_r = k_s$$

Weighted Average Cost of Capital *(WACC)*

$$k_a = w_i \times k_i + w_p \times k_p + w_s \times k_{r\,or\,n}$$

stock, common stock, and retained earnings) can be calculated individually. Only the cost of debt must be adjusted for taxes, since the costs of the other forms of financing are paid from after-tax cash flows.

● The cost of long-term debt is the after-tax cost today of raising long-term funds through borrowing. It can be approximated using a formula and a tax-adjustment calculation.

● The cost of preferred stock is the stated annual dividend expressed as a percentage of the net proceeds from the sale of preferred shares.

● The cost of common stock equity can be calculated using the constant growth valuation model or the capital asset pricing model *(CAPM)*. An adjustment in the cost of common stock equity to reflect underpricing and flotation costs is required to find the cost of new issues of common stock. The cost of retained earnings is equal to the cost of common stock equity.

● A firm's weighted average cost of capital *(WACC)* can be determined by combining the costs of specific types of capital after weighting each cost using historical book or market value weights or target book or market value weights. The theoretically preferred approach uses target weights based on market values.

- A firm's weighted marginal cost of capital *(WMCC)* function can be developed by finding the weighted average cost of capital for various levels of total new financing. The function relates the weighted average cost of capital to each level of total new financing.
- The investment opportunities schedule *(IOS)* presents a ranking of currently available investments from those with the highest returns to those with the lowest returns. It is used in combination with the *WMCC* to find the level of financing/investment that maximizes owners' wealth.

QUESTIONS

13-1 What is the *cost of capital?* What role does it play in making long-term investment decisions? Why is use of a weighted average cost rather than the specific cost recommended?

13-2 You have just been told, "Since we are going to finance this project with debt, its required rate of return must exceed the cost of debt." Do you agree or disagree? Explain.

13-3 Why is the cost of capital most appropriately measured on an after-tax basis? What effect, if any, does this have on specific cost components?

13-4 What is meant by the *net proceeds* from the sale of a bond? In which circumstances is a bond expected to sell at a discount or at a premium?

13-5 What sort of general approximation is used to find the before-tax cost of debt? How is the before-tax cost of debt converted into the after-tax cost?

13-6 How would you calculate the cost of preferred stock? Why do we concern ourselves with the net proceeds from the sale of the stock instead of the sale price?

13-7 What premise about share value underlies the constant growth valuation model (Gordon model) used to measure the cost of common stock equity, k_s? What does each component of the equation represent?

13-8 If retained earnings are viewed as a fully subscribed issue of additional common stock, why is the cost of financing a project with retained earnings technically less than the cost of using a new issue of common stock?

13-9 Describe the logic underlying the use of *target capital structure weights*, and compare and contrast this approach with the use of historic weights.

13-10 What does the *weighted marginal cost of capital (WMCC)* function represent? Why does this function increase?

13-11 What is the *investment opportunities schedule (IOS)?* Is it typically depicted as an increasing or decreasing function of the level of investment at a given point in time? Why?

13-12 Use a graph to show how the weighted marginal cost of capital *(WMCC)* and the investment opportunities schedule *(IOS)* can be used to find the level of financing/investment that maximizes owners' wealth.

PROBLEMS

13-1 **(Concept of Cost of Capital)** Wren Manufacturing is in the process of analyzing its investment decision-making procedures. The two projects evaluated by the firm during the past month were projects 263 and 264. The basic variables surrounding each project analysis and the resulting decision actions are summarized in the following table.

Basic variables	Project 263	Project 264
Cost	$64,000	$58,000
Life	15 years	15 years
Return	8%	15%
Least-cost financing		
Source	Debt	Equity
Cost (after-tax)	7%	16%
Decision		
Action	Accept	Reject
Reason	8% return > 7% cost	15% return < 16% cost

a Evaluate the firm's decision-making procedures and explain why the acceptance of project 263 and rejection of project 264 may not be in the owners' best interest.

b If the firm maintains a capital structure containing 40 percent debt and 60 percent equity, find its weighted average cost using the data in the table.

c Had the firm used the weighted average cost calculated in **b**, what actions would have been taken relative to projects 263 and 264?

d Compare and contrast the firm's actions with your findings in **c**. Which decision method seems most appropriate? Explain why.

13-2 **(Cost of Debt)** Currently Krick and Company can sell 15-year, $1,000 par-value bonds paying *annual interest* at a 12 percent stated rate. As a result of current interest rates, the bonds can be sold for $1,010 each; flotation costs of $30 per bond will be incurred in this process. The firm is in the 40 percent tax bracket.

a Find the net proceeds from sale of the bond, N_d.

b Estimate the before-tax cost of debt, k_d.

c Convert your finding in **b** into the after-tax cost of debt, k_i.

13-3 **(Cost of Debt)** For each of the following $1,000 par-value bonds, assuming *annual interest* payment and a 40 percent tax rate, calculate the *after-tax* cost.

Bond	Life	Underwriting fee	Discount (−) or premium (+)	Stated rate
A	20 years	$25	$−20	9%
B	16	40	$+10	10
C	15	30	$−15	12
D	25	15	Par	9
E	22	20	$−60	11

13-4 **(Cost of Preferred Stock)** The No-Tread Tire Company has just issued preferred stock. The stock has a 12 percent annual dividend and a $100 par value and was sold at $97.50 per share. In addition, flotation costs of $2.50 per share must be paid.

a Calculate the cost of the preferred stock.

b If the firm had sold the preferred stock with a 10 percent annual dividend and a $90.00 net price, what would its cost have been?

13-5 **(Cost of Preferred Stock)** Determine the cost for each of the following preferred stocks.

Preferred stock	Par value	Sale price	Flotation cost	Annual dividend
A	$100	$101	$9.00	11%
B	$ 40	$ 38	$3.50	8%
C	$ 35	$ 37	$4.00	$5.00
D	$ 30	$ 26	5% of par	$3.00
E	$ 20	$ 20	$2.50	9%

13-6 **(Cost of Common Stock Equity)** Delico Meat Packing wishes to measure its cost of common stock equity. The firm's stock is currently selling for $57.50. The firm expects to pay a $3.40 dividend at the end of the year. The dividends for the past five years were as follows:

Year	Dividend
1987	$3.10
1986	2.92
1985	2.60
1984	2.30
1983	2.12

After underpricing and flotation costs, the firm expects to net $52 per share on a new issue.

a Determine the growth rate of dividends.

b Determine the net proceeds, N_n, the firm actually receives.

c Using the constant growth valuation model, determine the cost of new common stock equity, k_n.

d Using the constant growth valuation model, determine the cost of retained earnings, k_r.

13-7 **(New Common Stock versus Retained Earnings)** Using the data for each firm in the table at the top of the next page, calculate the cost of new common stock and the cost of retained earnings using the constant growth valuation model.

Firm	Current market price per share	Dividend growth rate	Projected dividend per share next year	Underpricing per share	Flotation cost per share
A	$50.00	8%	$2.25	$2.00	$1.00
B	20.00	4	1.00	0.50	1.50
C	42.50	6	2.00	1.00	2.00
D	19.00	2	2.10	1.30	1.70

13-8 **(Cost of Equity — CAPM)** Tucker and Tucker (T&T) common stock has a beta, *b*, of 1.2. If the risk-free rate is 6 percent and the market return is 11 percent,

a Determine the risk premium on T&T common stock.

b Determine the required return T&T common stock should provide.

c Determine T&T's cost of common equity using the *CAPM*.

13-9 **(*WACC* — Book Weights)** Atlanta Tire has on its books the following amounts and specific (after-tax) costs for each source of capital:

Source of capital	Book value	Specific cost
Long-term debt	$700,000	5.25%
Preferred stock	50,000	12.00
Common stock equity	650,000	16.00

a Calculate the firm's weighted average cost of capital using book value weights.

b Explain how the firm can use this cost in the investment decision-making process.

13-10 **(*WACC* — Book Weights and Market Weights)** The Pure Air Company has compiled the following information:

Source of capital	Book value	Market value	After-tax cost
Long-term debt	$4,000,000	$3,840,000	6.00%
Preferred stock	40,000	60,000	13.00
Common stock equity	1,060,000	3,000,000	17.00
Totals	$5,100,000	$6,900,000	

a Calculate the weighted average cost of capital using book value weights.

b Calculate the weighted average cost of capital using market value weights.

c Compare the answers obtained in **a** and **b**. Explain the differences.

13-11 **(*WACC* and Target Weights)** After careful analysis, the Ellwood Company has determined that its optimal capital structure is composed of the following sources and target market value proportions:

Source of capital	Target market value proportions
Long-term debt	30%
Preferred stock	15
Common stock equity	55
Total	100%

The cost of debt is estimated to be 7.2 percent, the cost of preferred stock is estimated to be 13.5 percent, the cost of new common stock is estimated to be 16.5 percent, and the cost of retained earnings is estimated to be 16 percent. All these are after-tax rates. Currently, the company's debt represents 25 percent, the preferred stock represents 10 percent, and the common stock equity represents 65 percent of the capital structure based on market values of the three components. The company expects to have a significant amount of retained earnings available and does not expect to sell any new common stock.

a Calculate the weighted average cost of capital based on market value weights.

b Calculate the weighted average cost of capital based on target weights.

13-12 ■ **(Calculation of Specific Costs and the WACC)** Keystone Pump has charged Martin Drywater, its financial manager, with measuring the cost of each specific type of capital as well as the weighted average cost of capital. The weighted average cost is to be measured using the firm's target capital structure weights. The firm wishes to finance projects using 40 percent long-term debt, 10 percent preferred stock, and 50 percent common stock equity (retained earnings, new common stock, or both). The firm's tax rate is 40 percent on ordinary income.

Debt. The firm can sell a 10-year, $1,000 par-value, 10 percent (stated *annual* interest rate) bond for $980. A flotation cost of 3 percent of the face value would be required in addition to the discount of $20 per bond.

Preferred stock. 8 percent preferred stock having a par value of $100 can be sold for $65. An additional fee of $2 per share must be paid to the underwriters.

Common stock. The firm's common stock is currently selling for $50 per share. The dividend expected to be paid at the end of the coming year (1988) is $4. Dividend payments in each of the past five years were as follows:

Year	Dividend
1987	$3.75
1986	3.50
1985	3.30
1984	3.15
1983	2.85

It is expected that to sell, new common stock must be underpriced $3 per share and the firm must also pay $2 per share in flotation costs.

a Calculate the specific cost of each source of financing. (Assume that $k_r = k_s$.)

b Assuming the firm plans to pay out all of its earnings as dividends (i.e., retained earnings = $0), calculate its weighted average cost of capital.

13-13 **(Calculation of Specific Costs, *WACC*, and *WMCC*)** Cloak, Inc., is interested in measuring its overall cost of capital. Current investigation has gathered the following data. The firm is in the 40% tax bracket.

Debt. The firm can raise an unlimited amount of debt by selling $1,000 par-value, 8 percent (stated interest rate), 20-year bonds on which *annual* interest payments will be made. To sell the issue, an average discount of $30 per bond would have to be given. The firm also must pay flotation costs of $30 per bond.

Preferred stock. The firm can sell 8 percent preferred stock at its $95-per-share par value. The cost of issuing and selling the preferred stock is expected to be $5 per share. An unlimited amount of preferred stock can be sold under these terms.

Common stock. The firm's common stock is currently selling for $100 per share. The firm expects to pay cash dividends of $7 per share next year. The firm's dividends have been growing at an annual rate of 6 percent, and this is expected to continue into the future. The stock will have to be underpriced by $3 per share, and flotation costs are expected to amount to $5 per share. The firm can sell an unlimited amount of new common stock under these terms.

Retained earnings. The firm expects to have available a limited amount of retained earnings. Once retained earnings are exhausted, the firm will use new common stock to meet its common stock equity financing need.

a Calculate the specific cost of each source of financing. (Round answers to the nearest .10 percent.)

b The firm's target capital structure proportions used in calculating its weighted average cost of capital are given. (Round answers to the nearest .01 percent in this part.)

Source of capital	Target capital structure proportion
Long-term debt	30%
Preferred stock	20
Common stock equity	50
Total	100%

1 Calculate the weighted average cost of capital associated with total financing *up to* the point when retained earnings are exhausted.

2 Calculate the weighted average cost of capital associated with total financing *after* retained earnings are exhausted and new common stock is used as common stock equity financing.

13-14 **(Integrative — *WACC*, *WMCC*, and *IOS*).** The H. Grimmer Company has compiled the data on the cost of each source of capital over specified ranges of total new financing as shown in the table at the top of the next page.

Range of total new financing	COST OF GIVEN TYPE OF CAPITAL		
	Debt	Preferred	Common
$0 to $200,000	6%	17%	20%
$200,000 to $500,000	6	17	22
$500,000 to $750,000	7	19	22
$750,000 to $1,000,000	9	19	24
Greater than $1,000,000	9	19	26

The company's target capital structure proportions used in calculating its weighted average cost of capital are as follows:

Source of capital	Target capital structure
Long-term debt	40%
Preferred stock	20
Common stock equity	40
Total	100%

a Calculate the weighted average cost of capital *(WACC)* for each range of total new financing.
b Use the results in **a** to draw the firm's weighted marginal cost of capital *(WMCC)* function on a set of total new financing or investment (*x*-axis)–weighted average cost of capital and return (*y*-axis) axes.
c Using the following information, draw the firm's investment opportunities schedule *(IOS)* on the set of axes used in **b**.

Investment opportunity	Rate of return	Initial investment
A	19%	$200,000
B	15	300,000
C	22	100,000
D	14	600,000
E	23	200,000
F	13	100,000
G	21	300,000
H	17	100,000
I	16	400,000

d Which, if any, of the available investments would you recommend that the firm accept? Explain your answer.

13-15 ■ **(Integrative—Specific Costs, *WACC*, *WMCC*, and *IOS*)** Allport Manufacturing is interested in measuring its overall cost of capital. Current investigation has gathered the following data. The firm is in the 40 percent tax bracket.
Debt. The firm can raise an unlimited amount of debt by selling $1,000

par-value, 10 percent (stated interest rate), ten-year bonds on which *annual* interest payments will be made. To sell the issue, an average discount of $30 per bond would have to be given. The firm must also pay flotation costs of $20 per bond.

Preferred stock. The firm can sell 11 percent preferred stock at its $100-per-share par value. The cost of issuing and selling the preferred stock is expected to be $4 per share. An unlimited amount of preferred stock can be sold under these terms.

Common stock. The firm's common stock is currently selling for $80 per share. The firm expects to pay cash dividends of $6 per share next year. The firm's dividends have been growing at an annual rate of 6 percent, and this is expected to continue in the future. The stock will have to be underpriced by $4 per share, and flotation costs are expected to amount to $4 per share. The firm can sell an unlimited amount of new common stock under these terms.

Retained earnings. The firm expects to have a limited amount of retained earnings available. Once exhausted the firm will use new common stock to raise common stock equity financing.

a Calculate the specific cost of each source of financing. (Round answers to the nearest .10 percent.)

b The firm's target capital structure proportions used in calculating its weighted average cost of capital are given. (Round answers to the nearest .01 percent in this part.)

Source of capital	Target capital structure proportion
Long-term debt	40%
Preferred stock	15
Common stock equity	45
Total	100%

1 Calculate the firm's weighted average cost of capital *(WACC)* assuming the use of *retained earnings* as the source of common stock equity financing.

2 Calculate the firm's weighted average cost of capital *(WACC)* assuming the use of *new common stock* as the source of common stock equity financing.

c Assume that retained earnings will provide for *total* new financing up to $500,000; beyond $500,000 of *total* new financing, new common stock will be used as the source of common equity financing. Using your findings in **b**, draw the firm's weighted marginal cost of capital *(WMCC)* function on a set of total new financing or investment (*x*-axis)–weighted average cost of capital and return (*y*-axis) axes.

d Using the information in the table at the top of the next page, draw the firm's investment opportunities schedule *(IOS)* on the set of axes used in **c**.

Investment opportunity	Rate of return	Initial investment
A	11.2%	$100,000
B	9.7	500,000
C	12.9	150,000
D	16.5	200,000
E	11.8	450,000
F	10.1	600,000
G	10.5	300,000

e Which, if any, of the available investments would you recommend the firm accept? Explain your answer.

Part Five

LONG-TERM FINANCIAL DECISIONS

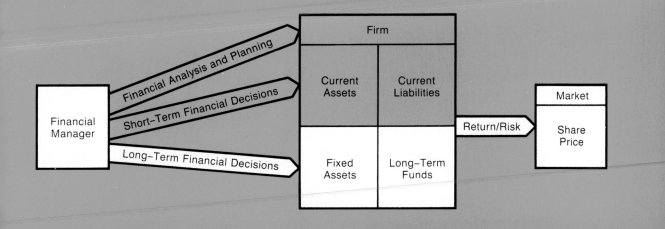

14

CAPITAL BUDGETING AND CASH FLOW PRINCIPLES

After studying this chapter, you should be able to:

- Understand the key capital expenditure motives and the steps in the capital budgeting process, beginning with proposal generation and concluding with follow-up.

- Define the basic terminology used to describe projects, funds availability, decision approaches, and cash flow patterns.

- Discuss the major components of relevant cash flows and the differences in the development of expansion-versus replacement-decision cash flows.

- Calculate the initial investment associated with a proposed capital expenditure given relevant cost, depreciation, and tax data.

- Determine the operating cash inflows relevant to a capital budgeting proposal using the income statement format.

capital budgeting The process of evaluating and selecting long-term investments, which for manufacturing firms are most commonly *fixed assets*, consistent with the firm's goal of owner wealth maximization.

Capital budgeting is the process of evaluating and selecting long-term investments consistent with the firm's goal of owner wealth maximization. Firms typically make a variety of long-term investments, but the most common such investment for the manufacturing firm is in *fixed assets*. These assets are a necessity since without them production would be impossible. Fixed assets are quite often referred to as *earning assets* because they generally provide the basis for the firm's earning power and value. The three major classes of fixed assets are property (land), plant, and equipment. Chapters 18 to 20 address the key issues in the long-term financing of fixed assets. We here concentrate on fixed-asset acquisition without regard to the specific method of financing used.

THE CAPITAL BUDGETING DECISION PROCESS

Since long-term investments represent sizable outlays of funds that commit a firm to some course of action, procedures are needed to analyze and select them properly. Attention must be given to the initial outlay and to subsequent cash flows associated with long-term or fixed-asset investments. As time passes, fixed assets may become obsolete or may require an overhaul; at these points, too, financial decisions may be required. This section of the chapter discusses capital expenditure motives and briefly describes the steps in the capital budgeting process.

Capital Expenditure Motives

capital expenditure An outlay of funds by the firm expected to produce benefits over a period *greater than* one year.

current expenditure An outlay of funds by the firm resulting in benefits received *within* one year.

A **capital expenditure** is an outlay of funds by the firm that is expected to produce benefits over a period of time greater than one year. A **current expenditure** is an outlay resulting in benefits received *within* one year. Fixed-asset outlays are capital expenditures, but not all capital expenditures are classified as fixed assets. A $60,000 outlay for a new machine with a usable life of 15 years is a capital expenditure that would appear as a fixed asset on the firm's balance sheet. A $60,000 outlay for advertising that produces benefits over a long period is also a capital expenditure. However, an outlay for advertising would rarely be shown as a fixed asset.

Capital expenditures are made for many reasons; but although the motives differ, the evaluation techniques are the same. The basic motives for capital expenditures are to expand, replace, or renew fixed assets or to obtain some other less tangible benefit over a long period.

EXPANSION Perhaps the most common motive for a capital expenditure is to expand the level of operations — usually through acquisition of fixed assets. A growing firm often finds it necessary to acquire new fixed assets rapidly. It is important to remember that fixed assets include property (land), plant, and equipment. In other words, the purchase of additional physical facilities, such as additional property and plant, is a capital expenditure.

REPLACEMENT   As a firm's growth slows and it reaches maturity, most of its capital expenditures will be for the replacement or renewal of obsolete or worn-out assets. This type of capital expenditure does not always result from the outright failure of a piece of equipment or the inability of an existing plant to function efficiently. The need to replace existing assets must be periodically examined by the firm's financial manager. A machine does not break down and say, "Please replace me!" But each time a machine requires a major repair, the outlay for the repair must be evaluated in terms of the outlay to replace the machine and the benefits of replacement.

RENEWAL   The renewal of fixed assets is often an alternative to replacement. Firms wishing to improve efficiency may find that both replacing and renewing existing machinery are suitable solutions. Renewal may involve rebuilding, overhauling, or retrofitting an existing machine or facility. Perhaps an existing drill press could be renewed by replacing its motor and adding a numeric control system. Perhaps a physical facility could be renewed by rewiring, adding air conditioning, and so on.

OTHER PURPOSES   Some capital expenditures do not result in the acquisition or transformation of tangible fixed assets that are shown on the firm's balance sheet. Instead, they involve a long-term commitment of funds by the firm in expectation of a future return. These expenditures include outlays for advertising, research and development, management consulting, and new products. Advertising outlays are expected to provide benefits in the form of increased future sales. Research and development outlays are expected to provide future benefits in the form of new product ideas. Management-consulting outlays are expected to provide returns in the form of increased profits from increased efficiency of operation. New products are expected to contribute to a product mix that maximizes overall returns. Many capital expenditure proposals—especially those such as the installation of pollution-control devices mandated by the government—are difficult to evaluate because it is difficult to measure the intangible returns they may generate.

Steps in the Process

The **capital budgeting process** can be viewed as consisting of five distinct but interrelated steps. It begins with proposal generation. This

capital budgeting process Consists of five distinct but interrelated steps beginning with proposal generation and followed by review and analysis, decision making, implementation, and follow-up.

is followed by review and analysis, decision making, implementation, and follow-up. Each step in the process is important; major time and effort, however, are devoted to review and analysis and decision making. These are the steps given the most attention in this and the following chapter.

PROPOSAL GENERATION Proposals for capital expenditures are made by people at all levels within a business organization. To stimulate a flow of ideas that could result in potential cost savings, many firms offer cash rewards to employees whose proposals are ultimately adopted and funded. Capital expenditure proposals typically travel from the originator to a reviewer at a higher level in the organization. For relatively minor expenditures, the review might be made at the next organizational level; major expenditure proposals go before a higher-level reviewer or review committee. Clearly proposals requiring large outlays will be much more carefully scrutinized than less costly ones.

REVIEW AND ANALYSIS Capital expenditure proposals—especially those requiring major outlays—are formally reviewed (1) to assess their appropriateness in light of the firm's overall objectives and plans and (2) more important, to evaluate their economic validity. Economic evaluation begins with an assessment of the costs and benefits. The proposed costs and benefits are then converted into a series of relevant cash flows to which various capital budgeting techniques are applied in order to measure the investment merit of the potential outlay. In addition, various aspects of the *risk* associated with the proposal are either incorporated into the economic analysis or somehow rated and recorded along with the economic measures. Once the economic analysis is completed, a summary report, often with a recommendation, is submitted to the decision maker or to a capital appropriations committee for action.

DECISION MAKING The size of proposed capital expenditures can vary significantly. Some expenditures, such as the purchase of a hammer that will provide benefits for three years, are by definition capital expenditures, even if the cost is only $15.[1] The purchase of a new machine costing $60,000 is also a capital expenditure because it is expected to

---

[1] Even though outlays to purchase items such as hammers are known to provide benefits over a period greater than a year, they are treated as expenditures in the year of purchase. There is a certain dollar limit beyond which outlays are *capitalized* (i.e., treated as a fixed asset) and *depreciated* rather than *expensed*. This dollar limit depends largely on what the U.S. Internal Revenue Service will permit. In accounting, the issue of whether to expense or capitalize an outlay is resolved using the *principle of materiality,* which suggests that any outlays deemed material (i.e., large) relative to the firm's scale of operations should be capitalized, whereas others should be expensed in the current period.

provide long-run returns. The actual dollar outlay and the importance of a capital item therefore determine the organizational level at which the expenditure decision is made.

Dollar Outlay. Firms delegate capital-expenditure authority on the basis of certain dollar limits. Generally, the board of directors reserves the right to make final decisions on capital expenditures requiring outlays beyond a certain dollar amount, while the authority for making smaller expenditures is delegated to other organizational levels. An example of a scheme for delegating capital-expenditure decision authority is presented in Table 14.1. As the size of expenditures decreases, the decision-making authority moves to lower levels within the organization. Of course, the detail and formality of the economic analysis on which the decision is based tend to increase in rigor with the dollar value of the proposal.

Importance. Firms operating under critical constraints with respect to time and production often find it necessary to provide for exceptions to a dollar-outlay scheme. In such cases the plant manager is often given the power to make decisions necessary to keep the production line moving, even though the outlays entailed are larger than he or she would normally be allowed to authorize. These exceptions must be allowed due to the high cost of interrupting production. It is wise to put some dollar limit on these critically important expenditures, but it can be set somewhat above the norm for that organizational level.

IMPLEMENTATION Once a proposal has been approved and funding has been made available,[2] the implementation phase begins. For minor outlays, implementation is relatively routine; the expenditure is made and payment is rendered. For major expenditures, greater control is typically required to make certain that what has been proposed and approved is actually acquired at the budgeted costs. Often the expendi-

---

TABLE 14.1 A Scheme for Delegating Capital Expenditure Decision Authority

Size of expenditure	Decision-making authority
Over $100,000	Board of directors or top management committee
$50,000 – $100,000	President and/or chair of board of directors
$20,000 – $50,000	Vice-president in charge of division
$5,000 – $20,000	Plant manager
Under $5,000	Persons designated by plant manager

---

[2] Capital expenditures are often approved as part of the annual budgeting process, although funding will not be made available until the budget is implemented—frequently as long as six months after approval.

THE MANAGER OF CAPITAL BUDGETING: A JOB DESCRIPTION

Basic Function

Responsible for budgeting and administering the company's capital asset expenditure program.

Primary Responsibilities and Duties

Compile and control the company's capital asset expenditures and construction program.

Analyze requests for capital appropriations.

Project future cash flow needs and analyze the resulting financing requirements.

Determine the amount and timing of future debt and equity needs.

Project and analyze financial statements.

Develop and maintain the computer system relating to capital asset analysis.

Prepare and present monthly reports on the capital expenditures program and cash flow projections.

Distribute information to and work with other corporate departments.

Supervise the identification of industrial revenue bond projects.

Supervise and review the calculation of various loan covenants and financial restrictions.

Obtain lease financing and assist in the issuance of industrial revenue bonds.

Negotiate terms of leases with lessors.

Education and Experience

MBA

3 years experience in accounting or management accounting.

3–4 years experience in financial analysis and reporting with emphasis on capital expenditure decisions and cash flow analysis.

Source: *Careers in Finance* (Tampa, Fl.: Financial Management Association, 1983), p. 5.

tures for a single proposal may occur in phases, with each outlay requiring the signed approval of specified company officers.

FOLLOW-UP Equally important in controlling the cost incurred during the implementation phase is the monitoring of results during the operating phase of a project. The comparisons of actual outcomes in terms of costs and benefits with those expected and those of previous projects are vital. When actual outcomes deviate from projected outcomes, action may be required to cut costs, improve benefits, or possibly to terminate the project. Follow-up is often ignored in practice, but it is an important activity that can contribute favorably to the firm's overall return, risk, and value.

CAPITAL BUDGETING TERMINOLOGY

Before beginning to develop the concepts, tools, and techniques related to the review and analysis and decision-making steps in the capital budgeting process, it is useful to understand some of the basic terminology of these areas. In addition, we present a number of key assumptions used to simplify the discussion in the remainder of this chapter as well as in Chapter 15.

Types of Projects

The firm may be confronted with a number of different types of projects. Depending on the types of projects being considered, different decision-making approaches may be required. The two most common project types are (1) independent and (2) mutually exclusive projects.

INDEPENDENT PROJECTS **Independent projects** do not compete with one another for the firm's investment; the acceptance of one *does not eliminate* the others from further consideration. If a firm has unlimited funds to invest, all the independent projects that meet its minimum investment criteria can be implemented.

> **independent projects** Projects that do not compete with one another for the firm's investment.

MUTUALLY EXCLUSIVE PROJECTS **Mutually exclusive projects** are projects that have the same function and therefore compete with one another. The acceptance of one of a group of mutually exclusive projects *eliminates* all other projects in the group from further consideration. For example, if a firm is confronted with three ways to achieve its goal of increasing productive capacity, the three alternatives would be considered mutually exclusive. If each of these alternatives meets the firm's minimum acceptance criteria, some technique must be used to determine the "best" one. Acceptance of this "best" alternative will eliminate the need for either of the other two.

> **mutually exclusive projects** Projects that compete with one another in such a way that acceptance of one eliminates all the others.

The Availability of Funds

The availability of funds for capital expenditures affects the firm's decision environment.

> **unlimited funds** Allow a firm to accept all independent projects that provide returns greater than some predetermined level.

UNLIMITED FUNDS If a firm has **unlimited funds** for investment, making capital budgeting decisions is quite simple. All independent projects that will provide returns greater than some predetermined level can be accepted. Most firms are not in such a situation. Typically only a certain number of dollars are allocated for making capital expenditures. Normally this amount is specified in the firm's annual budget.

capital rationing The availability of only a fixed number of dollars for allocation to competing capital expenditures.

CAPITAL RATIONING   Most firms operate under **capital rationing.** This means that they have only a fixed number of dollars available for capital expenditures and that numerous projects will compete for these limited dollars. The firm must therefore ration its funds by allocating them to projects that will maximize share value. Procedures for dealing with capital rationing are presented in Chapter 15. The discussions that follow assume unlimited funds.

Approaches to Decision Making

Two basic approaches to capital budgeting decisions are available. These approaches are somewhat dependent on whether or not the firm is confronted with capital rationing, and they are affected by the type of project involved. The two are the *accept-reject approach* and the *ranking approach.*

accept-reject approach The evaluation of capital expenditure proposals to determine their acceptability.

THE ACCEPT-REJECT APPROACH   The **accept-reject approach** involves evaluating capital expenditure proposals to determine whether they are acceptable. This is a simple approach because it requires merely comparing the projected return of the potential expenditure to the firm's minimum acceptable return. This approach can be used if the firm has unlimited funds available. The accept-reject decision is also a preliminary step in evaluating mutually exclusive projects or in a situation in which capital must be rationed. In these cases only acceptable projects should be considered.

ranking approach The ranking of projects under consideration on the basis of some predetermined measure such as the rate of return.

THE RANKING APPROACH   A second method, the **ranking approach,** involves ranking projects on the basis of some predetermined measure such as the rate of return. The project with the highest return is ranked first, and the project with the lowest return is ranked last. Only acceptable projects should be ranked. Ranking is useful in selecting the "best" of a group of mutually exclusive projects and in evaluating projects with a view to capital rationing.

When the firm is confronted with a number of projects, some of which are mutually exclusive and some of which are independent, it must first determine the best of each group of mutually exclusive alternatives. This reduces the mixed group of projects to a group of independent projects. The best of the acceptable independent projects can then be selected. All acceptable projects can be implemented if the firm has unlimited funds. If capital rationing is necessary, the mix of projects that maximizes the firm's overall value should be accepted. The following example illustrates the evaluation process.

EXAMPLE

A firm with unlimited funds must evaluate eight projects—A through H. Projects A, B, and C are mutually exclusive; projects G and H are also mutually exclusive; and projects D, E, and F are independent of the other projects. The projects are listed along with their returns:

Project	Status	Return (%)
A		16
B	Mutually exclusive	19
C		11
D	Independent	15
E	Independent	13
F	Independent	21
G		20
H	Mutually exclusive	17

To evaluate these projects, the best of the mutually exclusive groups must first be determined. On the basis of the given return figures, project B would be selected from mutually exclusive projects A, B, and C since it has the highest return of this group, and project G would be preferred to project H since it has the higher return. After the selection of the best of the two groups of mutually exclusive projects, the five remaining independent projects can be ranked on the basis of their respective returns:

Rank	Project	Return (%)
1	F	21
2	G	20
3	B	19
4	D	15
5	E	13

Given that the firm has unlimited funds, and assuming that all projects are acceptable, ranking in this case would not be necessary. If the firm were operating in an environment of capital rationing, however, ranking would be useful in determining which projects to accept. ■

Types of Cash Flow Patterns

Cash flow patterns associated with capital investment projects can be classified as *conventional* or *nonconventional*. Another classification is as an *annuity* or a *mixed stream*.

conventional cash flow pattern An initial outflow followed by a series of inflows.

CONVENTIONAL CASH FLOWS A **conventional cash flow pattern** consists of an initial outflow followed by a series of inflows. This pattern is associated with many types of capital expenditures. For example, a firm may spend $10,000 today and as a result expect to receive cash inflows of $2,000 each year for the next eight years. This conventional pattern is diagrammed in Figure 14.1. All conventional cash flow patterns can be diagrammed in this way.

nonconventional cash flow pattern Any pattern in which an initial outlay is *not* followed by a series of inflows.

NONCONVENTIONAL CASH FLOWS A **nonconventional cash flow pattern** is any pattern in which an initial outlay is *not* followed by a series of inflows. For example, the purchase of a machine may require an initial cash outflow of $20,000 and may generate cash inflows of $5,000 each year for four years. In the fifth year after purchase, an outlay of $8,000 may be required to overhaul the machine, after which it generates inflows of $5,000 each year for five years. This nonconventional pattern is illustrated in Figure 14.2.

Difficulties often arise in evaluating projects involving a nonconventional pattern of cash flows. The discussions in the remainder of this chapter and in the following chapter are therefore limited to the evaluation of conventional patterns.

annuity A stream of equal annual cash flows.

mixed stream A series of cash flows exhibiting any pattern other than an annuity.

ANNUITY OR MIXED STREAM As pointed out in Chapter 11, an **annuity** is a stream of equal annual cash flows. A series of cash flows exhibiting any pattern other than an annuity is a **mixed stream** of cash flows. The

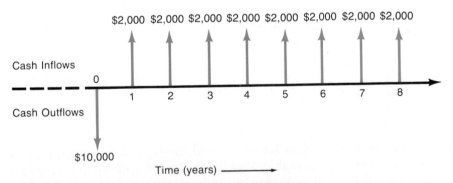

FIGURE 14.1 A Conventional Cash Flow Pattern
This conventional pattern of cash flow consists of an initial outflow ($10,000) followed by a series of inflows ($2,000 each year for eight years).

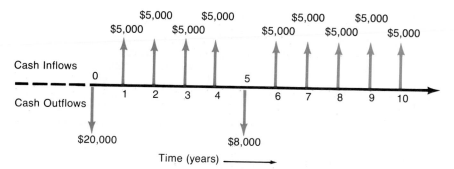

FIGURE 14.2 A Nonconventional Cash Flow Pattern
This nonconventional cash flow pattern consists of an initial outflow ($20,000)
followed by a series of inflows ($5,000 each year for 4 years) followed by another
outflow ($8,000 in year 5) followed by a final series of inflows ($5,000 each year
for 5 years).

cash inflows of $2,000 per year (for eight years) in Figure 14.1 are
inflows from an annuity, while the unequal pattern of inflows in Figure
14.3 (page 424) represents a mixed stream. As pointed out in Chapter
11, the techniques required to evaluate cash flows are much simpler to
use when the pattern of flows is an annuity.

THE RELEVANT CASH FLOWS

To evaluate capital expenditure alternatives, the **relevant cash flows,**
which are the *incremental after-tax cash outflow (investment) and re-*
sulting subsequent inflows, must be determined. The **incremental cash**
flows represent the *additional* cash flows — outflows or inflows —
expected to result from a proposed capital expenditure. As noted in
Chapter 3, cash flows, rather than accounting figures, are used because
it is these flows that directly affect the firm's ability to pay bills and
purchase assets. Furthermore, accounting figures and cash flows are
not necessarily the same due to the presence of certain noncash expenditures on the firm's income statement. The remainder of this chapter is devoted to the procedures for measuring the relevant cash flows
associated with proposed capital expenditures.

relevant cash flows The
incremental after-tax
cash outflow (invest-
ment) and resulting sub-
sequent inflows asso-
ciated with a proposed
capital expenditure.

incremental cash flows
The *additional* cash
flows — outflows or
inflows — expected to
result from a proposed
capital expenditure.

Major Cash Flow Components

The cash flows of any project having the *conventional pattern* include
two basic components: (1) an initial investment, and (2) operating cash
inflows. All projects, whether for expansion, replacement, renewal, or
some other purpose, have these components. Figure 14.3 depicts the
cash flows for a project. Each of the cash flow components is labeled.

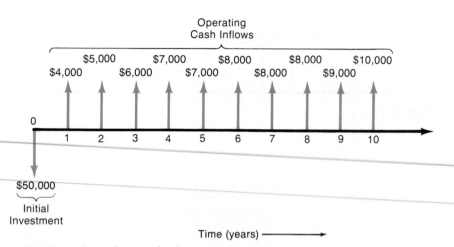

FIGURE 14.3 Major Cash Flow Components
The major cash flow components for this project consist of the initial investment of $50,000 at time zero and the operating cash inflows, which increase from $4,000 in the first year to $10,000 in the tenth and final year.

initial investment The relevant cash outflow for a capital expenditure at time zero.

The **initial investment,** which is the relevant cash outflow at time zero, is $50,000 for the proposed project. The **operating cash inflows,** which are the incremental after-tax cash inflows resulting from use of the project during its life, gradually increase from $4,000 in the first year to $10,000 in the tenth and final year of the project.

operating cash inflows The incremental after-tax cash inflows resulting from use of a project during its life.

Expansion Versus Replacement Cash Flows

The development of relevant cash flows is most straightforward in the case of *expansion decisions*. In this case the initial investment and operating cash inflows are merely the after-tax cash outflow and inflows, respectively, associated with the proposed outlay. When making *replacement decisions* the development of relevant cash flows is more complicated due to the need to find the *incremental* cash outflows and inflows that will result from the proposed replacement. The initial investment in this case would be found by subtracting any after-tax cash inflows expected from liquidation of the old asset being replaced from the initial investment needed to acquire the new asset. The operating cash inflows would be found by taking the difference between the operating cash inflows from the new asset and from the replaced asset.

EXAMPLE

Column 1 of Table 14.2 shows the initial investment and operating cash inflows for an *expansion decision* involving the acquisition of

TABLE 14.2 Expansion and Replacement Cash Flows

	EXPANSION	REPLACEMENT	
	New Asset A (1)	Old Asset A (2)	Relevant cash flows [(1) − (2)] (3)
Initial investment	$13,000	$3,000[a]	$10,000
Year		Operating cash inflows	
1	$ 5,000	$3,000	$ 2,000
2	5,000	2,500	2,500
3	5,000	2,000	3,000
4	5,000	1,500	3,500
5	5,000	1,000	4,000

[a] After-tax cash inflows expected from liquidation.

new asset A. It can be seen that as a result of a $13,000 initial investment, the firm would expect operating cash inflows of $5,000 in each of the next five years.

If new asset A is being considered as a *replacement* for old asset A, the relevant cash flows would be found by subtracting the cash flows attributed to old asset A from the cash flows for new asset A. The expected after-tax cash inflows from liquidating old asset A and the current operating cash inflows from the old asset are shown in column 2 of Table 14.2. It can be seen that if old asset A is liquidated, $3,000 of after-tax cash inflows would result initially, and in years one through five $3,000, $2,500, $2,000, $1,500, and $1,000 of operating cash inflows would be eliminated. Therefore the relevant cash flows resulting from the replacement decision would be the difference in cash flows between new asset A and old asset A, as shown in column 3 of Table 14.2. ■

Actually, all capital budgeting decisions can be viewed as replacement decisions. Expansion decisions are merely replacement decisions in which all cash flows from the old asset are zero. In light of this fact, the following discussions emphasize the more general replacement decisions.

◼ FINDING THE INITIAL INVESTMENT

As previously stated, the term *initial investment* as used here refers to the relevant cash outflow to be considered in evaluating a prospective capital expenditure. It is calculated by subtracting all cash inflows occurring at time zero from all cash outflows occurring at time zero (the time the expenditure is made). Since our discussion of capital budgeting is concerned only with investments exhibiting conventional cash flows, the initial investment must occur at time zero.

The basic variables that must be considered in determining the initial investment associated with a capital expenditure are the cost of the new asset, the installation costs (if any), the proceeds (if any) from the sale of an old asset, and the taxes (if any) resulting from the sale of an old asset. The basic format for determining the initial investment is given in Table 14.3.

The Cost of a New Asset

cost of a new asset The net outlay its acquisition requires.

The **cost of a new asset** is the net outlay it requires. Usually we are concerned with the acquisition of a fixed asset for which a definite purchase price is paid. If there are no installation costs and the firm is not replacing an existing asset, the purchase price of the asset is equal to the initial investment. Each capital expenditure decision should be checked to make sure installation costs have not been overlooked.

Installation Costs

installation costs Any added costs necessary to place an asset into operation.

Installation costs are any added costs necessary to place an asset into operation. They are considered part of the firm's capital expenditure. The Internal Revenue Service (IRS) requires the firm to add installation costs to the purchase price in order to determine the depreciable value of an investment, which is depreciated over a period of years.

Proceeds from the Sale of an Old Asset

proceeds from the sale of an old asset The net cash inflow resulting from the selling of an old asset.

If a new asset is intended to replace an existing asset that is being sold, the **proceeds from the sale of an old asset** are the net cash inflows it provides. If costs are incurred in the process of removing the old assets, the proceeds from the sale of the old assets are reduced by them. Proceeds received from the sale of an old asset decrease the firm's initial investment in the new asset.

TABLE 14.3 The Basic Format for Determining Initial Investment

Cost of new asset
+Installation costs
−Proceeds from sale of old asset
±Taxes on sale of old asset
Initial investment

Taxes

Taxes must be considered in calculating the initial investment whenever a new asset replaces an old asset that has been sold.[3] The proceeds from the sale of the replaced asset are normally subject to some type of tax. The amount of tax depends on the relationship between the sale price, initial purchase price, and the book value of the asset being replaced. An understanding of (1) book value and (2) basic tax rules is necessary to determine the taxes on the sale of an asset.

BOOK VALUE The **book value** of an asset is its strict accounting value. It can be calculated using the following equation:

Book value = installed cost of asset − accumulated depreciation   (14.1)

> **book value** The strict accounting value of an asset calculated by subtracting its accumulated depreciation from installed cost.

EXAMPLE

Kontra Industries acquired a machine tool with an installed cost of $100,000 two years ago. The asset was being depreciated under ACRS (see Chapter 3) using a five-year recovery period.[4] Referring to Table 3.6 (page 54), it can be seen that under ACRS for a five-year recovery period, 20 percent and 32 percent of the installed cost would be depreciated in years 1 and 2, respectively. In other words, 52 percent (20 percent + 32 percent) of the $100,000 cost, or $52,000 (.52 × $100,000), would represent the accumulated depreciation at the end of year 2. Substituting into Equation 14.1, we get:

Book value = $100,000 − $52,000 = $48,000

The book value of Kontra's asset at the end of year 2 is therefore $48,000. ∎

BASIC TAX RULES When selling an asset, four potential tax situations can occur. These situations differ, depending upon the relationship between the asset's sale price, its initial purchase price, and its book value. The three key forms of taxable income and their associated tax treatments are defined and summarized in Table 14.4. The assumed tax rates used throughout this text are noted in the final column of the same

---

[3] A brief discussion of the tax treatment of ordinary and capital gains income was presented in Chapter 2.

[4] Under the *Tax Reform Act of 1986* most manufacturing machinery and equipment has a 7-year recovery period as noted in Chapter 3 (Table 3.5). Using this recovery period results in 8 years of depreciation, which unnecessarily complicates examples and problems. To simplify, *machinery and equipment are treated as 5-year assets throughout this and the following chapters.*

TABLE 14.4 Tax Treatment on Sales of Assets

Type of taxable income	Definition	Tax treatment	Assumed tax rate
Capital gain	Portion of the sale price that is in excess of the initial purchase price.	Regardless of how long the asset has been held, the total capital gain is taxed as ordinary income.	40%
Recaptured depreciation	Portion of the sale price that is in excess of book value and represents a recovery of previously taken depreciation.	All recaptured depreciation is taxed as ordinary income.	40%
Loss on sale of asset	Amount by which sale price is *less than* book value.	If asset is depreciable and used in business, loss is deducted from ordinary income.	40% of loss is a tax savings.
		If asset is *not* depreciable or is *not* used in business, loss is deductible only against capital gains.	40% of loss is a tax savings.

table. The four possible tax situations resulting in one or more forms of taxable income are: (1) the asset is sold for more than its initial purchase price; (2) the asset is sold for more than its book value but less than its initial purchase price; (3) the asset is sold for its book value; and (4) the asset is sold for less than its book value. An example will illustrate.

EXAMPLE

The old asset purchased two years ago for $100,000 by Kontra Industries has a current book value of $48,000. What will happen if the firm now decides to sell the asset and replace it? The tax consequences associated with sale of the asset depend upon the sale price. Let us consider each of the four possible situations.

The sale of the asset for more than its initial purchase price   If Kontra sells the old asset for $110,000, it realizes a capital gain of $10,000 (the amount by which the sale price exceeds the initial purchase price of $100,000) which is taxed as ordinary income.[5] The firm also experiences ordinary income in the form of recaptured depreciation of $52,000 ($100,000 − $48,000). The taxes on the total gain of $62,000 are calculated as follows:

	Amount (1)	Rate (2)	Tax [(1) × (2)] (3)
Capital gain	$10,000	.40	$ 4,000
Recaptured depreciation	52,000	.40	20,800
Totals	$62,000		$24,800

These taxes should be used in calculating the initial investment in the new asset, using the format in Table 14.3. In effect, they raise the amount of the firm's initial investment in the new asset by reducing the proceeds from the sale of the old asset.

The sale of the asset for more than its book value but less than its initial purchase price   If Kontra sells the old asset for $70,000, which is less than its original purchase price but more than its book value, there is no capital gain. However, the firm still experiences a gain in the form of recaptured depreciation of $22,000 ($70,000 − $48,000), which is taxed as ordinary income. Since the firm is assumed to be in the 40 percent tax bracket, the taxes on the $22,000 gain are $8,800. This $8,800 in taxes should be used in calculating the initial investment in the new asset.

The sale of the asset for its book value   If the asset is sold for $48,000, which is its book value, the firm breaks even. Since *no tax results from selling an asset for its book value,* there is no effect on the initial investment in the new asset.

The sale of the asset for less than its book value   If Kontra sells the asset for $30,000, an amount less than its book value, it experiences a loss of $18,000 ($48,000 − $30,000). If this is a depreciable asset used in the business, the loss may be used to offset ordinary operating income. If the asset is *not* depreciable or *not* used in the business, the loss can be used only to offset capital gains. In both cases the loss will save the firm $7,200 ($18,000 × .40) in taxes. In either case, if current operating earnings or capital gains are not sufficient to offset the loss, the firm may be able to apply these losses to prior years' taxes or future years' taxes.[6] ■

---

[5] Although the *Tax Reform Act of 1986* requires corporate capital gains to be treated as ordinary income, the structure for corporate capital gains is retained under the law in order to facilitate a rate differential in the likely event of future tax revisions. Therefore, this distinction is made throughout the text discussions.

[6] The tax law provides detailed procedures for tax loss *carrybacks* and *carryforwards*. Coverage of such procedures is beyond the scope of this text, and they are therefore ignored in subsequent discussions.

Calculating the Initial Investment

It should be clear that a variety of tax and other considerations enter into the initial investment calculation. The following example illustrates how the basic variables described in the preceding discussion are used to calculate the initial investment according to the format in Table 14.3.

EXAMPLE

The Norman Company is trying to determine the initial investment required to replace an old machine with a new, much more sophisticated model. The proposed machine's purchase price is $380,000, and an additional $20,000 will be required to install it. It will be depreciated under ACRS using a five-year recovery period. The old machine was purchased three years ago at a cost of $240,000 and was being depreciated under ACRS using a five-year recovery period. The firm has found a buyer willing to pay $280,000 for the old machine and remove it at the buyer's own expense. Both ordinary income and capital gains are taxed at a rate of 40 percent.

The only component of the initial investment required by the proposed purchase that is difficult to obtain is taxes. Since the firm is planning to sell the old machine for $40,000 more than its purchase price, it will realize a *capital gain of $40,000*. The book value of the old machine can be found using the depreciation percentages from Table 3.6 (page 54) of 20 percent, 32 percent, and 19 percent for years 1 through 3, respectively. The resulting book value is $69,600 ($240,000 − [(.20 + .32 + .19) × $240,000]). An *ordinary gain of $170,400* ($240,000 − $69,600) in recaptured depreciation is also realized on the sale. The total taxes on the gain are $84,160 [($40,000 + $170,400) × .40]. Substituting these taxes along with the purchase price and installation cost of the new machine and the proceeds from the sale of the old machine into the format in Table 14.3 results in an initial investment of $204,160. This represents the net cash outflow required at time zero:

Cost of new machine	$380,000 ⎱ Depreciable
+Installation costs	20,000 ⎰ outlay
−Proceeds from sale of old machine	280,000
+Taxes on sale of old machine	84,160
Initial investment	$204,160

AMOCO'S CAPITAL BUDGET CUT TO 3.5 BILLION!

Amoco Corp. [in February 1986], citing the "severe drop in world crude oil prices," reduced its 1986 capital and exploration budget about 30% to $3.5 billion from $5 billion.

Amoco said the revised expenditure level is subject to further adjustments as developments in the oil industry dictate.

The collapse of world oil prices has led other major oil concerns, including Los Angeles-based Atlantic Richfield Co. and Bartlesville, Okla.-based Phillips Petroleum Co., to slash 1986 capital spending budgets. Arco, which two weeks ago cut its spending to $2 billion from $3 billion, said the move would preserve operating and financial flexibility. Last week Phillips cut its spending 30% to $1 billion.

In initially setting its 1986 budget at $5 billion, which was below the $5.4 billion budget in 1985, Amoco had cited "uncertainties in 1986 in the oil and gas business."

Amoco said the budget cuts will come mostly from exploration and production spending in U.S. and foreign programs. But Amoco said exploration and production activities will continue to be its major focus, adding that it didn't plan other cost-cutting measures.

About 80% of Amoco's original budget was designated for world-wide exploration and production activity.

An Amoco spokesman said various projects planned for 1986 are being reevaluated, but added that the budget's percentage breakdown hasn't been determined. Amoco wouldn't elaborate further regarding its decision.

As reported, the company had expected to spend about $150 million in 1986 for exploration and production in the Gulf of Mexico, a drop of about 25% from about $200 million in 1985. An even larger drop was expected for the company's spending in Alaska.

Source: Carlee R. Scott, "Amoco Reduces '86 Outlays 30% to $3.5 Billion," *The Wall Street Journal*, February 26, 1986, p. 5. Reprinted by permission of *The Wall Street Journal.* © Dow Jones & Company, Inc. 1986. All rights reserved.

◼ FINDING THE OPERATING CASH INFLOWS

The benefits expected from a capital expenditure are measured by its *operating cash inflows,* which are *incremental after-tax cash inflows.* In this section we use the income statement format to develop clear definitions of the terms *after-tax, cash inflows,* and *incremental.*

Interpreting the Term *After-Tax*

Benefits expected to result from proposed capital expenditures must be measured on an after-tax basis, since the firm will not have the use of any benefits until it has satisfied the government's tax claims. These claims depend on the firm's taxable income, so the deduction of taxes *prior to* making comparisons between proposed investments is necessary for consistency. Consistency is required in evaluating capital expenditure alternatives since the intention is to compare like benefits.

Interpreting the Term *Cash Inflows*

All benefits expected from a proposed project must be measured on a cash flow basis. Cash inflows represent dollars that can be spent, not merely "accounting profits," which are not necessarily available for paying the firm's bills. A simple technique for converting after-tax net profits into operating cash inflows was illustrated in Chapter 3. The basic calculation requires adding any *noncash charges* deducted as expenses on the firm's income statement back to net profits after taxes. Probably the most common noncash charge found on income statements is depreciation. It is the only noncash charge that will be considered in this section. The following example shows how after-tax operating cash inflows can be calculated for a present and a proposed project.

EXAMPLE

The Norman Company's estimates of its revenues and expenses (excluding depreciation), with and without the proposed capital expenditure described in the preceding example, are given in Table 14.5. Note that both the expected usable life of the proposed machine and the remaining usable life of the present machine is five years. The amount to be depreciated with the proposed machine is calculated by summing the purchase price of $380,000 and the installation costs of $20,000. Since the machine is to be depreciated under ACRS using a five-year recovery period, 20, 32, 19, 12, 12, and 5 percent would be recovered in years 1 through 6, respectively (see Chapter 3 and Table 3.6 on page 54 for more detail).[7] The resulting depreciation on this machine for each

---

[7] As noted in Chapter 3, it takes $n + 1$ years to depreciate an n-year class asset under the provisions of the *Tax Reform Act of 1986*. Therefore, ACRS percentages are given for each of six years for use in depreciating an asset with a five-year recovery period.

of the six years, as well as the remaining three years of depreciation on the old machine, are calculated in Table 14.6.[8]

The operating cash inflows in each year can be calculated using the following income statement format:

Revenue
−Expenses (excluding depreciation)
Profits before depreciation and taxes
−Depreciation
Net profits before taxes
−Taxes
Net profits after taxes
+Depreciation
Operating cash inflows

Substituting the data from Tables 14.5 and 14.6 into this format and assuming a 40 percent tax rate, Table 14.7 demonstrates the

TABLE 14.5 Norman Company's Revenue and Expenses (Excluding Depreciation) for Proposed and Present Machines

Year	Revenue (1)	Expenses (excl. depr.) (2)
With proposed machine		
1	$2,520,000	$2,300,000
2	2,520,000	2,300,000
3	2,520,000	2,300,000
4	2,520,000	2,300,000
5	2,520,000	2,300,000
With present machine		
1	$2,200,000	$1,990,000
2	2,300,000	2,110,000
3	2,400,000	2,230,000
4	2,400,000	2,250,000
5	2,250,000	2,120,000

[8] It is important to recognize that while both machines will provide five years of use, the proposed new machine will be depreciated over the six-year period, while the present machine—as noted in the preceding example—has been depreciated over three years and therefore has only its final three years (years 4, 5, and 6) of depreciation (i.e., 12, 12, and 5 percent, respectively, under ACRS) remaining.

calculation of operating cash inflows for each year for both the proposed and the present machine. It can be seen that since the proposed machine will be depreciated over six years, the analysis must be performed over the six-year period in order to fully capture the tax effect of depreciation in year 6 for the new asset. The resulting operating cash inflows are shown in column 8 of the table. The year 6 cash inflow for the proposed machine of $8,000 results from the tax benefit of the year 6 depreciation deduction. ■

Interpreting the Term *Incremental*

The final step in estimating the operating cash inflows to be used in evaluating a proposed project is to calculate the *incremental,* or *relevant,* cash inflows. Incremental operating cash inflows are needed, since our concern is *only* with how much more or less operating cash will flow into the firm as a result of the proposed project.

TABLE 14.6 Depreciation Expense for Proposed and Present Machines for the Norman Company

Year	Cost (1)	Applicable ACRS depreciation percentages (from Table 3.6) (2)	Depreciation [(1) × (2)] (3)
With proposed machine			
1	$400,000	20%	$ 80,000
2	400,000	32	128,000
3	400,000	19	76,000
4	400,000	12	48,000
5	400,000	12	48,000
6	400,000	5	20,000
Totals		100%	$400,000
With present machine			
1	$240,000	12% (year 4 depreciation)	$ 28,800
2	240,000	12 (year 5 depreciation)	28,800
3	240,000	5 (year 6 depreciation)	12,000
4	} Since the present machine is at the end of the third year of its cost recovery at the time the analysis is performed, it has only the final three years of depreciation (years 4, 5, and 6) yet applicable.		0
5			0
6			0
		Total	$ 69,600[a]

[a] The total of $69,600 represents the book value of the present machine at the end of the third year, which was calculated in the preceding example.

TABLE 14.7 Calculation of Operating Cash Inflows for Norman Company's Proposed and Present Machines

Year	Revenue[a] (1)	Expenses (excl. depr.)[b] (2)	Profits before depreciation and taxes [(1) − (2)] (3)	Depreciation[c] (4)	Net profits before taxes [(3) − (4)] (5)	Taxes [.40 × (5)] (6)	Net profits after taxes [(5) − (6)] (7)	Operating cash inflows [(4) + (7)] (8)
With proposed machine								
1	$2,520,000	$2,300,000	$220,000	$ 80,000	$140,000	$56,000	$ 84,000	$164,000
2	2,520,000	2,300,000	220,000	128,000	92,000	36,800	55,200	183,200
3	2,520,000	2,300,000	220,000	76,000	144,000	57,600	86,400	162,400
4	2,520,000	2,300,000	220,000	48,000	172,000	68,800	103,200	151,200
5	2,520,000	2,300,000	220,000	48,000	172,000	68,800	103,200	151,200
6	0	0	0	20,000	−20,000	−8,000	−12,000	8,000
With present machine								
1	$2,200,000	$1,990,000	$210,000	$ 28,800	$181,200	$72,480	$108,720	$137,520
2	2,300,000	2,110,000	190,000	28,800	161,200	64,480	96,720	125,520
3	2,400,000	2,230,000	170,000	12,000	158,000	63,200	94,800	106,800
4	2,400,000	2,250,000	150,000	0	150,000	60,000	90,000	90,000
5	2,250,000	2,120,000	130,000	0	130,000	52,000	78,000	78,000
6	0	0	0	0	0	0	0	0

[a] From column 1 of Table 14.5.

[b] From column 2 of Table 14.5.

[c] From column 3 of Table 14.6.

435

EXAMPLE

Table 14.8 demonstrates the calculation of Norman Company's incremental (relevant) operating cash inflows for each year. The estimates of operating cash inflows developed in Table 14.7 are given in columns 1 and 2. The column 2 values represent the amount of operating cash inflows the Norman Company will receive if it does not replace the present machine. If the proposed machine replaces the present machine, the firm's operating cash inflows for each year will be those shown in column 1. Subtracting the operating cash inflows with the present machine from the operating cash inflows with the proposed machine in each year results in the incremental operating cash inflows for each year in column 3 of Table 14.8. These are the relevant inflows to be considered in evaluating the benefits of making a capital expenditure for the proposed machine. ■

SUMMARIZING THE RELEVANT CASH FLOWS

The two cash flow components—the initial investment and the subsequent operating cash inflows—together represent a project's *relevant cash flows*. These cash flows can be viewed as the incremental, after-tax cash flows attributable to the proposed project; they represent, in a cash flow sense, how much better or worse off the firm will be if it chooses to implement the proposal.

TABLE 14.8 Incremental (Relevant) Operating Cash Inflows for the Norman Company

	OPERATING CASH INFLOWS		
Year	Proposed machine[a] (1)	Present machine[a] (2)	Incremental (relevant) [(1) − (2)] (3)
1	$164,000	$137,520	$26,480
2	183,200	125,520	57,680
3	162,400	106,800	55,600
4	151,200	90,000	61,200
5	151,200	78,000	73,200
6	8,000	0	8,000

[a] From column 8 of Table 14.7.

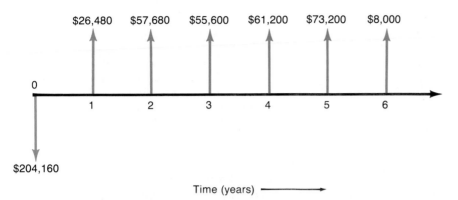

FIGURE 14.4 The Norman Company's Relevant Cash Flows with the Proposed Machine

The relevant cash flows for the Norman Company's proposed machine investment display a conventional pattern with an initial investment of $204,160 followed by operating cash inflows of $26,480, $57,680, $55,600, $61,200, $73,200, and $8,000 in years 1 through 6, respectively.

EXAMPLE

The relevant cash flows for the Norman Company's proposed replacement expenditure can now be presented. They are shown graphically in Figure 14.4. As the figure shows, they follow a conventional pattern (an initial outlay followed by a series of inflows). Techniques for analyzing this type of pattern to determine whether to undertake a proposed capital investment are discussed in Chapter 15. ▪

SUMMARY

● Capital budgeting is the process used to evaluate and select capital expenditures consistent with the goal of owner wealth maximization. Capital expenditures are long-term investments made to expand, replace, or renew fixed assets or to obtain some other less tangible benefit.

● The capital budgeting process contains five distinct but interrelated steps: proposal generation, review and analysis, decision making, implementation, and follow-up.

● Capital expenditure proposals may be independent or mutually exclusive. Most firms have only limited funds for capital investments and must ration them among carefully selected projects. To make investment decisions when proposals are mutually exclusive or when capital must be rationed, projects must be ranked; otherwise accept-reject decisions must be made.

● Conventional cash flow patterns consist of an initial outflow followed by a series of inflows; any other pattern is nonconventional. These patterns can be either annuities or mixed streams.

● The relevant cash flows necessary for making capital budgeting decisions are the initial investment and the operating cash inflows associated with a given proposal. For replacement decisions, these flows are found by determining the difference between the cash flows associated with the new asset and the old asset. Expansion decisions are viewed as replacement decisions in which all cash flows from the old asset are zero.

● The initial investment is the initial outlay required, taking into account the cost (including installation) of the new asset, proceeds from the sale of the old asset, and taxes on the sale of the old asset.

● The book value of an asset is its strict accounting value, which is used to determine what, if any, taxes are owed as a result of selling an asset. Any of three forms of taxable income—capital gain, recaptured depreciation, or a loss—can result from sale of an asset, depending upon whether it is sold (1) for more than its initial purchase price; (2) for more than book value but less than initially paid; (3) for book value; or (4) for less than book value.

● Incremental after-tax operating cash inflows are the additional cash flows received as a result of implementing a proposal. The income statement format can be conveniently used to estimate these "relevant" operating cash inflows.

QUESTIONS

14-1 What is *capital budgeting?* How do capital expenditures relate to the capital budgeting process? Do all capital expenditures involve fixed assets? Explain.

14-2 What are the basic motives described in the chapter for making capital expenditures? Discuss, compare, and contrast them.

14-3 Briefly describe each of the steps—proposal generation, review and analysis, decision making, implementation, and follow-up—involved in the capital budgeting process.

14-4 Define and differentiate between each of the following sets of capital budgeting terms.
  a Independent versus mutually exclusive projects
  b Unlimited funds versus capital rationing
  c Accept-reject versus ranking approach
  d Conventional versus nonconventional cash flows
  e Annuity versus mixed stream cash flows

14-5 Why is it important to evaluate capital budgeting projects on the basis of *incremental after-tax cash flows?* How can expansion decisions be treated as replacement decisions? Explain.

14-6 Describe each of the following components of the initial investment and explain how the initial investment is calculated using them.
  a Cost of new asset
  b Installation costs

c Proceeds from sale of old asset

d Taxes on sale of old asset

14-7 What is the *book value* of an asset, and how is it calculated? Describe the three key types of taxable income and their associated tax treatments.

14-8 What four tax situations may result from the sale of an asset that is being replaced? Describe the tax treatment in each situation.

14-9 Referring to the framework for calculating initial investment given in this chapter, explain how a firm would determine the *depreciable value* of the new asset.

14-10 How is the *Accelerated Cost Recovery System (ACRS)* used to depreciate an asset? How does depreciation enter into the operating cash inflow calculation?

14-11 Given the revenues, expenses (excluding depreciation), and depreciation associated with a present asset and a proposed replacement for it, how would the incremental (relevant) operating cash inflows associated with the decision be calculated?

14-12 Diagram and describe the two elements representing the *relevant cash flows* for a conventional capital budgeting project.

PROBLEMS

14-1 **(Classification of Expenditures)** Given the following list of outlays, indicate whether each would normally be considered a capital or a current expenditure. Explain your answers.

a An initial lease payment of $5,000 for electronic point-of-sale cash register systems.

b An outlay of $20,000 to purchase patent rights from the inventor.

c An outlay of $80,000 for a major research and development program.

d An $80,000 investment in a portfolio of marketable securities.

e A $300 outlay for an office machine.

f An outlay of $2,000 for a new machine tool.

g An outlay of $240,000 for a new building.

h An outlay of $1,000 for a marketing research report.

14-2 **(Basic Terminology)** A firm is considering the following three separate situations.

Situation A: Build either a small office building or a convenience store on a parcel of land located in a high-traffic area. Adequate funding is available, and both projects are known to be acceptable. The office building will require an initial investment of $620,000 and is expected to provide operating cash inflows of $40,000 per year for 20 years; the convenience store is expected to cost $500,000 and provide a growing stream of operating cash inflows over its 20-year-life. The initial operating cash inflow is $20,000 and will increase by 5 percent each year.

Situation B: Replace a machine with a new one requiring a $60,000 initial investment and providing operating cash inflows of $10,000 per year for the first five years. At the end of year 5, a machine overhaul costing $20,000 is required, and after it is completed, expected operating cash inflows are $10,000 in year 6, $7,000 in year 7, $4,000 in year 8, and $1,000 in year 9, at the end of which the machine will be scrapped.

   Situation C: Invest in any or all of the four machines whose relevant cash flows are given in the following table. The firm has $500,000 budgeted to fund these machines, all of which are known to be acceptable. Initial investment for each machine is $250,000.

	OPERATING CASH INFLOWS			
Year	Machine 1	Machine 2	Machine 3	Machine 4
1	$ 50,000	$70,000	$65,000	$90,000
2	70,000	70,000	65,000	80,000
3	90,000	70,000	80,000	70,000
4	−30,000	70,000	80,000	60,000
5	100,000	70,000	−20,000	50,000

For each situation or project, indicate

a Whether the *situation* is independent or mutually exclusive.

b Whether the availability of funds is unlimited or if capital rationing exists.

c Whether accept-reject or ranking decisions are required.

d Whether each *project's* cash flows are conventional or nonconventional.

e Whether each *project's* cash flow pattern is an annuity or mixed stream.

14-3 **(Expansion versus Replacement Cash Flows)** Nick Stamas, Inc. has estimated the cash flows over the five-year lives for two projects, A and B. These cash flows are summarized below:

	PROJECT	
	A	B
Initial investment	$40,000	$12,000[a]
Year	Operating cash inflows	
1	$10,000	$6,000
2	12,000	6,000
3	14,000	6,000
4	16,000	6,000
5	10,000	6,000

[a] After-tax cash inflows expected from liquidation.

a If project A were actually a *replacement* for project B and the $12,000 initial investment shown for B was the after-tax cash inflows expected from liquidating it, what would be the relevant cash flows for this replacement decision?

b How can an *expansion decision* such as project A be viewed as a special form of a replacement decision? Explain.

14-4 **(Relevant Cash Flow Pattern Fundamentals)** For each of the following projects, determine the *relevant cash flows*, classify the cash flow
pattern, and diagram the pattern.

    a A project requiring an initial investment of $120,000 that generates
annual operating cash inflows of $25,000 for the next 18 years. In each
of the 18 years, maintenance of the project will require a $5,000 cash
outflow.

    b A new machine having an installed cost of $85,000. Sale of the old
machine will yield $30,000 after taxes. Operating cash inflows gener-
ated by the replacement will amount to $20,000 in each year of a
six-year period.

    c An asset requiring an initial investment of $2 million that will yield
annual operating cash inflows of $300,000 for each of the next ten
years. Operating cash outlays will be $20,000 for each year except year
6, when an overhaul requiring an additional cash outlay of $500,000
will be required.

14-5 **(Book Value)** Find the book value for each of the assets below assuming that ACRS depreciation is being used. (Note: See Table 3.6 on page 54
for the applicable depreciation percentages.)

Asset	Installed cost	Recovery period	Elapsed time since purchase
A	$ 950,000	5 years	3 years
B	40,000	3 years	1 year
C	96,000	5 years	4 years
D	350,000	5 years	1 year
E	1,500,000	7 years	5 years

14-6 **(Book Value and Taxes on Sale of Assets)** Waters Manufacturing
purchased a new machine three years ago for $80,000. It is being depre-
ciated under ACRS with a five-year recovery period using the percentages given in Table 3.6 on page 54. Assume 40 percent ordinary and
capital gains tax rates.

    a What is the book value of the machine?

    b Calculate the firm's tax liability if it sells the machine for the following:
$100,000; $56,000; $23,200; $15,000.

14-7 **(Tax Calculations)** For each of the following cases, describe the various taxable components of the funds received through sale of the asset
and determine the total taxes resulting from the transaction. Assume 40
percent ordinary and capital gains tax rates. The asset was purchased for
$200,000 two years ago and is being depreciated under ACRS using a
five-year recovery period. (See Table 3.6 on page 54 for the applicable
depreciation percentages.)

    a The asset is sold for $220,000.

    b The asset is sold for $150,000.

    c The asset is sold for $105,600.

    d The asset is sold for $80,000.

14-8 ◼ (**Initial Investment—Basic Calculation**) M. Higgins, Inc., is considering the purchase of a new grading machine to replace the existing one. The existing machine was purchased three years ago at an installed cost of $20,000; it was being depreciated under ACRS using a five-year recovery period. (See Table 3.6 on page 54 for the applicable depreciation percentages.) The existing machine is expected to have a usable life of at least five more years. The new machine would cost $35,000 and require $5,000 in installation costs; it would be depreciated using a five-year recovery period under ACRS. The existing machine can currently be sold for $25,000 without incurring any removal costs. The firm pays 40 percent taxes on both ordinary income and capital gains. Calculate the *initial investment* associated with the proposed purchase of a new grading machine.

14-9 ◼ (**Initial Investment at Various Sale Prices**) Bolton Castings Corporation is considering replacement of one machine with another. The old machine was purchased three years ago for an installed cost of $10,000. The firm is depreciating the machine under ACRS using a five-year recovery period. (See Table 3.6 on page 54 for the applicable depreciation percentages.) The new machine costs $24,000 and requires $2,000 in installation costs. Assume the firm is subject to a 40 percent tax rate on both ordinary income and capital gains. In each of the following cases, calculate the initial investment for the replacement.
a Bolton Castings Corporation (BCC) sells the old machine for $11,000.
b BCC sells the old machine for $7,000.
c BCC sells the old machine for $2,900.
d BCC sells the old machine for $1,500.

14-10 (**Depreciation**) A firm is evaluating the acquisition of an asset that costs $64,000 and requires $4,000 in installation costs. If the firm depreciates the asset under ACRS using a five-year recovery period (see Table 3.6 on page 54 for the applicable depreciation percentages), determine the depreciation charge for each year.

14-11 (**Incremental Operating Cash Inflows**) A firm is considering renewing its equipment to meet increased demand for its product. The cost of equipment modifications will be $1.9 million plus $100,000 in installation costs. The firm will depreciate the equipment modifications under ACRS using a five-year recovery period. (See Table 3.6 on page 54 for the applicable depreciation percentages.) Additional sales revenue from the renewal should amount to $1.2 million per year, and additional operating expenses and other costs (excluding depreciation) will amount to 40 percent of the additional sales. The firm has an ordinary tax rate of 40 percent. (Note: Answer the following questions for each of the next *six* years.)
a What incremental earnings before depreciation and taxes will result from the renewal?
b What incremental earnings after taxes will result from the renewal?
c What incremental operating cash inflows will result from the renewal?

14-12 ◼ (**Incremental Operating Cash Inflows—Expense Reduction**) Tex-Tube Corporation is considering replacement of a machine. The replacement will reduce operating expenses (i.e., increase revenues) by $16,000 per year for each of the five years the new machine is expected to last. Although the old machine has zero book value, it can be used for five more years. The depreciable value of the new machine is $48,000; the firm will depreciate the machine under ACRS using a five-year recovery period (see Table 3.6 on page 54 for the applicable depreciation percentages) and is subject to a 40 percent tax rate on ordinary income. Estimate the incremental operating cash inflows generated by the replacement. (Note: Be sure to consider the depreciation in year 6.)

14-13   **(Incremental Operating Cash Inflows)**   The Fenton Tool Company has been considering purchasing a new lathe to replace a fully depreciated lathe that will last five more years. The new lathe is expected to have a five-year life and depreciation charges of $2,000 in year 1, $3,200 in year 2, $1,900 in year 3, $1,200 in both year 4 and year 5, and $500 in year 6. The firm estimates the revenues and expenses (excluding depreciation) for the new and the old lathe as shown in the following table. The firm has a 40 percent tax rate on ordinary income.

	NEW LATHE		OLD LATHE	
Year	Revenue	Expenses (excl. depr.)	Revenue	Expenses (excl. depr.)
1	$40,000	$30,000	$35,000	$25,000
2	41,000	30,000	35,000	25,000
3	42,000	30,000	35,000	25,000
4	43,000	30,000	35,000	25,000
5	44,000	30,000	35,000	25,000

a Calculate the operating cash inflows associated with each lathe. (Note: Be sure to consider the depreciation in year 6.)
b Calculate the incremental (relevant) operating cash inflows resulting from the proposed lathe replacement.
c Diagram the incremental operating cash inflows calculated in b.

14-14   **(Relevant Cash Flows)**   The Blake Company is considering replacing an existing piece of machinery with a more sophisticated machine. The old machine was purchased three years ago at a cost of $50,000, and this amount was being depreciated under ACRS using a five-year recovery period. The machine has five years of usable life remaining. The new machine being considered will cost $76,000 and requires $4,000 in installation costs. The new machine would be depreciated under ACRS using a five-year recovery period. The old machine can currently be sold for $55,000 without incurring any removal costs. The firm pays 40 percent taxes on both ordinary income and capital gains. The revenues and expenses (excluding depreciation) associated with the new and the old machine for the next five years are given in the table at the top of page 444. (Table 3.6 on page 54 contains the applicable ACRS depreciation percentages.)

		NEW MACHINE		OLD MACHINE	
Year	Revenue	Expenses (excl. depr.)	Revenue	Expenses (excl. depr.)
1	$750,000	$720,000	$674,000	$660,000
2	750,000	720,000	676,000	660,000
3	750,000	720,000	680,000	660,000
4	750,000	720,000	678,000	660,000
5	750,000	720,000	674,000	660,000

a Calculate the initial investment associated with replacement of the old machine by the new one.

b Determine the incremental operating cash inflows associated with the proposed replacement. (Note: Be sure to consider the depreciation in year 6.)

c Diagram the relevant cash flows found in **a** and **b** associated with the proposed replacement decision.

14-15 ■ **(Integrative—Determining Relevant Cash Flows)** A machine currently in use was originally purchased two years ago for $40,000. The machine is being depreciated under ACRS using a five-year recovery period; it has three years of usable life remaining. The current machine can be sold today to net $42,000. A new machine, using a three-year ACRS recovery period, can be purchased at a price of $140,000. It will require $10,000 to install and has a three-year usable life. *Profits before depreciation and taxes* are expected to be $70,000 for each of the next 3 years with the old machine and $120,000 in the first year and $130,000 in the second and third years with the new machine. Both ordinary corporate income and capital gains are subject to a 40 percent tax. (Table 3.6 on page 54 contains the applicable ACRS depreciation percentages.)

a Determine the initial investment associated with the proposed replacement decision.

b Calculate the incremental operating cash inflows for years 1 to 4 associated with the proposed replacement. (Note: Only depreciation cash flows must be considered in year 4.)

c Diagram the relevant cash flows found in **a** and **b** associated with the proposed replacement decision.

14-16 ■ **(Integrative—Determining Relevant Cash Flows)** The Sentry Company is contemplating the purchase of a new high-speed widget grinder to replace the existing grinder. The existing grinder was purchased two years ago at an installed cost of $60,000; it was being depreciated under ACRS using a five-year recovery period. The existing grinder is expected to have a usable life of five more years. The new grinder would cost $105,000 and require $5,000 in installation costs; it has a five-year usable life and would be depreciated under ACRS using a five-year recovery period. The existing grinder can currently be sold for $70,000 without incurring any removal costs. The firm pays 40 percent taxes on both ordinary income and capital gains. The estimated *profits* *before depreciation and taxes* over the five years for both the new and existing grinder are given below. (Table 3.6 on page 54 contains the applicable ACRS depreciation percentages.)

<table>
<tr><th colspan="3" align="center">PROFITS BEFORE
DEPRECIATION AND TAXES</th></tr>
<tr><th>Year</th><th>New grinder</th><th>Existing grinder</th></tr>
<tr><td>1</td><td>$43,000</td><td>$26,000</td></tr>
<tr><td>2</td><td>43,000</td><td>24,000</td></tr>
<tr><td>3</td><td>43,000</td><td>22,000</td></tr>
<tr><td>4</td><td>43,000</td><td>20,000</td></tr>
<tr><td>5</td><td>43,000</td><td>18,000</td></tr>
</table>

a Calculate the initial investment associated with the replacement of the existing grinder by the new one.

b Determine the incremental operating cash inflows associated with the proposed grinder replacement. (Note: Be sure to consider the depreciation in year 6.)

c Diagram the relevant cash flows associated with the proposed grinder replacement decision.

14-17 ■ **(Integrative — Determining Relevant Cash Flows)** East Coast Drydock is considering replacement of an existing hoist with one of two newer, more efficient pieces of equipment. The existing hoist is three years old, cost $32,000, and is being depreciated under ACRS using a five-year recovery period. Although the existing hoist has only three years (years 4, 5, and 6) of depreciation remaining under ACRS, it has a remaining usable life of five years. Hoist A, one of the two possible replacement hoists, costs $40,000 to purchase and $8,000 to install. It has a five-year usable life and will be depreciated under ACRS using a five-year recovery period. The other hoist, B, costs $54,000 to purchase and $6,000 to install. It also has a five-year usable life and it will be depreciated under ACRS using a five-year recovery period.

The projected *profits before depreciation and taxes* with each alternative hoist and the existing hoist are given in the following table. The

<table>
<tr><th colspan="4" align="center">PROFITS BEFORE
DEPRECIATION AND TAXES</th></tr>
<tr><th>Year</th><th>With
hoist A</th><th>With
hoist B</th><th>With
existing hoist</th></tr>
<tr><td>1</td><td>$21,000</td><td>$22,000</td><td>$14,000</td></tr>
<tr><td>2</td><td>21,000</td><td>24,000</td><td>14,000</td></tr>
<tr><td>3</td><td>21,000</td><td>26,000</td><td>14,000</td></tr>
<tr><td>4</td><td>21,000</td><td>26,000</td><td>14,000</td></tr>
<tr><td>5</td><td>21,000</td><td>26,000</td><td>14,000</td></tr>
</table>

existing hoist can currently be sold for $18,000 and will not incur any removal costs. The firm is subject to a 40 percent tax rate on both ordinary income and capital gains. (Table 3.6 on page 54 contains the applicable ACRS depreciation percentages.)

a Calculate the initial investment associated with each alternative.

b Calculate the incremental operating cash inflows associated with each alternative. (Note: Be sure to consider the depreciation in year 6.)

c Diagram the relevant cash flows associated with each alternative.

14-18 **(Integrative — Determining Relevant Cash Flows)** Doormaster Products Company expects its *net profits after taxes* for the next five years to be as shown in the following table.

Year	Net profits after taxes
1	$100,000
2	150,000
3	200,000
4	250,000
5	320,000

Consideration is currently being given to the renewal of Doormaster's *only* depreciable asset, a machine originally costing $30,000, having a current book value of zero, and that can now be sold for $20,000. The firm is subject to a 40 percent tax on both ordinary income and capital gains. The company uses ACRS depreciation. (See Table 3.6 on page 54 for the applicable depreciation percentages.)

Alternative 1: Renew the existing machine at a total depreciable cost of $90,000. The renewed machine would have a five-year usable life and be depreciated under ACRS using a five-year recovery period. Renewing the machine would allow the firm to achieve the following projected *profits before depreciation and taxes:*

Year	Profits before depreciation and taxes
1	$198,500
2	290,800
3	381,900
4	481,900
5	581,900

Alternative 2: Replace the existing machine with a new machine costing $100,000 and requiring installation costs of $10,000. The new machine would have a five-year usable life and be depreciated under ACRS

using a five-year recovery period. The firm's projected *profits before depreciation and taxes*, if it acquires the machine, are as follows:

Year	Profits before depreciation and taxes
1	$235,500
2	335,200
3	385,100
4	435,100
5	551,100

a Calculate the initial investment associated with each alternative.
b Calculate the incremental operating cash inflows associated with each alternative. (Note: Be sure to consider the depreciation in year 6.)
c Diagram the relevant cash flows associated with each alternative.

15

CAPITAL BUDGETING TECHNIQUES: CERTAINTY AND RISK

After studying this chapter, you should be able to:

● Calculate, interpret, and evaluate the two most popular unsophisticated capital budgeting techniques—average rate of return and payback period.

● Apply the sophisticated capital budgeting techniques — net present value *(NPV)*, profitability index *(PI)*, and internal rate of return *(IRR)*—to relevant cash flows to choose acceptable as well as preferred capital expenditures.

● Discuss whether the net present value or the internal rate of return technique is better, and describe popular techniques for choosing projects under capital rationing.

● Recognize the basic approaches—sensitivity analysis, statistical approaches, decision trees, and simulation —for dealing with project risk.

● Understand the calculation and practical aspects of the two basic risk-adjustment techniques—certainty equivalents *(CEs)* and risk-adjusted discount rates *(RADRs)*.

The cash flows developed in Chapter 14 must be analyzed to assess whether a project is acceptable or to rank projects. A number of techniques are available for performing such analyses. The preferred approaches integrate time value procedures (Chapter 11), risk, return, and valuation concepts (Chapter 12), and the cost of capital (Chapter 13) in order to select capital expenditures that are consistent with achievement of the firm's goals. The focus in this chapter is on the use of these techniques to evaluate capital expenditure proposals for decision-making purposes. Initially it is assumed that the firm has unlimited funds and that all projects' cash flows have the same level of risk. Since very few decisions are actually made under these conditions, it is important to understand the techniques for dealing with capital rationing and risk. The discussion begins with a look at both unsophisticated and sophisticated capital budgeting techniques.

◼ UNSOPHISTICATED CAPITAL BUDGETING TECHNIQUES

unsophisticated capital budgeting techniques Capital budgeting methods that do *not* explicitly consider the time value of money by discounting cash flows to find present value.

Unsophisticated capital budgeting techniques do *not* explicitly consider the time value of money by discounting cash flows to find present value. There are two basic unsophisticated techniques for determining the acceptability of capital expenditure alternatives. One is to calculate the average rate of return, and the other is to find the payback period.

We shall use the same basic problem to illustrate the application of all the techniques described in this chapter. The problem concerns the Blano Company, which is currently contemplating two projects—project A, which requires an initial investment of $42,000, and project B, which requires an initial investment of $45,000. The projected profits after taxes and incremental cash inflows associated with each of these projects for each year of their respective five-year lives[1] are presented in Table 15.1. The average profits after taxes and average cash inflows for each project are also indicated in the table. It can be seen that the projects exhibit conventional cash flow patterns, which are assumed throughout the text.

Average Rate of Return

Find the average rate of return is a popular approach for evaluating proposed capital expenditures. Its appeal stems from the fact that the average rate of return is typically calculated from accounting data (profits after taxes). The most common definition of the **average rate of**

---

[1] For simplification, these five-year-lived projects with five years of cash inflows are used throughout this chapter. Projects with usable lives equal to the number of years of cash inflows are also included in the end-of-chapter problems. It is important to recall from Chapter 14 that under the *Tax Reform Act of 1986* ACRS depreciation results in $n + 1$ years of depreciation for an n-year class asset. This means that in actual practice projects will typically have at least one year of cash flow beyond their recovery period.

TABLE 15.1 Capital Expenditure Data for the Blano Company

Initial investment	Project A		Project B	
	$42,000		$45,000	
Year	Profits after taxes	Cash inflows	Profits after taxes	Cash inflows
1	$7,700	$14,000	$21,250	$28,000
2	4,760	14,000	2,100	12,000
3	5,180	14,000	550	10,000
4	5,180	14,000	550	10,000
5	5,180	14,000	550	10,000
Averages	$5,600	$14,000	$ 5,000	$14,000

return for a given project is as follows:

$$\text{Average rate of return} = \frac{\text{average profits after taxes}}{\text{average investment}} \qquad (15.1)$$

Average profits after taxes are found by adding up the after-tax profits expected over the project's total life and dividing the total by the number of years of life. In the case of an annuity, the average after-tax profits are equal to any year's profits. The **average investment** is found by dividing the initial investment by 2. The average rate of return can be interpreted as the annual accounting rate of return expected on the average investment.

THE DECISION CRITERION The decision criterion when average rate of return is used to make accept-reject decisions is as follows: *If the average rate of return ≥ minimum acceptable average rate of return, accept the project; otherwise, reject the project.*

average rate of return For a given project, the average profits after taxes divided by the firm's average investment. Can be interpreted as the annual accounting rate of return expected on the average investment.

average profits after taxes The total after-tax profits expected over the project's life divided by the number of years of the project's life.

average investment The initial investment divided by 2.

EXAMPLE

The average profits expected for projects A and B (given in Table 15.1) are $5,600 and $5,000, respectively. The average investment for project A is $21,000 ($42,000 ÷ 2) and for project B is $22,500 ($45,000 ÷ 2). Dividing the average profits after taxes by the average investment results in the average rate of return for each project:

$$\text{Project A: } \frac{\$\,5,600}{\$21,000} = 26.67\%$$

$$\text{Project B: } \frac{\$\,5,000}{\$22,500} = 22.22\%$$

If Blano's minimum acceptable average rate of return is 24 percent, then project A would be accepted and project B rejected. If the minimum return is 28 percent, both projects would be rejected. If the projects were being ranked for profitability, project A would be preferred over project B because it has a higher average rate of return (26.67% versus 22.22%). ■

PROS AND CONS OF THE AVERAGE RATE OF RETURN The most favorable aspect of using the average rate of return to evaluate projects is its ease of calculation. The only input required is projected profit, a figure that should be easily obtainable. There are three major weaknesses of this approach, however. The key conceptual weakness is the inability to specify the appropriate average rate of return in light of the wealth maximization goal. The second weakness stems from the use of accounting profits rather than cash flow as a measure of return. (This weakness can be overcome by using average cash inflows in the numerator in Equation 15.1.) The third major weakness is that this method ignores the time factor in the value of money. The indifference to the time factor can be illustrated by the following example.

EXAMPLE

Each of the three projects for which data are given in Table 15.2 has an average rate of return of 40 percent. Although the average rates of return are the same for all three projects, the financial manager would *not* be indifferent to them; he or she would prefer project Z to project Y and project Y to project X because project Z has the most favorable profit flow pattern, project Y has the next most favorable flow pattern, and project X has the least attractive flow pattern. ■

TABLE 15.2 Calculation of the Average Rate of Return for Three Alternative Capital Expenditure Projects

	Project X	Project Y	Project Z
(1) Initial investment	$20,000	$20,000	$20,000
(2) Average investment [(1) ÷ 2]	$10,000	$10,000	$10,000
Year	**Profits after taxes**		
1	$2,000	$4,000	$6,000
2	3,000	4,000	5,000
3	4,000	4,000	4,000
4	5,000	4,000	3,000
5	6,000	4,000	2,000
(3) Average profits after taxes	$4,000	$4,000	$4,000
(4) Average rate of return [(3) ÷ (2)]	40%	40%	40%

Payback Period

Payback periods are another commonly used criterion for evaluating proposed investments. The **payback period** is the exact amount of time required for the firm to recover its initial investment as calculated from *cash inflows*. In the case of an *annuity* the payback period can be found by dividing the initial investment by the annual cash inflow, whereas for a *mixed stream* the yearly cash inflows must be accumulated until the initial investment is recovered.

payback period The exact amount of time required for the firm to recover its initial investment as calculated from *cash inflows*.

THE DECISION CRITERION   The decision criterion when payback is used to make accept-reject decisions is as follows: *If the payback period ≤ maximum acceptable payback period, accept the project; otherwise, reject the project.*

EXAMPLE

The data for Blano Company's projects A and B presented in Table 15.1 can be used to demonstrate the calculation of the payback period. For project A, which is an annuity, the payback period is 3.00 years ($42,000 initial investment ÷ $14,000 annual cash inflow). Since project B generates a mixed stream of cash inflows, the calculation of the payback period is not quite as clear-cut. In year 1, the firm will recover $28,000 of its $45,000 initial investment. At the end of year 2, $40,000 ($28,000 from year 1 plus $12,000 from year 2) will be recovered. At the end of year 3, $50,000 ($40,000 from years 1 and 2 plus $10,000 from year 3) will be recovered. Since the amount received by the end of year 3 is greater than the initial investment of $45,000, the payback period is somewhere between two and three years. Only $5,000 ($45,000 − $40,000) must be recovered during year 3. Actually, $10,000 is recovered, but only 50 percent of this cash inflow ($5,000 ÷ $10,000) is needed to complete the payback of the initial $45,000. The payback period for project B is therefore 2.50 years (2 years plus 50 percent of year 3).

   If Blano's maximum acceptable payback period is 2.75 years, project A would be rejected and project B would be accepted. If the maximum payback were 2.25 years, both projects would be rejected. If the projects were being ranked, project B would be preferred over project A since it has a shorter payback period (2.50 years versus 3.00 years). ■

PROS AND CONS OF PAYBACK PERIODS   The payback period is a more accurate measure than the average rate of return because it considers cash flows rather than accounting profits. The payback period is also a superior measure (compared to the average rate of return) in that it gives *some* implicit consideration to the timing of cash flows and therefore of the time value of money. A final reason many firms use the payback period as a decision criterion or as a supplement to sophisticated decision techniques is that it is a measure of *risk exposure*. The shorter the payback period the less exposure, and vice versa. The major weakness of payback is that, like the average rate of return, this method cannot specify the appropriate payback period in light of the wealth maximization goal. A second weakness is that this approach fails to take *fully* into account the time factor in the value of money; by measuring how quickly the firm recovers its initial investment, it only implicitly considers the timing of cash flows. A third weakness is the failure to recognize cash flows that occur *after* the payback period. This weakness can be illustrated by an example.

EXAMPLE

Data for two investment opportunities — X and Y — are given in Table 15.3. The payback period for project X is two years; for project Y it is three years. Strict adherence to the payback approach suggests that project X is preferable to project Y. However, if we look beyond the payback period, we see that project X returns only an additional $1,200 ($1,000 in year 3, $100 in year 4, and $100 in year 5), while project Y returns an additional $7,000 ($4,000 in year 4 and $3,000 in year 5). Based on this information, it appears that project Y is preferable to X. The payback approach ignores the cash inflows in years 3, 4, and 5 for project X and in years 4 and 5 for project Y. ■

■ SOPHISTICATED CAPITAL BUDGETING TECHNIQUES

sophisticated capital budgeting techniques
Capital budgeting methods that give explicit consideration to the time value of money, including net present value, the profitability index, and the internal rate of return.

Sophisticated capital budgeting techniques give explicit consideration to the time value of money. These techniques include net present

TABLE 15.3 Calculation of the Payback Period for Two Alternative Investment Projects

	Project X	Project Y
Initial investment	$10,000	$10,000
Year	Cash inflows	
1	$5,000	$3,000
2	5,000	4,000
3	1,000	3,000
4	100	4,000
5	100	3,000
Payback period	2 years	3 years

TIMOTHY L. TABOR: FINANCIAL WHIZ KID

Timothy L. Tabor's friends say he is a financial whiz kid who thrives on work, risk, controversy and making money. The 32-year-old Mr. Tabor is likely to find all four in his new job as head of Chemical Bank's stock-trading unit that will specialize in takeover speculation.

Although Chemical has declined to comment on the recently formed unit, banking sources expect Mr. Tabor's annual compensation to top that of Chairman Walter Shipley, possibly by a large margin. In 1984, Mr. Shipley earned $806,338.

A former Rhodes Scholar and class valedictorian at the University of Oklahoma, Mr. Tabor was wooed away from Kidder, Peabody & Co., where he was second in command of the securities firm's merger arbitrage unit. A source familiar with the Kidder operation said, "I don't know how much of its success was due to Tim or to the market, but it certainly did very well." Mr. Tabor joined Kidder in 1981 as director of corporate planning, but two years later moved to arbitrage, where he developed a computerized trading program.

"That was his idea of a great job," says Karen M. Schimpf, a former colleague of Mr. Tabor's at the accounting firm of Peat, Marwick, Mitchell & Co., where he worked for six years before joining Kidder. "He had the notion of arbitrage as a trench-coated spy-film type of thing, phoning in his trades from the waterfront," she says. "He said he wanted to be doing deals from a pay telephone at the end of a dock."

Mr. Tabor, who declined to be interviewed for this article, posted one of the highest scores in the country the year he took the certified public accountant exam, friends say. By often working around the clock several days in a row, Mr. Tabor set a Peat Marwick record for most hours billed in a year — 3,200.

Mr. Tabor's capacity for work showed up even earlier in life. While in high school in Oklahoma City, he worked at a drive-in restaurant and during summer vacations criss-crossed the Southwest selling women's hose.

A stringy six-footer, Mr. Tabor seemed drawn to risk and controversy at an early age. "He was a daredevil," says Libby Keating, a stepsister who lives in Edmond, Okla. She recalls that he was a member of the Kerr-McGee Corp. diving team and relished plunging from steep cliffs into Oklahoma lakes.

Source: Phillip L. Zweig, "Chemical Bank's Tabor Thrives on Risk and Likely Will Find It at Trading Unit," *The Wall Street Journal*, February 28, 1986, p. 11.

value, the profitability index, and the internal rate of return. They all discount the firm's cash flows using the cost of capital, which was discussed in detail in Chapter 13. The terms *discount rate* and *opportunity cost* are used interchangeably with *cost of capital* to refer to the minimum return that must be earned on a project in order to leave the firm's market value unchanged. Initially, all projects evaluated are assumed to be equally risky.

Net Present Value (NPV)

net present value (NPV)
Found by subtracting the initial investment from the present value of the cash inflows discounted at a rate equal to the firm's cost of capital.

Net present value (NPV), as noted in Equation 15.2, is found by subtracting the initial investment from the present value of the cash inflows discounted at a rate equal to the firm's cost of capital:

$$NPV = \text{present value of cash inflows} - \text{initial investment} \qquad (15.2)$$

THE DECISION CRITERION The criterion when *NPV* is used to make accept-reject decisions is as follows: *If NPV ≥ $0, accept the project; otherwise, reject the project.* If the *NPV* is greater than or equal to zero, the firm will earn a return greater than or equal to its cost of capital. Such action should enhance or maintain the wealth of the firm's owners.

EXAMPLE

The net present value (NPV) approach can be illustrated using the Blano Company data presented in Table 15.1. If the firm has a 10 percent cost of capital, the net present values for projects A (an

TABLE 15.4 The Calculation of NPVs for the Blano Company's Capital Expenditure Alternatives

Project A			
Annual cash inflow			$14,000
×PV annuity interest factor, PVIFA[a]			3.791
PV of cash inflows			$53,074
−Initial investment			42,000
Net present value (NPV)			$11,074

Project B

Year	Cash inflows (1)	PV interest factor, PVIF[b] (2)	Present value [(1) × (2)] (3)
1	$28,000	.909	$25,452
2	12,000	.826	9,912
3	10,000	.751	7,510
4	10,000	.683	6,830
5	10,000	.621	6,210
		PV of cash inflows	$55,914
		− Initial investment	45,000
		Net present value (NPV)	$10,914

[a] From Table D-4, for 5 years and 10 percent.

[b] From Table D-3, for given year and 10 percent.

annuity) and B (a mixed stream) can be calculated as in Table 15.4. These calculations are based on the application of the techniques presented in Chapter 11. The results show that the net present values of projects A and B are, respectively, $11,074 and $10,914. Both projects are acceptable, since the net present value of each is greater than zero. If the projects were being ranked, however, project A would be considered superior to B since it has a higher net present value ($11,074 versus $10,914) than that of B. ■

Profitability Index *(PI)*

The **profitability index *(PI)***, as noted in Equation 15.3, is calculated by dividing the present value of cash inflows by the initial investment in a project.

profitability index *(PI)* The present value of cash inflows divided by the initial investment.

$$PI = \frac{\text{present value of cash inflows}}{\text{initial investment}} \qquad (15.3)$$

THE DECISION CRITERION   The criterion when the *PI* is used to make accept-reject decisions is as follows: *If PI ≥ 1, accept the project; otherwise, reject the project.* When the *PI* is greater than or equal to 1, the net present value is greater than or equal to zero. Therefore, the *NPV* and the *PI* approaches give the same solution to accept-reject decisions. The acceptance of projects having *PI*s greater than or equal to 1 will enhance or maintain the wealth of the firm's owners.

EXAMPLE

Profitability indexes for the Blano Company can be easily determined using the present values calculated in Table 15.4. The *PI*s for projects A and B are, respectively, 1.26 ($53,074 ÷ $42,000) and 1.24 ($55,914 ÷ $45,000). Since both *PI*s are greater than 1, both projects are acceptable. Ranking the projects on the basis of *PI* indicates that project A is preferable to project B because A returns $1.26 present value for each dollar invested, while B returns only $1.24. This ranking is the same as that obtained using *NPV*s; however, *the condition of conflicting rankings by these two techniques is not unusual.* ■

Internal Rate of Return *(IRR)*

The **internal rate of return *(IRR)*** is defined as the discount rate that equates the present value of cash inflows with the initial investment associated with a project. The *IRR*, in other words, is the discount rate that causes the *NPV* of an investment opportunity to equal zero (since

internal rate of return *(IRR)* The discount rate that equates the present value of cash inflows with the initial investment thereby causing *NPV* = $0.

the present value of cash inflows equals the initial investment). The calculation of the *IRR* is no easy chore.

THE DECISION CRITERION   The criterion, when the *IRR* is used in making accept-reject decisions, is as follows: *If IRR ≥ cost of capital, accept the project; otherwise, reject the project.* This criterion guarantees that the firm is earning at least its required return and assures that the market value of the firm will increase or at least remain unchanged.

CALCULATING THE *IRR*   The *IRR* must be calculated using trial-and-error techniques. Calculating the *IRR* for an annuity is considerably easier than calculating it for a mixed stream of operating cash inflows. The steps involved in calculating the *IRR* in each case are given in Table 15.5. The application of these steps can be illustrated by the following example.

EXAMPLE

The two-step procedure given in Table 15.5 for finding the *IRR* of an *annuity* can be demonstrated using Blano Company's project A cash flows given in Table 15.1.

Step 1:   Dividing the initial investment of $42,000 by the annual cash inflow of $14,000 results in a payback period of 3.000 years ($42,000 ÷ $14,000 = 3.000).

Step 2:   According to Table D-4, the *PVIFA* factors closest to 3.000 for five years are 3.058 (for 19 percent) and 2.991 (for 20 percent). The value closest to 3.000 is 2.991; therefore, the *IRR* for project A, to the nearest 1 percent, is *20 percent*. (*Note:* For our purposes, values rounded to the nearest 1 percent are acceptable.)

Project A with an *IRR* of 20 percent is quite acceptable, since this *IRR* is above the firm's 10 percent cost of capital (20 percent *IRR* > 10 percent cost of capital).

   The application of the seven-step procedure given in Table 15.5 for finding the internal rate of return of a *mixed stream* of cash inflows can be illustrated using the Blano Company's project B cash flows given in Table 15.1.

Step 1:   Summing the cash inflows for years 1 through 5 results in total cash inflows of $70,000, which, when divided by the number of years in the project's life, results in an average annual cash inflow or "fake annuity" of $14,000 [($28,000 + $12,000 + $10,000 + $10,000 + $10,000) ÷ 5].

TABLE 15.5 Steps for Calculating the Internal Rates of Return (*IRRs*) of Annuities and Mixed Streams

FOR AN ANNUITY

Step 1: Calculate the payback period for the project.

Step 2: Use Table D-4 (the present-value interest factors for a $1 annuity, *PVIFA*) and find, for the life of the project, the factor closest to the payback value. This is the internal rate of return *(IRR)* to the nearest 1 percent.

FOR A MIXED STREAM[a]

Step 1: Calculate the average annual cash inflow to get a "fake annuity."

Step 2: Divide the average annual cash inflow into the initial investment to get a "fake payback period" (or present-value interest factor for a $1 annuity, *PVIFA*). The fake payback is needed to estimate the *IRR* for the fake annuity.

Step 3: Use Table D-4 *(PVIFA)* and the fake payback period in the same manner as described in step 2 for finding the *IRR* of an annuity. The result will be a *very rough* approximation of the *IRR*, based on the assumption that the mixed stream of cash inflows is an annuity.

Step 4:[b] Adjust the *IRR* obtained in step 3 subjectively by comparing the pattern of average annual cash inflows (calculated in step 1) to the actual mixed stream of cash inflows. If the actual cash flow stream seems to have higher inflows in the earlier years than the average stream, adjust the *IRR* up a few percentage points. If the actual cash inflows in the earlier years are below the average, adjust the *IRR* down a few percentage points. If the average cash inflows seem fairly close to the actual pattern, make no adjustment in the *IRR*.

Step 5: Using the *IRR* from step 4, calculate the net present value of the mixed-stream project. Be sure to use Table D-3 (the present-value interest factors for $1, *PVIF*), treating the estimated *IRR* as the discount rate.

Step 6: If the resulting *NPV* is greater than zero, subjectively raise the discount rate; if the resulting *NPV* is less than zero, subjectively lower the discount rate.

Step 7: Calculate the *NPV* using the new discount rate. Repeat step 6. Stop as soon as two *consecutive* discount rates that cause the *NPV* to be positive and negative, respectively, have been found. Whichever of these two rates causes the *NPV* to be closest to zero is the *IRR* to the nearest 1 percent.

---

[a] Note that subjective estimates are suggested in steps 4 and 6. After working a number of these problems, a "feel" for the appropriate subjective adjustment, or "educated guess," may result.

[b] The purpose of this step is to provide a more accurate first estimate of the *IRR*. This step can be skipped.

Step 2: Dividing the initial outlay of $45,000 by the average annual cash inflow of $14,000 (calculated in step 1) results in a "fake payback period" (or present value of an annuity factor, *PVIFA*) of 3.214 years.

Step 3: In Table D-4, the factor closest to 3.214 for five years is 3.199, the factor for a discount rate of 17 percent. The starting estimate of the *IRR* is therefore 17 percent.

Step 4: Since the actual early-year cash inflows are greater than the average cash inflows of $14,000, a *subjective* increase of 2 percent is made in the discount rate. This makes the estimated *IRR* 19 percent.

Step 5: Using the present-value interest factors *(PVIF)* for 19 percent and the correct year from Table D-3, the net present value of the mixed stream is calculated as follows:

Year(t)	Cash inflows (1)	$PVIF_{19\%,t}$ (2)	Present value at 19% [(1) × (2)] (3)
1	$28,000	.840	$23,520
2	12,000	.706	8,472
3	10,000	.593	5,930
4	10,000	.499	4,990
5	10,000	.419	4,190
		PV of cash inflows	$47,102
		−Initial investment	45,000
		Net present value (*NPV*)	$ 2,102

Steps 6 and 7: Since the net present value of $2,102, calculated in step 5, is greater than zero, the discount rate should be subjectively increased. Since the *NPV* is not close to zero, let's try an increase to 21 percent.

Year(t)	Cash inflows (1)	$PVIF_{21\%,t}$ (2)	Present value at 21% [(1) × (2)] (3)
1	$28,000	.826	$23,128
2	12,000	.683	8,196
3	10,000	.564	5,640
4	10,000	.467	4,670
5	10,000	.386	3,860
		PV of cash inflows	$45,494
		−Initial investment	45,000
		Net present value (*NPV*)	$ 494

These calculations indicate that the *NPV* of $494 for an *IRR* of 21 percent is reasonably close to, but still greater than, zero. Thus a higher discount rate should be tried. Since we are so close, let's try 22 percent. As the following calculations show, the net present value from a discount rate of 22 percent is −$256.

Year(t)	Cash inflows (1)	$PVIF_{22\%,t}$ (2)	Present value at 22% [(1) × (2)] (3)
1	$28,000	.820	$22,960
2	12,000	.672	8,064
3	10,000	.551	5,510
4	10,000	.451	4,510
5	10,000	.370	3,700
		PV of cash inflows	$44,744
		−Initial investment	45,000
		Net present value (*NPV*)	−$ 256

Since 21 and 22 percent are consecutive discount rates that give positive and negative net present values, the trial-and-error process can be terminated. The *IRR* we are seeking is the discount rate for which the *NPV* is closest to zero. For this project, 22 percent causes the *NPV* to be closer to zero than 21 percent, so 22 percent is the *IRR* we shall use. As indicated earlier, for our purposes the *IRR* rounded to the nearest 1 percent will suffice. Therefore, the *IRR* of project B is approximately *22 percent.*

Project B is acceptable since its *IRR* of approximately 22 percent is greater than the Blano Company's 10 percent cost of capital. This is the same conclusion reached using the *NPV* and *PI* as criteria. It is interesting to note that the *IRR* suggests that project B is preferable to A, which has an *IRR* of approximately 20 percent. This conflicts with the rankings of the projects obtained using *NPV* and *PI*. Such conflicts are not unusual; *there is no guarantee that these three techniques (NPV, PI, and IRR) will rank projects in the same order. However, all the methods should reach the same conclusion about the acceptability or nonacceptability of projects.* ■

Comparison of *NPV* and *IRR*

Of the three sophisticated capital budgeting techniques, net present value *(NPV)* and internal rate of return *(IRR)* deserve the greatest attention. *Both techniques will always generate the same accept-reject decision for a given project, but differences in their underlying assumptions can cause them to rank projects differently.* To understand the differences and preferences surrounding these techniques, we need to look at conflicting rankings and the question of which approach is better.

CONFLICTING RANKINGS The possibility of *conflicting rankings* of projects by *NPV* and *IRR* should be clear from the Blano Company example. Ranking is an important consideration when projects are mutually exclusive or when capital rationing is necessary. When projects are mutually exclusive, ranking enables the firm to determine the best project from a financial viewpoint. When capital rationing is necessary, ranking projects may not determine the group of projects to accept, but it will provide a logical starting point.

conflicting rankings
Conflicts in the ranking of a given project by *NPV* and *IRR* that result from differences in the magnitude and timing of cash flows.

intermediate cash inflows Cash inflows received prior to the termination of a project.

Conflicting rankings using *NPV* and *IRR* result from *differences in the magnitude and timing of cash flows.* Although these two factors can be used to explain conflicting rankings, the underlying cause results from the implicit assumption concerning the reinvestment of **intermediate cash inflows** — cash inflows received prior to termination of the project. *NPV* assumes that intermediate cash inflows are reinvested at the cost of capital, whereas *IRR* assumes that intermediate cash inflows can be invested at a rate equal to the project's *IRR*.

WHICH APPROACH IS BETTER? *On a purely theoretical basis, NPV is the better approach to capital budgeting.* Its theoretical superiority is attributed to a number of factors. Most important is the fact that the use of *NPV* implicitly assumes that any intermediate cash inflows generated by an investment are reinvested at the firm's cost of capital. The use of *IRR* assumes reinvestment at the often high rate specified by the *IRR*. Since the cost of capital tends to be a reasonable estimate of the rate at which the firm could actually reinvest intermediate cash inflows, the use of *NPV* with its more conservative and realistic reinvestment rate is in theory preferable. In addition, certain mathematical properties may cause a project with nonconventional cash flows to have zero or more than one *IRR;* this problem does not occur with the *NPV* approach.

Evidence suggests[2] that in spite of the theoretical superiority of *NPV,* financial managers prefer to use *IRR.* This preference for *IRR* is attributable to the general disposition of business people toward *rates of return* rather than actual *dollar returns.* Because interest rates, profitability, and so on are most often expressed as annual rates of return, the use of

---

[2] For example, see Lawrence J. Gitman and John R. Forrester, Jr., "A Survey of Capital Budgeting Techniques Used by Major U.S. Firms," *Financial Management,* 6 (Fall 1977), pp. 66–71, for a discussion of evidence with respect to capital budgeting decision-making practices in major U.S. firms.

IRR makes sense to financial decision makers. They tend to find *NPV* more difficult to use because it does not really measure benefits *relative to the amount invested*. Because a variety of methods and techniques are available for avoiding the pitfalls of the *IRR*, its widespread use should not be viewed as reflecting a lack of sophistication on the part of financial decision makers.

CAPITAL RATIONING

Firms commonly find a greater number of acceptable projects than they have the funds to undertake. The objective of *capital rationing* is to select the group of projects that provides the *highest overall net present value* and does not require more dollars than are budgeted. As a prerequisite to capital rationing, the best of any mutually exclusive projects must be chosen and placed in the group of independent projects. Two basic approaches to project selection under capital rationing are discussed here.

Internal Rate of Return Approach

The **internal rate of return approach** involves graphically plotting *IRR*s in descending order against total dollar investments. This graph, as noted in Chapter 13, is called the *investment opportunities schedule (IOS)*. By drawing the cost of capital line and then imposing a budget constraint, the group of acceptable projects can be determined. The problem with this technique is that it does not guarantee the maximum dollar return to the firm. It merely provides a satisfactory solution to capital rationing problems.

internal rate of return approach An approach to capital rationing that involves the graphic plotting of project *IRR*s in descending order against the total dollar investment.

EXAMPLE

The Gould Fuel Company is confronted with six projects competing for the firm's fixed budget of $250,000. The initial investment and *IRR* for each project are as follows:

Project	Initial investment	*IRR*
A	$ 80,000	12%
B	70,000	20
C	100,000	16
D	40,000	8
E	60,000	15
F	110,000	11

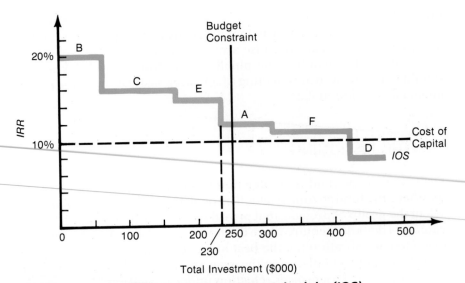

**FIGURE 15.1 Investment Opportunities Schedule (IOS)
for the Gould Fuel Company Projects**
Applying the *IRR* approach to capital rationing, Gould Fuel Company's $250,000
budget constraint would permit acceptance of only projects B, C, and E in spite of
the fact that projects A and F have *IRR*s greater than the 10 percent cost of capital.

The firm has a cost of capital of 10 percent. Figure 15.1 presents
the investment opportunities schedule (*IOS*) resulting from ranking the six projects in descending order based on *IRR*s. According
to the schedule, only projects B, C, and E should be accepted.
Together they will absorb $230,000 of the $250,000 budget.
Project D is not worthy of consideration since its *IRR* is less than
the firm's 10 percent cost of capital. The drawback of this approach, however, is that there is no guarantee that the acceptance
of projects B, C, and E will maximize *total dollar returns* and
therefore owners' wealth. ∎

Net Present Value Approach

**net present value
approach** An approach
to capital rationing that
involves the use of
present values to
determine the group of
projects that will
maximize owners' wealth.

The **net present value approach** is based on the use of present values to
determine the group of projects that will maximize owners' wealth. It is
implemented by ranking projects on the basis of *IRR*s or *PI*s (profitability indexes) and then evaluating the present value of the benefits from
each potential project to *determine the combination of projects with the
highest overall present value*. This is the same as maximizing net present
value, since whether the entire budget is used or not, it is viewed as the
total initial investment. The portion of the firm's budget that is not used
does not increase the firm's value. At best, the unused money can be

invested in marketable securities or returned to the owners in the form of cash dividends. In either case the wealth of the owners is not likely to be enhanced.

EXAMPLE

The group of projects described in the preceding example is ranked in Table 15.6 on the basis of *IRR*s. The present value of the cash inflows associated with the projects is also included in the table. Projects B, C, and E, which together require $230,000, yield a present value of $336,000. However, if projects B, C, and A were implemented, the total budget of $250,000 would be used and the present value of the cash inflows would be $357,000. This is greater than the return expected from selecting the projects on the basis of the highest *IRR*s. Implementing B, C, and A is preferable, since they maximize the present value for the given budget. *The firm's objective is to use its budget to generate the highest present value of inflows.* Assuming that any unused portion of the budget does not gain or lose money, the total *NPV* for projects B, C, and E would be $106,000 ($336,000 − $230,000), while for projects B, C, and A, the total *NPV* would be $107,000 ($357,000 − $250,000). Selection of projects B, C, and A will therefore maximize *NPV*. ■

APPROACHES FOR DEALING WITH RISK

In the context of capital budgeting, **risk** either refers to the chance that a project will prove unacceptable (i.e., $NPV < \$0$, $PI < 1$, or $IRR <$ cost of capital) or, more formally, the degree of variability of cash flows. Projects with a small chance of being acceptable and a broad range of expected cash flows are more risky than projects having a high chance of acceptance and a narrow range of expected cash flows. In the conventional capital budgeting projects assumed here, risk therefore stems

risk Either the chance that a project will prove unacceptable or, more formally, the degree of variability of cash flows.

TABLE 15.6 Rankings for the Gould Fuel Company Projects

Project	Initial investment	IRR	PV of inflows at 10%	
B	$ 70,000	20%	$112,000	
C	100,000	16	145,000	
E	60,000	15	79,000	
A	80,000	12	100,000	
F	110,000	11	126,500	Cutoff point
D	40,000	8	36,000	(*IRR* < 10%)

almost entirely from *cash inflows*, since the initial investment is generally known with relative certainty. Using the basic risk concepts presented in Chapter 12, we present here some approaches for dealing with risk in capital budgeting: sensitivity analysis, statistical approaches, decision trees, and simulation.

Sensitivity Analysis

One of the simplest approaches for getting a feel for project risk is *sensitivity analysis*. In capital budgeting, one of the most common sensitivity approaches is to estimate the *NPV*s associated with the pessimistic (worst), the most likely (expected), and the optimistic (best) cash inflow estimates. By subtracting the pessimistic-outcome *NPV* from the optimistic-outcome *NPV*, the *range* can be determined.

EXAMPLE

Treadwell Tire Company is considering investing in either of two mutually exclusive projects, A and B, each requiring a $10,000 initial outlay and expected to provide equal annual cash inflows over their 15-year lives. The firm's financial manager made pessi-

TABLE 15.7 Sensitivity Analysis of Treadwell's Projects A and B

	Project A	Project B
Initial investment	$10,000	$10,000
Annual cash inflows		
Outcome		
Pessimistic	$1,500	$ 0
Most likely	2,000	2,000
Optimistic	2,500	4,000
Range	$1,000	$4,000
Net present values[a]		
Outcome		
Pessimistic	$1,409	−$10,000
Most likely	5,212	5,212
Optimistic	9,015	20,424
Range	$7,606	$30,424

[a] These values were calculated using the corresponding annual cash inflows. A 10 percent cost of capital and a 15-year life for the annual cash inflows were used.

mistic, most likely, and optimistic estimates of the cash inflows for each project. The cash inflow estimates and resulting NPVs in each case are summarized in Table 15.7. Comparing the ranges of cash inflows ($1,000 for project A and $4,000 for project B) and, more important, the range of NPVs ($7,606 for project A and $30,424 for project B) makes it clear that project A is less risky than project B. The assumed risk-averse decision maker will take project A, thereby eliminating the possibility of loss. ■

Statistical Approaches

The use of the standard deviation and coefficient of variation to measure the risk of a single asset held in isolation were presented in Chapter 12. These measures can be applied to cash inflow or net present value (NPV) data in order to measure project risk statistically. The following example illustrates the calculation of these statistics using NPV data.

EXAMPLE

The Treadwell Tire Company estimated the probabilities of the pessimistic, most likely, and optimistic NPV outcomes for projects A and B shown in Table 15.8. To find the standard deviation of each project, the first step is to calculate the *expected net present value of each project*. The *expected NPV*, $\overline{NPV}$, can be calculated using Equation 12.1 from Chapter 12, rewritten as

$$\overline{NPV} = \sum_{i=1}^{n} NPV_i \times Pr_i \qquad (15.4)$$

TABLE 15.8 NPVs and Associated Probability Estimates for Treadwell's Projects A and B.

i	Outcome$_i$	NPV_i^a	Probability, Pr_i^b
Project A			
1	Pessimistic	$ 1,409	.25
2	Most likely	5,212	.50
3	Optimistic	9,015	.25
Project B			
1	Pessimistic	−$10,000	.25
2	Most likely	5,212	.50
3	Optimistic	20,424	.25

^{a} From Table 15.7.

^{b} Values estimated subjectively, based on past experience.

where

$$NPV_i = NPV \text{ for the } i\text{th outcome}$$
$$Pr_i = \text{probability of occurrence of the } i\text{th } NPV$$
$$n = \text{number of outcomes considered}$$

Substituting the data from Table 15.8, the expected NPV can be calculated for each project:

$$\overline{NPV}_A = \$1,409(.25) + \$5,212(.50) + \$9,015(.25)$$
$$= \$352.25 + \$2,606.00 + \$2,253.75 = \underline{\$5,212}$$

$$\overline{NPV}_B = -\$10,000(.25) + \$5,212(.50) + \$20,424(.25)$$
$$= -\$2,500 + \$2,606 + \$5,106 = \underline{\$5,212}$$

Note that both projects have expected NPVs of $5,212 which also equals their most likely estimates.

Once the expected NPV, $\overline{NPV}$, has been calculated, the *standard deviation of NPV*, σ_{NPV}, can be found using Equation 12.2 from Chapter 12, rewritten as

$$\sigma_{NPV} = \sqrt{\sum_{i=1}^{n} (NPV_i - \overline{NPV})^2 \times Pr_i} \qquad (15.5)$$

The calculation of the standard deviation of NPV for projects A and B using Equation 15.5 is given in Table 15.9. It can be seen that

TABLE 15.9 Calculation of the Standard Deviation of *NPV* for Treadwell's Projects A and B

i	NPV_i	$\overline{NPV}$	$NPV_i - \overline{NPV}$	$(NPV_i - \overline{NPV})^2$	Pr_i	$(NPV_i - \overline{NPV})^2 \times Pr_i$
Project A						
1	$1,409	$5,212	−$3,803	$14,462,809	.25	$3,615,702
2	5,212	5,212	0	0	.50	0
3	9,015	5,212	3,803	14,462,809	.25	3,615,702

$$\sum_{i=1}^{3} (NPV_i - \overline{NPV})^2 \times Pr_i = \$7,231,404$$

$$\sigma_{NPV_A} = \sqrt{\sum_{i=1}^{3} (NPV_i - \overline{NPV})^2 \times Pr_i} = \sqrt{\$7,231,404} = \underline{\$2,689}$$

i	NPV_i	$\overline{NPV}$	$NPV_i - \overline{NPV}$	$(NPV_i - \overline{NPV})^2$	Pr_i	$(NPV_i - \overline{NPV})^2 \times Pr_i$
Project B						
1	−$10,000	$5,212	$15,212	$231,400,000	.25	$ 57,850,000
2	5,212	5,212	0	0	.50	0
3	20,424	5,212	15,212	231,400,000	.25	57,850,000

$$\sum_{i=1}^{3} (NPV_i - \overline{NPV})^2 \times Pr_i = \$115,700,000$$

$$\sigma_{NPV_B} = \sqrt{\sum_{i=1}^{3} (NPV_i - \overline{NPV})^2 \times Pr_i} = \sqrt{\$115,700,000} = \underline{\$10,756}$$

project B's standard deviation of $10,756 is much higher than project A's standard deviation of $2,689. Project B is therefore clearly more risky than project A.

The *coefficient of variation, CV*, is an especially useful statistic for comparing the risk of projects of differing sizes. Since projects A and B have the same expected *NPV*, the coefficient of variation does not really improve the comparison. Applying Equation 12.3 from Chapter 12 to the *NPV* data, the coefficient of variation of *NPV*, CV_{NPV}, is defined as

$$CV_{NPV} = \frac{\sigma_{NPV}}{\overline{NPV}} \tag{15.6}$$

Substituting σ_{NPV} and $\overline{NPV}$ for projects A and B into Equation 15.6 yields

$$CV_{NPV_A} = \frac{\sigma_{NPV_A}}{NPV_A} = \frac{\$2,689}{\$5,212} = \underline{\underline{.516}}$$

$$CV_{NPV_B} = \frac{\sigma_{NPV_B}}{NPV_B} = \frac{\$10,756}{\$5,212} = \underline{\underline{2.064}}$$

Clearly project B, with a coefficient of variation of *NPV* of 2.064, is more risky than project A, which has a *CV* of .516. ■

Decision Trees

Decision trees are diagrams that permit the various investment decision alternatives and payoffs as well as their probabilities of occurrence to be mapped out in a clear fashion. Their name derives from their resemblance to a tree with a number of branches (see Figure 15.2). Decision trees rely on estimates of the probabilities associated with the outcomes (or payoffs) of competing courses of action. The payoffs associated with each course of action are weighted by the associated probability, the weighted payoffs for each course of action are summed, and the expected value of each course of action is then determined. The alternative providing the highest expected value would be preferred.

decision trees Diagrams that permit the mapping of the various investment decision alternatives and payoffs as well as their probabilities of occurrence.

EXAMPLE

Convy, Inc., wishes to choose between two equally risky projects, I and J. To make this decision, Convy's management has gathered the necessary data, which are depicted in the decision tree in Figure 15.2. Project I requires an initial investment of $120,000; a resulting expected present value of cash inflows of $130,000 is shown in column 4. Project I's expected net present value, which is calculated below the decision tree, is therefore $10,000. Since

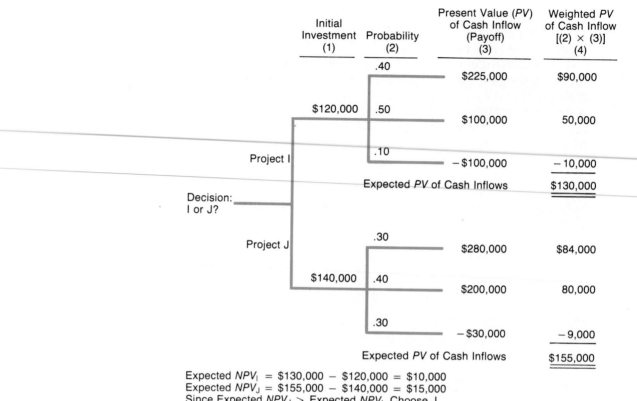

	Initial Investment (1)	Probability (2)	Present Value (PV) of Cash Inflow (Payoff) (3)	Weighted PV of Cash Inflow [(2) × (3)] (4)
		.40	$225,000	$90,000
	$120,000	.50	$100,000	50,000
Project I		.10	−$100,000	−10,000
			Expected PV of Cash Inflows	$130,000
		.30	$280,000	$84,000
Project J	$140,000	.40	$200,000	80,000
		.30	−$30,000	−9,000
			Expected PV of Cash Inflows	$155,000

Expected NPV_I = $130,000 − $120,000 = $10,000
Expected NPV_J = $155,000 − $140,000 = $15,000
Since Expected NPV_J > Expected NPV_I, Choose J.

FIGURE 15.2 Decision Tree for Convy, Inc.'s, Choice Between Projects I and J
The $10,000 expected *NPV* of project I ($130,000 expected present value of cash inflows − $120,000 initial investment) is less than the $15,000 expected *NPV* of project J ($155,000 expected present value of cash inflows − $140,000 initial investment). Project J is therefore preferred.

the $15,000 expected net present value of project J, which is determined in a similar fashion, is greater than that for project I, project J would be preferred. ■

Simulation

simulation A statistically based approach used in capital budgeting to get a feel for risk by applying predetermined probability distributions and random numbers to estimate risky outcomes.

Simulation is a statistically based approach used in capital budgeting to get a feel for risk by applying predetermined probability distributions and random numbers to estimate risky outcomes. By tying the various cash flow components together in a mathematical model and repeating the process numerous times, a probability distribution of project returns can be developed. Figure 15.3 presents a flowchart of the simula-

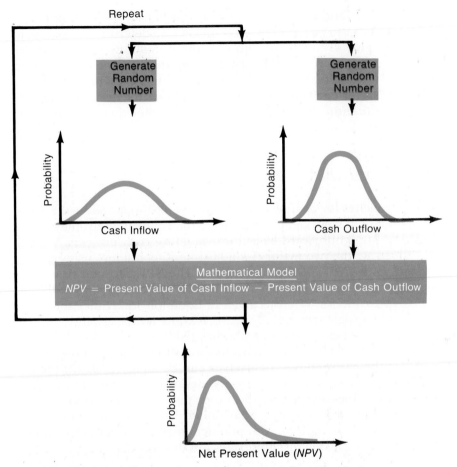

FIGURE 15.3 Flowchart of a Net Present Value Simulation
The basic *NPV* simulation uses random numbers with the probability distributions
to determine cash inflow and cash outflow, which are substituted into the
mathematical model to determine *NPV*. This process is repeated a large number of
times in order to create a probability distribution of *NPV*.

tion of the net present value of a project. The process of generating
random numbers and using the probability distributions for cash inflows and outflows allows values for each of these variables to be determined. Substituting these values into the mathematical model results
in an *NPV*. By repeating this process perhaps a thousand times, a probability distribution of net present values is created.

Although only gross cash inflows and outflows are simulated in Figure 15.3, more sophisticated simulations using individual inflow and
outflow components, such as sales volume, sales price, raw material
cost, labor cost, maintenance expense, and so on, are quite common.

From the distribution of returns, regardless of how they are measured (*NPV*, *IRR*, and so on), the decision maker can determine not only the expected value of the return but also the probability of achieving or surpassing a given return. The use of computers has made the simulation approach quite feasible. The output of simulation provides an excellent basis for decision making since it allows the decision maker to view a continuum of risk-return trade-offs rather than a single-point estimate.

RISK-ADJUSTMENT TECHNIQUES

The approaches for dealing with risk presented so far allow the financial manager to get a "feel" for project risk. Unfortunately, they do not provide a straightforward basis for evaluating risky projects. We will now illustrate the two major risk-adjustment techniques using the net present value *(NPV)* decision method.[3] The *NPV* decision rule of accepting only those projects with *NPV* ≥ $0 will continue to hold. The basic expression for *NPV* was given in Equation 15.2. Since the initial investment, which occurs at time zero, is known with certainty, only the present value of cash inflows embodies risk.

Two opportunities to adjust the present value of cash inflows for risk exist: (1) the cash inflows themselves can be adjusted, or (2) the discount rate can be adjusted. Here we describe and compare the two techniques — the cash inflow adjustment process using *certainty equivalents*, and the discount rate adjustment process using *risk-adjusted discount rates*. In addition, the practical aspects of certainty equivalents and risk-adjusted discount rates are discussed.

Certainty Equivalents (*CEs*)

certainty equivalents (*CEs*) Risk-adjustment factors that represent the percent of estimated cash inflow that investors would be satisfied to receive *for certain* rather than inflows that are *possible* for each year.

risk-free rate (*R_F*) The rate of return one would earn on a virtually riskless investment such as a U.S. Treasury bill.

The theoretically preferable approach for risk adjustment involves the use of **certainty equivalents (*CEs*)**, which represent the percent of estimated cash inflow that investors would be satisfied to receive *for certain* rather than the cash inflows that are *possible* for each year. The project under consideration is therefore adjusted for risk by first converting the expected cash inflows to certain amounts using the certainty equivalents and then discounting the cash inflows at the risk-free rate. The **risk-free rate (*R_F*)** is the rate of return one would earn on a virtually riskless investment such as a U.S. Treasury bill. It is used to discount the certain cash inflows and is not to be confused with a risk-adjusted discount rate. (If a risk-adjusted rate were used, the risk

[3] The *IRR* could just as well have been used, but since *NPV* is theoretically preferable, it is used instead.

SANDY McDONNELL'S RISK IS REWARDED

In shiny new offices on the perimeter of McDonnell Douglas Corp.'s sprawling facilities at the Long Beach, Calif. airport, a group of engineers is beginning work on a new generation of commercial airliners. By year-end [1985] there will be 200 engineers working segregated from the rest of the Douglas division staff. Why? Explains Louis Harrington, vice president and general manager for advanced products: "to put increased focus on the project."

The project is a plane that will enter service in the early 1990s, using the latest fuel-saving propfan engine. It has a three-year, $40 million-to-$50 million technology development budget. That's the current commitment. It will be 1987 before a formal proposal goes to the board of directors to spend the much larger sums needed to launch a new-technology aircraft.

But the active scene at Long Beach says loudly that the commitment to a long-term presence in commercial aviation has already been made at McDonnell Douglas, the $10 billion (revenues) St. Louis-based aerospace giant. Chairman Sanford N. McDonnell, 63, made that commitment three years ago when he gambled on leasing DC-9-80 airliners rather than shuttering the Long Beach plant. The leases were more or less profitless, but they kept the plant operating. And then business really picked up. Since 1980 McDonnell Douglas has sold close to 450 DC-9-80s — now marketed as the MD-80 — to 35 airlines and has an order backlog of $7 billion. Best of all, the MD-80 gives the company a leg up on the competition in this next aircraft generation with its promise of much lower fuel consumption. The design of the existing 155-seat MD-80, with its engines at the rear, can readily be adapted, in a relatively low-cost version, to use propfans. . . .

Way back in 1982 Sandy McDonnell got lots of free advice from Wall Street and elsewhere about why he should cut his losses and cede the commercial market to Boeing. He chose to be stubborn. Good thing.

Source: Howard Banks, "Risk Rewarded," *Forbes*, November 4, 1985, pp. 99–100.

would in effect be counted twice.) Although the process described here of converting risky cash inflows to certain cash inflows is somewhat subjective, the technique is theoretically sound.

EXAMPLE

The Blano Company wishes to consider risk in the analysis of two projects, A and B. The basic data for these projects were initially presented in Table 15.1, and the analysis of the projects using net present value and assuming the projects had equivalent risks was presented in Table 15.4. Ignoring risk differences and using net present value, it was shown earlier that at the firm's 10 percent cost of capital, project A was preferred over project B since its *NPV* of $11,074 was greater than B's *NPV* of $10,914. Assume, however, that on further analysis the firm found that project A was actually more risky than project B. To consider the differing risks, the firm estimated the certainty equivalents for each project's cash inflows for each year. Columns 2 and 7 of Table 15.10 show the estimated values for projects A and B, respectively. Multiplying the risky

TABLE 15.10 Analysis of the Blano Company's Projects A and B Using Certainty Equivalents

PROJECT A

Year(t)	Cash inflows (1)	Certainty equivalent factors[a] (2)	Certain cash inflows [(1) × (2)] (3)	$PVIF_{6\%,t}$ (4)	Present value [(3) × (4)] (5)
1	$14,000	.90	$12,600	.943	$11,882
2	14,000	.90	12,600	.890	11,214
3	14,000	.80	11,200	.840	9,408
4	14,000	.70	9,800	.792	7,762
5	14,000	.60	8,400	.747	6,275
			PV of cash inflows		$46,541
			−Initial investment		42,000
			Net present value *(NPV)*		$ 4,541

PROJECT B

Year(t)	Cash inflows (6)	Certainty equivalent factors[a] (7)	Certain cash inflows [(6) × (7)] (8)	$PVIF_{6\%,t}$ (9)	Present value [(8) × (9)] (10)
1	$28,000	1.00	$28,000	.943	$26,404
2	12,000	.90	10,800	.890	9,612
3	10,000	.90	9,000	.840	7,560
4	10,000	.80	8,000	.792	6,336
5	10,000	.70	7,000	.747	5,229
			PV of cash inflows		$55,141
			−Initial investment		45,000
			Net present value *(NPV)*		$10,141

NOTE: The basic cash flows for these projects were presented in Table 15.1, and the analysis of the projects using *NPV* and assuming equal risk was presented in Table 15.4.

[a] These values were estimated by management; they reflect the risk managers perceive in the cash inflows.

cash inflows (given in columns 1 and 6) by the corresponding certainty equivalents (*CE*s) (columns 2 and 7, respectively) gives the certain cash inflows for projects A and B shown in columns 3 and 8, respectively.

Upon investigation, Blano's management estimated the prevailing risk-free rate of return, R_F, to be 6 percent. Using the 6 percent risk-free rate to discount the certain cash inflows for each of the projects results in the net present values of $4,541 for project A and $10,141 for project B, as calculated in Table 15.10. Note that as a result of the risk adjustment, project B is now preferred. The usefulness of the certainty equivalent approach for risk adjustment should be quite clear; the only difficulty lies in the need to make subjective estimates of the certainty equivalents. ■

Risk-Adjusted Discount Rates (*RADR*s)

A more practical approach to risk adjustment involves the use of *risk-adjusted discount rates (RADRs)*. Instead of adjusting the cash inflows for risk, as was done using the certainty equivalent approach, this approach adjusts the discount rate. The **risk-adjusted discount rate (RADR)** reflects the return that must be earned on the given project to compensate the firm's owners adequately, thereby resulting in the maintenance or improvement of share price. The higher the risk of a project, the higher the *RADR* and therefore the lower the net present value for a given stream of cash inflows.

Using the coefficient of variation *(CV)* as a measure of project risk, the firm can develop some type of **market risk-return function** — a graph of the discount rates associated with each level of project risk. An example of such a function is given in Figure 15.4, which relates the risk-adjusted discount rate, *RADR*, to the project risk as measured by the coefficient of variation, *CV*. This function is similar to the capital asset pricing model (CAPM) presented in Chapter 12. The risk-return function in Figure 15.4 indicates that project cash inflows associated with a riskless event (*CV* = 0) should be discounted at a 6 percent rate. This rate of return therefore represents the risk-free rate, R_F (point *a* in the figure). For all levels of risk greater than certainty (*CV* > 0), the associated required rate of return is indicated. Points *b*, *c*, and *d* indicate that rates of return of approximately 9, 11, and 14 percent will be required on projects with coefficients of variation of 0.6, 1.0, and 1.5, respectively.

Figure 15.4 is a *risk-return function*, which means that investors will discount cash inflows with the given levels of risk at the corresponding rates. Therefore, in order not to damage its market value, the firm must use the correct discount rate for evaluating a project. If a firm discounts a risky project's cash inflows at too low a rate and accepts the project,

risk-adjusted discount rate (RADR) The rate of return that must be earned on a given project to compensate the firm's owners adequately, thereby resulting in the maintenance or improvement of share price.

market risk-return function A graph of the discount rates associated with each level of project risk.

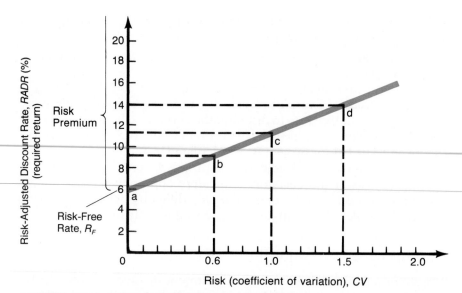

FIGURE 15.4 A Market Risk-Return Function
The market risk-return function shows the risk-adjusted discount rate, *RADR*, or required return associated with each level of risk measured by the coefficient of variation, *CV*. At *CV*s of 0 (no risk), 0.6, 1.0, and 1.5, the *RADR*s are approximately 6 percent (risk-free rate, R_F), 9 percent, 11 percent, and 14 percent, respectively.

the firm's market price may drop as investors recognize that the firm itself has become more risky. The amount by which the required discount rate exceeds the risk-free rate is called the **risk premium.** It of course increases with increasing project risk. A simple example will clarify the use of the risk-adjusted discount rate, *RADR*, in evaluating capital budgeting projects.

risk premium The amount by which the required discount rate exceeds the risk-free rate for a project.

EXAMPLE

The Blano Company wishes to use the risk-adjusted discount rate approach to determine, according to *NPV*, whether to implement project A or project B. In addition to the data presented earlier, Blano's management has estimated the coefficient of variation for project A as 1.5 and for project B as 1.0. According to Figure 15.4, the *RADR* for project A is approximately 14 percent; for project B, it is approximately 11 percent. Due to the riskier nature of project A, its risk premium is 8 percent (14 percent – 6 percent); for project B the risk premium is 5 percent (11 percent – 6 percent). The net present value of each project, using its *RADR*, is calculated in Table 15.11. The results clearly show that project B is preferable to project A, since its risk-adjusted net present value *(NPV)* of

TABLE 15.11 Analysis of the Blano Company's Projects A and B Using Risk-Adjusted Discount Rates

Project A			Project B		
		Year(t)	Cash inflows (1)	$PVIF_{11\%,t}$ (2)	Present value [(1) × (2)] (3)
Annual cash inflow	$14,000	1	$28,000	.901	$25,228
×$PVIFA_{14\%,5\,yrs}$	3.433	2	12,000	.812	9,744
PV of cash inflows	$48,062	3	10,000	.731	7,310
−Initial investment	42,000	4	10,000	.659	6,590
Net present value *(NPV)*	$ 6,062	5	10,000	.593	5,930
		PV of cash inflows			$54,802
		−Initial investment			45,000
		Net present value *(NPV)*			$ 9,802

NOTE: Using Figure 15.4 and the coefficients of variation of 1.5 and 1.0 for projects A and B, respectively, a discount rate of 14 percent is used for project A and 11 percent for project B.

$9,802 is greater than the $6,062 risk-adjusted *NPV* for project A. This is the same conclusion that resulted using certainty equivalents in the preceding example. As noted earlier (see Table 15.4), when the discount rates are not adjusted for risk, project A would be preferred to project B. The usefulness of risk-adjusted discount rates should now be clear; the real difficulty of this approach lies in estimating the market risk-return function. ■

CE Versus *RADR* in Practice

Certainty equivalents (CEs) are theoretically superior to risk-adjusted discount rates (RADRs) for project risk adjustment. However, due to the complexity of developing *CEs, RADRs are most often used in practice.* Their popularity stems from two major facts: (1) They are consistent with the general disposition of financial decision makers toward rates of return, and (2) they are easily estimated and applied to risky decision situations. The first reason is clearly a matter of personal preference, but the second is based on the computational convenience and well-developed procedures involved in the use of *RADRs.* In practice, risk is often subjectively categorized rather than related to a continuum of *RADRs* associated with each level of risk, as illustrated by the market risk-return function in Figure 15.4. Firms often establish a number of *risk classes,* with an *RADR* assigned to each. Each project is then subjectively placed in the appropriate risk class, and the corresponding *RADR* is used to evaluate it. An example will help to illustrate this approach.

EXAMPLE

Assume that the management of Blano Company decided to use a more subjective but practical *RADR* approach to analyze projects. Each project would be placed in one of four risk classes according to its perceived risk. The classes were ranged from I for the lowest-risk projects to IV for the highest-risk projects. Associated with each class was an *RADR* appropriate to the level of risk of projects in the class. A brief description of each class, along with the associated *RADR*, is given in Table 15.12. It shows that lower-risk projects tend to involve routine replacement or renewal activities, whereas higher-risk projects involve expansion, often into new or unfamiliar activities.

The financial manager of Blano has assigned project A to Class III and project B to Class II. The cash flows for project A would therefore be evaluated using a 14 percent *RADR*, and project B's would be evaluated using a 10 percent *RADR*.[4] The net present value of project A at 14 percent was calculated in Table 15.11 to be $6,062, and the *NPV* for project B at a 10 percent *RADR* was found to be $10,914 in Table 15.4. Clearly, with *RADR*s based on the use of risk classes, project B is preferred over project A. As noted

TABLE 15.12 Blano Company's Risk Classes and *RADR*s

Risk class	Description	Risk-adjusted discount rate, *RADR*
I	*Below-average risk:* Projects with low risk typically involve routine replacement without modernization of existing activities.	8%
II	*Average risk:* Projects similar to those currently implemented. Typically involve renewal or replacement of existing activities.	10%
III	*Above-average risk:* Projects with higher than normal, but not excessive, risk. Typically involve expansion of existing or similar activities.	14%
IV	*Highest risk:* Projects with very high risk. Typically involve expansion into new or unfamiliar activities.	20%

[4] Note that the 10 percent *RADR* for project B using the risk classes in Table 15.12 differs from the 11 percent *RADR* found earlier for project B using the market risk-return function. This difference is attributable to the less precise nature of the use of risk classes.

earlier, this result is contrary to the findings in Table 15.4, where no attention was given to the differing risk of projects A and B. ■

SUMMARY

- The key formulas/definitions and decision criteria for capital budgeting techniques are summarized in Table 15.13.
- Unsophisticated capital budgeting techniques include the average rate of return and the payback period. The average rate of return is calculated by dividing the average profits after taxes by the average investment. The payback period is the amount of time required for the firm to recover its initial investment from cash inflows.
- Sophisticated capital budgeting techniques use the cost of capital to consider the time factor in the value of money. They include the net present value *(NPV)*, profitability index *(PI)*, and internal rate of return *(IRR)*. All these techniques provide the same accept-reject decisions for a given project but often conflict when ranking projects.
- On a purely theoretical basis, *NPV* is preferred over *IRR*, since *NPV* assumes reinvestment of intermediate cash inflows at the cost of capital and does not exhibit the mathematical problems often occurring when calculating *IRRs* for nonconventional cash flows. In practice the *IRR* is more commonly used

TABLE 15.13 Summary of Key Formulas/Definitions and Decision Criteria for Capital Budgeting Techniques

Technique	Formula/definition	Decision criteria
UNSOPHISTICATED		
Average rate of return	$\dfrac{\text{average profits after taxes}}{\text{average investment}}$	*Accept* if greater than or equal to minimum acceptable average rate of return; otherwise *reject*.
Payback period	For annuity: $\dfrac{\text{initial investment}}{\text{annual cash inflow}}$ For mixed stream: Calculate cumulative cash inflows on year-to-year basis until the initial investment is recovered.	*Accept* if less than or equal to maximum acceptable payback period; otherwise *reject*.
SOPHISTICATED		
Net present value *(NPV)*	present value of cash inflows − initial investment	*Accept* if greater than or equal to $0; otherwise *reject*.
Profitability index *(PI)*	$\dfrac{\text{present value of cash inflows}}{\text{initial investment}}$	*Accept* if greater than or equal to 1; otherwise *reject*.
Internal rate of return *(IRR)*	The discount rate that equates the present value of cash inflows with the initial investment thereby causing $NPV = \$0$.	*Accept* if greater than or equal to the cost of capital; otherwise *reject*.

by major firms because it is consistent with the general preference of business people toward rates of return.

● Common techniques for solving capital rationing problems include the internal rate of return approach and the net present value approach. Of the two, the net present value approach best achieves the objective of using the budget to generate the highest present value of inflows.

● Risk in capital budgeting is concerned either with the chance that a project will prove unacceptable or, more formally, the degree of variability of cash flows. Sensitivity analysis is one of the simplest approaches for getting a "feel" for project risk. Statistical techniques for measuring project risk include the standard deviation and the coefficient of variation.

● A decision tree relies on estimates of probabilities associated with the outcomes of competing courses of action to determine the expected values used to select a preferred action. Simulation, which results in a probability distribution of project returns, usually requires a computer and allows the decision maker to understand the risk-return trade-offs involved in a proposed investment.

● The two major risk-adjustment techniques are certainty equivalents (CEs) and risk-adjusted discount rates (RADRs). Certainty equivalents (CEs) are used to adjust the risky cash inflows to certain amounts, which are discounted at a risk-free rate in order to find the NPV. The risk-adjusted discount rate (RADR) technique involves a market-based adjustment of the discount rate used to calculate NPV.

● Certainty equivalents are the theoretically superior risk-adjustment technique. Risk-adjusted discount rates are more commonly used in practice because decision makers prefer rates of return and they are easier to calculate.

QUESTIONS

15-1 What weaknesses are associated with the use of the *average rate of return* for evaluating a proposed capital expenditure? How can a tie in the rankings be resolved using this technique?

15-2 What is the *payback period?* How is it calculated? What weaknesses are commonly associated with the use of the payback period to evaluate a proposed investment?

15-3 What is the one characteristic that so-called sophisticated capital budgeting techniques have in common that the unsophisticated techniques do not? What are the names commonly used to describe the rate at which cash flows are discounted in order to find present values?

15-4 What is the formula for finding the *net present value (NPV)* of a project with conventional cash flows? What is the acceptance criterion for *NPV?*

15-5 How is the *profitability index (PI)* calculated? What is its acceptance criterion? Is this measure consistent with the use of *NPV?* Explain.

15-6 What is the *internal rate of return (IRR)* on an investment? How is it determined? What is its acceptance criterion?

15-7 Do the net present value *(NPV)*, profitability index *(PI)*, and internal rate of return *(IRR)* always agree with respect to accept-reject decisions? Ranking decisions? Explain.

15-8   What causes conflicts in the ranking of projects using net present value *(NPV)* and internal rate of return *(IRR)?* Explain how on a purely theoretical basis the assumption concerning the reinvestment of intermediate cash inflows tends to favor the use of net present value *(NPV)*.

15-9   In practice, which of the two major capital budgeting techniques—net present value *(NPV)* or internal rate of return *(IRR)*—is preferred? Explain the rationale for this preference in light of the fact that it is inconsistent with theory.

15-10 What is *capital rationing?* Is it unusual for a firm to ration capital? Compare and contrast the *internal rate of return approach* and *net present value approach* to capital rationing. Which is better? Why?

15-11 Define *risk* in terms of cash inflows from a project. Briefly describe each of the following and explain how they can be used to deal with project risk:
   a Sensitivity analysis
   b Statistics
   c Decision trees
   d Simulation

15-12 Describe the underlying logic and basic procedures involved in using (1) *certainty equivalents (CEs)* and (2) *risk-adjusted discount rates (RADRs)* in the risk-adjustment process.

15-13 Compare and contrast certainty equivalents *(CEs)* and risk-adjusted discount rates *(RADRs)* from both a theoretical and a practical point of view. In practice, how are *risk classes* often used to apply *RADRs?* Explain.

PROBLEMS

15-1   **(Average Rate of Return)**   A firm is considering the acquisition of an asset that requires an initial investment of $10,000 and will provide after-tax profits of $1,000 per year for five years. The firm has a minimum acceptable average rate of return of 25 percent.
   a Calculate the average rate of return.
   b Should the firm accept the project? Why?

15-2   **(Payback Period)**   The Lee Corporation is considering a capital expenditure that requires an initial investment of $42,000 and returns after-tax cash inflows of $7,000 per year for 10 years. The firm has a maximum acceptable payback period of eight years.
   a Determine the payback period for this project.
   b Should the company accept the project? Why, or why not?

15-3   **(Average Rate of Return, Cash Inflows, and Payback)**   Dandy's Sporting Equipment Company is evaluating a new machine. The initial investment of $20,000 will be depreciated under ACRS using a recovery period of five years. The machine will generate profits after taxes of $3,000 per year for each of the five years of its usable life.

a Determine the average rate of return for the machine, using the most common formula.

b Determine the after-tax cash inflows associated with the machine for years 1 through 6. (Note: Although no profits are given for year 6, the depreciation in year 6 will create cash inflow. See Equation 3.1 on page 52 and Table 3.6 on page 54.)

c Determine the payback period for the machine.

15-4 **(Payback Comparisons)**   Dallas Tool has a five-year maximum acceptable payback period. The firm is considering the purchase of a new machine and must choose between two alternative ones. The first machine requires an initial investment of $14,000 and generates annual after-tax cash inflows of $3,000 for each of the next seven years. The second machine requires an initial investment of $21,000 and provides an annual cash inflow after taxes of $4,000 for 20 years.

a Determine the payback period for each machine.

b Comment on the acceptability of the machines assuming they are independent projects.

c Which machine should the firm accept? Why?

d Do the machines in this problem illustrate any of the criticisms of using payback? Discuss.

15-5 **(*NPV* for Varying Required Returns)**   Cheryl's Beauty Aids is evaluating a new fragrance-mixing machine. The asset requires an initial investment of $24,000 and will generate after-tax cash inflows of $5,000 per year for eight years. For each of the required rates of return listed, (1) calculate the net present value, (2) indicate whether to accept or reject the machine, and (3) explain your decision.

a The cost of capital is 10 percent.

b The cost of capital is 12 percent.

c The cost of capital is 14 percent.

15-6 **(Net Present Value—Independent Projects)**   Using a 14 percent cost of capital, calculate the net present value for each of the following independent projects and indicate whether or not each is acceptable.

	Project A	Project B	Project C	Project D	Project E
Initial investment	$26,000	$500,000	$170,000	$950,000	$80,000
Year			Cash inflows		
1	$4,000	$100,000	$20,000	$230,000	$ 0
2	4,000	120,000	19,000	230,000	0
3	4,000	140,000	18,000	230,000	0
4	4,000	160,000	17,000	230,000	20,000
5	4,000	180,000	16,000	230,000	30,000
6	4,000	200,000	15,000	230,000	0
7	4,000		14,000	230,000	50,000
8	4,000		13,000	230,000	60,000
9	4,000		12,000		70,000
10	4,000		11,000		

15-7   (**Average Rate of Return, Payback, and *NPV***)   MacAllister Products has three projects under consideration. The cash flows for each of them are given below. The firm has a 16 percent cost of capital.

	Project A	Project B	Project C
Initial investment	$40,000	$40,000	$40,000
Year		Cash inflows	
1	$13,000	$ 7,000	$19,000
2	13,000	10,000	16,000
3	13,000	13,000	13,000
4	13,000	16,000	10,000
5	13,000	19,000	7,000

a *Using the cash inflows,* calculate the average rate of return for each project. Which project is preferred using this method?
b Calculate each project's payback period. Which project is preferred using this method?
c Calculate each project's net present value *(NPV)*. Which project is preferred using this method?
d Comment on your findings in **a**, **b**, and **c** and recommend the best project. Explain your recommendation.

15-8   (***NPV* and *PI***)   Calculate the net present value *(NPV)* and profitability index *(PI)* for the following 20-year projects. Comment on the acceptability of each. Assume that the firm has an opportunity cost of 14 percent.
a Initial investment is $10,000; cash inflows are $2,000 per year.
b Initial investment is $25,000; cash inflows are $3,000 per year.
c Initial investment is $30,000; cash inflows are $5,000 per year.

15-9   (***NPV* and *PI***)   A firm can purchase a fixed asset for a $13,000 initial investment. If the asset generates an annual after-tax cash inflow of $4,000 for four years:
a Determine the net present value *(NPV)* of the asset, assuming that the firm has a 10 percent cost of capital. Is the project acceptable?
b Determine the profitability index *(PI)* assuming that the firm has a 10 percent cost of capital. Is the project acceptable?
c Determine the maximum required rate of return (closest whole-percentage rate) the firm can have and still accept the asset. Discuss this finding in light of your responses to **a** and **b**.

15-10   (***NPV* and *PI*—Mutually Exclusive Projects**)   Jackson Enterprises is considering the replacement of one of its old drill presses. Three alternative replacement presses are under consideration. The relevant cash flows associated with each are given in the table at the top of the next page. The firm's cost of capital is 15 percent.

	Press A	Press B	Press C
Initial investment	$85,000	$60,000	$130,000
Year		Cash inflows	
1	$18,000	$12,000	$50,000
2	18,000	14,000	30,000
3	18,000	16,000	20,000
4	18,000	18,000	20,000
5	18,000	20,000	20,000
6	18,000	25,000	30,000
7	18,000	—	40,000
8	18,000	—	50,000

a Calculate the net present value *(NPV)* of each press.
b Calculate the profitability index *(PI)* for each press.
c Using both *NPV* and *PI*, evaluate the acceptability of each press. Do the two techniques agree with respect to each press?
d Rank the presses from best to worst using each technique, *NPV* and *PI*. Do the rankings agree? Explain your findings.

15-11 ■ **(Internal Rate of Return)** For each of the following projects, calculate the internal rate of return *(IRR)* and indicate for each project the maximum cost of capital the firm could have and find the *IRR* acceptable.

	Project A	Project B	Project C	Project D
Initial investment	$90,000	$490,000	$20,000	$240,000
Year		Cash inflows		
1	$20,000	$150,000	$7,500	$120,000
2	25,000	150,000	7,500	100,000
3	30,000	150,000	7,500	80,000
4	35,000	150,000	7,500	60,000
5	40,000	—	7,500	—

15-12 ■ **(*IRR*—Mutually Exclusive Projects)** Paulus Corporation is attempting to choose the better of two mutually exclusive projects available for expanding the firm's warehouse capacity. The relevant cash flows for the projects are given. The firm's cost of capital is 15 percent.

	Project X	Project Y
Initial investment	$500,000	$325,000
Year		Cash inflows
1	$100,000	$140,000
2	120,000	120,000
3	150,000	95,000
4	190,000	70,000
5	250,000	50,000

a Calculate the *IRR* to the nearest whole percent for each of the projects.

b Assess the acceptability of each project based on the *IRR*s found in **a**.

c Which project is preferred, based on the *IRR*s found in **a**?

15-13 **(IRR, Investment Life, and Cash Inflows)** Cincinnati Machine Tool (CMT) accepts projects earning more than the firm's 15 percent cost of capital. CMT is currently considering a ten-year project that provides annual cash inflows of $10,000 and requires an initial investment of $61,450. (*Note:* All amounts are after taxes.)

a Determine the *IRR* of this project. It is acceptable?

b Assuming that the cash inflows continue to be $10,000 per year, how many *additional years* would the flows have to continue to make the project acceptable (have an *IRR* of 15 percent)?

c With the given life, initial investment, and cost of capital, what is the minimum annual cash inflow the firm should accept?

15-14 **(NPV, PI, and IRR)** Lilo Manufacturing Enterprises has prepared the following estimates for a long-term project it is considering. The initial investment will be $18,250, and the project is expected to yield after-tax cash inflows of $4,000 per year for seven years. The firm has a 10 percent cost of capital.

a Determine the net present value *(NPV)* of the project.

b Determine the profitability index *(PI)* for the project.

c Determine the internal rate of return *(IRR)* for the project.

d Would you recommend that Lilo accept or reject the project? Explain your answer.

15-15 **(ARR, Payback, NPV, PI, and IRR)** Bruce Read Enterprises is attempting to evaluate the feasibility of investing $95,000 in a piece of equipment having a five-year life. The firm has estimated the *profits after taxes* and *cash inflows* associated with the proposal as follows:

Year	Profits after taxes	Cash inflows
1	$ 5,000	$20,000
2	3,000	25,000
3	9,000	30,000
4	14,000	35,000
5	19,000	40,000

The firm has a 12 percent cost of capital.

a Calculate the average rate of return *(ARR)* for the proposed investment.

b Calculate the payback period for the proposed investment.

c Calculate the net present value *(NPV)* for the proposed investment.

d Calculate the profitability index *(PI)* for the proposed investment.

e Calculate the internal rate of return *(IRR)*, rounded to the nearest whole percent, for the proposed investment.

f Evaluate the acceptability of the proposed investment using *NPV, PI,* and *IRR*. What recommendation would you make relative to implementation of the project? Why?

15-16 **(NPV, IRR, and Conflicting Rankings)** Candor Enterprises is considering two mutually exclusive projects. The firm, which has a

12 percent cost of capital, has estimated its cash flows as shown in the following table.

	Project A	Project B
Initial investment	$130,000	$85,000
Year	**Cash inflows**	
1	$25,000	$40,000
2	35,000	35,000
3	45,000	30,000
4	50,000	10,000
5	55,000	5,000

a Calculate the *NPV* of each project and assess its acceptability.
b Calculate the *IRR* for each project and assess its acceptability.
c Evaluate and discuss the rankings of the two projects based on your findings in **a** and **b**.

15-17 **(All Techniques—Mutually Exclusive Investment Decision)** The Easi Chair Company is attempting to select the best of three mutually exclusive projects for increasing its aluminum extrusion capacity. The initial investment and after-tax cash inflows associated with each project are given in the table.

Cash flow	Project A	Project B	Project C
Initial investment	$60,000	$100,000	$110,000
Cash inflow, years 1–5	$20,000	$ 31,500	$ 32,500

a Calculate the average rate of return for each project using the *cash inflows* rather than the after-tax profits.
b Calculate the payback period for each project.
c Calculate the net present value of each project assuming that the firm has a cost of capital equal to 13 percent.
d Calculate the internal rate of return for each project.
e Assuming that the cost of capital is 13 percent, which project would you recommend? Why?

15-18 **(All Techniques—Mutually Exclusive Projects)** The following two proposals of equal risk have been made for the purchase of new equipment. The firm's cost of capital is 13 percent. The cash flows for each project are given in the table at the top of the next page.

a Use the firm's *cash inflows* rather than after-tax profits to calculate the average rate of return *(ARR)* for each project.
b Calculate each project's payback period.
c Calculate the net present value *(NPV)* for each project.
d Calculate the profitability index *(PI)* for each project.
e Calculate the internal rate of return *(IRR)* for each project.

	Project A	**Project B**
Initial investment	$80,000	$50,000
Year	**Cash inflows**	
1	$15,000	$15,000
2	20,000	15,000
3	25,000	15,000
4	30,000	15,000
5	35,000	15,000

f Summarize the preferences dictated by each measure and indicate which project you would recommend if the firm has (1) unlimited funds and (2) capital rationing.

15-19 ■ **(Integrative — Complete Investment Decision)** Hot Springs Press is considering purchase of a new printing press. The total installed cost of the press would be $2.2 million. This outlay would be partially offset by the sale of an existing press. The old press has zero book value, cost $1 million ten years earlier, and can be sold currently for $1.2 million before taxes. As a result of the new press, sales in each of the next five years are expected to increase by $1.6 million, but product costs (excluding depreciation) will represent 50 percent of sales. The press will be depreciated under ACRS using a five-year recovery period (see Table 3.6 on page 54). The firm is subject to a 40 percent tax rate on both ordinary income and capital gains. Hot Springs Press's cost of capital is 11 percent.

a Determine the initial investment required by the new press.

b Determine the operating cash inflows attributable to the new press. (Note: Be sure to consider the depreciation in year 6.)

c Determine the payback period.

d Determine the net present value and the internal rate of return related to the proposed new press.

e Make a recommendation to accept or reject the new press and justify your answer.

15-20 **(Capital Rationing — _IRR_ and _NPV_ Approaches)** Bromley and Sons is attempting to select the best of a group of independent projects competing for the firm's fixed capital budget of $4.5 million. The firm recognizes that any unused portion of this budget will earn less than its 15 percent cost of capital, thereby resulting in a present value of inflows less than the initial investment. The firm has summarized the key data to be used in selecting the best group of projects in the table at the top of the next page.

a Use the _internal rate of return (IRR) approach_ to select the best group of projects.

b Use the _net present value (NPV) approach_ to select the best group of projects.

c Compare, contrast, and discuss your findings in **a** and **b**.

d Which projects should the firm implement? Why?

Project	Initial investment	IRR	Present value of inflows at 15%
A	$5,000,000	17%	$5,400,000
B	800,000	18	1,100,000
C	2,000,000	19	2,300,000
D	1,500,000	16	1,600,000
E	800,000	22	900,000
F	2,500,000	23	3,000,000
G	1,200,000	20	1,300,000

15-21 **(Capital Rationing—NPV Approach)** A firm must select the optimal group of projects from those in the table, given its capital budget of $1 million.

Project	Initial investment	NPV
A	$300,000	$ 84,000
B	200,000	10,000
C	100,000	25,000
D	900,000	90,000
E	500,000	70,000
F	100,000	50,000
G	800,000	160,000

a Calculate the *profitability index (PI)* associated with each project.
b Select the optimal group of projects using the *PIs* from **a** to prepare an initial ranking. Keep in mind that unused funds are costly.

15-22 **(Sensitivity Analysis)** Renaissance Pharmaceutical is in the process of evaluating two mutually exclusive additions to their processing capacity. The firm's financial analysts have developed pessimistic, most likely, and optimistic estimates of the annual cash inflows associated with each project. These estimates are given in the following table.

	Project A	Project B
Initial investment	$8,000	$8,000
Outcome	**Annual cash inflows**	
Pessimistic	$ 200	$ 900
Most likely	1,000	1,000
Optimistic	1,800	1,100

a Determine the range of annual cash inflows for each of the two projects.
b Assume that the firm's cost of capital is 10 percent and that both projects have 20-year lives. Construct a table similar to that above for the *NPVs* for each project. Include the *range* of *NPVs* for each project.

c Do **a** and **b** provide consistent views of the two projects? Explain.

d Which project would you recommend? Why?

15-23 **(Expected *NPV* and Risk)**   Using the net present values (*NPV*s) and associated probabilities for projects X and Y summarized in the table below,

a Calculate and compare the expected *NPV*s of the projects.

b Compare the riskiness of the two projects.

PROJECT X		PROJECT Y	
NPV ($)	Probability	*NPV* ($)	Probability
−15,000	.01	−20,000	.00
0	.03	−10,000	.02
15,000	.03	0	.04
25,000	.05	10,000	.06
30,000	.15	20,000	.08
35,000	.50	30,000	.15
40,000	.15	40,000	.35
45,000	.05	50,000	.20
55,000	.03	60,000	.05
70,000	.00	70,000	.03
		80,000	.01
		90,000	.01
		100,000	.00

15-24 **(Statistical Evaluation of *NPV*)**   A clothing manufacturer is considering a new line. The following table summarizes the net present values (*NPV*s) and associated probabilities for various outcomes for the two lines being considered.

Market outcome	Probability	NET PRESENT VALUE	
		Line S	Line T
Very poor	.05	−$ 6,000	$ 500
Poor	.15	2,000	4,500
Average	.60	8,500	8,000
Good	.15	15,000	12,500
Excellent	.05	23,000	16,500

a Calculate the expected *NPV* for each line.

b Calculate the range of *NPV*s for each line.

c Calculate the standard deviation of *NPV*, σ_{NPV}, for each line.

d Calculate the coefficient of variation of *NPV*, CV_{NPV}, for each line.

e Using the statistics developed in **a** through **d**, evaluate the risk and return of the lines. Which do you prefer? Why?

15-25 **(Decision Trees)**   The Ouija Board-Games Company can bring out one of two new games this season. The *Signs Away* game has a higher initial cost but also has a higher expected return. *Monopolistic Competition,* the alternative, has a slightly lower initial cost but also has a lower expected return. The present values (*PVs*) and probabilities associated with each game are listed in the following table.

Game	Initial investment	PV of cash inflows	Probabilities
Signs Away	$140,000		1.00
		$320,000	.30
		220,000	.50
		− 80,000	.20
Monopolistic Competition	$120,000		1.00
		$260,000	.20
		200,000	.45
		− 50,000	.35

a Construct a decision tree to analyze the games.
b Which game would you recommend (following a decision-tree analysis)?
c Has your analysis captured the differences in project risk? Explain.

15-26 **(Simulation)**   Wales Castings has compiled the following information on a capital expenditure proposal:

(1) The projected cash *inflows* are normally distributed with a mean of $36,000 and a standard deviation of $9,000.
(2) The projected cash *outflows* are normally distributed with a mean of $30,000 and a standard deviation of $6,000.
(3) The firm has an 11 percent cost of capital.
(4) The probability distributions of cash inflows and cash outflows are not expected to change over the project's 10-year life.

a Describe how the preceding data could be used to develop a simulation model for finding the net present value of the project.
b Discuss the advantages of using a simulation to evaluate the proposed project.

15-27 **(Certainty Equivalents — Accept-Reject Decision)**   Pleasantville Ball Valve has constructed a table, shown below, that gives expected cash inflows and certainty equivalents for these cash inflows. These measures are for a new machine that lasts five years and requires an initial investment of $95,000. The firm has a 15 percent cost of capital, and the risk-free rate is 10 percent.

Year	Cash inflows	Certainty equivalent
1	$35,000	1.0
2	35,000	.8
3	35,000	.6
4	35,000	.6
5	35,000	.2

a What is the net present value (unadjusted for risk)?

b What is the certainty equivalent net present value?

c Should the firm accept the project? Explain.

d Management has some doubts about the estimate of the certainty equivalent for year 5. There is some evidence that it may not be any lower than for year 4. What impact might this have on the decision you recommended in **c**? Explain.

15-28 **(Certainty Equivalents — Mutually Exclusive Decision)** JAN Ventures, Inc., is considering investing in either of two mutually exclusive projects, C and D. The firm has a 14 percent cost of capital, and the risk-free rate is currently 9 percent. The initial investment, expected cash inflows, and certainty equivalents associated with each of the projects are presented in the following table.

	PROJECT C		PROJECT D	
Initial investment	$40,000		$56,000	
Year	Cash inflows	Certainty equivalent	Cash inflows	Certainty equivalent
1	$20,000	.90	$20,000	.95
2	16,000	.80	25,000	.90
3	12,000	.60	15,000	.85
4	10,000	.50	20,000	.80
5	10,000	.40	10,000	.80

a Find the net present value (unadjusted for risk) for each project. Which is preferred using this measure?

b Find the certainty equivalent net present value for each project. Which is preferred using this risk-adjustment technique?

c Compare and discuss your findings in **a** and **b**. Which, if either, of the projects would you recommend that the firm accept? Explain.

15-29 **(Risk-Adjusted Discount Rates — Basic)** P. Ladew, Inc., is considering investment in one of three mutually exclusive projects, E, F, and G. The firm's cost of capital is 15 percent, and the risk-free rate, R_F, is 10 percent. The firm has gathered the following basic cash flow and risk index data for each project.

	PROJECT(j)		
	E	F	G
Initial investment	$15,000	$11,000	$19,000
Year	Cash inflows		
1	$6,000	$6,000	$ 4,000
2	6,000	4,000	6,000
3	6,000	5,000	8,000
4	6,000	2,000	12,000
Risk index (RI_j)	1.80	1.00	0.60

a Find the net present value *(NPV)* of each project using the firm's cost of capital. Which project is preferred in this situation?

b The firm uses the following equation to determine the risk-adjusted discount rate, $RADR_j$, for each project *j*.

$$RADR_j = R_F + RI_j \times (k - R_F)$$

where

R_F = risk-free rate of return
RI_j = risk index for project *j*
k = cost of capital

Substitute each project's risk index into this equation to determine its *RADR*.

c Use the *RADR* for each project to determine its risk-adjusted *NPV*. Which project is preferred in this situation?

d Compare and discuss your findings in **a** and **c**. Which project would you recommend that the firm accept?

15-30 **(Integrative — Certainty Equivalents and Risk-Adjusted Discount Rates)** After a careful evaluation of investment alternatives and opportunities, the Joely Company has determined that the following is the best estimate of the market risk-return function.

Risk index	Appropriate discount rate
0.0	7.0% (risk-free rate)
0.2	8.0
0.4	9.0
0.6	10.0
0.8	11.0
1.0	12.0
1.2	13.0
1.4	14.0
1.6	15.0
1.8	16.0
2.0	17.0

The firm is faced with two mutually exclusive projects, A and B. The following are the data the firm has been able to gather about the projects:

	Project A	Project B
Initial investment	$20,000	$30,000
Project life	5 years	5 years
Annual cash inflow	$ 7,000	$10,000
Risk index	0.2	1.4

Year	Certainty equivalents	
	Project A	Project B
0	1.00	1.00
1	0.95	0.90
2	0.90	0.80
3	0.90	0.70
4	0.85	0.70
Greater than 4	0.80	0.60

All the firm's cash inflows have already been adjusted for taxes.

a Evaluate the projects using *certainty equivalents.*

b Evaluate the projects using *risk-adjusted discount rates.*

c Discuss your findings in **a** and **b** and explain why the two approaches are alternative techniques for considering risk in capital budgeting.

15-31 **(Risk Classes and *RADR*)**   Attila Industries is attempting to select the best of three mutually exclusive projects, X, Y, and Z. Though all the projects have five-year lives, they possess differing degrees of risk. Project X is in Class V, the highest-risk class; project Y is in Class II, the below-average-risk class; and project Z is in Class III, the average-risk class. The basic cash flow data for each project and the risk classes and risk-adjusted discount rates (*RADR*s) used by the firm are given in the following tables.

	Project X	Project Y	Project Z
Initial investment	$180,000	$235,000	$310,000
Year		**Cash inflows**	
1	$80,000	$50,000	$90,000
2	70,000	60,000	90,000
3	60,000	70,000	90,000
4	60,000	80,000	90,000
5	60,000	90,000	90,000

Risk Classes and *RADR*s

Class	Description	Risk-adjusted discount rate (*RADR*)
I	Lowest risk	10%
II	Below-average risk	13
III	Average risk	15
IV	Above-average risk	19
V	Highest risk	22

a Find the risk-adjusted *NPV* for each project.

b Which, if any, project would you recommend the firm undertake?

16

CAPITAL STRUCTURE AND DIVIDEND POLICY

After studying this chapter, you should be able to:

● Understand capital structure, including the basic types of capital, external assessment of capital structure, and the concept of an optimal capital structure.

● Discuss the graphic presentation, risk considerations, and basic shortcoming of using the *EBIT-EPS* approach to compare capital structures.

● Describe cash dividend payment procedures, dividend reinvestment plans, the residual theory of dividends and related arguments, and the key factors that affect dividend policy.

● Describe and evaluate the three basic types of dividend policies—constant-payout-ratio, regular, and low-regular-and-extra—employed by firms.

● Contrast the basic features, objectives, and procedures for paying other forms of dividends, including stock dividends, stock splits, and stock repurchases.

Capital structure and dividend policy are important long-term financial decision areas. Both are deeply rooted in financial theory and play an important role in the maximization of shareholder wealth. The firm's **capital structure** — the mix of long-term debt and equity utilized by the firm — can significantly affect its value by affecting risk and return. Poor capital structure decisions can result in a high cost of capital, thereby making more investments unacceptable. Effective decisions can lower the cost of capital, resulting in more acceptable investments that will add to owners' wealth.

capital structure The mix of long-term debt and equity utilized by the firm.

As noted in Chapter 12, expected cash dividends are the key return variable from which owners and investors determine share value. In each period, any earnings that remain after satisfying obligations to creditors, the government, and preferred stockholders can be retained by the firm, paid out as cash dividends, or divided between retained earnings and cash dividends. Retained earnings can be invested in assets that will help the firm to expand or maintain its present rate of growth. On the other hand, the owners of the firm generally desire some current return on their equity investment — the payment of a cash dividend, which reduces the amount of earnings retained. Here we initially discuss the important aspects of capital structure followed by a comprehensive review of dividend policy.

THE FIRM'S CAPITAL STRUCTURE

Capital structure is one of the most complex areas of financial decision making due to its interrelationship with other financial decision variables. An ability to assess the firm's capital structure and to understand its relationship to risk, return, and value is a necessary skill. This and the following two sections link together the concepts presented in Chapters 4, 5, 12, and 13.

Types of Capital

The term **capital** denotes the long-term funds of the firm. All of the items on the right-hand side of the firm's balance sheet, excluding current liabilities, are sources of capital. The simplified balance sheet at the top of page 496 illustrates the basic breakdown of total capital into its two components — debt capital and equity capital.

capital The long-term funds of the firm; all items on the right-hand side of the firm's balance sheet, excluding current liabilities.

Debt capital includes all long-term borrowing incurred by the firm. The various types and characteristics of long-term debt will be discussed in detail in Chapter 18. In Chapter 13 the cost of debt was found to be less than the cost of other forms of financing. The relative inexpensiveness of debt capital is attributable to the fact that the lenders take the least risk of any long-term contributors of capital. This is be-

debt capital All long-term borrowing incurred by the firm.

Balance Sheet

Assets	Current liabilities				
	Long-term debt	}	Debt capital	}	Total capital
	Stockholders' equity 　Preferred stock 　Common stock equity 　　Common stock 　　Retained earnings	}	Equity capital		

cause (1) they have a higher priority of claim against any earnings or assets available for payment, (2) they have a far stronger legal pressure against the company to make payment than that of preferred or common stockholders, and (3) the tax-deductibility of interest payments lowers the debt cost to the firm substantially.

equity capital The long-term funds provided by the firm's owners, the stockholders.

　　Equity capital consists of the long-term funds provided by the firm's owners, the stockholders. Unlike borrowed funds that must be repaid at a specified future date, equity capital is expected to remain in the firm for an indefinite period of time. The two basic sources of equity capital are (1) preferred stock and (2) common stock equity, which includes common stock and retained earnings. As demonstrated in Chapter 13, common stock is typically the most expensive form of equity, followed by retained earnings and preferred stock, respectively. The characteristics of retained earnings are briefly discussed as part of the dividend presentation later in this chapter; preferred and common stock are discussed further in Chapter 19.

　　Our concern here is the relationship between debt and equity capital. Key differences between these two types of capital relative to voice in management, claims on income and assets, maturity, and tax treatment are summarized in Table 16.1. It should be clear that due to its secondary position relative to debt, suppliers of equity capital take greater risk and therefore must be compensated with higher expected returns than suppliers of debt capital.

External Assessment of Capital Structure

In Chapter 5 it was shown that *financial leverage* results from the use of fixed-payment financing, such as debt and preferred stock, to magnify return and risk. Debt ratios, which measure, directly and indirectly, the firm's degree of financial leverage were presented in Chapter 4. A direct measure of the degree of indebtedness is the *debt ratio*: The higher this ratio, the greater the firm's financial leverage. The measures of the firm's ability to meet fixed payments associated with debt include the *times interest earned ratio* and the *fixed-payment coverage ratio*. These ratios provide indirect information on leverage. The smaller these

TABLE 16.1 Key Differences Between Debt and Equity Capital

	TYPE OF CAPITAL	
Characteristic	Debt	Equity
Voice in management[a]	No	Yes
Claims on income and assets	Senior to equity	Subordinate to debt
Maturity	Stated	None
Tax treatment	Interest deduction	No deduction

[a] In default, debtholders and preferred stockholders *may* receive a voice in management; otherwise, only common stockholders have voting rights.

ratios, the less able the firm is to meet payments as they come due. In general, low-debt-payment ratios are associated with high degrees of financial leverage. The more risk a firm is willing to take, the greater will be its financial leverage. In theory, the firm should maintain financial leverage consistent with a capital structure that maximizes owners' wealth.

An acceptable degree of financial leverage for one industry or line of business can be highly risky in another due to differing operating characteristics between industries or lines of business. Table 16.2 presents the debt and times interest earned ratios for selected industries and lines of business. Significant industry differences can be seen in these data. For example, the debt ratio for electronic computing equipment manufacturers is 52.9 percent, while for auto retailers it is 71.6 percent. Of course, differences in debt positions are also likely to exist *within* an industry or line of business.

THE OPTIMAL CAPITAL STRUCTURE

A firm's capital structure is closely related to its cost of capital. Many debates over whether an "optimal" capital structure exists are found in the financial literature. This controversy began in the late 1950s, and there is as yet no resolution. Those who believe that an optimal capital structure exists follow the **traditional approach,** while those who believe such a structure does *not* exist are supporters of the **M and M approach,** named for its initial proponents, Franco Modigliani and Merton H. Miller.

To provide some insight into what is meant by an optimal capital structure, we will examine the traditional approach.[1] In the traditional

traditional approach
The theory that an optimal capital structure exists, and that the value of the firm is maximized when the cost of capital is minimized.

M and M approach
Named for its initial proponents, Franco Modigliani and Merton H. Miller, the theory that an optimal capital structure does *not* exist.

[1] You may wonder why attention is given only to the traditional approach and not to the Modigliani and Miller approach. The chief reason is that the M and M model is algebraically somewhat rigorous, and it is more important at this level to become familiar with the key concepts that affect managerial decisions than to delve deeply into the theory of finance. Business people tend to believe the traditional as opposed to the M and M approach.

TABLE 16.2 Debt Ratios for Selected Industries and Lines of Business (Fiscal Years Ended 6/30/84 through 3/31/85)

Industry or line of business	Debt ratio	Times interest earned ratio
Manufacturing industries		
Books: publishing and printing	63.1%	4.6×
Diary products	66.4	3.2
Electronic computing equipment	52.9	4.4
Fertilizers	64.1	1.8
Iron and steel foundries	61.0	2.8
Jewelry, precious metals	39.5	2.0
Motor vehicles	68.4	4.3
Wines, distilled liquors, liqueurs	64.1	1.5
Women's dresses	57.4	2.8
Wholesaling industries		
Furniture	66.3	2.9
General groceries	68.3	2.2
Hardware and paints	62.0	2.8
Men's and boys' clothing	64.4	2.7
Petroleum products	67.8	2.3
Retailing industries		
Autos, new and used	71.6	3.2
Department stores	55.6	2.6
Radio, television, record players	69.6	3.2
Restaurants	72.4	2.2
Shoes	67.9	2.7
Service industries		
Accounting, auditing, bookkeeping	49.7	6.1
Advertising agencies	74.7	4.4
Auto-repair shops	67.6	3.0
Insurance agents and brokers	80.8	2.7
Physicians	56.0	3.5
Travel agencies	71.6	4.0

SOURCE: *Annual Statement Studies, 1985* (fiscal years ended 6/30/84 through 3/31/85) (Philadelphia: Robert Morris Associates, 1985) Copyright © 1985 by Robert Morris Associates.

NOTE: Robert Morris Associates recommends that these ratios be regarded only as general guidelines and not as absolute industry norms. No claim is made as to the representativeness of their figures.

approach to capital structure, *the value of the firm is maximized when the cost of capital is minimized.* Using a simple zero growth valuation model (see Equation 12.11 in Chapter 12), the value of the firm, V, can be defined by Equation 16.1, where *EBIT* equals earnings before interest and taxes and k_a is the weighted average cost of capital:

$$V = \frac{EBIT}{k_a}$$

(16.1)

Clearly, if we assume that *EBIT* is constant, the value of the firm, V, is maximized by minimizing the weighted average cost of capital, k_a.

Cost Functions

It can be seen from Figure 16.1 that three cost functions—the cost of debt, k_i; the cost of equity, k_s; and the weighted average cost of capital, k_a—are plotted as a function of financial leverage measured by the debt ratio (debt-to-total assets). The *cost of debt*, k_i, remains constant as financial leverage increases from zero up to the point where lenders begin to raise interest rates to compensate for the increasing risk. At that point, the cost of debt will increase. The *cost of equity*, k_s, also increases with increasing financial leverage, but much more rapidly than the cost of debt. The faster increase in the cost of equity occurs because the firm's earnings are discounted at a higher rate as leverage increases in order to compensate for the higher degree of financial risk.

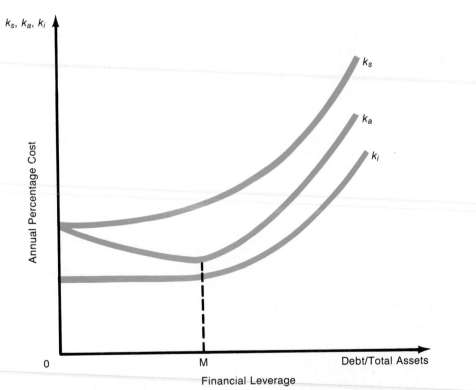

FIGURE 16.1 The Traditional Approach to Capital Structure
As financial leverage increases, the cost of debt, k_i, remains constant and then rises, while the cost of equity, k_s, always rises. The resulting weighted average cost of capital, k_a, is U-shaped or saucer-shaped causing the optimal capital structure to occur at its minimum, M, where the value of the firm is maximized.

The *weighted average cost of capital,* k_a, results from a weighted average of the firm's debt and equity capital. At a debt ratio of zero, the firm is 100 percent equity-financed. As debt is substituted for equity and as the debt ratio increases, the weighted average cost of capital declines because the debt cost is less than the equity cost ($k_i < k_s$). As the debt ratio continues to increase, the increased debt cost eventually causes the weighted average cost of capital to rise (after point M in Figure 16.1). This behavior results in a U-shaped, or saucer-shaped, weighted average cost of capital function, k_a.

A Graphic View of the Optimal Structure

optimal capital structure Under the *traditional approach* to capital structure, the capital structure for which the weighted average cost of capital is minimized, thereby maximizing the firm's possessive value.

Since the maximization of value, V, is achieved when the overall cost of capital, k_a, is at a minimum (see Equation 16.1), the **optimal capital structure** is therefore that at which the weighted average cost of capital, k_a, is minimized. In Figure 16.1 the point M represents the point of optimal financial leverage and hence of optimal capital structure for the firm, since it results in a minimum weighted average cost of capital, k_a. Generally, the lower the firm's weighted average cost of capital, the greater the difference between the return on a project and this cost, and therefore the greater the owners' return. These increased returns of course contribute to an increase in the firm's value.

THE *EBIT-EPS* APPROACH TO CAPITAL STRUCTURE

EBIT-EPS approach Involves selecting the capital structure that maximizes earnings per share *(EPS)* over the expected range of earnings before interest and taxes *(EBIT)*.

The graphic comparison of financing plans on a set of *EBIT-EPS* axes was briefly described in Chapter 5. Here, a similar *EBIT-EPS* approach is used to evaluate alternative capital structures. The **EBIT-EPS approach** to capital structure involves selecting the capital structure that maximizes earnings per share *(EPS)* over the expected range of earnings before interest and taxes *(EBIT)*. Since a key variable affecting the market value of a firm's shares is its earnings, *EPS* can be used to assess the effect of various capital structures on the shareholders' wealth.

Presenting a Financing Plan Graphically

To analyze the effects of a firm's capital structure on the owners' returns, we consider the relationship between earnings before interest and taxes *(EBIT)* and earnings per share *(EPS)*. A constant level of expected *EBIT* is assumed in order to isolate the impact on returns of the financing costs associated with alternative capital structures (financing plans). *EPS* is used to measure the owners' returns, which are expected to be closely related to share price.

THE DATA REQUIRED   To graph a financing plan, at least two *EBIT-EPS* coordinates are required. The approach for obtaining coordinates can be illustrated by the following example.

EXAMPLE

The JSG Company's current capital structure is as follows.

CURRENT CAPITAL STRUCTURE

Long-term debt	$ 0
Common stock equity (25,000 shares @ $20)	500,000
Total capital (assets)	$500,000

Note that JSG's capital structure currently contains only common stock equity; the firm has no debt or preferred stock. If we for convenience assume the firm has no current liabilities, its debt ratio (total liabilities ÷ total assets) is currently 0 percent ($0 ÷ $500,000); it therefore has *zero* financial leverage. Assume the firm is in the 40 percent tax bracket.

EBIT-EPS coordinates for JSG's current capital structure can be found using the technique presented in Chapter 5. Since the *EBIT-EPS* graph is a straight line, any two *EBIT* values can be used to find coordinates. Here we arbitrarily use values of $100,000 and $200,000.

EBIT (assumed)	$100,000	$200,000
−Interest (rate × $0 debt)	0	0
Earnings before taxes	$100,000	$200,000
−Taxes (.40)	40,000	80,000
Earnings after taxes	$ 60,000	$120,000
EPS	$\dfrac{\$60{,}000}{25{,}000 \text{ sh.}} = \$2.40$	$\dfrac{\$120{,}000}{25{,}000 \text{ sh.}} = \$4.80$

The two *EBIT-EPS* coordinates resulting from these calculations are (1) $100,000 *EBIT* and $2.40 *EPS* and (2) $200,000 *EBIT* and $4.80 *EPS*. ■

PLOTTING THE DATA   The two sets of *EBIT-EPS* coordinates developed for JSG Company's current zero leverage (debt ratio = 0 percent) situation can be plotted on a set of *EBIT-EPS* axes, as shown in Figure 16.2. Since our concern is only with positive levels of *EPS*, the graph has not

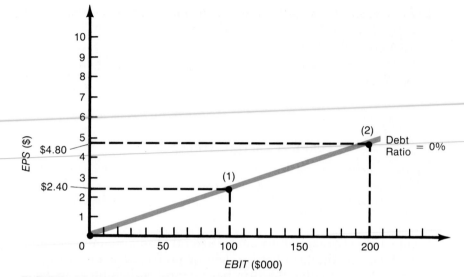

**FIGURE 16.2 Graphic Presentation of JSG Company's
Zero Leverage Financing Plan**

Plotting the two coordinates (1) $100,000 *EBIT* and $2.40 *EPS* and (2) $200,000
EBIT and $4.80 *EPS* on the *EBIT-EPS* axes results in a straight line representing JSG
Company's zero leverage (debt ratio = 0 percent) financing plan. The figure shows
the level of *EPS* for each level of *EBIT*.

been extended below the *x*-axis. The figure shows the level of *EPS*
expected for each level of *EBIT*.

Comparing Alternative Capital Structures

The graphic display of financing plans in a fashion similar to Figure 16.2
can be used to compare alternative capital structures. The following
example illustrates this procedure.

EXAMPLE

The JSG Company, whose current zero leverage capital structure
was described in the preceding example and Figure 16.2, is contemplating shifting its capital structure to either of two leveraged
positions. In order to maintain its $500,000 of total capital, JSG's
capital structure will be shifted to greater leverage by issuing debt
and using the proceeds to retire an equivalent amount of common
stock. The two alternative capital structures result in debt ratios of
30 percent and 60 percent, respectively. The basic information on
the current and two alternative capital structures is summarized
in Table 16.3.

TABLE 16.3 Basic Information on JSG Company's Current and Alternative Capital Structures

Capital structure debt ratio (1)	Total assets[a] (2)	Debt [(1) × (2)] (3)	Equity [(2) − (3)] (4)	Interest rate on debt[b] (5)	Annual interest [(3) × (5)] (6)	Shares of common stock outstanding [(4) ÷ $20][c] (7)
0% (current plan)	$500,000	$ 0	$500,000	0 %	$ 0	25,000
30	500,000	150,000	350,000	10	15,000	17,500
60	500,000	300,000	200,000	16.5	49,500	10,000

[a] Because the firm for convenience is assumed to have no current liabilities, total assets equals total capital of $500,000.

[b] The interest rate on all debt increases with increases in the debt ratio due to the greater leverage and risk associated with higher debt ratios.

[c] The $20 value represents the book value of common stock equity.

Using the data in Table 16.3, the coordinates needed to plot the 30 percent and 60 percent debt capital structures can be calculated. For convenience, using the same $100,000 and $200,000 *EBIT* values used earlier to plot the current capital structure, we get the following:

CAPITAL STRUCTURE

	30% Debt		60% Debt	
EBIT (assumed)	$100,000	$200,000	$100,000	$200,000
−Interest (Table 16.3)	15,000	15,000	49,500	49,500
Earnings before taxes	$ 85,000	$185,000	$ 50,500	$150,500
−Taxes (.40)	34,000	74,000	20,200	60,200
Earnings after taxes	$ 51,000	$111,000	$ 30,300	$ 90,300
EPS	$\frac{\$51,000}{17,500 \text{ sh.}} = \$2.91$	$\frac{\$111,000}{17,500 \text{ sh.}} = \$6.34$	$\frac{\$30,300}{10,000 \text{ sh.}} = \$3.03$	$\frac{\$90,300}{10,000 \text{ sh.}} = \$9.03$

The two sets of *EBIT-EPS* coordinates developed above along with those developed earlier for the current zero-leverage capital structure are summarized in Table 16.4. They are used to plot the 30 percent and 60 percent capital structures (along with the 0 percent structure) on the *EBIT-EPS* axes in Figure 16.3. An analysis of the figure shows that over certain ranges of *EBIT*, each capital structure reflects superiority over the others in terms of maximizing *EPS*. The zero-leverage capital structure (debt ratio = 0 percent) would be superior to either of the other capital structures for levels of *EBIT* between $0 and $50,000. Between $50,000 and $95,500 of *EBIT*, the capital structure associated with a debt ratio of 30 percent would be preferred. At a level of *EBIT* in

TABLE 16.4 *EBIT-EPS* Coordinates for JSG Company Selected Capital Structures

Capital structure debt ratio	EBIT	
	$100,000	$200,000
	Earnings per share *(EPS)*	
0%	$2.40	$4.80
30	2.91	6.34
60	3.03	9.03

excess of $95,500 the capital structure associated with a debt ratio of 60 percent would provide the highest earnings per share.[2] ■

Considering Risk in *EBIT-EPS* Analysis

When interpreting *EBIT-EPS* analysis, it is important to consider the risk of each capital structure alternative. Graphically, the risk of each capital structure can be viewed in light of the *financial breakeven point* (*EBIT*-axis intercept) and the *degree of financial leverage* reflected in the slope of the capital structure line. The higher the financial break-even point and the steeper the slope of the capital structure line, the greater the financial risk. Further assessment of risk can be performed using ratios. With increased financial leverage, as measured using the debt ratio, we would expect a corresponding decline in the firm's ability to make scheduled interest payments, as measured using the times interest earned ratio.

EXAMPLE

Reviewing the three capital structures plotted for the JSG Company in Figure 16.3, we can see that as the debt ratio increases, so does the financial risk of each alternative. Both the financial breakeven point and the slope of the capital structure lines increase with increasing debt ratios. If we use the $100,000 *EBIT* value, the times interest earned ratio (*EBIT* ÷ interest) for the zero-leverage capital structure is infinity ($100,000 ÷ 0), for the 30 percent debt case it is 6.67 ($100,000 ÷ $15,000), and for the 60 percent debt case it is 2.02 ($100,000 ÷ $49,500). Since lower

[2] Algebraic techniques are available for finding the *indifference points* between the capital structure alternatives. Due to their relative complexity, these techniques are not presented. Instead, emphasis here is given to the visual estimation of these points from the graph.

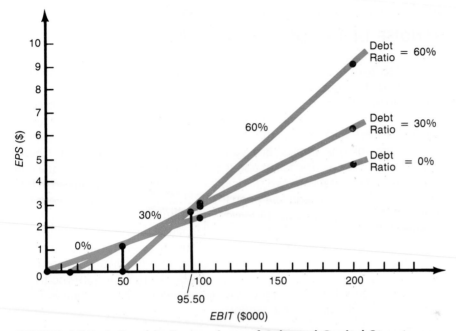

FIGURE 16.3 A Graphic Comparison of Selected Capital Structures for JSG Company

The zero leverage capital structure (debt ratio = 0 percent) maximizes *EPS* when *EBIT* is between $0 and $50,000; between $50,000 and $95,500 of *EBIT,* the capital structure with the 30 percent debt ratio is preferred; and for *EBIT* in excess of $95,500 the capital structure with the 60 percent debt ratio maximizes *EPS.*

times interest earned ratios reflect higher risk, these ratios support the earlier conclusion that the risk of the capital structures increases with increasing financial leverage. The capital structure for a debt ratio of 60 percent is more risky than that for a debt ratio of 30 percent, which in turn is more risky than the capital structure for a debt ratio of 0 percent. ▪

Basic Shortcoming of *EBIT-EPS* Analysis

The most important point to recognize when using *EBIT-EPS* analysis is that this technique tends to concentrate on *maximization of earnings rather than maximization of owners' wealth.* Although there may be a positive relationship between these two objectives, the use of an *EPS-*maximizing approach ignores risk. To select the best capital structure, both return *(EPS)* and risk (via the required return, k_s) must be integrated into a valuation framework in a fashion consistent with the capital structure theory presented earlier. While more sophisticated

---

MERCHANDISE DIVIDENDS: A HIDDEN PERK?

Irked to learn that the chairman of a company whose shares you own can use the corporate jet for sightseeing? Or that the president gets free weekends at the corporate hunting lodge? A slender booklet, *Shareholder Freebies,* may help you cool down. It lists various perks — gifts and merchandise discounts — that you can enjoy by merely being a stockholder in any of some 50 different companies.

Here are some examples. Buy your first 100 or more shares of Chesebrough-Pond's Inc. and get a gift pack of about $65 worth of products. Stop at a unit of Ramada Inns Inc., show that you own stock in the company, and you can earn a free upgrade to a better room. Attend the annual shareholders' meetings of PepsiCo, General Mills, or Shaklee, and you might leave with about $10 worth of samples.

Some of the freebies have been curtailed since the booklet ($9.50 from Buttonwood Press, 41 Park Ave., New York, N.Y. 10016) went to press. And you certainly won't want to figure in a "gift factor" along with the price-earnings ratio when you consider buying a particular stock. But the booklet may inspire you to ask companies in which you hold shares if they have similar deals. "Just by asking you may get them to offer something," say the authors.

Source: "Surprising Dividends from Owning Stock," *Business Week,* November 11, 1985, p. 142. Reprinted from the November 11, 1985, issue of *Business Week* by special permission, © 1985 by McGraw-Hill, Inc.

---

approaches that consider both return and risk are available, their complexity puts them beyond the scope of this basic text.

DIVIDEND FUNDAMENTALS

Dividend policy, like capital structure, can significantly affect the firm's share price. Dividends represent a source of cash flow to stockholders and provide them with information relative to the firm's current and future performance. Because **retained earnings** — earnings not distributed as dividends — are a form of *internal* financing, the dividend decision can significantly affect the firm's *external* financing requirements. In other words, if the firm needs financing, the larger the cash dividend paid, the greater the amount of financing that must be raised externally through borrowing or through the sale of preferred or common stock. To provide an understanding of the fundamentals of dividend policy, we discuss the procedures for paying cash dividends, dividend reinvestment plans, the residual theory of dividends, and the key factors affecting dividend policy.

retained earnings Those earnings of the firm that are not distributed as dividends. A form of *internal* financing.

Cash Dividend Payment Procedures

The payment of cash dividends to corporate stockholders is decided by the firm's board of directors. The directors normally hold a quarterly or semiannual dividend meeting at which they evaluate the past period's financial performance and future outlook to determine whether and in what amount dividends should be paid. The payment date of the cash dividend (if one is declared) must also be established.

AMOUNT OF DIVIDENDS   Whether dividends should be paid and, if they are, how large they should be are important decisions that depend largely on the firm's dividend policy. Most firms pay some cash dividends each period. The amount is generally fixed, although significant increases or decreases in earnings may justify changing it. Most firms have a set policy with respect to the amount of the periodic dividend, but the firm's directors can change this amount at the dividend meeting.

RELEVANT DATES   If the directors of the firm declare a dividend, they will also indicate the record and payment dates associated with the dividend. Typically, the directors issue a statement indicating their dividend decision, the record date, and the payment date. This statement is generally quoted in *The Wall Street Journal, Barron's,* and other financial news media.

   Record Date.   All persons whose names are recorded as stockholders on the **date of record,** which is set by the directors, will at a specified future time receive a declared dividend. These stockholders are often referred to as **holders of record.** Due to the time needed to make bookkeeping entries when a stock is traded, the stock will begin selling **ex dividend** four *business days* prior to the date of record. A simple way to determine the first day on which the stock sells ex dividend is to subtract four from the date of record; if a weekend intervenes, subtract six days. Purchasers of a stock selling ex dividend do not receive the current dividend.

   Payment Date.   The payment date is also set by the directors. It is generally set a few weeks after the record date. The **payment date** is the actual date on which the company will mail the dividend payment to the holders of record. An example will clarify the various dates and accounting entries.

date of record The date, set by the firm's directors, on which all persons whose names are recorded as stockholders will at a specified future time receive a declared dividend.

holders of record Owners of the firm's shares on the *date of record.*

ex dividend Period beginning four business days prior to the date of record during which a stock will be sold without paying the current dividend.

payment date The actual date on which the company will mail the dividend payment to the holders of record.

EXAMPLE

At the quarterly dividend meeting of the Junot Company, held June 10, the directors declared an $.80 per share cash dividend for holders of record on Monday, July 1. The firm had 100,000 shares of common stock outstanding. The payment date for the dividend was August 1. Before the dividend was declared, the key accounts of the firm were as follows:

| Cash | $200,000 | Dividends payable | $ 0 |
| | | Retained earnings | 1,000,000 |

When the dividend was announced by the directors, $80,000 ($.80 per share × 100,000 shares) of the retained earnings was transferred to the dividends payable account. The key accounts thus became

| Cash | $200,000 | Dividends payable | $ 80,000 |
| | | Retained earnings | 920,000 |

The Junot Company's stock sold ex dividend for four *business days* prior to the date of record, which was June 25. This date was found by subtracting six days (since a weekend intervenes) from the July 1 date of record. Purchasers of Junot's stock on June 24 or earlier received the rights to the dividends; those purchasing the stock on or after June 25 did not. When the August 1 payment date arrived, the firm mailed dividend checks to the holders of record as of July 1. This produced the following balances in the key accounts of the firm:

| Cash | $120,000 | Dividends payable | $ 0 |
| | | Retained earnings | 920,000 |

The net effect of declaration and payment of the dividend was to reduce the firm's total assets (and stockholders' equity) by $80,000. ■

Dividend Reinvestment Plans

dividend reinvestment plans Plans offered by firms that enable stockholders to use dividends to acquire full or fractional shares at little or no transaction (brokerage) cost.

A growing number of firms offer **dividend reinvestment plans,** which enable stockholders to use dividends to acquire shares—even fractional shares—at little or no transaction (brokerage) cost. Especially popular between 1982 and 1985 were the plans of public utilities, such as electric companies, telephone companies, and natural gas distributors, because participating shareholders received a special tax break that ended December 31, 1985. Today, cash dividends (or the value of the stocks received through a dividend reinvestment plan) from all plans are taxed as ordinary income. In addition, when the acquired shares are sold, if the proceeds are in excess of the original purchase price, the capital gain will also be taxed as ordinary income.

Dividend reinvestment plans can be handled by a company in either of two ways. Both allow the stockholder to elect to have dividends reinvested in the firm's shares. In one approach, a third-party trustee is paid a fee to buy the firm's *outstanding shares* in the open market on behalf of the shareholders who wish to reinvest their dividends. This type of plan benefits participating shareholders by allowing them to use their dividends to purchase shares generally at a lower transaction cost than they would otherwise pay. The second approach involves buying *newly issued shares* directly from the firm without paying any transaction costs. This approach allows the firm to raise new capital while at the same time permitting owners to reinvest their dividends, frequently at about 5 percent below the current market price. Clearly the existence of dividend reinvestment plans may enhance the appeal of a firm's shares.

The Residual Theory of Dividends

One school of thought — the **residual theory of dividends** — suggests that the dividend paid by a firm should be viewed as a residual — the amount left over after all acceptable investment opportunities have been undertaken. According to this approach, as long as the firm's equity need is in excess of the amount of retained earnings, no cash dividend would be paid. If an excess of retained earnings exists, the residual amount would then be distributed as a cash dividend. This view of dividends tends to suggest that the required return of investors, k_s, is *not* influenced by the firm's dividend policy — a premise that in turn suggests that dividend policy is irrelevant.

residual theory of dividends The theory that the dividend paid by the firm is considered a residual, an amount left over after all acceptable investment opportunities have been undertaken.

THE IRRELEVANCE OF DIVIDENDS   The residual theory of dividends suggests that dividends are irrelevant — that the value of the firm is not affected by its dividend policy. The major advocates of this view are Franco Modigliani and Merton H. Miller (commonly referred to as M and M). They argue that the way a firm splits its earnings between dividends and reinvestment has no direct effect on value. Modigliani and Miller suggest the existence of a **clientele effect:** A firm will attract stockholders whose preferences with respect to the payment and stability of dividends correspond to the payment pattern and stability of the firm itself. Since the shareholders get what they expect, M and M argue that the value of the firm's stock is unaffected by changes in dividend policy.

clientele effect The theory that a firm will attract stockholders whose preferences with respect to the payment and stability of dividends correspond to the payment pattern and stability of the firm itself.

However, recognizing that dividends do somehow affect stock prices, M and M suggest that the positive effects of dividend increases are attributable not to the dividend itself but to the **informational content** of dividends with respect to future earnings. The information provided by the dividends causes owners to bid up the price of the stock based on future expectations. M and M argue that when acceptable

informational content The information provided by the dividends of a firm that causes owners to bid up the price of the stock based on future earnings expectations.

investment opportunities are not available, the firm should distribute the unneeded funds to the owners, who can invest the money in other firms that have acceptable investment alternatives. They conclude that since dividends are irrelevant to the firm's value, the firm does not need to have a dividend policy.

THE RELEVANCE OF DIVIDENDS The key argument of those supporting dividend relevance is that because current dividend payments reduce investor uncertainty, investors will discount the firm's earnings at a lower rate, k_s, thereby placing a higher value on the firm's stock. If dividends are not paid, investor uncertainty will increase, raising the required rate of return, k_s, and lowering the stock's value.

The dividend relevance school's leading proponent, Myron J. Gordon, suggests that stockholders prefer current dividends and that there is, in fact, a direct relationship between the dividend policy of a firm and its market value. Gordon's "bird-in-the-hand" argument suggests that investors are generally risk averters and attach less risk to current as opposed to future dividends or capital gains.

In practice, the actions of financial managers and stockholders alike support the belief that dividend policy affects stock value. Since our concern is with the day-to-day behavior of business firms, the remainder of this chapter is consistent with the widely held belief that dividends *are relevant* — that each firm must develop a dividend policy that fulfills the goals of owners and maximizes their wealth in the long run.

Factors Affecting Dividend Policy

Before discussing the basic types of dividend policies, we should consider the factors involved in formulating dividend policy. These include legal constraints, contractual constraints, internal constraints, the firm's growth prospects, owner considerations, and market considerations.

LEGAL CONSTRAINTS Most states prohibit corporations from paying out as cash dividends any portion of the firm's "legal capital," which is measured by the par value of common stock. Other states define legal capital to include not only the par value of the common stock but also any paid-in capital in excess of par. These "capital impairment restrictions" are generally established to provide a sufficient equity base to protect creditors' claims. An example will clarify the differing definitions of capital.

EXAMPLE

The Miller Flour Company's stockholders' equity account is presented below.

Miller Flour Company's Stockholders' Equity

Common stock at par	$100,000
Paid-in capital in excess of par	200,000
Retained earnings	140,000
Total stockholders' equity	$440,000

In states where the firm's legal capital is defined as the par value of its common stock, the firm could pay out $340,000 ($200,000 + $140,000) in cash dividends without impairing its capital. In states where the firm's legal capital includes all paid-in capital, the firm could pay out only $140,000 in cash dividends. ■

An earnings requirement limiting the amount of dividends to the sum of the firm's present and past earnings is sometimes imposed. In other words, the firm cannot pay more in cash dividends than the sum of its most recent and past retained earnings. However, *the firm is not prohibited from paying more in dividends than its current earnings.*[3]

EXAMPLE

Assume the Miller Flour Company, presented in the preceding example, in the year just ended has $30,000 in earnings available for common stock dividends. An analysis of the stockholders' equity account above indicates that the firm has past retained earnings of $140,000. Thus it could legally pay dividends of up to $170,000. ■

If a firm has overdue liabilities or is legally insolvent or bankrupt (if the fair market value of its assets is less than its liabilities), most states prohibit its payment of cash dividends. In addition, the Internal Revenue Service prohibits firms from accumulating earnings in order to reduce the owners' taxes. A firm's owners must pay income taxes on dividends when received, but the owners are not taxed on capital gains in market value until the stock is sold. A firm may retain a large portion of earnings in order to delay the payment of taxes by the owners. If the

---

[3] A firm having an operating loss in the current period could still pay cash dividends as long as sufficient retained earnings were available and, of course, as long as it had the cash with which to make the payments.

excess earnings accumulation tax The tax levied by the IRS on retained earnings above $250,000, when it has determined that the firm has accumulated an excess of earnings in order to allow owners to delay paying ordinary income taxes.

IRS can determine that a firm has accumulated an excess of earnings in order to allow owners to delay paying ordinary income taxes, it may levy an **excess earnings accumulation tax** on any retained earnings above $250,000—the amount currently exempt from this tax for all firms except personal corporations.

CONTRACTUAL CONSTRAINTS Often the firm's ability to pay cash dividends is constrained by certain restrictive provisions in a loan agreement. Generally, these constraints prohibit the payment of cash dividends until a certain level of earnings has been achieved or limit the amount of dividends paid to a certain amount, or percentage, of earnings. Constraints on dividend payments help to protect creditors from losses due to insolvency on the part of the firm. The violation of a contractual constraint is generally grounds for a demand of immediate payment by the funds supplier affected.

INTERNAL CONSTRAINTS The firm's ability to pay cash dividends is generally constrained by the amount of excess cash available. Although it is possible for a firm to borrow funds to pay dividends, lenders are generally reluctant to make such loans since they produce no tangible or operating benefits that will help the firm repay the loan. Although a firm may have high earnings, its ability to pay dividends may be constrained by a low level of liquid assets (cash and marketable securities).

EXAMPLE

The Miller Flour Company's stockholders' equity account presented earlier indicates that if the firm's legal capital is defined as all paid-in capital, the firm can pay $140,000 in dividends. If the firm has total liquid assets of $50,000 ($20,000 in cash plus marketable securities worth $30,000) and $35,000 of this is needed for operations, the maximum dividend the firm can pay is $15,000 ($50,000 − $35,000). ▪

GROWTH PROSPECTS The firm's financial requirements are directly related to the degree of asset expansion anticipated. If the firm is in a growth stage, it may need all the funds it can get to finance capital expenditures. A growing firm also requires funds to maintain and improve its assets. High-growth firms typically find themselves constantly in need of funds. Their financial requirements may be characterized as large and immediate. Firms exhibiting little or no growth may periodically need funds to replace or renew assets.

A firm must evaluate its financial position from the standpoint of profitability and risk in order to develop insight into its ability to raise capital externally. It must determine not only its ability to raise funds but also the cost and speed with which financing can be obtained. Generally, a large, mature firm has adequate access to new capital, whereas the funds available to a rapidly growing firm may not be sufficient to support the numerous acceptable projects. A growth firm is likely to have to depend heavily on internal financing through retained earnings to take advantage of profitable projects, and is likely to pay out only a very small percentage of its earnings as dividends. A more stable firm that needs capital funds only for planned outlays is better advised to pay out a large proportion of its earnings, especially if it has ready sources of financing.

OWNER CONSIDERATIONS In establishing a dividend policy, the primary concern of the firm should be to maximize owners' wealth. Although it is impossible to establish a policy that will maximize each owner's wealth, the firm must establish a policy that has a favorable effect on the wealth of the *majority* of owners.

One consideration is the tax status of a firm's owners. If a firm has a large percentage of wealthy stockholders who are in a high tax bracket, it may decide to pay out a *lower* percentage of its earnings in order to allow the owners to delay the payment of taxes until they sell the stock. Of course, when the stock is sold, if the proceeds are in excess of the original purchase price, the capital gain will be taxed as ordinary income. Lower-income shareholders, however, who need dividend income, will prefer a *higher* payout of earnings.

A second consideration is the owners' investment opportunities. A firm should not retain funds for investment in projects yielding lower returns than the owners could obtain from external investments of equal risk. The firm should evaluate the returns expected on its own investment opportunities and, using present-value techniques, determine whether greater returns are obtainable from external investments such as government securities or other corporate stocks. If it appears that the owners would have better opportunities externally, the firm should pay out a higher percentage of its earnings. If the firm's investment opportunities are at least as good as similar-risk external investments, a lower payout is justifiable.

A final consideration is the potential dilution of ownership. If a firm pays out a higher percentage of earnings, new equity capital will have to be raised with common stock, which may result in the dilution of both control and earnings for the existing owners. By paying out a low percentage of its earnings, the firm can minimize such possibility of dilution.

MARKET CONSIDERATIONS Since the wealth of the firm's owners is reflected in the market price of the firm's shares, an awareness of the market's probable response to certain types of policies is helpful in formulating a suitable dividend policy. Stockholders are believed to value a fixed or increasing level of dividends as opposed to a fluctuating pattern of dividends. In addition, stockholders generally value a policy of continuous dividend payment. Since paying a fixed or increasing dividend eliminates uncertainty about the magnitude of dividends, the earnings of the firm are likely to be discounted at a lower rate. This should result in an increase in the market value of the stock and therefore increased owners' wealth.

A final market consideration is the *informational content* of dividends. Shareholders often view the firm's dividend payments as an indicator of future success. A stable and continuous dividend conveys to the owners that the firm is in good health and that there is no reason for concern. If the firm skips a dividend payment in a given period due to a loss or to very low earnings, shareholders are likely to react unfavorably. The nonpayment of the dividend creates uncertainty about the future, and this uncertainty is likely to result in lower stock values. Owners and investors generally construe a dividend payment during a period of losses as an indication that the loss is merely temporary.

TYPES OF DIVIDEND POLICIES

dividend policy The firm's plan of action to be followed whenever a decision concerning dividends must be made.

The firm's **dividend policy** represents a plan of action to be followed whenever the dividend decision must be made. The dividend policy must be formulated with two basic objectives in mind: maximizing the wealth of the firm's owners and providing for sufficient financing. These two objectives are interrelated. They must be fulfilled in light of a number of factors — legal, contractual, internal, growth, owner-related, and market-related — that limit the policy alternatives. Three of the more commonly used dividend policies are described below. A particular firm's cash dividend policy may incorporate elements of each.

payout ratio Calculated by dividing the firm's cash dividend per share by its earnings per share, thereby indicating the percentage of each dollar earned that is distributed to the owners in the form of cash.

Constant-Payout-Ratio Dividend Policy

One type of dividend policy occasionally adopted by firms is the use of a constant payout ratio. The **payout ratio,** calculated by dividing the firm's cash dividend per share by its earnings per share, indicates the percentage of each dollar earned that is distributed to the owners in the form of cash. With a **constant-payout-ratio dividend policy,** the firm establishes that a certain percentage of earnings will be paid to owners in each dividend period. The problem with this policy is that if the firm's earnings drop or if a loss occurs in a given period, the dividends may be low or even nonexistent. Since dividends are often considered an indi-

constant-payout-ratio dividend policy A dividend policy based on the payment of a certain percentage of earnings to owners in each dividend period.

cator of the firm's future condition and status, the firm's stock may thus be adversely affected by this type of action. An example will clarify the problems stemming from a constant-payout-ratio policy.

EXAMPLE

The Nader Motor Company has a policy of paying out 40 percent of earnings in cash dividends. In periods when a loss occurs, the firm's policy is to pay no cash dividends. Nader's earnings per share, dividends per share, and average price per share for the past six years were as follows:

Year	Earnings/share	Dividends/share	Average price/share
1982	$4.50	$1.80	$50.00
1983	2.00	0.80	46.00
1984	−1.50	0.00	38.00
1985	1.75	0.70	48.00
1986	3.00	1.20	52.00
1987	−0.50	0.00	42.00

Dividends increased in 1984–1985 and in 1985–1986 and decreased in 1982–1983, 1983–1984, and 1986–1987. It can be seen from the data that in years of decreasing dividends the firm's stock price dropped; when dividends increased, the price of the stock increased. Nader's sporadic dividend payments appear to make its owners uncertain about the returns they can expect from their investment in the firm and therefore tend to generally depress the stock's price. Although a constant-payout-ratio-dividend policy is used by some firms, it is *not* recommended. ■

Regular Dividend Policy

Another type of dividend policy, the **regular dividend policy,** is based on the payment of a fixed-dollar dividend in each period. The *regular dividend policy* provides the owners with generally positive information, indicating that the firm is okay and thereby minimizing their uncertainty. Often, firms using this policy will increase the regular dividend once a *proven* increase in earnings has occurred. Under this policy, dividends are almost never decreased.

regular dividend policy
A dividend policy based on the payment of a fixed-dollar dividend in each period.

EXAMPLE

The Norman Oil Company's dividend policy is to pay annual dividends of $1.00 per share until per-share earnings have exceeded

$4.00 for three consecutive years, at which time the annual dividend is raised to $1.50 per share and a new earnings plateau is established. The firm does not anticipate decreasing its dividend unless its liquidity is in jeopardy. Norman's earnings per share, dividends per share, and average price per share for the past 12 years were as follows:

Year	Earnings/share	Dividends/share	Average price/share
1976	$2.85	$1.00	$35.00
1977	2.70	1.00	33.50
1978	0.50	1.00	33.00
1979	0.75	1.00	33.00
1980	3.00	1.00	36.00
1981	6.00	1.00	38.00
1982	2.00	1.00	38.50
1983	5.00	1.00	42.00
1984	4.20	1.00	43.00
1985	4.60	1.50	45.00
1986	3.90	1.50	46.50
1987	4.50	1.50	47.50

It can be seen that regardless of the level of earnings, Norman Oil paid dividends of $1.00 per share through 1984. In 1985 the dividend was raised to $1.50 per share, since earnings of $4.00 per share had been achieved for three years. In 1985 the firm would also have had to establish a new earnings plateau for further dividend increases. Norman Oil Company's average price per share exhibited a stable, increasing behavior in spite of a somewhat volatile pattern of earnings. ■

target dividend-payout ratio A policy under which the firm attempts to pay out a certain percentage of earnings as a stated dollar dividend adjusted toward a target payout as proven earnings increases occur.

Often, a regular dividend policy is built around a **target dividend-payout ratio.** Under this policy the firm attempts to pay out a certain percentage of earnings, but rather than let dividends fluctuate, it pays a stated dollar dividend and adjusts it toward the target payout as proven increases in earnings occur. For instance, the Norman Oil Company appears to have a target payout ratio of around 35 percent. The payout was about 35 percent ($1.00 ÷ $2.85) when the dividend policy was set in 1976, and when the dividend was raised to $1.50 in 1985 the payout ratio was about 33 percent ($1.50 ÷ $4.60).

low-regular-and-extra dividend policy A dividend policy based on paying a low regular dividend, supplemented by an additional dividend when earnings warrant it.

Low-Regular-and-Extra Dividend Policy

Some firms establish a **low-regular-and-extra dividend policy,** paying a low regular dividend, supplemented by an additional dividend when earnings warrant it. If earnings are higher than normal in a given pe-

DIVIDEND NEWS

    The Wall Street Journal reports "Corporate Dividend News" daily. The following excerpts from this report for February 25, 1986 show announcements of *passed dividends* by New Orleans Public Service Inc., a *stock split* by National Computer Systems Inc., and a *stock dividend* by Borg-Warner Corp., along with some announced dividends.

    NEW ORLEANS PUBLIC SERVICE INC., a unit of Middle South Utilities Inc., said its board voted to omit the April 1 quarterly on all its preferred and common stock. The action marked the second consecutive quarter that the New Orleans-based electric utility has failed to pay a dividend. All the concern's common shares are held by Middle South.

* * *

    NATIONAL COMPUTER SYSTEMS INC. declared a 3-for-2 stock split and a quarterly of four cents a share on the post-split shares. Both are payable March 19 to stock of record March 7. The Eden Prairie, Minn.-based maker of computer products last paid a quarterly of five cents a share. The new rate represents a 20% increase in the payout.

* * *

    BORG-WARNER CORP. said its board declared as a special dividend the distribution of shares of York International Corp., the company's air conditioning unit, payable March 24 to stock of record March 10. Holders will receive one share of York common for every 10 shares of Borg-Warner common. As previously reported, Borg-Warner's board approved a plan to spin off the unit, which had been marginally profitable and hurt by effects of the strong U.S. dollar. Borg-Warner is a Chicago-based manufacturing and services concern.

* * *

Dividends Reported February 25

Company	Period	Amt.	Payable date	Record date
Regular				
Apache Corp	Q	.07	4-30-86	3-31
Brockway Inc	Q	.33	3-31-86	3- 7
Chase Manhattan pfD	Q	1.31¼	3-31-86	3-14
Chase Manhattan pfE	Q	1.306	3-31-86	3-14
Culbro Corp	Q	.20	4- 1-86	3-18
Dallas Corp	Q	.16½	4- 3-86	3-20
Dynalectron Corp	A	.27	4- 4-86	3-19
Florida Progress Corp	Q	.57	3-20-86	3- 5
Georgia Power	Q	.63	4- 1-86	3-14

* * *

Source: "Corporate Dividend News," *The Wall Street Journal*, February 26, 1986, p. 21. Reprinted by permission of *The Wall Street Journal*. © Dow Jones & Company, Inc. 1986. All rights reserved.

extra dividend An additional dividend optionally paid by the firm if earnings are higher than normal in a given period.

riod, the firm may pay this additional dividend, which will be designated an **extra dividend.** By designating the amount by which the dividend exceeds the regular payment as an extra dividend, the firm avoids giving shareholders false hopes. The use of the "extra" designation is especially common among companies that experience cyclical shifts in earnings.

By establishing a low regular dividend that is paid each period, the firm gives investors the stable income necessary to build confidence in the firm, while the extra dividend permits them to share in the spoils if the firm experiences an especially good period. Firms using this policy must raise the level of the regular dividend once proven increases in earnings have been achieved. The extra dividend should not be a regular event, or it becomes meaningless. The use of a target dividend-payout ratio in establishing the regular dividend level is advisable.

OTHER FORMS OF DIVIDENDS

A number of other forms of dividends are available to the firm. Here, we will discuss two other methods of paying dividends—stock dividends and stock repurchases—as well as a closely related topic, stock splits.

Stock Dividends

stock dividend The payment of a dividend by the firm in the form of stock to existing owners.

A **stock dividend** is the payment of a dividend in the form of stock to existing owners. Often, firms pay stock dividends as a replacement for or a supplement to cash dividends. Although stock dividends do not have a real value, stockholders may perceive them to represent something they did not have before and therefore have value.

ACCOUNTING ASPECTS   In an accounting sense, the payment of a stock dividend is a shifting of funds between capital accounts rather than a use of funds. When a firm declares a stock dividend, the procedures with respect to announcement and distribution are the same as those described earlier for a cash dividend. The accounting entries associated with the payment of stock dividends are given in the following example.

EXAMPLE

The Wieta Company's current stockholders' equity on its balance sheet is as follows:

Preferred Stock	$ 300,000
Common stock (100,000 shares at $4 par)	400,000
Paid-in capital in excess of par	600,000
Retained earnings	700,000
Total stockholders' equity	$2,000,000

If Wieta declares a 10 percent stock dividend and the market price of its stock is $15 per share, $150,000 (10% × 100,000 shares × $15 per share) of retained earnings will be capitalized. The $150,000 will be distributed between common stock and paid-in capital in excess of par accounts based on the par value of the common stock. The resulting account balances are as follows:

Preferred Stock	$ 300,000
Common stock (110,000 shares at $4 par)	440,000
Paid-in capital in excess of par	710,000
Retained earnings	550,000
Total stockholders' equity	$2,000,000

Since 10,000 (10 percent of 100,000) new shares have been issued and the prevailing market price is $15 per share, $150,000 ($15 per share × 10,000 shares) has been shifted from retained earnings to the common stock and paid-in capital accounts. A total of $40,000 ($4 par × 10,000 shares) has been added to common stock, and the remaining $110,000 [($15 − $4) × 10,000 shares] has been added to the paid-in capital in excess of par. The firm's total stockholders' equity has not changed; funds have only been *redistributed* among stockholders' equity accounts. ■

THE SHAREHOLDER'S VIEWPOINT The shareholder receiving a stock dividend receives nothing of value. After the dividend is paid, the per-share value of the shareholder's stock will decrease in proportion to the dividend in such a way that the market value of his or her total holdings in the firm will remain unchanged. The shareholder's proportion of ownership in the firm will also remain the same, and as long as the firm's earnings remain unchanged, so will his or her share of total earnings. A continuation of the preceding example will clarify this point.

EXAMPLE

Mr. X owned 10,000 shares of the Wieta Company's stock. The company's most recent earnings were $220,000, and earnings are not expected to change in the near future. Before the stock dividend, Mr. X owned 10 percent (10,000 shares ÷ 100,000 shares) of the firm's stock, which was selling for $15 per share. Earnings per share were $2.20 ($220,000 ÷ 100,000 shares). Since Mr. X owns 10,000 shares, his earnings were $22,000 ($2.20 per share × 10,000 shares). After receiving the 10 percent stock dividend, Mr. X has 11,000 shares, which again is 10 percent (11,000 shares ÷ 110,000 shares) of the ownership. The market price of the stock can be expected to drop to $13.64 per share [$15 × (1.00 ÷ 1.10)], which means that the market value of Mr. X's holdings will be $150,000 (11,000 shares × $13.64 per share). This is the same as the initial value of his holdings (10,000 shares × $15 per share). The future earnings per share will drop to $2 ($220,000 ÷ 110,000 shares), since the same $220,000 in earnings must now be divided among 110,000 shares. Since Mr. X still owns 10 percent of the stock, his share of total earnings is still $22,000 ($2 per share × 11,000 shares). In summary, if the firm's earnings remain constant and total cash dividends do not increase, a stock dividend will result in a lower per-share market value for the firm's stock. ■

THE COMPANY'S VIEWPOINT   Stock dividends are more costly to issue than cash dividends, but the advantages generally outweigh these costs. Firms find the stock dividend a means of giving owners something without having to use cash. Generally, when a firm is growing rapidly and needs internal financing to perpetuate this growth, a stock dividend is used. As long as the stockholders recognize that the firm is reinvesting its earnings in a manner that should tend to maximize future earnings, the market value of the firm should at least remain unchanged. If the stock dividend is paid so that cash can be retained to satisfy past-due bills, a decline in market value may result.

Stock Splits

stock split A method commonly used to lower the market price of a firm's stock by increasing the number of shares belonging to each shareholder.

Although not a type of dividend, *stock splits* have an effect on a firm's share price similar to that of stock dividends. **A stock split** is a method commonly used to lower the market price of a firm's stock by increasing the number of shares belonging to each shareholder. Quite often, a firm believes that its stock is priced too high and that lowering the market price will enhance trading activity. Stock splits are often made prior to new issues of a stock to enhance the marketability of the stock and stimulate market activity.

A stock split has no effect on the firm's capital structure. It commonly increases the number of shares outstanding and reduces the stock's per-share par value. In other words, when a stock is split, a specified number of new shares are exchanged for a given number of outstanding shares. In a 2-for-1 split, two new shares are exchanged for each old share; in a 3-for-2 split, three new shares are exchanged for each two old shares, and so on.

EXAMPLE

The Brandt Company had 200,000 shares of $2 par-value common stock and no preferred stock outstanding. Since the stock is selling at a high market price, the firm has declared a 2-for-1 stock split. The total before- and after-split stockholders' equity is given below.

BEFORE SPLIT

Common stock (200,000 shares at $2 par)	$ 400,000
Paid-in capital in excess of par	4,000,000
Retained earnings	2,000,000
Total stockholders' equity	$6,400,000

AFTER 2-FOR-1 SPLIT

Common stock (400,000 shares at $1 par)	$ 400,000
Paid-in capital in excess of par	4,000,000
Retained earnings	2,000,000
Total stockholders' equity	$6,400,000

The insignificant effect of the stock split on the firm's books is obvious. ■

Stock can be split in any way desired. Sometimes a **reverse stock split** is made: a certain number of outstanding shares are exchanged for one new share. For example, in a 1-for-2 split, one new share is exchanged for two old shares; in a 2-for-3 split, two new shares are exchanged for three old shares, and so on. Reverse stock splits are initiated when a stock is selling at too low a price to appear respectable.

reverse stock split A method used to raise the market price of a firm's stock by exchanging a certain number of outstanding shares for one new share of stock.

It is not unusual for a stock split to cause a slight increase in the market value of the stock. This is attributable to the informational content of stock splits and the fact that *total* dividends paid commonly increase slightly after a split.

Stock Repurchases

In the recent past, firms have increased their repurchasing of shares of outstanding common stock in the marketplace. A **stock repurchase** is made for a number of reasons: to obtain shares to be used in acquisitions, to have shares available for employee stock option plans, to achieve a gain in the book value of equity when shares are selling below their book value, or merely to retire outstanding shares. This section is concerned with the repurchase of shares for retirement, since this type of repurchase is similar to the payment of cash dividends.

stock repurchase The repurchasing by the firm of outstanding shares of its common stock in the marketplace.

ACCOUNTING ENTRIES The accounting entries that result when common stock is repurchased are a reduction in cash and the establishment of an asset account called "treasury stock," which is shown as a deduction from stockholders' equity. The label **treasury stock** is used to

treasury stock The term used to designate repurchased shares of stock on the firm's balance sheet.

indicate the presence of repurchased shares on the balance sheet. The repurchase of stock can be viewed as a cash dividend, since it involves the distribution of cash to the firm's owners, who are the sellers of the shares.

MOTIVES FOR THE RETIREMENT OF SHARES When common stock is repurchased for retirement, the underlying motive is to distribute excess cash to the owners. Retiring stock means that the owners receive cash for their shares. The general rationale for this action is that as long as earnings remain constant, the repurchase of shares reduces the number of outstanding shares, raising the earnings per share and therefore the market price per share. In addition, certain owner tax benefits may result from the use of stock repurchases. The retirement of common stock can be viewed as a type of reverse dilution, since the earnings per share and the market price of stock are increased by reducing the number of shares outstanding. A simple example will clarify this point.

EXAMPLE

The Farrell Company has released the following financial data:

Earnings available for common stockholders	$1,000,000
Number of shares of common outstanding	400,000
Earnings per share ($1,000,000 ÷ 400,000)	$2.50
Market price per share	$50
Price/earnings (P/E) ratio ($50 ÷ $2.50)	20

The firm is contemplating declaring cash dividends of $2 per share, which will raise the price of the stock to $52 (since the market price is currently $50) after the declaration and before the ex dividend date. The total amount of dividends to be paid by the firm will be $800,000 (400,000 shares × $2 per share). However, instead of paying $800,000 in cash dividends, the firm could repurchase stock at $52 per share. With $800,000, it could repurchase approximately 15,385 shares ($800,000 ÷ $52 per share). As a result of this repurchase, 384,615 shares (400,000 shares − 15,385 shares) of common stock would remain outstanding. Earnings per share *(EPS)* would rise to $2.60 ($1,000,000 ÷ 384,615). If the stock still sold at 20 times earnings (P/E = 20), applying the price/earnings (P/E) multiples approach presented in Chapter 12, its market price would rise to $52 per share ($2.60 × 20). The market price per share would be the same, $52, regardless of whether the cash dividend was paid or stock was repurchased. ■

The advantages of stock repurchases are an increase in per-share earnings and certain owner tax benefits. The tax advantage stems from the fact that if the cash dividend is paid, the owners will have to pay ordinary income taxes on it, whereas the $2 increase in the market value of the stock due to the repurchase will not be taxed until the owner sells the stock. Of course, when the stock is sold, if the proceeds are in excess of the original purchase price, the capital gain will be taxed as ordinary income. The IRS allegedly watches firms that regularly repurchase stock and levies a penalty if it believes the repurchases have been made to delay the payment of taxes by the stockholders. Enforcement in this area appears to be relatively lax.

SUMMARY

- A firm's capital structure is determined by the mix of long-term debt and equity it uses in financing its operations. Debt and equity capital differ with respect to voice in management, claims on income and assets, maturity, and tax treatment. Capital structure can be externally assessed using the debt ratio, times interest earned, and the fixed-payment coverage ratio.
- Under the traditional approach to capital structure, as financial leverage increases, the cost of debt remains constant and then rises, whereas the cost of equity always rises. The optimal capital structure is that for which the weighted average cost of capital is minimized, thereby maximizing share value.
- The *EBIT-EPS* approach can be used to evaluate various capital structures in light of the returns they provide the firm's owners and their degree of financial risk. Using the *EBIT-EPS* approach, the preferred capital structure would be the one expected to provide maximum *EPS* over the firm's expected range of *EBIT*. Graphically, this approach reflects risk in terms of the financial breakeven point and the slope of the capital structure line. The major shortcoming of *EBIT-EPS* analysis is that by ignoring risk it concentrates on maximization of earnings rather than maximization of owners' wealth.
- The cash dividend decision is normally a quarterly decision made by the corporate board of directors. The amount (if any) of dividends is set by the board, which establishes the record date and payment date. Because the dividend decision affects the level of retained earnings, it can significantly affect the firm's external financing requirements.
- Many firms offer dividend reinvestment plans that allow stockholders to acquire shares in lieu of cash dividends, often at an attractive price. A company offering such a plan can either have a trustee buy outstanding shares on behalf of participating shareholders or it can issue new shares to plan participants.
- The residual theory of dividends suggests that the dividend paid by the firm would be the amount, if any, left after all acceptable investment opportunities have been undertaken. This theory implies that dividend policy does not

affect the value of the firm and therefore is irrelevant. However, the more widely accepted school of thought maintains that dividend policy is relevant. It argues that paying dividends reduces the owners' uncertainty, causing them to discount earnings at a lower rate and thereby raise the market value of the firm's stock.

● Certain factors must be considered in setting dividend policy. Most state laws prohibit paying out legal capital or limit dividends to the amount of present and past retained earnings. They also prohibit insolvent or bankrupt firms from paying cash dividends. The IRS prohibits excess earnings accumulation. Loan provisions often limit dividends. The amount of cash and marketable securities a firm has often acts as an internal dividend constraint. In addition, growth prospects, owner considerations, and certain market considerations affect dividend policy.

● The firm's dividend policy should maximize the wealth of its owners while providing for sufficient financing. Commonly used dividend policies include a constant-payout-ratio, regular dividends, or low-regular-and-extra dividends.

● Occasionally firms may pay stock dividends by shifting funds between capital accounts. Stock splits, which bear some similarity to stock dividends, are sometimes used to enhance trading activity in a firm's shares. Stock repurchases can be made in lieu of cash dividend payments in order to allow owners to delay the payment of taxes until the stock is sold.

QUESTIONS

16-1 What is a firm's *capital structure?* How do *debt* and *equity* capital differ?

16-2 What ratios are commonly used to externally assess the degree of financial leverage in a firm's capital structure?

16-3 Under the traditional approach to capital structure, what happens to the cost of debt and the cost of equity as the firm's financial leverage increases? Describe the resulting weighted average cost of capital. Is there an *optimal capital structure* under this approach?

16-4 Explain the *EBIT-EPS approach* to capital structure. Include in your explanation a graph indicating the financial breakeven point; label the axes. Is this approach consistent with maximization of value? Explain.

16-5 How do the date of record and the holders of record relate to the payment of cash dividends? What does the term *ex dividend* mean? Who sets the dividend payment date?

16-6 What is a *dividend reinvestment plan?* What benefit is available to plan participants? Describe the two ways companies can handle such plans.

16-7 Describe the *residual theory of dividends.* Would following this approach lead to a stable dividend? What are the two key positions with respect to the relevance of dividend policy? Explain.

16-8 Briefly describe each of the following factors affecting dividend policy:
    a Legal constraints
    b Contractual constraints
    c Internal constraints

d Growth prospects

e Owner considerations

f Market considerations

16-9 What are (1) a constant-payout-ratio dividend policy, (2) a regular dividend policy, and (3) a low-regular-and-extra dividend policy? What are the effects of these policies?

16-10 What is a *stock dividend?* If it is more costly to issue stock than to pay cash dividends, why do firms issue stock dividends?

16-11 What is a *stock split?* What is a *reverse stock split?* Compare a stock split with a stock dividend.

16-12 What is the logic behind *repurchasing shares* of common stock to distribute excess cash to the firm's owners? How might this raise the per-share earnings and market price of outstanding shares?

PROBLEMS

16-1 **(Various Capital Structures)** The Zachary Corporation currently has $1 million in total assets and is totally equity-financed. It is contemplating a change in capital structure. Compute the amount of debt and equity that would be outstanding if the firm were to shift to one of the following debt ratios (the amount of total assets would not change): 10; 20; 30; 40; 50; 60; and 90 percent. Is there a limit to the debt ratio's value?

16-2 **(*EBIT* and *EPS*)** Western Oil Corporation has a current capital structure consisting of $250,000 of 16 percent (annual interest) debt and 2,000 shares of common stock. The firm pays taxes at the rate of 40 percent on ordinary income.

a Using *EBIT* values of $80,000 and $120,000, determine the associated earnings per share *(EPS)*.

b Graph the firm's current capital structure on a set of *EBIT-EPS* axes.

16-3 **(*EBIT-EPS* and Capital Structure)** Parker Petroleum is considering two capital structures. The key information follows. Assume a 40 percent tax rate on ordinary income.

Source of capital	Structure A	Structure B
Long-term debt	$100,000, annual interest at 16% stated rate	$200,000, annual interest at 17% stated rate
Common stock	4,000 shares	2,000 shares

a Calculate two *EBIT-EPS* coordinates for each of the structures.

b Plot the two capital structures on a set of *EBIT-EPS* axes.

c Indicate over what *EBIT* range, if any, each structure is preferred.

d Discuss the leverage and risk aspects of each structure.

e If the firm is fairly certain its *EBIT* will exceed $75,000, which structure would you recommend? Why?

16-4 **(*EBIT-EPS* and Capital Structure)**   Wonder Diaper is considering two possible capital structures, A and B, below. Assume a 40 percent tax rate on ordinary income.

Source of capital	Structure A	Structure B
Long-term debt	$75,000, annual interest at 16% stated rate	$50,000, annual interest at 15% stated rate
Common stock	8,000 shares at $20	10,000 shares at $20

a Calculate two *EBIT-EPS* coordinates for each of the structures.
b Graph the two capital structures on the same set of *EBIT-EPS* axes.
c Discuss the leverage and risk associated with each of the structures.
d Over what range of *EBIT* would each structure be preferred?
e Which structure would you recommend if the firm expects its *EBIT* to be $35,000? Explain.

16-5 **(Integrative—*EBIT-EPS* and Alternative Capital Structures)**   Triple D Corporation wishes to analyze five possible capital structures—0; 15; 30; 45; and 60 percent debt ratios. The firm's total assets of $1 million are assumed constant. Its common stock is valued at $25 per share, and the firm is in the 40 percent tax bracket. The following additional data has been gathered for use in analyzing the five capital structures under consideration.

Capital structure debt ratio	Interest rate on debt
0%	0.0%
15	8.0
30	10.0
45	13.0
60	17.0

a Calculate the amount of debt, the amount of equity, and the number of shares of common stock outstanding for each of the capital structures being considered.
b Calculate the annual interest on the debt under each of the capital structures being considered. (*Note:* The interest rate given is applicable to *all* debt associated with the corresponding debt ratio.)
c Calculate *EPS* associated with $150,000 and $250,000 of *EBIT* for each of the five capital structures.
d Using the *EBIT-EPS* data developed in **c**, plot the five capital structures on the same set of *EBIT-EPS* axes.
e Evaluate the relative degrees of leverage of the plans and discuss the range of *EBIT* (from the graph in **d**) over which each capital structure is preferred.

    f What is the major problem with the use of *EBIT-EPS* analysis to select the best capital structure? Explain.

16-6 **(Dividend Payment Procedures)** Dayton Widget, at the quarterly dividend meeting, declared a cash dividend of $1.10 per share for holders of record on Monday, July 10. The firm has 300,000 shares of common stock outstanding and has set a payment date of July 31. Prior to the dividend declaration, the firm's key accounts were as follows:

Cash	$500,000	Dividends payable	$ 0
		Retained earnings	2,500,000

    a Show the entries after the meeting adjourned.
    b When is the ex dividend date?
    c After the July 31 payment date, what values would the key accounts have?
    d What effect, if any, will the dividend have on the firm's total assets?

16-7 **(Dividend Constraints)** The Boulder Company's stockholders' equity account is as follows:

Common stock (400,000 shares at $4 par)	$1,600,000
Paid-in capital in excess of par	1,000,000
Retained earnings	1,900,000
Total stockholders' equity	$4,500,000

The earnings available for common stockholders from this period's operations are $100,000, which have been included as part of the $1.9 million retained earnings.

    a What is the maximum dividend per share the firm can pay? (Assume that legal capital includes *all* paid-in capital.)
    b If the firm has $160,000 in cash, what is the largest per-share dividend it can pay without borrowing?
    c Indicate the accounts and changes, if any, that will result if the firm pays the dividends indicated in **a** and **b**.
    d Indicate the effects of an $80,000 cash dividend on stockholders' equity.

16-8 **(Dividend Constraints)** A firm has $800,000 in paid-in capital, retained earnings of $40,000 (including the current year's earnings), and 25,000 shares of common stock outstanding. In the most recent year it has $29,000 of earnings available for the common stockholders.

    a What is the most the firm can pay in cash dividends to each common shareholder? (Assume that legal capital includes *all* paid-in capital.)
    b What effect would a cash dividend of $.80 per share have on the firm's balance sheet entries?
    c If the firm cannot raise any new funds from external sources, what do you consider the key constraint with respect to the magnitude of the firm's dividend payments? Why?

16-9 **(Alternative Dividend Policies)** A firm has had the earnings per share over the past 10 years shown in the table at the top of page 528.

Year	Earnings per share
1987	$4.00
1986	3.80
1985	3.20
1984	2.80
1983	3.20
1982	2.40
1981	1.20
1980	1.80
1979	−0.50
1978	0.25

a If the firm's dividend policy was based on a constant payout ratio of 40 percent for all years with positive earnings and a zero payout otherwise, determine the annual dividend for each year.

b If the firm had a dividend payout of $1.00 per share, increasing by $.10 per share whenever the dividend payout fell below 50 percent for two consecutive years, what annual dividend did the firm pay each year?

c If the firm's policy was to pay $.50 per share each period except when earnings per share exceed $3.00, when an extra dividend equal to 80 percent of earnings beyond $3.00 would be paid, what annual dividend did the firm pay each year?

d Discuss the pros and cons of each dividend policy described in **a** through **c**.

16-10 **(Alternative Dividend Policies)** Given the following earnings per share over the period 1980–1987, determine the annual dividend per share under each of the policies set forth in **a** through **d**.

Year	Earnings per share
1987	$1.40
1986	1.56
1985	1.20
1984	−0.85
1983	1.05
1982	0.60
1981	1.00
1980	0.44

a Pay out 50 percent of earnings in all years with positive earnings.

b Pay $.50 per share and increase to $.60 per share whenever earnings per share rise above $.90 per share for two consecutive years.

c Pay $.50 per share except when earnings exceed $1.00 per share, when there would be an extra dividend of 60 percent of earnings above $1.00 per share.

d Combine policies in **b** and **c**. When the dividend is raised (in **b**), raise the excess dividend base (in **c**) from $1.00 to $1.10 per share.

    e Compare and contrast each of the dividend policies described in **a** through **d**.

16-11 **(Stock Dividend—Firm)** TFS has a stockholders' equity account, given here. The firm's common stock has a current market price of $30 per share.

Preferred stock	$100,000
Common stock (10,000 shares at $2 par)	20,000
Paid-in capital in excess of par	280,000
Retained earnings	100,000
Total stockholders' equity	$500,000

    a Show the effects on TFS of a 5 percent stock dividend.
    b Show the effects of (1) a 10 percent and (2) a 20 percent stock dividend.
    c In light of your answers to **a** and **b**, discuss the effects of stock dividends on stockholders' equity.

16-12 **(Cash versus Stock Dividend)** Nimms Steel has a stockholders' equity account as given. The firm's common stock currently sells for $4 per share.

Preferred stock	$ 100,000
Common stock (400,000 shares at $1 par)	400,000
Paid-in capital in excess of par	200,000
Retained earnings	320,000
Total stockholders' equity	$1,020,000

    a Show the effects on the firm of a $.01, $.05, $.10, and $.20 per-share *cash* dividend.
    b Show the effects on the firm of a 1 percent, 5 percent, 10 percent, and 20 percent *stock* dividend.
    c Compare the effects in **a** and **b**. What are the significant differences in the two methods of paying dividends?

16-13 **(Stock Dividend—Investor)** Dana Bond currently holds 400 shares of Mountain Grown Coffee. The firm has 40,000 shares outstanding. The firm most recently had earnings available for common stockholders of $80,000, and its stock has been selling for $22 per share. The firm intends to retain its earnings and pay a 10 percent stock dividend.
    a How much does the firm currently earn per share?
    b What proportion of the firm does Dana Bond currently own?
    c What proportion of the firm will Ms. Bond own after the stock dividend? Explain your answer.
    d At what market price would you expect the stock to sell after the stock dividend?
    e Discuss what effect, if any, the payment of stock dividends will have on Ms. Bond's share of the ownership and earnings of Mountain Grown Coffee.

16-14 **(Stock Dividend — Investor)** The Mission Company has outstanding 50,000 shares of common stock currently selling at $40 per share. The firm most recently had earnings available for common stockholders of $120,000, but it has decided to retain these funds and is considering either a 5 percent or a 10 percent stock dividend in lieu of a cash dividend.

a Determine the firm's current earnings per share.

b If Jack Frost currently owns 500 shares of the firm's stock, determine his proportion of ownership currently and under each of the proposed dividend plans. Explain your findings.

c Calculate and explain the market price per share under each of the stock dividend plans.

d For each of the proposed stock dividends, calculate the earnings per share after payment of the stock dividend.

e How much would the value of Jack Frost's holdings be under each of the plans? Explain.

f As Mr. Frost, would you have any preference with respect to the proposed stock dividends? Why or why not?

16-15 **(Stock Split — Firm)** The U.S. Oil Company's current stockholders' equity account is as follows:

Preferred stock	$ 400,000
Common stock (600,000 shares at $3 par)	1,800,000
Paid-in capital in excess of par	200,000
Retained earnings	800,000
Total stockholders' equity	$3,200,000

a Indicate the change, if any, expected if the firm declares a 2-for-1 stock split.

b Indicate the change, if any, expected if the firm declares a 1-for-1½ *reverse* stock split.

c Indicate the change, if any, expected if the firm declares a 3-for-1 stock split.

d Indicate the change, if any, expected if the firm declares a 6-for-1 stock split.

e Indicate the change, if any, expected if the firm declares a 1-for-4 *reverse* stock split.

16-16 **(Stock Split — Firm)** The Big Company is considering a 3-for-2 stock split. It currently has the stockholders' equity position shown below. The current stock price is $120 per share. The most recent period's earnings available for common is included in retained earnings.

Preferred stock	$ 1,000,000
Common stock (100,000 shares at $3 par)	300,000
Paid-in capital in excess of par	1,700,000
Retained earnings	10,000,000
Total stockholders' equity	$13,000,000

a What effects on Big Company would result from the stock split?

b What change in stock price would you expect to result from the stock split?

c What is the maximum cash dividend *per share* the firm could pay on common stock before and after the stock split? (Assume that legal capital includes *all* paid-in capital.)

d Contrast your answers to **a** through **c** with the circumstances surrounding a 50 percent stock dividend.

e Explain the differences between stock splits and stock dividends.

16-17 **(Stock Repurchase)**   The following financial data on the Victor Stock Company are available:

Earnings available for common stockholders	$800,000
Number of shares of common outstanding	400,000
Earnings per share ($800,000 ÷ 400,000)	$2
Market price per share	$20
Price/earnings *(P/E)* ratio ($20 ÷ $2)	10

The firm is currently contemplating paying cash dividends of $1 per share, which will raise the stock price to $21 after the announcement and before the ex dividend date.

a Approximately how many shares of stock can the firm repurchase at the $21-per-share price using the funds that would have gone to pay the cash dividend?

b Calculate earnings per share *(EPS)* after the repurchase. Explain your calculations.

c If the stock still sells at 10 times earnings, how much will the market price be after the repurchase?

d Compare and contrast the pre- and post-repurchase earnings per share. Discuss the tax implications of this action.

e Compare and contrast the pre- and post-repurchase market price. Discuss your findings.

16-18 **(Stock Repurchase)**   The Off Shore Steel Company has earnings available for common stockholders of $2 million and 500,000 shares of common stock outstanding at $60 per share. The firm is currently contemplating the payment of $2 per share in cash dividends.

a Calculate the firm's current earnings per share *(EPS)* and price/earnings *(P/E)* ratio.

b The firm's stock is expected to sell at $62 per share after the dividend announcement and before the ex dividend date. If the firm can repurchase shares at that price, how many shares can be purchased in lieu of making the proposed cash dividend payment?

c How much will the *EPS* be after the proposed repurchase? Why?

d If the stock will sell at the old *P/E* ratio, what will the market price be after repurchase?

e Compare and contrast the earnings per share and market price per share before and after the proposed repurchase.

17

EXPANSION
AND
FAILURE

After studying this chapter, you should be able to:

● Understand the key types of business combinations and the most common motives for combining businesses.

● Demonstrate the procedures used to analyze and negotiate cash purchases of companies (acquired either as a collection of assets or as a going concern) and stock-exchange acquisitions.

● Describe leveraged buyouts, the basic methods used to negotiate a merger, and the major advantages and disadvantages of holding companies.

● Understand the types and major causes of business failure and the use of voluntary settlements to sustain or liquidate the failed firm.

● Explain bankruptcy legislation and the procedures involved in reorganizing or liquidating a bankrupt firm under current bankruptcy laws.

Business combinations are sometimes used by firms to externally expand in order to rapidly increase productive capacity, liquidity, sales, earnings, or share price. Such combinations can be used to acquire a collection of needed assets or another going concern. A major boom in the use of business combinations as a form of external expansion began in 1980 and continues today. The most popular forms of business combinations are consolidations, mergers, and holding companies. Unfortunately not all firms are able to sustain themselves indefinitely; many fail each year. In some instances they can be reorganized voluntarily or under bankruptcy law with the cooperation of outsiders. If reorganization is not feasible, voluntary or legal procedures can be used to liquidate the firm in an orderly fashion. It is important that the financial manager understand the fundamental aspects of both expansion through business combinations and business failure. Here we first discuss business combinations followed by a brief review of business failure.

FUNDAMENTALS OF BUSINESS COMBINATIONS

Types of Business Combinations

The key forms of business combinations are *consolidations, mergers,* and *holding companies*. These arrangements have certain basic similarities and differences.

CONSOLIDATIONS   A **consolidation** involves the combination of two or more companies to form a completely new corporation. The new corporation normally absorbs the assets and liabilities of the companies from which it is formed. The former corporations cease to exist. Consolidations normally occur when the firms to be combined are of similar size. They are carried out by issuing to shareholders in the old firms a certain number (or fraction) of shares of stock in the new firm in exchange for each share of the old firm.

> **consolidation** The combination of two or more companies to form a completely new corporation.

MERGERS   A **merger** is quite similar to a consolidation except that when two or more firms are merged, the resulting firm maintains the identity of one of the firms. Mergers are generally confined to combinations of two firms that are unequal in size; the identity of the larger of the two firms is normally maintained. Usually the assets and liabilities of the smaller firm are consolidated into those of the larger. The larger firm pays for its acquisition of the assets or common stock of the smaller firm with cash or with its preferred or common stock. Due to the similarity between consolidations and mergers, in the remainder of this chapter the term *merger* will be used to refer to both.

> **merger** Generally, the combination of two firms of unequal size, in which the identity of the larger of the two firms is maintained.

holding company
A corporation that has voting control of one or more other corporations.

subsidiaries The companies controlled by a holding company.

HOLDING COMPANIES   A **holding company** is a corporation that has voting control of one or more other corporations. Having control in large, widely held companies generally requires ownership of between 10 and 20 percent of the outstanding stock. The companies controlled by a holding company are normally referred to as its **subsidiaries.** Control of a subsidiary is typically obtained by purchasing (generally for cash) a sufficient number of shares of its stock.

Motives for Combinations

Firms combine through mergers or holding company arrangements in order to fulfill certain objectives. The most common motives for combination include growth or diversification, synergistic effects, fund raising, increased managerial skills, tax considerations, and increased ownership liquidity.

GROWTH OR DIVERSIFICATION   Companies that desire rapid growth in *size* or *market share* or diversification in *the range of their products* may find that some form of combination will fulfill this objective. Instead of going through the time-consuming process of internal growth or diversification, the firm may achieve the same objective in a short period of time by acquiring or combining with an existing firm. If a firm that wants to expand operations in existing or possibly new product areas can find a suitable going concern, it may avoid many of the risks associated with the design, manufacture, and sale of additional or new products. Moreover, when a firm expands or extends its product line by acquiring another firm, it also removes a potential competitor.[1] Mergers and holding companies may be used to achieve horizontal, vertical, or congeneric growth, or conglomerate diversification. Each of these situations is briefly described in Table 17.1.

SYNERGISTIC EFFECTS   The *synergistic effects* of business combinations are certain economies of scale resulting from the combined firms' lower overhead. Synergistic effects are said to be present when a whole is greater than the sum of the parts ("1 plus 1 equals 3"). The economies of scale that generally result from combination lower combined overhead, thereby increasing earnings to a level greater than the sum of the earnings of each of the independent firms. Synergistic effects are most obvious when firms merge with other firms in the same line of business, since many redundant functions and employees can thereby be elimi-

---

[1] Certain legal constraints on growth—especially where the elimination of competition is expected—exist. The various antitrust laws, which are closely enforced by the Federal Trade Commission (FTC) and the Justice Department, prohibit business combinations that eliminate competition, especially when the resulting enterprise would be a monopoly.

TABLE 17.1 Key Types of Growth or Diversification

Type of growth or diversification	Description
Horizontal growth	Results from combination of firms in the *same line of business*. For example, the merger of two machine-tool manufacturers. Used to expand operations in an existing product line and at the same time eliminate a competitor.
Vertical growth	When a firm *acquires a supplier or a customer*. For example, the merger of a machine-tool manufacturer with its supplier of castings. Economic benefit stems from greater control over the acquisition of raw materials or the distribution of finished goods.
Congeneric growth	Achieved by acquiring a firm in the *same general industry* but neither in the same line of business nor a supplier or customer. For example, the merger of a machine-tool manufacturer with the manufacturer of industrial conveyor systems. The benefit results from the ability to use the same sales and distribution channels to reach customers of both businesses.
Conglomerate diversification	Involves the combination of firms in *unrelated businesses*. For example, the merger of a machine-tool manufacturer with a chain of fast-food restaurants. The key benefit of conglomerates lies in their ability to *reduce risk* by combining firms with differing seasonal or cyclical patterns of sales and earnings.

nated. Staff functions, such as purchasing and sales, are probably most greatly affected by this type of combination.

FUND RAISING Often firms combine to enhance their fund-raising ability. A firm may be unable to obtain funds for its own internal expansion but able to obtain funds for external business combinations. Quite often one firm may combine with another that has high liquid assets and low levels of liabilities. The acquisition of this type of "cash-rich" company immediately increases the firm's borrowing power by decreasing its financial leverage. This should enable the raising of funds externally at more favorable rates.

INCREASED MANAGERIAL SKILLS   Occasionally a firm will have good potential that it finds itself unable to develop fully due to deficiencies in certain areas of management. If the firm cannot hire the management it needs, it might combine with a compatible firm that has the needed managerial personnel. Of course any combination, regardless of the specific motive for it, should contribute to the maximization of owners' wealth.

tax loss carryforward In a combination or merger, the tax loss of one of the firms that can be applied against a limited amount of future income of the combined firm over the shorter of either 15 years or until the total tax loss has been exhausted.

TAX CONSIDERATIONS   Quite often tax considerations are a key motive for combination. In such a case the tax benefit generally stems from the fact that one of the firms has a **tax loss carryforward.** This means that the company's tax loss can be applied against a limited amount[2] of future income of the combined firm over the shorter of either 15 years or until the total tax loss has been exhausted. Two situations could actually exist. A company with a tax loss could acquire a profitable company in order to utilize the tax loss. In this case the acquiring firm would boost the combination's after-tax earnings by reducing the taxable income of the acquired firm. A tax loss may also be useful when a profitable firm acquires a firm that has such a loss. In either situation, however, the merger must be justified not only on the basis of the tax benefits but also on grounds consistent with the goal of owners' wealth maximization. Moreover, the tax benefits described are useful only in mergers—not in the formation of holding companies—since only in the case of mergers are operating results reported on a consolidated basis. An example will clarify the use of the tax loss carryforward.

EXAMPLE

The Maxwell Company has a total of $450,000 in tax loss carryforwards resulting from operating tax losses of $150,000 a year in each of the past three years. To use these losses and to diversify its operations, the C. B. Company has acquired Maxwell through a merger. C. B. expects to have *earnings before taxes* of $300,000 per year. We assume that these earnings are realized, they fall within the annual limit legally allowed for application of the tax loss carryforward resulting from the merger (see footnote 2 below), the Maxwell portion of the merged firm just breaks even, and C. B. is in the 40 percent tax bracket. The total taxes paid by the two firms and their after-tax earnings without and with the merger are calculated as shown in the table at the top of the next page.

[2] The *Tax Reform Act of 1986*, in order to deter firms from combining solely to take advantage of tax loss carryforwards, initiated an annual limit on the amount of taxable income against which such losses can be applied. The annual limit is determined by formula and is tied to the value of the loss corporation before the combination. While not fully eliminating this motive for combination, the act is expected to make it more difficult for firms to justify combinations solely on the basis of tax loss carryforwards.

TOTAL TAXES AND AFTER-TAX EARNINGS WITHOUT MERGER

	Year			Total for 3 years
	1	2	3	
(1) Earnings before taxes	$300,000	$300,000	$300,000	$900,000
(2) Taxes [.40 × (1)]	120,000	120,000	120,000	360,000
(3) Earnings after taxes [(1) − (2)]	$180,000	$180,000	$180,000	$540,000

TOTAL TAXES AND AFTER-TAX EARNINGS WITH MERGER

	Year			Total for 3 years
(4) Earnings before losses	$300,000	$300,000	$300,000	$900,000
(5) Tax loss carryforward	300,000	150,000	0	450,000
(6) Earnings before taxes [(4) − (5)]	$ 0	$150,000	$300,000	$450,000
(7) Taxes [.40 × (6)]	0	60,000	120,000	180,000
(8) Earnings after taxes [(4) − (7)]	$300,000	$240,000	$180,000	$720,000

With the merger the total tax payments are less—$180,000 (total of line 7) versus $360,000 (total of line 2). With the merger the total after-tax earnings are more—$720,000 (total of line 8) versus $540,000 (total of line 3). The combined firms are able to deduct the tax loss either for 15 years subsequently or until the total tax loss has been exhausted, whichever period is shorter. In this example the shorter is at the end of year 2. ■

INCREASED OWNERSHIP LIQUIDITY   In the case of mergers the combination of two small firms or a small and a larger firm into a larger corporation may provide the owners of the small firm(s) with greater liquidity. This is due to the higher marketability associated with the shares of larger firms. Instead of holding shares in a small firm that has a very "thin" market, the owners will receive shares that are traded in a broader market and can thus be liquidated more readily. Not only does the ability to convert shares into cash quickly have appeal, but owning shares for which market price quotations are readily available provides owners with a better sense of the value of their holdings. Especially in the case of small, closely held firms, the improved liquidity of ownership obtainable through a merger with an acceptable firm may have considerable appeal.

ANALYZING AND NEGOTIATING BUSINESS COMBINATIONS

This portion of the chapter describes the procedures used to analyze and negotiate business combinations. Initially attention is given to the analysis of mergers using cash purchases and stock-exchange acquisitions. Next, leveraged buyouts (LBOs) and the merger negotiation process are described. Finally, the major advantages and disadvantages of holding companies are reviewed.

Cash Purchases

When one firm acquires another firm for cash (debt is assumed to be the same as cash here), the use of simple capital budgeting procedures is required. Whether the second firm is being acquired for its assets or as a going concern, the basic approach is similar.

ACQUISITIONS OF ASSETS In some instances a firm is acquired not for its income-earning potential but as a collection of assets (generally fixed assets) that are needed by the acquiring firm. The cash price paid for this type of acquisition depends largely on which assets are being acquired; consideration must also be given to the value of any tax losses. To determine whether the purchase of assets is financially justified, the firm must estimate both the costs and benefits of the assets. This is a capital budgeting problem (see Chapters 14 and 15) since an initial cash outlay is made to acquire assets and, as a result, future cash inflows are expected.

EXAMPLE

The PR Company is interested in acquiring certain fixed assets of the Zoom Company. Zoom, which has tax loss carryforwards from losses over the past five years, is interested in selling out, but it wishes to sell out entirely, not just in getting rid of certain fixed assets. A condensed balance sheet for the Zoom Company follows.

Balance Sheet for Zoom Company

Assets		Liabilities and stockholders' equity	
Cash	$ 2,000	Total liabilities	$ 80,000
Marketable securities	0	Stockholders' equity	120,000
Accounts receivable	8,000	Total liabilities and	
Inventories	10,000	stockholders' equity	$200,000
Machine A	10,000		
Machine B	30,000		
Machine C	25,000		
Land and buildings	115,000		
Total assets	$200,000		

PR Company needs only machines B and C and the land and buildings. However, it has made some inquiries and has arranged to sell the accounts receivable, inventories, and machine A for $23,000. Since there is also $2,000 in cash, PR will get $25,000 for the excess assets. Zoom wants $20,000 for the entire company, which means that PR will have to pay the firm's creditors $80,000 and its owners $20,000. The actual outlay required by PR after liquidating the unneeded assets will be $75,000 [($80,000 + $20,000) − $25,000]. In other words, to obtain the use of the desired assets (machines B and C and the land and buildings) and the benefits of Zoom's tax losses, PR must pay $75,000. The *after-tax cash inflows* expected to result from the new assets and applicable tax losses are $14,000 per year for the next five years and $12,000 per year for the following five years. The desirability of this acquisition can be determined by calculating the net present value of this outlay using the PR Company's 11 percent cost of capital, as shown in Table 17.2. Since the net present value of $3,072 is greater than zero, PR's value should be increased by acquiring the Zoom Company. ■

ACQUISITIONS OF GOING CONCERNS Cash acquisitions of going concerns are best analyzed using capital budgeting techniques such as those described for asset acquisitions. The basic difficulty in applying the capital budgeting approach to the cash acquisition of a going concern is the *estimation of cash flows* and certain *risk considerations*. The methods of estimating expected cash flows from an acquisition are no different from those used in estimating cash flows in any capital budgeting decision. Whenever a firm considers acquiring for cash another firm that has different risk behaviors, it should adjust the cost of capital appropriately (see Chapter 15) prior to applying capital budgeting techniques. An example will clarify this procedure.

TABLE 17.2 An Analysis of the Zoom Company Acquisition by the PR Company

Year(s)	Cash flow (1)	Present value factor at 11% (2)	Present value [(1) × (2)] (3)
0	($75,000)	1.000[a]	($75,000)
1–5	14,000	3.696[b]	51,744
6	12,000	0.535[a]	6,420
7	12,000	0.482[a]	5,784
8	12,000	0.434[a]	5,208
9	12,000	0.391[a]	4,692
10	12,000	0.352[a]	4,224
		Net present value	$ 3,072

[a] The present-value interest factor, *PVIF*, for $1 discounted at 11 percent for the corresponding year obtained from Table D-3.

[b] The present-value interest factor for an annuity, *PVIFA*, with a five-year life discounted at 11 percent obtained from Table D-4.

EXAMPLE

The Edge Company is contemplating the acquisition of the Wall Company, which can be purchased for $60,000 in cash. Edge currently has a high degree of financial leverage, which is reflected in its 13 percent cost of capital. Because of the low financial leverage of the Wall Company, Edge estimates that its overall cost of capital will drop to 10 percent after the acquisition. Since the effect of the less risky capital structure resulting from the acquisition of Wall Company cannot be reflected in the expected cash flows, the post-acquisition cost of capital (10 percent) must be used to evaluate the cash flows expected from the acquisition. The incremental cash inflows forecast from the proposed acquisition are expected over a 30-year time horizon. These estimated inflows are $5,000 for years 1 through 10, $13,000 for years 11 through 18, and $4,000 for years 19 through 30. The net present value of the acquisition is calculated in Table 17.3.

Since the net present value of the acquisition is greater than zero ($2,357), the acquisition is acceptable. It is interesting to note that had the effect of the changed capital structure on the cost of capital not been considered, the acquisition would have been found unacceptable since the net present value *at a 13 percent cost of capital* is − $11,864, which is less than zero. ■

TABLE 17.3 An Analysis of the Wall Company Acquisition by the Edge Company

Year(s)	Cash flow (1)	Present value factor at 10%[a] (2)	Present value [(1) × (2)] (3)
0	($60,000)	1.000	($60,000)
1–10	5,000	6.145	30,725
11–18	13,000	(8.201 − 6.145)[b]	26,728
19–30	4,000	(9.427 − 8.201)[b]	4,904
		Net present value	$ 2,357

[a] Present-value interest factors for annuities, *PVIFA*, obtained from Table D-4.

[b] These factors are found using a shortcut technique that can be applied to annuities for periods of years beginning at some point in the future. By finding the appropriate interest factor for the present value of an annuity given for the last year of the annuity and subtracting the present-value interest factor of an annuity for the year immediately preceding the beginning of the annuity, the appropriate interest factor for the present value of an annuity beginning sometime in the future can be obtained. You can check this shortcut by using the long approach and comparing the results.

Stock-Exchange Acquisitions

Quite often a firm is acquired through the exchange of common stock. The acquiring firm exchanges its shares for shares of the firm being acquired according to a predetermined ratio. The *ratio of exchange* of shares is determined in the merger negotiations. This ratio affects the various financial yardsticks that are used by existing and prospective shareholders in valuing the merged firm's shares.

RATIO OF EXCHANGE When one firm trades its stock for the shares of another firm, the number of shares of the acquiring firm to be exchanged for each share of the acquired firm must be determined. The first requirement, of course, is that the acquiring company have sufficient shares available to complete the transaction. Often a firm's repurchase of shares, which was discussed in Chapter 16, is necessary to obtain sufficient shares for such a transaction. The acquiring firm generally offers more for each share of the acquired firm than the current market price of its publicly traded shares. The actual **ratio of exchange** is merely the ratio of the amount *paid* per share of the acquired firm to the per-share market price of the acquiring firm. It is calculated in this manner since the acquiring firm pays the acquired firm in stock, which has a value equal to its market price. An example will clarify the calculation.

> **ratio of exchange** The ratio of the amount *paid* per share of the acquired firm to the per-share market price of the acquiring firm.

EXAMPLE

The Bigge Company, whose stock is currently selling for $80 per share, is interested in acquiring the Tiny Company. To prepare for the acquisition, Bigge has been repurchasing its own shares over the past three years. Tiny's stock is currently selling for $75 per share, but in the merger negotiations, Bigge has found it necessary to offer Tiny $110 per share. Since Bigge does not have sufficient financial resources to purchase the firm for cash, and it does not wish to raise these funds, Tiny has agreed to accept Bigge's stock in exchange for its shares. As stated, Bigge's stock currently sells for $80 per share and it must pay $110 per share for Tiny's stock. Therefore the ratio of exchange is 1.375 ($110 ÷ $80). This means that the Bigge Company must exchange 1.375 shares of its stock for each share of Tiny's stock. ■

EFFECT ON EARNINGS PER SHARE Ordinarily the resulting earnings per share differ from the premerger earnings per share for both the acquiring firm and the acquired firm. They depend largely on the ratio of exchange and the premerger earnings per share of each firm. It is best to view the initial and long-run effects of the ratio of exchange on earnings per share *(EPS)* separately.

Initial Effect. When the ratio of exchange is equal to 1 and both the acquiring and the acquired firm have the *same* premerger earnings per share, the merged firm's earnings per share will initially remain constant. In this rare instance, both the acquiring and the acquired firm would also have equal price/earnings *(P/E)* ratios. In actuality the earnings per share of the merged firm are generally above the premerger earnings per share of one firm and below the premerger earnings per share of the other, after making the necessary adjustment for the ratio of exchange. These differences can be illustrated by a simple example.

EXAMPLE

The Bigge Company is contemplating acquiring the Tiny Company by exchanging 1.375 shares of its stock for each share of Tiny's stock. The current financial data related to the earnings and market price for each of these companies are given in Table 17.4. Although Tiny's stock currently has a market price of $75 per share, Bigge has offered it $110 per share. As seen in the preceding example, this results in a ratio of exchange of 1.375.

To complete the merger and retire the 20,000 shares of Tiny Company stock outstanding, Bigge will have to issue and (or) use treasury stock totaling 27,500 shares (1.375 × 20,000 shares). Once the merger is completed, Bigge will have 152,500 shares of common stock (125,000 + 27,500) outstanding. If the earnings of each of the firms remain constant, the merged company will be expected to have earnings available for the common stockholders of $600,000 ($500,000 + $100,000). The earnings per share of the merged company should therefore equal approximately $3.93 per share ($600,000 ÷ 152,500 shares).

It would appear at first that the Tiny Company's shareholders

TABLE 17.4 Bigge Company and Tiny Company Financial Data

Item	Bigge Company	Tiny Company
(1) Earnings available for common stock	$500,000	$100,000
(2) Number of shares of common stock outstanding	125,000	20,000
(3) Earnings per share [(1) ÷ (2)]	$4	$5
(4) Market price per share	$80	$75
(5) Price/earnings (P/E)ratio [(4) ÷ (3)]	20	15

have sustained a decrease in per-share earnings from $5 to $3.93, but since each share of the Tiny Company's original stock is equivalent to 1.375 shares of the merged company, the equivalent earnings per share are actually $5.40 ($3.93 × 1.375). In other words, as a result of the merger the Bigge Company's original shareholders experience a decrease in earnings per share from $4 to $3.93 to the benefit of the Tiny Company's shareholders, whose earnings per share increase from $5 to $5.40. These results are summarized in Table 17.5. ■

The postmerger earnings per share for owners of the acquiring and acquired company can be explained by comparing the price/earnings (P/E) ratio paid by the acquiring company with its initial P/E ratio. This relationship is summarized in Table 17.6 on page 545. By paying more than its current value per dollar of earnings to acquire each dollar of earnings (P/E paid > P/E of acquiring company), the acquiring firm transfers the claim on a portion of its premerger earnings to the owners of the acquired firm. Therefore, on a postmerger basis the acquired firm's *EPS* increases and the acquiring firm's *EPS* decreases. If the acquiring company were to pay less than its current value per dollar of earnings to acquire each dollar of earnings (P/E paid < P/E of acquiring company), the opposite effects would result. The P/E ratios associated with the Bigge-Tiny merger can be used to explain the effect of the merger on earnings per share.

EXAMPLE

The Bigge Company's P/E ratio is 20, while the P/E ratio based on the share price paid the Tiny Company was 22 ($110 ÷ $5). Since

TABLE 17.5 Summary of the Effects on Earnings per Share of a Merger Between the Bigge Company and the Tiny Company at $110 per Share

Stockholders	Earnings Per Share	
	Before merger	After merger
Bigge Company	$4.00	$3.93[a]
Tiny Company	5.00	5.40[b]

[a] $\dfrac{\$500{,}000 + \$100{,}000}{(1.375 \times 20{,}000) + 125{,}000} = \$3.93$

[b] $\$3.93 \times 1.375 = \$5.40$

MERGERSPEAK: GREENMAIL, GOLDEN PARACHUTES, LADY MACBETH STRATEGIES . . .

Greenmail, golden parachutes, scorched-earth defenses, shark repellents, poison pills, Lady Macbeth strategies, white knights, and Pac-Man defenses sound more like video-game tactics than serious moves by adult masters of business administration in the world of corporate takeovers.

But serious they are. Despite their joy-stick titles, these are not the product of 20-year-old software moguls but of pin-striped strategists in the hostile takeover wars. And the effect of some of the tactics has become a poison pill for 42 million average stockholders.

Many corporate mergers are logical. As more industries enter a world market, mergers can add to efficiency and productive capacity in the competition for that vast market.

What does not make sense, in terms of the long-term health of the capitalist system, is the unfair practice called greenmail and its associated gambits.

Shark repellents and poison pills are schemes that protect corporate management against raiders, sometimes to the detriment of stockholders. Golden parachutes guarantee big payoffs to executives in case repellents don't work. A Lady Macbeth strategy is (pardon the gender change) a white knight who gallops up to save a company, then joins with the raider to do in the king and take control. Lady Macbeth, in this case, wants all the perfumes of Arabia not for spot cleaning but to rival Saudi assets.

Greenmail, in case you have missed some recent takeover battles, occurs when a corporate raider or group of raiders buys a minority position in the stock of a target company. This threat to win control then provokes a buy-back offer from the worried executives of the threatened corporation. The buy-back typically gives the greenmailers a sharply higher price per share than the other, more common holders of common stock can get for theirs. To add insult to injury, this extra expenditure of company (i.e., stockholders') money dilutes the value of the other shares. No Mafia protection seller could fail to admire the quick and unfair results of this system.

Source: Earl W. Foell, "Takeover May Not Be Fair Game," May 21, 1984. Reprinted by permission from *The Christian Science Monitor.* © 1984 The Christian Science Publishing Society. All rights reserved.

the *P/E* based on the share price paid for the Tiny Company was greater than the *P/E* for the Bigge Company (22 versus 20), the effect of the merger was to decrease the *EPS* for original holders of shares in the Bigge Company (from $4.00 to $3.93) and to increase the effective *EPS* of original holders of shares in the Tiny Company (from $5.00 to $5.40). ∎

TABLE 17.6 Effect of Price/Earnings (P/E) Ratios on Earnings per Share (EPS)

Relationship between P/E paid and P/E of acquiring company	EFFECT ON EPS	
	Acquiring company	Acquired company
P/E paid > P/E of acquiring company	Decrease	Increase
P/E paid = P/E of acquiring company	Constant	Constant
P/E paid < P/E of acquiring company	Increase	Decrease

Long-Run Effect. The long-run effect of a merger on the earnings per share of the merged company depends largely on whether the earnings of the merged firm grow. Often, although a decrease in the per-share earnings of the stock held by the original owners of the acquiring firm is expected initially, the long-run effects of the merger on earnings per share are quite favorable. Since growth in earnings is generally expected by a business firm, the key factor enabling the acquiring company, which initially experiences a decrease in *EPS*, to experience higher future *EPS* than it would have without the merger is the fact that the earnings attributable to the acquired company's assets grow at a faster rate than those resulting from the acquiring company's pre-merger assets. An example will clarify this point.

EXAMPLE

In 1987 the Bigge Company acquired the Tiny Company by exchanging 1.375 shares of its common stock for each share of the Tiny Company. Other key financial data and the effects of this exchange ratio were discussed in the preceding example. The total earnings of the Bigge Company were expected to grow at an annual rate of 3 percent without the merger, while the Tiny Company's earnings were expected to grow at a 7 percent annual rate without the merger. The same growth rates are expected to apply to the component earnings streams with the merger.[3] Table 17.7 shows the future effects on *EPS* for the Bigge Company without and with the proposed Tiny Company merger, based on these growth rates.

Table 17.7 indicates that the earnings per share without the merger will be greater than the *EPS* with the merger for the years 1987 through 1989. After 1989, however, the *EPS* will be higher than they would have been without the merger as a result of the

[3] Sometimes, due to synergistic effects the combined earnings stream is greater than the sum of the individual earnings streams. This possibility is ignored here.

TABLE 17.7 Effects of Earnings Growth on *EPS* for the Bigge Company without and with the Tiny Company Merger

	WITHOUT MERGER		WITH MERGER	
Year	Total earnings[a]	Earnings per share[b]	Total earnings[c]	Earnings per share[d]
1987	$500,000	$4.00	$600,000	$3.93
1988	515,000	4.12	622,000	4.08
1989	530,450	4.24	644,940	4.23
1990	546,364	4.37	668,868	4.39
1991	562,755	4.50	693,835	4.55
1992	579,638	4.64	719,893	4.72

[a] Based on a 3 percent annual growth rate.

[b] Based on 125,000 shares outstanding.

[c] Based on 3 percent annual growth in the Bigge Company's earnings and 7 percent annual growth in the Tiny Company's earnings.

[d] Based on 152,500 shares outstanding [(1.375 × 20,000 shares) + 125,000 shares].

faster earnings growth rate of the Tiny Company (7 percent versus 3 percent). Although a few years are required for this difference in the growth rate of earnings to pay off, it can be seen that in the future the Bigge Company will receive an earnings benefit as a result of merging with the Tiny Company at a 1.375 ratio of exchange. The relationships in Table 17.7 are graphed in Figure 17.1. The long-run earnings advantage of the merger is clearly depicted by this graph. ■

EFFECT ON MARKET PRICE PER SHARE   The market price per share does not necessarily remain constant after the acquisition of one firm by another. Adjustments take place in the marketplace in response to changes in expected earnings, the dilution of ownership, changes in risk, and certain other operating and financial changes. Using the ratio of exchange, a **ratio of exchange in market price** can be calculated. It indicates the market price per share of the acquiring firm *paid* for each dollar of market price per share of the acquired firm. This ratio, the *MPR*, is defined by Equation 17.1.

ratio of exchange in market price The ratio indicating the market price per share of the acquiring firm *paid* for each dollar of market price per share of the acquired firm.

$$MPR = \frac{MP_{acquiring} \times RE}{MP_{acquired}} \tag{17.1}$$

where

$$
\begin{aligned}
MPR &= \text{market price ratio of exchange} \\
MP_{acquiring} &= \text{market price per share for the acquiring firm} \\
MP_{acquired} &= \text{market price per share for the acquired firm} \\
RE &= \text{ratio of exchange}
\end{aligned}
$$

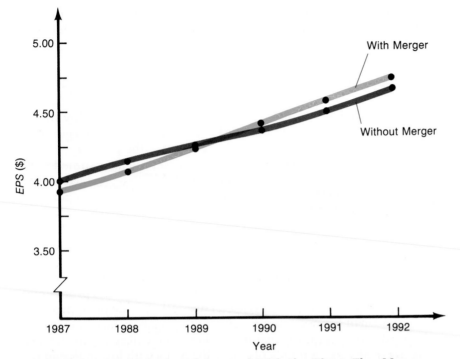

FIGURE 17.1 Future *EPS* without and with the Bigge-Tiny Merger
The earnings per share *(EPS)* for the Bigge Company in the 1987 through 1989
period will be lower with the proposed Tiny Company merger than without it.
After 1989 the postmerger *EPS* will be greater with rather than without the
proposed merger.

The following example can be used to illustrate the calculation of
this ratio.

EXAMPLE

In the Bigge-Tiny example, the market price of the Bigge Company's stock was $80 and that of the Tiny Company's was $75. The
ratio of exchange was 1.375. Substituting these values into Equation 17.1 yields a ratio of exchange in market price of 1.47 [($80 ×
1.375) ÷ $75]. This means that $1.47 of the market price of the
Bigge Company is given in exchange for every $1.00 of the market
price of the Tiny Company.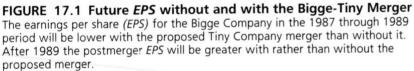

The ratio of exchange in market price is normally always greater than
1, which indicates that to acquire a firm, a premium above its market
price must be paid by the acquirer. Even so, the original owners of the
acquiring firm may still gain because the merged firm's stock may sell

at a price/earnings ratio above the individual premerger ratios. This results due to the improved risk and return relationship perceived by shareholders and other investors.

EXAMPLE

The financial data developed earlier for the Bigge-Tiny merger can be used to explain the market price effects of a merger. If the earnings of the merged company remain at the premerger levels, and if the stock of the merged company sells at an assumed multiple of 21 times earnings, the values in Table 17.8 can be expected. In spite of the fact that the Bigge Company's earnings per share decline from $4.00 to $3.93 (see Table 17.5), the market price of its shares will increase from $80.00 (see Table 17.4) to $82.53 as a result of the merger. ■

Although the kind of behavior exhibited in this example is not unusual, the financial manager must recognize that only with proper management of the merged enterprise can its market value be improved. If the merged firm cannot achieve sufficiently high earnings in view of its risk, there is no guarantee that its market price will reach the forecast value. Nevertheless, a policy of acquiring firms with low *P/E*s can produce favorable results for the owners of the acquiring firm. Acquisitions are especially attractive when the acquiring firm's stock price is high, since fewer shares must be exchanged to acquire a given firm.

Leveraged Buyouts (*LBOs*)

leveraged buyout *(LBO)*
An acquisition technique in which a large amount of debt is used to purchase a firm.

A popular technique currently used to make acquisitions is the **leveraged buyout** *(LBO)*, which involves the use of a large amount of debt to purchase a firm. Typically the debt represents 90 percent or more of the purchase price. A large part of the borrowing is secured by the acquired firm's assets, and the lenders, due to the high risk, take a portion of the

TABLE 17.8 Postmerger Market Price of the Bigge Company Using a *P/E* Ratio of 21

Item	Merged company
(1) Earnings available for common stock	$600,000
(2) Number of shares of common stock outstanding	152,500
(3) Earnings per share [(1) ÷ (2)]	$3.93
(4) Price/earnings *(P/E)* ratio	21
(5) Expected market price per share [(3) × (4)]	$82.53

firm's equity. The acquirers in *LBO*s are other firms or groups of investors that frequently include key members of existing management.

An attractive candidate for acquisition through leveraged buyout should possess three basic attributes:

1. It must have a good position in its industry with a solid profit history and reasonable expectations for growth.
2. The firm should have a relatively low level of debt and a high level of "bankable" assets that can be used as loan collateral.
3. It must have stable and predictable cash flows that are adequate to meet interest and principal payments on the debt and provide adequate working capital.

Of course, a willingness on the part of existing ownership and management to sell the company on a leveraged basis is also needed.

The leveraged buyout of Gibson Greeting Cards by a group of investors and managers headed by William Simon, former secretary of the treasury, demonstrates the popularity of *LBO*s. In the early 1980s Simon's group, Wesray, purchased Gibson from RCA for $81 million. The group put up $1 million and borrowed the remaining $80 million, using the firm's assets as collateral. Within three years after Gibson had been acquired, Wesray had publicly sold 50 percent of the company for $87 million. Wesray still owned 50 percent of Gibson and had earned $87 million on a $1 million investment. While this cannot be cited as the typical outcome of a leveraged buyout, it does point out the potential rewards from the use of *LBO*s to finance acquisitions.

The Merger Negotiation Process

Mergers are often handled by **investment bankers** hired by the prospective participants to find a suitable merger partner and assist in negotiations. A firm seeking a potential acquisition can hire an investment banker to find firms meeting their requirements. Once located, the investment banker negotiates with the management or the investment banker of the potential acquisition. Frequently when management wishes to sell the firm or a division of the firm, it will hire an investment banker to seek out potential buyers. In the event that attempts to negotiate with the management of an acquisition candidate break down, the firm, often with the aid of its investment banker, can make a direct appeal to shareholders by using tender offers (as explained below). The investment banker is typically compensated with a fixed fee, a commission tied to the transaction price, or with a combination of fees and commissions.

investment bankers
Hired by the prospective participants in a merger to find a suitable partner and assist in negotiations.

MANAGEMENT NEGOTIATIONS   To initiate the negotiation process, the acquiring firm must make an offer based on a certain ratio of exchange.

The merger candidate must then review the offer and, in light of alternative offers, accept or reject the terms presented. A desirable merger candidate usually receives more than a single offer. Normally, certain nonfinancial issues relating to the disposition and compensation of the existing management, product-line policies, financing policies, and the independence of the acquired firm must be resolved. The key factor, of course, is the per-share price offered, which is reflected in the ratio of exchange. Although the negotiations are generally based on the expectation of a merger, sometimes negotiations will break down.

TENDER OFFERS When management negotiations for an acquisition break down, *tender offers* may be used to negotiate a merger directly with the firm's stockholders. A **tender offer** is a formal offer to purchase a given number of shares of a firm's stock at a specified price. The offer is made at a premium above the market price to all the stockholders. The stockholders are advised of this proposal through announcements in financial newspapers or through direct communications from the offering firm. Sometimes a tender offer is made in order to add pressure to existing merger negotiations. In other cases the tender offer may be made without warning as an attempt at an abrupt corporate takeover.

tender offer A formal offer to purchase a given number of shares of a firm's stock at a specified price, often in order to acquire the firm.

If the management of a firm does not favor a merger or considers the premium in a projected tender offer too low, it is likely to take certain defensive actions to ward off the tender offer. Common strategies include declaring an attractive dividend, informing stockholders of alleged damaging effects of being taken over, or attempting to sue the acquiring firm. These actions may deter or delay a tender offer. Deterring the tender offer by filing suit gives the management that is fearful of a takeover time to find and negotiate a merger with a firm it would prefer to be acquired by.

Holding Companies

As defined earlier, a *holding company* is a corporation that has voting control of one or more other corporations. The holding company may need to own only a small percentage of the outstanding shares to have this voting control. In the case of companies with a relatively small number of shareholders, as much as 30 to 40 percent of the stock may be required. In the case of firms with a widely dispersed ownership, 10 to 20 percent of the shares may be sufficient to gain voting control. A holding company desirous of obtaining voting control of a firm may use direct market purchases or tender offers to obtain needed shares.

ADVANTAGES OF HOLDING COMPANIES The primary advantage of the holding company arrangement is the *leverage effect* that permits the firm to control a large amount of assets with a relatively small dollar investment. In other words, the owners of a holding company can *control* significantly larger amounts of assets than they could *acquire* through mergers. The following example may help illustrate the leverage effect.

EXAMPLE

The Hauck Company currently holds voting control of two subsidiaries — company X and company Y. The balance sheets for the Hauck Company and its two subsidiaries are presented in Table 17.9. It owns approximately 17 percent ($10 ÷ $60) of company X and 20 percent ($14 ÷ $70) of company Y. It is assumed that these holdings are sufficient for voting control.

The owners of the Hauck Company's $12 worth of equity have control over $260 worth of assets (company X's $100 worth and company Y's $160 worth). This means that the owners' equity represents only about 4.6 percent ($12 ÷ $260) of the total assets controlled. From the discussions of ratio analysis, leverage, and capital structure in Chapters 4, 5, and 16, you should recognize

TABLE 17.9 Balance Sheets for the Hauck Company and Its Subsidiaries

Assets		Liabilities and stockholders' equity	
HAUCK COMPANY			
Common stock holdings		Long-term debt	$ 6
Company X	$10	Preferred stock	6
Company Y	14	Common stock equity	12
Total	$24	Total	$24
COMPANY X			
Current assets	$ 30	Current liabilities	$ 15
Fixed assets	70	Long-term debt	25
Total	$100	Common stock equity	60
		Total	$100
COMPANY Y			
Current assets	$ 20	Current liabilities	$ 10
Fixed assets	140	Long-term debt	60
Total	$160	Preferred stock	20
		Common stock equity	70
		Total	$160

that this is quite a high degree of leverage. If an individual stockholder or even another holding company owns $3 of Hauck Company's stock, which is assumed sufficient for its control, it will in actuality control the whole $260 of assets. The investment itself in this case would represent only 1.15 percent ($3 ÷ $260) of the assets controlled. ■

The high leverage obtained through a holding company arrangement greatly magnifies earnings and losses for the holding company. Quite often a **pyramiding** of holding companies occurs when one holding company controls other holding companies, thereby causing an even greater magnification of earnings and losses. The greater the leverage, the greater the risk involved. The risk-return trade-off is a key consideration in the holding company decision.

pyramiding An arrangement among holding companies wherein one holding company controls other holding companies, thereby causing an even greater magnification of earnings and losses.

Another commonly cited advantage of the holding company arrangement is the *risk protection* resulting from the fact that failure of one of the companies (such as Y in the preceding example) does not result in the failure of the entire holding company. Since each subsidiary is a separate corporation, the failure of one company should cost the holding company, at maximum, no more than its investment in that subsidiary. Other advantages include the fact that certain state *tax benefits* may be realized by each subsidiary in its state of incorporation, *lawsuits or legal actions* against a subsidiary will not threaten the remaining companies, and it is *generally easy to gain control* of a firm since stockholder or management approval is not generally necessary.

DISADVANTAGES OF HOLDING COMPANIES   A major disadvantage of the holding company arrangement is the *increased risk* resulting from the leverage effect. When general economic conditions are unfavorable, a loss by one subsidiary may be magnified. For example, if subsidiary company X in Table 17.9 experiences a loss, its inability to pay dividends to the Hauck Company could result in the Hauck Company's inability to meet its scheduled payments.

Another disadvantage is *double taxation*. Prior to paying dividends a subsidiary must pay federal and state taxes on its earnings. Although an 80 percent tax exemption is allowed on dividends received by one corporation from another, the remaining 20 percent received is taxable. (In the event that the holding company owns 80 percent or more of the stock in the subsidiary, 100 percent of the dividends are tax exempt.) If a subsidiary were part of a merged company, double taxation would *not* exist.

A final disadvantage of holding companies is the generally *high cost of administration* resulting from maintaining each subsidiary company as a separate entity. A merger, on the other hand, would likely result in certain administrative economies of scale. The need for coordination and communication between the holding company and its subsidiaries may further elevate these costs.

THE TYPES AND CAUSES OF BUSINESS FAILURE[4]

A business failure is an unfortunate circumstance. Although the majority of firms that fail do so within the first year or two of life, other firms grow, mature, and fail much later. The failure of a business can be viewed in a number of ways and can result from one or more causes.

Types of Business Failure

A firm may fail because its *returns are negative or low*. A firm that consistently reports operating losses will probably experience a decline in market value. If the firm fails to earn a return greater than its cost of capital, it can be viewed as having failed. Negative or low returns, unless remedied, are likely to result eventually in one of the following more serious types of failure.

A second type of failure, **technical insolvency,** occurs when a firm is unable to pay its liabilities as they come due. When a firm is technically insolvent, its assets are still greater than its liabilities, but it is confronted with a *liquidity crisis*. If some of its assets can be converted into cash within a reasonable period, the company may be able to escape complete failure. If not, the result is the third and most serious type of failure, **bankruptcy.** Bankruptcy occurs when a firm's liabilities exceed the fair market value of its assets. A bankrupt firm has a *negative* stockholders' equity.[5] This means that the claims of creditors cannot be satisfied unless the firm's assets can be liquidated for more than their book value. Although bankruptcy is an obvious form of failure, *the courts treat technical insolvency and bankruptcy in the same way.* They are both considered to indicate the financial failure of the firm.

technical insolvency
Occurs when a firm is unable to pay its liabilities as they come due.

bankruptcy Occurs when a firm's liabilities exceed the fair market value of its assets.

Major Causes of Business Failure

The primary cause of business failure is *mismanagement*, which accounts for more than 50 percent of all cases. Numerous specific mana-

[4] Occasionally a division or subsidiary of an otherwise profitable firm will fail. In such an event the firm is faced with a *divestiture decision:* it must estimate and compare the economic costs and benefits of sustaining versus selling or liquidating the poorly performing operation. Although the procedures involved in divestiture decisions are similar to those used to evaluate business failure, they are beyond the scope of this basic text.

[5] Since on a balance sheet the firm's assets equal the sum of its liabilities and stockholders' equity, the only way a firm that has more liabilities than assets can balance its balance sheet is to have a *negative* stockholders' equity.

gerial faults can cause the firm to fail. Overexpansion, poor financial actions, an ineffective sales force, and high production costs can all singly, or in combination, cause the ultimate failure of the firm. Since all major corporate decisions are eventually measured in terms of dollars, the financial manager may play a key role in avoiding or causing a business failure. It is his or her duty to monitor the firm's financial pulse.

Economic activity—especially economic downturns—can contribute to the failure of a firm. If the economy goes into a recession, sales may decrease abruptly, leaving the firm with high fixed costs and insufficient revenues to cover them. In addition, rapid rises in interest rates during a recession can further contribute to cash flow problems and make it more difficult for the firm to obtain and maintain needed financing. If the recession is prolonged, the likelihood of survival decreases even further.

A final cause of business failure is *corporate maturity*. Firms, like individuals, do not have infinite lives. Like a product, a firm goes through the stages of birth, growth, maturity, and eventual decline. The firm's management should attempt to prolong the growth stage through business combinations, research, and the development of new products. Once the firm has matured and has begun to decline, it should seek to be acquired by another firm or liquidate before it fails. Effective management planning should help the firm to postpone decline and ultimate failure.

VOLUNTARY SETTLEMENTS

voluntary settlement An arrangement between a technically insolvent or bankrupt firm and its creditors enabling it to bypass many of the costs involved in legal bankruptcy proceedings.

When a firm becomes technically insolvent or bankrupt, it may arrange with its creditors a **voluntary settlement,** which enables it to bypass many of the costs involved in legal bankruptcy proceedings. The settlement is normally initiated by the debtor firm, since such an arrangement may enable it to continue to exist or to be liquidated in a manner that gives the owners the greatest chance of recovering part of their investment. The debtor, possibly with the aid of a key creditor, arranges a meeting between itself and all its creditors. At the meeting a committee of creditors is selected to investigate and analyze the debtor's situation and recommend a plan of action. The recommendations of the committee are discussed with both the debtor and the creditors, and a plan for sustaining or liquidating the firm is drawn up.

Voluntary Settlement to Sustain the Firm

Normally the rationale for sustaining a firm is that it is reasonable to believe the firm's recovery is feasible. By sustaining the firm the creditor can continue to receive business from it. A number of strategies are commonly used. An **extension** is an arrangement whereby the firm's creditors receive payment in full, although not immediately. Normally when creditors grant an extension, they agree to require cash payments for purchases until all past debts have been paid. A second arrangement, called **composition,** is a pro rata cash settlement of creditor claims. Instead of receiving full payment of their claims, as in the case of an extension, creditors receive only a partial payment. A uniform percentage of each dollar owed is paid in satisfaction of each creditor's claim. A third arrangement is **creditor control.** In this case the committee may decide that the only circumstance in which maintaining the firm is feasible is if the operating management is replaced. The creditor committee may then take control of the firm and operate it until all claims have been settled. Sometimes, a plan involving some combination of extension, composition, and creditor control will result. An example of this would be a settlement whereby the debtor agrees to pay a total of 75 cents on the dollar in three equal annual installments of 25 cents on the dollar, while the creditors agree to sell additional merchandise to the firm on 30-day terms if the existing management is replaced by a new management acceptable to them.

extension An arrangement whereby the firm's creditors receive payment in full, although not immediately.

composition A pro rata cash settlement of creditor claims by the debtor firm; a uniform percentage of each dollar owed is paid.

creditor control An arrangement in which the creditor committee replaces the firm's operating management and operates the firm until all claims have been settled.

Voluntary Settlement Resulting in Liquidation

After the situation of the firm has been investigated by the creditor committee, recommendations have been made, and talks among the creditors and the debtor have been held, the only acceptable course of action may be liquidation of the firm. Liquidation can be carried out in two ways—privately or through the legal procedures provided by bankruptcy law. If the debtor firm is willing to accept liquidation, legal procedures may not be required. Generally, the avoidance of litigation enables the creditors to obtain *quicker* and *higher* settlements. However, all the creditors must agree to a private liquidation in order for it to be feasible.

The objective of the voluntary liquidation process is to recover as much per dollar owed as possible. Under voluntary liquidation common stockholders, who are the firm's true owners, cannot receive any funds until the claims of all other parties have been satisfied. A common procedure is to have a meeting of the creditors at which they make an **assignment** by passing the power to liquidate the firm's assets to an adjustment bureau, trade association, or a third party, which becomes the *assignee.* The assignee's job is to liquidate the assets, obtaining the best price possible. The assignee is sometimes referred to as the *trustee,* since it is entrusted with the title to the company's assets and the responsibility to liquidate them efficiently. Once the trustee has liquidated the assets, it distributes the recovered funds to the creditors and

assignment A voluntary liquidation procedure by which a firm's creditors pass the power to liquidate the firm's assets to an adjustment bureau, trade association, or a third party, which is designated the *assignee.*

owners (if any funds remain for the owners). The final action in a private liquidation is for the creditors to sign a release attesting to the satisfactory settlement of their claims.

REORGANIZATION AND LIQUIDATION IN BANKRUPTCY

If a voluntary settlement for a failed firm cannot be agreed upon, the firm can be forced into bankruptcy by its creditors. As a result of bankruptcy proceedings, the firm may be either reorganized or liquidated.

Bankruptcy Legislation

As already stated, *bankruptcy* in the legal sense occurs when the firm cannot pay its bills or when its liabilities exceed the fair market value of its assets. In either of these situations a firm may be declared legally bankrupt. However, creditors generally attempt to avoid forcing a firm into bankruptcy if it appears to have opportunities for future success.

Bankruptcy Reform Act of 1978 The current governing bankruptcy legislation in the United States.

The governing bankruptcy legislation in the United States today is the **Bankruptcy Reform Act of 1978,** which significantly modified earlier bankruptcy legislation. This law contains eight odd-numbered chapters (1 through 15). A number of these chapters would apply in the instance of failure; the two key sections are Chapters 7 and 11. **Chapter 7** of the Bankruptcy Reform Act of 1978 details the procedures to be followed when liquidating a failed firm. This chapter typically comes into play once it has been determined that a fair, equitable, and feasible basis for the reorganization of a failed firm does not exist (although a firm may of its own accord choose not to reorganize and may instead go directly into liquidation). **Chapter 11** outlines the procedures for reorganizing a failed firm, whether its petition is filed voluntarily or involuntarily. If a workable plan for reorganization cannot be developed, the firm will be liquidated under Chapter 7.

Chapter 7 The portion of the Bankruptcy Reform Act of 1978 that details the procedures to be followed when liquidating a failed firm.

Chapter 11 The portion of the Bankruptcy Reform Act of 1978 that outlines the procedures for reorganizing a failed firm, whether its petition is filed voluntarily or involuntarily.

Reorganization in Bankruptcy

voluntary reorganization A petition filed by a failed firm in its own behalf for reorganizing its structure and paying its creditors.

There are two basic types of reorganization petitions — voluntary and involuntary. Any firm that is not a municipal or financial institution or a railroad can file a petition for **voluntary reorganization** on its own behalf. **Involuntary reorganization** is initiated by an outside party, usually a creditor. An involuntary petition against a firm can be filed if one of three conditions is met:

involuntary reorganization A petition initiated by an outside party, usually a creditor, for the reorganization and payment of creditors of a failed firm.

1. The firm has past-due debts of $5,000 or more.
2. Three or more creditors can prove they have aggregate unpaid claims of $5,000 against the firm. If the firm has fewer than 12 creditors, any creditor owed more than $5,000 can file the petition.

SUGGESTIONS FOR AVOIDING BANKRUPTCY

How can a company in trouble avoid bankruptcy proceedings? Here are some suggestions from Edmond P. Freiermuth, a Santa Monica, Calif., consultant who was a banker for 10 years, making many loans to small and medium-size businesses.

The first thing to do, he says, is analyze the extent of the company's financial difficulties and their causes. Then an estimate should be made of cash receipts and disbursements for the next three to six months.

The projection of cash in and out will probably show disbursements exceeding receipts. "Typically," Mr. Freiermuth says, "management hasn't been as aggressive as it could be in collecting accounts receivable and has let accounts payable go."

The remedy is to cut expenses as quickly as possible. "You have to take a hard look at all expenditures," he says, especially payroll. Usually, he finds more employees than are necessary because small-business owners tend to be reluctant to fire people.

One client hadn't cut its work force even though sales had plunged 50%. "It was incredible," Mr. Freiermuth says. And the concern had been threatened with legal action by creditors who, he says, "were furious."

He convinced the owners that they had to let go half the employees — 50 people — for the company to avoid bankruptcy. The owners were able to placate the creditors by honestly stating the condition of the company and explaining what was being done to turn it around. It's a mistake to mislead creditors, Mr. Freiermuth says. They know something is wrong because they haven't been paid, and their cooperation is needed to keep the business out of bankruptcy proceedings.

Chapter 11 of the Bankruptcy Code offers a business protection from creditors while it tries to work out a settlement with them, but it is an expensive process, Mr. Freiermuth says. It involves legal fees that the business can ill afford, and it consumes time that the owners should spend turning the business around. Says the banker-turned-consultant, "I'm a strong believer in avoiding Chapter 11."

3. The firm is *insolvent*, which means (a) that it is not paying its debts as they come due, (b) that within the immediately preceding 120 days a custodian (a third party) was appointed or took possession of the debtor's property, or (c) that the fair market value of the firm's assets is less than the stated value of its liabilities.

PROCEDURES The procedures for the initiation and execution of corporate reorganizations entail five separate steps: filing; appointment;

development and approval of a reorganization plan; acceptance of the plan; and payment of expenses.

Filing. A reorganization petition under Chapter 11 must be filed in a federal bankruptcy court. In the case of an involuntary petition, if it is challenged by the debtor, a hearing must be held to determine whether the firm is insolvent. If so, the court enters an "Order for Relief" that formally initiates the process.

Appointment. The judge before whom the reorganization petition is submitted will evaluate it and, upon finding it acceptable, will enter an order approving it. If it is approved, the judge will appoint the filing firm the **debtor in possession (DIP)** of the assets. If creditors object to the appointment of the debtor in possession, they can ask the judge to appoint a trustee.

debtor in possession (DIP) The designation assigned to a failed firm that has petitioned for, and received, permission to reorganize under Chapter 11.

Reorganization Plan. After reviewing its situation, the debtor in possession submits a plan of reorganization to the court. The plan and a disclosure statement summarizing the plan are filed, and a hearing is held to determine whether they are sufficient. The main requirement is that the plan be *fair, equitable,* and *feasible.* The court's approval or disapproval is based on its evaluation of the plan in light of these standards. A plan is considered *fair and equitable* if it *maintains the priorities* of the contractual claims of the creditors, preferred stockholders, and common stockholders. The court must also find the reorganization plan *feasible,* meaning it must be *workable.* The reorganized corporation must have sufficient working capital, sufficient funds to cover fixed charges, sufficient credit prospects, and sufficient ability to retire or refund debts as proposed by the plan.

Acceptance of the Reorganization Plan. Once approved, the disclosure statement, along with the plan, are given to the firm's creditors and shareholders for their acceptance. Under the Bankruptcy Reform Act, creditors and owners are separated into groups with similar types of claims. In the case of creditor groups, approval by holders of at least two-thirds of the claims as well as a numerical majority of creditors in the group is required. In the case of ownership groups (preferred and common stockholders), two-thirds of the shares in each group must approve the reorganization plan for it to be accepted. Once accepted, the plan is put into effect as soon as possible.

Payment of Expenses. After the reorganization plan has been approved or disapproved, all parties to the proceedings whose services were beneficial or contributed to the approval or disapproval of the plan file a statement of expenses. If the court finds these claims acceptable, the debtor must pay these expenses within a reasonable period of time.

ROLE OF THE DEBTOR IN POSSESSION (DIP) Since reorganization activities are largely in the hands of the debtor in possession (DIP), it is useful to understand the DIP's responsibilities. The DIP's first responsibility is the valuation of the firm to determine whether reorganization is appropriate. To do this, the DIP must estimate both the *liquidation value* of the enterprise and its value as a *going concern*. If the DIP finds that its value as a going concern is less than its liquidation value, it will recommend liquidation. If the opposite is found to be true, the DIP will recommend reorganization. If the reorganization of the firm is recommended by the DIP, a plan of reorganization must be drawn up. The key portion of the reorganization plan generally concerns the firm's capital structure. Since most firms' financial difficulties result from high fixed charges, the company's capital structure is generally *recapitalized,* or altered, in order to reduce these charges. Under **recapitalization** debts are generally exchanged for equity, or the maturities of existing debts are extended. The DIP, in recapitalizing the firm, places a great deal of emphasis on building a mix of debt and equity that will allow it to meet its debts and provide a reasonable level of earnings for its owners.

recapitalization The reorganization procedure under which a failed firm's debts are generally exchanged for equity or the maturities of existing debts are extended.

Once the optimal capital structure has been determined, the DIP must establish a plan for exchanging outstanding obligations for new securities. The guiding principle is to *observe priorities*. Senior claims (those with higher legal priority) must be satisfied prior to junior claims (those with lower legal priority). To comply with this principle, senior suppliers of capital must receive a claim on new capital equal to their previous claims. The common stockholders are the last to receive any new securities. (It is not unusual for them to receive nothing.) Security holders do not necessarily have to receive the same type of security they held before; often they receive a combination of securities. Once the debtor in possession has determined the new capital structure and distribution of capital, it will submit the reorganization plan and disclosure statement to the court as described.

Liquidation in Bankrupty

The liquidation of a bankrupt firm usually occurs once the courts have determined that reorganization is not feasible. A petition for reorganization must normally be filed by the managers or creditors of the bankrupt firm. If no petition is filed, if a petition is filed and denied, or if the reorganization plan is denied, the firm must be liquidated. Three important aspects of liquidation in bankruptcy are the procedures, the priority of claims, and the final accounting.

PROCEDURES When a firm is adjudged bankrupt, the judge may appoint a *trustee* to perform the many routine duties required in administering the bankruptcy. The trustee takes charge of the property of the bankrupt firm and protects the interest of its creditors. Once the firm has been adjudged bankrupt, a meeting of creditors must be held between 20 and 40 days thereafter. At this meeting the creditors are made aware of the prospects for the liquidation. The meeting is presided over by the bankruptcy court clerk. The trustee is then given the responsibility to liquidate the firm, keep records, examine creditors' claims, disburse money, furnish information as required, and make final reports on the liquidation. In essence the trustee is responsible for the liquidation of the firm. Occasionally the court will call subsequent creditor meetings, but only a final meeting for closing the bankruptcy is required.

PRIORITY OF CLAIMS   It is the trustee's responsibility to liquidate all the firm's assets and to distribute the proceeds to the holders of *provable claims*. The courts have established certain procedures for determining the provability of claims. The priority of claims, which is specified in Chapter 7 of the Bankruptcy Reform Act, must be maintained by the trustee in distributing the funds from liquidation. It is important to recognize that any **secured creditors** have specific assets pledged as collateral and in liquidation receive proceeds from the sale of those assets. If these proceeds are inadequate to meet their claim, the secured creditors become **unsecured, or general, creditors** for the unrecovered amount since specific collateral no longer exists. These and all other unsecured creditors will divide up on a pro rata basis the funds, if any, remaining after all prior claims have been satisfied. If the proceeds from the sale of secured assets are in excess of the claims against them, the excess funds become available to meet claims of unsecured creditors. The complete order of priority of claims is as follows:

secured creditors Creditors who have specific assets pledged as collateral and in liquidation of the failed firm receive proceeds from the sale of those assets.

unsecured, or general, creditors Creditors having a general claim against all the firm's assets other than those specifically pledged as collateral.

1. The expenses of administering the bankruptcy proceedings.
2. Any unpaid interim expenses incurred in the ordinary course of business between filing the bankruptcy petition and the entry of an Order for Relief in an involuntary proceeding. (This step is *not* applicable in a voluntary bankruptcy.)
3. Wages of not more than $2,000 per worker that have been earned by workers in the 90-day period immediately preceding the commencement of bankruptcy proceedings.
4. Unpaid employee benefit plan contributions that were to be paid in the 180-day period preceding the filing of bankruptcy or the termination of business, whichever occurred first. For any employee, the sum of this claim plus eligible unpaid wages (item 3) cannot exceed $2,000.
5. Claims of farmers or fishermen in a grain-storage or fish-storage facility, not to exceed $2,000 for each producer.
6. Unsecured customer deposits, not to exceed $900 each, resulting from purchasing or leasing a good or service from the failed firm.
7. Taxes legally due and owed by the bankrupt firm to the federal

government, state government, or to any other governmental sub-division.

8. Claims of secured creditors, who receive the proceeds from the sale of collateral held, regardless of the priorities above. If the proceeds from the liquidation of the collateral are insufficient to satisfy the secured creditors' claims, the secured creditors become unsecured creditors for the unpaid amount.

9. Claims of unsecured creditors. The claims of unsecured, or general, creditors and unsatisfied portions of secured creditors' claims (item 8) are all treated equally.

10. Preferred stockholders, who receive an amount up to the par, or stated, value of their preferred stock.

11. Common stockholders, who receive any remaining funds, which are distributed on an equal per-share basis. If different classes of common stock (see Chapter 19) are outstanding, priorities may exist.

It can be seen from this list that the expenses of administering the bankruptcy proceedings, certain unpaid interim expenses, wages, un-

TABLE 17.10 Balance Sheet for the Dempsey Company

Assets		Liabilities and stockholders' equity	
Cash	$ 10,000	Accounts payable	$ 200,000
Marketable securities	5,000	Notes payable—bank	1,000,000
Accounts receivable	1,090,000	Accrued wages[a]	320,000
Inventories	3,100,000	Unpaid employee benefits[b]	80,000
Prepaid expenses	5,000	Unsecured customer deposits[c]	100,000
Total current assets	$4,210,000	Taxes payable	300,000
Land	$2,000,000	Total current liabilities	$2,000,000
Net plant	1,810,000	First mortgage[d]	$1,800,000
Net equipment	80,000	Second mortgage[d]	1,000,000
Total fixed assets	$3,890,000	Unsecured bonds	800,000
Total	$8,100,000	Total long-term debt	$3,600,000
		Preferred stock (5,000 shares)	$ 400,000
		Common stock (10,000 shares)	500,000
		Paid-in capital in excess of par	1,500,000
		Retained earnings	100,000
		Total stockholders' equity	$2,500,000
		Total	$8,100,000

[a] Represents wages of $800 per employee earned within 90 days of filing bankruptcy for 400 of the firm's employees.

[b] These unpaid employee benefits were due in the 180-day period preceding the firm's bankruptcy filing, which occurred simultaneously with the termination of its business.

[c] Unsecured customer deposits not exceeding $900 each.

[d] The first and second mortgages are on the firm's total fixed assets.

paid employee benefits, certain claims of farmers or fishermen, unsecured customer deposits, and taxes must be paid first. In spite of these priorities, secured creditors have first claim on proceeds from the sale of their collateral. The claims of unsecured creditors, including the unpaid claims of secured creditors, are satisfied next and, finally, the claims of preferred and common stockholders. The application of these priorities by the trustee in bankruptcy liquidation proceedings can be illustrated by a simple example.

EXAMPLE

The Dempsey Company has the balance sheet presented in Table 17.10 on page 561. The trustee, as was her obligation, has liquidated the firm's assets, obtaining the highest amounts she could get. She managed to obtain $2.3 million for the firm's current assets and $2 million for the firm's fixed assets. The total proceeds from the liquidation were therefore $4.3 million. It should be clear that the firm is legally bankrupt, since its liabilities of $5.6 million dollars exceed the $4.3 million fair market value of its assets.

The next step is to distribute the proceeds to the various creditors. The only liability not shown on the balance sheet is $800,000 in expenses for administering the bankruptcy proceedings and satisfying unpaid bills incurred between the time of filing the bankruptcy petition and the entry of an Order for Relief. The distribution of the $4.3 million among the firm's creditors is shown in Table 17.11. It can be seen from the table that once all prior claims on the proceeds from liquidation have been satisfied, the unsecured creditors get the remaining funds. The pro rata distribution of the $700,000 among the unsecured creditors is given in Table 17.12. The disposition of funds in the Dempsey

TABLE 17.11 Distribution of the Liquidation Proceeds of the Dempsey Company

Proceeds from liquidation	$4,300,000
— Expenses of administering bankruptcy and paying interim bills	$ 800,000
— Wages owed workers	320,000
— Unpaid employee benefits	80,000
— Unsecured customer deposits	100,000
— Taxes owed governments	300,000
Funds available for creditors	$2,700,000
— First mortgage, paid from the $2 million proceeds from the sale of fixed assets	$1,800,000
— Second mortgage, partially paid from the remaining $200,000 of fixed asset proceeds	200,000
Funds available for unsecured creditors	$ 700,000

TABLE 17.12 Pro Rata Distribution of Funds Among Unsecured Creditors of the Dempsey Company

Unsecured creditors' claims	Amount	Settlement at 25%[a]
Unpaid balance of second mortgage	$ 800,000[b]	$200,000
Accounts payable	200,000	50,000
Notes payable—bank	1,000,000	250,000
Unsecured bonds	800,000	200,000
Totals	$2,800,000	$700,000

[a] The 25 percent rate is calculated by dividing the $700,000 available for unsecured creditors by the $2.8 million owed unsecured creditors. Each is entitled to a pro rata share.

[b] This figure represents the difference between the $1 million second mortgage and the $200,000 payment on the second mortgage from the proceeds from the sale of the collateral remaining after satisfying the first mortgage.

Company liquidation should be clear from Tables 17.11 and 17.12. Since the claims of the unsecured creditors have not been fully satisfied, the preferred and common stockholders receive nothing. ■

FINAL ACCOUNTING   After the trustee has liquidated all the bankrupt firm's assets and distributed the proceeds to satisfy all provable claims in the appropriate order of priority, he or she makes a final accounting to the bankruptcy court and creditors. Once the court approves the final accounting, the liquidation is complete.

SUMMARY

● The three key types of business combinations are consolidations, mergers, and holding companies. Motives for business combinations include growth or diversification, synergistic effects, fund raising, increased managerial skills, tax considerations, and increased ownership liquidity.
● In cash purchases of assets or going concerns, traditional capital budgeting procedures using net present value can be applied to evaluate the economic feasibility of the transaction. In a stock-exchange acquisition, a ratio of exchange must be established. The resulting relationship between the price/earnings (P/E) ratio paid by the acquiring firm and its initial P/E ratio affects the merged firm's earnings per share and market price.
● A popular technique currently used in making acquisitions is the leveraged buyout, which involves the use of a large amount of debt to purchase a firm.
● Investment bankers are commonly hired by prospective participants to find a suitable merger partner and assist in negotiations. A merger can be nego-

tiated with a firm's management or directly with the firm's stockholders by using tender offers to purchase their stock.

● A holding company can be created by one firm gaining control of other companies, often by owning as little as 10 to 20 percent of their stock. The chief advantages of holding companies are the leverage effect, risk protection, tax benefits, protection against lawsuits, and the fact that it generally is easy to gain control of a subsidiary. The disadvantages commonly cited include increased risk due to the magnification of losses, double taxation, and the high cost of administration.

● A firm may fail because it has negative or low returns, because it is technically insolvent, or because it is bankrupt. The major causes of business failure are mismanagement, downturns in economic activity, and corporate maturity.

● Voluntary settlements are initiated by the debtor and can result in sustaining the firm through an extension, a composition, creditor control of the firm, or a combination of these strategies. If creditors do not agree to a plan to sustain a firm, they may recommend voluntary liquidation, which bypasses many of the legal requirements of bankruptcy.

● A failed firm that cannot or does not want to arrange a voluntary settlement can voluntarily or involuntarily file in federal bankruptcy court for reorganization under Chapter 11 or liquidation under Chapter 7 of the Bankruptcy Reform Act of 1978. Under Chapter 11 the judge will appoint the debtor in possession, who with court supervision develops, if feasible, a reorganization plan.

● A firm that cannot be reorganized under Chapter 11 of the bankruptcy law or does not petition for reorganization is liquidated under Chapter 7. The responsibility for liquidation is placed in the hands of a court-appointed trustee, whose responsibilities include the liquidation of assets, the distribution of the proceeds, and making a final accounting.

QUESTIONS

17-1   Describe and differentiate between *consolidations, mergers,* and *holding companies.* How does the holding company arrangement differ from both consolidations and mergers?

17-2   Briefly describe each of the four key types of growth or diversification. Why and in what situations may the acquisition of a firm with a *tax loss carryforward* be attractive?

17-3   Describe the procedures typically used when a firm is acquiring for cash either assets or a going concern.

17-4   What is the *ratio of exchange?* Is it based on the current market prices of the shares of the acquiring and acquired firm? Why, or why not?

17-5   What are the important considerations in evaluating the long-run impact of a merger on the combined firm's earnings per share? Why may a long-run view change a merger decision?

17-6   What is a *leveraged buyout (LBO)?* What are the three key attributes of an attractive candidate for acquisition using an *LBO?*

17-7   What role do *investment bankers* often play in the merger negotiation process? What is a *tender offer?* When and how is it used?

17-8 What are the key advantages and disadvantages cited for the holding company arrangement? What is *pyramiding,* and what are its consequences?

17-9 What are the three types of business failure? What is the difference between *technical insolvency* and *bankruptcy?* What are the major causes of business failure?

17-10 Define an *extension* and a *composition,* and explain how they might be combined to form a voluntary settlement plan to sustain the firm. How is a voluntary settlement resulting in liquidation handled?

17-11 What is the concern of Chapter 11 of the Bankruptcy Reform Act of 1978? How is the *debtor in possession (DIP)* involved in (1) the valuation of the firm, (2) the recapitalization of the firm, and (3) the exchange of obligations using the priority rule?

17-12 What is the concern of Chapter 7 of the Bankruptcy Reform Act of 1978? Under which conditions is a firm liquidated in bankruptcy? Describe the procedures (including the role of the trustee) involved in liquidating the bankrupt firm.

17-13 In which order would the following claims be settled in distributing the proceeds from liquidating a bankrupt firm?

a Claims of preferred stockholders

b Claims of secured creditors

c Expenses of administering the bankruptcy

d Claims of common stockholders

e Claims of unsecured, or general, creditors

f Taxes legally due

g Unsecured deposits of customers

h Certain eligible wages

i Unpaid employee benefit plan contributions

j Unpaid interim expenses incurred between the time of filing and the entry of an Order for Relief

k Claims of farmers or fishermen in a grain-storage or fish-storage facility

PROBLEMS

17-1 **(Tax Effects of Acquisition)** The Overtime Watch Company is contemplating the acquisition of the Sport Watch Company, a firm that has shown large operating tax losses over the past few years. As a result of the acquisition, Overtime believes the total pretax profits of the consolidation will not change from their present level for 15 years. The tax loss carryforward of Sport Watch is $800,000, while Overtime projects annual earnings before taxes to be $280,000 per year for each of the next 15 years. These earnings are assumed to fall within the annual limit legally allowed for application of the tax loss carryforward resulting from the proposed acquisition (see footnote 2 on page 536). The firm is in the 40 percent tax bracket.

a If Overtime does not make the acquisition, what are the company's tax liability and earnings after taxes each year over the next 15 years?

b If the acquisition is made, what are the company's tax liability and earnings after taxes each year over the next 15 years?

c If Sport Watch can be acquired for $350,000 in cash, should Overtime make the acquisition, based on tax considerations? (Ignore present value.)

17-2 **(Tax Effects of Acquisition)** The Gourmette Corporation is evaluating the acquisition of Student Prince Hot Dog Stands. Student Prince has a tax loss carryforward of $1.8 million. Gourmette can purchase Student Prince for $2.1 million. It can sell the assets for $1.6 million — their book value. Gourmette expects earnings before taxes in the five years after the acquisition to be as follows:

Year	Earnings before taxes
1	$150,000
2	400,000
3	450,000
4	600,000
5	600,000

The expected earnings given above are assumed to fall within the annual limit legally allowed for application of the tax loss carryforward resulting from the proposed acquisition (see footnote 2 on page 536). Gourmette is in the 40 percent tax bracket.

a Calculate the firm's tax payments and earnings after taxes for each of the next five years *without* the acquisition.

b Calculate the firm's tax payments and earnings after taxes for each of the next five years *with* the acquisition.

c What are the total benefits associated with the tax losses from the acquisition? (Ignore present value.)

d Discuss whether you would recommend the proposed acquisition. Support your decision with figures.

17-3 **(Tax Benefits and Price)** Painted Pants has a tax loss carryforward of $800,000. Two firms are interested in acquiring Painted for the tax loss advantage. Studs Duds has expected earnings before taxes of $200,000 per year for each of the next seven years and a cost of capital of 15 percent. Glitter Threads has expected earnings before taxes for the next seven years as indicated:

GLITTER THREADS

Year	Earnings before taxes
1	$ 80,000
2	120,000
3	200,000
4	300,000
5	400,000
6	400,000
7	500,000

Both Studs Duds' and Glitter Threads' expected earnings are assumed to fall within the annual limit legally allowed for application of the tax loss carryforward resulting from the proposed acquisition (see footnote 2 on page 536). Glitter Threads has a cost of capital of 15 percent. Both firms are subject to 40 percent tax rates on ordinary income.

a What is the tax advantage of the acquisition each year for Studs Duds?

b What is the tax advantage of the acquisition each year for Glitter Threads?

c What is the maximum cash price each interested firm would be willing to pay for Painted Pants? (*Hint:* Calculate the present value of the tax advantages.)

d Use your answers in **a** through **c** to explain why an acquisition candidate can have different values to different potential acquiring firms.

17-4 **(Asset Acquisition Decision)** The Blue Printing Company is considering the acquisition of Multicolor Press at a cash price of $60,000. Multicolor Press has liabilities of $90,000. Multicolor has a large press that Blue needs; the remaining assets would be sold to net $65,000. As a result of acquiring the press, Blue would experience an increase in cash inflow of $20,000 per year over the next ten years. The firm has a 14 percent cost of capital.

a What is the effective or net cost of the large press?

b If this is the only way Blue can obtain the large press, should the firm go ahead with the acquisition? Explain your answer.

c If the firm could purchase a press that would provide slightly better quality and $26,000 annual cash inflow for ten years for a price of $120,000, which alternative would you recommend? Explain your answer.

17-5 **(Cash Acquisition Decision)** The Toma Fish Company is contemplating acquisition of Seaside Packing Company for a cash price of $180,000. Toma currently has high financial leverage and therefore has a cost of capital of 14 percent. As a result of acquiring Seaside Packing, which is financed entirely with equity, the firm expects its financial leverage to be reduced and its cost of capital therefore to drop to 11 percent. The acquisition of Seaside Packing is expected to increase Toma's cash inflows by $20,000 per year for the first three years and by $30,000 per year for the following 12 years.

a Determine whether the proposed cash acquisition is desirable. Explain your answer.

b If the firm's financial leverage would actually remain unchanged as a result of the proposed acquisition, would this alter your recommendation? Support your answer with numerical data.

17-6 **(Cash Acquisition Decision)** Cathcart Oil is being considered for acquisition by Onagonda Oil. The combination, Onagonda believes, would increase its cash inflows by $25,000 for each of the next five years and $50,000 for each of the following five years. Cathcart has high financial leverage, and Onagonda can expect its cost of capital to increase from 12 to 15 percent if the acquisition is made. The cash price of Cathcart is $125,000.

a Would you recommend the acquisition?

b Would you recommend the acquisition if the Onagonda firm could use the $125,000 to purchase equipment returning cash inflows of $40,000 per year for each of the next ten years?

17-7   **c** If the cost of capital does not change with the acquisition, would your decision in **b** be different? Explain.

    (**Ratio of Exchange and *EPS***)   McBell's Public House is attempting to acquire the Moon Bar and Private Club. Certain financial data on these corporations are summarized as follows:

Item	McBell's Public House	Moon Bar and Private Club
Earnings available for common stock	$20,000	$8,000
Number of shares of common stock outstanding	20,000	4,000
Market price per share	$12	$24

McBell's has sufficient authorized but unissued shares to carry out the proposed acquisition.

a If the ratio of exchange is 1.8, what will be the earnings per share (*EPS*) based on the original shares of each firm?

b If the ratio of exchange is 2.0, what will be the earnings per share (*EPS*) based on the original shares of each firm?

c If the ratio of exchange is 2.2, what will be the earnings per share (*EPS*) based on the original shares of each firm?

d Discuss the principle illustrated by your answers to **a** through **c**.

17-8   (***EPS* and Merger Terms**)   Dodd Manufacturing Company is interested in acquiring the Talbot Machine Company by exchanging four-tenths shares of its stock for each share of Talbot stock. Certain financial data on these companies are given.

Item	Dodd Manufacturing	Talbot Machine
Earnings available for common stock	$200,000	$50,000
Number of shares of common stock outstanding	50,000	20,000
Earnings per share (*EPS*)	$4.00	$2.50
Market price per share	$50.00	$15.00
Price/earnings (*P/E*) ratio	12.5	6

Dodd has sufficient authorized but unissued shares to carry out the proposed acquisition.

a How many new shares of stock will Dodd have to issue in order to make the proposed acquisition?

b If the earnings for each firm remain unchanged, what will the post-merger earnings per share be?

c How much, effectively, has been earned on behalf of each of the original shares of Talbot stock?

d How much, effectively, has been earned on behalf of each of the original shares of Dodd's stock?

17-9   (**Ratio of Exchange**)   Calculate the ratio of exchange (1) of shares and

	CURRENT MARKET PRICE PER SHARE		
Case	Acquiring firm	Acquired firm	Price per share offered
A	$50	$25	$ 30.00
B	80	80	100.00
C	40	60	70.00
D	50	10	12.50
E	25	20	25.00

(2) in market price for each of the following cases. What does each ratio signify? Explain.

17-10 (Expected *EPS*—Merger Decision) At the end of 1987, Badger Enterprises had 80,000 shares of common stock outstanding and had earnings available for common of $160,000. The Potut Company, at the end of 1987, had 10,000 shares of common stock outstanding and had earned $20,000 for common shareholders. Badger earnings are expected to grow at an annual rate of 5 percent, while Potut's growth rate in earnings should be 10 percent per year.

a Calculate earnings per share (*EPS*) for Badger Enterprises for each of the next five years, assuming there is no merger.

b Calculate the next five years' earnings per share (*EPS*) for Badger if it acquires Potut at a ratio of exchange of 1.3.

c Calculate the next five years' earnings per share (*EPS*) for Badger if it acquires Potut at a ratio of exchange of 1.1.

d Graph the *EPS* figures from **a**, **b**, and **c** on a set of year (*x*-axis)–*EPS* (*y*-axis) axes. Explain the differences.

e Which plan—**b** or **c**—is preferable from the viewpoint of each of the firms? Why?

17-11 (Expected *EPS*—Merger Decision) O. T. Books wishes to evaluate a proposed merger into Plain Cover Publications. O. T. had 1987 earnings of $200,000, has 100,000 shares of common stock outstanding, and expects earnings to grow at an annual rate of 7 percent. Plain Cover had 1987 earnings of $800,000, has 200,000 shares of common stock outstanding, and expects its earnings to grow at 3 percent per year.

a Calculate the expected earnings per share (*EPS*) for O. T. Books for each of the next five years without the merger.

b What would O. T. Books's stockholders earn in each of the next five years on each of their O. T. Books shares converted into Plain Cover shares at a ratio of (1) .6 and (2) .8 shares of Plain Cover for one share of O. T. Books?

c Graph the pre- and postmerger *EPS* figures developed in **a** and **b** on a set of year (*x*-axis)–*EPS* (*y*-axis) axes.

d If you were the financial manager for O. T. Books, what would you recommend from **b**, (1) or (2)? Explain your answer.

17-12 (*EPS* and Postmerger Price) Data for the Vinco Company and the Lyle Company are given. The Vinco Company is considering the acquisition of the Lyle Company by exchanging 1.25 shares of its stock for each share of Lyle Company stock. The Vinco Company expects to sell at the same price/earnings (P/E) multiple after the merger as before merging.

Item	Vinco Company	Lyle Company
Earnings available for common stock	$225,000	$50,000
Number of shares of common stock outstanding	90,000	15,000
Market price per share	$45	$50

  a Calculate the ratio of exchange of market prices.
  b Calculate the earnings per share (EPS) and price/earnings (P/E) ratio for each company.
  c Calculate the price/earnings (P/E) ratio used to purchase the Lyle Company.
  d Calculate the postmerger earnings per share (EPS) for the Vinco Company.
  e Calculate the expected market price per share of the merged firm. Discuss this result in light of your findings in **a**.

17-13 (Holding Company) The Summa Company holds stock in company A and company B. A simplified balance sheet is presented for the companies. Summa has voting control over both company A and company B.

Assets		Liabilities and stockholders' equity	
SUMMA COMPANY			
Common stock holding		Long-term debt	$ 40,000
Company A	$ 40,000	Preferred stock	25,000
Company B	60,000	Common stock equity	35,000
Total	$100,000	Total	$100,000
COMPANY A			
Current assets	$100,000	Current liabilities	$100,000
Fixed assets	400,000	Long-term debt	200,000
Total	$500,000	Common stock equity	200,000
		Total	$500,000
COMPANY B			
Current assets	$180,000	Current liabilities	$100,000
Fixed assets	720,000	Long-term debt	500,000
Total	$900,000	Common stock equity	300,000
		Total	$900,000

  a What percentage of the total assets controlled by the Summa Company does its common stock equity represent?
  b If another company owns 15 percent of the common stock of the Summa Company and by virtue of this fact has voting control, what

percentage of the total assets controlled does the outside company's equity represent?

c How does a holding company effectively provide a great deal of control for a small dollar investment?

d Answer questions **a** and **b** in light of the following additional facts.

  (1) Company A's fixed assets consist of $20,000 of common stock in company C. This provides voting control.

  (2) Company C, which has total assets of $400,000, has voting control of company D, which has $50,000 of total assets.

  (3) Company B's fixed assets consist of $60,000 of stock in both company E and company F. In both cases, this gives it voting control. Companies E and F have total assets of $300,000 and $400,000, respectively.

17-14 (**Voluntary Settlements**)   Classify each of the following voluntary settlements as an extension, a composition, or a combination of the two.

a Paying all creditors 30 cents on the dollar in exchange for complete discharge of the debt.

b Paying all creditors in full in three periodic installments.

c Paying a group of creditors with claims of $10,000 in full over two years and immediately paying the remaining creditors 75 cents on the dollar.

17-15 (**Voluntary Settlements**) For a firm with outstanding debt of $125,000, classify each of the following voluntary settlements as an extension, a composition, or a combination of the two.

a Paying a group of creditors in full in four periodic installments and paying the remaining creditors in full immediately.

b Paying a group of creditors 90 cents on the dollar immediately and paying the remaining creditors 80 cents on the dollar in two periodic installments.

c Paying all creditors 15 cents on the dollar.

d Paying all creditors in full in 180 days.

17-16 (**Voluntary Settlements — Payments**)   The Limetree Business Forms Company recently ran into certain financial difficulties that have resulted in the initiation of voluntary settlement procedures. The firm currently has $150,000 in outstanding debts and approximately $75,000 in liquidable short-term assets. Indicate, for each plan below, whether the plan is an extension, a composition, or a combination of the two. Also indicate the cash payments and timing of the payments required of the firm under each plan.

a Each creditor will be paid 50 cents on the dollar immediately, and the debts will be considered fully satisfied.

b Each creditor will be paid 80 cents on the dollar in two quarterly installments of 50 cents and 30 cents. The first installment is to be paid in 90 days.

c Each creditor will be paid the full amount of its claims in three installments of 50 cents, 25 cents, and 25 cents on the dollar. The installments will be made in 60-day intervals, beginning in 60 days.

d A group of creditors having claims of $50,000 will be immediately paid in full; the remainder will be paid 85 cents on the dollar, payable in 90 days.

17-17 (Unsecured Creditors) A firm has $450,000 in funds to distribute to its unsecured creditors. Three possible sets of unsecured creditor claims are presented. Calculate the settlement, if any, to be received by each creditor in each case.

Unsecured creditors' claims	Case I	Case II	Case III
Unpaid balance of 2d mortgage	$300,000	$200,000	$ 500,000
Accounts payable	200,000	100,000	300,000
Notes payable — bank	300,000	100,000	500,000
Unsecured bonds	100,000	200,000	500,000
Total	$900,000	$600,000	$1,800,000

17-18 (Liquidation and Priority of Claims) The Castelli Company recently failed and was left with the following balance sheet.

Assets		Liabilities and stockholders' equity	
Cash	$ 80,000	Accounts payable	$ 400,000
Marketable securities	10,000	Notes payable — bank	800,000
Accounts receivable	1,090,000	Accrued wages[a]	500,000
Inventories	2,300,000	Unpaid employee benefits[b]	100,000
Prepaid expenses	20,000	Unsecured customer deposits[c]	50,000
Total current assets	$3,500,000	Taxes payable	250,000
Land	$1,000,000	Total current liabilities	$2,100,000
Net plant	2,000,000	First mortgage[d]	$2,000,000
Net equipment	1,500,000	Second mortgage[d]	800,000
Total fixed assets	$4,500,000	Unsecured bonds	500,000
Total	$8,000,000	Total long-term debt	$3,300,000
		Preferred stock (10,000 shares)	$ 300,000
		Common stock (5,000 shares)	300,000
		Paid-in capital in excess of par	1,500,000
		Retained earnings	500,000
		Total stockholders' equity	$2,600,000
		Total	$8,000,000

[a] Represents wages of $250 per employee earned within 90 days of filing bankruptcy for 2,000 of the firm's employees.

[b] These unpaid employee benefits were due in the 180-day period preceding the firm's bankruptcy filing, which occurred simultaneously with the termination of its business.

[c] Unsecured customer deposits not exceeding $900 each.

[d] The first and second mortgages are on the firm's total fixed assets.

  a The trustee liquidated the firm's assets, obtaining net proceeds of $2.2 million from the current assets and $2.5 million from the fixed assets. In the process of liquidating the assets, the trustee incurred expenses totaling $400,000. Because of the speed with which the Order for Relief was entered, no interim expenses were incurred.

    (1) Prepare a table indicating the amount, if any, to be distributed to each claimant except unsecured creditors. Indicate the amount to be paid, if any, to the group of unsecured creditors.

(2) After all claims other than those of unsecured creditors have been satisfied, how much, if any, is still owed the second-mortgage holders? Why?

(3) Prepare a table showing how the remaining funds, if any, would be distributed to the firm's unsecured creditors.

b Rework **a**, assuming that the trustee liquidated the firm's assets for $4.2 million—$2.2 million from the current assets and $2 million from the fixed assets.

c Compare, contrast, and discuss your findings in **a** and **b**.

17-19 (Liquidation and Priority of Claims) The Windy Corporation recently failed and was liquidated by a court-appointed trustee who charged $200,000 for her services. Between the time of filing of the bankruptcy petition and the entry of an Order for Relief, a total of $100,000 in unpaid bills was incurred and remain unpaid. The preliquidation balance sheet is as follows:

Assets		Liabilities and stockholders' equity	
Cash	$ 40,000	Accounts payable	$ 200,000
Marketable securities	30,000	Notes payable—bank	300,000
Accounts receivable	620,000	Accrued wages[a]	50,000
Inventories	1,200,000	Unsecured customer deposits[b]	30,000
Prepaid expenses	10,000	Taxes payable	20,000
Total current assets	$1,900,000	Total current liabilities	$ 600,000
Land	$ 300,000	First mortgage[c]	$ 700,000
Net plant	400,000	Second mortgage[c]	400,000
Net equipment	400,000	Unsecured bonds	300,000
Total fixed assets	$1,100,000	Total long-term debt	$1,400,000
Total	$3,000,000	Preferred stock (15,000 shares)	$ 200,000
		Common stock (10,000 shares)	200,000
		Paid-in capital in excess of par	500,000
		Retained earnings	100,000
		Total stockholders' equity	$1,000,000
		Total	$3,000,000

[a] Represents wages of $500 per employee earned within 90 days of filing bankruptcy for 100 of the firm's employees.

[b] Unsecured customer deposits not exceeding $900 each.

[c] The first and second mortgages are on the firm's total fixed assets.

a If the trustee liquidated the assets for $2.5 million—$1.3 million from current assets and $1.2 million from fixed assets,

(1) Prepare a table indicating the amount to be distributed to each claimant. Indicate if the claimant is an unsecured creditor.

(2) Prior to satisfying unsecured creditor claims, how much is owed to first-mortgage holders and second-mortgage holders?

(3) Do the firm's owners receive any funds? If so, in what amounts?

b If the trustee liquidated the assets for $1.8 million—$1.2 million from current assets and $600,000 from fixed assets—rework your answers in **a**.

c Compare, contrast, and discuss your findings in **a** and **b**.

Part Six

SOURCES OF LONG-TERM FINANCING

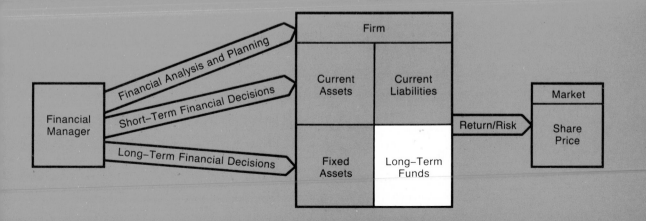

18

LONG-TERM DEBT AND LEASING

After studying this chapter, you should be able to:

● Describe the basic characteristics of long-term debt financing, including standard debt provisions, restrictive debt provisions, and cost.

● Understand the characteristics of term (long-term) loan agreements and the various financial institutions, agencies, and other organizations that make them available to business.

● Discuss the legal aspects of corporate bonds, general features of a bond, bond ratings, popular types of bonds, selling bonds, and bond-refunding options.

● Review the basic types of leases, leasing arrangements, the legal requirements of a lease, and the lease contract.

● Analyze the lease-versus-purchase decision, the effects of leasing on future financing, and the advantages and disadvantages of leasing.

long-term financing
Financing with an initial
maturity of more than
one year.

Long-term debt and leasing are important forms of **long-term financing**—financing with an initial maturity of more than one year. Long-term debt can be obtained with a *term loan,* which is negotiated from a financial institution, or through the sale of *bonds,* which are marketable debt sold to a number of institutional and individual lenders. Long-term debt provides financial leverage (see Chapter 5) and is a desirable component of capital structure (see Chapter 16) since it tends to lower the weighted average cost of capital[1] (see Chapter 13).

Leasing, like long-term debt, allows the firm to obtain use, but not ownership, of fixed assets in exchange for a series of contractual, periodic lease payments. The use of leasing has grown in popularity over the past 25 years due to the increased understanding and availability of this financing tool. We begin this chapter with discussions of long-term debt financing followed by a review of leasing.

CHARACTERISTICS OF LONG-TERM DEBT FINANCING

The long-term debts of a business typically have maturities of between 5 and 20 years. When a long-term debt is within one year of its maturity, accountants will show the balance of the long-term debt as a current liability because at that point it becomes a short-term obligation. Similar treatment is given to portions of long-term debts payable in the coming year. These entries are normally labeled "current portion of long-term debt."

Standard Debt Provisions

standard debt provisions Provisions in
long-term debt agreements specifying certain
criteria of satisfactory
record keeping and
reporting, tax payment,
and general business
maintenance on the part
of the borrowing firm.

A number of **standard debt provisions** are included in long-term debt agreements. These provisions specify certain criteria of satisfactory record keeping and reporting, tax payment, and general business maintenance on the part of the borrowing firm. Standard debt provisions do not normally place a burden on the financially sound business. Commonly included standard provisions are listed below.

1. The borrower is required to *maintain satisfactory accounting records* in accordance with generally accepted accounting principles (GAAP).
2. The borrower is required to periodically *supply audited financial statements* that are used by the lender to monitor the firm and enforce the debt agreement.

---

[1] Of course, as noted in Chapter 16, the introduction of large quantities of debt into the firm's capital structure can result in high levels of financial risk, which can cause the weighted average cost of capital to rise.

3. The borrower is required to *pay taxes and other liabilities when due.*
4. The borrower is required to *maintain all facilities in good working order,* thereby behaving as a "going concern."

Restrictive Debt Provisions

Long-term debt agreements, whether resulting from a term loan or a bond issue, normally include certain **restrictive covenants,** contractual clauses placing certain operating and financial constraints on the borrower. Since the lender is committing funds for a long period, it of course seeks to protect itself. Restrictive covenants remain in force for the life of the debt agreement. The most common restrictive covenants are listed below.

restrictive covenants In long-term debt agreements, contractual clauses placing certain operating and financial constraints on the borrower.

1. The borrower is required to *maintain a minimum level of net working capital.* Net working capital below the minimum is considered indicative of inadequate liquidity, a common prerequisite to loan default and ultimate failure.
2. Borrowers are *prohibited from selling accounts receivable* to generate cash, since this could cause a long-run cash shortage if proceeds are used to meet current obligations.
3. Long-term lenders commonly impose *fixed-asset restrictions* on the firm. These constrain the firm with respect to the liquidation, acquisition, and encumbrance of fixed assets, since any of these actions could damage the firm's ability to repay its debt.
4. Many debt agreements *constrain subsequent borrowing* by prohibiting additional long-term debt, or by requiring that additional borrowing be *"subordinated"* to the original loan. **Subordination** means that all subsequent or less important creditors agree to wait until all claims of the *senior debt* are satisfied prior to having their claims satisfied.

subordination In a long-term debt agreement, the stipulation that all subsequent or less important creditors agree to wait until all claims of the *senior debt* are satisfied before having their claims satisfied.

5. Borrowers may be *prohibited from entering into certain types of leases* in order to limit additional fixed-payment obligations.
6. Occasionally the lender *prohibits combinations* by requiring the borrower to agree not to consolidate, merge, or combine in any way with another firm, since such an action could significantly change the borrower's business and financial risk.
7. To prevent liquidation of assets through large salary payments, the lender may *prohibit or limit salary increases* for specified employees.
8. The lender may include *management restrictions* requiring the borrower to maintain certain "key employees" without whom the future success of the firm would be uncertain.
9. Occasionally the lender includes a covenant *limiting the borrower's security investment* alternatives. This restriction protects

the lender by controlling the risk and marketability of the borrower's security investments.

10. Occasionally a covenant specifically requires the borrower to *spend the borrowed funds on a proven financial need.*

11. A relatively common provision *limits the firm's annual cash dividend payments* to a maximum of 50 to 70 percent of its net earnings or a specified dollar amount.

In the process of negotiating the terms of long-term debt, borrower and lender must ultimately agree to acceptable restrictive covenants. A good financial manager will know in advance the relative impact of proposed restrictions and will "hold the line" on those that may have a severely negative or damaging effect. The violation of any standard or restrictive provision by the borrower gives the lender the right to demand immediate repayment of the debt. Generally the lender will evaluate any violation in order to determine whether it is serious enough to jeopardize the loan. On the basis of such an evaluation the lender may demand immediate repayment of the loan, waive the violation and continue the loan, or waive the violation but alter the terms of the initial debt agreement.

Cost of Long-Term Debt

The cost of long-term debt is generally greater than that of short-term borrowing. In addition to standard and restrictive provisions, the long-term debt agreement specifies the interest rate, the timing of payments, and the dollar amount of payments. The major factors affecting the cost, or interest rate, of long-term debt are loan maturity, loan size, and more importantly, borrower risk and the basic cost of money.

LOAN MATURITY Generally long-term loans have higher interest rates than short-term loans. The longer the term of a loan, the less accuracy there is in predicting future interest rates and therefore the greater the risk of forgoing an opportunity to loan money at a higher rate. In addition, the longer the term, the greater the repayment risk associated with the loan. To compensate for both the uncertainty of future interest rates and the fact that the longer the term of a loan the higher the probability that the borrower will default, the lender typically charges a higher interest rate on long-term loans.

LOAN SIZE The size of the loan affects the interest cost of borrowing in an inverse manner. Loan administration costs per dollar borrowed are likely to decrease with increasing loan size. On the other hand, the risk to the lender increases since larger loans result in less diversification. The size of the loan sought by each borrower must therefore be evaluated to determine the net administrative cost–risk trade-off.

BORROWER RISK As noted in Chapter 5, the higher the firm's operating leverage the greater its business risk. Also, the higher the borrower's debt ratio (or the lower its times interest earned ratio), the greater its financial risk. The lender's main concern is with the ability of the borrower to repay the loan. The overall assessment of the borrower's business and financial risk, along with information on past payment patterns, is used by the lender in setting the interest rate on any loan.

BASIC COST OF MONEY The cost of money is the basis for determining the actual interest rate charged. Generally the rate on U.S. Treasury securities with *equivalent maturities* is used as the basic standard for the risk-free cost of money. To determine the actual interest rate to be charged, the lender will add premiums for loan size and borrower risk to this basic cost of money for the given maturity.

TERM LOANS

A **term (long-term) loan** is a loan made by a financial institution to a business and having an initial maturity of more than one year. These loans generally have maturities of 5 to 12 years; shorter maturities are available, but minimum five-year maturities are common. These loans are often made to finance *permanent* working capital needs, to pay for machinery and equipment, or to liquidate other loans.

term (long-term) loan
A loan made by a financial institution to a business and having an initial maturity of more than one year.

Characteristics of Term Loan Agreements

The actual **term loan agreement** is a formal contract ranging from a few to a few hundred pages. The following items are commonly specified in the document: the amount and maturity of the loan; payment dates; interest rate; standard provisions; restrictive provisions; collateral (if any); purpose of the loan; action to be taken in the event the agreement is violated; and stock-purchase warrants. Of these, only payment dates, collateral requirements, and stock-purchase warrants require further discussion.

term loan agreement
A formal contract, ranging from a few to a few hundred pages, specifying the conditions under which a financial institution has made a long-term loan.

PAYMENT DATES Term loan agreements generally require monthly, quarterly, semiannual, or annual payments. Generally these equal payments fully repay the interest and principal over the life of the loan. Occasionally a term loan agreement will require periodic payments over the life of the loan followed by a large lump-sum payment at maturity. This so-called **balloon payment** represents the entire loan principal if the periodic payments represent only interest.

balloon payment At the maturity of a loan, a large lump-sum payment representing the entire loan principal if the periodic payments represent only interest.

COLLATERAL REQUIREMENTS Term lending arrangements may be unsecured or secured in a fashion similar to that for short-term loans.

Whether collateral is required depends on the lender's evaluation of the borrower's financial condition. Common types of collateral include machinery and equipment, plant, pledges of accounts receivable, and pledges of securities. Any collateral and its disposition under various circumstances is specifically described in the term loan agreement.

STOCK-PURCHASE WARRANTS   A trend in term lending is for the corporate borrower to give the lender certain financial perquisites in addition to the payment of interest and repayment of principal. **Stock-purchase warrants** are warrants that allow the holder to purchase a certain number of shares of the firm's common stock at a specified price over a certain period of time. These are used to entice institutional lenders to make long-term loans, possibly under more than normally favorable terms. Stock-purchase warrants are discussed in greater detail in Chapter 20.

stock-purchase warrants Warrants allowing the holder to purchase a certain number of shares of the firm's common stock at a specified price over a certain period of time.

Term Lenders

The primary financial institutions making term loans to businesses are commercial banks; insurance companies; pension funds; regional development companies; the Small Business Administration; small business investment companies; commercial finance companies; and equipment manufactures' financing subsidiaries. Although the characteristics and provisions of term lending agreements made by these institutions are quite similar, a number of basic differences exist. Table 18.1 summarizes the key characteristics and types of loans offered.

CORPORATE BONDS

corporate bond A certificate indicating that a corporation has borrowed a certain amount of money from an institution or an individual and promises to repay it in the future under clearly defined terms.

A **corporate bond** is a certificate indicating that a corporation has borrowed a certain amount of money from an institution or an individual and promises to repay it in the future under clearly defined terms. Most bonds are issued with maturities of 10 to 30 years and with a par, or face, value of $1,000. The stated interest rate on a bond represents the percentage of the bond's par value that will be paid annually, typically in two equal semiannual installments. The bondholders, who are the lenders, are promised the semiannual interest payments and, at maturity, the principal amount (par value) loaned.

Legal Aspects of Corporate Bonds

Since a corporate bond issue may be for millions of dollars obtained by selling portions of the debt to numerous unrelated persons, certain legal arrangements are required to protect purchasers. Bondholders are protected legally primarily through the indenture and the trustee.

TABLE 18.1 Characteristics and Types of Loans Made by Major Financial Institutions

Institution	Characteristics	Types of loans
Commercial bank	Makes some term loans to businesses.	Generally less than 12-year maturity except for real estate. Primarily to small firms and secured by collateral.
Insurance company	Life insurers are most active lenders.	Maturities of 10 to 20 years. Generally to larger firms and in larger amounts than commercial bank loans. Both unsecured and secured loans.
Pension fund	Invests a small portion of its funds in term loans to business.	Generally mortgage loans to large firms. Similar to insurance company loans.
Regional development companies	An association generally attached to local or regional governments. Attempts to promote business development in a given area by offering attractive financing deals. Obtains funds from various governmental bodies and through sale of tax-exempt bonds.	Term loans are made at competitive rates.
Small Business Administration (SBA)	An agency of the federal government that makes loans to "eligible" small and minority-owned businesses.	Joins with private lender and lends or guarantees repayment of all or part of the loan. Most loans are made for less than $500,000 at or below commercial bank interest rates.
Small business investment company (SBIC)	Licensed by the government, and makes both debt and equity investments in small firms.	Makes loans to small firms with high growth potential. Term loans with 5- to 20-year maturities and interest rates above those on bank loans. Generally receives, in addition, an equity interest in the borrowing firm.
Commercial finance company (CFC)	Involved in financing equipment purchases. Often a subsidiary of the manufacturer of equipment.	Makes secured loans for purchase of equipment. Typically installment loans with less-than-10-year maturities at higher-than-bank interest rates.
Equipment manufacturers' financing subsidiary	A type of "captive finance company" owned by the equipment manufacturer.	Makes long-term installment loans on equipment sales. Similar to commercial finance companies.

CREDIT RATINGS NEWS

The Wall Street Journal reports "Credit Ratings" daily. The following excerpt from the February 12, 1986, *Journal* explains the possible lowering of credit ratings by Standard & Poor's of a group of oil concerns.

Standard & Poor's Corp. said it may lower the credit ratings of 13 oil and oil-service companies that are particularly vulnerable to falling oil prices.

S&P said the companies are vulnerable because of "past financing or operational strategies." The rating concern said the companies' common traits are "aggressive leverage structures, uncertain cash flow prospects, or both."

S&P noted that the oil industry "faces a bleak near-term outlook." It added: "With continued weak demand, overproduction by OPEC," and new pricing policies, "much of the oil market's discipline is gone."

The companies added to S&P's Credit-Watch list are: Diamond Shamrock Corp., Dallas, single-A-minus senior debt; Forest Oil Corp., Bradford, Pa., single-B subordinated debt; Freeport-McMoRan Inc., New Orleans, double-B-plus subordinated debt; Gearhart Industries Inc., Fort Worth, Texas, triple-B-plus subordinated debt; Kerr-McGee Corp., Oklahoma City, single-A senior debt; and McDermott Inc., New Orleans, single-A senior debt.

Also, Noble Affiliates Inc., Ardmore, Okla., single-A senior debt; NRM Energy Co. LP, Dallas, double-B-minus preferred stock; Phillips Petroleum Co., Bartlesville, Okla., triple-B senior debt; Smith International Inc., Newport Beach, Calif., triple-B senior debt; Templeton Energy Inc., Houston, single-B subordinated debt; Tidewater Inc., New Orleans, triple-B-minus subordinated debt; and Zapata Corp., Houston, single-B-minus subordinated debt.

In New Orleans, officials of Freeport-McMoRan and McDermott International Inc., parent of McDermott Inc., couldn't be reached for comment.

BOND INDENTURE A **bond indenture** is a complex and lengthy legal document stating the conditions under which a bond has been issued. It specifies both the rights of the bondholders and the duties of the issuing corporation. In addition to specifying the interest and principal payments and dates, it contains various standard and restrictive provisions, sinking-fund requirements, and provisions with respect to a security interest (if the bond is secured).

> **bond indenture** A complex and lengthy legal document stating the conditions under which a bond has been issued.

Sinking-Fund Requirements. The standard and restrictive provisions for long-term debt (loans) and for bond issues have already been described in an earlier section of this chapter. However, an additional restrictive provision often included in a bond indenture is a **sinking-fund requirement.** Its objective is to provide for the systematic retirement of bonds prior to their maturity. To carry out this requirement, the corporation makes semiannual or annual payments to a *trustee*, who uses these funds to retire bonds by purchasing them in the marketplace. This process is simplified by inclusion of a *call feature*, which permits the issuer to repurchase bonds at a stated price prior to maturity. The trustee will "call" bonds only when sufficient bonds cannot be purchased in the marketplace or when the market price of the bond is above the stated (call) price.

> **sinking-fund requirement** A restrictive provision often included in a bond indenture providing for the systematic retirement of bonds prior to their maturity.

Security Interest. The bond indenture is similar to a loan agreement in that any collateral pledged against the bond is specifically identified in the document. Usually, the title to the collateral is attached to the indenture, and the disposition of the collateral in various circumstances is specifically described. The protection of bond collateral is crucial to increase the safety and thereby enhance the marketability of a bond issue.

TRUSTEE A **trustee** is a third party to a bond indenture. The trustee can be an individual, a corporation, or, most often, a commercial bank trust department. The trustee, who is paid for its services, acts as a "watchdog" on behalf of the bondholders, making sure that the issuer does not default on its contractual responsibilities. The trustee is empowered to take specified actions on behalf of the bondholders if the terms of the indenture are violated.

> **trustee** A paid individual, corporation, or commercial bank trust department that acts as the third party to a bond indenture in order to ensure that the issuer does not default on its contractual responsibilities to the bondholders.

General Features of a Bond Issue

Three common features of a bond issue are (1) a conversion feature, (2) a call feature, and (3) stock-purchase warrants. These features provide both the issuer and the purchaser with certain opportunities for replacing, retiring, and (or) supplementing the bond with some type of equity issue.

conversion feature
A feature of so-called *convertible bonds* allowing bondholders to change each bond into a stated number of shares of stock.

CONVERSION FEATURE The **conversion feature** of certain so-called *convertible bonds* allows bondholders to change each bond into a stated number of shares of stock. Bondholders will convert their bonds only when the market price of the stock is greater than the conversion price, hence providing a profit for the bondholder. Chapter 20 discusses convertible bonds in detail.

call feature A feature included in almost all corporate bond issues giving the issuer the opportunity to repurchase bonds prior to maturity at a stated price.

call price The stated price at which bonds may be repurchased using a call feature prior to maturity.

call premium The amount by which a bond's call price exceeds its par value.

CALL FEATURE The **call feature** is included in almost all corporate bond issues. It gives the issuer the opportunity to repurchase bonds prior to maturity. The **call price** is the stated price at which bonds may be repurchased prior to maturity. Sometimes the call privilege is exercisable only during a certain period. As a rule, the call price exceeds the par value of a bond by an amount equal to one year's interest. For example, a $1,000, 10 percent bond would be callable for around $1,100 [$1,000 + (10% × $1,000)]. The amount by which the call price exceeds the bond's par value is commonly referred to as the **call premium.** The call feature is generally advantageous to the issuer, since it permits it to retire outstanding debt prior to maturity. Thus when interest rates fall, an issuer can call an outstanding bond and reissue a new bond at a lower interest rate. When interest rates rise, the call privilege will not be exercised, except possibly to meet sinking-fund requirements.

STOCK-PURCHASE WARRANTS Like term loans, warrants are occasionally attached to bonds as "sweeteners" to make them more attractive to prospective buyers. As noted earlier, a stock-purchase warrant gives its holder the right to purchase a certain number of shares of common stock at a specified price over a certain period of time. An in-depth discussion of stock-purchase warrants is included in Chapter 20.

Bond Ratings

The riskiness of publicly traded bond issues is assessed by independent agencies such as Moody's and Standard & Poor's. Moody's has 9 ratings; Standard & Poor's has 12. The ratings are derived by these agencies using financial ratio and cash flow analyses. Table 18.2 summarizes these ratings. There is normally an inverse relationship between the quality or rating of a bond and the rate of return it must provide bondholders. High-quality (high-rated) bonds provide lower returns than lower-quality (low-rated) bonds. This reflects the risk-return trade-off for the lender. When considering bond financing, the financial manager must therefore be concerned with the expected ratings of the firm's bond issue since these ratings can significantly affect salability and cost.

TABLE 18.2 Moody's and Standard & Poor's Bond Ratings

Moody's	Interpretation	Standard & Poor's	Interpretation
Aaa	Prime quality	AAA	Bank investment quality
Aa	High grade	AA	
A	Upper medium grade	A	
Baa	Medium grade	BBB	
Ba	Lower medium grade or speculative	BB	Speculative
B	Speculative	B	
Caa	From very speculative	CCC	
Ca	to near or in default	CC	
C	Lowest grade	C	Income Bond
		DDD	In default (rating
		DD	indicates the relative
		D	salvage value)

SOURCE: Moody's Investors Service, Inc., and Standard & Poor's N.Y.S.E. Reports.

Popular Types of Bonds

Bonds can be classified in a variety of ways. The popular types of bonds are summarized in terms of key characteristics and priority of lender's claim in Table 18.3. Note that the first three types—debentures, subordinated debentures, and income bonds—are unsecured; the next three—mortgage bonds, collateral trust bonds, and equipment trust certificates—are secured; and the last two—deep discount bonds and variable-rate bonds—can take either form, although they are most commonly unsecured. In addition, deep discount and variable-rate bonds are relatively new innovations in bond financing. They were developed to meet the needs of investors for tax deferral and as protection against changing interest rates. In order to more effectively raise debt financing at a reasonable cost, new innovations in bond financing are expected to continue.

Selling Bonds

A firm can sell bonds either through a *public offering* or through a *private (direct) placement*. The public sale of bonds employing the services of an investment banker is most common. These sales are closely regulated by the *Securities and Exchange Commission (SEC)* as well as by state securities commissions. As noted in Chapter 2, an **investment banker** is neither an investor nor a banker but an institution that pur-

investment banker
Neither an investor nor a banker, but an institution that purchases securities from corporate and government issuers for sale to the public.

TABLE 18.3 Summary of Characteristics and Priority of Claim of Popular Types of Bonds

Bond type	Characteristics	Priority of lender's claim
Debentures	Only creditworthy firms can issue debentures. Convertible bonds are normally debentures.	Claims are same as those of any general creditor. May have other unsecured bonds subordinated to them.
Subordinated debentures	Claims are not satisfied until those of the creditors holding certain (senior) debts have been fully satisfied.	Claim is that of a general creditor but not as good as a senior debt claim.
Income bonds	Payment of interest is required only when earnings are available from which to make such payment. Commonly issued in reorganization of a failed or failing firm.	Claim is that of a general creditor. Not in default when interest payments are missed since they are contingent only on earnings being available.
Mortgage bonds	Secured by real estate or buildings. Can be *open-end* (other bonds issued against collateral), *limited open-end* (a specified amount of additional bonds can be issued against collateral), or *closed-end;* may contain an *after-acquired clause* (property subsequently acquired becomes part of mortgage collateral).	Claim on proceeds from sale of mortgaged assets; if not fully satisfied, lender becomes a general creditor. The *first-mortgage* claim must be fully satisfied prior to distribution of proceeds to *second-mortgage* holders, and so on. A number of mortgages can be issued against the same collateral.
Collateral trust bonds	Secured by stock and (or) bonds that are owned by the issuer. Collateral value is generally 25 percent to 35 percent greater than bond value.	Claim on proceeds from stock and (or) bond collateral; if not fully satisfied, becomes a general creditor.
Equipment trust certificates	Used to finance "rolling stock"—airplanes, trucks, boats, railroad cars. A mechanism whereby a trustee buys equipment with funds raised through the sale of trust certificates and then leases the asset to the firm, which, after the final scheduled lease payment, receives title to the asset. A type of leasing.	Claim is on proceeds from sale of asset; if proceeds do not satisfy outstanding debt, trust certificate holders become general creditors.
Deep discount (and zero coupon) bonds	Issued with very low or no (zero) coupon (stated interest) rate and sell at a large discount from par. A significant portion (or all) of the investor's return therefore comes from gain in value (i.e., par value minus purchase price). Generally callable at par value.	Claims vary, depending on the other features of the bond. Can be unsecured or secured.
Variable-rate bonds	Stated interest rate is adjusted periodically within stated limits in response to changes in specified money or capital market rates. Popular when future inflation and interest rates are uncertain. Tends to sell at close to par as a result of the automatic adjustment to changing market conditions.	Claims vary, depending on the other features of the bonds. Can be unsecured or secured.

chases securities from corporate and government issuers for sale to the public. Investment bankers provide advice in designing and pricing a bond or stock issue and guarantee the issuer that it will receive at least a specified minimum amount from that issue. Their compensation comes from the discount they receive from the proposed sale price. In addition, the issuer must pay administrative costs related to legal, accounting, printing, and so forth.

Typically for large public bond offerings, the combined selling and administrative costs total between 1 and 5 percent of the amount of funds raised. If the issuer wishes to place the bond issue with a single lender, such as an insurance company, it will make a private placement. In such a case an investment banker is frequently employed to provide pricing and other advice, and to assist in finding a buyer.

◼ Bond-Refunding Options

A firm that wishes to retire or refund a bond prior to maturity has two options. Both require some foresight on the part of the issuer.

SERIAL ISSUES   The borrower can issue **serial bonds,** a certain proportion of which matures each year. When serial bonds are issued, a schedule showing the interest rate associated with each maturity is given. An example would be a $30 million, 20-year bond issue for which $1.5 million of the bonds ($30 million ÷ 20 years) mature each year. The interest rates associated with shorter maturities would, of course, differ from the rates associated with longer maturities. Although serial bonds cannot necessarily be retired at the option of the issuer, they do permit the issuer to systematically retire the debt.

serial bonds An issue of bonds of which a certain proportion matures each year.

REFUNDING BONDS BY EXERCISING A CALL   If interest rates drop following the issuance of a bond, the issuer may wish to refund (refinance) the debt with new bonds at the lower interest rate. If a call feature has been included in the issue, the issuer can easily retire the issue. The desirability of such an action is not necessarily obvious but can be determined using present-value techniques. The process used in making these decisions can be illustrated by a simple example. However, a few tax-related points should be clarified first.

Call Premiums.   The amount by which the call price exceeds the par value of the bond is the *call premium*. It is paid by the issuer to the bondholder to buy back outstanding bonds prior to maturity. The call premium is treated as a tax-deductible expense in the year of the call.

Bond Discounts and Premiums.   When bonds are sold at a discount or at a premium, the firm is required to amortize (write off) the discount or premium in equal portions over the life of the bond. The

($3,738,812) yields a net present value of $1,198,812. Since a positive net present value results, the proposed refunding plan is recommended.

CHARACTERISTICS OF LEASES

leasing The process by which a firm can avail itself of the use of certain fixed assets for which it must make a series of contractual, periodic, tax-deductible payments.

lessee The receiver of the services of the assets under a lease contract.

lessor The owner of the assets being leased to the lessee.

Through **leasing** a firm can avail itself of the use of certain fixed assets for which it must make a series of contractual, periodic, tax-deductible payments. The **lessee** is the receiver of the services of the assets under the lease contract, whereas the **lessor** is the owner of the assets. Leasing can take a number of forms. Here we discuss the basic types of leases and leasing arrangements, with special emphasis on the effects of leasing on the corporation. The legal requirements of a lease and the lease contract are also briefly described.

Basic Types of Leases

The two basic types of leases available to a business are *operating* and *financial* leases, the latter of which are often called *capital leases* by accountants. Each is briefly described below.

operating lease
A *cancelable* contractual arrangement whereby the lessee agrees to make periodic payments to the lessor for five or fewer years for an asset's services.

OPERATING LEASES   An **operating lease** is normally a contractual arrangement whereby the lessee agrees to make periodic payments to the lessor for five or fewer years for an asset's services. Such leases are generally *cancelable* at the option of the lessee, who may be required to pay a predetermined penalty for cancellation. Assets leased under operating leases generally have a usable life *longer* than the term of the lease. Usually, however, they would become less efficient and technologically obsolete if leased for a longer period of years. Computer systems are prime examples of assets whose relative efficiency is expected to diminish with new technological developments. The operating lease is therefore a common arrangement for obtaining such systems, as well as for other relatively short-lived assets such as automobiles.

If an operating lease is held to maturity, the lessee at that time returns the leased asset to the lessor, who may lease it again or sell the asset. Normally the asset still has a positive market value at the termination of the lease. In some instances, the lease contract will give the lessee the opportunity to purchase the leased asset. Generally the total payments made by the lessee to the lessor are *less* than the initial cost of the leased asset paid by the lessor.

financial (or capital) lease A *longer-term* lease than an operating lease that is *noncancelable* and obligates the lessee to make payments for the use of an asset over a predefined period of time.

FINANCIAL (OR CAPITAL) LEASES   A **financial (or capital) lease** is a *longer-term* lease than an operating lease. Financial leases are *noncancelable* and therefore obligate the lessee to make payments for the use

SALOMON BROTHERS IS LEADING UNDERWRITER

The table below shows the leading underwriters for U.S. issuers of both debt and equity during 1985. Salomon Brothers was clearly the leading underwriter.

Leading Underwriters for U.S. Issuers

Manager	Total amount managed (in billions of dollars)	In U.S. Debt (in billions of dollars)	Equity[1] (in billions of dollars)	Outside U.S[2] (in billions of dollars)	Fees (in millions of dollars)
Salomon Bros.	$34.2	$23.9	$4.9	$5.4	$402
First Boston	25.7	17.2	3.3	5.7	272
Goldman Sachs	19.9	10.9	5.0	4.1	348
Merrill Lynch	17.6	9.3	5.5	2.8	333
Drexel Burnham Lambert	13.3	9.9	3.3	.1	402
Morgan Stanley	12.7	6.6	3.0	3.0	196
Shearson Lehman	10.3	5.1	4.4	.8	212
Kidder Peabody	3.9	1.7	1.8	.3	95
Union Bank of Switzerland	3.0	—	—	3.0	59
Paine Webber	2.9	1.9	1.0	—	65

[1] Includes equity and equity-related offerings.

[2] Includes non-dollar issues.

SOURCE: IDD Information Services.

Source: Table from Ann Monroe, "Salomon Leads '85 List of Underwriters of Securities Offerings by U.S. Issuers," *The Wall Street Journal,* January 2, 1986, p. 12. Reprinted by permission of *The Wall Street Journal.* © Dow Jones & Company Inc. 1986. All rights reserved.

of an asset over a predefined period of time. Even if the lessee does not require the service of the leased asset, it is contractually obligated to make payments over the life of the lease contract. Financial leases are commonly used for leasing land, buildings, and large pieces of fixed equipment. The noncancelable feature of the financial lease makes it quite similar to certain types of long-term debt. The lease payment becomes a fixed, tax-deductible expenditure that must be paid at predefined dates over a definite period. Failing to make the contractual payments may in some instances mean bankruptcy for the lessee.

Another distinguishing characteristic of the financial lease is that the total payments over the lease period are *greater* than the cost of the leased asset to the lessor. Because the lease term is closely aligned with the economic life of the asset, the lessor must receive more than the asset's purchase price in order to earn its required return on the investment. The emphasis here and in the following sections is on financial leases, since they result in inescapable long-term financial commitments by the firm. Some financial leases give the lessee a purchase option at maturity.

Leasing Arrangements

Lessors use three primary techniques for obtaining assets to be leased. The method depends largely on the desires of the prospective lessee. A **direct lease** results when a lessor owns or acquires the assets that are leased to a given lessee. In other words, the lessee did not previously own the assets it is leasing. A second technique commonly used by lessors to acquire leased assets is to purchase assets already owned by the lessee and lease them back. A **sale-leaseback arrangement** is normally initiated by a firm that needs funds for operations. By selling an existing asset to a lessor and then *leasing it back*, the lessee receives cash for the asset immediately while at the same time obligating itself to make fixed periodic payments for use of the leased asset. Leasing arrangements that include one or more third-party lenders are *leveraged leases*. Unlike direct and sale-leaseback arrangements, under a **leveraged lease** the lessor acts as an equity participant, supplying only about 20 percent of the cost of the asset, and a lender supplies the balance. In recent years leveraged leases have become especially popular in structuring leases of very expensive assets.

A lease agreement normally specifies whether the lessee is responsible for maintenance of the leased assets. Operating leases normally include **maintenance clauses** requiring the lessor to maintain the assets and make insurance and tax payments. Financial leases almost always require the lessee to pay maintenance and other costs. The lessee is usually given the option to renew a lease at its expiration. **Renewal options,** which grant lessees the right to re-lease assets at expiration, are especially common in operating leases, since their term is generally shorter than the usable life of the leased assets.

The lessor can be one of a number of parties. In operating lease arrangements, the lessor is quite likely to be the manufacturer's leasing subsidiary or an independent leasing company. Financial leases are frequently handled by independent leasing companies or the leasing subsidiaries of large financial institutions such as commercial banks and life insurance companies. Life insurance companies are especially active in real estate leasing. Pension funds, like commercial banks, have also been increasing their leasing activities.

---

direct lease A lease under which a lessor owns or acquires the assets that are leased to a given lessee.

sale-leaseback arrangement A lease under which the lessee sells an asset for cash to a prospective lessor and then leases back the same asset, making periodic payments for its use.

leveraged lease A lease under which the lessor acts as an equity participant, supplying only about 20 percent of the cost of the asset, while a lender supplies the balance.

maintenance clauses Provisions within an operating lease requiring the lessor to maintain the assets and make insurance and tax payments.

renewal options Provisions especially common in operating leases that grant the lessee the option to re-lease assets at their expiration.

Legal Requirements of a Lease

To prevent firms from using a leasing arrangement as a disguise for what is actually an installment loan, the Internal Revenue Service specifies certain conditions under which lease payments are tax-deductible. If a lease arrangement does not meet these basic requirements, then the lease payments are not completely tax-deductible.[3] To conform with the IRS code, a leasing arrangement must meet the following major conditions:[4]

1. The lessor must own the property and anticipate earning a pretax profit from leasing it.
2. The lessor and lessee must agree that the transaction is a lease, the term of the lease must conform to IRS requirements, and the lessor must specify it as "designated lease property" on its income tax return.
3. The lease must be entered into within 90 days after the property is placed in service.
4. The lessee can be given the option to purchase the property, but the price must be equal to or greater than 10 percent of the original purchase price.

The Lease Contract

The key items of the lease contract normally include the term, or duration, of the lease, provisions for its cancellation, lease payment amounts and dates, renewal features, purchase options, maintenance and associated cost provisions, and other provisions specified in the lease negotiation process. While some provisions are optional, the leased assets, the terms of the agreement, the lease payment, and the payment interval must all be clearly specified in every lease agreement. Furthermore, the consequences of the lessee missing a payment or the violation of any other lease provisions by either the lessee or lessor must be clearly stated in the contract.

---

[3] The IRS's concern stems from the fact that the full lease payment is tax-deductible, while in the case of an installment loan only the interest component of the payment is tax-deductible. To obtain high current tax deductions, the firm would lease the asset over a specified period, at the end of which it could purchase the asset for a nominal amount. Such a scheme would permit the firm to maximize its tax deductions and still ultimately own the asset.

[4] This is not an exhaustive listing of the conditions, but it reflects the most important and limiting requirements.

LEASING AS A SOURCE OF FINANCING

Leasing is considered a source of financing provided by the lessor to the lessee. The lessee receives the service of a certain fixed asset for a specified period of time, in exchange for which the lessee commits itself to a fixed periodic payment. The only other way the lessee could obtain the services of the given asset would be to purchase it outright; and the outright purchase of the asset would require financing. The following discussions of the lease-versus-purchase decision, the effects of leasing on future financing, and the advantages and disadvantages of leasing should better explain the role of leasing as a source of financing.

The Lease-Versus-Purchase Decision

The lease-versus-purchase, or lease-versus-buy, decision is one that commonly confronts firms contemplating the acquisition of new fixed assets. The alternatives available are (1) lease the assets, (2) borrow funds to purchase the assets, or (3) purchase the assets using available liquid cash. Alternatives 2 and 3, although they differ, are analyzed in a similar fashion. Even if the firm has the liquid resources with which to purchase the assets, the use of these funds is viewed as equivalent to borrowing. Therefore, here we need to compare only the leasing and purchasing alternatives.

The lease-versus-purchase decision is made using basic present-value techniques. The following steps are involved in the analysis:

Step 1: Find the *after-tax cash outflows for each year under the lease* alternative. This step generally involves a fairly simple tax adjustment of the annual lease payments.

Step 2: Find the *after-tax cash outflows for each year under the purchase* alternative. This step involves adjusting the scheduled loan payment for the tax shields resulting from the tax deductions attributable to interest and depreciation.

Step 3: Calculate the *present value of the cash outflows* associated with the lease (from step 1) and purchase (from step 2) alternatives using the *after-tax cost of debt* as the discount rate. The after-tax cost of debt is used since this decision involves very low risk.

Step 4: Choose the alternative with the *lowest present value* of cash outflows from step 3. This will be the *least cost* financing alternative.

Due to the relative complexity of the tax adjustments required to determine the after-tax lease and purchase outflows in steps 1 and 2, only steps 3 and 4 are demonstrated in the following example.

EXAMPLE

The Moore Company is contemplating acquiring a new machine-tool costing $24,000. Discussions with various financial institutions have shown that leasing or purchasing arrangements can be made to obtain the use of the machine. The firm is in the 40 percent tax bracket, and its after-tax cost of debt is approximately 6 percent.

Leasing: The firm would obtain a five-year lease requiring annual end-of-year lease payments of $6,132.[5] All maintenance, insurance, and other costs would be borne by the lessee.

Purchasing: The firm would finance the purchase of the machine with a 9 percent, five-year loan requiring equal end-of-year installment payments of $6,170. The machine would be depreciated using ACRS over its five-year normal recovery period.

After applying various tax, interest, and depreciation adjustments, the after-tax cash outflows associated with leasing and purchasing, respectively, were determined. These values are shown for leasing and purchasing, respectively, in columns 1 and 4 of Table 18.6. Applying the appropriate 6 percent present-value interest factors (columns 2 and 5) to the lease and purchase cash

TABLE 18.6 A Comparison of the Cash Outflows Associated with Leasing versus Purchasing for the Moore Company

	LEASING			PURCHASING		
End of year	After-tax cash outflows[a] (1)	Present-value factors[b] (2)	Present value of outflows [(1) × (2)] (3)	After-tax cash outflows[a] (4)	Present-value factors[b] (5)	Present value of outflows [(4) × (5)] (6)
1	$3,679	.943	$ 3,469	$3,866	.943	$ 3,646
2	3,679	.890	3,274	3,338	.890	2,971
3	3,679	.840	3,090	3,592	.840	3,017
4	3,679	.792	2,914	3,763	.792	2,980
5	3,679	.747	2,748	3,950	.747	2,951
	PV of cash outflows		$15,495	PV of cash outflows		$15,565

[a] Values developed using techniques beyond the scope of this basic text.

[b] From Table D-3, *PVIF*, for 6 percent and the corresponding year.

[5] Lease payments are generally made at the beginning of the year. In order to simplify the following discussions, end-of-year lease payments have been assumed.

outflows in columns 1 and 4 results in the present values of these outflows shown in columns 3 and 6, respectively, of Table 18.6. The sum of the present values of the cash outflows for the leasing alternative is given in column 3 of Table 18.6, and the sum for the purchasing alternative is given in column 6 of Table 18.6. Since the present value of cash outflows for leasing ($15,495) is lower than that for purchasing ($15,565), the leasing alternative is preferred. Leasing results in an incremental savings of $70 ($15,565 − $15,495) and is therefore the less costly alternative. ■

Effects of Leasing on Future Financing

Since leasing is considered a type of financing, it affects the firm's future financing. Lease payments are shown as a tax-deductible expense on the firm's income statement. Anyone analyzing the firm's income statement would probably recognize that an asset is being leased, although the actual details of the amount and term of the lease would be unclear. The following sections discuss the lease disclosure requirements established by the Financial Accounting Standards Board (FASB) and the effect of leases on financial ratios.

LEASE DISCLOSURE REQUIREMENTS   After many years of debate and controversy, the *Financial Accounting Standards Board (FASB)* in November 1976 in Standard No. 13, "Accounting for Leases," finally established requirements for the explicit disclosure of certain types of lease obligations on the firm's balance sheet. Standard No. 13 established criteria for classifying various types of leases and set reporting standards for each class. The standard defines a financial (capital) lease as one having *any* of the following elements:

1.   The lease transfers ownership of the property to the lessee by the end of the lease term.
2.   The lease contains an option to purchase the property at a "bargain" price.
3.   The lease term is equal to 75 percent or more of the estimated economic life of the property.
4.   At the beginning of the lease, the present value of the lease payments is equal to 90 percent or more of the fair market value of the leased property less any investment tax credit received by the lessor.

capitalized lease
A *financial (capital) lease* that has the present value of all its payments included as an asset and corresponding liability on the firm's balance sheet, as required by *Financial Accounting Standards Board (FASB)* Standard No. 13.

If a lease meets any of the above criteria, it is shown as a **capitalized lease,** meaning the present value of all its payments is included as an asset and corresponding liability on the firm's balance sheet. If a lease meets none of the above criteria it is an operating lease and need not be capitalized, but its basic features must be disclosed in a footnote to the financial statements. Standard No. 13, of course, establishes detailed guidelines to be used in capitalizing leases to reflect them as an asset and corresponding liability on the balance sheet. Subsequent standards have further refined lease capitalization and disclosure procedures. Let us look at an example.

EXAMPLE

The Graber Company is leasing an asset under a 10-year lease requiring annual end-of-year payments of $15,000. The lease can be capitalized merely by calculating the present value of the lease payments over the life of the lease. However, the rate at which the payments should be discounted is difficult to determine.[6] If 10 percent were used, the present, or capitalized, value of the lease would be $92,175 ($15,000 × 6.145). This value would be shown as an asset and corresponding liability on the firm's balance sheet, which should result in an accurate reflection of the firm's true financial position.

LEASES AND FINANCIAL RATIOS Since the consequences of missing a financial lease payment are the same as those of missing an interest or principal payment on debt, a financial analyst must view the lease as a long-term financial commitment of the lessee. With FASB No. 13, the inclusion of financial (capital) leases as an asset and corresponding liability (i.e., long-term debt) provides for a balance sheet that more accurately reflects the firm's financial status and thereby permits various types of financial ratio analyses to be performed directly on the statement by any interested party.

Advantages and Disadvantages of Leasing

Leasing has a number of commonly cited advantages and disadvantages that should be considered in making a lease-versus-purchase decision. Although not all these advantages and disadvantages hold in every case, it is not unusual for a number of them to apply in a given situation.

ADVANTAGES OF LEASING The commonly cited advantages of leasing are listed on page 600.

---

[6] The Financial Accounting Standards Board in Standard No. 13 established certain guidelines for the appropriate discount rate to use when capitalizing leases. Most commonly, the rate that the lessee would have incurred to borrow the funds to buy the asset with a secured loan under terms similar to the lease repayment schedule would be used. This simply represents the *before-tax cost of a secured debt.*

1. Leasing allows the lessee, in effect, to *depreciate land*, which is prohibited if the land were purchased. Since the lessee who leases land is permitted to deduct the *total lease payment* as an expense for tax purposes, the effect is the same as if the firm had purchased the land and then depreciated it.

2. Since it results in the receipt of service from an asset possibly without increasing the assets or liabilities on the firm's balance sheet, leasing may result in misleading *financial ratios*. With the passage of FASB No. 13, this advantage no longer applies to financial leases, although in the case of operating leases it remains a potential advantage.

3. The use of sale-leaseback arrangements may permit the firm to *increase its liquidity* by converting an *existing* asset into cash, which can then be used as working capital. A firm short of working capital or in a liquidity bind can sell an owned asset to a lessor and lease the asset back for a specified number of years.

4. Leasing provides *100 percent financing*. Most loan agreements for the purchase of fixed assets require the borrower to pay a portion of the purchase price as a down payment. As a result the borrower is able to borrow only 90 to 95 percent of the purchase price of the asset.

5. When a *firm becomes bankrupt* or is reorganized, the maximum claim of lessors against the corporation is three years of lease payments. If debt is used to purchase an asset, the creditors have a claim equal to the total outstanding loan balance.

6. In a lease arrangement, the firm may *avoid the cost of obsolescence* if the lessor fails to accurately anticipate the obsolescence of assets and sets the lease payment too low. This is especially true in the case of operating leases, which generally have relatively short lives.

7. A lessee *avoids many of the restrictive covenants* that are normally included as part of a long-term loan. Requirements with respect to minimum net working capital, subsequent borrowing, changes in management, and so on are *not* normally found in a lease agreement.

8. In the case of low-cost assets that are infrequently acquired, leasing—especially operating leases—may provide the firm with needed *financing flexibility*. That is, the firm does not have to arrange other financing for these assets and can somewhat conveniently obtain them through a lease.

DISADVANTAGES OF LEASING   The commonly cited disadvantages of leasing are the following:

1. A lease does not have a stated interest cost. Thus in many leases the *return to the lessor is quite high*, so the firm might be better off borrowing to purchase the asset.

2. At the end of the term of the lease agreement, the *salvage value* of an asset, if any, is realized by the lessor. If the lessee had purchased the asset, it could have claimed its salvage value.

3. Under a lease, the lessee is generally *prohibited from making improvements* on the leased property or asset without the approval of the lessor. If the property were owned outright, this difficulty would not arise.

4. If a lessee leases (under a financial lease) an *asset that subsequently becomes obsolete*, it still must make lease payments over the remaining term of the lease. This is true even if the asset is unusable.

SUMMARY

- Standard and restrictive provisions are included in long-term debt agreements in order to protect the lender. Standard debt provisions do not ordinarily place a burden on a financially sound business. Restrictive covenants tend to place certain operating and financial constraints on the borrower.

- The cost (interest rate) of long-term debt is normally higher than the cost of short-term borrowing. Major factors affecting the cost of long-term debt are loan maturity, loan size, and more importantly, borrower risk and the basic cost of money.

- The conditions of a term (long-term) loan are specified in the term loan agreement. Term loans generally require periodic installment payments; some require balloon payments at maturity. Term loans may be either unsecured or secured. Some term lenders receive stock-purchase warrants. Term loans can be obtained from a number of types of major financial institutions.

- Corporate bonds are certificates indicating that a corporation has borrowed a certain amount that it promises to repay in the future under clearly defined terms. Most bonds are issued with maturities of 10 to 30 years and a par value of $1,000. All conditions of the bond issue are detailed in the indenture, which is enforced by the trustee.

- A bond may include a conversion feature, a call feature, or stock-purchase warrants. Bond ratings by independent agencies indicate the risk of a bond issue. A variety of unsecured, secured, and innovative bonds are available. Bonds are sold by the firm either through a public offering or a private placement, generally with the aid of an investment banker.

- Firms sometimes retire or refund (refinance) bonds prior to their maturity. When serial bonds are issued, retirement is on a planned basis. A call feature is used to refund bonds when there is a drop in interest rates sufficient to create a positive net present value.

- A lease is a contractual arrangement under which the lessee makes periodic lease payments in order to obtain the use of fixed assets owned by the lessor. Operating leases are generally for a term of 5 years or less, are cancelable, provide for maintenance of the asset by the lessor, and are renewable. Financial leases tend to be of longer term, noncancelable, require the lessee to maintain the asset, and are not renewable.

- A lessor can obtain assets to be leased through a direct lease, a sale-leaseback arrangement, or a leveraged lease. It can be a manufacturer's leasing subsidiary, an independent leasing company, or the leasing subsidiary of a large financial institution.
- The IRS specifies conditions under which lease payments are tax-deductible. In addition, Standard No. 13 of the Financial Accounting Standards Board (FASB) requires the firm to disclose the existence of leases on its financial statements.
- A lease-versus-purchase decision can be evaluated by calculating the after-tax cash outflows associated with the leasing and purchasing alternatives. The most desirable alternative is the one that has the lower present value of after-tax cash outflows. In addition, a number of commonly cited advantages and disadvantages should be considered in making lease-versus-purchase decisions.

QUESTIONS

18-1 What are the two key methods of raising long-term debt financing? What motives does the lender have for including certain *restrictive covenants* in a debt agreement? How do these covenants differ from so-called *standard debt provisions?*

18-2 What is the general relationship between the cost of short-term and long-term debt? What are the major factors affecting the cost, or interest rate, of long-term debt?

18-3 What types of payment dates are generally required in a term (long-term) loan agreement? What is a *balloon payment?*

18-4 What role do commercial banks, insurance companies, pension funds, regional development companies, the Small Business Administration, small business investment companies, commercial finance companies, and equipment manufacturers play in lending long-term funds to businesses?

18-5 What types of maturities, denominations, and interest payments are associated with a typical corporate bond? Describe the role of the *bond indenture* and the *trustee.*

18-6 What does it mean if a bond has a *conversion feature?* A *call feature? Stock-purchase warrants?* How are bonds rated, and why? How can a firm sell its bonds?

18-7 Describe the basic characteristics of each of the following popular types of bonds:
  a Debentures
  b Subordinated debentures
  c Income bonds
  d Mortgage bonds
  e Collateral trust bonds
  f Equipment trust certificates
  g Deep discount (and zero coupon) bonds
  h Variable-rate bonds

18-8   What two options may be available to a firm that wants to retire or refund an outstanding bond issue prior to maturity? Must these options be provided for in advance of issuance? Why might the issuer wish to retire or refund a bond prior to its maturity?

18-9   What is *leasing*? Describe, compare, and contrast *operating leases* and *financial (or capital) leases*.

18-10 Describe and compare the following three methods used by lessors to acquire assets to be leased:
    a Direct lease
    b Sale-leaseback arrangement
    c Leveraged lease

18-11 Describe the four basic steps involved in the lease-versus-purchase decision process. Why must present-value techniques be used in this process?

18-12 According to FASB Standard No. 13, under what conditions must a lease be treated as a *capitalized lease* on the balance sheet? How does the financial manager capitalize a lease?

18-13 List and discuss the commonly cited advantages and disadvantages that should be considered in making a lease-versus-purchase decision.

PROBLEMS

18-1   **(Bond Discounts or Premiums)**   The initial proceeds per bond, the size of the issue, the initial maturity of the bond, and the years remaining to maturity are given for a number of bonds. In each case the firm is in the 40 percent tax bracket and the bond has a $1,000 par value.

Bond	Proceeds per bond	Size of issue	Initial maturity of bond	Years remaining to maturity
A	$ 980	20,000 bonds	25 years	20
B	1,020	14,000 bonds	20 years	12
C	1,000	10,500 bonds	10 years	8
D	950	9,000 bonds	30 years	21
E	1,030	3,000 bonds	30 years	15

    a Indicate whether each bond was sold at a discount, at a premium, or at its par value.
    b Determine the total discount or premium for each issue.
    c Determine the annual amount of discount or premium amortized for each bond.
    d Calculate the unamortized discount or premium for each bond.
    e Determine the after-tax cash flow associated with the retirement now of each of these bonds, using the values developed in **d**.

18-2   **(Cost of a Call)**   For each of the callable bond issues in the table, calculate the after-tax cost of calling the issue. Each bond has a $1,000 par value; the various issue sizes and call prices are summarized in the table at the top of page 604. The firm is in the 40 percent tax bracket.

Bond	Size of issue	Call price
A	8,000 bonds	$1,080
B	10,000 bonds	1,060
C	6,000 bonds	1,010
D	3,000 bonds	1,050
E	9,000 bonds	1,040
F	13,000 bonds	1,090

18-3 **(Amortization of Issue Cost)** The initial issuance cost, the initial maturity, and the number of years remaining to maturity are given for a number of bonds. The firm is in the 40 percent tax bracket.

Bond	Initial issuance cost	Initial maturity of bond	Years remaining to maturity
A	$500,000	30 years	24
B	200,000	20 years	5
C	40,000	25 years	10
D	100,000	10 years	2
E	80,000	15 years	9

a Calculate the annual amortization of the issuance cost for each bond.
b Determine the after-tax cash inflow, if any, expected to result from the unamortized issuance cost if the bond were called today.

18-4 **(Refunding Decision)** The Schuyler Company is contemplating calling an outstanding $30 million bond issue and replacing it with a new $30 million bond issue. The firm wishes to do this to take advantage of the decline in interest rates that has occurred since the initial bond issuance. The old and new bonds are described below. The firm is in the 40 percent tax bracket.

Old bonds: The outstanding bonds have a $1,000 par value and a 14 percent stated interest rate. They were issued five years ago with a 25-year maturity. They were initially sold for their par value of $1,000, and the firm incurred $250,000 in issuance costs. They are callable at $1,140.

New bonds: The new bonds would have a $1,000 par value and a 12 percent stated interest rate. They would have a 20-year maturity and could be sold at their par value. The issuance cost of the new bonds would be $400,000.

a Calculate the after-tax cash inflow expected from the unamortized portion of the old bonds' issuance cost.
b Calculate the annual after-tax cash inflow from the issuance cost of the new bonds, assuming the 20-year amortization.
c Calculate the after-tax cash outflow from the call premium required to retire the old bonds.
d Determine the incremental initial outlay required to issue the new bonds.

    e Calculate the annual cash flow savings, if any, expected from the bond refunding.

    f If the firm has a 7 percent after-tax cost of debt, would you recommend the proposed refunding? Why or why not?

18-5 **(Refunding Decision)** Lawrence Furniture is considering calling an outstanding bond issue of $10 million and replacing it with a new $10 million issue. The firm wishes to do this to take advantage of the decline in interest rates that has occurred since the original issue. The two bond issues are described below; the firm is in the 40 percent tax bracket.

Old bonds: The outstanding bonds have a $1,000 par value and a 17 percent stated interest rate. They were issued five years ago with a 20-year maturity. They were initially sold at a $20-per-bond discount, and a $120,000 issuance cost was incurred. They are callable at $1,170.

New bonds: The new bonds would have a 15-year maturity, a par value of $1,000, and a 14 percent stated interest rate. It is expected that these bonds can be sold at par for a flotation cost of $200,000.

    a Calculate the incremental initial outlay required to issue the new bonds.

    b Calculate the annual cash flow savings, if any, expected from the bond refunding.

    c If the firm uses its after-tax cost of debt of 8 percent to evaluate low-risk decisions, would you recommend refunding? Explain your answer.

18-6 **(Refunding Decision—Advanced)** The Korrect Kopy Company is considering the calling of an outstanding bond issue of $14 million and replacing it with a new $14 million issue. The details of both bond issues are outlined below. The firm has a 40 percent tax rate.

Old bonds: Korrect's old issue has a stated interest rate of 14 percent, was issued six years ago, and had a 30-year maturity. The bonds sold at a $15 discount from their $1,000 par value, flotation costs were $120,000, and their call price is $1,140.

New bonds: The new issue is expected to sell at par ($1,000), have a 24-year maturity, and have a flotation cost of $360,000.

    a What is the incremental initial outlay required to issue the new bonds?

    b What are the annual cash flow savings, if any, from refunding if (1) the new bonds have a 12.5 percent stated interest rate; (2) the new bonds have a 13 percent stated interest rate.

    c Construct a table showing the net benefits of refunding under the two circumstances given in **b**, when (1) the firm has an after-tax cost of debt of 6 percent; (2) the firm has an after-tax cost of debt of 8 percent.

    d Discuss the set(s) of circumstances operating when refunding is favorable and when it is not.

18-7 **(Lease versus Purchase)** The Haunted House Restaurant wishes to evaluate two plans, leasing and borrowing to purchase, for financing an oven. The firm has an after-tax cost of debt of 9 percent and plans to use a 5-year time horizon for comparing the lease and purchase alternatives. The estimated after-tax cash outflows associated with the lease and purchase alternatives are given in the table at the top of page 606.

End of year	AFTER-TAX CASH OUTFLOWS	
	Lease	Purchase
1	$3,450	$3,570
2	3,450	3,200
3	3,450	3,470
4	3,450	3,700
5	3,450	3,970

a Calculate the present value of the lease outflows.

b Calculate the present value of the purchase outflows.

c Use your findings in a and b to recommend either the lease or purchase alternative. Justify your recommendation.

18-8 **(Lease versus Purchase)** The Tony Corporation is attempting to determine whether to lease or purchase (by borrowing) a new light-duty truck. The firm's after-tax cost of debt is 8 percent, and it plans to use a 3-year time horizon for comparing the lease and purchase alternatives. The estimated after-tax cash outflows for the lease and purchase alternatives are as follows:

End of year	AFTER-TAX CASH OUTFLOWS	
	Lease	Purchase
1	$18,400	$16,480
2	16,000	14,340
3	14,600	15,690

a Calculate the present value of the lease outflows.

b Calculate the present value of the purchase outflows.

c Use your findings in a and b to recommend either the lease or purchase alternative. Justify your recommendation.

18-9 **(Lease versus Purchase)** The Tucson Tube Company needs to expand its facilities. To do so the firm must acquire an $80,000 machine either through leasing or purchasing by borrowing. The firm has a 9 percent after-tax cost of debt and plans to compare the two financing alternatives over a 5-year time horizon. The after-tax cash outflows associated with each alternative are as follows:

End of year	AFTER-TAX CASH OUTFLOWS	
	Lease	Purchase
1	$11,700	$14,020
2	12,700	12,460
3	13,700	13,550
4	14,700	14,430
5	15,700	15,440

a Calculate the present value of the lease outflows.

b Calculate the present value of the purchase outflows.

c Use your findings in **a** and **b** to recommend either the lease or purchase alternative. Justify your recommendation.

18-10 **(Capitalized Lease Values)**   Given the following lease payments, terms remaining until the leases expire, and discount rates, calculate the capitalized value of each lease, assuming that lease payments are made annually at the end of each year.

Lease	Lease payment	Remaining term	Discount rate
A	$ 40,000	12 years	10%
B	120,000	8 years	12
C	9,000	18 years	14
D	16,000	3 years	9
E	47,000	20 years	11

19

PREFERRED
AND
COMMON
STOCK

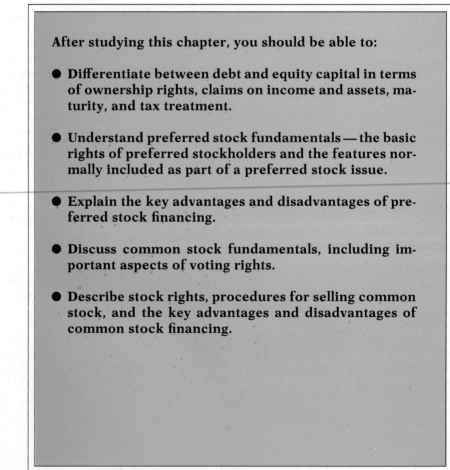

After studying this chapter, you should be able to:

● Differentiate between debt and equity capital in terms of ownership rights, claims on income and assets, maturity, and tax treatment.

● Understand preferred stock fundamentals — the basic rights of preferred stockholders and the features normally included as part of a preferred stock issue.

● Explain the key advantages and disadvantages of preferred stock financing.

● Discuss common stock fundamentals, including important aspects of voting rights.

● Describe stock rights, procedures for selling common stock, and the key advantages and disadvantages of common stock financing.

A firm needs to maintain an equity base large enough to allow it to take advantage of low-cost debt and build an optimal capital structure (see Chapter 16). Equity capital can be raised *internally* through retained earnings, which were briefly discussed as they related to dividend policy in Chapter 16, or *externally* by selling preferred or common stock. Although preferred stock, as noted in the discussion of cost of capital in Chapter 13, is a less costly form of financing than common stock and retained earnings, it is not frequently used to raise equity capital. This chapter begins with brief discussions of equity capital and preferred stock, and then concentrates its attention on the characteristics, features, and role of common stock.

THE NATURE OF EQUITY CAPITAL

The key differences between debt and equity capital have been summarized in Chapter 16 (see, specifically, Table 16.1). These differences relate to ownership rights, claims on the firm's income and assets, maturity, and tax treatment.

Ownership Rights

Unlike creditors (lenders), holders of equity capital (preferred and common stockholders) are owners of the firm. Holders of equity capital often have voting rights that permit them to select the firm's directors and to vote on special issues. In contrast, debtholders may receive voting privileges only when the firm has violated the conditions of a *term loan agreement* or *bond indenture*.

Claims on Income and Assets

Holders of equity capital receive claims on both income and assets that are secondary to the claims of creditors.

CLAIMS ON INCOME The claims of equity holders on income cannot be paid until the claims of all creditors have been satisfied. These claims include both interest and scheduled principal payments. Once these claims have been satisfied, the firm's board of directors can decide whether to distribute dividends to the owners. Of course as noted in Chapter 16, a firm's ability to pay dividends may be limited by legal, contractual, or internal constraints.

CLAIMS ON ASSETS The claims of equity holders on the firm's assets are secondary to the claims of creditors. As noted in Chapter 17, when the firm becomes bankrupt, assets are sold and the proceeds distributed first to employees and customers, then to the government, then to secured creditors, then to unsecured creditors, and finally to equity holders. Because equity holders are the last to receive any distribution of assets during bankruptcy proceedings, they expect greater compensation in the form of dividends or rising stock prices.

Maturity

Unlike debt, equity capital is a permanent form of financing. It does not "mature," and therefore repayment of the initial amount paid in is not required. Since equity does not mature and will be liquidated only during bankruptcy proceedings, the owners must recognize that although a ready market may exist for the firm's shares, the price that can be realized may fluctuate. This potential fluctuation of the market price of equity makes the overall returns to a firm's owners even more risky.

Tax Treatment

As noted in Chapter 2, interest payments to debtholders are treated as tax-deductible expenses on the firm's income statement, whereas dividend payments to preferred and common stockholders are not tax-deductible. The tax-deductibility of interest, as pointed out in Chapter 13, primarily accounts for the fact that the cost of debt is generally less than the cost of equity.

PREFERRED STOCK FUNDAMENTALS

par-value preferred stock Preferred stock with a stated face value that is used with the stated dividend percentage to determine the annual dollar dividend.

no-par preferred stock Preferred stock with no stated face value but that has a stated annual dollar dividend.

adjustable-rate (or floating-rate) preferred stock (ARPS) Preferred stock whose dividend rate is tied to interest rates on specific government securities.

Preferred stock gives its holders certain privileges that make them senior to common stockholders. Because of this, firms generally do not issue large quantities of preferred stock. Preferred stockholders are assured a fixed periodic return, which is stated either as a percentage or as a dollar amount. In other words, a 5 percent preferred stock or a $5 preferred stock can be issued. The way the dividend is stated depends on whether or not the preferred stock has a par value. **Par-value preferred stock** has a stated face value. The annual dividend is stated as a percentage on par-value preferred stock and in dollars on **no-par preferred stock,** which does not have a stated face value. Thus a 5 percent preferred stock with a $100 par value is expected to pay $5 (5 percent of $100) in dividends per year, while a $5 preferred stock with no par value is also expected to pay its $5 stated dividend each year.

Most preferred stock has a fixed dividend, but some firms issue **adjustable-rate (or floating-rate) preferred stock (ARPS).** Such stocks have a dividend rate tied to interest rates on specific government securities. Rate adjustments are commonly made quarterly, and typically the rate must be maintained within certain preset limits. The appeal of ARPS is the protection offered investors against sharp rises in interest rates, since the dividend rate on ARPS will rise with interest rates. From the firm's perspective, adjustable-rate preferreds have appeal since they can be sold at an initially lower dividend rate and the scheduled dividend rate will fall if interest rates decline.

Basic Rights of Preferred Stockholders

The basic rights of preferred stockholders with respect to voting, the distribution of earnings, and the distribution of assets are somewhat more favorable than the rights of common stockholders. Because preferred stock is a form of ownership and has no maturity date, its claims on income and assets are secondary to those of the firm's creditors.

Voting rights Preferred stock is often considered a *quasi-debt* since, much like interest on debt, it yields a fixed periodic (dividend) payment. Of course, as ownership preferred stock is unlike debt in that it has no maturity date. Because their claim on the firm's income is fixed and takes precedence over the claim of common stockholders, preferred stockholders are therefore not exposed to the same degree of risk as common stockholders. They are consequently *not* normally given the right to vote.

Distribution of earnings Preferred stockholders are given preference over common stockholders with respect to the distribution of earnings. If the stated preferred stock dividend is *passed* (not paid) by the board of directors, the payment of dividends to common stockholders is prohibited. It is this preference in dividend distribution that makes common stockholders the true risk takers with respect to receipt of periodic returns.

Distribution of assets Preferred stockholders are usually given preference over common stockholders in the liquidation of assets as a result of a firm's bankruptcy, although they must wait until all creditors have been satisfied. The amount of the claim of preferred stockholders in liquidation is normally equal to the par, or stated, value of the preferred stock. The preferred stockholder's preference over the common stockholder places the common stockholder in the more risky position with respect to recovery of investment.

Features of Preferred Stock

A number of features are generally included as part of a preferred stock issue. These features, along with a statement of the stock's par value, the

WESTERN UNION PASSES 6th DIVIDEND: PREFERRED GETS 2 DIRECTORS

Western Union Corp. directors voted to again omit quarterly common and preferred dividends, a decision that will allow preferred shareholders to elect two additional board members.

Analysts said, however, that because of the company's fundamental problems, they didn't expect the election of new directors by preferred shareholders to markedly affect the effort that is under way to turn around the company.

"What is a preferred shareholder director going to do?" said Glenn R. Pafumi, an analyst for Dean Witter Reynolds Inc. "I'm not sure they're going to make that much of a difference."

In an interview last month, Robert S. Leventhal, Western Union's chairman, suggested that he didn't consider the consequence of the dividend decision significant, saying, "You know, having new directors on the board isn't the most terrible thing."

The company, which currently has eight board members, said it expects to nominate the additional candidates for election by preferred shareholders at Western Union's May 15 [1986] annual meeting.

Western Union has four issues of preferred shares outstanding, as well as four issues of preferred shares for its major subsidiary, Western Union Telegraph Co. The communications and information services company saves $6.2 million quarterly by deferring preferred dividends, which are cumulative. With yesterday's [February 25, 1986] action, Western Union will owe $37.2 million in dividend payouts to its preferred holders.

Under the company's charter, preferred holders are allowed to elect two directors to Western Union's board, as well as up to eight directors to the company's Western Union Telegraph unit, if the company fails to pay six consecutive dividends for either concern. Directors voted to eliminate the sixth dividend yesterday on the parent company's stock, as well as on common and preferred shares of the telegraph unit. Currently, both the parent company and the subsidiary share the same board.

Source: Peter W. Barnes, "Western Union Again Omits Dividends, Permitting Election of 2 More Directors," *The Wall Street Journal*, February 26, 1986, p. 10. Reprinted by permission of *The Wall Street Journal*. © Dow Jones & Company Inc. 1986. All rights reserved.

amount of dividend payments, the dividend payment dates, and any restrictive covenants, are specified in an agreement similar to a *term loan agreement* or *bond indenture* (see Chapter 18).

RESTRICTIVE COVENANTS The restrictive covenants commonly found in a preferred stock issue are aimed at assuring the continued existence of the firm and, most important, regular payment of the stated dividend.

These covenants include provisions related to passing dividends, the sale of senior securities, mergers, sales of assets, working capital requirements, and the payment of common stock dividends or common stock repurchases. The violation of preferred stock covenants usually permits preferred stockholders to force the retirement of their stock at or above its par, or stated, value.

CUMULATION   Most preferred stock is **cumulative** with respect to any dividends passed. That is, all dividends in arrears must be paid prior to the payment of dividends to common stockholders. If preferred stock is **noncumulative,** passed (unpaid) dividends do not accumulate. In this case only the most recent dividend must be paid prior to paying dividends to common stockholders. Since the common stockholders, who are the firm's true owners, can receive dividends only after the dividend claims of preferred stockholders have been satisfied, it is in the firm's best interest to pay preferred dividends when they are due.[1] The following example will help clarify the distinction between cumulative and noncumulative preferred stock.

cumulative preferred stock Preferred stock for which all passed (unpaid) dividends in arrears must be paid prior to paying dividends to common stockholders.

noncumulative preferred stock Preferred stock for which passed (unpaid) dividends do not accumulate.

EXAMPLE

The Utley Company currently has outstanding an issue of $6 preferred stock on which quarterly dividends of $1.50 are to be paid. Due to a cash shortage, the last two quarterly dividends were passed. The directors of the company have been receiving a large number of complaints from common stockholders, who have of course not received any dividends in the past two quarters either. If the preferred stock is cumulative, the company will have to pay its preferred shareholders $4.50 per share ($3.00 of dividends in arrears plus the current $1.50 dividend) prior to paying dividends to its common stockholders. If the preferred stock is noncumulative, however, the firm must pay only the current $1.50 dividend to its preferred stockholders prior to paying dividends to its common stockholders. ■

PARTICIPATION   Most issues of preferred stock are **nonparticipating,** which means that preferred stockholders receive only the specified dividend payments. Occasionally, **participating preferred stock** is issued. This type provides for dividend payments based on certain formulas allowing preferred stockholders to participate with common

nonparticipating preferred stock Preferred stock whose stockholders receive only the specified dividend payments.

participating preferred stock Preferred stock that provides for dividend payments based on certain formulas allowing preferred stockholders to participate with common stockholders in the receipt of dividends beyond a specified amount.

[1] Most preferred stock is cumulative since it is difficult to sell noncumulative stock. The common stockholders will obviously prefer noncumulative preferred to be issued, since it does not place them in quite as risky a position. But they must recognize that it is often in the best interest of the firm to sell *cumulative* preferred stock.

stockholders in the receipt of dividends beyond a specified amount. This feature is included only when the firm considers it absolutely necessary to obtain badly needed funds.

CALL FEATURE Preferred stock is generally *callable*, which means that the issuer can retire outstanding stock within a certain period of time at a specified price. The call option generally cannot be exercised until a period of years has elapsed since the issuance of the stock. The call price is normally set above the initial issuance price, but may decrease according to a predetermined schedule as time passes. Making preferred stock callable provides the issuer with a method of bringing the fixed-payment commitment of the preferred issue to an end.

conversion feature
A provision in convertible preferred stock permitting its transference into a specified number of shares of common stock.

CONVERSION FEATURE Preferred stock quite often contains a **conversion feature** that permits its transference into a specified number of shares of common stock. Sometimes the conversion ratio, or time period for conversion, changes according to a prespecified formula. A detailed discussion of conversion is presented in Chapter 20.

ADVANTAGES AND DISADVANTAGES OF PREFERRED STOCK

It is difficult to generalize about the advantages and disadvantages of preferred stock due to the variety of features that may be incorporated in a preferred stock issue. The attractiveness of preferred stock is also affected by current interest rates and the firm's existing capital structure. Nevertheless, some key advantages and disadvantages are often cited.

Advantages

One commonly cited advantage of preferred stock is its *ability to increase leverage*. Since preferred stock obligates the firm to pay only fixed dividends to its holders, its presence helps to increase the firm's financial leverage. (The effects of preferred stock on a firm's financial leverage were discussed in Chapter 5.) Increased financial leverage will magnify the effects of increased earnings on common stockholders' returns.

A second advantage is the *flexibility* provided by preferred stock. Although preferred stock provides added leverage in much the same way as bonds, it differs from bonds in that the issuer can pass a dividend payment without suffering the consequences that result when an interest payment is missed on a bond. Preferred stock allows the issuer to keep its levered position without running as great a risk of being forced out of business in a lean year as it might if it missed interest payments on actual debt.

A third advantage of preferred stock has been its *use in mergers*. Often preferred stock is exchanged for the common stock of an acquired firm, with the preferred dividend set at a level equivalent to the historic dividend of the acquired firm. This allows the acquiring firm to state at the time of the acquisition that only a fixed dividend will be paid. All other earnings can be reinvested to perpetuate the growth of the merged enterprise. In addition, this permits the owners of the acquired firm to be assured of a continuing stream of dividends equivalent to that which may have been provided prior to acquisition.

Disadvantages

Two major disadvantages are often cited for preferred stock. One is the *seniority of the preferred stockholder's claim*. Since holders of preferred stock are given preference over common stockholders with respect to the distribution of earnings and assets, the presence of preferred stock in a sense jeopardizes common stockholders' returns. If a firm has preferred stockholders to pay, and if the firm's after-tax earnings are quite variable, its ability to pay at least token dividends to common stockholders may be seriously impaired.

A second disadvantage of preferred stock is cost. The *cost of preferred stock financing is generally higher than that of debt financing*. This is because, unlike the payment of interest to bondholders, the payment of dividends to preferred stockholders is not guaranteed. Since preferred shareholders are willing to accept the added risk of purchasing preferred stock rather than long-term debt, they must be compensated with a higher return. Another factor causing the cost of preferred stock to be significantly greater than that of long-term debt is the fact that interest on debt is tax-deductible, whereas preferred stock dividends must be paid from after-tax earnings.

COMMON STOCK FUNDAMENTALS

The true owners of business firms are the common stockholders, who invest their money in the firm only because of their expectation of future returns. A common stockholder is sometimes referred to as a *residual owner*, since in essence he or she receives what is left after all other claims on the firm's income and assets have been satisfied. As a result of this generally uncertain position, the common stockholder expects to be compensated with adequate dividends and, ultimately, capital gains. Here we discuss the fundamental aspects of common stock: ownership; par value; authorized, outstanding, and issued stock;

voting rights; dividends; stock repurchases; and the distribution of earnings and assets.

Ownership

privately owned All common stock of a firm owned by a single individual.

closely owned All common stock of a firm owned by a small group of investors such as a family.

publicly owned Common stock of a firm owned by a broad group of unrelated individual and (or) institutional investors.

The common stock of a firm can be **privately owned** by a single individual, **closely owned** by a small group of investors, such as a family, or **publicly owned** by a broad group of unrelated individual and (or) institutional investors. Typically, small corporations are privately or closely owned, and if their shares are traded this occurs privately or on the over-the-counter exchange (see Chapter 2). Large corporations, which are emphasized in the following discussions, are publicly owned, and their shares are generally actively traded on the organized or over-the-counter exchanges, which were briefly described in Chapter 2.

Par Value

par value A relatively useless value arbitrarily placed on stock in the corporate charter.

no par value Used to describe stock issued without a par value, in which case the stock may be assigned a value or placed on the books at the price at which it is sold.

Common stock may be sold with or without a par value. A **par value** is a relatively useless value arbitrarily placed on the stock in the firm's corporate charter. It is generally quite low, somewhere in the range of $1. Firms often issue stock with **no par value,** in which case they may assign it a value or place it on the books at the price at which it is sold. A low par value may be advantageous in states where certain corporate taxes are based on the par value of stock; if a stock has no par value, the tax may be based on an arbitrarily determined per-share figure. The accounting entries resulting from the sale of common stock can be illustrated by a simple example.

EXAMPLE

The Moxie Company has issued 1,000 shares of $2 par-value common stock, receiving proceeds of $50 per share. This results in the following entries on the firm's books:

Common stock (1,000 shares at $2 par)	$ 2,000
Paid-in capital in excess of par	48,000
Common stock equity	$50,000

Sometimes the entry labeled "paid-in capital in excess of par" may be labeled "capital surplus." As noted in Chapter 16, firms are often prohibited by state law from distributing any paid-in capital as dividends. ■

Authorized, Outstanding, and Issued Stock

A corporate charter must state the number of shares of common stock the firm is *authorized* to issue. Not all authorized shares will necessarily be **outstanding**—that is, currently under ownership of the firm's shareholders. Since it is often difficult to amend the charter to authorize the issuance of additional shares, firms generally attempt to authorize more shares than they plan to issue. It is possible for the corporation to have *issued* more shares of common stock than are currently outstanding if it has repurchased stock. Repurchased stock, as noted in Chapter 16, is called *treasury stock*. The amount of treasury stock is therefore found by subtracting the number of outstanding shares from the number of shares issued.

outstanding Shares of common stock currently under ownership of the firm's shareholders.

Voting Rights

Generally, each share of common stock entitles the holder to one vote in the election of directors and in other special elections. Votes are generally assignable and must be cast at the annual stockholders' meeting. Occasionally, **nonvoting common stock** is issued when the firm's present owners wish to raise capital through the sale of common stock but do not want to give up any voting power. When this is done, the common stock will be classed. Class A common is typically designated as nonvoting, while class B common would have voting rights. Because class A shares are not given voting rights, they generally are given preference over class B shares in the distribution of earnings and assets. Treasury stock, which resides within the corporation, generally *does not* have voting rights. Three aspects of voting require special attention — proxies, majority voting, and cumulative voting.

nonvoting common stock Common stock that carries no voting rights; typically designated as class A common stock.

PROXIES Since most small stockholders cannot attend the annual meeting to vote, they may sign a **proxy statement** giving their votes to another party. The solicitation of proxies from shareholders is closely controlled by the Securities and Exchange Commission, since there is a possibility that proxies will be solicited on the basis of false or misleading information. The existing management generally receives the stockholders' proxies, since it is able to solicit them at company expense. Occasionally, when the ownership of the firm is widely disseminated, outsiders may attempt to gain control by waging a **proxy battle.** This requires soliciting a sufficient number of votes to unseat the existing management. To win a corporate election, votes from a majority of the shares voted are required. Proxy battles generally occur when the existing management is performing poorly; however, the odds of a nonmanagement group winning a proxy battle are generally slim.

proxy statement A statement conferring the votes of a stockholder or stockholders to another party or parties.

proxy battle The attempt by a nonmanagement group to gain control of the management of a firm through the solicitation of a sufficient number of corporate votes.

majority voting system
The system whereby in the election of the board of directors each stockholder is entitled to one vote for each share of stock owned.

MAJORITY VOTING   In the **majority voting system,** each stockholder is entitled to one vote for each share of stock owned. The stockholders vote for each position on the board of directors separately, and each stockholder is permitted to vote all of his or her shares for *each* director he or she favors. The directors receiving the majority of the votes are elected. It is impossible for minority interests to select a director, since each shareholder can vote his or her shares for as many of the candidates as he or she wishes. As long as management controls a majority of the votes, it can elect all the directors. An example will clarify this point.

EXAMPLE

The Dill Company is in the process of electing three directors. There are 1,000 shares of stock outstanding, of which management controls 60 percent. The management-backed candidates are A, B, and C; the minority candidates are D, E, and F. By voting its 600 shares (60 percent of 1,000) for *each* of its candidates, management can elect A, B, and C; the minority shareholders, with only 400 votes for each of their candidates, cannot elect any directors. Management's candidates will receive 600 votes each, and other candidates will receive 400 votes each. ■

cumulative voting system The system under which each share of common stock is allotted a number of votes equal to the total number of corporate directors to be elected and votes can be given to *any* director.

CUMULATIVE VOTING   Some states require, and others permit, the use of a **cumulative voting system** to elect corporate directors. This system gives a number of votes equal to the number of directors to be elected to each share of common stock. The votes can be given to *any* director(s) the stockholder desires. The advantage of this system is that it provides the minority shareholders with an opportunity to elect at least some directors.

EXAMPLE

The Esco Company, like the Dill Company, is in the process of electing three directors. In this case, however, each share of common stock entitles the holder to three votes, which may be voted in any manner desired. Again, there are 1,000 shares outstanding, and management controls 600. It therefore has a total of 1,800 votes (3 × 600), while the minority shareholders have 1,200 votes (3 × 400). In this situation, the majority shareholders can elect only two directors, and the minority shareholders can elect at least one director. The majority shareholders can split their votes evenly among the three candidates (give them 600 votes each); but if the minority shareholders give all their votes to one of their candidates, he or she will win. ■

A commonly cited formula for determining the number of shares necessary to elect a certain number of directors, *NE*, under cumulative voting is given by Equation 19.1:

$$NE = \frac{O \times D}{T + 1} + 1 \qquad (19.1)$$

where

NE = number of shares needed to elect a certain number of directors
O = total number of shares of common stock outstanding
D = number of directors desired
T = total number of directors to be elected

EXAMPLE

Substituting the values in the preceding example for O (1,000) and T (3) into Equation 19.1 and letting $D = 1, 2$, and 3 yields values of *NE* equal to 251, 501, and 751. Since the minority stockholders control only 400 shares, they can elect only one director. ■

The advantage of cumulative voting from the viewpoint of minority shareholders should be clear from the example. However, even with cumulative voting, certain election procedures such as staggered terms for directors can be used to prevent minority representation on a board. Also, the majority shareholders may control a large enough number of shares or the total number of directors to be elected may be small enough to prevent minority representation.

Dividends

The payment of corporate dividends is at the discretion of the board of directors. Most corporations pay dividends quarterly. Dividends may be paid in cash, stock, or merchandise. Cash dividends are the most common; merchandise dividends are the least common. *Stock splits,* which have some similarity to *stock dividends,* are sometimes used to enhance the trading activity of a stock (see Chapter 16). The common stockholder is not promised a dividend, but he or she grows to expect certain payments from the historical dividend pattern of the firm. Before dividends are paid to common stockholders, the claims of all creditors, the government, and preferred stockholders must be satisfied. Because of the importance of the dividend decision to the growth and valuation of the firm, a portion of Chapter 16 was devoted to a discussion of dividend policy.

Stock Repurchases

Another characteristic of common stock, alluded to earlier in the discussion of authorized, outstanding, and issued stock, is the repurchase of stock. Firms occasionally repurchase stock in order to change their capital structure or to increase the returns to the owners. The effect of repurchasing common stock is similar to that of the payment of cash dividends to stockholders. The repurchase of stock is popular among firms that are in a very liquid position with no attractive investment opportunities. Since stock repurchases are similar to cash dividend payments, they too were given coverage in Chapter 16.

Distribution of Earnings and Assets

As mentioned in previous sections, holders of common stock have no guarantee of receiving any periodic distribution of earnings in the form of dividends, nor are they guaranteed anything in the event of liquidation. However, one thing they are assured of is that they cannot lose any more than they have invested in the firm. Moreover, the common stockholder can receive unlimited returns through dividends and through the appreciation in the value of his or her holdings. In other words, although nothing is guaranteed, the *possible* rewards for providing risk capital can be considerable and even great.

STOCK RIGHTS AND OTHER CONSIDERATIONS

In addition to common stock fundamentals, stock rights, selling common stock, and the advantages and disadvantages of common stock are important considerations.

Stock Rights

stock rights Provide stockholders with the privilege to purchase additional shares of stock based on their number of owned shares.

Stock rights provide stockholders with the privilege to purchase additional shares of stock based on their number of owned shares. Rights are an important tool of common stock financing without which shareholders would run the risk of losing their proportionate control of the corporation.

preemptive rights Allow common stockholders to maintain their *proportionate* ownership in the corporation when new issues are made.

PREEMPTIVE RIGHTS Many issues of common stock provide shareholders with **preemptive rights,** which allow stockholders to maintain their *proportionate* ownership in the corporation when new issues are made. Most states permit shareholders to be extended this privilege in the corporate charter. Preemptive rights allow existing shareholders to maintain their voting control and protect against the dilution of their ownership and earnings. **Dilution of ownership** usually results in the dilution of earnings, since each present shareholder will have a claim on a *smaller* part of the firm's earnings than previously. Of course, if total earnings simultaneously increase, the long-run effect may be an overall increase in earnings per share.

From the firm's viewpoint, the use of rights offerings to raise new equity capital may be cheaper than a public offering of stock. An example may help clarify the use of rights.

dilution of ownership
Occurs when a new stock issue results in each present stockholder having a claim on a *smaller* part of the firm's earnings than previously.

EXAMPLE

The Dominic Company currently has 100,000 shares of common stock outstanding and is contemplating issuing an additional 10,000 shares through a rights offering. Each existing shareholder will receive one right per share, and each right will entitle the shareholder to purchase one-tenth of a share of new common stock (10,000 ÷ 100,000), so 10 rights will be required to purchase one share of the stock. The holder of 1,000 shares of existing common stock will receive 1,000 rights, each permitting the purchase of one-tenth of a share of new common stock, for a total of 100 shares of new common stock. If the shareholder exercises his or her rights, he or she will end up with a total of 1,100 shares of common stock, or 1 percent of the total number of shares outstanding (110,000). This is the same proportion the shareholder had prior to the rights offering.

MECHANICS OF RIGHTS OFFERINGS   When a company makes a rights offering, the board of directors must set a *date of record*, which is the last date on which the recipient of a right must be the legal owner indicated in the company's stock ledger. Due to the time needed to make bookkeeping entries when a stock is traded, stocks usually begin selling **ex rights** — without the rights being attached to the stock — four *business days* prior to the date of record.

ex rights The condition under which stock is sold for a period without announced rights being attached to the stock.

The issuing firm sends rights to *holders of record*, who are free to exercise their rights, sell them, or let them expire. Rights are transferable, and many are traded actively enough to be listed on the various securities exchanges. They are exercisable for a specified period of time, generally not more than a few months, at a price, which is called the **subscription price**, set somewhat below the prevailing market price. Since fractions of shares are not always issued, it is sometimes necessary to purchase additional rights or sell any extra rights. The value of a right depends largely on the number of rights needed to purchase a share of stock and the amount by which the right subscription price is below the current market price. If the rights have a very low

subscription price The price below the prevailing market price at which stock rights may be exercisable for a specified period of time.

EMPLOYEE OWNERS ARE TIGHT-FISTED MANAGERS

Employees at Marquette Electronics Inc. aren't the gold diggers that they might appear to be. It's not that they don't enjoy the cushy atmosphere in which they work. But it wasn't their idea to build a weight room, a restaurant selling beer and wine, or a company theater.

In fact, Marquette's employees take a pretty flinty-eyed view of it when president Mike Cudahy indulges his sugar-daddy tendencies. That's because it's not just his money he's spending. Some of it — in the form of company contributions to an employee stock ownership trust (ESOT) — is theirs. Since the plan was begun about 12 years ago, contributions to the ESOT have ranged from 5% of pretax profits in the early years of the plan (the minimum allowed under the ESOT plan) to about 20% (or $2.1 million) in 1985. Individual contributions to the ESOT vary widely, according to salary. The money is paid out as cash each quarter or invested in mutual funds for the future.

It is no surprise, then, that the employees ask questions — *lots* of questions — every time the quarterly numbers come out. Nor are they shy about challenging expenditures. When they noticed that Cudahy had ordered the pouring of sidewalks and a patio outside the manufacturing facility, there were plenty of skeptical employees complaining about the high cost of concrete. Not everyone is thrilled with a day-care center that is subsidized by the company but benefits only a fraction of the work force. Cracks about the company's idyllic research center have a jagged edge to them. And last spring, when Cudahy was considering building a million-dollar health center — with gym, swimming pool, racquetball and tennis courts, an exercise room, and a domed courtyard — there was so much advance grumbling that Cudahy felt obligated to hand out ballots with the blueprints. Did his employees want to see 10% to 15% of the company's annual ESOT contribution for the foreseeable future go toward such a "magnificent facility?" By a vote of three-to-one, they did not. . . .

Source: "The Pool Would be Nice Boss, But We'd Rather Have the Cash," *INC.*, March 1986, p. 84. Reprinted with permission of INC. magazine, March, 1986. Copyright © 1986 by INC. Publishing Company, 38 Commercial Wharf, Boston, MA 02110.

value and an individual owns only a small number of shares, the rights may be allowed to expire.

MANAGEMENT DECISIONS   A firm's management must make two basic decisions when preparing for a rights offering. The first is the price at which the right holders can purchase a new share of common stock.

The subscription price must be set *below* the current market price, but how far below depends on management's evaluation of the sensitivity of the market demand to a price change, the degree of dilution in ownership and earnings expected, and the size of the offering. Management will consider the rights offering successful if approximately 90 percent of the rights are exercised.

Once management has determined the subscription price, it must determine the number of rights required to purchase a share of stock. Since the amount of funds to be raised is known in advance, the subscription price can be divided into this value to get the total number of shares that must be sold. Dividing the total number of shares outstanding by the total number of shares to be sold will give management the number of rights required to purchase a share of stock.

EXAMPLE

The Lorne Company intends to raise $1 million through a rights offering. The firm currently has 160,000 shares outstanding, which have been most recently trading for $53 to $58 per share. The company has consulted an investment banking firm, which has recommended setting the subscription price for the rights at $50 per share. It believes that at this price the offering will be fully subscribed. The firm must therefore sell an additional 20,000 shares ($1,000,000 ÷ $50 per share). This means that 8 rights (160,000 ÷ 20,000) will be needed to purchase a new share at $50. Each right will entitle its holder to purchase one-eighth of a share of common stock. ■

VALUE OF A RIGHT   Theoretically, the value of a right should be the same if the stock is selling *with rights* or *ex rights*. In either case, the market value of a right may differ from its theoretical value.

With Rights.   Once a rights offering has been declared, shares will trade with rights for only a few days. Equation 19.2 is used to find the value of a right when the stock is trading with rights, R_w:

$$R_w = \frac{M_w - S}{N + 1} \qquad (19.2)$$

where

R_w = theoretical value of a right when stock is selling with rights
M_w = market value of the stock with rights
S = subscription price of the stock
N = number of rights needed to purchase one share of stock

EXAMPLE

The Lorne Company's stock is currently selling with rights at a price of $54.50 per share, the subscription price is $50 per share, and 8 rights are required to purchase a new share of stock. According to Equation 19.2, the value of a right is $.50 [($54.50 − $50.00) ÷ (8 + 1)]. A right should therefore be worth $.50 in the marketplace. ■

Ex Rights. When a share of stock is traded ex rights, meaning that the value of the right is no longer included in the stock's market price, the share price of the stock is expected to drop by the value of a right. Equation 19.3 is used to find the market value of the stock trading ex rights, M_e. The same notation is used as in Equation 19.2:

$$M_e = M_w - R_w \qquad (19.3)$$

The value of a right when the stock is trading ex rights, R_e, is given by Equation 19.4:

$$R_e = \frac{M_e - S}{N} \qquad (19.4)$$

The use of these equations can be illustrated by returning to the Lorne Company example.

EXAMPLE

According to Equation 19.3, the market price of the Lorne Company stock selling ex rights is $54 ($54.50 − $.50). Substituting this value into Equation 19.4 gives the value of a right when the stock is selling ex rights, which is $.50 [($54.00 − $50.00) ÷ 8]. The theoretical value of the right when the stock is selling with rights or ex rights is therefore the same. ■

MARKET BEHAVIOR OF RIGHTS As indicated earlier, stock rights are negotiable instruments, often traded on securities exchanges. The market price of a right will generally differ from its theoretical value. The extent to which it will differ will depend on how the firm's stock price is expected to behave during the period when the right is exercisable. By buying rights instead of the stock itself, investors can achieve much higher returns on their money when stock prices rise.

Selling Common Stock

Aside from the sale of new common stock through a rights offering, the firm may be able to sell new shares of common stock directly through some type of stock option or stock-purchase plan. **Stock options** are generally extended to management and permit it to purchase a certain number of shares of their firm's common stock at a specified price over a certain period of time. **Stock-purchase plans** are fringe benefits occasionally offered to employees that allow them to purchase the firm's stock at a discount or on a matching basis, with the firm absorbing part of the cost.

New issues of common stock, like bonds, can also be sold publicly through an *investment banker*. Of course, these sales are closely regulated by the *Securities and Exchange Commission (SEC)* as well as by state securities commissions. Public sale is commonly used in situations in which rights offerings are not required or are unsuccessful. The *public offering* of common stock through an investment banker is generally more expensive than any type of *private placement*, but the investment banker provides useful advice as well as a convenient forum for selling new common stock. For large public stock offerings, the total cost of investment banking services and administration (legal, accounting, printing, and so forth) ranges between 3 and 10 percent of the amount of funds raised. (A brief discussion of the role of the investment banker was presented in Chapter 2.)

stock options Privileges generally extended to management permitting the purchase of a certain number of shares of their firm's common stock at a specified price over a certain period of time.

stock-purchase plans Fringe benefits occasionally offered to employees, allowing the purchase of the firm's stock at a discount or on a matching basis with the firm absorbing part of the cost.

Advantages and Disadvantages of Common Stock

A number of key advantages and disadvantages of common stock are often cited.

ADVANTAGES   The basic advantages of common stock stem from the fact that it is a source of financing that places a *minimum of constraints* on the firm. Since dividends do not *have* to be paid on common stock and their nonpayment does not jeopardize the receipt of payment by other security holders, common stock financing is quite attractive. The fact that common stock has *no maturity,* thereby eliminating a future repayment obligation, also enhances its desirability as a form of financing. Another advantage of common stock over other forms of long-term financing is its *ability to increase the firm's borrowing power.* The more common stock a firm sells, the larger its equity base and therefore the more easily and cheaply long-term debt financing can be obtained.

DISADVANTAGES   The disadvantages of common stock financing include the *potential dilution of ownership and earnings.* Only when rights are offered and exercised by their recipients can this be avoided. Of course, the dilution of ownership and earnings resulting from new issues of common stock may go unnoticed by the small shareholder. Another disadvantage of common stock financing is its *high cost.* In Chapter 13 common stock equity was shown to be, normally, the most expensive form of long-term financing. This is because dividends are not tax-deductible and because common stock is a riskier security than either debt or preferred stock.

SUMMARY

- Preferred and common stock are external sources of equity capital. They have claims on income and assets that are secondary to the claims of creditors, have no maturity date, and do not receive tax benefits similar to those given debtholders.
- Preferred stockholders are given preference over common stockholders with respect to the distribution of earnings and assets. Preferred stock is similar to debt in that though some adjustable-rate (or floating-rate) issues exist, it generally has a fixed annual dividend. Because preferred stockholders' claims are given preference over the claims of common stockholders, they do not normally receive voting privileges.
- Preferred stock issues may have certain restrictive covenants, cumulative dividends, participation in earnings, a call feature, and a conversion feature.
- The basic advantages for the use of preferred stock financing include its ability to increase the firm's leverage, the flexibility of the obligation, and its use in mergers. Disadvantages include the seniority of its claim over the common stockholders and its relatively high cost compared to debt financing.
- The common stock of a firm can be privately owned, closely owned, or publicly owned. It can be sold with or without a par value. Not all shares authorized in the corporate charter will be outstanding. If the firm has treasury stock, it will have issued more shares than are outstanding.
- Some firms issue various classes of common stock, in which class A shares have no voting rights but are given preference over class B voting shares with respect to the distribution of earnings and assets. Proxies can be used to transfer voting rights from one party to another. Either majority voting or cumulative voting, which provides minority shareholders with an opportunity to elect at least some directors, may be used by the firm.
- Holders of common stock may receive a preemptive right that gives them an opportunity to purchase new common stock on a pro rata basis. Stock rights are used to pass this option to the owners. A certain number of rights are required to purchase shares at a reduced price, which causes each right to have a monetary value. Rights may be exercised, sold, purchased, or allowed to expire.
- In addition to rights offerings, new common stock can be sold directly through stock options, a stock-purchase plan, or publicly through an investment banker.
- Basic advantages of common stock include the minimum of constraints it places on the firm, its lack of a maturity date, and its ability to increase the firm's borrowing power. Disadvantages include the potential dilution of ownership and earnings and its high cost.

QUESTIONS

19-1 How do debt and equity capital differ? What are the key differences between them with respect to ownership rights, claims on income and assets, maturity, and tax treatment?

19-2 What is *preferred stock?* What claims do preferred stockholders have with respect to the distribution of earnings and assets? How are dividends on preferred stock typically stated? What is an *adjustable-rate (or floating-rate) preferred stock (ARPS)?*

19-3 What are *cumulative* and *noncumulative* preferred stock? Which form is most common? Why?

19-4 What is a *call feature* in a preferred stock issue? When and at what price does the call usually take place? What benefit does the call offer the issuer of preferred stock?

19-5 What are the key advantages and disadvantages of using preferred stock financing as a source of new capital funds?

19-6 Why is the common stockholder considered the true owner of a firm? What risks do common stockholders take that other suppliers of long-term capital do not?

19-7 What are *proxies?* How are they used? What are *proxy battles*, and why are they initiated? Why is it difficult for minority shareholders to win such battles?

19-8 How do majority and cumulative voting systems differ? Which of these voting systems would be preferred by the minority shareholders? Why?

19-9 What is a right *subscription price?* How is it determined? Given the subscription price, what must the firm know to determine the number of rights to offer?

19-10 How is the theoretical value of a right found if the stock is selling *with rights?* When a share is trading *ex rights?* How do these two values compare? Do they typically equal their market price?

19-11 How are *stock options* and *stock-purchase plans* used to directly sell new common stock? How is new common stock sold publicly?

19-12 What are the key advantages and disadvantages of using common stock financing as a source of new capital funds?

PROBLEMS

19-1 **(Preferred Dividends)** Pickering, Hardwood, and Rap has an outstanding issue of preferred stock with an $80 par value and an 11 percent annual dividend.

a What is the annual dollar dividend? If it is paid quarterly, how much will be paid each quarter?

b If the preferred stock is *noncumulative* and the board of directors has passed the preferred dividend for the last three years, how much must be paid to preferred stockholders prior to paying dividends to common stockholders?

    c If the preferred stock is *cumulative* and the board of directors has passed the preferred dividend for the last three years, how much must be paid to preferred stockholders prior to paying dividends to common stockholders?

19-2 **(Preferred Dividends)** In each case in the table, how many dollars of preferred dividends per share must be paid to preferred stockholders prior to paying common stock dividends?

Case	Type	Par value	Dividend per share per period	Periods of dividends passed
A	Cumulative	$ 80	$5	2
B	Noncumulative	110	8%	3
C	Noncumulative	100	$11	1
D	Cumulative	60	8.5%	4
E	Cumulative	90	9%	0

19-3 **(Participating Preferred Stock)** The Crumpled Kan Company has outstanding an issue of 3,000 shares of participating preferred stock that has a $100 par value and an 8 percent annual dividend. The preferred stockholders participate fully (on an equal per-share basis) with common shareholders in annual dividends of more than $9 per share for common stock. The firm has 5,000 shares of common stock outstanding.

    a If the firm pays preferred stockholders their dividends and then declares an additional $100,000 in dividends, how much will be the total dividend per share for preferred and common stock, respectively?

    b If the firm pays preferred stockholders their dividends and then declares an additional $40,000 in dividends, what is the total dividend per share for each type of shareholder?

    c If the firm's preferred stock is cumulative and the past two years' dividends have been passed, what dividends will be received by each type of shareholder if the firm declares a *total* dividend of $30,000?

    d Rework **c** assuming that the total dividend payment is $20,000.

    e Rework **a** and **b** assuming that the preferred stock is nonparticipating.

19-4 **(Accounting for Common Stock)** What accounting entries on the firm's balance sheet would result from the following cases?

    a A firm sells 10,000 shares of $1-par common stock at $13 per share.

    b A firm sells 20,000 shares of $2-par common and receives $100,000.

    c A firm sells 200,000 shares of no-par common stock for $8 million.

    d A firm sells 14,000 shares of common stock for the par value of $5 per share.

19-5 **(Majority versus Cumulative Voting)** Cobbie's Place, a fast-food franchise, is electing five new directors to the board. The company has 1,000 shares of common stock outstanding. The management, which controls 54 percent of the common shares outstanding, backs candidates A through E; the minority shareholders are backing candidates F through J.

    a If the firm uses a *majority voting system*, how many directors will each group elect?

b If the firm uses a *cumulative voting system,* how many directors will each group elect?

c Discuss the differences between these two approaches and the resulting election outcomes.

19-6 **(Majority versus Cumulative Voting)** Determine the number of directors that can be elected by the *minority shareholders* using (1) majority voting and (2) cumulative voting in each of the following cases.

Case	Number of shares outstanding	Percentage of shares held by minority	Number of directors to be elected
A	140,000	20%	3
B	100,000	40	7
C	175,000	30	4
D	880,000	40	5
E	1,000,000	18	9

19-7 **(Number of Rights)** Indicate (1) how many shares of stock one right is worth and (2) the number of shares a given stockholder, X, can purchase in each of the following cases:

Case	Number of shares outstanding	Number of new shares to be issued	Number of shares held by stockholder X
A	900,000	30,000	600
B	1,400,000	35,000	200
C	800,000	40,000	2,000
D	60,000	12,000	1,200
E	180,000	36,000	1,000

19-8 **(Theoretical Value of Rights)** Determine the theoretical value of the right when the stock is selling (1) *with rights* and (2) *ex rights* in each of the following cases:

Case	Market value of stock *with rights*	Subscription price of stock	Number of rights needed to purchase one share of stock
A	$20.00	$17.50	4
B	56.00	50.00	3
C	41.00	30.00	6
D	50.00	40.00	5
E	92.00	82.00	8

19-9 **(Value of a Right)** Your sister-in-law is a stockholder in a corporation that just recently declared a rights offering. In need of cash, she has offered to sell you her rights for 30 cents each. The key data relative to the stock and associated rights are as follows:

Current stock price *with rights*	$37.25/share
Subscription price of stock rights	$36.00/share
Number of rights needed to purchase one share of common stock	4

a Determine the theoretical value of the rights when the stock is selling *with rights*.

b Determine the theoretical value of the rights when the stock is trading *ex rights*.

c Discuss your findings in **a** and **b**. Would you accept your sister-in-law's offer?

19-10 **(Sale of Common Equity — Rights)** Bulah Gas wishes to raise $1 million in common equity financing using a rights offering. The company has 500,000 shares of common stock outstanding that have recently traded for $25 to $28 per share. The firm believes that if the subscription price is set at $25, the shares will be fully subscribed.

a Determine the number of new shares the firm must sell to raise the desired amount of capital.

b How many shares will each right entitle a holder of one share to purchase?

c Rework **a** and **b** assuming that the subscription price is $10.

d What is the theoretical value of a right if the current market price is $27 *with rights* and the subscription price is $25? Answer for both when the stock is selling *with rights* and *ex rights*.

e Rework **d** assuming that the subscription price is $10.

f Which subscription price ($25 or $10) will be more likely to assure complete subscription? Why?

19-11 **(Sale of Common Equity — Rights)** The Scroll Paper Corporation is interested in raising $600,000 of new equity capital through a rights offering. The firm currently has 300,000 shares of common stock outstanding. It expects to set the subscription price at $25 and anticipates that the stock will sell for $29 *with rights*.

a Calculate the number of new shares the firm must sell to raise the desired amount of funds.

b How many rights will be needed to purchase one share of stock at the subscription price?

c Cogburn Jones holds 48,000 shares of Scroll Paper common stock. If he exercises his rights, how many additional shares can he purchase?

d Determine the theoretical value of a right when the stock is selling (1) *with rights* and (2) *ex rights*.

e Approximately how much could Jones get for his rights immediately after the stock goes *ex rights*?

f If the date of record for the Scroll Paper Company was Monday, March 15, on what dates would the stock sell (1) *with rights* and (2) *ex rights*?

20

CONVERTIBLES, WARRANTS, AND OPTIONS

After studying this chapter, you should be able to:

● Describe the basic types of convertible securities, their general features, the key motives for using them, and other considerations.

● Demonstrate the procedures for determining the straight bond value, conversion (or stock) value, and market value of a convertible bond.

● Explain the basic characteristics of stock-purchase warrants and compare them with convertibles and rights.

● Calculate the theoretical value of a warrant and use its market value to determine the warrant premium.

● Define options and discuss the basics of calls and puts, options markets, options trading, and the role of call and put options in managerial finance.

Chapters 18 and 19 have presented the various methods of raising long-term financing externally—term loans, bonds, leasing, preferred stock, and common stock. In addition, three vehicles—the conversion feature, stock-purchase warrants, and options—are available for use by the firm in its long-term financing activities.

The *conversion feature*, which can be part of either a bond or preferred stock, permits the firm's capital structure to be changed without increasing the total financing. *Stock-purchase warrants* can be attached to either a long-term loan or a bond. These permit the firm to raise additional funds at some point in the future by selling common stock, thereby shifting the company's capital structure to a less highly levered position. *Options* are a special type of security that provide the holder with the right to purchase or sell specified assets at a stated price on or before a set expiration date. Here we focus on the characteristics and role in long-term financing of convertibles, warrants, and options.

CHARACTERISTICS OF CONVERTIBLE SECURITIES

conversion feature An option included as part of a bond or a preferred stock issue permitting its holder to convert the security into a specified number of shares of common stock.

A **conversion feature** is an option included as part of a bond or a preferred stock issue that permits the holder to convert the security into a specified number of shares of common stock. The conversion feature typically enhances the marketability of an issue.

Types of Convertible Securities

Corporate bonds or preferred stocks may be convertible into common stock. The most common type of convertible security is the bond. Convertibles normally have an accompanying *call feature*. This feature permits the issuer to retire or encourage conversion of outstanding convertibles when appropriate.

convertible bond A bond that at some future time can be converted into a specified number of shares of common stock.

straight bonds Bonds that are nonconvertible, having no conversion feature.

CONVERTIBLE BONDS   A **convertible bond** is a bond that at some future time can be converted into a specified number of shares of common stock. It is almost always a *debenture*—an unsecured bond—with a call feature. Because the conversion feature provides the purchaser of a convertible bond with the possibility of becoming a stockholder on favorable terms, convertible bonds are generally a less expensive form of financing than similar-risk nonconvertible or **straight bonds.** The conversion feature adds a degree of speculation to a bond issue, although the issue still maintains its value as a bond. Convertible bonds are normally convertible only for a specified period of years.

convertible preferred stock Preferred stock that at some future time can be converted into a specified number of shares of common stock.

CONVERTIBLE PREFERRED STOCK   **Convertible preferred stock** can normally be sold with a lower stated dividend than a similar-risk nonconvertible or **straight preferred stock.** This is because the convertible preferred holder is assured of the fixed dividend payment associated with a preferred stock and also may receive the appreciation resulting from increases in the market price of the underlying common stock. Convertible preferred stocks are usually convertible over an unlimited time horizon. Although convertible preferred stock behaves in a fashion similar to convertible bonds, the following discussions will concentrate on the more popular convertible bonds.

straight preferred stock
Preferred stock that is nonconvertible, having no conversion feature.

General Features of Convertibles

The general features of convertible securities include the conversion ratio, the conversion period, and the conversion (or stock) value.

CONVERSION RATIO The **conversion ratio** is the ratio at which a convertible security can be exchanged for common stock. The conversion ratio can be stated in two ways.

conversion ratio The ratio at which a convertible security can be exchanged for common stock.

1. Sometimes the conversion ratio is stated by indicating that the security is convertible into a given number of shares of common stock. In this situation the conversion ratio is *given*. To find the **conversion price,** which is the per-share price effectively paid for common stock as the result of conversion, the par value (not the market value) of the convertible security must be divided by the conversion ratio.

conversion price The per-share price effectively paid for common stock as the result of conversion of a convertible security.

EXAMPLE

International Widget Company has outstanding a bond with a $1,000 par value and convertible into 25 shares of common stock. The bond's conversion ratio is 25. The conversion price for the bond is $40 per share ($1,000 ÷ 25). ▪

2. Sometimes, instead of the conversion ratio, the conversion price is given. The conversion ratio can be obtained by dividing the par value of the convertible by the conversion price.

EXAMPLE

The Ginsberg Company has outstanding a convertible 20-year bond with a par value of $1,000. The bond is convertible at $50 per share into common stock. The conversion ratio is 20 ($1,000 ÷ $50). ▪

The issuer of a convertible security normally establishes a conversion ratio or conversion price that sets the conversion price per share at the time of issuance above the current market price of the firm's stock. If the prospective purchasers do not expect conversion ever to be feasible, they will purchase a straight security or some other convertible issue. A predictable chance of conversion must be provided for in order to enhance the marketability of a convertible security.

CONVERSION PERIOD   Convertible securities are often convertible only within or after a certain period of time. Sometimes conversion is not permitted until two to five years have passed. In other instances conversion is permitted only for a limited number of years, say for five or ten years after issuance of the convertible. Other issues are convertible at any time during the life of the security.

conversion (or stock) value The value of the convertible security measured in terms of the market price of the common stock into which it can be converted.

CONVERSION (OR STOCK) VALUE   The **conversion (or stock) value** is the value of the convertible measured in terms of the market price of the common stock into which it can be converted. The conversion value can be found simply by multiplying the conversion ratio by the current market price of the firm's common stock.

> ### EXAMPLE
>
> The Sperling Electronics Company has outstanding a $1,000 bond that is convertible into common stock at $62.50 a share. The conversion ratio is therefore 16 ($1,000 ÷ $62.50). Since the current market price of the common stock is $65 per share, the conversion value is $1,040 (16 × $65). Since the conversion value is above the bond value of $1,000, conversion is a viable option for the owner of the convertible security. ∎

Motives for Convertible Financing

Using convertible securities to raise long-term funds can help the firm achieve its capital structure (see Chapter 16) and cost of capital (see Chapter 13) goals. Specifically, convertibles can be used as a form of deferred common stock financing, as a "sweetener" for financing, and for raising temporarily cheap funds.

DEFERRED COMMON STOCK FINANCING   The use of convertible securities provides for future common stock financing. When a convertible security is issued, both issuer and purchaser expect the security to be converted into common stock at some point in the future. If the purchaser did not have this expectation, he or she would not accept the lower interest rate normally associated with convertible issues. Since the convertible security is initially sold with a conversion price above the current market price of the firm's stock, conversion is initially not feasible.

The issuer of a convertible could sell common stock instead, but it could be issued only at or below its current market price. By selling the convertible, the issuer in effect makes a *deferred sale* of common stock. As the market price of the firm's common stock rises to a higher level, conversion may occur. By deferring the issuance of new common stock until the market price of the stock has increased, the firm is able to decrease the dilution of both ownership and earnings. The earnings benefit of using convertible securities as a form of deferred common stock financing can be illustrated by the following example.

EXAMPLE

The Mitton Manufacturing Company needs $1 million of new long-term financing. The firm is considering the sale of common stock or a convertible bond. The current market price of the common stock is $20 per share. To sell the new issue, the stock would have to be underpriced by $1 and sold for $19 per share. This means that approximately 52,632 shares ($1,000,000 ÷ $19 per share) would have to be sold. The alternative would be to issue 30-year, 12 percent, $1,000 par-value convertible bonds. The conversion price would be set at $25 per share, and the bond could be sold at par (for $1,000). Thus 1,000 bonds ($1,000,000 ÷ $1,000 per bond) would have to be sold. The firm currently has outstanding 200,000 shares of common stock. Most recently the earnings available for common stock were $500,000 or $2.50 per share ($500,000 ÷ 200,000 shares).

If we assume that the earnings available for common stock will remain at the $500,000 level, the dilution benefit of using a convertible security to defer common stock financing can easily be illustrated. The earnings per share with both common stock financing and a convertible bond are given in the following table.

Financing alternative	Number of shares outstanding	Earnings per share
Common stock	252,632	$1.98
Convertible bond		
Before conversion	200,000	$2.50[a]
After conversion[b]	240,000	$2.08

[a] To simplify this example, the additional interest expense on the convertible bond has been ignored.

[b] Assuming that all bonds are converted.

AN AESTHETICALLY APPEALING DEBENTURE

A brawny man on a couch is flanked by a blonde in a flimsy nightgown and a brunette in a blue slip and black leather jacket.

Sound like the cover of a bad detective novel? Actually, it's a debenture.

Most debentures are bland, paper documents on which companies promise to repay investors. This one is a 4-by-5-foot oil painting in aqua, magenta and gold leaf.

It's a $10,000 debenture of Minsky Finances Inc., a newly formed company in the New York City borough of Queens that plans to buy and sell art. The painting is due in 1994 and yields 10% interest — well below the current rate [March 1984] of about 12.4% on 10-year U.S. Treasury notes.

Richard Minsky, a 37-year-old artist, hit on the idea of a series of oil-painted debentures as a way to raise $2 million over the next few years. "A lot of people would want to hang this type of financial instrument on their walls," he says. "It's museum quality."

Painted above the trio on the couch on the first debenture — which is still drying — is the name of the company in gold leaf. Below the couch are the words "Love Me Tender" in white. Bordering the canvas are 10 smaller scenes of couples swimming, dancing and wrestling.

To receive the $1,000 interest each year, the investor must clip one of the smaller scenes and send it to Mr. Minsky. Of course, this would create a series of holes. "The investor may find that the painting is more likely to appreciate in value if he doesn't redeem the coupons," Mr. Minsky says.

When the painting "matures" in 10 years, he says, Minsky Finances will buy it back for $10,000. Or the investor could try to sell it to someone else for a higher price.

Next in the series will be a more abstract debenture with swirls of red, white and blue. Then Mr. Minsky plans to offer a convertible debenture, featuring a gold Cadillac Eldorado convertible and convertible into Minsky Finances common shares.

Source: Kathleen A. Hughes "New Company Issues a Debenture That's Secured by a Picture Frame," *The Wall Street Journal*, March 26, 1984, p. 27. Reprinted by permission of *The Wall Street Journal*. © Dow Jones & Company Inc. 1984. All rights reserved.

After conversion of the convertible bond, 40,000 additional shares of common stock are outstanding. The use of the convertible bond has not only resulted in a smaller dilution of earnings per share ($2.08 per share versus $1.98 per share) but also in a smaller number of shares outstanding (240,000 versus 252,632), thereby preserving the voting control of the owners. ■

A "SWEETENER" FOR FINANCING   The conversion feature often makes a bond issue more attractive to the purchaser. The convertible bond-holder is given an opportunity both to become a common stockholder and to share in the potential growth of the firm. Since the purchaser of the convertible is given the opportunity to share in the firm's future success, *convertibles can normally be sold with lower interest rates than nonconvertibles*. Therefore, from the firm's viewpoint, including a conversion feature reduces the effective interest cost of debt. The purchaser of the issue sacrifices a portion of his or her interest return for the potential opportunity to become a common stockholder in the future.

RAISING TEMPORARILY CHEAP FUNDS   The discussion of the cost of capital in Chapter 13 indicated that the cost of debt is less than the cost of common stock. By using convertible bonds, the firm can temporarily raise cheap funds to finance projects. Once such projects are on line, the firm may wish to shift its capital structure to a less highly levered position. A conversion feature gives the issuer the opportunity, through actions of convertible holders, to shift its capital structure at a future point in time.

Other Considerations

Two other considerations with respect to convertible security issues require discussion — forcing conversion and overhanging issues.

FORCING CONVERSION   When the price of the firm's common stock rises above the conversion price, the market price of the convertible security will normally rise to a level close to its conversion value. When this happens, many convertible holders will not convert since they already have the market price benefit obtainable from conversion and can still receive fixed periodic interest payments. Because of this behavior, virtually all convertible securities have a call feature that enables the issuer to encourage or "force" conversion. The call price of the security generally exceeds the security's par value by an amount equal to one year's stated interest on the security. Although the issuer must pay a premium for calling a security, the call privilege is generally not exercised until the conversion value of the security is 10 to 15 percent *above the call price*. This type of premium above the call price helps to assure the issuer that when the call is made, the holders of the convertible will convert it instead of accepting the call price.

EXAMPLE

The Armstead Company currently has outstanding a 12 percent, $1,000 convertible bond. The bond is convertible into 50 shares of common stock at a conversion price of $20 per share ($1,000 ÷ 50 shares) and callable at $1,120. Since the bond is convertible into 50 shares of common stock, calling it would be equivalent to paying each bondholder $22.40 per share ($1120 ÷ 50 shares). If the firm issues the call when the stock is selling for $24 per share, a convertible bondholder is likely to take the $1,120 instead of converting the bond even though he or she realizes only $22.40 per share instead of $24. This is because the holder recognizes that the stock price is likely to drop as soon as the conversion occurs. Also, if the holder wishes to sell the stock after conversion, he or she will have to pay brokerage fees and taxes on the transaction.

If the Armstead Company waited until the market price exceeded the call price by 10 to 15 percent—if, say, the call was made when the market price of the stock reached $25—most of the convertible holders would probably convert the bond. The market price of $25 per share would be approximately 11.6 percent above the call price per share of $22.40—high enough to cover any movements in the stock price or brokerage fees and taxes associated with conversion. At least 30 days' advance notice is normally given prior to a call. ■

OVERHANGING ISSUES   There are instances when the market price of a security does not reach a level sufficient to stimulate the conversion of associated convertibles. A convertible security that cannot be forced into conversion using the call feature is an **overhanging issue.** An overhanging issue can be quite detrimental to a firm. If the firm were to call the issue, the bondholders would accept the call price rather than convert the bonds and effectively pay an excessive price for the stock. In this case the firm would not only have to pay the call premium, but it would require additional financing to pay for the call itself. If the firm raised these funds through the sale of equity, a large number of shares would have to be issued due to their low market price. This, in turn, could result in the dilution of existing ownership. Another source of financing the call would be the use of debt or preferred stock, but this would leave the firm's capital structure no less levered than prior to the call. An example can be used to demonstrate the problems associated with an overhanging issue.

overhanging issue A convertible security that cannot be forced into conversion using the call feature.

EXAMPLE

The Armstead Company's 12 percent, $1,000 convertible bond described in the preceding example is convertible into 50 shares of common stock at a conversion price of $20 per share, and callable at $1,120. At the $1,120 call price, calling the bonds would be equivalent to paying each bondholder $22.40 per share ($1,120 ÷ 50 shares). If the common stock were selling for less than this amount, say at $21 per share, and the firm wished to force conversion, such an action would be impossible. Calling the bond would *not* force conversion since the bondholders would accept the $1,120 call price rather than the 50 shares of common stock which would be worth only $1,050 ($21/share × 50 shares). Furthermore, the firm would have to finance the call by selling common stock, additional bonds, or preferred stock. Clearly, this convertible bond is an overhanging issue since the firm cannot force its bondholders to convert to common stock. ▪

DETERMINING THE VALUE OF A CONVERTIBLE BOND

The key characteristic of convertible securities that greatly enhances their marketability is their ability to minimize the possibility of a loss while providing a possibility of capital gains. This section discusses the three values of a convertible bond: (1) the straight bond value, (2) the conversion (or stock) value, and (3) the market value.

Straight Bond Value

The **straight bond value** of a convertible bond is the price at which it would sell in the market without the conversion feature. This value is found by determining the value of a nonconvertible bond with similar payments issued by a firm having the same risk. The straight bond value is typically the *floor*, or minimum, price at which the convertible bond would be traded. The straight bond value equals the present value of the bond's interest and principal payments discounted at the interest rate the firm would have to pay on a nonconvertible bond.

straight bond value The price at which a convertible bond would sell in the market without the conversion feature.

EXAMPLE

The Rich Company has just sold a $1,000, 20-year convertible bond with a 12 percent stated interest rate. The bond interest will be paid at the end of each year, and the principal will be repaid at maturity.[1] A straight bond could have been sold with a 14 percent stated interest rate, but the conversion feature compensates for the lower rate on the convertible. The straight bond value of the convertible is calculated as shown in the table at the top of page 640.

---

[1] Consistent with Chapter 12, we continue to assume the payment of annual rather than semiannual bond interest. This assumption simplifies the calculations involved while maintaining the conceptual accuracy of the procedures presented.

Year(s)	Payments (1)	Present-value interest factor at 14 percent (2)	Present value [(1) × (2)] (3)
1–20	$ 120[a]	6.623[b]	$794.76
20	1,000	.073[c]	73.00
		Straight bond value	$867.76

[a] $1,000 at 12% = $120 interest per year.

[b] Present-value interest factor for an annuity, *PVIFA*, discounted at 14% for 20 years, from Table D-4.

[c] Present-value interest factor for $1, *PVIF*, discounted at 14% for year 20, from Table D-3.

This value, $867.76, is the minimum price at which the convertible bond is expected to sell. Generally, only in certain instances where the stock's market price is below the conversion price will the bond be expected to sell at this level. ■

Conversion (or Stock) Value

The *conversion (or stock) value* of a convertible security has been defined earlier as the value of the convertible measured in terms of the market price of the common stock into which the security can be converted. When the market price of the common stock exceeds the conversion price, the conversion (or stock) value exceeds the par value. An example will clarify the point.

EXAMPLE

The Rich Company's convertible bond described earlier is convertible at $50 per share. This means each bond can be converted into 20 shares, since each bond has a $1,000 par value. The conversion values of the bond when the stock is selling at $30, $40, $50, $60, $70, and $80 per share are shown in the following table.

Market price of stock	Conversion value
$30	$ 600
40	800
50 (conversion price)	1,000 (par value)
60	1,200
70	1,400
80	1,600

It can be seen that when the market price of the common stock exceeds the $50 conversion price, the conversion value exceeds the $1,000 par value. Since the straight bond value (calculated in the preceding example) is $867.76, the bond will, in a stable environment, never sell for less than this amount, regardless of how low its conversion value is. If the market price per share were $30, the bond would still sell for $867.76 — not $600 — because its value as a bond would dominate. ■

Market Value

The market value of a convertible is likely to be greater than its straight value or its conversion value. The amount by which the market value exceeds its straight or conversion value is often called the **market premium.** The closer the straight value is to the conversion value, the larger the market premium. The premium is attributed to the convertible security purchaser's expectations relative to future stock price movements. The general relationship of the straight bond value, conversion value, market value, and market premium for the Rich Company's convertible bond is shown in Figure 20.1. The straight bond value acts as a floor for the security's value up to the point **X**, where the share price is high enough to cause the conversion value to exceed the straight bond value. The market value of the convertible often exceeds both its straight and conversion values, thus resulting in a market premium.

market premium The amount by which the market value exceeds the straight or conversion value of a convertible security.

CHARACTERISTICS OF STOCK-PURCHASE WARRANTS

Stock-purchase warrants are quite similar to stock rights, which were described in detail in Chapter 19. A **stock-purchase warrant** gives the holder an option to purchase a certain number of shares of common stock at a specified price over a certain period of time. Warrants also bear some similarity to convertibles in that they provide for the injection of additional equity capital into the firm at some future date. Some of the basic characteristics of stock-purchase warrants are discussed here.

stock-purchase warrant An instrument that gives its holder an option to purchase a certain number of shares of common stock at a specified price over a certain period of time.

Warrants as "Sweeteners"

Warrants are often attached to debt issues as "sweeteners," or added benefits. When a firm makes a large issue of debt, the attachment of stock-purchase warrants may add to the marketability of the issue while

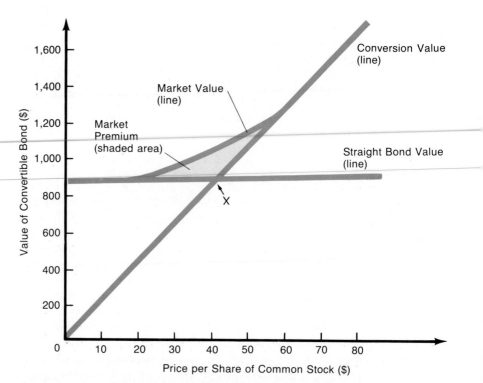

FIGURE 20.1 The Values and Market Premium for the Rich Company's Convertible Bond
The $867.76 straight value of Rich Company's convertible bond acts as a floor for its value up to point X where the stock price is high enough to cause the conversion value to exceed the straight bond value. The market value of the convertible exceeds these values creating a market premium.

lowering the required interest rate. As sweeteners, warrants are similar to conversion features. Often, when a new firm is raising its initial capital, suppliers of debt will require warrants to permit them to share in whatever success the firm achieves.

Exercise Prices

exercise price (option price) The price at which holders of warrants can purchase a specified number of shares of common stock.

The price at which holders of warrants can purchase a specified number of shares of common stock is normally referred to as the **exercise price** or **option price**. This price is normally set at 10 to 20 percent above the market price of the firm's stock at the time of issuance. Until the market price of the stock exceeds the exercise price, holders of warrants would not be advised to exercise them, since they could purchase the stock more cheaply in the marketplace.

Life of a Warrant

Warrants normally have a life of no more than 10 years, although some have infinite lives. While unlike convertible securities, warrants cannot be called, their limited life stimulates holders to exercise them when the exercise price is below the market price of the firm's stock.

Warrant Trading

A warrant is usually *detachable,* which means that the bondholder may sell the warrant without selling the security to which it is attached. Many detachable warrants are listed and actively traded on organized securities exchanges and on the over-the-counter exchange. The majority of actively traded warrants are listed on the American Stock Exchange. Warrants, as demonstrated in a later section, often provide investors with better opportunities for gain (with increased risk) than the underlying common stock.

Comparison of Warrants and Convertibles

The exercise of a warrant shifts the firm's capital structure to a less highly levered position because new common stock is issued without any change in debt. If a convertible bond were converted, the reduction in leverage would be even more pronounced, since common stock would be issued in exchange for a reduction in debt. In addition, the exercise of a warrant provides an influx of new capital; with convertibles the new capital is raised when the securities are originally issued rather than when converted. The influx of new equity capital resulting from the exercise of a warrant does not occur until the firm has achieved a certain degree of success that is reflected in an increased price for its stock. In this instance, the firm conveniently obtains needed funds.

Comparison of Warrants and Rights

The similarity between a warrant and a right should be clear. Both result in new equity capital, although the warrant provides for *deferred* equity financing. The life of a right is typically not more than a few months; a warrant is generally exercisable for a period of years. Rights are issued at a subscription price below the prevailing market price of the stock, while warrants are generally issued at an exercise price 10 to 20 percent above the prevailing market price.

WARRANTS AS DIVIDENDS . . . WHAT NEXT?

How does a penny-pinching public company raise a new dose of equity without paying all those fees to underwriters and attorneys? Calumet Industries Inc., a $55-million maker of specialty lubricating oils, tackled this question last winter [1984] and thinks it has found an intriguing method. . . .

President and chief executive officer Peter Salvino investigated the possibility of doing a $2-million or $3-million equity offering, but to him the costs of a small public offering seemed staggering; together, the underwriters and attorneys would claim about 8¢ for every new dollar raised (about $160,000 on $2 million). On the other hand, there was no getting around the fact that Calumet needed to attract money. So Salvino began searching for alternatives.

Early in 1984, Salvino conjured up an idea for, in effect, killing two birds with one stone. He suggested that Calumet raise the new equity capital directly from its existing shareholders. The investors had been without dividends since the end of 1981. Why couldn't the company design an attractive offer just for them — something to reward the shareholders for standing by Calumet during tough times but, at the same time, encourage them to buy *new* shares?

Salvino asked the company's law firm to explore the technicalities of declaring a special type of dividend — one consisting not of cash but of a warrant to purchase new stock at a favorable price. Much to Salvino's surprise, the attorneys were unable to locate any company that had successfully raised capital in this way. At the same time, although unconventional, the technique seemed perfectly legal as far as Securities and Exchange Commission regulations were concerned. If it worked, it would be tens of thousands of dollars cheaper than selling a secondary stock offering through an investment bank.

Last spring [1984], Calumet decided to give it a try. The company prepared an eight-page prospectus and mailed it to shareholders. For every five shares owned, a shareholder received a warrant to buy one share at the discounted price. Shareholders have [had] until May 1, 1985, to purchase a total of 332,693 new shares. When and if all of the warrants are converted, Calumet stands to raise a bit more than $2 million, even after printing and legal expenses of about $35,000.

Last December [1984], with the stock trading at $7.75 per share on the over-the-counter market, Calumet's financing strategy seemed to be on track. . . .

THE VALUE OF WARRANTS

Like a convertible security, a warrant has both a theoretical and a market value. The difference between these values, or the **warrant premium,** depends largely on investor expectations and the ability of the investors to get more leverage from the warrants than from the underlying stock.

warrant premium The difference between the actual and theoretical market value of a warrant.

Theoretical Value of a Warrant

The *theoretical value* of a stock-purchase warrant is the amount one would expect the warrant to sell for in the marketplace. Equation 20.1 gives the theoretical value of a warrant:

$$TVW = (P_o - E) \times N \qquad (20.1)$$

where

TVW = theoretical value of a warrant
P_o = current market price of a share of common stock
E = exercise price of the warrant
N = number of shares of common stock obtainable with one warrant

The use of Equation 20.1 can be illustrated by the following example.

EXAMPLE

The Sassy Car Company has outstanding warrants that are exercisable at $40 per share and entitle holders to purchase three shares of common stock. The warrants were initially attached to a bond issue to sweeten the bond. The common stock of the firm is currently selling for $45 per share. Substituting $P_o = \$45$, $E = \$40$, and $N = 3$ into Equation 20.1 yields a theoretical warrant value of $15 [(\$45 - \$40) \times 3]$. Therefore, Sassy's warrants should sell for $15 in the marketplace. ■

Market Value of a Warrant

The market value of a stock-purchase warrant is generally above the theoretical value of the warrant. Only when the theoretical value of the warrant is very high are the market and theoretical values close. The general relationship between the theoretical and market values of the Sassy Car Company's warrants is presented graphically in Figure 20.2. The market value of the warrants generally exceeds the theoretical value by the greatest amount when the stock's market price is close to the warrant exercise price per share.

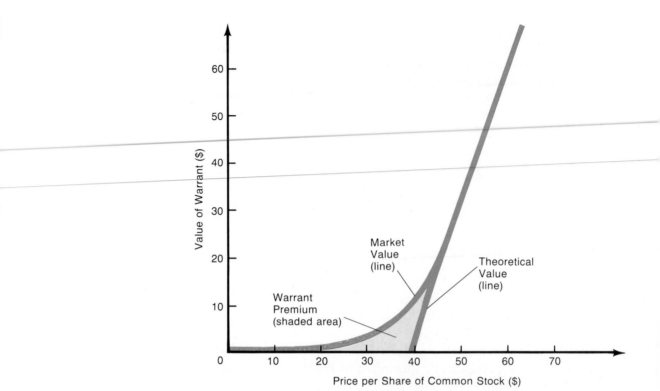

FIGURE 20.2 The Values and Warrant Premium for the Sassy Car Company's Stock-Purchase Warrants

The theoretical value of Sassy Car Company's warrants is zero when the market price of the common stock is below the $40 exercise price, and greater than zero beyond that point. The market value of the warrant exceeds the theoretical value creating a warrant premium.

Warrant Premium

The *warrant premium,* or amount by which the market value of the Sassy Car Company's warrants exceeds the theoretical value of these warrants, is also shown in Figure 20.2. This premium results from a combination of investor expectations and the ability of the investor with a fixed sum to invest to obtain much larger potential returns (and risk) by trading in warrants rather than the underlying stock. An example will clarify the effect of expectations of stock price movements on warrant market values.

EXAMPLE

John Investor has $2,430 he is interested in investing in the Sassy Car Company. Sassy's stock is currently selling for $45 per share, and its warrants are selling for $18 per warrant. Each warrant entitles the holder to purchase three shares of Sassy's common stock at $40 per share. Since Sassy's stock is selling for $45 per share, the theoretical warrant value, calculated in the preceding example using Equation 20.1, is $15 [($45 − $40) × 3].

The warrant premium is believed to result from investor expectations and leverage opportunities. John Investor could spend his $2430 in either of two ways. Ignoring brokerage fees, he could purchase 54 shares of common stock at $45 per share or 135 warrants at $18 per warrant. If Mr. Investor purchases the stock, its price rises to $48, and if he then sells the stock, he will gain $162 ($3 per share × 54 shares). If instead of purchasing the stock he purchases the 135 warrants and the stock price increases by $3 per share, Mr. Investor will make approximately $1,215. Since the price of a share of stock rises by $3, the price of each warrant can be expected to rise by $9, since each warrant can be used to purchase three shares of common stock. A gain of $9 per warrant on 135 warrants means a total gain of $1,215 on the warrants. ■

The greater leverage associated with trading warrants should be clear from the preceding example. Of course, since leverage works both ways it results in greater risk. If the market price fell by $3, the loss on the stock would be $162, while the loss on the warrants would be close to $1,215. Clearly, the use of warrants by investors is more risky.

OPTIONS

In the most general sense, an **option** can be viewed as an instrument that provides its holder with an opportunity to purchase or sell a specified asset at a stated price on or before a set *expiration date*. Today the interest in options centers on options on common stock. The development of organized options exchanges has created markets in which to trade these options, which themselves are securities. Three basic forms of options are rights, warrants, and calls and puts. Rights were discussed in Chapter 19, and warrants have been described in the preceding section.

Calls and Puts

The two most common types of options are calls and puts. A **call option** is an option to *purchase* a specified number of shares (typically 100) of a stock on or before some future date at a stated price. Call options usually have initial lives of one to nine months, occasionally one year. The **striking price** is the price at which the holder of the option can buy

option An instrument that provides its holder with an opportunity to purchase or sell a specified asset at a stated price on or before a set *expiration date*.

call option An option to *purchase* a specified number of shares (typically 100) of a stock on or before some future date at a stated price.

striking price The price at which the holder of a call option can purchase (or holder of a put option can sell) a specified amount of stock at any time prior to the option's expiration date.

the stock at any time prior to the option's expiration date; it is generally set at or near the prevailing market price of the stock at the time the option is issued. For example, if the stock of Altex Corporation is currently selling for $50 per share, a call option on the stock initiated today would likely have a striking price set at $50 per share. To purchase a call option, a specified price of normally a few hundred dollars must be paid.

put option An option to *sell* a given number of shares (typically 100) of stock on or before a specified future date at a stated striking price.

A **put option** is an option to *sell* a given number of shares (typically 100) of stock on or before a specified future date at a stated striking price. Like the call option, the striking price of the put is close to the market price of the underlying stock at the time of issuance. The lives and costs of puts are similar to those of calls.

How the Options Markets Work

There are two ways of making options transactions. The first involves making a transaction through one of 20 or so call and put options dealers with the help of a stockbroker. The other, more popular mechanism is the organized options exchanges. The main exchanges are the *Chicago Board Options Exchange (CBOE)* and the *American Stock Exchange (AMEX)*. Both exchanges now provide organized marketplaces in which purchases and sales of both call and put options can be made in an orderly fashion. The options traded on the options exchanges are standardized and are considered registered securities. Each option is for 100 shares of the underlying stock. The price at which options transactions can be made is determined by the forces of supply and demand.

Logic of Options Trading

The most common motive for purchasing call options is the expectation that the market price of the underlying stock will rise by more than enough to cover the cost of the option and thereby allow the purchaser of the call to profit.

EXAMPLE

Assume that Sam Peters pays $250 for a three-month *call option* on Altex Corporation at a striking price of $50. This means that by paying $250 Sam is guaranteed that he can purchase 100 shares of Altex at $50 per share at any time during the next three months. Ignoring any brokerage fees or dividends, the stock price must climb $2.50 per share ($250 ÷ 100 shares) to $52.50 per share to cover the cost of the option. If the stock price were to rise to $60 per share during the period, Sam's net profit would be $750 [(100 shares × \$60/share) − (100 shares × \$50/share) − \$250]. Since this return would be earned on a \$250 investment, it illustrates the high potential return on investment that options offer. Of course, had the stock price not risen above \$50 per share, Sam would have lost the \$250 since there would have been no reason to exercise the option. Had the stock price risen to between \$50 and \$52.50 per share, Sam probably would have exercised the option in order to reduce his loss to an amount less than \$250. ■

Put options are purchased in the expectation that the share price of a given security will decline over the life of the option. Purchasers of puts commonly own the shares and wish to protect a gain they have realized since their initial purchase. By buying a put, they lock in the gain because it enables them to sell their shares at a known price during the life of the option. Investors gain from put options when the price of the underlying stock declines by more than the per-share cost of the option. The logic underlying the purchase of a put is exactly the opposite of that underlying the use of call options.

Role of Call and Put Options in Managerial Finance

Although call and put options are an extremely popular investment vehicle, they play *no* direct role in the fund-raising activities of the financial manager. These options are issued by investors, not businesses. *They are not a source of financing to the firm.* Corporate pension managers, whose job it is to invest and manage corporate pension funds, may use call and put options as part of their investment activities to earn a return or to protect or lock in returns already earned on securities. The presence of options trading in the firm's stock could — by increasing trading activity — stabilize the firm's share price in the marketplace, but the financial manager has no direct control over this. Buyers of options do not have any say in the firm's management or any voting rights; only stockholders are given these privileges. Despite the popularity of call and put options as an investment vehicle, the financial manager has very little need to deal with them, especially as part of fund-raising activities.

SUMMARY

- Corporate bonds or preferred stocks may both be convertible into common stock. Most convertibles have a call feature. The conversion ratio indicates the number of shares a convertible can be exchanged for and determines the conversion price. A conversion privilege may have a limited life.
- The key motives for the use of convertibles are to obtain deferred common

stock financing, to "sweeten" bond issues, and to raise temporarily cheap funds.

● When conversion becomes attractive the firm may use the call feature to encourage or "force" conversion. When conversion cannot be forced, the firm has an "overhanging issue."

● Typically the minimum value at which a convertible bond will trade is its straight (nonconvertible) bond value. The conversion (or stock) value of a convertible is its value measured in terms of the common stock into which it may be converted. The market value of a convertible generally exceeds these values, thereby creating a market premium.

● Stock-purchase warrants are often attached to debt issues to "sweeten" them and lower their interest cost. A warrant provides the holder with the privilege of purchasing a certain number of shares of common stock at the specified exercise price. Warrants generally have limited lives, are detachable, and may be listed and traded on securities exchanges.

● Warrants are similar to convertibles, but exercising them has a less pronounced effect on the firm's leverage and brings in new funds. Warrants are also similar to stock rights, except that the life of a warrant is generally longer than that of a right, and the exercise price of a warrant is initially set above the underlying stock's current market price.

● The market value of a warrant usually exceeds its theoretical value, creating a warrant premium. The premium results from investor expectations and the ability of investors to obtain considerably more leverage (and risk) from trading warrants than from trading the underlying stock.

● An option provides its holder with an opportunity to purchase or sell a specified asset at a stated price on or before a set expiration date. Rights, warrants, and calls and puts are all options. Calls are options to purchase common stock, and puts are options to sell common stock. Call and put options do not play a direct role in the fund-raising activities of the financial manager.

QUESTIONS

20-1 What is the *conversion feature?* What types of securities typically have this feature?

20-2 What is a *conversion ratio?* How is it related to the *conversion price?* How are conversion periods commonly described?

20-3 Briefly describe each of the following motives for using convertible financing:
   a Deferred common stock financing
   b A "sweetener" for financing
   c Raising temporarily cheap funds

20-4 When the market price of the stock rises above the conversion price, why may a convertible security *not* be converted? How can the *call feature* be used to force conversion in this situation? What is an *overhanging issue?*

20-5 What is meant by the *straight bond value* of a convertible security? How is this value calculated, and why is it often viewed as a floor for the convertible's value?

20-6   What is the *conversion (or stock) value* of a convertible security? How can the conversion value be calculated if you know the conversion ratio and the current market price of the firm's stock?

20-7   Describe the general relationship among the straight bond value, conversion value, market value, and market premium associated with a convertible bond.

20-8   What are *stock-purchase warrants?* What are the similarities and key differences between the effects of warrants and convertibles on the firm's capital structure and its ability to raise new capital?

20-9   What are the similarities and key differences between the effects of warrants and rights on the firm's capital structure and its ability to raise new capital?

20-10 What is the general relationship between the theoretical and market values of a warrant? In what circumstances are these values quite close? What is a *warrant premium?*

20-11 What is an *option?* Define the *striking price* of an option. Are rights and warrants options?

20-12 Define *calls* and *puts.* What is the logic of buying a call and buying a put? What role, if any, do call and put options play in the fund-raising activities of the financial manager?

PROBLEMS

20-1   **(Conversion Price)**   Calculate the conversion price for each of the following convertible bonds:

  a A $1,000-par-value bond convertible into 20 shares of common stock.
  b A $500-par-value bond convertible into 25 shares of common stock.
  c A $1,000-par-value bond convertible into 50 shares of common stock.

20-2   **(Conversion Ratio)**   What is the conversion ratio for each of the following bonds?

  a A $1,000-par-value bond convertible into common stock at $43.75 per share.
  b A $1,000-par-value bond convertible into common stock at $25 per share.
  c A $600-par-value bond convertible into common stock at $30 per share.

20-3   **(Conversion (or Stock) Value)**   What is the conversion (or stock) value for each of the following convertible bonds?

  a A $1,000-par-value bond convertible into 25 shares of common stock. The common stock is currently selling at $50 per share.
  b A $1,000-par-value bond convertible into 12.5 shares of common stock. The common stock is currently selling for $42 per share.
  c A $1,000-par-value bond convertible into 100 shares of common stock. The common stock is currently selling for $10.50 per share.

20-4   **(Conversion (or Stock) Value)**   Find the conversion (or stock) value for each of the convertible bonds described in the table at the top of page 652.

Convertible	Conversion ratio	Current market price of stock
A	25	$42.25
B	16	50.00
C	20	44.00
D	5	19.50

20-5 **(Convertibles and *EPS*)** The Chutney Company is considering two alternatives for raising a needed $1 million. The first involves a sale of common stock at $37 per share, underpriced by $3 relative to the current market price of $40. The second alternative would be to sell $1,000-par-value convertible bonds. These carry a 13 percent stated annual interest rate and can be sold at par value. The conversion ratio would be 22. The firm currently has 150,000 shares of common stock outstanding. The earnings available for common stockholders are expected to be $600,000 per year for each of the next several years.

a Determine the number of shares of common stock outstanding and the earnings per share *(EPS)* under the common stock financing alternative.

b Determine the number of shares of common stock outstanding and the earnings per share *(EPS)* associated with the bond *prior to its conversion* under the convertible bond financing alternative. (Ignore bond interest.)

c Determine the number of shares outstanding and the earnings per share *(EPS)* associated with the bond alternative *once all bonds have been converted.*

d Discuss which of the two alternatives, stock or convertible bonds, is preferable in terms of maximizing earnings per share *(EPS)*.

20-6 **(Convertibles and *EPS*)** Chatsworth Ice must decide whether to obtain a needed $2 million of financing by selling common stock at its currently depressed price or selling convertible bonds. The firm's common stock is currently selling for $32 per share; new shares can be sold for $30 per share, an underpricing of $2 per share. The firm currently has 100,000 shares of common stock outstanding. Convertible bonds can be sold for their $1,000 par value and would be convertible at $34. The firm expects its earnings available for common stockholders to be $200,000 each year over the next several years.

a Calculate the earnings per share *(EPS)* of common stock resulting from
(1) The sale of common stock.
(2) The sale of the convertible bonds *prior to conversion.* (Ignore bond interest.)
(3) The sale of convertible bonds *after all bonds have been converted.*

b Which of the two financing alternatives, stock or convertible bonds, would you recommend the company adopt? Why?

20-7 **(Straight Bond Values)** Calculate the straight bond value for each of the bonds described in the table at the top of page 653.

Bond	Par value	Stated interest rate (paid annually)	Stated interest rate on equal-risk straight bond	Years to maturity
A	$1,000	10%	14%	20
B	800	12	15	14
C	1,000	13	16	30
D	1,000	14	17	25

20-8 **(Determining Values—Convertible Bond)** The Western Clock Company has an outstanding issue of convertible bonds with a $1,000 par value. These bonds are convertible into 40 shares of common stock. They have a 12 percent stated annual interest rate and a 20-year maturity. The interest rate on a straight bond of similar risk is currently 15 percent.
a Calculate the straight bond value of the bond.
b Calculate the conversion (or stock) values of the bond when the market prices of the common stock are $20, $25, $28, $35, and $50 per share, respectively.
c For each of the stock prices given in b, at what price would you expect the bond to sell? Why?
d What is the least you would expect the bond to sell for, regardless of the common stock price behavior?

20-9 **(Determining Values—Convertible Bond)** Mrs. Tom's Fish Company has an outstanding issue of 15-year convertible bonds with a $1,000 par value. These bonds are convertible into 80 shares of common stock. They have a 13 percent stated annual interest rate, whereas the interest rate on straight bonds of similar risk is 16 percent.
a Calculate the straight bond value of this bond.
b Calculate the conversion (or stock) values of the bond when the market price is $9, $12, $13, $15, and $20 per share of common stock, respectively.
c For each of the common stock prices given in b, at which price would you expect the bond to sell? Why?
d Graph the conversion value and straight value of the bond for each common stock price given. Plot the per-share common stock prices on the x-axis and the bond values on the y-axis. Use this graph to indicate the minimum market value of the bond associated with each common stock price.

20-10 **(Warrant Values)** Joan's Electronics has warrants that allow the purchase of three shares of its outstanding common stock at $50 per share. The common stock price per share and the market value of the warrant associated with that stock price are summarized in the table at the top of page 654.
a For each of the common stock prices given, calculate the theoretical warrant value.
b Graph on a set of per-share common stock price (x-axis)–warrant value (y-axis) axes the theoretical and market values of the warrant.
c If the warrant value is $12 when the market price of common stock is

Common stock price per share	Market value of warrant
$42	$ 2
46	8
48	9
54	18
58	28
62	38
66	48

$50, does this contradict or support the graph you have constructed? Explain why or why not.

d Specify the area of *warrant premium*. Why does this premium exist?

e If the expiration date of the warrants is quite close, would you expect your graph to look different? Explain.

20-11 **(Common Stock versus Warrants)**   Gayle Graham is evaluating the Ever-On Battery Company's common stock and warrants in order to choose the best investment. The firm's stock is currently selling for $50 per share; its warrants to purchase three shares of common stock at $45 per share are selling for $20. Ignoring transactions costs, Ms. Graham has $8,000 to invest. She is quite optimistic with respect to Ever-On because she has certain "inside information" about the firm's prospects with respect to a large government contract.

a How many shares of stock and how many warrants can Ms. Graham purchase?

b Suppose Ms. Graham purchased the stock, held it one year, then sold it for $60 per share. Ignoring brokerage fees and taxes, what total gain would she realize?

c Suppose Ms. Graham purchased warrants and held them for one year, and the market price of the stock increased to $60 per share. Ignoring brokerage fees and taxes, what would be her total gain if the market value of warrants increased to $45 and she sold out?

d What benefit, if any, would the warrants provide? Are there any differences in the risk of these two alternative investments? Explain.

20-12 **(Common Stock versus Warrants)**   Mark Christian can invest $5,000 in the common stock or the warrants of Kettering Engineering Center, Inc. The common stock is currently selling for $30 per share; its warrants, which provide for the purchase of two shares of common stock at $28 per share, are currently selling for $7. The stock is expected to rise to a market price of $32 within the next year, so the expected theoretical value of a warrant over the next year is $8. The expiration date of the warrant is one year from the present.

a If Mr. Christian purchases the stock, holds it for one year, and then sells it for $32, what is his total gain? (Ignore brokerage fees and taxes.)

b If Mr. Christian purchases the warrant and converts to common stock in one year, what is his total gain if the market price of common shares is actually $32? (Ignore brokerage fees and taxes.)

c Repeat **a** and **b** assuming that the market price of the stock in one year is (1) $30 and (2) $28.

d Discuss the two alternatives and the trade-offs associated with them.

20-13 **(Options Profits and Losses)** For each of the following *100-share options*, use the underlying stock price at expiration and other information to determine the amount of profit or loss an investor would have had, ignoring brokerage fees.

Option	Type of option	Cost of option	Striking price per share	Underlying stock price per share at expiration
A	Call	$200	$50	$55
B	Call	350	42	45
C	Put	500	60	50
D	Put	300	35	40
E	Call	450	28	26

20-14 **(Call Option)** Jack Butler is considering buying 100 shares of Iris, Inc., at $62 per share. Because he has read that the firm will likely soon receive certain large orders from abroad, he expects the price of Iris, Inc., to increase to $70 per share. As an alternative, Jack is considering purchase of a call option for 100 shares of Iris, Inc., at a striking price of $60. The 90-day option will cost $600. Ignore any brokerage fees or dividends.

a What would Jack's profit be on the stock transaction if its price does rise to $70 and he sells?

b How much would Jack earn on the option transaction if the underlying stock price rises to $70?

c How high must the stock price rise in order for Jack to break even on the option transaction?

d Compare, contrast, and discuss the relative profit and risk from the stock and the option transactions.

20-15 **(Put Option)** Charles Vogel, the pension fund manager for Jayson Industries, is considering purchase of a put option in anticipation of a price decline in the stock of Stick, Inc. The option to sell 100 shares of Stick, Inc., at any time during the next 90 days at a striking price of $45 can be purchased for $380. The stock of Stick, Inc., is currently selling for $46 per share.

a Ignoring any brokerage fees or dividends, what profit or loss would Charles make if he buys the option and the lowest price of Stick, Inc. stock during the 90 days is $46, $44, $40, $35, respectively?

b What effect would the fact that the price of Stick, Inc.'s stock slowly rose from its initial $46 level to $55 at the end of 90 days have on Charles's purchase?

c In light of your findings, discuss the potential risks and returns from using put options to attempt to profit from an anticipated decline in share price.

APPENDIXES

Appendix A
INTERNATIONAL PERSPECTIVES

After studying this Appendix, you should be able to:

- Discuss the financial markets, legal forms of business, and tax considerations faced by multinational companies (MNCs) operating in their global environment.

- Identify some of the major features that differentiate domestically oriented financial statements from internationally based reports.

- Describe the international short-term financial decisions related to cash management and short-term sources of financing.

- Understand the impact of both foreign exchange and political risks on MNCs and the means by which multinationals can attempt to lessen these risks.

- Discuss international long-term financial decisions as related to capital budgeting, business combinations, long-term debt, and equity capital.

multinational companies (MNCs) Firms that have substantial assets and operations in foreign markets, and that draw part of their total revenues and profits from such markets.

In recent years, international finance has become an increasingly important element in the management of **multinational companies (MNCs).** These firms, based in the United States, Western Europe, Japan, and elsewhere abroad, have substantial assets and operations in foreign markets and draw part of their total revenues and profits from such markets. The basics of managerial finance presented in this text are applicable to the management not only of domestic companies but of MNCs as well. However, certain factors unique to the international setting tend to complicate the financial management of a multinational company. From the comparison between a U.S. domestic firm (firm A) and a U.S.-based MNC (firm B) in Table A.1, it can be seen that interna-

TABLE A.1 International Factors and Their Influence on MNCs' Operations

Factor	Firm A (Domestic)	Firm B (MNC)
Multinational financial markets	All debt and equity structures based on the domestic financial market	Opportunities and challenges arise from the existence of different financial markets where debt and equity can be issued
Foreign ownership	All assets owned by domestic entities	Portions of equity of foreign investments owned by foreign partners, thus affecting foreign decision making and profits
Multinational accounting	All consolidation of financial statements based on one currency	The existence of different currencies and of specific translation rules influences the consolidation of financial statements into one currency
Foreign exchange risks	All operations in one currency	Fluctuations in foreign exchange markets can affect foreign revenues and profits as well as the overall value of the firm

tional factors related to markets, ownership, accounting, and risk have a significant influence on MNCs' operations. This appendix highlights the major factors of the international environment, financial statements, short-term financial decisions, risk, and long-term financial decisions.

THE MULTINATIONAL COMPANY AND ITS ENVIRONMENT

The MNC's operating environment cuts across national boundaries, thereby creating opportunities and challenges for the financial manager. Accompanying an expanded financial marketplace in which to borrow and invest are a variety of laws, restrictions, and taxes that are significantly different from those affecting a purely domestic firm. Here we take a brief look at international financial markets, legal forms, and taxes.

International Financial Markets

During the last two decades the **Euromarket** has rapidly grown into a major financial forum. This market provides multinational companies with opportunities for borrowing and investing currencies outside their country of origin; and furthermore it provides the additional feature of less financial regulation by domestic governments.

Euromarket The major financial forum that provides multinational companies with opportunities for borrowing and investing currencies outside their country of origin; it provides the added feature of less financial regulation by domestic governments.

GROWTH OF THE EUROMARKET Several reasons can be offered as to why the Euromarket has grown to such a magnitude. First, beginning in the early 1960s, the USSR wanted to maintain its dollar earnings outside the legal jurisdiction of the United States, mainly due to the Cold War. Second, consistently large U.S. balance-of-payments deficits helped "scatter" dollars around the world. Third, the existence of specific regulations and controls on dollar deposits in the United States, including interest-rate ceilings imposed by the government, helped send such deposits outside the United States.

Certain cities around the world—so-called **offshore centers**—have achieved prominence and are considered pivotal points of Euromarket business. (These include London, Singapore, Bahrain, Nassau, Hong Kong, and Luxembourg.) The availability of communication and transportation facilities, along with the importance of language, costs, time zones, taxes, and local banking regulations, are among the main reasons for the importance of these centers.

offshore centers Certain cities around the world (including London, Singapore, Bahrain, Nassau, Hong Kong, and Luxembourg) that are considered pivotal points of Euromarket business.

MAJOR PARTICIPANTS The Euromarket is dominated by the dollar, and major American banks have been among the most important participants in this market. In recent years, however, powerful banks in Europe, Japan, and Canada have increased their participation. From 1977 to 1980, for instance, U.S. bank lending to foreign countries grew at an annual rate of 13.4 percent, while non-U.S. bank lending abroad grew at a rate of 32.7 percent.

Since the oil embargo of 1973, massive amounts of dollars have been placed in short-term Euromarket bank deposits. Eurobanks, in turn, have been lending to various groups of borrowers, led in recent years by the less-developed countries. Although developing countries are now major borrowers, the industrialized nations also continue to borrow actively in international markets. Included in the latter group's borrowing are the funds obtained by multinational companies. In addition, MNCs use the Euromarket for investing excess cash. (Further details on MNCs' Euromarket activities are given below.)

Legal Forms of Business

In many countries outside the U.S., operating a foreign business as a subsidiary or affiliate can take two forms, both of which are similar to the U.S. corporation. In German-speaking nations, the two forms are the *Aktiengesellschaft* (A.G.) and the *Gesellschaft mit beschrankter Haftung* (GmbH). In many countries the similar forms are the *Société Anonyme* (S.A.) and the *Société Responsibilité Limitée* (S.A.R.L.). The A.G. and the S.A. are the most common form, but the GmbH and the S.A.R.L. offer much greater freedom and require fewer formalities for formation and operation.

While establishing a business in a form like the S.A. can involve most of the provisions governing a U.S.-based corporation, in order to operate in many foreign countries—especially in most of the less-developed nations—it is often essential for the MNC to enter into joint-venture business agreements with private investors or with government-based agencies of the host country. A **joint venture** is a partnership under which the participants have contractually agreed to contribute specified amounts of money and expertise in exchange for stated proportions of ownership and profit. The governments of numerous countries, such as Brazil, Colombia, Mexico, and Venezuela in Latin America, and Indonesia, Malaysia, the Philippines, and Thailand in Southeast Asia, have in recent years instituted new laws and regulations governing MNCs. The basic rule introduced by most of these nations requires that majority ownership (i.e., at least 51 percent of the total equity) of MNCs' joint-venture projects be held by domestically based investors.

The existence of joint-venture laws and restrictions has certain implications for the operation of foreign-based subsidiaries. First, majority foreign ownership may result in a substantial degree of management and control by host-country participants, which in turn can influence

joint venture A partnership between a multinational company and a foreign investor (private or government) in which contractually specified amounts of money and expertise are contributed by the participants for stated proportions of ownership and profit.

day-to-day operations in a manner detrimental to the managerial policies and procedures normally pursued by the MNC. Next, foreign ownership may result in disagreements among the partners as to the exact distribution of profits and the portion to be allocated for reinvestment. Moreover, the governments of a number of countries, including Argentina, Brazil, Nigeria, and Thailand, among others, have in the past imposed ceilings not only on the return of invested funds to MNCs but also on profit remittances by these firms back to the parent companies. From a "positive" point of view, however, it can be argued that to operate in many currently less-developed countries, it is beneficial for MNCs to enter into joint-venture agreements, given the potential risks stemming from political instability in the host countries. (This issue will be addressed later in this Appendix.)

International Taxes

International taxation is quite complex because national governments follow a variety of tax policies. In general, from the point of view of a U.S.-based MNC, several factors must be taken into account.

First, the *level* of foreign taxes needs to be examined. Certain countries are known for their "low" tax levels, including the Bahamas, Switzerland, Liechtenstein, Luxembourg, Panama, and Bermuda. These nations, unlike some of the major industrialized countries, typically have no withholding taxes on *intra-MNC dividends*, which are dividends paid by a foreign subsidiary of a MNC to the parent company. Next, there is a question as to the definition of *taxable income*. While some governments may regard profits to be taxable as received on a cash basis, others may treat the same profits as taxable as earned on an accrual basis. Differences can also exist on treatments of noncash charges, such as depreciation, amortization, and depletion. Finally, the existence of tax agreements between the United States and other governments can influence the total tax bill of the parent MNC. For a U.S.-based MNC, it must be noted that the U.S. government claims jurisdiction over *all* of its income, wherever earned. (Special rules apply to foreign corporations conducting business in the U.S.). However, it may be possible for the multinational to take foreign income taxes as a direct credit against its U.S. tax liabilities. Additional provisions apply to tax deferrals by MNCs on foreign income; to operations set up in American possessions, such as the U.S. Virgin Islands, Guam, and American Samoa; to capital gains from the sale of stock in a foreign corporation; and to withholding taxes.

A final point to be noted is that a number of individual state governments in the United States have in recent years introduced new measures—in the form of special tax formulas—that tax multinationals (American and foreign alike) on a percentage of their *total*

unitary tax laws Laws in some states that provide for a tax against multinationals (both American and foreign) on a percentage of a MNC's *total* worldwide income, rather than the usual approach of taxing only an MNC's earnings within a given state.

worldwide income rather than, as is generally accepted elsewhere, on their earnings arising within the jurisdiction of each respective government. In the U.S., the state governments of Alaska, California, Idaho, Montana, New Hampshire, and North Dakota have applied so-called **unitary tax laws.** MNCs, meanwhile, may face overlapping taxation of income by states and by foreign governments, since U.S. federal tax treaties with other countries do not apply to state taxation of MNCs. As part of their response to unitary tax laws, multinationals have already pressured a number of state governments—including Colorado, Florida, Indiana, Massachusetts, and Oregon—into abolishing these laws, while many MNCs have in the last year relocated their investments from those states that continue to apply them.

INTERNATIONAL FINANCIAL STATEMENTS

Several features distinguish domestically oriented financial statements from internationally based reports. Among these are the issues of consolidation, translation of individual accounts within the financial statements, and overall reporting of international profits.

Consolidation

At present U.S. rules require the *consolidation* of the financial statements of subsidiary companies according to the percentage of ownership by the parent firm of the subsidiary. Table A.2 illustrates this point.

As indicated, the regulations range from requiring a one-line income-item reporting of dividends, to a pro rata inclusion of profits and

TABLE A.2 United States Rules for Consolidation of Financial Statements

Percentage of beneficial ownership by parent in subsidiary	Consolidation for financial reporting purposes
0–19%	Dividends as received
20–49%	Pro rata inclusions of profits and losses
50–100%	Full consolidation[a]

[a] Consolidation may be avoided in the case of some majority-owned foreign operations if the parent can convince its auditors that it does not have control of the subsidiary or there are substantial restrictions on the repatriation of cash.

SOURCE: Rita M. Rodriguez and E. Eugene Carter, *International Financial Management*, 3rd ed. (Englewood Cliffs, N.J.: Prentice-Hall, 1984), p. 492.

losses, to a full disclosure in the balance sheet and income statement. (When ownership is less than 50 percent, since the balance sheet, and thus the subsidiary's financing, are not reported, it is possible for the parent MNC to have off-balance-sheet financing.)

Translation of Individual Accounts

Unlike domestic items in financial statements, international items require translation from the original currency back into U.S. dollars before the financial statements of a subsidiary are submitted to the parent firm for consolidation. Since December 15, 1982, all financial statements of American MNCs are required to conform to Statement No. 52, issued by the Financial Accounting Standards Board (FASB).

Under **FASB No. 52,** the *current-rate method* is implemented in a two-step process. (See Figure A.1.) First, each entity's balance sheet and income statement are measured in terms of their functional currency using generally accepted accounting principles (GAAP). In other words, foreign-currency elements are first translated by each subsidiary into its **functional currency** — the currency of the economic environment in which that entity primarily generates and expends cash, and in which its accounts are maintained. In the second step, as shown in

FASB No. 52 Statement issued by the Financial Accounting Standards Board (FASB) requiring American MNCs to first convert the financial statement accounts of foreign subsidiaries into the country's *functional currency* and then translate the accounts into the parent firm's currency using the *all-current-rate method.*

functional currency The currency of the economic environment in which a financial entity primarily generates and expends cash, and in which its accounts are maintained.

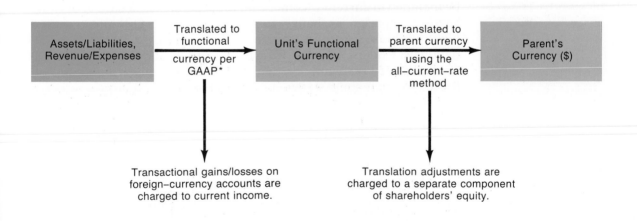

*Generally accepted accounting principles.

FIGURE A.1 Details of FASB No. 52
Under FASB No. 52, financial statement accounts are first translated using GAAP into the country's functional currency, which is then translated using the all-current-rate method into the parent firm's currency. The first translation can result in transaction (cash) gains or losses, and the second can result in translation (accounting) adjustments. (*Source:* John B. Giannotti, "FAS 52 Gives Treasurers the Scope FAS 8 Denied Them," *Euromoney,* April 1982, pp. 141 – 151.)

all-current-rate method
The method by which the *functional currency*-denominated financial statements of a multinational's subsidiary are translated into the parent company's currency.

Figure A.1, by using the **all-current-rate method** (which requires the translation of all balance sheet items at the closing rate and all income statement items at average rates), the functional currency-denominated financial statements are translated into the parent's currency.

Each of these steps can result in certain gains or losses. The first step can lead to transaction (cash) gains or losses, which, whether realized or not, are charged directly to current income. The second step can result in translation (accounting) adjustments. The latter are excluded from current income and are instead disclosed and charged to a separate component of stockholders' equity.

International Profits

Prior to January 1976, the practice for most American multinationals was to utilize a special account called the *reserve account* to show "smooth" international profits. Excess international profits due to favorable exchange fluctuations were deposited in this account. Withdrawals were made during periods of high losses stemming from unfavorable exchange movements. Thus the overall result was to display a smooth, or unvarying, pattern in an MNC's international profits.

Between 1976 and 1982, however, the existence of *FASB No. 8* required that both transaction gains or losses and translation adjustments be included in current income, with the separate disclosure of only the aggregate foreign exchange gain or loss. This requirement caused highly visible swings, or variations, in the reported profits of U.S. multinationals. Under FASB No. 52, which replaced FASB No. 8, effective December 15, 1982, only certain transactional gains or losses are reflected in the income statement. Overall, assuming a positive income flow for a subsidiary, the income statement risk will be positive and will be similarly enhanced or reduced by an appreciation or depreciation of the functional currency.

INTERNATIONAL SHORT-TERM FINANCIAL DECISIONS

The basic short-term financial decision techniques discussed in Part Three of the text are generally applicable in an international setting. The key differences result from the fact that a multinational company in its international financial activities has access to the international financial markets and is exposed to many currencies.

International Cash Management

In its international cash management, an MNC can respond to foreign exchange risks by protecting (hedging) its undesirable cash and marketable securities exposures or by certain adjustments in its operations. The first approach involves actions to be taken in the international financial markets in the form of borrowing or lending in different currencies and also undertaking contracts in the futures markets. (More details about this approach will be given later in this appendix.) The second procedure involves adjustments to assets and liabilities in order to protect international cash flows from exchange-rate fluctuations. This can be accomplished either through third parties or through intra-MNC accounts.

THIRD PARTIES   This approach centers on the operating relationships that a subsidiary of an MNC maintains with *other* firms — "third parties." Depending on management's expectation of a local currency's position, adjustments in operations would involve the increase or decrease of financial assets. Thus if a U.S.-based MNC with a subsidiary in Mexico expects the Mexican currency to *appreciate* in value relative to the U.S. dollar, local customers' accounts receivable would be *increased* and accounts payable *reduced* if at all possible. Since the dollar is the currency in which the MNC parent must prepare consolidated financial statements, the net result in this case would be to favorably increase the Mexican subsidiary's resources in local currency.

INTRA-MNC ACCOUNTS   This approach focuses on the operating relationship a subsidiary has with its parent or with other subsidiaries within the same MNC. In dealing with exchange risks, a subsidiary can rely on "intra-MNC" accounts. Specifically, undesirable foreign exchange exposures can be corrected to the extent that the subsidiary can take the following steps:

1. In appreciation-prone countries, intra-MNC accounts receivable are collected as soon as possible, while payment of intra-MNC accounts payable is delayed as long as possible.
2. In devaluation-prone countries, intra-MNC accounts receivable are not collected for as long as possible, while intra-MNC accounts payable are paid as soon as possible.

Again using the example of a Mexican subsidiary, the net result of step 1 or step 2 would be the potential increase or decrease of the subsidiary's resources in the Mexican currency, depending on whether that currency is appreciating or depreciating relative to the parent MNC's main currency, the U.S. dollar.

From a *global* point of view and as far as MNC's consolidated intracompany accounts are concerned, the manipulation of such accounts by one subsidiary can produce the opposite results for another subsidiary or the parent firm. If an MNC's subsidiaries in, for instance, Brazil and Mexico are dealing with each other, the Brazilian subsidiary's manipulations of intra-MNC accounts in anticipation of an appreciation of that country's currency relative to that of Mexico can mean exchange gains for the Brazilian subsidiary but losses for the Mexican one. The exact degree and direction of the actual manipulations, however, may depend on the tax status of each country, the MNC obviously wanting to have the exchange losses in the country with the higher tax rate. Finally, changes in intra-MNC accounts can also be subject to restrictions and regulations by the respective host countries of various subsidiaries.

International Short-Term Sources of Financing

In international operations the usual domestic sources of short-term financing, along with other sources, are available to MNCs. Included are accounts payable as well as accruals, bank and nonbank sources in each subsidiary's local environment, and the Euromarket, as discussed earlier. Our emphasis here is on the "foreign" sources.

For the subsidiary of a multinational company, its local economic market is a basic source of both short- and long-term financing. Moreover, the subsidiary's borrowing and lending status, relative to a local firm in the same economy, can be superior, since the subsidiary can rely on the potential backing and guarantee of its parent MNC. One drawback, however, is that most local markets and local currencies are regulated by local authorities. Thus a subsidiary may ultimately choose to turn to the Euromarket and take advantage of borrowing and investing in an unregulated financial forum.

Eurocurrency markets
The portion of the Euromarket providing short-term foreign-currency financing to MNCs' subsidiaries.

The Euromarket offers nondomestic financing opportunities for both the short term (Eurocurrency) and the long term (Eurobonds). (Eurobonds will be discussed later.) In the case of short-term financing, the forces of supply and demand are among the main factors determining exchange rates in **Eurocurrency markets,** with each currency's nominal interest rate being influenced by economic policies pursued by the respective "home" governments. In other words, the interest rates offered in the Euromarket on, for example, the U.S. dollar are greatly affected by the prime rate inside the United States, and the dollar's exchange rates with other major currencies are in turn influenced by the supply and demand forces acting in such markets (and in response to interest rates).

nominal interest rate
The stated interest rate charged on financing when only the MNC parent's currency is involved.

effective interest rates
In the international context, equal to nominal rates plus (or minus) any forecast appreciation (or depreciation) of a foreign currency relative to the currency of the MNC parent.

Unlike borrowing in the domestic markets, where only one currency and a **nominal interest rate** is involved, financing activities in the Euromarket can involve several currencies and both nominal and effective interest rates. **Effective interest rates** are equal to nominal rates plus (or minus) any forecast appreciation (or depreciation) of a currency relative to the currency of the MNC parent—say, the U.S. dollar. An example will illustrate the issues involved.

EXAMPLE

A multinational company, MNC, Inc., has subsidiaries in Switzerland (local currency, Swiss franc, Sf) and Belgium (local currency, Belgian franc, Bf). Based on each subsidiary's forecast operations, the short-term financial needs of each (in equivalent U.S. dollars) are as follows:

Switzerland: $80 million excess cash to be invested (lent)
Belgium: $60 million funds to be raised (borrowed)

Based on all available information, the parent firm has provided each subsidiary with the following figures regarding exchange rates and interest rates. (The figures for the effective rates shown are derived by adding the forecast % change numbers to the nominal rates.)

		CURRENCY	
Item	US$	Sf	Bf
Current exchange rates		Sf2.09/US$	Bf50.1/US$
Forecast % change		+5.2%	−6.3%
Interest rates			
Nominal			
Euromarket	14.0%	4.0%	17.5%
Domestic	12.8	3.6	16.7
Effective			
Euromarket	14.0%	9.2%	11.2%
Domestic	12.8	8.8	10.4

From the point of view of a multinational, the effective rates of interest, which take into account each currency's forecast % change (appreciation or depreciation) relative to the U.S. dollar, are the main items to be considered for investment and borrowing decisions. (It is assumed here that due to local regulations, a subsidiary is *not* permitted to use the domestic market of *any other* subsidiary.) The relevant question is, where should funds be invested and borrowed?

For investment purposes, the highest available rate of interest is the effective rate for the U.S. dollar in the Euromarket. Therefore, the Swiss subsidiary should invest its $80 million dollars in the Euromarket. In the case of raising funds, the cheapest source *open* to the Belgian subsidiary is the 9.2 percent in the Sf Euromarket. The subsidiary should therefore raise the $60 million in Swiss francs. These two transactions will result in the most revenues and least costs, respectively.

Several points should be made with respect to the preceding example. First of all, this is a simplified case of the actual workings of the Eurocurrency markets. The example ignores taxes, intersubsidiary investing or borrowing, and periods longer or shorter than a year. Nevertheless, it shows how the existence of many currencies can provide both challenges and opportunities for MNCs. Next, the focus has been solely on accounting values; of greater importance would be the impact of these actions on market value. Finally, it is important to note the following details about the figures presented. The forecast % change (appreciation or depreciation) data are regarded as those normally supplied by the MNC's international financial managers. The management may have a range of forecasts, from the most likely to the least likely. In addition, the company's management is likely to take a specific position in terms of its response to any remaining foreign exchange exposures. If any action is to be taken, certain amounts of one or more currencies will be borrowed and then invested in other currencies in the hope of realizing potential gains to offset potential losses associated with the exposures.

INTERNATIONAL RISKS

The concepts of risk and return on domestic investments discussed in this text are applicable to international investments as well. For the latter, however, additional factors must be taken into account, including both foreign exchange (economic) and political risks.

Foreign Exchange Risks

Since multinational companies operate in many different foreign markets, portions of these firms' revenues and costs are based on foreign currencies. In order to understand the **foreign exchange risk** caused by varying exchange rates between two currencies, we examine both the relationship that exists among various currencies and the impact of currency fluctuations.

foreign exchange risk The risk created by the varying exchange rate between two currencies.

RELATIONSHIP AMONG CURRENCIES Since the mid-1970s, the major currencies of the world have had a *floating*—as opposed to *fixed*—relationship to the U.S. dollar and to one another. The currencies regarded as major (or "hard") include the British pound (£), Swiss franc (Sf), Deutsche mark (DM), French franc (Ff), Japanese yen (Y), Canadian dollar (C$), and, of course, the U.S. dollar (US$). The value of two currencies with respect to one another, or their **foreign exchange rate,** is expressed as follows:

foreign exchange rate The value of two currencies with respect to one another.

$$US\$ \ 1.00 = Sf \ 2.09$$
$$Sf \ 1.00 = US\$ \ .47$$

The usual exchange quotation in international markets is given as Sf2.09/US$, where the unit of account is the Swiss franc and the unit of currency being priced is one U.S. dollar.

For the major currencies, the existence of a **floating relationship** means that the value of any two currencies with respect to one another is allowed to fluctuate on a daily basis. On the other hand, many of the nonmajor currencies of the world attempt to maintain a constant, or nonfluctuating, **fixed relationship** with respect to one of the major currencies, a combination of major currencies, or relative to some kind of international foreign exchange standard.

On any given day, the relationship between any two of the major currencies will contain two sets of figures, one reflecting the **spot exchange rate** (the rate on that date), and the other indicating the **forward exchange rate** (the rate at some specified future date). The foreign exchange rates given in Figure A.2 can be used to illustrate these concepts. For instance, the figure shows that on Wednesday, January 8, 1986, the spot rate for the Swiss franc was Sf 2.0940/US$, while the forward (future) rate was Sf 2.0866/US$ for 30-day delivery. In

floating relationship The fluctuating relationship of the values of two currencies with respect to one another.

fixed relationship The constant, or nonfluctuating, relationship of the values of two currencies with respect to one another.

spot exchange rate The rate of exchange between two currencies on any given date.

forward exchange rate The rate of exchange between two currencies at some specified future date.

FOREIGN EXCHANGE

Wednesday, January 8, 1986
The New York foreign exchange selling rates below apply to trading among banks in amounts of $1 million and more, as quoted at 3 p.m. Eastern time by Bankers Trust Co. Retail transactions provide fewer units of foreign currency per dollar.

Country	U.S. $ equiv. Wed.	Tues.	Currency per U.S. $ Wed.	Tues.
Argentina (Austral) ...	1.2484	1.2484	.801	.801
Australia (Dollar) ...	.6885	.6895	1.4524	1.4503
Austria (Schilling)	.05794	.05838	17.26	17.13
Belgium (Franc)				
Commercial rate	.01997	.02004	50.06	49.89
Financial rate	.01970	.01983	50.75	50.43
Brazil (Cruzeiro)	.00009615	.0009615	10400.00	10400.00
Britain (Pound)	1.4420	1.4430	.6935	.6930
30-Day Forward	1.4363	1.4386	.6962	.6951
90-Day Forward	1.4260	1.4295	.7013	.6995
180-Day Forward ...	1.4115	1.4155	.7085	.7065
Canada (Dollar)	.7139	.7153	1.4007	1.3980
30-Day Forward	.7128	.7143	1.4029	1.3999
90-Day Forward	.7108	.7125	1.4069	1.4036
180-Day Forward ...	.7081	.7102	1.4122	1.4080
Chile (Official rate) ...	.005479	.005479	182.50	182.50
China (Yuan)	.3131	.3131	3.1935	3.1935
Colombia (Peso)	.005837	.005837	171.32	171.32
Denmark (Krone)	.1119	.1124	8.9380	8.8950
Ecuador (Sucre)				
Official rate	.01504	.01504	66.48	66.48
Floating rate	.007952	.007952	125.75	125.75
Finland (Markka)	.1852	.1853	5.4000	5.3975
France (Franc)	.1323	.1336	7.5600	7.4825
30-Day Forward	.1321	.1334	7.5700	7.4975
90-Day Forward	.1311	.1322	7.6300	7.5650
180-Day Forward ...	.1298	.1308	7.7025	7.6450
Greece (Drachma)	.006780	.006803	147.50	147.00
Hong Kong (Dollar) ..	.1281	.1281	7.8050	7.8050
India (Rupee)	.08237	.08258	12.14	12.11
Indonesia (Rupiah) ...	.0008881	.0008881	1126.00	1126.00
Ireland (Punt)	1.2440	1.2525	.8039	.7984
Israel (Shekel)	.0006739	.0006739	1484.00	1484.00
Italy (Lira)	.0005984	.0006020	1671.00	1661.00
Japan (Yen)	.004941	.004964	202.40	201.45
30-Day Forward	.004966	.004970	202.16	201.21
90-Day Forward	.004952	.004989	201.93	200.46
180-Day Forward ...	.004978	.005003	200.87	199.90
Jordan (Dinar)	2.8265	2.8265	.3538	.3538

Country	U.S. $ equiv. Wed.	Tues.	Currency per U.S. $ Wed.	Tues.
Kuwait (Dinar)	3.4542	3.4542	.2895	.2895
Lebanon (Pound)	.05540	.05540	18.05	18.05
Malaysia (Ringgit)	.4114	.4115	2.4310	2.4300
Malta (Lira)	2.3781	2.3781	.4205	.4205
Mexico (Peso)				
Floating rate	z	z	z	z
Netherland(Guilder) .	.3621	.3644	2.7620	2.7440
New Zealand (Dollar)	.4965	.5250	2.0141	1.9048
Norway (Krone)	.1328	.1330	7.5320	7.5200
Pakistan (Rupee)	.06341	.06349	15.77	15.75
Peru (Sol)	.0007173	.0007173	13942.00	13942.00
Philippines (Peso)	.05263	.05263	19.00	19.00
Portugal (Escudo)	.006410	.006410	156.00	156.00
Saudi Arabia (Riyal)	.2740	.2740	3.6500	3.6490
Singapore (Dollar)	.4719	.4729	2.1190	2.1145
South Africa (Rand)				
Commercial rate	.4045	.4025	2.4721	2.4845
Financial rate	.2960	.2865	3.3783	3.4904
South Korea (Won)	.001123	.001123	890.60	890.60
Spain (Peseta)	.006549	.006570	152.70	152.20
Sweden (Krona)	.1318	.1325	7.5875	7.5500
Switzerland (Franc) .	.4776	.4836	2.0940	2.0680
30-Day Forward	.4792	.4854	2.0866	2.0603
90-Day Forward	.4822	.4883	2.0738	2.0479
180-Day Forward ...	.4866	.4930	2.0550	2.0285
Taiwan (Dollar)	.02508	.02508	39.87	39.87
Thailand (Baht)	.03752	.03752	26.65	26.65
United Arab(Dirham)	.2723	.2723	3.6730	3.6730
Uruguay (New Peso)				
Financial	.008008	.008008	124.875	124.875
Venezuela (Bolivar)				
Official rate	.1333	.1333	7.50	7.50
Floating rate	.06752	.06752	14.81	14.81
W. Germany (Mark) ..	.4057	.4100	2.4650	2.4390
30-Day Forward	.4069	.4113	2.4575	2.4314
90-Day Forward	.4090	.4134	2.4447	2.4189
180-Day Forward ...	.4125	.4168	2.4240	2.3992

FIGURE A.2 Spot and Forward Exchange Rate Quotations

On each business day the exchange rate between the U.S. dollar and other currencies is reported as a spot rate on either a floating- or fixed-rate basis, depending on the currency. For major currencies, forward exchange rates are also reported. (*Source: The Wall Street Journal*, January 9, 1986, p. 23.)

other words, on January 8, 1986, one could take a contract on Swiss francs for 30 days hence at an exchange rate of Sf 2.0866/US$. *Forward delivery rates* are also available for 90-day and 180-day contracts. For all such contracts, the agreements and signatures are completed on, say, January 8, 1986, whereas the actual exchange of dollars and Swiss francs between buyers and sellers will take place on the future date, say, 30 days later.

Figure A.2 can also be used to illustrate the differences between floating and fixed currencies. All the major currencies previously mentioned have spot and forward rates with respect to the U.S. dollar. Moreover, a comparison of the exchange rates prevailing on January 8, 1986, versus those on Tuesday, January 7, 1986, indicates that the floating major currencies (or other currencies that also float in relation to the U.S. dollar, such as the Austrian schilling and the Indian rupee) have experienced changes in rates. Fixed currencies, such as the Chinese yuan and the Peruvian sol, do not fluctuate on a daily basis with respect to the currency or currencies to which they are pegged. (I.e., they have very limited movements with respect to either the U.S. dollar or other currencies.)

A final point to note is the concept of changes in the value of a currency with respect to the U.S. dollar or another currency. For the floating currencies, changes in the value of foreign exchange rates are called *appreciation* and *depreciation*. For example, referring to Figure A.2, it can be said that the value of the French franc has *depreciated* from Ff 7.4825 on Tuesday to Ff 7.5600 on Wednesday. In other words, it takes more francs to buy one dollar on Wednesday than on the preceding day. For the fixed currencies, changes in values are called official **revaluation** and **devaluation**, but these terms have the same meanings as appreciation and depreciation, respectively.

revaluation The appreciation in value in a fixed currency.

devaluation The depreciation in value of a fixed currency.

IMPACT OF CURRENCY FLUCTUATION Multinational companies face foreign exchange risks under both floating and fixed arrangements. Returning to the U.S. dollar–Swiss franc relationship, we note that the forces of international supply and demand as well as internal and external economic and political elements help shape both the spot rates and the forward rates between these two currencies. Since a typical MNC cannot control much (or most) of these "outside" elements, the company faces potential changes in exchange rates in the form of appreciation or depreciation that can in turn affect its revenues, costs, and profits as measured in U.S. dollars. For currencies fixed in relation to each other, the risks come from the same set of elements as indicated above. Again, these official changes, like the ones brought about by the market in the case of floating currencies, can affect the MNC's operations and its dollar-based financial position.

The risks stemming from changes in exchange rates can be illustrated by examining the balance sheet and income statement of MNC, Inc. We will focus on its subsidiary in Switzerland.

EXAMPLE

MNC, Inc., has a Swiss subsidiary that at the end of 1987 has the financial statements shown in Table A.3. The figures for the balance sheet and income statement are given in the local currency, Swiss francs (Sf). Using the foreign exchange rate of Sf 2.10/US$ for December 31, 1987, the statements have been translated into U.S. dollars. For simplicity it is assumed that all the local figures are expected to remain the same during 1988. As a result, as of January 1, 1988, the subsidiary expects to show the same dollar figures on 12/31/88 as on 12/31/87. However, due to the change in the value of the Swiss franc relative to the dollar, from Sf 2.10/US$ to Sf 2.25/US$, it is clear that the translated dollar values of the

TABLE A.3 MNC, Inc.'s Swiss Subsidiary's Financial Statements

Translation of balance sheet

	12/31/87		12/31/88
Assets	Sf	US$	US$
Cash	8.00	3.81	3.55
Inventory	60.00	28.57	26.66
Plant and equipment (net)	32.00	15.23	14.22
Total	100.00	47.61	44.43
Liabilities and equity			
Debt	48.00	22.86	21.33
Paid-in capital	40.00	19.04	17.77
Retained earnings	12.00	5.71	5.33
Total	100.00	47.61	44.43

Translation of income statement

	12/31/87		12/31/88
	Sf	US$	US$
Sales	600.00	285.71	266.66
Cost of goods sold	550.00	261.90	244.44
Operating profits	50.00	23.81	22.22

NOTE: This example is simplified to show how the balance sheet and income statement are subject to exchange fluctuations. For the applicable rules on the translation of foreign accounts, review the discussion of international financial statements presented earlier.

items in the balance sheet, along with the dollar profit value on 12/31/88, are lower than those of the previous year, the changes being due only to fluctuations in foreign exchange. ■

There are additional complexities attached to each individual account in the international financial statements. For instance, it is important whether a subsidiary's debt is all in the local currency, in U.S. dollars, or in several currencies. Moreover, it is important which currency (or currencies) the revenues and costs are denominated in. The risks exemplified so far relate to what is called the **accounting exposure.** In other words, foreign exchange fluctuations affect individual accounts in the financial statements. A different, and perhaps more important, risk element concerns **economic exposure,** which is the potential impact of exchange rate fluctuations on the firm's value. Given that all future cash flows are subject to exchange rate changes, it is obvious that their present value, and therefore the value of the firm, will change with unexpected changes in exchange rates.

What can MNC's management do about these risks? The actions will depend on the management's attitude toward risk. This attitude, in turn, translates into how aggressively management wants to hedge (protect against) the company's undesirable positions and exposures. The money markets, the forward (futures) markets, and the foreign-currency options markets can be used — either individually or in conjunction with one another — to hedge foreign exchange exposures. Because of their complexity, further discussion of hedging strategies is not included in this appendix.

Political Risks

Another important risk facing MNCs is political risk. **Political risk** refers to the implementation by a host government of specific rules and regulations that can result in the discontinuity or seizure of the operations of a foreign company in that country. Political risk usually occurs in the form of nationalization, expropriation, and confiscation. Under such circumstances, the assets and operations of a foreign firm are taken over by the host government, usually without proper (or any) compensation.

Political risk has two basic forms: *macro* and *micro*. **Macro political risk** means that due to political change, a revolution, or the adoption of new policies by a host government, *all* foreign firms in the country will be subjected to political risk. In other words, no individual country or firm is treated differently; all assets and operations of foreign firms are totally taken over. An example of this is China in 1949 or Cuba in 1959–1960. **Micro political risk,** on the other hand, refers to the case in which an individual firm, a specific industry, or companies from a

accounting exposure The risk resulting from the effects of changes in foreign exchange rates on the translated value of a firm's accounts denominated in the given foreign currency.

economic exposure The risk resulting from the effects of changes in foreign exchange rates on the firm's value.

political risk The potential discontinuity or seizure of an MNC's operations in a host country due to the host's implementation of specific rules and regulations (such as nationalization, expropriation, and confiscation).

macro political risk The subjection of *all* foreign firms to political risk by a host country, due to political change, revolution, or the adoption of new policies.

micro political risk The subjection of an individual firm, a specific industry, or companies from a particular foreign country to political risk (takeover) by the host country.

particular foreign country will be subjected to takeover. Examples include the nationalizations by a majority of the oil-exporting countries of the assets of the international oil companies in their territories.

Although political risk can occur in any country — even in the United States — the political instability of the so-called Third World generally makes the positions of multinational companies most vulnerable there. At the same time, some of the countries in this group have the most promising markets for the goods and services being offered by MNCs. The main question, therefore, is how to engage in operation and foreign investment in such countries and yet avoid or minimize the potential political risk.

Table A.4 shows some of the available approaches for coping with political risk that MNCs may be able to adopt. The negative approaches are generally used by firms in extractive industries. The external approaches are also of limited use. The best policies MNCs can follow are the positive approaches, which have both economic and political aspects.

In recent years MNCs have been relying on a variety of complex forecasting techniques whereby "international experts," using the available historical data, predict the chances for political instability in a host country and the potential effects on MNC operations. Events in

TABLE A.4 Approaches for Coping with Political Risk

Positive approaches		Negative approaches
Prior negotiation of controls and operating contracts Prior agreement for sale Joint venture with government or local private sector	Direct	License or patent restrictions under international agreements Control of external raw materials Control of transportation to (external) markets Control of downstream processing Control of external markets
Use of locals in management Joint venture with local banks Equity participation by middle class Local sourcing Local retail outlets	Indirect	

External approaches to minimize loss
International insurance or investment guarantees Thinly capitalized firms: 　Local financing 　External financing secured only by the local operation

SOURCE: Rita M. Rodriguez and E. Eugene Carter, *International Financial Management,* 3rd ed. (Englewood Cliffs, N.J.: Prentice-Hall, 1984), p. 512.

Iran and Nicaragua, among others, however, point to the limited use of such techniques and tend to reinforce the usefulness of the positive approaches.

INTERNATIONAL LONG-TERM FINANCIAL DECISIONS

In addition to the long-term financial concepts and techniques described in the text, certain aspects unique to the international setting require discussion. First, some concepts specific to international capital budgeting will be highlighted. Next we will consider international business combinations; then international long-term debt and its use by multinational companies. And finally, a brief discussion of international equity capital is presented.

International Capital Budgeting

Several factors unique to international capital budgeting need to be examined. First, the elements relating to a parent company's *investment* in a subsidiary and the concept of taxes must be considered. For example, in the case of manufacturing investments, questions may arise as to the value of the equipment a parent may contribute to the subsidiary. Is the value based on the market conditions in the parent country or in the local host economy? In general, the market value of an asset in the host country is its relevant "price."

The existence of different taxes—as pointed out earlier—can complicate the measurement of the *cash flows* to be received by the parent from a subsidiary, because different definitions of taxable income can arise. There are still other complications when it comes to measuring actual cash flows. From a parent firm's viewpoint, the cash flows are those refunded (repatriated) by the subsidiary. In some countries, however, such cash flows may be totally or partially blocked. Obviously, depending on the life of the project in the host country, the returns and net present values (NPVs) associated with such projects can significantly vary from the subsidiary's and the parent's point of view. For instance, for a project of only five years' duration, if all yearly cash flows are blocked by the host government, the subsidiary may show a "normal" or even superior return and NPV, while the parent may show no return at all. On the other hand, for a project of longer life, even if cash flows are blocked for the first few years, the remaining years' cash flows can contribute toward the parent's returns and NPV.

Finally, there is the issue of *risk* attached to international cash flows. The three basic types of risk categories are (1) business and financial risks, (2) inflation and foreign exchange risks, and (3) political risks. The first category relates to the type of industry the subsidiary is in as well as to its financial structure (more details on financial risks are presented below). As for the other two categories, we have already discussed both the risks of having investments, profits, and assets/liabilities in different currencies, as well as the potential impacts of political risks and how MNCs can combat them.

It is to be noted here that the presence of such risks will influence the discount rate (or the cost of capital) to be used in evaluating international cash flows. The basic rule, however, is that the *local cost of equity capital* is the starting discount rate to which risks stemming from foreign exchange and political factors should be added, and from which benefits reflecting the parent's lower capital costs should be subtracted.

International Business Combinations

The motives for domestic business combinations stated in the text—growth or diversification, synergistic effects, fund raising, increased managerial skills, tax considerations, and increased ownership liquidity—as well as the factors emphasized in earlier sections of this Appendix are all applicable to MNCs' international combinations. Several additional points nevertheless need attention.

First, international joint ventures and acquisitions, especially those involving U.S. firms, have increased significantly in recent years. MNCs based in North America, Western Europe, and Japan have made substantial contributions to this increase. Moreover, a fast-growing group of MNCs has emerged in the past two decades, operating from such home bases as India, Pakistan, Mexico, Argentina, Brazil, Singapore, and Hong Kong, and this has added further to the number and value of international acquisitions.

Foreign direct investments in the United States have gained popularity in the past few years, although the amount represents still less than half the value of investments by American companies abroad. Most of the foreign direct investors in the United States come from one of seven countries: Britain, Canada, France, the Netherlands, Japan, Switzerland, and West Germany, with the heaviest investments concentrated in manufacturing, followed by the petroleum and trade sectors. Another interesting trend is the current increase in the number of joint ventures between companies based in Japan and firms domiciled elsewhere in the industrialized world, especially U.S.-based MNCs. While Japanese authorities continue their discussions and debates with other governments regarding Japan's international trade surpluses as well as perceived trade barriers, joint ventures and other forms of business combinations, acquisitions, and agreements continue to take place. According to the judgment of some U.S. corporate executives, such business ventures are viewed as a "ticket into the Japanese market" as well as a way to curb a potentially tough competitor.

Developing countries, too, have been attracting foreign direct investments in both horizontal and vertical industries. Meanwhile, during the last two decades a number of these nations have adopted specific policies and regulations aimed at controlling the inflows of foreign investments, a major provision being the 49 percent ownership limitation applied to MNCs. Of course, international competition among differently based MNCs has been of benefit to some developing countries in their attempts at extracting concessions from multinationals. However, an increasing number of such nations have shown greater flexibility in their recent dealings with MNCs as the latter group has become more reluctant to form joint ventures under the stated conditions. Furthermore, given the present as well as the expected international economic and trade status, it is likely that as more Third World countries recognize the need for foreign capital and technology, they will exhibit even greater flexibility in their business agreements with MNCs.

A final point here relates to the existence of international *holding companies*. Places such as Liechtenstein and Panama have long been considered favorable spots for forming holding companies due to their conducive legal, corporate, and tax environments. International holding companies control many business entities in the form of subsidiaries, branches, joint ventures, and other agreements. For international legal (especially tax-related) reasons, as well as anonymity, such holding companies have become increasingly popular in recent years.

International Long-Term Debt

MNCs, in conducting their global operations, have access to a variety of international financial instruments, with international bonds being among the most widely used. Since the discussion of international financial markets provided information on international loans, the focus here is on international bonds used by MNCs in their global operations.

international bond
A bond initially sold outside the country of the borrower and often distributed in several countries.

foreign bond An international bond sold primarily in the country of the currency of the issue.

Eurobond An international bond sold primarily in countries other than the country of the currency in which the issue is denominated.

INTERNATIONAL BONDS In general, an **international bond** initially sold outside the country of the borrower is often distributed in several countries. When a bond is sold primarily in the country of the currency of the issue, it is called a **foreign bond.** For example, an MNC based in West Germany might float a bond issue in the French capital market underwritten by a French syndicate and denominated in French francs. When an international bond is sold primarily in countries other than the country of the currency in which the issue is denominated, it is called a **Eurobond.** Thus an MNC based in the United States might float a Eurobond in several European capital markets, underwritten by an international syndicate and denominated in U.S. dollars.

Foreign companies, along with international organizations, tend to dominate the foreign bond market, with the Swiss franc being the dominant currency in recent years. In the case of new issues of Eurobonds, companies outside the United States have shown consistent dominance during the 1979–1983 period, with the U.S. dollar the most desired currency.

SELLING INTERNATIONAL BONDS   The institutions assisting the issuers of foreign bonds are those that handle bond issues in the respective countries in which such bonds are issued. For Eurobonds, a number of financial institutions in the United States and Western Europe form international syndicates to sell the bonds. The selling and administrative costs for Eurobonds are comparable to those for bond flotation in the U.S. domestic market.

In order to raise funds through international bond issues, many MNCs establish their own financial subsidiaries. Many American-based MNCs, for example, have created subsidiaries in the United States and Western Europe, especially in Luxembourg. Such subsidiaries can be used to raise large amounts of funds in "one move," with the funds redistributed wherever MNCs need them. (Special tax rules applicable to such subsidiaries also make them desirable to MNCs.)

INTEREST RATES   In the case of foreign bonds, interest rates are usually directly correlated with the domestic rates prevailing in the respective countries. For Eurobonds, several interest rates may be influential. For instance, for a Eurodollar bond, the interest rate will reflect the U.S. long-term rate, the Eurodollar rate, and long-term rates in other countries.

International Equity Capital

International capital markets provide multinational companies with a setting in which equity funds can be raised. Several characteristics of such a setting distinguish it from a domestic one.

The basic aspects of foreign ownership of international operations have been discussed earlier in this Appendix. Recent laws and regulations enacted by a number of host countries require MNCs to maintain less than 50 percent ownership in their subsidiaries in those countries. For a U.S.-based MNC, for example, establishing foreign subsidiaries in the form of joint ventures means that a certain portion of the firm's total international equity stock is held by foreign owners. Some of the advantages and disadvantages of joint ventures have been highlighted earlier.

A number of MNCs have the parent firm's equity stock distributed internationally and owned by stockholders of different nationalities. Capital markets in Western Europe and in Japan are the usual channels used by U.S.-based MNCs that desire international ownership of their equity. For MNCs based elsewhere, United States capital markets serve a similar function.

In establishing a foreign subsidiary, an MNC may wish to have as little equity and as much debt as possible, with the debt coming either from local sources in the host country or from the MNC itself. Each of these actions has advantages. A host country may allow more-than-normal *local debt* for a subsidiary; and for the latter this is a good protective measure in terms of lessening the potential impact of political risk. In other words, if local sources are involved in the capital structure of a subsidiary, there may be fewer threats from local authorities in the event of changes in government or the enactment of new regulations imposed on foreign business.

In support of the other action, having more *MNC-based debt* in a subsidiary's capital structure, it is true that many host governments are less restrictive — in terms of taxation and the actual return of capital — toward intra-MNC interest payments than toward intra-MNC dividend remittances. Under certain circumstances, the parent firm may therefore be in a better position if it has more MNC-based debt than equity in the capital structure of its subsidiaries.

A final point to note is that in international capital markets, as in domestic capital markets, different *classes* of equity — such as preferred and common — can be issued.

SUMMARY

- The existence and expansion of dollars held outside the United States have contributed in recent years to the development of a major international financial market, the Euromarket. The large international banks, developing and industrialized nations, and multinational companies participate as borrowers and lenders in this market.
- Setting up operations in foreign countries can entail special problems due to, among other things, the legal form of business organization chosen, the degree of ownership allowed by the host country, possible restrictions and regulations on the return of capital and profits, and international taxation.
- Certain regulations that apply to international operations tend to complicate the preparation of foreign-based financial statements. Included are rulings that pertain to consolidation, translation of accounts, and reporting international profits.
- The foreign exchange risks that complicate international cash management can be overcome through manipulations of accounts receivable and accounts payable from and to third parties and intra-MNC accounts. The existence of the Eurocurrency markets, in particular, allows multinationals to take advantage of unregulated financial markets to invest (lend) and raise

short-term funds (borrow) in a variety of currencies and to protect themselves against foreign exchange risk exposures.

● Operating in international markets involves certain factors that can influence the risk and return characteristics of an MNC. Economic exposure from foreign exchange risk results from the existence of different currencies and the potential impact they can have on the value of foreign operations. Political risks stem mainly from political instability in a number of countries and from the associated implications for the assets and operations of MNCs with subsidiaries located in such countries.

● International cash flows can be subject to a variety of factors, including local taxes in host countries, host-country regulations that may block the return (repatriation) of MNCs' cash flow, the usual business and financial risks, risks stemming from different currency and political actions by host governments, and the application of a local cost of capital.

● International business combinations—joint ventures and acquisitions, along with international holding companies—have come to exist for reasons similar to those leading to the creation of their domestic counterparts. Special factors affecting these combinations relate to international taxation and various regulations imposed on MNCs by host countries.

● International capital markets provide MNCs with an opportunity to raise long-term debt through the issuance of international bonds in various currencies. Foreign bonds are sold primarily in the country of the currency of issue, while Eurobonds are sold primarily in countries other than the country of the currency in which the issue is denominated.

● Multinational companies can use international capital markets to raise equity. In establishing foreign subsidiaries, it may be more advantageous to issue debt (either local or MNC-based) than MNC-owned equity.

QUESTIONS

A-1 Discuss the major reasons for the growth of the Euromarket.

A-2 What is an *offshore center*? Name the major participants in the Euromarket.

A-3 What is a *joint venture*? Why is it often essential to use this arrangement? What effect do joint-venture laws and restrictions have on the operation of foreign-based subsidiaries?

A-4 From the point of view of a U.S.-based MNC, what key tax factors need to be considered? What is the *unitary tax*?

A-5 State the rules for consolidation of foreign subsidiaries. Under *FASB No. 52*, what are the translation rules for financial statement accounts?

A-6 Discuss the steps to be followed in adjusting a subsidiary's accounts relative to *third parties* when that subsidiary's local currency is expected to appreciate in value in relation to the currency of the parent MNC.

A-7 Outline the changes to be undertaken in *intra-MNC accounts* if a subsidiary's currency is expected to depreciate in value relative to the currency of the parent MNC.

A-8 Define *spot* and *forward* exchange rates. Define and compare *accounting exposures* and *economic exposures* to exchange rate fluctuations.

A-9 Discuss macro and micro political risk. Describe some techniques for dealing with political risk.

A-10 Indicate how net present value (NPV) can differ whether measured from the parent's point of view or that of the foreign subsidiary when cash flows may be blocked by local authorities.

A-11 What are some of the major reasons for the rapid expansion in international business combinations of firms?

A-12 Describe and differentiate between *foreign bonds* and *Eurobonds*. Explain how each is sold and discuss the determinant(s) of their interest rates.

A-13 What are the long-run advantages of having more *local* debt and less MNC-based equity in the capital structure of a foreign subsidiary?

PROBLEM

A-1 **(Euromarket Investment and Fund Raising)** A multinational company has two subsidiaries, one in France (local currency, French franc, Ff) and the other in West Germany (local currency, Deutsche mark, DM). Forecasts of business operations indicate the following short-term financial needs for each subsidiary (in equivalent U.S. dollars):

France: $70 million excess cash to be invested (lent)
West Germany: $50 million funds to be raised (borrowed)

The management has the following data:

		CURRENCY	
Item	US$	Ff	DM
Current exchange rates		Ff8.50/US$	DM2.60/US$
Forecast % change		−3.8%	+2.5%
Interest rates			
Nominal			
Euromarket	13.8%	12.3%	9.9%
Domestic	11.9	12.1	8.7
Effective			
Euromarket	13.8%		
Domestic	11.9		

Determine the effective rates of interest for Ff and DM in both the Euromarket and the domestic market; then indicate where the funds should be invested and raised. (Note: Assume that due to local regulations, a subsidiary is *not* permitted to use the domestic market of *any other* subsidiary.)

Appendix B

CAREER OPPORTUNITIES IN FINANCE

If you have an interest in the dollars and cents of running a business, like to follow the daily ups and downs of the financial markets, have a knack for numbers, and would like to land a job with a salary ranking among the highest of all business graduates, finance might be the career for you. Opportunities for the new graduate are abundant; there are over 1,000,000 positions in the general field of finance. This appendix focuses on careers in finance; what they are, where to find them, and what they are paying.

WHAT ARE THE JOBS?

There are two basic career paths in finance. The first is *managerial finance,* which involves managing the finance function for businesses in the manufacturing and trade industries. These industries make and sell consumer and commercial products. The second is a career in the *financial services* industry, which creates and sells intangible financial products or services. Banking, securities, real estate, and insurance are all financial service industries.

The job descriptions that follow are divided into two career paths: managerial finance and financial services. A mixture of entry-level positions available to the recent college graduate and advanced positions available after a number of years of work experience and/or an advanced degree are presented. Although many of the top positions in finance are not available to the recent graduate, firms frequently hire new graduates as "assistants" to these positions. (Note: One * designates an entry-level position and two **s designate an advanced position.) A review of the job descriptions below should help you understand the many exciting career opportunities available in finance.

CAREER PATH 1:
MANAGERIAL FINANCE

A career in managerial finance can lead to the executive suite. According to a study of the CEOs of the nation's largest businesses, the majority have risen to the top after an average of 15 years in various financial management positions in the firm.[1] One explanation of why many CEOs are chosen from financial management may be that the language of business is dollars, and those managing dollars generally have the full attention of a firm's top management. Exposure to these top policy makers can speed an effective financial manager's climb in the organization.

Capital Budgeting Analyst**/Manager**

The capital budgeting analyst/manager is responsible for the evaluation and selection of proposed projects and for the allocation of funds for these projects. In the evaluation process, the analyst compiles relevant data and makes cash flow projections about proposed projects. The analyst evaluates the project's acceptability based on the firm's return criteria and assesses the project's impact on the firm's asset structure. Upon selection of acceptable projects, the analyst/manager oversees the financial aspects of the implementation of the projects; this sometimes includes analyzing and arranging the necessary financing.

> Salary: Junior analyst: $25,000–$30,000
> Manager: $30,000–$60,000

Cash Manager**

The cash manager is responsible for maintaining and controlling the daily cash balances of the firm. In a large company, this involves coordinating national or international banking relationships, compensating balances, lockbox arrangements, cash transfers, and establishing and maintaining lines of credit. An understanding of the business and cash cycles of the firm is essential in projecting the firm's daily cash surplus or deficit. The cash manager is responsible for investing surplus funds in short-term marketable securities, while a deficit requires that the manager arrange necessary short-term financing through trade credit,

---

[1] Louis E. Boone and James C. Johnson, "Profiles of the 801 Men and 1 Woman at the Top," *Business Horizons*, February 1980, pp. 47–52.

bank notes or lines, accounts receivable or inventory loans, factoring, commercial paper, or other sources.

    Salary: $40,000–$75,000

Property Manager **

A property manager acquires, finances, manages, promotes, and markets properties for a firm that is not otherwise in the real estate business. Real estate can be both a substantial source and use of cash to a firm. By developing existing property or refinancing property using various leasing techniques, the earnings performance of the firm can be significantly enhanced. Property managers are employed by large firms, insurance companies, pension funds, and banks.

    Salary: Entry-level: $15,000–$20,000
                Experienced corporate property manager: up to $70,000

Credit Analyst*/Manager**

The general credit analyst/manager administers the firm's credit policy by analyzing or managing two basic activities: the evaluation of credit applications and the collection of accounts receivable. Routine duties involve analyzing the financial condition of applicants, checking credit histories, and determining the appropriate amount of credit and credit terms to offer the applicant. The manager also supervises the collection of current and past-due accounts receivable. By 1995, the demands for credit analysts and credit managers are expected to increase by about 41 percent and 33 percent, respectively.[2]

    Salary: Analyst: $13,000–$20,000
             Manager: $25,000 and up

Financial Analyst*

A financial analyst may be responsible for a variety of financial tasks. Primarily, the analyst is involved in preparing and analyzing the firm's financial plans and budgets. This function requires a close working relationship with the accounting activity. Other duties may include financial forecasting, assisting in preparation of pro forma statements,

[2] Steven S. Ross, "Careers: What's Hot, What's Not," *Business Week's Guide to Careers, Job Trak* (Special Edition), 1985, pp. 13–18.

and analyzing other aspects of the firm such as its liquidity, short-term borrowing, fixed assets, and capital structure. The degree of specialization of the analyst's duties is generally dependent upon the size of the firm. Larger firms tend to have specialized analysts, while smaller firms assign the analyst a number of areas of responsibility.

Many students headed for a career in managerial finance will begin as a financial, or "budget," analyst, doing financial planning and budgeting. According to the chief financial officers (CFOs) of firms in the *Fortune* 1000, financial planning and budgeting is the biggest career growth area in managerial finance.[3] In addition, these CFOs indicated it is also the most important and time-consuming managerial finance task. By 1995, the demand for financial analysts is expected to increase by about 37 percent.[4]

Salary:	Entry-level:	$15,000 – $20,000
	MBA:	$20,000 – $40,000

Pension Fund Manager**

The pension fund manager is responsible for coordinating the management of the earning assets of the employees' pension fund. The fund may be managed by the firm or by a bank trust department, insurance company, or investment firm. If the pension fund is managed within the firm, the manager prudently assesses the suitability of investments, develops a diversified investment portfolio, monitors both the financial markets and the firm's portfolio, and administers all financial transactions involved in the investment management process. If all or part of the pension fund is managed outside the firm, the pension fund manager monitors the performance of the external fund managers and oversees the employee-related aspects of the fund.

Salary: $40,000 and up

Project Finance Manager**

Project finance manager is a position that generally exists only at the largest firms. Responsibilities include arranging financing for capital expenditures that meet the firm's capital-structure objectives. The manager of project finance coordinates the activities of consultants, investment bankers, and legal counsel. An essential skill of this manager is the

---

[3] Lawrence J. Gitman and Charles E. Maxwell, "Financial Activities of Major U.S. Firms: Survey and Analysis of *Fortune's* 1000," *Financial Management*, Winter 1985, pp. 57–65.

[4] See note 2 above.

ability to evaluate and forecast financial market conditions and to assess their impact on future project financing.

Salary: $40,000 – $50,000

CAREER PATH 2:
FINANCIAL SERVICES

The financial services industry is the fastest-growing area in finance. It offers career opportunities in banking, securities, real estate, and insurance. Most of the jobs in the financial services industry can be obtained by qualified candidates upon graduation from college. To be successful in financial services, the graduate must understand the financial aspects of a product or service and also be able to sell that service. The majority of entry-level positions in this career path are sales-oriented.

BANKING

Loan Officer**

A loan officer evaluates the credit of personal and business loan applicants. Loan officers may specialize in commercial, installment, or mortgage loans. The commercial loan officer develops and monitors the credit relationship between the business customer and the bank. Responsibilities include evaluation of the creditworthiness of the business, negotiating credit terms, monitoring the firm's financial condition, cross-selling the bank's other corporate services, and acting as a financial adviser to smaller firms.

Salary: Entry-level: $20,000 – $30,000
Experienced: $30,000 – $50,000

Retail Bank Manager*

Retail banking involves the bank's branch offices, which deal directly with the public. The branch manager supervises the programs offered by the bank to its customers — installment loans, mortgages, checking, savings, retirement accounts, and other financial products. Due to the competitive nature of banking since the industry's deregulation, the successful retail banker must aggressively market the bank's new products as well as possess a certain degree of financial savvy.

The outlook for employment in the banking industry looks favorable over the next decade. Banks are hiring graduates with degrees in finance or accounting with a marketing emphasis as well as finance graduates with a technical background in management information systems and computers.[5] Many banks have management training programs that provide the entry-level trainee with experience in retail banking. According to *Business Week's Guide to Careers*, the bank-trainee position is one of the top 20 entry-level jobs in terms of ultimate salary potential and number of openings expected in the coming decade.

Salary: Entry-level: $13,200–$17,000
MBA: $20,000–$28,000

Trust Officer**

Trust officers manage portfolios of investments for individuals, foundations, institutions, and corporate pension and profit-sharing plans. The trust officer and his or her staff research, analyze, and monitor both currently held and potential investment vehicles for retention or inclusion in the portfolios they manage.

Salary: $20,000–$50,000

SECURITIES

Financial Planner*

A financial planner works in an advisory capacity to individuals. The planner advises the client about budgeting, securities, insurance, real estate, taxes, retirement and estate planning, and devises a comprehensive financial plan to meet the client's life objectives. This position has been included in the securities industry section but could as well have been in the banking, real estate, or insurance sections of this appendix. Eighty percent of all financial planners are employed by the financial services industry and serve as a complement to the sales function in their firm. The other 20 percent are self-employed and sell advice rather than financial products, such as securities, tax shelters, or insurance.

Salary: Entry-level: $18,000–$25,000
Experienced: up to $100,000

Investment Banker**

Investment bankers are considered the financial "movers and shakers" on Wall Street. They act as brokers between the issuers and buyers of

[5] John Stodden, "Job Map," *Business Week's Guide to Careers, Job Trak* (Special Edition), 1985, pp. 4–9.

newly issued stocks and bonds. Generally, the investment banker purchases the security issue and then markets it to the public, bearing all the risk of selling the issue. Considerable experience and expertise are necessary to land a job in a Wall Street investment banking firm, but the rewards are worth the effort.

Salary: Entry-level MBA: $30,000 – $50,000
After 10 years' experience: $250,000 – $300,000

Securities Analyst**

Securities analysts are the financial experts on Wall Street who study stocks and bonds, usually in specific industries. They are specialists with respect to a particular firm or industry, and understand the economic impact of changes in the competitive, financial, and foreign markets on that firm or industry. They are employed by and act as advisers to securities firms, fund managers, and insurance companies.

Salary: Junior analyst with MBA: $25,000 – $30,000
Experienced analyst: up to $100,000

Stockbroker* or Account Executive*

A stockbroker or account executive's responsibilities include handling orders to buy and sell securities, counseling customers on financial matters, supplying the latest stock and bond quotations, and responding to customer inquiries. Stockbrokers are usually hired by brokerage firms, investment banks, mutual funds, and insurance companies. Job opportunities for brokers are also emerging in traditional financial institutions such as banks and savings and loans. Most firms offer a training program at the entry level that prepares the stockbroker to take the required standardized licensing examination. According to *Business Week's Guide to Careers*, the broker trainee position is one of the top 12 entry-level jobs in terms of ultimate salary potential and number of openings expected in the coming decade. Out of 200,000 people employed in the securities market, over one-half are stockbrokers or securities salespeople. However, the turnover rate is very high among these positions, being 95 percent within the first two years.[6]

Salary: Trainee: $12,000 – $16,000 plus commissions
Experienced broker: $50,000 – $100,000 or more

[6] Nicholas Basta, "Securities Industry," *Business Week's Guide to Careers*, February/March 1984, p. 75.

REAL ESTATE

Real Estate Agent*/Broker*

Most property is sold or leased with the aid of a real estate agent who is generally employed by a broker. Some of the agent's and broker's duties include finding potential buyers and lessees for listed property, showing property, and negotiating sale or lease terms agreeable to both parties. Additionally, a broker is generally an independent businessperson experienced in the field of real estate; he or she supports the sales staff, providing office space and a budget for advertising and promoting listed properties. Many real estate agents and brokers are also certified property managers, real estate appraisers, and real estate developers. By 1995, the demand for real estate brokers is expected to increase by about 30 percent in economically developing regions of the country.[7]

Salary: Beginner: $10,000 – $15,000
         Experienced: $25,000 – $75,000

INSURANCE

Insurance Agent*/Broker*

Insurance agents and brokers develop programs to fit customers' needs, interview insurance prospects, help with claims and settlements, and collect premiums. An agent is usually employed by a single insurance company, whereas a broker is independent and represents no particular company but can sell policies from many. Getting a job as an insurance agent is easy; being successful is much more difficult. The turnover rate is similar to that for stockbrokers; approximately 90 percent of the newly employed in this field leave after two years.[8]

Salary: Trainee: $15,000 – $22,500
         Experienced agent: $30,000 – $50,000

Underwriter**

Underwriters appraise and select the risks their company will insure. This includes the appraisal of the risks of individuals after analyzing insurance applications, reports from loss-control consultants, medical reports, and actuarial studies. Commercial underwriting involves insuring a firm's major fixed assets, such as heavy equipment. When

[7] See note 2 above.

[8] See note 6 above.

deciding whether an applicant is an acceptable risk, an underwriter may outline the terms of the contract, including the amount of the premium. By 1995, the demand for underwriters is expected to increase by about 21 percent.[9]

   Salary: $30,000 – $50,000

WHERE ARE THE JOBS?

Locating the fastest-growing job opportunities in managerial finance requires targeting the regions of the country where manufacturing and trade industries are flourishing. Figure B.1 shows where the jobs are. The best overall job markets in managerial finance currently are all in

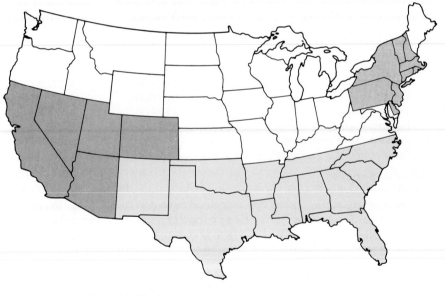

Best Job Markets

Managerial Finance

Financial Services

Managerial Finance and Financial Services

FIGURE B.1 Where Are the Jobs?
The best overall job markets for managerial finance are in the southern half of the country, while the best markets for first jobs in financial services are in New England, the Middle Atlantic, and the Pacific Southwest.

[9] See note 2 above.

the southern half of the country. However, there are still many opportunities in the north.

The best job markets for first jobs in financial services are in New England, the Middle Atlantic, and the Pacific Southwest. In New England and the Middle Atlantic region, the growth in the service industry is resulting in the rapid expansion of opportunities in finance and insurance since most firms in these industries are headquartered in those regions. In the Pacific Southwest, demographics show that the rising population and industrial activity are causing an increase in the demand for accountants, financial analysts, and associated managers and administrative staffs.[10] (see Figure B.1).

TABLE B.1 Salaries of Various Career Opportunities in Finance

Job Title	Entry-level salary	Potential salary
Managerial Finance		
Capital budgeting analyst	$25,000–$30,000	$ 60,000
Cash manager	—	$ 75,000
Property manager	$15,000–$20,000	$ 70,000
Credit analyst	$13,000–$15,000	$ 20,000
Credit manager	$25,000–$40,000	$ 80,000
Financial analyst	$15,000–$20,000	$ 40,000
Pension fund manager	—	$100,000
Project finance manager	—	$ 50,000
Financial Services		
Banking		
Loan officer	$20,000–$30,000	$ 50,000
Retail bank manager	$13,200–$22,500	$ 28,000
Trust officer	$20,000–$30,000	$ 50,000
Securities		
Financial planner	$18,000–$25,000	$100,000
Investment banker	$30,000–$50,000	$250,000
Securities analyst	$25,000–$30,000	$100,000
Stockbroker or account executive	$12,000–$16,000	$100,000
Real Estate		
Real estate agent/broker	$10,000–$15,000	$ 75,000
Insurance		
Agent/broker	$15,000–$22,500	$ 50,000
Underwriter	$17,000–$25,000	$ 50,000

[10] See note 5 above.

WHAT ARE THE JOBS PAYING?

The finance graduate can expect top salary offers among business graduates. In finance, entry-level job offers averaged $19,506 in 1985.[11] The best offers are going to the business majors with a technical background. The salaries summarized in Table B.1 are expressed in ranges and are only guidelines. Many factors may affect the salary level of a job: the geographic region, the employee's work experience and educational background, and the size of the company.

SOURCES OF INFORMATION

Nicholas Basta, "Securities Industry," *Business Week's Guide to Careers*, February/March 1984, p. 75.

Louis E. Boone and James C. Johnson, "Profiles of the 801 Men and 1 Woman at the Top," *Business Horizons*, February 1980, pp. 47–52.

Careers in Finance, Financial Management Association, 1983.

Career Information Center, Second Edition, Glencoe Publishing, 1984.

College Placement Council, *CPC Salary Survey*, December 1985.

Anita Gates, *90 Most Promising Careers for the 80s*, Monarch Press, 1982.

Lawrence J. Gitman and Charles E. Maxwell, "Financial Activities of Major U.S. Firms: Survey and Analysis of *Fortune's* 1000," *Financial Management*, Winter 1985, pp. 57–65.

Occupational Outlook Handbook, U.S. Department of Labor, Bureau of Labor Statistics, April 1984.

Steven S. Ross, "Careers: What's Hot, What's Not," *Business Week's Guide to Careers*, *Job Trak* (Special Edition), McGraw-Hill, 1985, pp.13–18.

John D. Shingleton and L. Patrick Scheetz, *Recruiting Trends, 1984–1985*, Placement Services, Michigan State University, East Lansing, Michigan.

Robert O. Snelling and Anne M. Snelling, *JOBS!*, New York, Simon and Schuster, 1985.

John Stodden, "Job Map," *Business Week's Guide to Careers, Job Trak* (Special Edition), McGraw-Hill, 1985, pp. 4–9.

---

[11] John Shingleton and L. Patrick Scheetz, *Recruiting Trends, 1984–1985*, Placement Services, Michigan State University, East Lansing, Michigan.

Appendix C

INSTRUCTIONS FOR USING *THE BASIC MANAGERIAL FINANCE (BMF) DISK*

OVERVIEW

The Basic Managerial Finance (BMF) Disk is a collection of financial routines designed to accompany *Basic Managerial Finance*. The disk is available for use in Apple II and IBM-PC microcomputers. All routines are written in BASIC and may be transferred easily to other computers with little or no modification.

The purpose of *The BMF Disk* is to aid the student's learning and understanding of managerial finance by providing a fast and easy method for performing the often time-consuming mathematical computations required. It is not the intent of this computer package to eliminate the need for learning the various concepts, but to assist in solving the problems once the appropriate formulas have been studied. The routines on the disk are arranged in the same order as the text discussions; for convenience, text page references are shown on the screen for each associated computational routine. As noted in the text Preface as well as in Chapter 1, applicability of the disk throughout the text and study guide is always keyed to related text discussions and end-of-chapter problems by the printed disk symbol ▰. This should allow the user to integrate the procedures on the disk with the corresponding text discussions.

TECHNICAL INFORMATION

Because of differences in their operating systems, there are certain technical differences between the Apple II and IBM-PC versions of *The BMF Disk*.

Apple II Version

The Apple II version of *The BMF Disk* as supplied is ready to use. This means it can be placed in the disk drive and booted without any reconfiguring. The disk contains the operating system and all necessary programs. Since the programs are written in Applesoft BASIC, those with earlier Apple IIs without autostart ROM will have to load Applesoft and then 'RUN HELLO' or transfer FPBASIC (Applesoft) to *The BMF Disk* and then make the needed changes in the Hello program. (Refer to *Apple II Reference Manual*.) With all other Apple IIs (II+, IIe, and IIc), as well as most Apple compatibles, you will be able to place the disk in the disk drive, close the door, boot the disk (or turn on computer), and proceed with a session of interactive financial problem solving (i.e., homework).

The BMF Disk contains a high-speed operating system called Diversi-DOS™, which is licensed for use with this program only. To legally use Diversi-DOS with other programs, you may send $30 directly to: DSR, Inc., 5848 Crampton Ct., Rockford, Illinois 61111. In return you will be sent a Diversi-DOS utility disk with documentation.

IBM-PC Version

The IBM-PC version of *The BMF Disk* is written in IBM BASIC (DOS 2.1) and is as similar to the Applesoft version as possible. The main difference, from a user's point of view, is that the IBM version does not contain an operating system or the BASIC program (BASICA.COM). Before the financial programs can be accessed, PC DOS or a compatible operating system must be loaded into the computer. After DOS is loaded, BASIC must be loaded. When this process is complete, the main program (START.BAS) may be run. This is accomplished by typing RUN "START after BASIC is "up."

To simplify this process, copy all programs to a formatted system disk with BASICA.COM already installed, or copy COMMAND.COM and BASICA.COM to *The BMF Disk* (preferably a backup copy). An autoboot procedure (AUTOEXEC.BAT) has been included to enable the IBM version to run in a "turnkey" fashion, as does the Apple version. This turnkey system will only operate if the programs are on a system disk that includes BASIC.

GENERAL PROGRAMMING CONVENTIONS

The user should become familiar with several conventions employed in the display portion of the programs. These deal with the way responses to prompts or queries are answered. Keep in mind that answers to computer-generated prompts are basically of two types. These are single-character responses and multiple-character responses.

Most responses are of the multiple-character variety. That is, they require the user to enter one or more numbers or letters followed by the RETURN key. (*Note:* The RETURN key is used to refer to the *carriage return key*—often noted as ⟨CR⟩—which may be labeled RETURN, ENTER, or ⟵, depending on the specific microcomputer being used.) These responses usually involve entering data. The remainder of responses will be mainly for program control and choice of options. Where practical, responses have been reduced to single-character entries not requiring the use of the RETURN key. Therefore it is important not to be too quick to hit the RETURN key after answering a prompt that requires only a single-character response.

Responses that have been reduced to single characters involve such prompts as (Y/N), which means a yes-or-no answer is required. Press Y for Yes and N for No. In most instances, Y is the default answer that is assumed if no other answer is given. This default will usually mean "everything is OK, so continue." For example, at the end of a screen of data the user will be asked "Are all values correct (Y/N)" where the Y(es) response is assumed. If the user enters anything other than N, the program will continue as if a Y were entered. (*Note:* The ⟨CR⟩ response refers to the carriage return key described above. Also, on the IBM-PC version, uppercase and lowercase letters are treated the same.)

The statement "Hit any key to continue ⟨ESC⟩ for menu" will be displayed at points where the program is pausing to permit the user to examine the screen. Almost any key stroke will allow the program to continue. Keys that do not have their own function codes will not allow the program to continue. Examples of these keys are the shift key and the control key. All other keys will allow the program to continue, but the ESCape key will bring up the current menu, thus permitting the user to return to the main menu or possibly end the session. (*Note:* Only at specified points in the program can escape be achieved using the ESC key.)

PROCEDURES

The major procedures for using the start-up program, main menu, and a review of each of the main menu items will acquaint you with the use of this user-friendly menu-driven disk. After the descriptions of each of the following routines, the file names for the given routine for both computers (Apple II and IBM-PC) are given. These file names could prove helpful if program enhancements are desired. For those unfamiliar with programming, these file names need not be of concern.

Start-Up Program

This program will perform an initializing function. Here the user enters his or her name and is given the option of using a printer. If the printer option is used, there must be a printer attached to the system and it must be turned on. Otherwise a reboot of the disk may be necessary.

File Name
Apple II--HELLO
IBM-PC--START.BAS

Main Menu

After answering the prompts in the start-up program, the main menu will be displayed. This menu controls *The BMF Disk* and is used as the starting point for all of the financial routines. The Main Menu appears as follows:

```
****The Basic Managerial Finance (BMF) Disk****
                    to accompany
    Basic Managerial Finance by Lawrence J. Gitman

         (1)  Financial Ratios
         (2)  Breakeven Analysis
         (3)  Cash Budget
         (4)  Pro Forma Statements
         (5)  Time Value of Money
         (6)  Bond & Stock Valuation
         (7)  Cost of Capital
         (8)  Capital Budgeting Cash Flows
         (9)  Capital Budgeting Techniques
        (10)  Bond Refunding Decision
         (0)  End Program
```

File Name
Apple II--MENU
IBM-PC--MENU.BAS

Review of Main Menu Items

By entering one of the numbers within the parentheses followed by the RETURN key, the chosen routine is brought up. The next screen displayed will be a menu giving the options available in that routine. Each of the ten menu routines is described below:

(1) Financial Ratios

Used for calculating financial ratios as described in Chapter 4. The menu is:

(1) Individual Ratios
Allows a single ratio to be calculated.
(2) Families of Ratios
Gives a choice of the four different groups of ratios: liquidity, activity, debt, and profitability.
(3) All Ratios
Gives all financial ratios as described in the text.
(4) Return to Main Menu

File Name
Apple II--RATIO ANALYSIS
IBM-PC--RATIO.BAS

(2) Breakeven Analysis

Used to determine the operating level at which a firm's breakeven point is reached, as described in Chapter 5. The menu is:

(1) Operating Breakeven Point
(2) Return to Main Menu

File Name
Apple II--BREAKEVEN ANALYSIS
IBM-PC--BREAKEVN.BAS

(3) Cash Budget

Used for creating cash budgets as described in Chapter 6. The menu is:

(1) Cash Budget
(2) Return to Main Menu

File Name
Apple II--CASH BUDGET
IBM-PC--CASHBUDG.BAS

(4) Pro Forma Statements

Used for creating simple pro forma statements as described in Chapter 6. The menu is:

(1) Pro Forma Statements
(2) Return to Main Menu

File Name
Apple II--PRO FORMA STATEMENTS
IBM-PC--PROFORMA.BAS

(5) Time Value of Money

Used for calculating present and future values as described in Chapter 11. The menu is:

(1) Present and Future Value of a Single Payment
(2) Present and Future Value of an Annuity
    Perpetuities may be calculated by entering any number of periods greater than or equal to 100.
(3) Present Value of a Mixed Stream
(4) Return to Main Menu

These routines may also be used to amortize or estimate growth rates. Enter known information as it is asked for, leaving one item blank. The blank item is the unknown calculated by the computer.

File Name
Apple II--TIME VALUE OF MONEY
IBM-PC--TIMEVALU.BAS

(6) Bond & Stock Valuation

Used to determine the value of bonds and stocks as described in Chapter 12. The menu is:

(1) Bond Valuation
(2) Common Stock Valuation
(3) Return to Main Menu

File Name
Apple II--STOCK BOND VALUATION
IBM-PC--STOCBOND.BAS

(7) Cost of Capital

Calculates the costs of long-term debt (bonds), preferred stock, common stock, and the weighted average and weighted marginal costs of capital as described in Chapter 13. The menu is:

(1) Long-Term Debt (Bonds)
(2) Preferred Stock
(3) Common Stock
(4) Weighted Average Cost of Capital
(5) Weighted Marginal Cost of Capital
(6) Return to Main Menu

File Name
Apple II--COST OF CAPITAL
IBM-PC--COSTCAP.BAS

(8) Capital Budgeting Cash Flows

Used to determine the initial investment only or all relevant cash flows for capital budgeting projects as described in Chapter 14. The menu is:

(1) Determining Initial Investment
(2) Determining Relevant Cash Flows
(3) Return to Main Menu

File Name
Apple II--CASH FLOW
IBM-PC--CASHFLOW.BAS

(9) Capital Budgeting Techniques
Used to compare multiple projects using capital budgeting techniques as described in Chapter 15. The menu is:

(1) Average Rate of Return
(2) Payback Period
    Net Present Value *(NPV)*
    Profitability Index *(PI)*
    Internal Rate of Return *(IRR)*
(3) Return to Main Menu

File Name
Apple II--CAPITAL BUDGETING
IBM-PC--CAPBUDG.BAS

(10) Bond Refunding Decision
Used to evaluate the option of retiring a bond issue with a new issue as described in Chapter 18. The menu is:

(1) Bond Refunding
(2) Return to Main Menu

File Name
Apple II--BOND REFUNDING DECISION
IBM-PC--BONDRFND.BAS

Appendix D
FINANCIAL TABLES

Table D-1 Future-Value Interest Factors for One Dollar Compounded at k Percent for n Periods: $FVIF_{k,n} = (1 + k)^n$

Period	1%	2%	3%	4%	5%	6%	7%	8%	9%	10%
1	1.010	1.020	1.030	1.040	1.050	1.060	1.070	1.080	1.090	1.100
2	1.020	1.040	1.061	1.082	1.102	1.124	1.145	1.166	1.188	1.210
3	1.030	1.061	1.093	1.125	1.158	1.191	1.225	1.260	1.295	1.331
4	1.041	1.082	1.126	1.170	1.216	1.262	1.311	1.360	1.412	1.464
5	1.051	1.104	1.159	1.217	1.276	1.338	1.403	1.469	1.539	1.611
6	1.062	1.126	1.194	1.265	1.340	1.419	1.501	1.587	1.677	1.772
7	1.072	1.149	1.230	1.316	1.407	1.504	1.606	1.714	1.828	1.949
8	1.083	1.172	1.267	1.369	1.477	1.594	1.718	1.851	1.993	2.144
9	1.094	1.195	1.305	1.423	1.551	1.689	1.838	1.999	2.172	2.358
10	1.105	1.219	1.344	1.480	1.629	1.791	1.967	2.159	2.367	2.594
11	1.116	1.243	1.384	1.539	1.710	1.898	2.105	2.332	2.580	2.853
12	1.127	1.268	1.426	1.601	1.796	2.012	2.252	2.518	2.813	3.138
13	1.138	1.294	1.469	1.665	1.886	2.133	2.410	2.720	3.066	3.452
14	1.149	1.319	1.513	1.732	1.980	2.261	2.579	2.937	3.342	3.797
15	1.161	1.346	1.558	1.801	2.079	2.397	2.759	3.172	3.642	4.177
16	1.173	1.373	1.605	1.873	2.183	2.540	2.952	3.426	3.970	4.595
17	1.184	1.400	1.653	1.948	2.292	2.693	3.159	3.700	4.328	5.054
18	1.196	1.428	1.702	2.026	2.407	2.854	3.380	3.996	4.717	5.560
19	1.208	1.457	1.753	2.107	2.527	3.026	3.616	4.316	5.142	6.116
20	1.220	1.486	1.806	2.191	2.653	3.207	3.870	4.661	5.604	6.727
21	1.232	1.516	1.860	2.279	2.786	3.399	4.140	5.034	6.109	7.400
22	1.245	1.546	1.916	2.370	2.925	3.603	4.430	5.436	6.658	8.140
23	1.257	1.577	1.974	2.465	3.071	3.820	4.740	5.871	7.258	8.954
24	1.270	1.608	2.033	2.563	3.225	4.049	5.072	6.341	7.911	9.850
25	1.282	1.641	2.094	2.666	3.386	4.292	5.427	6.848	8.623	10.834
30	1.348	1.811	2.427	3.243	4.322	5.743	7.612	10.062	13.267	17.449
35	1.417	2.000	2.814	3.946	5.516	7.686	10.676	14.785	20.413	28.102
40	1.489	2.208	3.262	4.801	7.040	10.285	14.974	21.724	31.408	45.258
45	1.565	2.438	3.781	5.841	8.985	13.764	21.002	31.920	48.325	72.888
50	1.645	2.691	4.384	7.106	11.467	18.419	29.456	46.900	74.354	117.386

TABLE D-1 FUTURE-VALUE INTEREST FACTORS FOR ONE DOLLAR

Table D-1 Future-Value Interest Factors for One Dollar Compounded at k Percent for n Periods: $FVIF_{k,n} = (1 + k)^n$ (continued)

Period	11%	12%	13%	14%	15%	16%	17%	18%	19%	20%
1	1.110	1.120	1.130	1.140	1.150	1.160	1.170	1.180	1.190	1.200
2	1.232	1.254	1.277	1.300	1.322	1.346	1.369	1.392	1.416	1.440
3	1.368	1.405	1.443	1.482	1.521	1.561	1.602	1.643	1.685	1.728
4	1.518	1.574	1.630	1.689	1.749	1.811	1.874	1.939	2.005	2.074
5	1.685	1.762	1.842	1.925	2.011	2.100	2.192	2.288	2.386	2.488
6	1.870	1.974	2.082	2.195	2.313	2.436	2.565	2.700	2.840	2.986
7	2.076	2.211	2.353	2.502	2.660	2.826	3.001	3.185	3.379	3.583
8	2.305	2.476	2.658	2.853	3.059	3.278	3.511	3.759	4.021	4.300
9	2.558	2.773	3.004	3.252	3.518	3.803	4.108	4.435	4.785	5.160
10	2.839	3.106	3.395	3.707	4.046	4.411	4.807	5.234	5.695	6.192
11	3.152	3.479	3.836	4.226	4.652	5.117	5.624	6.176	6.777	7.430
12	3.498	3.896	4.334	4.818	5.350	5.936	6.580	7.288	8.064	8.916
13	3.883	4.363	4.898	5.492	6.153	6.886	7.699	8.599	9.596	10.699
14	4.310	4.887	5.535	6.261	7.076	7.987	9.007	10.147	11.420	12.839
15	4.785	5.474	6.254	7.138	8.137	9.265	10.539	11.974	13.589	15.407
16	5.311	6.130	7.067	8.137	9.358	10.748	12.330	14.129	16.171	18.488
17	5.895	6.866	7.986	9.276	10.761	12.468	14.426	16.672	19.244	22.186
18	6.543	7.690	9.024	10.575	12.375	14.462	16.879	19.673	22.900	26.623
19	7.263	8.613	10.197	12.055	14.232	16.776	19.748	23.214	27.251	31.948
20	8.062	9.646	11.523	13.743	16.366	19.461	23.105	27.393	32.429	38.337
21	8.949	10.804	13.021	15.667	18.821	22.574	27.033	32.323	38.591	46.005
22	9.933	12.100	14.713	17.861	21.644	26.186	31.629	38.141	45.923	55.205
23	11.026	13.552	16.626	20.361	24.891	30.376	37.005	45.007	54.648	66.247
24	12.239	15.178	18.788	23.212	28.625	35.236	43.296	53.108	65.031	79.496
25	13.585	17.000	21.230	26.461	32.918	40.874	50.656	62.667	77.387	95.395
30	22.892	29.960	39.115	50.949	66.210	85.849	111.061	143.367	184.672	237.373
35	38.574	52.799	72.066	98.097	133.172	180.311	243.495	327.988	440.691	590.657
40	64.999	93.049	132.776	188.876	267.856	378.715	533.846	750.353	1051.642	1469.740
45	109.527	163.985	244.629	363.662	538.752	795.429	1170.425	1716.619	2509.583	3657.176
50	184.559	288.996	450.711	700.197	1083.619	1670.669	2566.080	3927.189	5988.730	9100.191

Table D-1   Future-Value Interest Factors for One Dollar Compounded at k Percent for n Periods: $FVIF_{k,n} = (1 + k)^n$ (continued)

Period	21%	22%	23%	24%	25%	26%	27%	28%	29%	30%
1	1.210	1.220	1.230	1.240	1.250	1.260	1.270	1.280	1.290	1.300
2	1.464	1.488	1.513	1.538	1.562	1.588	1.613	1.638	1.664	1.690
3	1.772	1.816	1.861	1.907	1.953	2.000	2.048	2.097	2.147	2.197
4	2.144	2.215	2.289	2.364	2.441	2.520	2.601	2.684	2.769	2.856
5	2.594	2.703	2.815	2.932	3.052	3.176	3.304	3.436	3.572	3.713
6	3.138	3.297	3.463	3.635	3.815	4.001	4.196	4.398	4.608	4.827
7	3.797	4.023	4.259	4.508	4.768	5.042	5.329	5.629	5.945	6.275
8	4.595	4.908	5.239	5.589	5.960	6.353	6.767	7.206	7.669	8.157
9	5.560	5.987	6.444	6.931	7.451	8.004	8.595	9.223	9.893	10.604
10	6.727	7.305	7.926	8.594	9.313	10.086	10.915	11.806	12.761	13.786
11	8.140	8.912	9.749	10.657	11.642	12.708	13.862	15.112	16.462	17.921
12	9.850	10.872	11.991	13.215	14.552	16.012	17.605	19.343	21.236	23.298
13	11.918	13.264	14.749	16.386	18.190	20.175	22.359	24.759	27.395	30.287
14	14.421	16.182	18.141	20.319	22.737	25.420	28.395	31.691	35.339	39.373
15	17.449	19.742	22.314	25.195	28.422	32.030	36.062	40.565	45.587	51.185
16	21.113	24.085	27.446	31.242	35.527	40.357	45.799	51.923	58.808	66.541
17	25.547	29.384	33.758	38.740	44.409	50.850	58.165	66.461	75.862	86.503
18	30.912	35.848	41.523	48.038	55.511	64.071	73.869	85.070	97.862	112.454
19	37.404	43.735	51.073	59.567	69.389	80.730	93.813	108.890	126.242	146.190
20	45.258	53.357	62.820	73.863	86.736	101.720	119.143	139.379	162.852	190.047
21	54.762	65.095	77.268	91.591	108.420	128.167	151.312	178.405	210.079	247.061
22	66.262	79.416	95.040	113.572	135.525	161.490	192.165	228.358	271.002	321.178
23	80.178	96.887	116.899	140.829	169.407	203.477	244.050	292.298	349.592	417.531
24	97.015	118.203	143.786	174.628	211.758	256.381	309.943	374.141	450.974	542.791
25	117.388	144.207	176.857	216.539	264.698	323.040	393.628	478.901	581.756	705.627
30	304.471	389.748	497.904	634.810	807.793	1025.904	1300.477	1645.488	2078.208	2619.936
35	789.716	1053.370	1401.749	1861.020	2465.189	3258.053	4296.547	5653.840	7423.988	9727.598
40	2048.309	2846.941	3946.340	5455.797	7523.156	10346.879	14195.051	19426.418	26520.723	36117.754
45	5312.758	7694.418	11110.121	15994.316	22958.844	32859.457	46897.973	66748.500	94739.937	134102.187
50	13779.844	20795.680	31278.301	46889.207	70064.812	104354.562	154942.687	229345.875	338440.000	497910.125

TABLE D-1 FUTURE-VALUE INTEREST FACTORS FOR ONE DOLLAR

Table D-1 Future-Value Interest Factors for One Dollar Compounded at k Percent for n Periods: $FVIF_{k,n} = (1 + k)^n$ (continued)

Period	31%	32%	33%	34%	35%	36%	37%	38%	39%	40%
1	1.310	1.320	1.330	1.340	1.350	1.360	1.370	1.380	1.390	1.400
2	1.716	1.742	1.769	1.796	1.822	1.850	1.877	1.904	1.932	1.960
3	2.248	2.300	2.353	2.406	2.460	2.515	2.571	2.628	2.686	2.744
4	2.945	3.036	3.129	3.224	3.321	3.421	3.523	3.627	3.733	3.842
5	3.858	4.007	4.162	4.320	4.484	4.653	4.826	5.005	5.189	5.378
6	5.054	5.290	5.535	5.789	6.053	6.328	6.612	6.907	7.213	7.530
7	6.621	6.983	7.361	7.758	8.172	8.605	9.058	9.531	10.025	10.541
8	8.673	9.217	9.791	10.395	11.032	11.703	12.410	13.153	13.935	14.758
9	11.362	12.166	13.022	13.930	14.894	15.917	17.001	18.151	19.370	20.661
10	14.884	16.060	17.319	18.666	20.106	21.646	23.292	25.049	26.924	28.925
11	19.498	21.199	23.034	25.012	27.144	29.439	31.910	34.567	37.425	40.495
12	25.542	27.982	30.635	33.516	36.644	40.037	43.716	47.703	52.020	56.694
13	33.460	36.937	40.745	44.912	49.469	54.451	59.892	65.830	72.308	79.371
14	43.832	48.756	54.190	60.181	66.784	74.053	82.051	90.845	100.509	111.119
15	57.420	64.358	72.073	80.643	90.158	100.712	112.410	125.366	139.707	155.567
16	75.220	84.953	95.857	108.061	121.713	136.968	154.002	173.005	194.192	217.793
17	98.539	112.138	127.490	144.802	164.312	186.277	210.983	238.747	269.927	304.911
18	129.086	148.022	169.561	194.035	221.822	253.337	289.046	329.471	375.198	426.875
19	169.102	195.389	225.517	260.006	299.459	344.537	395.993	454.669	521.525	597.625
20	221.523	257.913	299.937	348.408	404.270	468.571	542.511	627.443	724.919	836.674
21	290.196	340.446	398.916	466.867	545.764	637.256	743.240	865.871	1007.637	1171.343
22	380.156	449.388	530.558	625.601	736.781	866.668	1018.238	1194.900	1400.615	1639.878
23	498.004	593.192	705.642	838.305	994.653	1178.668	1394.986	1648.961	1946.854	2295.829
24	652.385	783.013	938.504	1123.328	1342.781	1602.988	1911.129	2275.564	2706.125	3214.158
25	854.623	1033.577	1248.210	1505.258	1812.754	2180.063	2618.245	3140.275	3761.511	4499.816
30	3297.081	4142.008	5194.516	6503.285	8128.426	10142.914	12636.086	15716.703	19517.969	24201.043
35	12719.918	16598.906	21617.363	28096.695	36448.051	47190.727	60983.836	78660.188	101276.125	130158.687
40	49072.621	66519.313	89962.188	121388.437	163433.875	219558.625	294317.937	393684.687	525508.312	700022.688

Table D-1 Future-Value Interest Factors for One Dollar Compounded at k Percent for n Periods: $FVIF_{k,n} = (1 + k)^n$ (continued)

Period	41%	42%	43%	44%	45%	46%	47%	48%	49%	50%
1	1.410	1.420	1.430	1.440	1.450	1.460	1.470	1.480	1.490	1.500
2	1.988	2.016	2.045	2.074	2.102	2.132	2.161	2.190	2.220	2.250
3	2.803	2.863	2.924	2.986	3.049	3.112	3.177	3.242	3.308	3.375
4	3.953	4.066	4.182	4.300	4.421	4.544	4.669	4.798	4.929	5.063
5	5.573	5.774	5.980	6.192	6.410	6.634	6.864	7.101	7.344	7.594
6	7.858	8.198	8.551	8.916	9.294	9.685	10.090	10.509	10.943	11.391
7	11.080	11.642	12.228	12.839	13.476	14.141	14.833	15.554	16.304	17.086
8	15.623	16.531	17.486	18.488	19.541	20.645	21.804	23.019	24.293	25.629
9	22.028	23.474	25.005	26.623	28.334	30.142	32.052	34.069	36.197	38.443
10	31.059	33.333	35.757	38.337	41.085	44.007	47.116	50.421	53.934	57.665
11	43.793	47.333	51.132	55.206	59.573	64.251	69.261	74.624	80.361	86.498
12	61.749	67.213	73.119	79.496	86.380	93.806	101.813	110.443	119.738	129.746
13	87.066	95.443	104.560	114.475	125.251	136.956	149.665	163.456	178.410	194.620
14	122.763	135.529	149.521	164.843	181.614	199.956	220.008	241.914	265.831	291.929
15	173.095	192.451	213.814	237.374	263.341	291.936	323.411	358.033	396.088	437.894
16	244.064	273.280	305.754	341.819	381.844	426.226	475.414	529.888	590.170	656.841
17	344.130	388.057	437.228	492.219	553.674	622.289	698.859	784.234	879.354	985.261
18	485.224	551.041	625.235	708.794	802.826	908.541	1027.321	1160.666	1310.236	1477.892
19	684.165	782.478	894.086	1020.663	1164.098	1326.469	1510.161	1717.785	1952.252	2216.838
20	964.673	1111.118	1278.543	1469.754	1687.942	1936.642	2219.936	2542.321	2908.854	3325.257
21	1360.188	1577.786	1828.315	2116.445	2447.515	2827.496	3263.304	3762.633	4334.188	4987.883
22	1917.865	2240.455	2614.489	3047.679	3548.896	4128.137	4797.051	5568.691	6457.941	7481.824
23	2704.188	3181.443	3738.717	4388.656	5145.898	6027.078	7051.660	8241.664	9622.324	11222.738
24	3812.905	4517.641	5346.355	6319.656	7461.547	8799.523	10365.934	12197.656	14337.258	16834.109
25	5376.191	6415.047	7645.289	9100.305	10819.242	12847.297	15237.914	18052.516	21362.508	25251.164
30	29961.941	37037.383	45716.496	56346.535	69348.375	85226.375	104594.938	128187.438	156885.438	191751.000

TABLE D-2 FUTURE-VALUE INTEREST FACTORS FOR A ONE-DOLLAR ANNUITY

Table D-2 Future-Value Interest Factors for a One-Dollar Annuity Compounded at k Percent for n Periods: $FVIFA_{k,n} = \sum_{t=1}^{n} (1+k)^{t-1}$

Period	1%	2%	3%	4%	5%	6%	7%	8%	9%	10%
1	1.000	1.000	1.000	1.000	1.000	1.000	1.000	1.000	1.000	1.000
2	2.010	2.020	2.030	2.040	2.050	2.060	2.070	2.080	2.090	2.100
3	3.030	3.060	3.091	3.122	3.152	3.184	3.215	3.246	3.278	3.310
4	4.060	4.122	4.184	4.246	4.310	4.375	4.440	4.506	4.573	4.641
5	5.101	5.204	5.309	5.416	5.526	5.637	5.751	5.867	5.985	6.105
6	6.152	6.308	6.468	6.633	6.802	6.975	7.153	7.336	7.523	7.716
7	7.214	7.434	7.662	7.898	8.142	8.394	8.654	8.923	9.200	9.487
8	8.286	8.583	8.892	9.214	9.549	9.897	10.260	10.637	11.028	11.436
9	9.368	9.755	10.159	10.583	11.027	11.491	11.978	12.488	13.021	13.579
10	10.462	10.950	11.464	12.006	12.578	13.181	13.816	14.487	15.193	15.937
11	11.567	12.169	12.808	13.486	14.207	14.972	15.784	16.645	17.560	18.531
12	12.682	13.412	14.192	15.026	15.917	16.870	17.888	18.977	20.141	21.384
13	13.809	14.680	15.618	16.627	17.713	18.882	20.141	21.495	22.953	24.523
14	14.947	15.974	17.086	18.292	19.598	21.015	22.550	24.215	26.019	27.975
15	16.097	17.293	18.599	20.023	21.578	23.276	25.129	27.152	29.361	31.772
16	17.258	18.639	20.157	21.824	23.657	25.672	27.888	30.324	33.003	35.949
17	18.430	20.012	21.761	23.697	25.840	28.213	30.840	33.750	36.973	40.544
18	19.614	21.412	23.414	25.645	28.132	30.905	33.999	37.450	41.301	45.599
19	20.811	22.840	25.117	27.671	30.539	33.760	37.379	41.446	46.018	51.158
20	22.019	24.297	26.870	29.778	33.066	36.785	40.995	45.762	51.159	57.274
21	23.239	25.783	28.676	31.969	35.719	39.992	44.865	50.422	56.764	64.002
22	24.471	27.299	30.536	34.248	38.505	43.392	49.005	55.456	62.872	71.402
23	25.716	28.845	32.452	36.618	41.430	46.995	53.435	60.893	69.531	79.542
24	26.973	30.421	34.426	39.082	44.501	50.815	58.176	66.764	76.789	88.496
25	28.243	32.030	36.459	41.645	47.726	54.864	63.248	73.105	84.699	98.346
30	34.784	40.567	47.575	56.084	66.438	79.057	94.459	113.282	136.305	164.491
35	41.659	49.994	60.461	73.651	90.318	111.432	138.234	172.314	215.705	271.018
40	48.885	60.401	75.400	95.024	120.797	154.758	199.630	259.052	337.872	442.580
45	56.479	71.891	92.718	121.027	159.695	212.737	285.741	386.497	525.840	718.881
50	64.461	84.577	112.794	152.664	209.341	290.325	406.516	573.756	815.051	1163.865

Table D-2 Future-Value Interest Factors for a One-Dollar Annuity Compounded at k Percent for n Periods: $FVIFA_{k,n} = \sum_{t=1}^{n} (1 + k)^{t-1}$ (continued)

Period	11%	12%	13%	14%	15%	16%	17%	18%	19%	20%
1	1.000	1.000	1.000	1.000	1.000	1.000	1.000	1.000	1.000	1.000
2	2.110	2.120	2.130	2.140	2.150	2.160	2.170	2.180	2.190	2.200
3	3.342	3.374	3.407	3.440	3.472	3.506	3.539	3.572	3.606	3.640
4	4.710	4.779	4.850	4.921	4.993	5.066	5.141	5.215	5.291	5.368
5	6.228	6.353	6.480	6.610	6.742	6.877	7.014	7.154	7.297	7.442
6	7.913	8.115	8.323	8.535	8.754	8.977	9.207	9.442	9.683	9.930
7	9.783	10.089	10.405	10.730	11.067	11.414	11.772	12.141	12.523	12.916
8	11.859	12.300	12.757	13.233	13.727	14.240	14.773	15.327	15.902	16.499
9	14.164	14.776	15.416	16.085	16.786	17.518	18.285	19.086	19.923	20.799
10	16.722	17.549	18.420	19.337	20.304	21.321	22.393	23.521	24.709	25.959
11	19.561	20.655	21.814	23.044	24.349	25.733	27.200	28.755	30.403	32.150
12	22.713	24.133	25.650	27.271	29.001	30.850	32.824	34.931	37.180	39.580
13	26.211	28.029	29.984	32.088	34.352	36.786	39.404	42.218	45.244	48.496
14	30.095	32.392	34.882	37.581	40.504	43.672	47.102	50.818	54.841	59.196
15	34.405	37.280	40.417	43.842	47.580	51.659	56.109	60.965	66.260	72.035
16	39.190	42.753	46.671	50.980	55.717	60.925	66.648	72.938	79.850	87.442
17	44.500	48.883	53.738	59.117	65.075	71.673	78.978	87.067	96.021	105.930
18	50.396	55.749	61.724	68.393	75.836	84.140	93.404	103.739	115.265	128.116
19	56.939	63.439	70.748	78.968	88.211	98.603	110.283	123.412	138.165	154.739
20	64.202	72.052	80.946	91.024	102.443	115.379	130.031	146.626	165.417	186.687
21	72.264	81.698	92.468	104.767	118.809	134.840	153.136	174.019	197.846	225.024
22	81.213	92.502	105.489	120.434	137.630	157.414	180.169	206.342	236.436	271.028
23	91.147	104.602	120.203	138.295	159.274	183.600	211.798	244.483	282.359	326.234
24	102.173	118.154	136.829	158.656	184.166	213.976	248.803	289.490	337.007	392.480
25	114.412	133.333	155.616	181.867	212.790	249.212	292.099	342.598	402.038	471.976
30	199.018	241.330	293.192	356.778	434.738	530.306	647.423	790.932	966.698	1181.865
35	341.583	431.658	546.663	693.552	881.152	1120.699	1426.448	1816.607	2314.173	2948.294
40	581.812	767.080	1013.667	1341.979	1779.048	2360.724	3134.412	4163.094	5529.711	7343.715
45	986.613	1358.208	1874.086	2590.464	3585.031	4965.191	6879.008	9531.258	13203.105	18280.914
50	1668.723	2399.975	3459.344	4994.301	7217.488	10435.449	15088.805	21812.273	31514.492	45496.094

Table D-2 Future-Value Interest Factors for a One-Dollar Annuity Compounded at k Percent for n Periods: $FVIFA_{k,n} = \sum_{t=1}^{n} (1 + k)^{t-1}$ (continued)

Period	21%	22%	23%	24%	25%	26%	27%	28%	29%	30%
1	1.000	1.000	1.000	1.000	1.000	1.000	1.000	1.000	1.000	1.000
2	2.210	2.220	2.230	2.240	2.250	2.260	2.270	2.280	2.290	2.300
3	3.674	3.708	3.743	3.778	3.813	3.848	3.883	3.918	3.954	3.990
4	5.446	5.524	5.604	5.684	5.766	5.848	5.931	6.016	6.101	6.187
5	7.589	7.740	7.893	8.048	8.207	8.368	8.533	8.700	8.870	9.043
6	10.183	10.442	10.708	10.980	11.259	11.544	11.837	12.136	12.442	12.756
7	13.321	13.740	14.171	14.615	15.073	15.546	16.032	16.534	17.051	17.583
8	17.119	17.762	18.430	19.123	19.842	20.588	21.361	22.163	22.995	23.858
9	21.714	22.670	23.669	24.712	25.802	26.940	28.129	29.369	30.664	32.015
10	27.274	28.657	30.113	31.643	33.253	34.945	36.723	38.592	40.556	42.619
11	34.001	35.962	38.039	40.238	42.566	45.030	47.639	50.398	53.318	56.405
12	42.141	44.873	47.787	50.895	54.208	57.738	61.501	65.510	69.780	74.326
13	51.991	55.745	59.778	64.109	68.760	73.750	79.106	84.853	91.016	97.624
14	63.909	69.009	74.528	80.496	86.949	93.925	101.465	109.611	118.411	127.912
15	78.330	85.191	92.669	100.815	109.687	119.346	129.860	141.302	153.750	167.285
16	95.779	104.933	114.983	126.010	138.109	151.375	165.922	181.867	199.337	218.470
17	116.892	129.019	142.428	157.252	173.636	191.733	211.721	233.790	258.145	285.011
18	142.439	158.403	176.187	195.993	218.045	242.583	269.885	300.250	334.006	371.514
19	173.351	194.251	217.710	244.031	273.556	306.654	343.754	385.321	431.868	483.968
20	210.755	237.986	268.783	303.598	342.945	387.384	437.568	494.210	558.110	630.157
21	256.013	291.343	331.603	377.461	429.681	489.104	556.710	633.589	720.962	820.204
22	310.775	356.438	408.871	469.052	538.101	617.270	708.022	811.993	931.040	1067.265
23	377.038	435.854	503.911	582.624	673.626	778.760	900.187	1040.351	1202.042	1388.443
24	457.215	532.741	620.810	723.453	843.032	982.237	1144.237	1332.649	1551.634	1805.975
25	554.230	650.944	764.596	898.082	1054.791	1238.617	1454.180	1706.790	2002.608	2348.765
30	1445.111	1767.044	2160.459	2640.881	3227.172	3941.953	4812.891	5873.172	7162.785	8729.805
35	3755.814	4783.520	6090.227	7750.094	9856.746	12527.160	15909.480	20188.742	25596.512	32422.090
40	9749.141	12936.141	17153.691	22728.367	30088.621	39791.957	52570.707	69376.562	91447.375	120389.375
45	25294.223	34970.230	48300.660	66638.937	91831.312	126378.937	173692.875	238384.312	326686.375	447005.062

Table D-2 Future-Value Interest Factors for a One-Dollar Annuity Compounded at k Percent for n Periods: $FVIFA_{k,n} = \sum\limits_{t=1}^{n} (1 + k)^{t-1}$ (continued)

Period	31%	32%	33%	34%	35%	36%	37%	38%	39%	40%
1	1.000	1.000	1.000	1.000	1.000	1.000	1.000	1.000	1.000	1.000
2	2.310	2.320	2.330	2.340	2.350	2.360	2.370	2.380	2.390	2.400
3	4.026	4.062	4.099	4.136	4.172	4.210	4.247	4.284	4.322	4.360
4	6.274	6.362	6.452	6.542	6.633	6.725	6.818	6.912	7.008	7.104
5	9.219	9.398	9.581	9.766	9.954	10.146	10.341	10.539	10.741	10.946
6	13.077	13.406	13.742	14.086	14.438	14.799	15.167	15.544	15.930	16.324
7	18.131	18.696	19.277	19.876	20.492	21.126	21.779	22.451	23.142	23.853
8	24.752	25.678	26.638	27.633	28.664	29.732	30.837	31.982	33.167	34.395
9	33.425	34.895	36.429	38.028	39.696	41.435	43.247	45.135	47.103	49.152
10	44.786	47.062	49.451	51.958	54.590	57.351	60.248	63.287	66.473	69.813
11	59.670	63.121	66.769	70.624	74.696	78.998	83.540	88.335	93.397	98.739
12	79.167	84.320	89.803	95.636	101.840	108.437	115.450	122.903	130.822	139.234
13	104.709	112.302	120.438	129.152	138.484	148.474	159.166	170.606	182.842	195.928
14	138.169	149.239	161.183	174.063	187.953	202.925	219.058	236.435	255.151	275.299
15	182.001	197.996	215.373	234.245	254.737	276.978	301.109	327.281	355.659	386.418
16	239.421	262.354	287.446	314.888	344.895	377.690	413.520	452.647	495.366	541.985
17	314.642	347.307	383.303	422.949	466.608	514.658	567.521	625.652	689.558	759.778
18	413.180	459.445	510.792	567.751	630.920	700.935	778.504	864.399	959.485	1064.689
19	542.266	607.467	680.354	761.786	852.741	954.271	1067.551	1193.870	1334.683	1491.563
20	711.368	802.856	905.870	1021.792	1152.200	1298.809	1463.544	1648.539	1856.208	2089.188
21	932.891	1060.769	1205.807	1370.201	1556.470	1767.380	2006.055	2275.982	2581.128	2925.862
22	1223.087	1401.215	1604.724	1837.068	2102.234	2404.636	2749.294	3141.852	3588.765	4097.203
23	1603.243	1850.603	2135.282	2462.669	2839.014	3271.304	3767.532	4336.750	4989.379	5737.078
24	2101.247	2443.795	2840.924	3300.974	3833.667	4449.969	5162.516	5985.711	6936.230	8032.906
25	2753.631	3226.808	3779.428	4424.301	5176.445	6052.957	7073.645	8261.273	9642.352	11247.062
30	10632.543	12940.672	15737.945	19124.434	23221.258	28172.016	34148.906	41357.227	50043.625	60500.207
35	41028.887	51868.563	65504.199	82634.625	104134.500	131082.625	164818.438	206998.375	259680.313	325394.688

TABLE D-2 FUTURE-VALUE INTEREST FACTORS FOR A ONE-DOLLAR ANNUITY

Table D-2   Future-Value Interest Factors for a One-Dollar Annuity Compounded at k Percent for n Periods: $FVIFA_{k,n} = \sum_{t=1}^{n}(1+k)^{t-1}$ (continued)

Period	41%	42%	43%	44%	45%	46%	47%	48%	49%	50%
1	1.000	1.000	1.000	1.000	1.000	1.000	1.000	1.000	1.000	1.000
2	2.410	2.420	2.430	2.440	2.450	2.460	2.470	2.480	2.490	2.500
3	4.398	4.436	4.475	4.514	4.552	4.592	4.631	4.670	4.710	4.750
4	7.201	7.300	7.399	7.500	7.601	7.704	7.807	7.912	8.018	8.125
5	11.154	11.366	11.581	11.799	12.022	12.247	12.477	12.710	12.947	13.188
6	16.727	17.139	17.560	17.991	18.431	18.881	19.341	19.811	20.291	20.781
7	24.585	25.337	26.111	26.907	27.725	28.567	29.431	30.320	31.233	32.172
8	35.665	36.979	38.339	39.746	41.202	42.707	44.264	45.874	47.538	49.258
9	51.287	53.510	55.825	58.235	60.743	63.352	66.068	68.893	71.831	74.887
10	73.315	76.985	80.830	84.858	89.077	93.494	98.120	102.961	108.028	113.330
11	104.374	110.318	116.586	123.195	130.161	137.502	145.236	153.383	161.962	170.995
12	148.168	157.651	167.719	178.401	189.734	201.752	214.497	228.007	242.323	257.493
13	209.916	224.865	240.837	257.897	276.114	295.558	316.310	338.449	362.062	387.239
14	296.982	320.308	345.397	372.372	401.365	432.514	465.975	501.905	540.471	581.858
15	419.744	455.837	494.918	537.215	582.980	632.470	685.983	743.819	806.302	873.788
16	592.839	648.288	708.732	774.589	846.321	924.406	1009.394	1101.852	1202.390	1311.681
17	836.903	921.568	1014.486	1116.408	1228.165	1350.631	1484.809	1631.740	1792.560	1968.522
18	1181.034	1309.625	1451.714	1608.626	1781.838	1972.920	2183.667	2415.974	2671.914	2953.783
19	1666.257	1860.666	2076.949	2317.421	2584.665	2881.461	3210.989	3576.640	3982.150	4431.672
20	2350.422	2643.144	2971.035	3338.084	3748.763	4207.926	4721.148	5294.422	5934.402	6648.508
21	3315.095	3754.262	4249.574	4807.836	5436.703	6144.566	6941.082	7836.742	8843.254	9973.762
22	4675.281	5332.047	6077.887	6924.281	7884.215	8972.059	10204.383	11599.375	13177.441	14961.645
23	6593.145	7572.500	8692.375	9971.957	11433.109	13100.195	15001.434	17168.066	19635.383	22443.469
24	9297.332	10753.941	12431.090	14360.613	16579.008	19127.273	22053.094	25409.730	29257.707	33666.207
25	13110.234	15271.582	17777.445	20680.270	24040.555	27926.797	32419.027	37607.387	43594.965	50500.316
30	73075.500	88181.938	106315.250	128058.125	154105.313	185273.000	222540.625	267055.375	320172.750	383500.000

Table D-3 Present-Value Interest Factors for One Dollar Discounted at k Percent for n Periods: $PVIF_{k,n} = \dfrac{1}{(1+k)^n}$

Period	1%	2%	3%	4%	5%	6%	7%	8%	9%	10%
1	.990	.980	.971	.962	.952	.943	.935	.926	.917	.909
2	.980	.961	.943	.925	.907	.890	.873	.857	.842	.826
3	.971	.942	.915	.889	.864	.840	.816	.794	.772	.751
4	.961	.924	.888	.855	.823	.792	.763	.735	.708	.683
5	.951	.906	.863	.822	.784	.747	.713	.681	.650	.621
6	.942	.888	.837	.790	.746	.705	.666	.630	.596	.564
7	.933	.871	.813	.760	.711	.665	.623	.583	.547	.513
8	.923	.853	.789	.731	.677	.627	.582	.540	.502	.467
9	.914	.837	.766	.703	.645	.592	.544	.500	.460	.424
10	.905	.820	.744	.676	.614	.558	.508	.463	.422	.386
11	.896	.804	.722	.650	.585	.527	.475	.429	.388	.350
12	.887	.789	.701	.625	.557	.497	.444	.397	.356	.319
13	.879	.773	.681	.601	.530	.469	.415	.368	.326	.290
14	.870	.758	.661	.577	.505	.442	.388	.340	.299	.263
15	.861	.743	.642	.555	.481	.417	.362	.315	.275	.239
16	.853	.728	.623	.534	.458	.394	.339	.292	.252	.218
17	.844	.714	.605	.513	.436	.371	.317	.270	.231	.198
18	.836	.700	.587	.494	.416	.350	.296	.250	.212	.180
19	.828	.686	.570	.475	.396	.331	.277	.232	.194	.164
20	.820	.673	.554	.456	.377	.312	.258	.215	.178	.149
21	.811	.660	.538	.439	.359	.294	.242	.199	.164	.135
22	.803	.647	.522	.422	.342	.278	.226	.184	.150	.123
23	.795	.634	.507	.406	.326	.262	.211	.170	.138	.112
24	.788	.622	.492	.390	.310	.247	.197	.158	.126	.102
25	.780	.610	.478	.375	.295	.233	.184	.146	.116	.092
30	.742	.552	.412	.308	.231	.174	.131	.099	.075	.057
35	.706	.500	.355	.253	.181	.130	.094	.068	.049	.036
40	.672	.453	.307	.208	.142	.097	.067	.046	.032	.022
45	.639	.410	.264	.171	.111	.073	.048	.031	.021	.014
50	.608	.372	.228	.141	.087	.054	.034	.021	.013	.009

TABLE D-3 PRESENT-VALUE INTEREST FACTORS FOR ONE DOLLAR

Table D-3 Present-Value Interest Factors for One Dollar Discounted at k Percent for n Periods: $PVIF_{k,n} = \dfrac{1}{(1+k)^n}$ (continued)

Period	11%	12%	13%	14%	15%	16%	17%	18%	19%	20%
1	.901	.893	.885	.877	.870	.862	.855	.847	.840	.833
2	.812	.797	.783	.769	.756	.743	.731	.718	.706	.694
3	.731	.712	.693	.675	.658	.641	.624	.609	.593	.579
4	.659	.636	.613	.592	.572	.552	.534	.516	.499	.482
5	.593	.567	.543	.519	.497	.476	.456	.437	.419	.402
6	.535	.507	.480	.456	.432	.410	.390	.370	.352	.335
7	.482	.452	.425	.400	.376	.354	.333	.314	.296	.279
8	.434	.404	.376	.351	.327	.305	.285	.266	.249	.233
9	.391	.361	.333	.308	.284	.263	.243	.225	.209	.194
10	.352	.322	.295	.270	.247	.227	.208	.191	.176	.162
11	.317	.287	.261	.237	.215	.195	.178	.162	.148	.135
12	.286	.257	.231	.208	.187	.168	.152	.137	.124	.112
13	.258	.229	.204	.182	.163	.145	.130	.116	.104	.093
14	.232	.205	.181	.160	.141	.125	.111	.099	.088	.078
15	.209	.183	.160	.140	.123	.108	.095	.084	.074	.065
16	.188	.163	.141	.123	.107	.093	.081	.071	.062	.054
17	.170	.146	.125	.108	.093	.080	.069	.060	.052	.045
18	.153	.130	.111	.095	.081	.069	.059	.051	.044	.038
19	.138	.116	.098	.083	.070	.060	.051	.043	.037	.031
20	.124	.104	.087	.073	.061	.051	.043	.037	.031	.026
21	.112	.093	.077	.064	.053	.044	.037	.031	.026	.022
22	.101	.083	.068	.056	.046	.038	.032	.026	.022	.018
23	.091	.074	.060	.049	.040	.033	.027	.022	.018	.015
24	.082	.066	.053	.043	.035	.028	.023	.019	.015	.013
25	.074	.059	.047	.038	.030	.024	.020	.016	.013	.010
30	.044	.033	.026	.020	.015	.012	.009	.007	.005	.004
35	.026	.019	.014	.010	.008	.006	.004	.003	.002	.002
40	.015	.011	.008	.005	.004	.003	.002	.001	.001	.001
45	.009	.006	.004	.003	.002	.001	.001	.001	*	*
50	.005	.003	.002	.001	.001	.001	*	*	*	*

*$PVIF$ is zero to three decimal places.

Table D-3 Present-Value Interest Factors for One Dollar Discounted at k Percent for n Periods: $PVIF_{k,n} = \dfrac{1}{(1+k)^n}$ (continued)

Period	21%	22%	23%	24%	25%	26%	27%	28%	29%	30%
1	.826	.820	.813	.806	.800	.794	.787	.781	.775	.769
2	.683	.672	.661	.650	.640	.630	.620	.610	.601	.592
3	.564	.551	.537	.524	.512	.500	.488	.477	.466	.455
4	.467	.451	.437	.423	.410	.397	.384	.373	.361	.350
5	.386	.370	.355	.341	.328	.315	.303	.291	.280	.269
6	.319	.303	.289	.275	.262	.250	.238	.227	.217	.207
7	.263	.249	.235	.222	.210	.198	.188	.178	.168	.159
8	.218	.204	.191	.179	.168	.157	.148	.139	.130	.123
9	.180	.167	.155	.144	.134	.125	.116	.108	.101	.094
10	.149	.137	.126	.116	.107	.099	.092	.085	.078	.073
11	.123	.112	.103	.094	.086	.079	.072	.066	.061	.056
12	.102	.092	.083	.076	.069	.062	.057	.052	.047	.043
13	.084	.075	.068	.061	.055	.050	.045	.040	.037	.033
14	.069	.062	.055	.049	.044	.039	.035	.032	.028	.025
15	.057	.051	.045	.040	.035	.031	.028	.025	.022	.020
16	.047	.042	.036	.032	.028	.025	.022	.019	.017	.015
17	.039	.034	.030	.026	.023	.020	.017	.015	.013	.012
18	.032	.028	.024	.021	.018	.016	.014	.012	.010	.009
19	.027	.023	.020	.017	.014	.012	.011	.009	.008	.007
20	.022	.019	.016	.014	.012	.010	.008	.007	.006	.005
21	.018	.015	.013	.011	.009	.008	.007	.006	.005	.004
22	.015	.013	.011	.009	.007	.006	.005	.004	.004	.003
23	.012	.010	.009	.007	.006	.005	.004	.003	.003	.002
24	.010	.008	.007	.006	.005	.004	.003	.003	.002	.002
25	.009	.007	.006	.005	.004	.003	.003	.002	.002	.001
30	.003	.003	.002	.002	.001	.001	.001	.001	*	*
35	.001	.001	.001	.001	*	*	*	*	*	*
40	*	*	*	*	*	*	*	*	*	*
45	*	*	*	*	*	*	*	*	*	*
50	*	*	*	*	*	*	*	*	*	*

*$PVIF$ is zero to three decimal places.

TABLE D-3 PRESENT-VALUE INTEREST FACTORS FOR ONE DOLLAR

Table D-3 Present-Value Interest Factors for One Dollar Discounted at k Percent for n Periods: $PVIF_{k,n} = \dfrac{1}{(1+k)^n}$ (continued)

Period	31%	32%	33%	34%	35%	36%	37%	38%	39%	40%
1	.763	.758	.752	.746	.741	.735	.730	.725	.719	.714
2	.583	.574	.565	.557	.549	.541	.533	.525	.518	.510
3	.445	.435	.425	.416	.406	.398	.389	.381	.372	.364
4	.340	.329	.320	.310	.301	.292	.284	.276	.268	.260
5	.259	.250	.240	.231	.223	.215	.207	.200	.193	.186
6	.198	.189	.181	.173	.165	.158	.151	.145	.139	.133
7	.151	.143	.136	.129	.122	.116	.110	.105	.100	.095
8	.115	.108	.102	.096	.091	.085	.081	.076	.072	.068
9	.088	.082	.077	.072	.067	.063	.059	.055	.052	.048
10	.067	.062	.058	.054	.050	.046	.043	.040	.037	.035
11	.051	.047	.043	.040	.037	.034	.031	.029	.027	.025
12	.039	.036	.033	.030	.027	.025	.023	.021	.019	.018
13	.030	.027	.025	.022	.020	.018	.017	.015	.014	.013
14	.023	.021	.018	.017	.015	.014	.012	.011	.010	.009
15	.017	.016	.014	.012	.011	.010	.009	.008	.007	.006
16	.013	.012	.010	.009	.008	.007	.006	.006	.005	.005
17	.010	.009	.008	.007	.006	.005	.005	.004	.004	.003
18	.008	.007	.006	.005	.005	.004	.003	.003	.003	.002
19	.006	.005	.004	.004	.003	.003	.003	.002	.002	.002
20	.005	.004	.003	.003	.002	.002	.002	.002	.001	.001
21	.003	.003	.003	.002	.002	.002	.001	.001	.001	.001
22	.003	.002	.002	.002	.001	.001	.001	.001	.001	.001
23	.002	.002	.001	.001	.001	.001	.001	.001	.001	*
24	.002	.001	.001	.001	.001	.001	.001	*	*	*
25	.001	.001	.001	.001	.001	*	*	*	*	*
30	*	*	*	*	*	*	*	*	*	*
35	*	*	*	*	*	*	*	*	*	*
40	*	*	*	*	*	*	*	*	*	*
45	*	*	*	*	*	*	*	*	*	*
50	*	*	*	*	*	*	*	*	*	*

*$PVIF$ is zero to three decimal places.

Table D-3 Present-Value Interest Factors for One Dollar Discounted at k Percent for n Periods: $PVIF_{k,n} = \dfrac{1}{(1+k)^n}$ (continued)

Period	41%	42%	43%	44%	45%	46%	47%	48%	49%	50%
1	.709	.704	.699	.694	.690	.685	.680	.676	.671	.667
2	.503	.496	.489	.482	.476	.469	.463	.457	.450	.444
3	.357	.349	.342	.335	.328	.321	.315	.308	.302	.296
4	.253	.246	.239	.233	.226	.220	.214	.208	.203	.198
5	.179	.173	.167	.162	.156	.151	.146	.141	.136	.132
6	.127	.122	.117	.112	.108	.103	.099	.095	.091	.088
7	.090	.086	.082	.078	.074	.071	.067	.064	.061	.059
8	.064	.060	.057	.054	.051	.048	.046	.043	.041	.039
9	.045	.043	.040	.038	.035	.033	.031	.029	.028	.026
10	.032	.030	.028	.026	.024	.023	.021	.020	.019	.017
11	.023	.021	.020	.018	.017	.016	.014	.013	.012	.012
12	.016	.015	.014	.013	.012	.011	.010	.009	.008	.008
13	.011	.010	.010	.009	.008	.007	.007	.006	.006	.005
14	.008	.007	.007	.006	.006	.005	.005	.004	.004	.003
15	.006	.005	.005	.004	.004	.003	.003	.003	.003	.002
16	.004	.004	.003	.003	.003	.002	.002	.002	.002	.002
17	.003	.003	.002	.002	.002	.002	.001	.001	.001	.001
18	.002	.002	.002	.001	.001	.001	.001	.001	.001	.001
19	.001	.001	.001	.001	.001	.001	.001	.001	.001	*
20	.001	.001	.001	.001	.001	.001	*	*	*	*
21	.001	.001	.001	*	*	*	*	*	*	*
22	.001	*	*	*	*	*	*	*	*	*
23	*	*	*	*	*	*	*	*	*	*
24	*	*	*	*	*	*	*	*	*	*
25	*	*	*	*	*	*	*	*	*	*
30	*	*	*	*	*	*	*	*	*	*
35	*	*	*	*	*	*	*	*	*	*
40	*	*	*	*	*	*	*	*	*	*
45	*	*	*	*	*	*	*	*	*	*
50	*	*	*	*	*	*	*	*	*	*

*$PVIF$ is zero to three decimal places.

TABLE D-4 PRESENT-VALUE INTEREST FACTORS FOR A ONE-DOLLAR ANNUITY

Table D-4 Present-Value Interest Factors for a One-Dollar Annuity Discounted at k Percent for n Periods: $PVIFA_{k,n} = \sum_{t=1}^{n} \dfrac{1}{(1+k)^t}$

Period	1%	2%	3%	4%	5%	6%	7%	8%	9%	10%
1	.990	.980	.971	.962	.952	.943	.935	.926	.917	.909
2	1.970	1.942	1.913	1.886	1.859	1.833	1.808	1.783	1.759	1.736
3	2.941	2.884	2.829	2.775	2.723	2.673	2.624	2.577	2.531	2.487
4	3.902	3.808	3.717	3.630	3.546	3.465	3.387	3.312	3.240	3.170
5	4.853	4.713	4.580	4.452	4.329	4.212	4.100	3.993	3.890	3.791
6	5.795	5.601	5.417	5.242	5.076	4.917	4.767	4.623	4.486	4.355
7	6.728	6.472	6.230	6.002	5.786	5.582	5.389	5.206	5.033	4.868
8	7.652	7.326	7.020	6.733	6.463	6.210	5.971	5.747	5.535	5.335
9	8.566	8.162	7.786	7.435	7.108	6.802	6.515	6.247	5.995	5.759
10	9.471	8.983	8.530	8.111	7.722	7.360	7.024	6.710	6.418	6.145
11	10.368	9.787	9.253	8.760	8.306	7.887	7.499	7.139	6.805	6.495
12	11.255	10.575	9.954	9.385	8.863	8.384	7.943	7.536	7.161	6.814
13	12.134	11.348	10.635	9.986	9.394	8.853	8.358	7.904	7.487	7.013
14	13.004	12.106	11.296	10.563	9.899	9.295	8.745	8.244	7.786	7.367
15	13.865	12.849	11.938	11.118	10.380	9.712	9.108	8.560	8.061	7.606
16	14.718	13.578	12.561	11.652	10.838	10.106	9.447	8.851	8.313	7.824
17	15.562	14.292	13.166	12.166	11.274	10.477	9.763	9.122	8.544	8.022
18	16.398	14.992	13.754	12.659	11.690	10.828	10.059	9.372	8.756	8.201
19	17.226	15.679	14.324	13.134	12.085	11.158	10.336	9.604	8.950	8.365
20	18.046	16.352	14.878	13.590	12.462	11.470	10.594	9.818	9.129	8.514
21	18.857	17.011	15.415	14.029	12.821	11.764	10.836	10.017	9.292	8.649
22	19.661	17.658	15.937	14.451	13.163	12.042	11.061	10.201	9.442	8.772
23	20.456	18.292	16.444	14.857	13.489	12.303	11.272	10.371	9.580	8.883
24	21.244	18.914	16.936	15.247	13.799	12.550	11.469	10.529	9.707	8.985
25	22.023	19.524	17.413	15.622	14.094	12.783	11.654	10.675	9.823	9.077
30	25.808	22.396	19.601	17.292	15.373	13.765	12.409	11.258	10.274	9.427
35	29.409	24.999	21.487	18.665	16.374	14.498	12.948	11.655	10.567	9.644
40	32.835	27.356	23.115	19.793	17.159	15.046	13.332	11.925	10.757	9.779
45	36.095	29.490	24.519	20.720	17.774	15.456	13.606	12.108	10.881	9.863
50	39.196	31.424	25.730	21.482	18.256	15.762	13.801	12.233	10.962	9.915

Table D-4 Present-Value Interest Factors for a One-Dollar Annuity Discounted at k Percent for n Periods: $PVIFA_{k,n} = \sum_{t=1}^{n} \dfrac{1}{(1+k)^t}$ (continued)

Period	11%	12%	13%	14%	15%	16%	17%	18%	19%	20%
1	.901	.893	.885	.877	.870	.862	.855	.847	.840	.833
2	1.713	1.690	1.668	1.647	1.626	1.605	1.585	1.566	1.547	1.528
3	2.444	2.402	2.361	2.322	2.283	2.246	2.210	2.174	2.140	2.106
4	3.102	3.037	2.974	2.914	2.855	2.798	2.743	2.690	2.639	2.589
5	3.696	3.605	3.517	3.433	3.352	3.274	3.199	3.127	3.058	2.991
6	4.231	4.111	3.998	3.889	3.784	3.685	3.589	3.498	3.410	3.326
7	4.712	4.564	4.423	4.288	4.160	4.039	3.922	3.812	3.706	3.605
8	5.146	4.968	4.799	4.639	4.487	4.344	4.207	4.078	3.954	3.837
9	5.537	5.328	5.132	4.946	4.772	4.607	4.451	4.303	4.163	4.031
10	5.889	5.650	5.426	5.216	5.019	4.833	4.659	4.494	4.339	4.192
11	6.207	5.938	5.687	5.453	5.234	5.029	4.836	4.656	4.486	4.327
12	6.492	6.194	5.918	5.660	5.421	5.197	4.988	4.793	4.611	4.439
13	6.750	6.424	6.122	5.842	5.583	5.342	5.118	4.910	4.715	4.533
14	6.982	6.628	6.302	6.002	5.724	5.468	5.229	5.008	4.802	4.611
15	7.191	6.811	6.462	6.142	5.847	5.575	5.324	5.092	4.876	4.675
16	7.379	6.974	6.604	6.265	5.954	5.668	5.405	5.162	4.938	4.730
17	7.549	7.120	6.729	6.373	6.047	5.749	5.475	5.222	4.990	4.775
18	7.702	7.250	6.840	6.467	6.128	5.818	5.534	5.273	5.033	4.812
19	7.839	7.366	6.938	6.550	6.198	5.877	5.584	5.316	5.070	4.843
20	7.963	7.469	7.025	6.623	6.259	5.929	5.628	5.353	5.101	4.870
21	8.075	7.562	7.102	6.687	6.312	5.973	5.665	5.384	5.127	4.891
22	8.176	7.645	7.170	6.743	6.359	6.011	5.696	5.410	5.149	4.909
23	8.266	7.718	7.230	6.792	6.399	6.044	5.723	5.432	5.167	4.925
24	8.348	7.784	7.283	6.835	6.434	6.073	5.746	5.451	5.182	4.937
25	8.422	7.843	7.330	6.873	6.464	6.097	5.766	5.467	5.195	4.948
30	8.694	8.055	7.496	7.003	6.566	6.177	5.829	5.517	5.235	4.979
35	8.855	8.176	7.586	7.070	6.617	6.215	5.858	5.539	5.251	4.992
40	8.951	8.244	7.634	7.105	6.642	6.233	5.871	5.548	5.258	4.997
45	9.008	8.283	7.661	7.123	6.654	6.242	5.877	5.552	5.261	4.999
50	9.042	8.304	7.675	7.133	6.661	6.246	5.880	5.554	5.262	4.999

TABLE D-4 PRESENT-VALUE INTEREST FACTORS FOR A ONE-DOLLAR ANNUITY

Table D-4 Present-Value Interest Factors for a One-Dollar Annuity Discounted at k Percent for n Periods: $PVIFA_{k,n} = \sum_{t=1}^{n} \dfrac{1}{(1+k)^t}$ (continued)

Period	21%	22%	23%	24%	25%	26%	27%	28%	29%	30%
1	.826	.820	.813	.806	.800	.794	.787	.781	.775	.769
2	1.509	1.492	1.474	1.457	1.440	1.424	1.407	1.392	1.376	1.361
3	2.074	2.042	2.011	1.981	1.952	1.923	1.896	1.868	1.842	1.816
4	2.540	2.494	2.448	2.404	2.362	2.320	2.280	2.241	2.203	2.166
5	2.926	2.864	2.803	2.745	2.689	2.635	2.583	2.532	2.483	2.436
6	3.245	3.167	3.092	3.020	2.951	2.885	2.821	2.759	2.700	2.643
7	3.508	3.416	3.327	3.242	3.161	3.083	3.009	2.937	2.868	2.802
8	3.726	3.619	3.518	3.421	3.329	3.241	3.156	3.076	2.999	2.925
9	3.905	3.786	3.673	3.566	3.463	3.366	3.273	3.184	3.100	3.019
10	4.054	3.923	3.799	3.682	3.570	3.465	3.364	3.269	3.178	3.092
11	4.177	4.035	3.902	3.776	3.656	3.544	3.437	3.335	3.239	3.147
12	4.278	4.127	3.985	3.851	3.725	3.606	3.493	3.387	3.286	3.190
13	4.362	4.203	4.053	3.912	3.780	3.656	3.538	3.427	3.322	3.223
14	4.432	4.265	4.108	3.962	3.824	3.695	3.573	3.459	3.351	3.249
15	4.489	4.315	4.153	4.001	3.859	3.726	3.601	3.483	3.373	3.268
16	4.536	4.357	4.189	4.033	3.887	3.751	3.623	3.503	3.390	3.283
17	4.576	4.391	4.219	4.059	3.910	3.771	3.640	3.518	3.403	3.295
18	4.608	4.419	4.243	4.080	3.928	3.786	3.654	3.529	3.413	3.304
19	4.635	4.442	4.263	4.097	3.942	3.799	3.664	3.539	3.421	3.311
20	4.657	4.460	4.279	4.110	3.954	3.808	3.673	3.546	3.427	3.316
21	4.675	4.476	4.292	4.121	3.963	3.816	3.679	3.551	3.432	3.320
22	4.690	4.488	4.302	4.130	3.970	3.822	3.684	3.556	3.436	3.323
23	4.703	4.499	4.311	4.137	3.976	3.827	3.689	3.559	3.438	3.325
24	4.713	4.507	4.318	4.143	3.981	3.831	3.692	3.562	3.441	3.327
25	4.721	4.514	4.323	4.147	3.985	3.834	3.694	3.564	3.442	3.329
30	4.746	4.534	4.339	4.160	3.995	3.842	3.701	3.569	3.447	3.332
35	4.756	4.541	4.345	4.164	3.998	3.845	3.703	3.571	3.448	3.333
40	4.760	4.544	4.347	4.166	3.999	3.846	3.703	3.571	3.448	3.333
45	4.761	4.545	4.347	4.166	4.000	3.846	3.704	3.571	3.448	3.333
50	4.762	4.545	4.348	4.167	4.000	3.846	3.704	3.571	3.448	3.333

Table D-4 Present-Value Interest Factors for a One-Dollar Annuity Discounted at k Percent for n Periods: $PVIFA_{k,n} = \sum_{t=1}^{n} \dfrac{1}{(1+k)^t}$ (continued)

Period	31%	32%	33%	34%	35%	36%	37%	38%	39%	40%
1	.763	.758	.752	.746	.741	.735	.730	.725	.719	.714
2	1.346	1.331	1.317	1.303	1.289	1.276	1.263	1.250	1.237	1.224
3	1.791	1.766	1.742	1.719	1.696	1.673	1.652	1.630	1.609	1.589
4	2.130	2.096	2.062	2.029	1.997	1.966	1.935	1.906	1.877	1.849
5	2.390	2.345	2.302	2.260	2.220	2.181	2.143	2.106	2.070	2.035
6	2.588	2.534	2.483	2.433	2.385	2.339	2.294	2.251	2.209	2.168
7	2.739	2.677	2.619	2.562	2.508	2.455	2.404	2.355	2.308	2.263
8	2.854	2.786	2.721	2.658	2.598	2.540	2.485	2.432	2.380	2.331
9	2.942	2.868	2.798	2.730	2.665	2.603	2.544	2.487	2.432	2.379
10	3.009	2.930	2.855	2.784	2.715	2.649	2.587	2.527	2.469	2.414
11	3.060	2.978	2.899	2.824	2.752	2.683	2.618	2.555	2.496	2.438
12	3.100	3.013	2.931	2.853	2.779	2.708	2.641	2.576	2.515	2.456
13	3.129	3.040	2.956	2.876	2.799	2.727	2.658	2.592	2.529	2.469
14	3.152	3.061	2.974	2.892	2.814	2.740	2.670	2.603	2.539	2.478
15	3.170	3.076	2.988	2.905	2.825	2.750	2.679	2.611	2.546	2.484
16	3.183	3.088	2.999	2.914	2.834	2.757	2.685	2.616	2.551	2.489
17	3.193	3.097	3.007	2.921	2.840	2.763	2.690	2.621	2.555	2.492
18	3.201	3.104	3.012	2.926	2.844	2.767	2.693	2.624	2.557	2.494
19	3.207	3.109	3.017	2.930	2.848	2.770	2.696	2.626	2.559	2.496
20	3.211	3.113	3.020	2.933	2.850	2.772	2.698	2.627	2.561	2.497
21	3.215	3.116	3.023	2.935	2.852	2.773	2.699	2.629	2.562	2.498
22	3.217	3.118	3.025	2.936	2.853	2.775	2.700	2.629	2.562	2.498
23	3.219	3.120	3.026	2.938	2.854	2.775	2.701	2.630	2.563	2.499
24	3.221	3.121	3.027	2.939	2.855	2.776	2.701	2.630	2.563	2.499
25	3.222	3.122	3.028	2.939	2.856	2.776	2.702	2.631	2.563	2.499
30	3.225	3.124	3.030	2.941	2.857	2.777	2.702	2.631	2.564	2.500
35	3.226	3.125	3.030	2.941	2.857	2.778	2.703	2.632	2.564	2.500
40	3.226	3.125	3.030	2.941	2.857	2.778	2.703	2.632	2.564	2.500
45	3.226	3.125	3.030	2.941	2.857	2.778	2.703	2.632	2.564	2.500
50	3.226	3.125	3.030	2.941	2.857	2.778	2.703	2.632	2.564	2.500

Table D-4 Present-Value Interest Factors for a One-Dollar Annuity Discounted at k Percent for n Periods: $PVIFA_{k,n} = \sum_{t=1}^{n} \frac{1}{(1+k)^t}$ (continued)

Period	41%	42%	43%	44%	45%	46%	47%	48%	49%	50%
1	.709	.704	.699	.694	.690	.685	.680	.676	.671	.667
2	1.212	1.200	1.188	1.177	1.165	1.154	1.143	1.132	1.122	1.111
3	1.569	1.549	1.530	1.512	1.493	1.475	1.458	1.441	1.424	1.407
4	1.822	1.795	1.769	1.744	1.720	1.695	1.672	1.649	1.627	1.605
5	2.001	1.969	1.937	1.906	1.876	1.846	1.818	1.790	1.763	1.737
6	2.129	2.091	2.054	2.018	1.983	1.949	1.917	1.885	1.854	1.824
7	2.219	2.176	2.135	2.096	2.057	2.020	1.984	1.949	1.916	1.883
8	2.283	2.237	2.193	2.150	2.109	2.069	2.030	1.993	1.957	1.922
9	2.328	2.280	2.233	2.187	2.144	2.102	2.061	2.022	1.984	1.948
10	2.360	2.310	2.261	2.213	2.168	2.125	2.083	2.042	2.003	1.965
11	2.383	2.331	2.280	2.232	2.185	2.140	2.097	2.055	2.015	1.977
12	2.400	2.346	2.294	2.244	2.196	2.151	2.107	2.064	2.024	1.985
13	2.411	2.356	2.303	2.253	2.204	2.158	2.113	2.071	2.029	1.990
14	2.419	2.363	2.310	2.259	2.210	2.163	2.118	2.075	2.033	1.993
15	2.425	2.369	2.315	2.263	2.214	2.166	2.121	2.078	2.036	1.995
16	2.429	2.372	2.318	2.266	2.216	2.169	2.123	2.079	2.037	1.997
17	2.432	2.375	2.320	2.268	2.218	2.170	2.125	2.081	2.038	1.998
18	2.434	2.377	2.322	2.270	2.219	2.172	2.126	2.082	2.039	1.999
19	2.435	2.378	2.323	2.270	2.220	2.172	2.126	2.082	2.040	1.999
20	2.436	2.379	2.324	2.271	2.221	2.173	2.127	2.083	2.040	1.999
21	2.437	2.379	2.324	2.272	2.221	2.173	2.127	2.083	2.040	2.000
22	2.438	2.380	2.325	2.272	2.222	2.173	2.127	2.083	2.040	2.000
23	2.438	2.380	2.325	2.272	2.222	2.174	2.127	2.083	2.041	2.000
24	2.438	2.380	2.325	2.272	2.222	2.174	2.127	2.083	2.041	2.000
25	2.439	2.381	2.325	2.272	2.222	2.174	2.128	2.083	2.041	2.000
30	2.439	2.381	2.326	2.273	2.222	2.174	2.128	2.083	2.041	2.000
35	2.439	2.381	2.326	2.273	2.222	2.174	2.128	2.083	2.041	2.000
40	2.439	2.381	2.326	2.273	2.222	2.174	2.128	2.083	2.041	2.000
45	2.439	2.381	2.326	2.273	2.222	2.174	2.128	2.083	2.041	2.000
50	2.439	2.381	2.326	2.273	2.222	2.174	2.128	2.083	2.041	2.000

Appendix E

USING
YOUR
CALCULATOR

INTRODUCTION

Within the last few years numerous technological advances have affected all aspects of our lives. Nowhere has this been more noticeable than in the development of computational aids. Calculators have become commonplace in the world of finance and business. In fact, several hand-held calculators currently available are more powerful than a roomful of first-generation computers. With proper use, the calculator can help you learn and apply the financial techniques presented in this book. Of course, you must recognize that a calculator will not make a decision for you; effective financial decision making requires an ability to interpret computed results.

CALCULATOR TYPES

If you have not yet acquired a calculator or are thinking about purchasing an additional one, the following comments may help. There are basically two broad types of calculators on the market with respect to operations. One uses the algebraic entry method; the other uses what is called reverse polish notation (RPN). For example, of the available financial calculators, the Texas Instruments (TI) business series use the algebraic entry method and the Hewlett-Packard (HP) business series use RPN. It is probably easier to learn to use a calculator that operates on the algebraic entry method, whereas calculators using the less popular RPN method allow for faster computations. More powerful calculators capable of performing specific financial computations in a single step are generally more expensive than those with only the four basic math functions. Like many things you will learn in finance, tradeoffs are likely to be involved in choosing a calculator. When shopping for a calculator, carefully compare calculator features and prices to your needs to ensure that you get the right calculator for the best price. While you may decide to acquire a more advanced business calculator, many of the techniques below, which assume only a four-function model, can be applied to all calculators.*

SIMPLIFYING ROUTINE CALCULATIONS

A simple calculator having only the four standard math functions and operating with the algebraic entry method is assumed in the examples of routine financial calculations given below. Persons having calculators using RPN will need to adjust the keystrokes accordingly. The examples that follow are aimed at minimizing input data and allowing the calculator to do most of the work. Although the methods presented may be different from those with which you are familiar, they provide for quicker computations with less chance of error. In the illustrations given, the boxed-in operators — $\boxed{\times}$, $\boxed{=}$, $\boxed{\div}$, etc. — indicate calculator keys; $\boxed{C}$ is the clear key.

Example 1: Mark-ups and Discounts

Suppose you just purchased inventory for resale. You plan to mark up the items 20 percent over cost. The first item costs $347.85. What is the retail price? You could calculate the mark-up and then add it to the cost as follows:

$\boxed{C}$ 347.85 $\boxed{\times}$ .20 $\boxed{=}$ 69.57 $\boxed{+}$ 347.85 $\boxed{=}$ 417.42   (answer)

Notice that the $347.85 was entered into the calculator twice (two chances to make a mistake). Instead, you could have obtained the same result by adding 20 percent to cost, which is 100 percent; thus the retail price would be 120 percent of cost. Using this method, you get the answer by the following computation:

$\boxed{C}$ 347.85 $\boxed{\times}$ 1.2 $\boxed{=}$ 417.42   (answer)

---

* In rare instances, a calculator may not have the capability of doing chain calculations, and therefore the methodology presented here will not work. To determine whether your calculator is one of the exceptions, check the operating instructions in your owner's guide, or do the following calculation:

$\boxed{C}$ 12 $\boxed{+}$ 8 $\boxed{\times}$ 5 $\boxed{\div}$ 4 $\boxed{=}$ 25

If you get the correct answer *without having to push the "equals" key between operations,* your calculator has chain capability.

Try it. You will discover that it is faster and easier. And if you think of the general principle involved, you will see many applications for this technique. If you get a 10 percent discount on an item with a list price of $543.77, what is the price you pay?

$$\boxed{C}\ 543.77\ \boxed{\times}\ .9\ \boxed{=}\ 489.39 \qquad \text{(answer)}$$

Example 2: Sequential Calculations

You wish to calculate a company's earnings after taxes. Its sales equal $75,950; cost of goods sold represents 75 percent of sales; interest expense is $1,000; and the tax rate is 40 percent. Using the usual method, the keystrokes would be:

$$\boxed{C}\ 75950\ \boxed{\times}\ .75\ \boxed{=}\ 56962.50 \qquad\qquad\qquad \text{(write down this number)}$$

$$\boxed{C}\ 75950\ \boxed{-}\ 56962.50\ \boxed{=}\ 18987.50\ \boxed{-}\ 1000\ \boxed{=}\ 17987.50\ \boxed{\times}\ .4\ \boxed{=}\ 7195$$
$$\qquad\qquad\qquad\qquad\qquad\qquad\qquad\qquad\qquad \text{(write down this number)}$$

$$\boxed{C}\ 17987.50\ \boxed{-}\ 7195\ \boxed{=}\ 10792.50 \qquad\qquad \text{(answer)}$$

Using the method described above, the same answer could have been determined by:

$$\boxed{C}\ 75950\ \boxed{\times}\ .25\ \boxed{-}\ 1000\ \boxed{\times}\ .6\ \boxed{=}\ 10792.50 \qquad \text{(answer)}$$

This method does *not* give you any of the intermediate answers, although they could, in part, be obtained by pushing the $\boxed{=}$ key after each operation.

Suppose you wanted to find the cost of goods sold and the gross profit. The standard method would involve the following:

$$\boxed{C}\ 75950\ \boxed{\times}\ .75\ \boxed{=}\ 56962.50 \qquad \text{(write down number—the cost of goods sold)}$$

$$\boxed{C}\ 75950\ \boxed{-}\ 56962.50\ \boxed{=}\ 18987.50 \qquad \text{(gross profit)}$$

The alternative method would be as follows:

$$\boxed{C}\ 75950\ \boxed{\times}\ .75\ \boxed{=}\ 56962.50 \qquad \text{(cost of goods sold)}$$

$$\boxed{\div}\ .75\ \boxed{\times}\ .25\ \boxed{=}\ 18987.50 \qquad \text{(gross profit)}$$

Notice that by remembering that all steps can be reversed mathematically by performing the opposite mathematical computation, you avoid the problem of having to enter long numbers more than once.

Example 3: Future Value of Cash Flow Streams

Suppose you need to find the future value of $100 one period from now, given a 10 percent interest rate—i.e., $100 \times (1 + .10) =$ future value. The keystrokes are:

$$\boxed{C}\ 100\ \boxed{\times}\ 1.1\ \boxed{=}\ 110 \qquad \text{(answer)}$$

This calculation is simple. Expanding the problem, we can compute the future value of the three flows at the end of the third period. The first flow of $150 is received today; the next flow of $200 is received one period from today; and the third flow of $300 is received two periods from today. The keystrokes using the standard method are:

| C | 150 | × | 1.1 | × | 1.1 | × | 1.1 | = | 199.65   (write down this number; it compounds three periods)

| C | 200 | × | 1.1 | × | 1.1 | = | 242.00   (write down this number; it compounds two periods)

| C | 300 | × | 1.1 | = | 330.00 | + | 199.65 | + | 242.00 | = | 771.65   (answer)
(note—last flow compounds one period)

Instead, we could also have done the following:

| C | 150 | × | 1.1 | + | 200 | × | 1.1 | + | 300 | × | 1.1 | = | 771.65   (answer)

Again, it was not necessary to write down any intermediate results.

In the above example the future value was calculated under the assumption that all of the cash flows occurred at the beginning of the period. If, instead, the cash flows were to occur at the end of the period, it would be necessary to make a slight adjustment in the calculations. Assume that the cash flows from the above example occur at the *end of periods* one, two, and three. What is the future value of these flows at the end of the third period? The keystrokes for the standard method are:

| C | 150 | × | 1.1 | × | 1.1 | = | 181.50   (write down this number; flow compounds for only two periods)

| C | 200 | × | 1.1 | = | 220   (write down this number; flow compounds for only one period)

| C | 181.50 | + | 220 | + | 300 | = | 701.50   (answer) (the last flow does not earn any interest—it was just deposited)

The difference of $70.15 is caused by the fact that each flow earns interest for one period less. If these had been annuities, the first case would have been called an *annuity due* and the latter case an *ordinary annuity* (the *FVIFA* table in this book is for ordinary annuities). The alternative method would use the following keystrokes to get the same answer:

| C | 150 | × | 1.1 | + | 200 | × | 1.1 | + | 300 | = | 701.50   (answer)

Example 4: Present Value of Cash Flow Streams

For present values, a methodology that is the inverse of future value is applied. The present value of $1,000 due in two periods discounted at 10 percent is equal to:

C 1000 ÷ 1.1 ÷ 1.1 = 826.44   (answer)

Again, it is easy to expand this technique to find the present value of a stream of cash flows. Assume you want to find the present value of the following cash flow stream using a 9 percent discount rate:

End of period	1	2	3
Cash flow	$200	$300	$400

Assume in this case you are going to use the present-value interest factors given in the PVIF table in this book. The following keystrokes would solve the problem:

C 200 × .917 = 183.40   (write down this
                                                                  number)
C 300 × .842 = 252.60   (write down this
                                                                  number)
C 400 × .772 + 183.40 + 252.60 = 744.80   (answer)

Although this method will give you the answer, it requires that you write down intermediate calculations and reenter data. An alternative method is to start with period 3 and work backward. The value of 400 measured at the end of period 2 is 400 ÷ 1.09, to which we can add 300 (the cash flow at the end of period 2) since they are now in the same time period. Continuing this process eventually works back to period 0 as shown below:

End of period	0	1	2	3
Cash flow		200.00	300.00	⌐ 400.00
		611.90 ←	366.97 ←	
(answer)	744.86 ←	811.90	└ 666.97	
	End ←			Start

Notice that by working backward, it is not necessary to write down any intermediate calculations. The keystrokes would be:

C 400 ÷ 1.09 + 300 ÷ 1.09 + 200 ÷ 1.09 = 744.86   (answer)
                                                                          (note slight
                                                                          rounding
                                                                          difference
                                                                          from
                                                                          earlier
                                                                          answer)

With a little practice, you will find this a very fast method for calculating the present value of cash flow streams — mixed streams or annuities.

You can also use it to find the internal rate of return by simply trying different rates until one that yields a zero NPV is found.

Example 5: Present Value with Varying Discount Rates

Frequently it is necessary to find the present value of future flows when you expect the discount rate to vary. If you expect the following future cash flows, what is the present value?

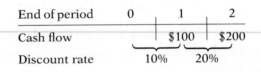

End of period	0	1	2
Cash flow		$100	$200
Discount rate		10%	20%

The discount rate from period 0 to 1 is 10 percent, and from period 1 to 2 is 20 percent. The following are the keystrokes used to solve this problem:

$$\boxed{C}\ 200\ \boxed{\div}\ 1.20\ \boxed{+}\ 100\ \boxed{\div}\ 1.10\ \boxed{=}\ 242.42 \quad \text{(answer)}$$

This type of problem can be extremely time-consuming to solve using financial tables. This technique can be just as readily applied to find future values when the interest rate varies.

PREPROGRAMMED FINANCIAL CALCULATORS

Many business calculators have financial function keys. They also have excellent instruction booklets that explain the calculators' operations. One hint you might find useful is to remember that you can work problems on the assumption of $1 being the amount (the same assumption financial tables make) and then multiply this result by the cash flow to get the final answer. This is a simple way to make sure you have punched the correct keys. You should be able to determine if the "factor" looks reasonable (e.g., *PVIFA* should always be less than the number of years).

With a little practice, you will discover that a preprogrammed financial calculator can be very handy. However, avoid becoming so dependent on it that you cannot work problems by hand. You must be able to assess the reasonableness of your answers. An understanding of the underlying financial concepts is necessary to make these judgments.

Appendix F

ANSWERS TO SELECTED END-OF-CHAPTER PROBLEMS

The following list of answers to selected problems (and portions of problems) is included to provide "check figures" for use in preparing detailed solutions to end-of-chapter problems requiring calculations. For problems that are relatively straightforward, the key answer is given; for more complex problems, answers to a number of parts of the problem are included. Detailed calculations are not shown—only the final and, in some cases, intermediate answers, which should help to confirm whether or not the correct solution is being developed. For problems containing a variety of cases for which similar calculations are required, the answers for only one or two cases have been included. The only verbal answers included are simple yes-or-no or "choice of best alternative" responses; answers to problems requiring detailed explanations or discussions are not given.

The problems (and portions of problems) for which answers have been included were selected randomly; therefore, there is no discernible pattern to the choice of problem answers given. The answers given are based on what are believed to be the most obvious and reasonable assumptions related to the given problem; in some cases, other reasonable assumptions could result in equally correct answers.

2-4	a		Actual return	Expected return
		Security A	13.3%	15%
		Security E	−2.7%	10%

2-6   a Tax liability $19,700
       c Average tax rate 21.3%
2-9   a Asset X: $250
       b Asset X: $100
3-3   Earnings available for common stockholders = $29,000
3-4   b $21,460

3-8   **a** $1.9375 earnings per share
      b Total assets $926,000
3-10 $80,000
3-16   **a** Total sources $3,700
      c Total sources $3,000
3-17   **a** Total sources $90,800
      c Total sources $72,900
4-2   **a** Average age of inventory 97.6 days
4-8   Total assets $1,500,000

4-10

	Industry average	Actual 1986	Actual 1987
Current ratio	1.80	1.84	1.04
Average collection period	37 days	36 days	57 days
Debt ratio	65%	67%	61%
Net profit margin	3.5%	3.6%	4.1%
Return on equity	9.5%	8.0%	11.3%

5-3   **a** $21,000
      d $5,250
5-7   **a** $Q = 8,000$ units
       $D = \$508,000$ or $[(\$63.50) \times (8,000)]$
      e 5.00
5-9   **a** $EPS = .375$
5-10   **a** $DFL = 1.5$
5-12   **a** $DFL_{BOND} = 1.32$
       $DFL_{STOCK} = 1.25$
      c Above $19,200 of *EBIT* the Bond Plan will be preferred, while below
        $19,200 of *EBIT* the Stock Plan is preferable.
5-14   **a** (1) 175,000 units
         (2) 233,333 units
      d $DTL = 2.40$
5-16   **a** $416,667
      b (1) $1.60 per share; (2) $4.30 per share
      e *DTL* 8.46; % change in *EPS* 4.23% increase

6-4

	February	March	April
a Ending cash	$37,000	$67,000	($22,000)
b Required total financing			$37,000
Excess cash balance	$22,000	$52,000	

      c Line of credit should be at least $37,000 to cover borrowing needs for
        the month of April.
6-7   **a** Net profits after taxes $577,200
       To retained earnings $257,200
6-8   **a** Net profits after taxes $216,857
      b Net profits after taxes $227,400
6-10   **a** Accounts receivable $1,440,000
       Net fixed assets $4,820,000
       Total current liabilities $2,260,000
       External funds required $775,000
       Total assets $9,100,000

6-11 **a** Net profits after taxes $67,500

	Percent-of-sales	Judgmental method
b Total assets	$729,000	$697,500
External funds required	$ 9,000	$ 11,250

7-1 **a** (3) Net working capital $2,000
c (3) Net working capital $4,000

7-5 **b** (1) $36,000
(2) $10,333

7-6 Annual loan cost $1,200

7-8 **b** Aggressive $788,917
Conservative $1,036,000

7-11 **a** Aggressive $30,000
Conservative $35,000

8-1 **a** 120 days
b 3 times
c $10,000,000

8-2 **a** 35 days
c $97,087

8-4 Plan E is best since it results in largest reduction in the cash cycle.

8-8 **a** 7 days collection float
b $21,450 opportunity cost

8-10 Yes. $108,000 annual savings versus $90,000 cost.

8-15 $22,500 annual savings

9-1 **a** Credit score Applicant B 81.5

9-2 **b** $75,000
c $9,000

9-4 **b** $28,000

9-6
Additional profit contribution from sales	$9,000
Cost of marginal investment in accounts receivable	($5,042)
Cost of marginal bad debts	($9,200)
Net profit from changing the policy	($5,242)

9-7 Net profit of the proposal $23,373

9-9 **a** $14,000 additional profit
b $32,500 marginal investment in accounts receivable
$ 8,034 cost of financing marginal investment in accounts receivable
$ 3,150 cost of marginal bad debts

9-13 **b** $52,000 net savings

9-16 **a** $EOQ = 4,899$ units
b Reorder point = 3,333 units

10-1 **a** December 25

10-2 **a** 36.73%
d 31.81%
g 8.82%

10-4 **a** X: 8.08%
b X: forgo

10-6 $1,300,000

10-7 $375

10-10 **a** 9.0%
       b 13.06%
10-12 Total $886,900
11-3 A $530.60
       D $78,450
11-5 **a** Annual $8,810
         Semiannual $8,955
         Quarterly $9,030
11-8 A $3,862.50
       B $138,450.00
       C $6,956.80
11-11 $408
11-13 **a** A $109,890
11-14 C $52,410
11-16 E $85,297.50
11-20 Future value of retirement home in 20 years = $272,595; Annual deposit = $4,759.49

11-22

Year	Interest	Principal
2	$1,489.61	$4,970.34

11-25 $PVIFA_{k,5\,yrs.} = 5.303$
       $13\% < k < 14\%$
11-28 **b** $A = 3,764.82$
11-29 The corporation must make a $15,575.10 annual end-of-year deposit in years 1 through 12 in order to provide a retirement annuity of $42,000 per year in years 13 through 32.

12-2 **a**

	Expansion A	Expansion B
Range	8	20

12-5 **a** Project 257
       (1) Range = 1.100
       (2) Expected value of return = 0.452
       (3) Standard deviation = 0.16538
       (4) Coefficient of variation = 0.366
12-10 **c** Asset B because it will have the highest increase in return.
12-12 Case A 8.9%
12-17 Asset A $10,870
       Asset D $9,717
12-19 **a** $1,156.88
12-21 **a** (3) $1,225.96
12-24 Firm A $18.60
       Firm C $22.68
12-26 Firm B $40.00
       Firm D $600.00
12-28 **a** $236,111
       b $413,409
12-30 **b** $P_0 = \$29.55$

13-1   **b** 12.4%
13-3   Bond A: $k_d = 9.44\%$; $k_i = 5.66\%$
        Bond E: $k_d = 11.84\%$; $k_i = 7.10\%$
13-6   **c** 16.54%
        d 15.91%
13-10   **a** Weighted Cost 8.344%
        b Weighted Cost 10.848%
13-13   **a** $k_i = .0513 \sim 5.1\%$
        $k_n = .1361 \sim 13.6\%$
        $k_r = 13\%$
        $k_p = .0844 \sim 8.4\%$
        b (1) $k_a = 9.71\%$
        (2) $k_a = 10.01\%$
13-15   **b** (1) Weighted Cost 10.41%
        (2) Weighted Cost 10.77%
        e Projects D, C, E, and A should be accepted because their respective
        rates of return exceed the *WMCC*.
14-1   **a** Current expenditure
        d Current expenditure
        f Capital expenditure
14-5   Asset A Book Value $275,500
        Asset B Book Value $ 26,800
14-7   **a** Taxes due $49,600
        d Taxes due −$6,400
14-8   Initial Investment $22,680
14-9   **a** Initial Investment $18,240
        c Initial Investment $20,640
14-11   **a** Cash Inflow Year 3 $584,000
14-14   **a** Initial Investment $41,200

b Year	1	2	3	4	5	6
Incremental Operating Cash Inflows	$13,600	$16,240	$11,080	$11,040	$13,440	$1,600

14-16   **a** Initial Investment $56,480

b Year	1	2	3	4	5	6
Incremental Operating Cash Inflows	$14,440	$22,600	$18,080	$17,880	$20,280	$2,200

14-18   Alternative 1
        a Initial Investment $90,000

b Year	1	2	3	4	5	6
Incremental Operating Cash Inflows	$26,300	$36,000	$35,980	$43,460	$33,460	$1,800

15-1   **a** .20 or 20%

15-4   **a** Machine 1: 4 years, 8 months
        Machine 2: 5 years, 3 months

15-7   **a** Project A .65 or 65%
        Project C .65 or 65%

        b Project A 3.08 years
        Project C 2.39 years

15-9   **a** $NPV = -\$320$; reject
        b $PI = 0.975$; reject

15-11   Project A: 17.43%
        Project D: 21.16%

15-14   **a** $NPV = \$1,222$
        b $PI = 1.067$
        c $IRR = 12\%$

15-16   Project A
        $NPV = \$15,245$
        $IRR = 16.06\%$

15-19   **a** Initial Investment $1,480,000

        b | Year | Cash Inflow |
        | --- | --- |
        | 1 | $656,000 |
        | 2 | 761,600 |
        | 3 | 647,200 |
        | 4 | 585,600 |
        | 5 | 585,600 |
        | 6 | 44,000 |

        c 3.2 years
        d $NPV = \$959,289$
        $IRR = 35\%$

15-20   **d** B, F, & G should be chosen.

15-24   **a** Line S; $E(NPV) = \$8,500$
        c Line S; Standard Deviation $= \$5,805.17$
        d Line S; $CV = .683$

15-27   **a** $NPV = \$22,320$
        b $NPV = -\$5,596$

15-29   **a** Project E: $NPV = \$2,130$
        Project F: $NPV = \$1,678$
        Project G: $NPV = \$1,144$
        c Project E: $NPV = \$834$
        Project F: $NPV = \$1,678$
        Project G: $NPV = \$2,138$

15-31   **b** Projects X and Z are acceptable with positive NPVs while Project Z
        with a negative NPV is not. Project X with the highest NPV should be
        undertaken.

16-1 | Debt ratio | Debt | Equity |
        | --- | --- | --- |
        | 40% | $400,000 | $600,000 |

16-3   **a** Financial breakeven points:

Structure A	**Structure B**
$16,000	$34,000

   c If *EBIT* is expected to be below $52,000, Structure A is preferred.
   If *EBIT* is expected to be above $52,000, Structure B is preferred.
   e At an *EBIT* level of $75,000, Structure B is recommended since the
   EPS is maximized.

16-5   **a** Debt ratio 15%; Debt = $150,000, Equity = $850,000, Number of
   shares of common stock = 34,000
   c Debt ratio 15%; *EBIT* $250,000, *EPS* = $4.20
   Debt ratio 60%; *EBIT* $250,000, *EPS* = $5.55

16-7   **a** $4.75/share
   b $0.40/share
   d A decrease in retained earnings and hence stockholder's equity by
   $80,000.

16-10   **a** 1985 = $0.60   **c** 1985 = $0.62
   b 1985 = $0.50   **d** 1985 = $0.62

16-11   **a** Retained earnings = $85,000
   b (1) Retained earnings = $70,000
     (2) Retained earnings = $40,000
   c Stockholders' equity has not changed. Funds have only been redistributed between the stockholders' equity accounts.

16-13   **a** *EPS* = $2
   b 1%
   c 1%; stock dividends do not have a real value.

16-18   **a** *EPS* = $4.00/share
   P/E = 15.00 times
   b 16,129 shares
   c $4.13/share; because there are fewer shares outstanding, which
   causes earnings per share to be higher.
   d $61.95/share

17-1   **a** Total tax liability = $1,680,000
   b Tax liability: Year 1 = $0
               Year 2 = $0
               Year 3 = $16,000
            Years 4 – 15 = $112,000/year

17-3   **a** Total tax advantage = $320,000; Years 1 – 4 = $80,000/year
   b Total tax advantage = $320,000:

Year	Tax advantage
1	$ 32,000
2	48,000
3	80,000
4	120,000
5	40,000
6	0
7	0

   c Studs Duds: $228,400
   Glitter Threads: $205,288

17-6   **a** Yes, the *NPV* = $42,150
        b Yes, the *NPV* = $101,000

17-7   **a** *EPS* merged firm = $1.029
        b *EPS* McBell's = $1.00
        c *EPS* Moon Bar = ($0.972)(2.2) = $2.139

17-9   (1) Ratio of Exchange; (2) Market Price
        A: 0.60; 1.20
        D: 0.25; 1.25
        E: 1.00; 1.25

17-12   **a** 1.125
        b Vinco Co.: EPS = $2.50, P/E = 18 times
        c 16.89 times

17-17   Case II:

Unpaid balance of 2nd Mortgage:	$150,000
Accounts payable:	$ 75,000
Notes payable:	$ 75,000
Unsecured bonds:	$150,000

17-19   **a** (1)

1st mortgage:	$700,000
2nd mortgage:	$400,000
Unsecured bonds:	$300,000
Preferred stock:	$200,000
Common stock:	$ 0

        (2) Zero
        b (1)

1st mortgage	$661,539
2nd mortgage	$246,154
Unsecured bonds	$184,615

18-1   Bond A: **a** Discount; **b** $400,000; **c** $16,000; **d** $320,000; **e** $128,000

18-3   Bond B: $20,000

18-4   **d** Incremental Initial Outlay: $2,840,000
        e Annual Cash Outflows with Old Bond: $2,516,000
           Annual Cash Outflows with New Bond: $2,152,000
        f Yes, Net Savings: $1,016,216

18-6   **b** (2) Annual Cash Flow Savings from New Bond: $85,600
        c (1) 12.5%: *PV* = $170,980
             13%:   *PV* = −$356,120
        d The reissue is favorable at a 12.5% stated interest rate if the discount rate is 6%. At a 13% stated interest rate the refunding of the bond should be rejected.

18-9   **a** *PV* of Lease Outflows: $52,611
        b *PV* of Purchase Outflows: $54,060
        c Since the present value of leasing is less than the present value of purchasing, the lease is recommended.

18-10

Lease	Capitalized value
A	$272,560
C	$ 58,203
E	$374,261

19-3 **a** Preferred dividends = $14.875/share
Common dividends = $15.875/share
c Preferred dividends = $10.00/share
Common dividends = $0.00/share

19-4 **a**

Common Stock (10,000 shares @ $1 par)	$ 10,000
Paid in capital in excess of par	120,000
Common stock equity	$130,000

19-5 **a** Majority: A, B, C, D, E: (.54)(1,000) = 540
b Majority can elect 3, and Minority can elect 2.

19-8 Case E: (1) With rights $1.11
(2) Ex rights $1.11

19-11 **a** 24,000 shares
b 12.5 rights
c 3,840 shares
d (1) $R_w = \$0.296$
(2) $M_e = \$28.704$
$R_e = \$0.296$

20-1 **a** $50
20-2 **b** 40 shares
20-3 **c** $1,050
20-6 **a** (1) $EPS = \$1.20$ per share
(2) $EPS = \$2.00$ per share
(3) $EPS = \$1.26$ per share

20-9 **a** Straight bond value = $832.75
b At $9.00: $720
c At $9.00: $832.75*
* The bond will not sell below the straight bond value.

20-11 **a** 160 shares, 400 warrants
b 20%
c 125%

20-14 **a** $800 profit
b $200
c $6/share

A-1

Effective rates	**Ff**	**DM**
Euromarket	8.5%	12.4%
Domestic	8.3	11.2

INDEX

Page numbers in **boldface** indicate glossary terms.